MW00816518

North American Odyssey

North American Odyssey

Historical Geographies for the Twenty-first Century

Edited by

Craig E. Colten and Geoffrey L. Buckley

ROWMAN & LITTLEFIELD
Lanham • Boulder • New York • Toronto • Plymouth, UK

Published by Rowman & Littlefield
4501 Forbes Boulevard, Suite 200, Lanham, Maryland 20706
www.rowman.com

10 Thornbury Road, Plymouth PL6 7PP, United Kingdom

British Library Cataloguing in Publication Information Available

Library of Congress Cataloging-in-Publication Data

North American odyssey : historical geographies for the twenty-first century / edited by Craig E. Colten and Geoffrey L. Buckley.
pages ; cm
Includes bibliographical references and index.
ISBN 978-1-4422-1584-9 (cloth : alk. paper) — ISBN 978-1-4422-1585-6 (pbk. : alk. paper) — ISBN 978-1-4422-1586-3 (electronic) 1. North America—Historical geography. I. Colten, Craig E. II. Buckley, Geoffrey L., 1965–
E40.5.N726 2014
911'.73—dc23

2013048468

™ The paper used in this publication meets the minimum requirements of American National Standard for Information Sciences—Permanence of Paper for Printed Library Materials, ANSI/NISO Z39.48-1992.

Printed in the United States of America

To our mentors who introduced us to this vast panorama that is historical geography, Don Meinig, Sam Hilliard, Bob Mitchell, and Paul Groves

Contents

PART III. TRANSFORMING THE LAND

PART IV. SHAPING THE LANDSCAPE

PART V. URBANIZING THE LAND

Figures, Table, and Textboxes

FIGURES

TABLE

TEXTBOXES

Introduction

Craig E. Colten and Geoffrey L. Buckley

Historical geography in North America—both as an academic pursuit and an avenue of inquiry—has a proud, if somewhat checkered, past. Like other subfields with which it is closely aligned, such as cultural geography, it has managed to survive—and even thrive—by adapting to ever-shifting intellectual terrain. In the early years of the twentieth century, however, its future was anything but certain. At the time, geographers such as Ellen Churchill Semple (1903) and Albert Brigham (1903) rose to prominence by exploring the influence of the physical environment on American history. When this approach lost favor, geographers not only abandoned their experiment with environmental determinism but largely dispensed with the historical perspective as well. In his 1940 presidential address to the Association of American Geographers, Carl Sauer (1941) lamented such shortsightedness. His vision of human geography as a thoroughly cultural-historical endeavor breathed fresh life into the subfield. It also inspired a new generation of scholars to view human geography as a product of cultural processes and dynamic interactions that take place over time as well as across space.

In more recent years, the so-called cultural turn of the twentieth century has influenced historical geography. While this development has diminished our reliance on Sauer's principal geographical tool—the map—it has sharpened the critical-thinking powers of human geographers in general and historical geographers in particular. Changes in methodologies and topical foci notwithstanding, recognition that a historical perspective allows us to better identify the forces—and make sense of the processes—that produce the geographies and landscapes we are familiar with today has remained constant since Sauer's day. Indeed, as the chapters in this volume demonstrate, the historical perspective is alive and well in North America.

A CONTINENTAL PERSPECTIVE

In the years between Sauer's 1940 address and the introduction of various critical approaches in the late 1990s, only a handful of authors attempted to synthesize the historical geography of North America. The first significant effort was Ralph Brown's *Historical Geography of the United States* (1948). Presenting a series of "geographies of the past," from first effective settlement until 1870, Brown used eyewitness accounts and contemporary maps to reconstruct the past. In so doing he strengthened the archival tradition that, to a great extent, distinguishes historical geography from other subfields. Although something of an outlier, his book nevertheless represented an important first step in the development of historical geography in North America. Significantly, Brown's work came out just as historical geography began to emerge as a standard offering of fully staffed departments throughout the country.

Twenty-five years later, Cole Harris and John Warkentin's *Canada before Confederation: A Study in Historical Geography* (1974) appeared on the scene. It differed from earlier volumes on Canada by emphasizing the geographical over the historical (see, e.g., Lucas 1901–1911). Like Brown's opus, *Canada before Confederation* was organized by region. More important, it served as a benchmark against which other volumes on Canada would inevitably be measured. Meanwhile, during the quarter century that separated the publication of these two works, historical geography flourished on university campuses. Trained by leading lights such as Carl Sauer at the University of California, Berkeley, and Andrew Hill Clark at the University of Wisconsin, historical geographers populated departments throughout the United States and Canada, providing geographic insights into the continent's changing past.

Historical geography's florescence continued with the release of *North America: The Historical Geography of a Changing Continent* (1987), edited by Robert Mitchell and Paul Groves. Asserting that their volume was "a response to a felt need in the discipline for an up-to-date, comprehensive treatment of the evolving geography of North America during the past four centuries" (1987, xi), Mitchell and Groves recruited some of the field's most accomplished and notable figures to contribute essays that, taken together, offered a more thorough overview of the historical geography of North America, in terms of territory and time, than any other volume to date. For the first time, historical geographers had extended their expertise across the continent and from prehistory to the more recent past. Organized chronologically, *North America*'s four sections began with the colonial period and carried through to the twentieth century. Each section in turn contained chapters organized by region. Publication of a revised edition in 2001 reflects the impact of this volume. Edited by Thomas McIlwraith and Edward Muller, the updated version of the book included many of the original authors but also several new authors and collaborators. In addition, the editors added chapters to address recent developments in the field. The volume retained its hybrid chronological/regional framework and continued to emphasize geographical change on a continental scale.

In 1990, Michael Conzen published the first edition of *The Making of the American Landscape*, also an edited volume featuring contributions by many of the discipline's most prominent practitioners. Rather than adopt a purely chronological or regional approach, however, Conzen elected to present his work as "an unabashedly evolutionary interpretation of the American landscape" ([1990]

2010, ix). It emphasized historical process, while showcasing particular landscapes. Whereas some chapters focused on physical features such as forests and waterways, others concentrated on purely human subject matter, such as the inscription of ethnicity, power, and central authority on the land. Updated in 2010, this collection offered a clear contrast to the Mitchell and Groves volume and remains essential reading in the field today.

At about the same time that Mitchell and Groves were working on the first edition of *North America: The Historical Geography of a Changing Continent*, Donald Meinig, a historical geographer at Syracuse University, was penning the first volume of a four-part series titled *The Shaping of America.* Meinig completed the first book in 1986 and the final volume twenty years later (Meinig 1986, 1995, 2000, and 2006). Like the other prominent national-scale treatments, Meinig's work adopted a chronological approach, further dividing the subject matter by region. Ambitious in breadth and scope, his books emphasize the sequence of events and processes that shaped the geography of the United States. His underlying theme was "the creation of a vast Atlantic circuit, a new human network of points and passages binding together four continents, three races, and a great diversity of regional parts" (Meinig 1986, 3). Employing a historical perspective enabled him to capture and chronicle the dynamic nature of these processes.

While Meinig's multivolume masterwork was in production, Carville Earle and Cole Harris were busy working on two national-level historical geographies. In *The American Way* (2003), Earle traces geopolitical and economic processes from colonial times to the twenty-first century. Referring to his work as geographical history, he makes a concerted effort to distinguish it from that of Meinig by eschewing a regional approach. In a dense and conceptually sophisticated treatment, he identifies temporal periods in the development of the American state and organizes geographic history according to long-wave policy and economic cycles. In *The Reluctant Land* (2008), Cole Harris synthesizes the scholarship of historical geographers and historians writing on Canada since publication of *Canada before Confederation* in 1974. In this comprehensive and authoritative work, Harris utilizes a regional approach to study Canada's past, tracing the country's emerging geography from prehistory to confederation. He also offers a more thoroughgoing reconstruction of precolonial indigenous society than had been available previously. Throughout this period, publication of numerous articles and books focused on more localized areas reveals the depth and breadth of historical geography in North America (see, e.g., Earle et al. 1989; Colten et al. 2003).

AN EVOLVING FIELD

Like Mitchell and Groves in 1987, we felt the time was right to make an assessment of historical geography—to see how it is changing and evolving. Our initial thought was simply to update the chapters in the McIlwraith and Muller volume. As we surveyed the field, however, the need for a fresh tack became apparent.

Rather than request authors to prepare chapters constrained regionally and temporally, we opted to use an entirely different framework. Given the direction of historical geography over the past twenty-five years, we decided to develop chapters based on topical and methodological approaches. This approach more closely reflected the research our contributors were conducting and the overall direction of the field.

Our hope is that this volume will complement, not replace, the Mitchell and Groves and McIlwraith and Muller volumes. Truth be told, their work was an inspiration to us. Like many of their contemporaries, the authors of this volume received their training from the generation who wrote chapters for the original Mitchell and Groves text. Indeed, many of us cut our academic teeth on this collection of essays. The topical treatments contained here reveal the extent to which these two enterprises are related as well as different. As historical geographers we are always rethinking the past, exploring new intellectual ground, and asking novel questions. We hope budding historical geographers will find inspiration in our book, just as the work of our predecessors inspired us.

We chose the title *North American Odyssey* to serve multiple purposes. It reflects the movement of indigenous peoples, Europeans, Africans, and Asians as they settled and resettled this continent. Their movements were unquestionably odysseys. The title also captures the vibrant nature of the field for it is suggestive of the intellectual peregrinations of scholars over the past three-quarters of a century. From Sauer's address in 1940, around the cultural turn, to the present, historical geographers have used the tools at their disposal—new methods, new theories, newly recognized sources—to push the boundaries of the discipline. This makes the field exciting, if not cohesive. We hope this volume captures some of this dynamism, encouraging more detailed investigations by the authors contained here as well as by those of our colleagues whom we could not include.

Of course, we encourage others—beyond geography and outside academia—to read these chapters. Now more than ever, long-term perspectives are exceptionally valuable and find support in government agencies as well as academic departments. Climate change is the most obvious issue today requiring our understanding of past patterns and processes. Using historical records to reconstruct landforms and plant geographies that existed long ago illustrates the value of sources and methods employed by historical geographers working in other specialties. A historical perspective is also essential when taking into account the human dimensions of long-term physical processes. For this reason, we encourage departments to restore faculty lines lost in the wake of tight budgets and increasing emphasis on practical, job-oriented skills. In our experience, historical geographers have much to contribute when it comes to discussions about local-global issues, and the field indeed has practical applications in disciplines like environmental geography and cultural resource management, to name just two. Finally, a fundamental plank of sustainability science asks us to consider how humans will prevail in the long term. Forecasting depends on deep temporal understanding of past human interactions with the environment. Historical geography offers a clear path to deciphering and depicting past geographies and unraveling the long-term trends.

ORGANIZATION AND STRUCTURE

Perhaps the key contribution that historical geography can make is to explore, expose, and explain processes at work in shaping geographies at different scales. In organizing this volume, we sought to emphasize that strength. We selected five key themes that showcase the dynamic processes that have guided the evolution of human geography in North America over the past several hundred years. Part I draws on Cole Harris's term "settling and resettling" and treats the "settling and resettling" of the land. This acknowledges the extensive and lasting imprint of indigenous societies and underscores the role of Europeans and Africans as secondary settlers.

Part II considers how, as European and African arrivals came to dominate the human landscape, society was remade, particularly during the nineteenth century. Chapters consider the emerging geographies of native peoples under federal management, immigrant groups in an industrializing nation, and the realignment of African Americans after the Civil War. Part III emphasizes the nature-society relations that transformed the continent in a European American dominated society. Chapters on transportation systems, resource extraction, water-resources management, and preservation fill out this portion of the book.

Part IV considers the many facets of landscape perception and interpretation. Chapters cover a wide variety of topics, including land division, regionalism, tourism, race, and gender. Additionally, authors examine the use of photographs and narrative to create and represent landscapes, both mythic and otherwise. Finally, in part V, a set of chapters addresses urban issues in North America. Specific topics include the evolving urban morphology of cities and the role of urban planning in directing the form and vitality of cities. A chapter on environmental justice in the city examines the inequities built into those processes.

REFERENCES

Brigham, Albert P. 1903. *Geographic Influences in American History.* Boston: Ginn and Co.

Brown, Ralph H. 1948. *Historical Geography of the United States.* New York: Harcourt, Brace and World.

Colten, Craig E., Peter J. Hugill, Terence Young, and Karen M. Morin. 2003. Historical Geography. In *Geography in America at the Dawn of the 21st Century*, edited by Gary L. Gaile and Cort J. Willmott, 149–63. Oxford: Oxford University Press.

Conzen, Michael P., ed. [1990] 2010. *The Making of the American Landscape.* New York: Routledge.

Earle, Carville. 2003. *The American Way: A Geographical History of Crisis and Recovery.* Lanham, MD: Rowman & Littlefield.

Earle, Carville, et al. 1989. Historical Geography. In *Geography in America*, edited by Gary Gale and Court Willmott, 156–91. Columbus, OH: Merrill Publishing.

Harris, Cole. 2008. *The Reluctant Land: Society, Space, and Environment in Canada before Confederation.* Vancouver: University of British Columbia Press.

Harris, R. Cole, and John Warkentin. 1974. *Canada before Confederation: A Study in Historical Geography.* New York: Oxford University Press.

Lucas, Charles P. 1901–1911. *Historical Geography of the British Colonies*. Vol. 5: *Canada*. Oxford: Clarendon Press.

McIlwraith, Thomas F., and Edward K. Muller, eds. 2001. *North America: The Historical Geography of a Changing Continent*. 2nd ed. Lanham, MD: Rowman & Littlefield.

Meinig, Donald W. 1986. *The Shaping of America: A Geographical Perspective on 500 Years of History*. Vol. 1: *Atlantic America, 1492–1800*. New Haven, CT: Yale University Press.

———. 1995. *The Shaping of America: A Geographical Perspective on 500 Years of History*. Vol. 2: *Continental America, 1800–1867*. New Haven, CT: Yale University Press.

———. 2000. *The Shaping of America: A Geographical Perspective on 500 Years of History*. Vol. 3: *Transcontinental America, 1850–1915*. New Haven, CT: Yale University Press.

———. 2006. *The Shaping of America: A Geographical Perspective on 500 Years of History*. Vol. 4: *Global America, 1915–2000*. New Haven, CT: Yale University Press.

Mitchell, Robert D., and Paul A. Groves, eds. 1987. *North America: The Historical Geography of a Changing Continent*. Lanham, MD: Rowman & Littlefield.

Sauer, Carl O. 1941. Foreword to Historical Geography. *Annals of the Association of American Geographers* 31: 1–24.

Semple, Ellen Churchill. 1903. *American History and Its Geographic Condition*. Boston: Houghton Mifflin.

I

SETTLING AND RESETTLING THE LAND

1

The New Narrative on Native Landscape Transformations

Michael D. Myers and William E. Doolittle

This chapter studies human-environment geography of the past. It deals with current portrayals of the pre–1492 CE landscape of North America and focuses on land-management practices and humanized or cultural landscapes, particularly cultivated fields. This chapter both addresses select theoretical and methodological issues and illustrates the diversity of ways in which we now know how native North Americans managed and transformed their environment. In so doing, we address the value gained from historical studies and what they tell us about the present and the prospects for the future. We operate under the assumption that most readers' understanding of native North America is based on an old narrative that is now largely mythical—small, sparse populations with limited technological, social, cultural, and economic accomplishments living in harmony with nature. The new narrative we present here draws on recent research, conducted mostly by geographers but also by archaeologists (e.g., Redman 2001) and historians (e.g., Krech 1999). It reveals larger populations than previously thought, as well as agricultural practices involving sophisticated knowledge and technology that altered the biophysical environment in such fundamental ways that they facilitated European colonization efforts and eventual dominance. The new narrative as presented here is, by necessity, selective and brief. A recent best-selling book by Charles C. Mann, *1491: New Revelations of the Americas before Columbus* (2011), although meant for a lay readership, is a more thorough treatise (that also includes South America), which we highly recommend to readers.

Today is an exciting time for pre-European research on the Americas and its landscapes, as many important issues remain the subject of debate. Most of these, such as migrations and the origins of Native American populations, the domestication of crops, and the development of agricultural technologies, are beyond the scope of this chapter. Here, we focus on what we now know about how native North Americans transformed the environment in order to make it productive.

GROWTH OF THE NEW NARRATIVE: THEORY AND METHOD

The new narrative began taking shape during the second half of the twentieth century, in large part due to the growing interest of geographers in landscape, particularly the historical landscapes of the Americas. At the forefront of this movement was the so-called Berkeley School of Geography that came about under the direction of Carl O. Sauer (Spencer 1976). Sauer, his students, their students, and their students contributed greatly to rewriting the narrative on pre-European America, its peoples, and their environments (Brown and Mathewson 1999). This research came to a crescendo in 1992 for the quincentennial of the 1492 encounter. Of particular importance was a special issue of the *Annals of the Association of American Geographers* (Butzer 1992). This publication focused attention on landscape transformations and their demographic (population) correlates. It was well received by historical demographers and epidemiologists who had also begun to question long-held assumptions about pre-Hispanic populations and the effects of European-introduced infectious diseases to which the Native American population had no immunity. Researchers interested in indigenous population numbers began to project population size estimates back in time, from more recent and more reliable numbers to those before 1492 based on assumptions of mortality, ranging anywhere from a 50 percent depopulation to more than 90 percent (e.g., Dobyns 1983). These efforts utilized documentary records from numerous archives throughout the New World and in Spain (e.g., Cook and Borah 1979); more recently, they included sophisticated computer models (e.g., Whitmore 1996). Archaeological investigations helped corroborate both the documentary evidence and computer models (e.g., Doolittle 1988a). In concert, these data and methods projected larger pre-European populations than previously thought and ultimately transformed interpretations of pre-European Native American demography. Scholars began to understand that reconstructing pre-European population figures for the Americas was indeed "one of the great inquiries of history" (Denevan 1992c, xxxix) and that postcontact depopulation was one of "the greatest destructions of lives in Human history" (Lovell 1992, 426). It also became clear, from a geographic perspective on human-induced environmental change, that the surprising discovery was "not that many people died but that many people lived" (Fenn 2001, cited in Mann 2005, 133).

As is currently understood, the amount of land under cultivation and the level of agricultural intensity—defined as the output (yield) per unit area per unit time (Turner and Doolittle 1978)—not only have a demographic correlate but tend to have a demographic causation (Boserup 1965; Turner, Hanham, and Portararo 1977). Generally speaking, agriculture tends to expand into new lands before it is intensified on currently cultivated land because expansion does not usually require new technology, whereas intensification on existing fields typically does (Boserup 1981; Doolittle 1980). Expansion of agriculture axiomatically requires the clearing of natural vegetation to create new fields, and agricultural intensification implies the increased sophistication of techniques. Conversely, decreases in population generally result in field abandonment, as an obvious consequence, and also tend to result in disintensification of production on existing fields given reduced production requirements (Doolittle 1988b). Over time and with reduced population after 1500, production declined and abandoned fields became overgrown with vegetation. The resulting landscapes associated with depopulation then appeared natural to observers who lacked modern training and experience. This difference between what was once thought to be natural vegetation and what is now known to be revegetation following field abandonment, along with the marked difference between pre-European Native American subsistence practices and what later European observers actually saw, distinguishes the old from the new narrative. Indigenous American agricultural systems were the products of long-term development, involving both expansion and intensification. With population declines at, shortly after, and even in waves preceding actual native contact with Europeans, formerly cultivated landscapes reverted to a more "pristine" appearance (Denevan 1992a). Further, relatively more intensive Native American production technologies reverted to what most scholars to this day classify as "horticulture" (belittling, given the more appropriate term "agriculture"), despite how impressed the early European explorers were with the *agriculture* of their New World counterparts. The native depopulation and accompanying field abandonment and agricultural disintensification across the North American continent, prior to the arrival of influential naturalists (e.g., Kalm 1972) and ethnographers (e.g., Wilson 1917), shaped their detailed commentaries, but their interpretations of a pristine wilderness were wrong and are now accepted as mythical.

Scholars educated in the new narrative now recognize that the regional diversity of agricultural practices for native North America has been a function of numerous groups of people developing a variety of new technologies, techniques, and practices to exploit a mosaic of biophysical environments, with sophistication comparable to their Old World counterparts, despite the absence of domesticated livestock. When Europeans began arriving in the New World in around 1500 CE and later, native peoples also responded in myriad ways. Not only did many die, but many moved, and almost all adopted, to one degree or another, new technologies. Contributors to the new narrative demonstrate most convincingly that many practices long thought to be ancient and indigenous to the New World were in fact adaptations to the postcontact world created by the introduction of technologies such as the steel axe, many of which were, in fact, incorporated into less intensive, less sophisticated agricultural practices (e.g., Denevan 1992b).

The approach most responsible for creating the new narrative was simply attention to as many types of data and as many previous contributions as possible (e.g., Butzer and Butzer 1993). Inductive work therefore held precedence over such deductive generalizations as the notion of environmental limits to development (Meggers 1954; see also Ferndon 1959; Hirshberg and Hirshberg 1957). Even the conceptual principles of intensification, disintensification, cultural adaptation to new circumstances, and systemic change, which helped shape the new narrative, were only modes of explanation or organizational principles to help guide research. Specific details of environmental management, of change and adjustment, and of long-term trends still had to be addressed to support any explanations. Invoking any of those conceptual principles alone was not to be confused with formulating an explanation itself (Harvey 1969), lest one be guilty of committing the fallacy of misplaced concreteness (Whitehead 1925). In philosophical terms, the approach was characteristically Aristotelian.

EXPLORING THE NEW NARRATIVE: ENVIRONMENT NOT PRISTINE

Certain writers (e.g., Sale 1991) have described the pre-European New World as a "paradise," with its biophysical environments little disturbed by people who lived in harmony with nature, in an almost timeless, natural state. That simplistic image of the noble savage long permeated the collective psyche of political philosophers, anthropologists, environmentalists, government officials, and lay people alike. However, that romantic and simultaneously pejorative image of Native Americans—as not full participants in the human condition—is more myth than reality (Thompson and Smith 1971), and in not being truthful, it probably did more harm than good (Martin 1981). That image gave rise to what has been called the "pristine myth" (e.g., Denevan 1992a) and has been the focus of many a rebuttal within the scholarship of the new narrative, not because of politics but because research has shown it to be false. Although it might take a moment to realize, this is a fact to celebrate, especially among Native Americans.

Philosophy and theory are fine in outlining the premises on which old and new narratives are framed, but more important are substantive facts, meaning data and evidence. We can treat landscapes as intellectual creations (e.g., Cosgrove 1998), but their composition involves real and tangible factors, including vegetation, soils, slopes, water, and myriad related phenomena (Olwig 1996). Accordingly, the remainder of this chapter deals with such evidence in order to provide a better understanding of the historical geography of landscape change and the new narrative. These related perspectives include the role of strategic burning as a widespread land-management practice, the existence of large expanses of cultivated fields prior to 1492, and the diversity of pre-European cultivated landscapes on the North American continent. For brevity, we have taken the descriptions and assessments offered here largely from *Cultivated Landscapes of Native North America* (Doolittle 2000), the most thorough examination of the topic to date. That book utilized early explorers' documentary accounts, assessments by ethnographers, cross-cultural comparisons, and archaeological and paleoenvironmental data. Each type of evidence has limitations, and employing them has required caution. Nevertheless, taken as a whole, they provide a compelling picture of the sophistication of North American agriculture and landscape transformation prior to 1492.

OF FIRE AND FIELDS

Fire can transform a landscape more quickly and more thoroughly than anything else (Pyne 1982). Although normally represented as an environmental destroyer, fire can actually have a positive effect both on vegetation and on other forms of life. Early European settlers in the Americas and their descendants feared fire's threat to what they had built, particularly homes. Their earlier native counterparts, however, used fire to their advantage. They did not typically attempt to extinguish wild fires but rather accommodated them, often for strategic purposes. Native peoples also set fires intentionally and controlled them to create new environments on both local and regional scales. For example, after harvesting wild grass seeds and various berries, natives burned the remaining plants to promote a more abundant yield the following year. They also burned trees felled for the creation of new fields, and before the next year's planting, they burned both the crop residue left from the year before and the weeds that had subsequently invaded the fields.

The old narrative maintained that native farmers practiced slash-and-burn shifting cultivation in the Eastern Woodlands and relied on early explorers' accounts as evidence. The new narrative uses the same data but, rather than proverbially jumping to simple conclusions based on any single individual account, addresses the complete documentary record from a critical perspective. It concludes that fields once cleared by slashing and burning were kept cleared and cultivated with limited fallows for a long time (Doolittle 2000, 174–90; 2004). Using perhaps the most widely cited reference as an example, John Smith of Pocahontas fame noted of natives in 1607 Virginia that

> the greatest labour they take, is in planting their corne, for the Country naturally is overgrowne with wood. To prepare the ground they bruise the barke of the trees neare the roote, then doe they scortch the roots with fire that they grow no more. The next yeare with a crooked peece of wood they beat up the weeds by the rootes, and in that they plant their Corne. (1910, 357)

Although this account mentions slashing and burning, neither Smith nor others so much as hint at field abandonment, forest regrowth, or rotational agriculture. And they mention the removal of roots, a labor-intensive practice not employed in slash-and-burn shifting cultivation. When taken in concert, therefore, such accounts indicate that once native populations cleared forests for planting, they kept them clear. The descriptions indicate the presence of permanent agriculture, not a simpler, slash-and-burn shifting cultivation. Adding further credence to this are accounts that mention preparation of existing fields already devoid of wood; these mention the tillage and/or burning of weeds and stubble, grass, or brush, but none mention removing trees that had regrown. These were fields under long-term permanent cultivation. They were not allowed to regrow forests and at most lay fallow for only short periods. The expansion of cultivated fields and areas under cultivation as the population grew transformed many formerly wooded areas into permanent fields.

Many accounts of native North American agriculture mention the use of fire and include observations from southern Canada through the Southeast, from the Atlantic coast inland, around the Great Lakes, and up the Mississippi River watershed as far north as Wisconsin and the Ohio River valley and as far west as western Oklahoma and the Texas panhandle. Farther west, where the paucity of rainfall limited forest ranges, agriculture in the localized and wetter higher elevations also required the clearing of trees. Not all cultivated fields required forest clearance, but indigenous farmers used fire to clear brush and grasses that impeded cultivation. The narrative on landscape transformations has long recognized the importance of burning, particularly for driving game, facilitating sight and travel, and defense (Day 1953). The new narrative now includes the use of burning for agricultural field clearance and maintenance.

At the forest edge, fires kept trees from invading open lands, especially formerly forested lands that had been already cleared. Burning removed burdensome undergrowth, both natural and postclearing regrowth. Early accounts of burning extensive areas may indicate maintenance of grassy tracts previously wooded. Setting fires can remove unwanted understory but also set the conditions for its growth and may require annual, or at least frequent, burning to maintain those benefits. In some parts of the Eastern Woodlands, burning resulted in open, parklike savannas. To create such a setting from an old-growth forest would require at least occasional fires that burned more than just the understory, then repeated fires to maintain that landscape. Overall, fire was an important factor in the human transformation of the North American landscape, including the Eastern Woodlands. Forests began to return to a more "natural state" only after the Native American population declined.

In order to grasp fully the role of burning by humans in forest landscapes, it is important to understand that not all trees were removed and their regrowth suppressed by fire, even if they were in the way of cultivation. There is much evidence that trees of certain species were valued and protected within otherwise cleared and cultivated fields. Trees protected for a nut harvest include walnut, chestnut, butternut, hickory nut, and pecan. Accounts discuss protection of smooth alder for its bark for medicinal purposes and of plum, crab apple, and wild grapevines for their fruit. Accounts also document protection of the same species within forests during annual burns or even in case of natural fire. An abundance of documentary evidence indicates that nuts and fruits were an important part of the Native American diet, and over time the landscape included a higher frequency of economic tree species both within fields and within adjacent forests than natural distribution would account for. There is also much evidence that tree species were actually transplanted in pre-European times, as many have been found outside their native range. Some early explorers' accounts of indigenous farmers cultivating both New and Old World trees together imply that tree planting was probably a familiar, if not a common, practice in pre-European times (Doolittle 2000, 62–66).

Finally, the use of fire to clear fields and transform landscapes was not simply some wholesale assault on nature. More was happening than simply clearing and burning, and for good reason. Native agriculturists protected and encouraged some species. Burning frequently made the land more productive with fresh growth of valued plants. Protecting and encouraging economically valued species within a particular habitat can actually protect that habitat by increasing biodiversity. Indeed, such strategies could be used to improve land use today.

LARGE FIELDS, FEW IN FALLOW

The old narrative that maintained the presence of slash-and-burn shifting cultivation made no mention of field sizes. Evidence from around the world has long indicated that slash-and-burn shifting cultivators tend to have small plots of land under cultivation at any one time, with numerous other small plots in various stages of fallow and forest regrowth and large tracts of land still in forest. Contributing to the myth perpetuated by the old narrative is the failure of previous scholars to mention details about the fields they actually saw.

An abundance of documentary evidence describes large fields and expansive areas currently under cultivation. Some fields were hundreds of hectares in areal extent, and in many places explorers mention trekking several days past seemingly countless numbers of such fields. To wit, writing of New England in 1605, Samuel de Champlain said that "all along the shore there is a great deal of land cleared up and planted with Indian corn" (1907, 66). Descriptions of small fields being either cultivated or in fallow are so few as to be rare exceptions (Doolittle 2000, 121–62).

The early European accounts of large fields should not be treated lightly. Explorers were clearly impressed with what they saw. These chroniclers lived in an era when the agricultural landscape of Europe differed greatly from that of today. During the 1500s and 1600s Europe had not yet felt even the "*early* agricultural revolution" of the late eighteenth and nineteenth centuries (Myers 2002). It is indeed plausible that Native Americans had an agriculture landscape comparable to their European contemporaries. That native farmers in North America had neither oxen nor plows simply makes large fields more impressive.

We cannot interpret explicit descriptions of fields not in cultivation when observed by early European explorers as indicating fields in fallow, as the old narrative of slash-and-burn shifting cultivation would hold. Instead, these reports tend to come from later European explorers, not the earliest ones, and well after the native population declines resulting from the introduction of Old World diseases. For example, William Bartram wrote in 1775 of the area near what is today Macon, Georgia, "On the east banks of the Oakmulge, this trading road runs nearly two miles through ancient Indian fields, which are called the Oakmulge fields: they are the rich low lands of the river. Their old fields and planting land extend up and down the river, fifteen or twenty miles" (1940, 68). Pehr Kalm, also writing in the late 1700s, noted of contemporary traveler accounts that "all of those who had made long journeys in *Canada* to the south, but chiefly westward, agreed that there were many great plains destitute of trees, where the land was furrowed, as if it had been ploughed. In what manner this happened no one knows. . . . Those furrowed plains sometimes continue for several days journey" (1972, 421–22).

It is certainly doubtful that ancient American farmers plowed their fields since there is no evidence of either plows or draft animals. However, abundant evidence from the upper Midwest indicates that ancient farmers did indeed reshape the surface of the land by creating series of ridges and furrows (figure 1.1) for a multitude of purposes, including ameliorating cold air drainage (Riley and Freimuth 1977), wetland drainage (Gallagher 1992), and ease of cultivation (Gartner 2003).

In summary, a sufficient number of early European documentary accounts of large fields and extensive tracts of land cultivated by indigenous farmers suggests that permanent cultivation was the norm, not some form of slash-and-burn shifting cultivation as the old narrative held. The latter type of agriculture

Figure 1.1. Relict ridged fields as they appeared in 1915 near Lake Winnebago, Wisconsin. Photograph by George R. Fox; used with permission of the State Historical Society of Wisconsin.

implies expansive forests surrounding a few nearly isolated, small, partially cleared fields and some abandoned fields lying fallow in some stage of forest regrowth. Such descriptions are almost nonexistent for native North America. Conversely, the plethora of descriptions of numerous large tracts of fully cleared and cultivated land contributes greatly to the new narrative of native farmers as accomplished models for developing a sustainable agricultural base to feed a large and settled (even urban) population.

DIVERSE AGRICULTURAL LANDSCAPES

Attention thus far has focused primarily on the eastern half of the continent, in part because the pristine myth does. In these forested areas, rainfall was normally adequate in both amount and distribution for crop production during the growing season. However, there were, and still are, diverse Native American cultivated landscapes in the western and especially the southwestern regions of the continent.

In the dry West, native farmers had to devise either means to conserve scant and unpredictable moisture that fell on their fields or methods to capture water from distant sources to transport to their fields. In some cases they did both. As in the East, they had to clear cultivated plots of natural vegetation, even if the land was not forested, although many fields were.

The simplest means of conserving moisture is to plant in relatively relief-free sandy areas where soil holds water below the surface. Two diverse examples should suffice. On the edge of the Colorado Plateau of northern Arizona, the Hopi cultivate sand dunes, as did their ancestors. Here there is little summer rain but abundant winter snowfall. Snow accumulates on the dunes, and as it melts in the spring, moisture percolates downward to be trapped beneath the sand, which then acts as a mulch during the hot summer months of the growing season. Crops take advantage of these waters (Hack 1942). In other localities, farmers cultivate the sandy floors of arroyos (washes) that appear dry on the surface but actually contain subsurface water that originates at seeps or springs further upslope in the drainage basin. Here again, crops benefit from these unseen waters (Bradfield 1971).

Ancient North American farmers also created mulch fields. In 1066 CE a volcano in northern Arizona, Sunset Crater, erupted, spreading a thin layer of volcanic ash across the landscape. Farmers raked the ash into ridges thirty centimeters high and planted beans and maize. The ridges not only acted as mulch, conserving soil moisture, but the ash contained nutrients that allowed farmers to cultivate the ridges for more than one hundred years (Colton 1960). Further south, near what is today Tucson, farmers gathered rocks strewn naturally across the surface of Pleistocene terraces, creating landscapes dominated by largely bare soil but containing a strange distribution of scattered rock piles. These features mystified archaeologists for more than a century. Finally, an inquisitive team undertook a systematic study and discovered that the bare areas between the rock piles had not been cultivated; the rock piles themselves, however, were micro-environments for growing agave. Like the previously discussed sands, the rock piles acted as mulch (Fish et al. 1985); further, rock stays cool as morning temperatures rise, creating condensation at the atmospheric dew point, which contributes sporadically to the availability of water to the crop.

In addition to rock piles, curious alignments of rocks also characterize parts of the southwestern landscape. In some places the lines of piled rocks are parallel. In other locales they also run perpendicular to each other, forming grids (figure 1.2). A multidisciplinary team conducted the most comprehensive study of such features to date. It found no evidence of staple crops such as maize, but the rock alignments served as mulch, facilitating the cultivation of agave (Doolittle and Neely 2004). Taking this technology one step further, ancient farmers in northern New Mexico excavated materials from naturally occurring gravel deposits and spread them across the surface, creating a mulched layer ten centimeters thick (figure 1.3). In some places these conserved soil moisture (Lightfoot and Eddy 1995); in others they apparently also retained daytime heat and extended the growing season, in addition to providing dew-point moisture (Maxwell and Anschuetz 1992). Regardless of the specific function, these features illustrate the ingenuity of native farmers and how their actions transformed the landscape.

It is a small step from rock piles to rock alignments and, by extension, from rock alignments on slopes to terraces and from rock alignments across gullies to water-controlling check dams. Hardly a slope near ancient habitation sites in the Southwest is not covered to one degree or another with vestiges of rock-faced terraces (figure 1.4). Terraces exist in a variety of sizes, ranging up to three meters high, up to forty meters long, and up to five meters wide. Although they can serve a multitude of functions, often simultaneously, they exist principally to create

Figure 1.2. Rock-bordered grids near Safford, Arizona. Photograph by William E. Doolittle.

relatively level field surfaces with deep soils that retain moisture (Herold 1965; Donkin 1979).

Much smaller terrace-like features that are nothing more than short rock alignments (less than five meters) across small gullies and ephemeral stream channels are typically called check dams—they literally check the flow of

Figure 1.3. A prehistoric pebble-mulched field in the Chama valley of New Mexico. Photograph by William E. Doolittle.

Figure 1.4. Ancient agricultural terraces on Tumamoc Hill, Tucson, Arizona. Photograph by William E. Doolittle.

water—and serve principally to slow periodic runoff and inhibit soil erosion. Although small and frequently almost invisible, such features across the southwestern landscape, doubtless numbering in the millions, have cumulatively had a major impact on transforming the landscape (Doolittle, Neely, and Pool 1993). Innocuous as they are individually, together they bespeak a monumental human presence in times past.

In the lower reaches of a few southwestern drainages, where stream gradients are slight (less than 1 percent), check dam–like features, albeit higher, wider, and at an angle, end in what are clearly the remains of small canals. These features appear to have been diversion weirs to redirect ephemeral stream flow or flash floods into canals that carried irrigation water to fields. More abundant than these diversion devices are canals themselves. Rapid stream flow clearly obliterated most of the diversion devices over time, but then logs, branches, brush, and earth were probably more commonly used than rocks. These structures were easy to construct but also easily destroyed, thus didn't survive.

Almost every wash in the Southwest contains such vestiges, but in the larger, permanently flowing river valleys with relatively broad alluvial plains, there is archaeological evidence of pre-European canal irrigation systems. The size of the respective system is largely a function of the size of the river. In some locales, such as northern New Mexico, where river valleys are rather narrow, they were single canals to individual fields. In other places, such as along the expansive Salt and Gila Rivers of central Arizona, the systems were mind-bogglingly huge. Some of these irrigation networks had main canals more than five meters wide, three meters deep, and twenty kilometers long. They had multiple branches, forming a reverse dendritic pattern that allowed for an elaborate distribution and water-sharing scheme covering approximately one hundred thousand hectares. These canals transported water downstream via gravity. Most were earth lined, but in a few places there is clear evidence of plaster lining, most commonly where bank erosion would have been a problem. Toward their upstream ends, farmers excavated these canals below the ground surface, but to function properly canals had to be elevated on earthen embankments so that water would flow out of them and down onto the field surfaces (Masse 1981).

Archaeological evidence indicates that southwestern farmers developed canal irrigation independently in the Southwest at approximately the same time as it developed farther south in Mesoamerica and Peru, around four thousand years ago (Damp, Hall, and Smith 2002; Doolittle 2006; Zimmerer 1995). Most of the southwestern irrigation systems had been abandoned and were derelict by the time Europeans arrived in the region. These interlopers did, however, report seeing irrigation canals functioning in a few areas, testifying to their longevity and hence sustainability (Doolittle 2000). For example, the Francisco de Ibarra expedition of 1565 reported that in Sonora, the entourage marched through "a valley two leagues long planted with corn fields, beans, calabashes, and melons, all irrigated" and through another "valley one league in extent entirely given over to irrigated fields" (Obregón 1928, 159, 175). In Chihuahua, Ibarra described a valley "inhabited by a great number of people, with much food, and as skillful in the cultivation of their fields and in the irrigation of them as one can find in the world" (Mecham 1927, 81). Evidence suggests this canal remains in use today (Doolittle 1993).

Paradoxically, remnants of one of the largest ancient canal systems in the region remain clearly visible on the landscape within meters of the Phoenix, Arizona, airport, in the heart of the urban area. These ancient canal features parallel a modern concrete-lined canal that carries irrigation waters to cotton fields well west of the city (figure 1.5). One should, therefore, never assume that intensive urbanization obliterated all remnants of ancient human activities. In this case, the canal is evidence of a vast and intensive agricultural system.

Finally, across the entire North American continent, not all agricultural production was on the types of fields described above, which we might consider "outfields," to use European parlance. Wherever Native Americans practiced agriculture, there were also "infields," that is, gardens adjacent to or near dwellings. These gardens were economically important to their users and an important component of the cultural landscape. More than just smaller versions of outfields, they served a number of important, independent functions, including increasing the variety of cultivated plants, easing watering and fertilizing from household waste, providing greater protection to the plants and generally reducing the risk of outfield failure, experimenting, producing seed crop, and even

Figure 1.5. Aerial view of spoil banks of prehistoric irrigation canals at the east end of the Phoenix, Arizona, airport. Photograph by, and used with permission of, Adriel Heisey.

providing protected beds for sprouting plants to transplant to larger fields (Doolittle 1992). Overall, between their sophisticated systems of outfield and infield production, Native American farmers managed productive cultivated fields and altered the natural vegetation, soils, and hydrology of the continent's landscapes on both local and regional scales.

We have drawn examples for this chapter almost exclusively from early European explorer accounts and archaeological excavations. However, many types of data, including ethnography, experimental archaeology, and cross-cultural comparisons, also informed the preceding discussion (Doolittle 2000; Myers 2002). The same level of synthesis, but from an even more inclusive range of data, methodologies, and analogues, will be required to address questions about Native American populations immediately prior to European contact. How many people did these diverse agricultural technologies feed over the many generations of their existence? What were the population growth rates within these farming societies? What analogues do we have for population growth rates for farming societies free of European infectious diseases? Today, in less developed countries, in rural agricultural areas, following the inoculation campaigns that began in the mid-twentieth century, we see population-doubling rates that stagger the imagination. Are these more applicable as analogues than pre-inoculation growth rates for disease-ridden European populations? What baseline can we even use for pre-Columbian populations when archaeological data demonstrate that growth rates were regionally variable and showed major long-term fluctuations? Of course, debates will continue about what constitute appropriate data and methods, and, again, new contributions will be needed before we have answers.

WHAT VALUE THE NEW NARRATIVE?

In conclusion, it is simply a truism that many, if not most, people today are concerned about the quality of the environment for their own and future generations, that many hold in high esteem a worldview that perceives the environment as sacred, and that many, perhaps rightfully, ascribe such a worldview to Native Americans. As attractive as such an ideal may be, equally impressive is a demonstrated early Native American sophistication in land management, and the two are not mutually exclusive. Our modern world requires both: not only must we preserve natural areas separate from our landscapes of production, but we must also express a sacred worldview together with sophisticated land management within those very landscapes that produce for our modern lives. Both ideals can be, and sometimes have been, achieved within the same landscapes. As Mann expressed in *1491* based on pre-European land-use data, and as many others have observed based on similar research, we can combine preservation of biodiversity, soil fertility, and water quality with productive agriculture, including forestry, within the same culturally managed landscapes, which we need not strip of either culture or nature.

Much has also been made of the need to distinguish between native North America, especially eastern North America, on the one hand, and the more populous and more urbanized pre-European societies in Mexico and South America. The new narrative, however, with its revelations about cultivated landscapes in native North America, including the Eastern Woodlands, has greatly reduced the need to emphasize that distinction. The concepts of intensification and disintensification, as well as the modern principle of cultural adaptation and selection, do not hold that members of one society are "more evolved" or at a "higher stage" than another. Instead, the systems that people are born into, help to reproduce, and sometimes help to demonstrate either evolution or devolution and differentiate levels of integration and "development." All people are complex actors within intricate social and natural environments, no less so a pre-European native North American than any other individual who has lived on this earth. Indeed, for all involved in reconstructing its history and for all whose ancestors created that world, the new historical narrative of pre-European North America should be a source of pride. That new narrative needs to be emphasized, as it has been here, in contrast with the old. We must dismiss the long-held belief that Native Americans, especially within forested regions, lived in a timeless harmony with the land, having little impact on their environment. Nevertheless, debates will continue about the spatial extent to which that environment was transformed: Did it happen everywhere, more or less, or only in a complex mosaic of essentially natural and essentially cultural landscapes? Could plant species domesticated in native North America or specific practices utilized benefit us today? Again, these are just some of the questions that call for continued contributions to the study of pre-European North America.

REFERENCES

Bartram, W. 1940. *The Travels of William Bartram*, edited by M. V. Doren. New York: Facsimile Library.

Boserup, E. 1965. *The Conditions of Agricultural Growth: The Economics of Agrarian Change under Population Press.* Chicago: Aldine.

———. 1981. *Population and Technological Change: A Study of Long-Term Trends.* Chicago: University of Chicago Press.

Bradfield, M. 1971. *The Changing Pattern of Hopi Agriculture.* Occasional Paper 30. London: Royal Anthropological Institute of Great Britain and Ireland.

Brown, S., and K. Mathewson. 1999. Sauer's Descent? Or, Berkeley Roots Forever? *Yearbook of the Association of Pacific Coast Geographers* 61: 137–57.

Butzer, K. W. 1982. *Archaeology as Human Ecology.* Cambridge: Cambridge University Press.

———, ed. 1992. The Americas before and after 1492: Current Geographical Research. *Annals of the Association of American Geographers* 82, no. 3: 345–68.

Butzer, K. W., and E. K. Butzer. 1993. The Sixteenth-Century Environment of the Central Mexican Bajío: Archival Reconstruction from Colonial Land Grants and the Question of Spanish Ecological Impact. In *Culture, Form, and Place: Essays in Cultural and Historical Geography*, edited by K. Mathewson. *Geoscience and Man* 32: 89–124.

Champlain, S. de. 1907. *Voyages of Samuel de Champlain*, edited by W. L. Grant. New York: Charles Scribner's Sons.

Colton, H. S. 1960. *Black Sand: Prehistory of Northern Arizona.* Albuquerque: University of New Mexico Press.

Cook, S. F., and W. W. Borah. 1979. Royal Revenues and Indian Population in New Spain, ca. 1620–1646. In *Essays in Population History.* Vol. 3: *Mexico and California*, 1–128. Berkeley: University of California Press.

Cosgrove, D. E. 1998. *Social Formation and Symbolic Landscape.* Madison: University of Wisconsin Press.

Damp, J. E., S. A. Hall, and S. J. Smith. 2002. Early Irrigation on the Colorado Plateau Near Zuni Pueblo, New Mexico. *American Antiquity* 67: 665–76.

Darwin, C. 1859. *On the Origin of Species by Means of Natural Selection, or the Preservation of Favoured Races in the Struggle for Life.* London: John Murray.

Darwin, C., and A. Wallace. 1858. Three Papers on the Tendency of Species to form Varieties; and on the Perpetuation of Varieties and Species by Natural Means of Selection. *Zoologist* 16: 6263–308.

Day, G. M. 1953. The Indian as an Ecological Factor in the Northeastern Forest. *Ecology* 34: 329–46.

Denevan, W. M. 1983. Adaptation, Variation, and Cultural Geography. *Professional Geographer* 35: 399–407.

———. 1992a. The Pristine Myth: The Landscape of the Americas in 1492. *Annals of the Association of American Geographers* 82, no. 3: 369–85.

———. 1992b. Stone vs. Metal Axes: The Ambiguity of Shifting Cultivation in Prehistoric Amazonia. *Journal of the Steward Anthropological Society* 20: 153–65.

———, ed. 1992c. *The Native Population of the Americas in 1492.* Madison: University of Wisconsin Press.

———. 2003. The Native Population of Amazonia in 1492 Reconsidered. *Revista de Indias* 43: 175–88.

Denevan, W. M., and K. Mathewson, eds. 2009. *Carl Sauer on Culture and Landscape: Readings and Commentaries.* Baton Rouge: Louisiana State University Press.

Dobyns, H. F. 1983. *Their Numbers Became Thinned: Native American Population Dynamics in Eastern North America.* Knoxville: University of Tennessee Press.

Donkin, R. A. 1979. *Agricultural Terracing in the Aboriginal New World.* Viking Fund Publications in Anthropology 56. Tucson: Wenner-Gren Foundation and University of Arizona Press.

Doolittle, W. E. 1980. Aboriginal Agricultural Development in the Valley of Sonora, Mexico. *Geographical Review* 70: 328–42.

———. 1983. Agricultural Expansion in a Marginal Area of Mexico. *Geographical Review* 73: 301–13.

———. 1988a. *Pre-Hispanic Occupance in the Valley of Sonora, Mexico: Archaeological Confirmation of Early Spanish Reports.* Anthropological Papers of the University of Arizona 48. Tucson: University of Arizona Press.

———. 1988b. Intermittent Use and Agricultural Change on Marginal Lands: The Case of Smallholders in Eastern Sonora, Mexico. *Geografiska Annaler* 70B: 255–66.

———. 1992. House-Lot Gardens in the Gran Chichimeca: Ethnographic Cause for Archaeological Concern. In *Gardens of Prehistory: The Archaeology of Settlement Agriculture in Greater Mesoamerica,* edited by T. W. Killion, 69–91. Tuscaloosa: University of Alabama Press.

———. 1993. Canal Irrigation at Casas Grandes: A Technological and Developmental Assessment of Its Origins. In *Culture and Contact: Charles C. DiPeso's Gran Chichimeca,* edited by A. I. Woosley and J. C. Ravesloot, 133–51. Dragoon and Albuquerque: The Amerind Foundation and the University of New Mexico Press.

———. 1998. Innovation and Diffusion of Sand- and Gravel-Mulch Agriculture in the American Southwest: A Product of the Eruption of Sunset Crater. *Quaternaire* 9: 61–69.

———. 2000. *Cultivated Landscapes of Native North America.* Oxford: Oxford University Press.

———. 2004. Permanent vs. Shifting Cultivation in Eastern Woodlands of North American prior to European Contact. *Agriculture and Human Values* 21: 181–89.

———. 2006. An Epilogue and Bibliographic Supplement to *Canal Irrigation in Prehistoric Mexico: The Sequence of Technological Change. Mono y Conejo* 4: 3–15.

Doolittle, W. E., and J. A. Neely, eds. 2004. *The Safford Valley Grids: Prehistoric Cultivation in the Southern Arizona Desert.* Anthropological Papers of the University of Arizona 70. Tucson: University of Arizona Press.

Doolittle, W. E., J. A. Neely, and M. D. Pool. 1993. A Method for Distinguishing between Prehistoric and Recent Water and Soil Control Features. *Kiva* 59: 7–25.

Fenn, E. 2001. *Pox Americana: The Great Smallpox Epidemic, 1775–82.* New York: Hill and Wang.

Ferndon, E. N. 1959. Agricultural Potential and the Development of Cultures. *Southwestern Journal of Anthropology* 15: 1–19.

Fish, S. K., P. R. Fish, C. Miksicek, and J. H. Madson. 1985. Prehistoric Agave Cultivation in Arizona. *Desert Plants* 7: 107–113.

Gallagher, J. P. 1992. Prehistoric Field Systems in the Upper Midwest. In *Late Prehistoric Agriculture: Observations from the Midwest,* edited by W. I. Woods, 95–135. Studies in Illinois Archaeology 8. Springfield: Illinois Historic Preservation Agency.

Gartner, W. G. 2003. Raised Field Landscapes of Native North America. Unpublished PhD diss., University of Wisconsin, Madison.

Hack, J. T. 1942. *The Changing Physical Environment of the Hopi Indians of Arizona*. Papers of the Peabody Museum of American Archaeology and Ethnology 35, no. 1. Cambridge, MA: Harvard University Press.

Harvey, D. 1969. *Explanation in Geography*. London: Edward Arnold.

Herold, L. C. 1965. *Trincheras and Physical Environment along the Rio Gavilan, Chihuahua, Mexico*. Publications in Geography 65–1. Denver: Department of Geography, University of Denver.

Hirshberg, R. I., and J. F. Hirshberg. 1957. Meggars' Law of Environmental Limitation on Culture. *American Anthropologist* 59: 890–92.

Holmberg, A. R. 1969. *Nomads of the Longbow: The Siriono of Eastern Bolivia*. New York: Natural History Press.

Kalm, P. 1972. *Travels into North America*. Translated by J. R. Forster. Barre, MA: Imprint Society.

Krech, S., III. 1999. *The Ecological Indian: Myth and History*. New York: W. W. Norton.

Lightfoot, D., and F. W. Eddy. 1995. The Construction and Configuration of Anasazi Pebble-Mulch Gardens in the Northern Rio Grande. *American Antiquity* 60: 459–70.

Lovell, W. G. 1992. "Heavy Shadows and Black Night": Disease and Depopulation in Colonial Spanish America. *Annals of the Association of American Geographers* 82: 426–43.

Mann, C. C. 2005. *1491: New Revelations of the Americas before Columbus*. New York: Vintage Books.

Martin, C. 1981. The American Indian as Miscast Ecologist. *The History Teacher* 14: 243–52.

Masse, W. B. 1981. Prehistoric Irrigation Systems in the Salt River Valley. *Science* 214: 408–15.

Mathewson, K., and M. S. Kenzer, eds. 2003. *Culture, Land, and Legacy: Perspectives on Carl Sauer and Berkeley School Geography*. Baton Rouge, LA: Geoscience Publications.

Maxwell, T. D., and K. F. Anschuetz. 1992. The Southwestern Ethnographic Record and Prehistoric Agricultural Diversity. In *Gardens of Prehistory: The Archaeology of Settlement Agriculture in Greater Mesoamerica*, edited by T. W. Killion, 35–68. Tuscaloosa: University of Alabama Press.

Mecham, J. L. 1927. *Francisco de Ibarra and Nueva Vizcaya*. Durham, NC: Duke University Press.

Meggers, B. J. 1954. Environmental Limitation on the Development of Culture. *American Anthropologist* 56: 801–24.

Myers, M. D. 2002. Which Way to Till This Field? The Cultural Selection of Surface Form in the Rise and Fall of Cultivation Ridges in Northwestern Europe. *Journal of Cultural Geography* 19: 65–94.

Obregón, B. 1928. *Obregón's History of 16th Century Explorations in Western America Entitled Chronicle, Commentary, or Relation of the Ancient and Modern Discoveries in New Spain and New Mexico, Mexico, 1584*. Translated, edited, and annotated by G. P. Hammond and A. Rey. Los Angeles, CA: Wetzel.

Olwig, K. R. 1996. Recovering the Substantive Nature of Landscape. *Annals of the Association of American Geographers* 86: 630–53.

Pyne, S. J. 1982. *Fire in America: A Cultural History of Wildland and Rural Fire*. Princeton, NJ: Princeton University Press.

Redman, C. L. 2001. *Human Impact on Ancient Environments*. Tucson: University of Arizona Press.

Riley, T. J., and G. Freimuth. 1977. Field Systems and Frost Drainage in the Prehistoric Agriculture of the Upper Great Lakes. *American Antiquity* 44: 271–85.

Sale, K. 1991. *The Conquest of Paradise: Christopher Columbus and the Columbian Legacy*. New York: Alfred A. Knopf.

Smith, J. 1910. The Sixth Voyage: To Another Part of Virginia. In *Travels and Works of Captain John Smith*, edited by E. Arber, 343–82. New York: Burt Franklin.

Spencer, J. E. 1976. What's in a Name—the Berkeley School. *Historical Geography Newsletter* 6: 7–11.

Thompson, D. Q., and R. H. Smith. 1971. The Forest Primeval in the Northeast—a Great Myth? In *Proceedings of the Annual Tall Timbers Fire Ecology Conference*, 255–265. Tallahassee, FL: Tall Timbers Research Station.

Turner, B. L., II, and W. E. Doolittle. 1978. The Concept and Measure of Agricultural Intensity. *Professional Geographer* 30: 297–301.

Turner, B. L., II, R. Q. Hanham, and A. V. Portararo. 1977. Population Pressure and Agricultural Intensity. *Annals of the Association of American Geographers* 67: 384–96.

Whitehead, A. N. 1925. *An Enquiry Concerning the Principles of Natural Knowledge*. Cambridge: Cambridge University Press.

Whitmore, T. M. 1996. Population Geography of Calamity: The 16th and 17th Century Yucatán. *International Journal of Population Geography* 2: 291–311.

Wilson, G. L. 1917. Agriculture of the Hidatsa Indians: An Indian Interpretation. *Studies in the Social Sciences* 9. Minneapolis: University of Minnesota.

Zimmerer, K. S. 1995. The Origins of Andean Irrigation. *Nature* 378: 481–83.

2

North America's Colonial European Roots, 1492 to 1867

Jeffrey S. Smith

At the turn of the twenty-first century, the majorities of the U.S. and Canadian populations were overwhelmingly of European origin. In fact, 62.6 percent of all people in the United States and 90.2 percent of all Canadians could trace their individual ancestries back to Europe (Brittingham and de la Cruz 2004; Statcan 2007). Within the United States, people of German background comprise the largest ancestral group, followed by the Irish, English/British, Italian, and Polish (table 2.1). Within Canada, for the most part, the same European ancestral groups

Table 2.1. Ten Largest Ancestral Groups in the United States (2000) and Canada (2001)

United States (2000[a])		Canada (2001)	
Ancestral Group	Percentage of the Population	Ancestral Group	Percentage of the Population
Total population	281,421,906		31,050,700
German	15.2	Canadian	37.6
Irish	10.8	English/British	19.3
English/British	9.1	French	15.0
African American	8.8	Scottish	13.4
American	7.2	Irish	12.3
Mexican	6.5	German	8.8
Italian	5.6	Italian	4.1
Polish	3.2	Chinese	3.5
French	3.0	Ukrainian	3.4
North American Indian	2.8	North American Indian	3.2
Percentage of the population with European ancestry	62.6		90.2

Source: Brittingham and de la Cruz 2004; Statcan 2007.

[a] The year 2000 marked the last census for which the U.S. government asked its population to identify their ethnic or ancestral background.

are well represented (English/British, Scottish, Irish, and German). The notable difference, however, is Canada's much larger French population. The dominant European populations within both countries are excellent examples of host societies.[1] The central question this chapter asks is, How did North America (United States and Canada) become dominated by a stock population that is so overwhelmingly European in origin? To answer that question we must go back five hundred years and chart the pattern of North America's European settlement. Furthermore, because historical geographers seek to understand processes and spatial variability, this chapter provides answers to such queries as, Which leading European groups first settled the lands we now know as the United States and Canada? How did the major colonial European powers differ in their intended use of North American lands? And how did those uses influence settlement patterns? Unfortunately, this chapter only partially answers its central question. Subsequent chapters will provide a more contemporary and complete explanation.

EUROPEAN CONTEXT FOR EXPLORATION

Historical records indicate that Europeans first set foot on North American soil in the late 900s. Leif Ericson, the most famous of the Viking Norsemen who traversed the north Atlantic, sailed west in 1000 CE from Greenland to present-day Newfoundland and perhaps to the shores of modern-day New England. Over the course of three hundred years, a series of settlements (including L'Anse aux Meadows) dotted a vast Viking territory. By 1347 Nordic seafarers had abandoned the outposts, most likely because of the great distance from Greenland and Iceland as well as the inhospitable climate. Europeans would not set foot on North American soil again for another 150 years.

Europe's discovery of the New World was largely the culmination of a series of fortuitous events both within and outside its boundaries (Boal and Royle 1999). First, as the spirit of the Renaissance and the Age of Discovery swept over Europe, royal leaders funded explorations to uncharted lands hoping to find abundant riches. Second, centuries of ethnic and religious conflict both domestically (e.g., Spanish expulsion of the Moors from Iberia) and abroad (e.g., the Crusades in Southwest Asia) gave European powers hard-won skills and a heightened confidence that emboldened them on their ventures to previously unknown parts of the world.[2] Third, northern and western Europeans' growing fondness for exotic spices and merchandise originating in the Spice Islands (Indonesia), China, and India encouraged them to find a new passage to Southeast Asia. Last, as a handful of European monarchs gradually wrested authority from local feudal lords and modern nation-states emerged, a new economic mind-set swept across Europe. Mercantilism[3] became the guiding force that steered the decisions of Europe's rulers. As life under the modern nation-states became more secure, landed elites also looked to expand their wealth by investing their riches in joint-stock companies (precursors to modern-day corporations), which they hoped would return handsome dividends. These events and transformations unfolding within Europe set the stage for the discovery of the New World.

James Vance (1970) and Donald Meinig (1986) explain that Europe's interaction with the New World progressed in three main stages (figure 2.1). Stage I (exploration) involves the general search for information and new knowledge. Spain led the way when it commissioned the four voyages of Christopher Columbus (1492 to 1506). Shortly thereafter, the British funded a series of expeditions also in search of a shortcut to the Orient. Their list of notable explorers begins with John Cabot, who sailed from the British Isles to the shores of Newfoundland in 1497. Not to be outdone by their archenemy, the French also sent explorers to the New World, including Giovanni da Verrazzano (1523) and Jacques Cartier (1534). Each successive voyage improved European geographic understanding of North America.

As Europe's leaders' and adventurers' comprehension of the New World came into focus, their perspective changed as well. No longer was North America simply an obstacle on the way to the Orient; it held its own potential as a source of wealth. This marks the beginning of Stage II (fixation) (figure 2.1). After establishing an initial settlement to serve as an entrepôt,[4] European investors began looking to the interior of the continent for riches (particularly gold and silver). Unfortunately, the vast stores of gold found among the Aztecs did not materialize farther north. Instead, animal products (cod and beaver pelts) and timber became valued commodities. Settlers sent these back to Europe in exchange for supplies and manufactured goods that would sustain the New World's small population.

Over time the trade became incredibly diverse and evolved into what is now referred to as the Columbian Exchange[5] (Crosby 1972). Goods and merchandise previously seen as exotic eventually helped revolutionize societies throughout the world. For example, the Americas offered maize (corn), potatoes, tomatoes, beans, chilies, and cacao (chocolate), all of which greatly diversified diets throughout the Eastern Hemisphere. Not all of the exchanges were benevolent, however. Europeans introduced communicable diseases, including malaria, measles, and smallpox, to which the indigenous population had no natural immunity. Within a century of first European contact, nearly 90 percent of Indians had perished. Even more important than the exchange of goods and merchandise was the blending of cultures. Countless European men (especially Spanish and French) reproduced with indigenous women, creating an entirely new segment of New World society.[6] We cannot overestimate the magnitude of this exchange between the hemispheres (Crosby 1972).

In the third and final stage (colonial expansion), European governments began populating the New World. A series of settlements (towns, villages, or outposts) radiated out from a port of entry in a classic dendritic pattern that followed along trade or transportation routes (figure 2.1). Gradually the colonial population expanded into the hinterland. During this stage, the leading colonial European governments differed greatly in their regard for the New World. The varying imperial objectives help explain not only the different settlement patterns but also the foundation of modern-day Anglo North America's population composition. The remainder of this chapter looks at the three major European powers, beginning with the Spanish, followed by the French, and finishing with the British.

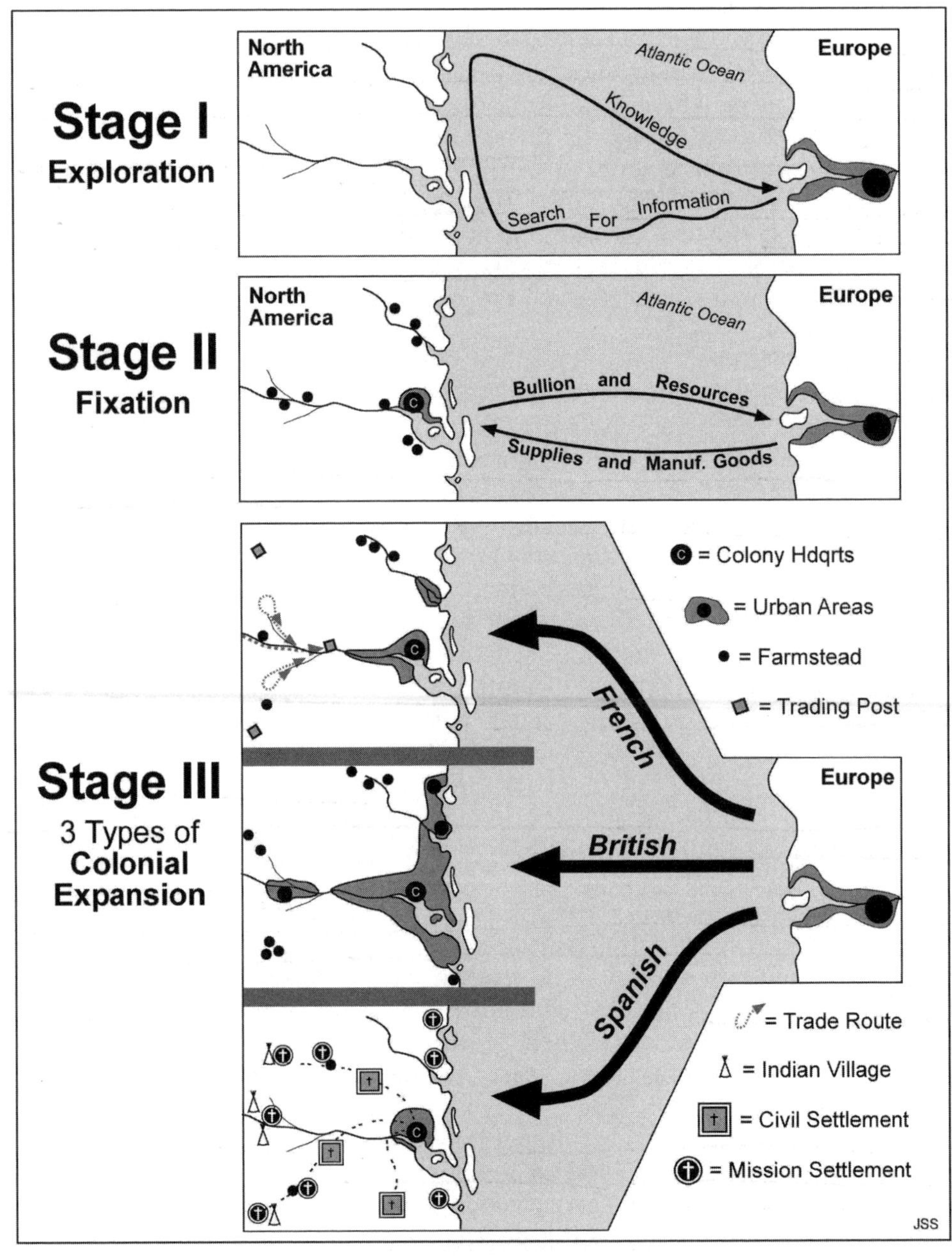

Figure 2.1. Three stages of mercantilism in colonial North America. Adapted from Vance (1970) and Meinig (1986).

EUROPEAN COLONIAL SETTLEMENTS

New Spain

In the years following Christopher Columbus's first voyage, Spain's presence in the Caribbean basin expanded rapidly (Sauer 1966). By 1515 Spain had established its colonial seat of power in Havana, Cuba, and exploration of the North American mainland proceeded at a fairly rapid pace. By 1520 Hernando Cortes's army had toppled the Aztec ruler (Moctezuma II), secured the vast stores of gold, and converted Tenochtitlan, the Aztec capital, into Spain's own capital city (Mexico City), which served as the seat of government or viceroyalty of New Spain.

From Mexico City various expeditions headed north to explore Spain's newly acquired lands and search for more wealth. During his search for the Seven Cities of Cibola, the fabled cities of gold, Francisco Vasquez de Coronado's travels in 1540 took him through present-day New Mexico and Colorado and as far northeast as Kansas. The information he and other Spanish explorers gathered helped open four main areas of northern New Spain to permanent settlement: coastal Florida, the upper Rio Grande, the lower Rio Grande, and coastal California (figure 2.2).

As convoys of Spanish galleons carried bullion from Havana to Spain, the Spanish crown established the fortified settlement of St. Augustine (1565) in present-day Florida to guard against piracy and resupply the ships' crews (figure 2.2). It is Spain's most lasting legacy on the Atlantic coast and North America's oldest European-founded settlement (Bolton 1921). Beginning in 1573 Franciscan missionaries extended Spain's influence north, founding mission Santa Elena, and west toward modern-day Alabama. None of these settlements was altogether successful. When captured by British forces in 1763, the weakly held fort at St. Augustine had only thirty-five hundred occupants. Twenty years later Britain gave it back to Spain, which retained control until 1819, when Spain ceded all of Florida to the United States under the Adams-Onis Treaty. Overall, Spain's imprint on Florida's landscape was very small.

Spain's impact on the landscape to the west was more lasting and consisted of three main northerly thrusts (Spicer 1962; Weber 1992). Juan de Oñate led the first prong in 1598 when he guided 129 soldiers (plus their families) and twenty priests north from Zacatecas to settle among local Indians at a community he named San Juan de los Caballeros (Barrett 2012) (figure 2.3). By 1607 the vanguard Spanish settlers had grown discontent with life in such an arid environment with few prospects of becoming rich. When Spanish authorities recalled Oñate on charges of mistreating the local Indians, the seat of government relocated to Santa Fe (the oldest capital city in the present-day United States), where many settlers had already moved. Santa Fe (1609) became Nuevo Mexico's most important community and the only Spanish settlement to reach the size and importance to merit the term *villa* (town).

From Santa Fe, Spanish authorities slowly expanded their presence throughout the upper Rio Grande region, providing religious guidance to the local Indian populations and securing Spain's northern frontier. By 1629 the core of Spanish influence extended along the Camino Real down the Rio Grande to Paso del Norte (present-day El Paso, Texas). Through a process described by Richard

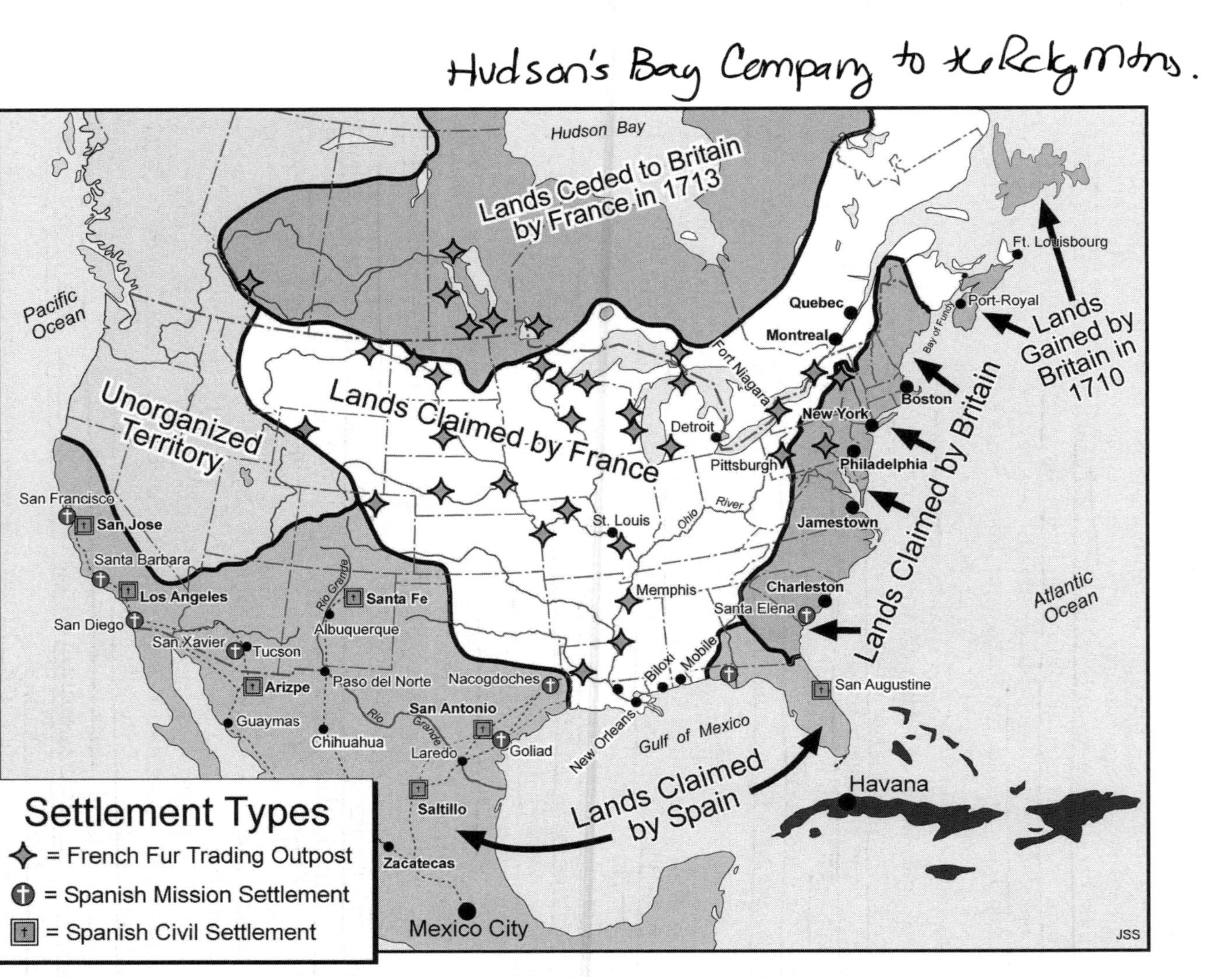

Figure 2.2. **European land claims in North America, 1763. U.S. states and Canadian provinces provided for reference only. Cartography by Jeffrey S. Smith.**

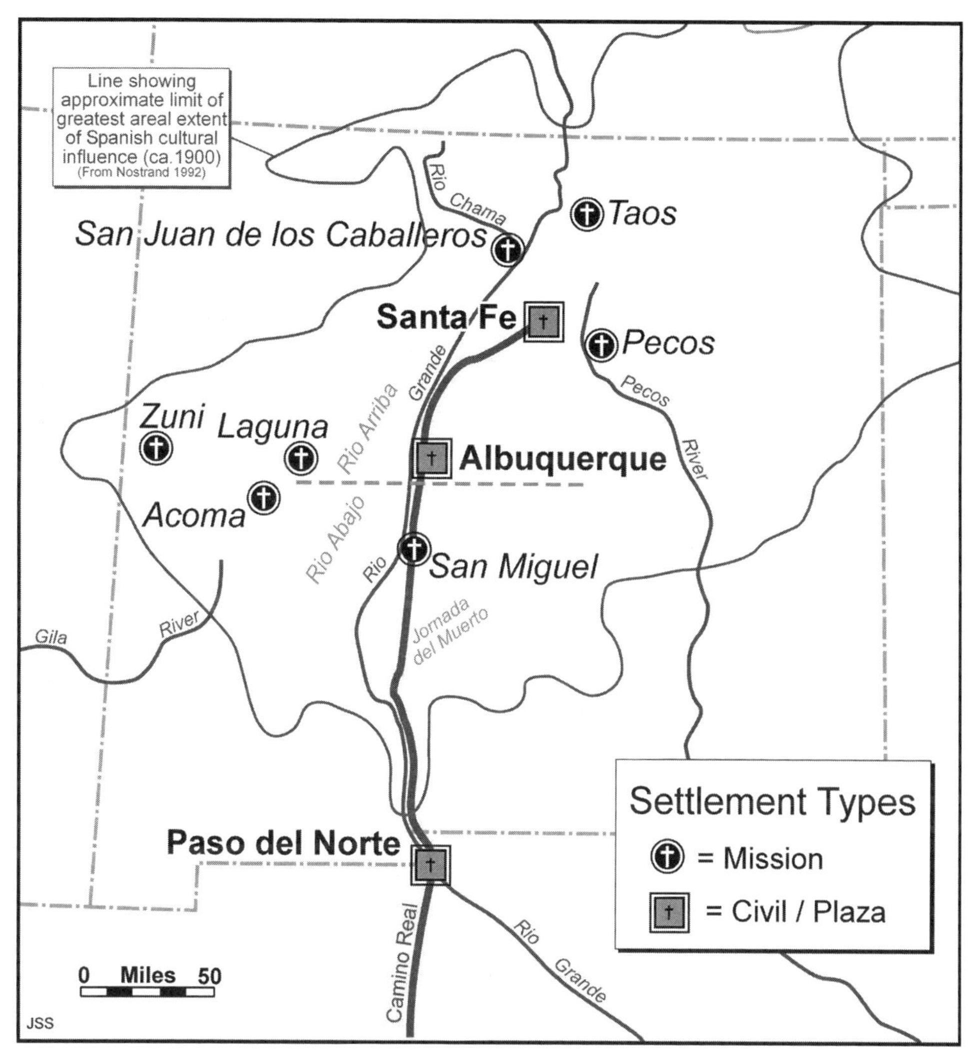

Figure 2.3. Colonial Spanish settlements in the upper Rio Grande region, ca. 1750. U.S. states provided for reference only. Cartography by Jeffrey S. Smith.

Nostrand (1992) as splinter diffusion,[7] Spanish missionaries and Castilian settlers steadily extended Spain's reach in all four cardinal directions. Alburquerque (1706; the U.S. government later dropped the first *r*) became the principal population center of the *rio abajo* (downstream region). The primary zone of expansion, however, was the *rio arriba* (upstream region) to the north. Spanish families settled in valley after valley, eventually reaching present-day south-central Colorado in 1851 (Smith 1999). At its greatest areal extent in 1900, the zone of Spain's cultural influence covered an area the size of the state of Utah and spilled onto the high plains of Oklahoma and Texas, west into Arizona, and north into southern Colorado (figure 2.3).

The second major thrust north by Spain into modern Anglo America occurred in Tejas (Texas) (figure 2.4). As French fur trappers and traders increased their presence in the Mississippi River basin in the 1680s, Spain felt compelled to secure its northeastern borderlands from encroachment. By 1690 Spanish officials had begun encouraging Spain's citizens to settle on lands within the Mississippi and Red River drainage areas. In tit-for-tat fashion, each new settlement by one country prompted a corresponding settlement by the other. For example, when France established Natchitoches in 1714 on the eastern side of the Red River, Spain countered with Los Adaes and Nacogdoches in 1716 (figure 2.4). Eventually, Spain's settlements became concentrated in three main complexes all linked by the eastern branch of the Camino Real (Nacogdoches, San Antonio de Bexar [1718], and Goliad [1749]) (Meinig 1969). As the threat from France diminished in the middle of the eighteenth century, Spain moved its provincial capital from Los Adaes to San Antonio because the area appeared more conducive to population growth. From there Spain established a series of mission settlements throughout the lower Rio Grande region. In 1819, under the Adams-Onis Treaty, the Sabine River became the international boundary between Spanish territories and the United States. Two years later Mexico gained its independence from a weakened Spanish government. Tejas entered a new era in its history, and Spain's time under the Texas sun came to an end.

The final thrust of Spanish influence in modern Anglo North America occurred along the Pacific coast (figure 2.5). After moderate success by Father Eusebio Kino in establishing mission settlements among the Pima Indians in northern Sonora and southern Arizona, Spain shifted its attention to the northwest coast (Meinig 1971). To address the steady encroachment of Russian fur traders upon its lands, the Spanish crown established numerous *mission* (religious), *plaza* (civil), and *presidio* (fortress) settlements along a third branch of the Camino Real. Most noteworthy were the twenty-one Franciscan missions, starting with San Diego (1769) in the south and continuing along the Pacific coast to San Luis Obispo (1772), San Francisco (1776), Santa Barbara (1786), and San Jose (1797) (Gentilcore 1961). Not only did the thin ribbon of settlements stem the Russian tide from the north, but the missions helped convert some of the local Indians to Christianity. In fact, Spain focused mainly on attending to the needs of the local Indians since only about three thousand Spaniards were living in coastal California at the time of Mexico's independence in 1821.

Spain's approach to settling its North American lands was stubbornly consistent. It began by exploring the uncharted territory, seeking great concentrations of wealth (especially gold) and collections of Indians to convert to Christianity. Next, Spain moved to secure its far-flung lands with population settlements. Spain's effort to settle Florida was largely unsuccessful; yet in the region between Tejas and California, where a more familiar arid climate prevailed, Spain succeeded in establishing principal administrative centers (e.g., Los Angeles, Santa Fe, and San Antonio) that served as anchors for settlement expansion (both civil and mission) along local trade and transportation routes. However, because distance to Mexico City was great and overland supply trains along the Camino Real were intermittent at best, few Spaniards were willing to settle on Spain's

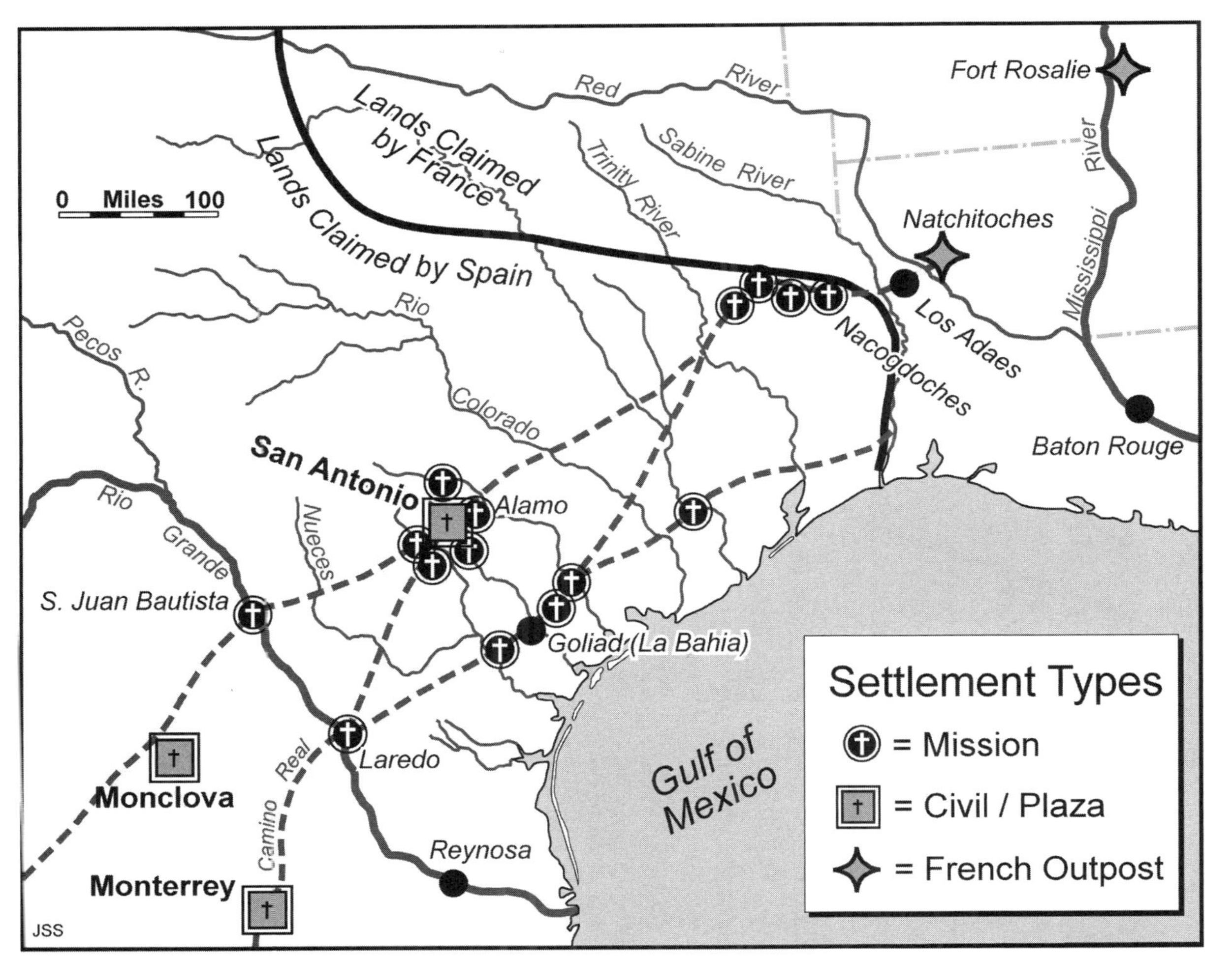

Figure 2.4. **Colonial Spanish settlements in the lower Rio Grande region, 1820. U.S. states provided for reference only. Cartography by Jeffrey S. Smith.**

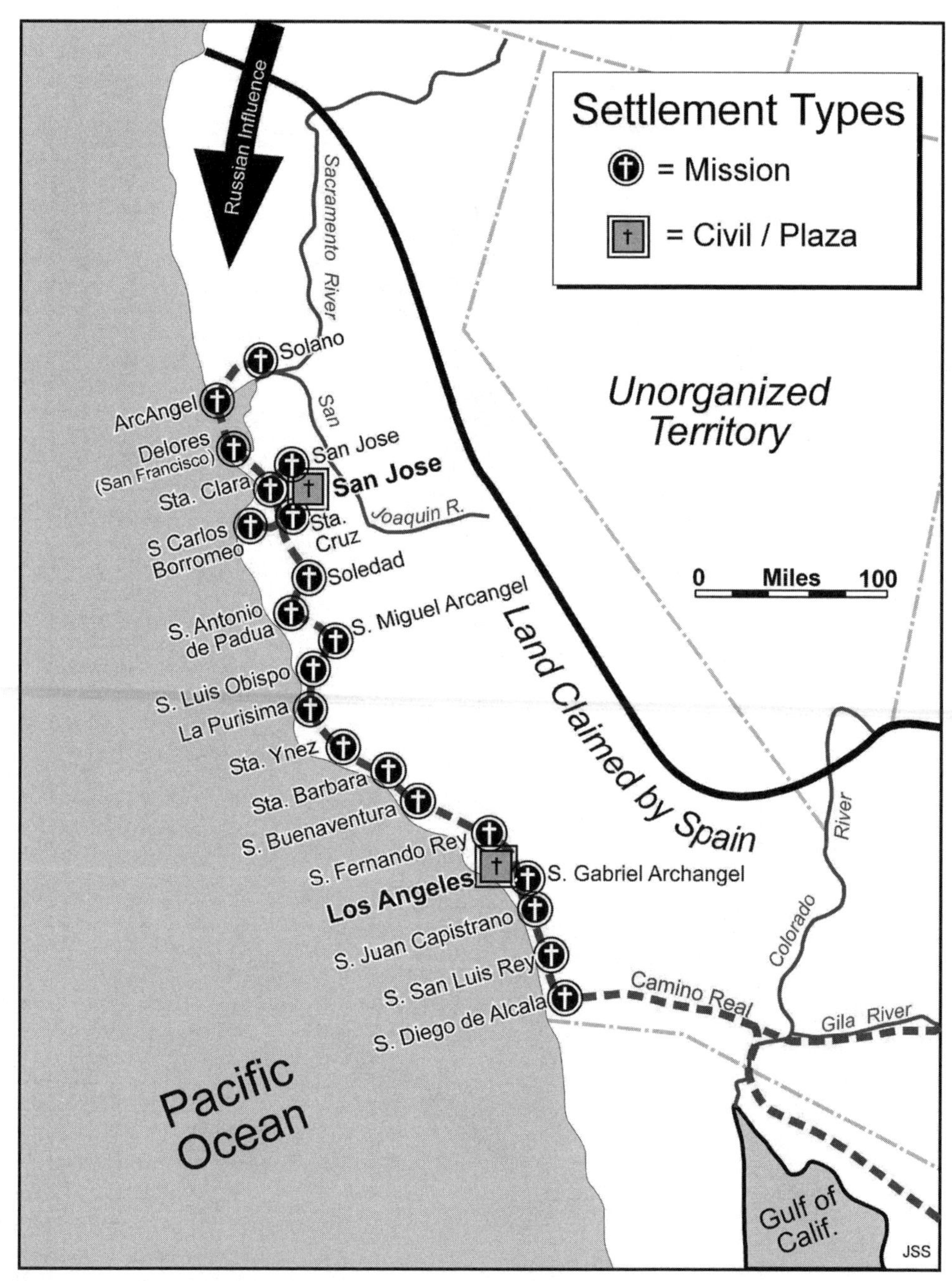

Figure 2.5. Colonial Spanish settlements in Alta California, 1820. U.S. states provided for reference only. Cartography by Jeffrey S. Smith.

northern frontier. Thus, the land remained thinly populated, and most settlements were largely self-sufficient. When the U.S. government began assuming political control of the borderland region in 1845, it encountered a culture dating back to colonial Spain (Nostrand 1992; Stoddard, Nostrand, and West 1983; Arreola 2002). That culture has served as host to all subsequent peoples entering the region.

New France

Notwithstanding Britain's discovery of rich fishing waters off the coast of Newfoundland (now known as the Grand Banks) in 1497, France showed little interest in the New World. Instead, France was striving to find a shortcut to Asia. Beginning in 1523 the king of France commissioned numerous explorers to find that undiscovered passage (e.g., Giovanni da Verrazzano [1523] and Jacques Cartier [1534–1541]), but to no avail. Aside from the rich cod fishing waters off the coast of Labrador, there was little to hold the French government's interest (Trudel 1973). Had it not been for French merchants who agreed to establish permanent settlements in exchange for exclusive fishing and fur-trading rights, France probably would have withdrawn its presence from the New World (Finlay and Sprague 1999).

King Henry IV's perspective changed in 1604 when he realized that he could use France's lands across the Atlantic to resettle the French Huguenots (Protestants) who were being persecuted in Catholic-dominated France. With his support the Huguenots planted the city of Port Royal (present-day Annapolis, Nova Scotia) on the Bay of Fundy (figure 2.2). In 1608, Samuel de Champlain ("Father of New France") founded the city of Quebec on the St. Lawrence River, and by 1642 French settlers had established Trois Rivieres and Montreal farther upstream. As settlement expanded, the French developed an alliance with the local Algonquin and Huron Indians, enabling hundreds of *voyageurs* to develop a dense fur-trading network. In 1663 King Louis XIV made New France a royal province and officially declared all the lands extending to the eastern bank of the Mississippi River French.

By the 1680s, French trappers and traders had extended France's influence upstream well beyond the Great Lakes, down the Mississippi River to the Gulf of Mexico, west toward modern Manitoba and Saskatchewan, and up the Missouri, Platte, and Arkansas Rivers to the Rocky Mountains. As the beaver trade extended farther into the interior, France needed outposts to store equipment, supplies, and pelts during the winter months (figure 2.2). They built a series of fortified settlements in the continent's interior, including Fort Niagara (1678), Cahokia (St. Louis, 1698), Biloxi (1699), Fort Detroit (1701), Mobile (1702), Fort Assumption (Memphis, 1739), and Fort Duquesne (Pittsburgh, 1754). In 1718 a settlement fortress at present-day New Orleans served the twofold purpose of discouraging Spanish ships from sailing up the Mississippi and acting as entrepôt for all upriver territory (Finlay and Sprague 1999). The vast French empire resembled a crescent spanning much of North America (Warkentin and Harris 1991); yet it was thinly populated and would prove difficult to defend when invaded by a foreign army.

In 1700 New France's population distribution was distinctly bifurcated, with most of its colonists concentrated along the St. Lawrence River from Quebec to Montreal (totaling roughly thirteen thousand people). The Acadian region around the Bay of Fundy was much smaller, with approximately fifteen hundred people, most of them farmers. Although the fur trade needed urban centers where pelts could be deposited, the trade network contributed little to urban growth because most of the goods were sent directly back to the lucrative markets in Europe. Quebec and Montreal were little more than small, preindustrial towns. In fact, the French settlers purchased most of the materials needed for construction from New England rather than producing them locally.

New France's greatest challenge was protecting its vast territory from foreign encroachment and effectively controlling its shipping lanes. Quebec and Montreal helped regulate trade along the St. Lawrence River, New Orleans controlled trade up the Mississippi River, and Detroit served as entrepôt for the Great Lakes region. In 1717 France built Fort Louisbourg at the mouth of the St. Lawrence River to serve as principal trade center between New France and the mother country.

At the midpoint of the eighteenth century, France's position along the St. Lawrence valley seemed secure. Although British loyalists from New England captured Port Royal in Acadia from the French in 1710 and the British gained control of all lands surrounding Hudson Bay under the Treaty of Utrecht (1713), France had the New World's largest military fort (Fort Louisbourg), the largest military presence, the strongest alliance with the local Indians, and control of strategic access points to the vast interior of the continent. Over seven short years, however, things would change rapidly for French interests in the New World.

The biggest source of contention between French and British interests rested on who controlled the Ohio River valley (figure 2.2), which France coveted because it served as the linchpin for its vast trading empire. The British saw the Ohio River valley as the natural extension of westward settlement.

In 1754, Lieutenant Colonel George Washington's attack on Fort Duquesne started the French and Indian War (also called the Seven Years' War in Europe), which pitted France, Spain, Austria, and Russia against Britain and Prussia (Finlay and Sprague 1999). Fearing a French insurrection in Acadia, in 1755 British officials expelled nearly four thousand people. The French Acadians scattered all over Anglo North America, some landing as far south as present-day Louisiana (their descendants are known today as Cajuns). In 1758 the British captured Fort Louisbourg and gained control of the mouth of the St. Lawrence River. By 1760 both Quebec and Montreal had succumbed to British forces. At the Treaty of Paris (1763), France gave the Louisiana Territory to Spain and ceded nearly all of its North American colonies to Britain. As part of the treaty, Britain agreed to honor the religious, political, and social freedoms of the French-speaking population (later known as the Quebec Act of 1774).

The final chapter of colonial Canada was written after the Napoleonic Wars in Europe (1803 to 1815). Because the United States placed restrictions on British immigration, British North America (present-day Canada) became a viable alternative, attracting as many as eight hundred thousand immigrants (mainly from

ON MAPS AND MAPPING

Stephen J. Hornsby

In his presidential address to the Association of American Geographers in 1956, distinguished American geographer Carl Sauer ruminated on "the education of a geographer." "The first . . . most primitive and persistent trait" of being a geographer, he thought, "is liking maps and thinking by means of them. We are empty-handed without them in the lecture room, in the study, in the field. Show me a geographer who does not need them constantly and want them about him, and I shall have my doubts as to whether he has made the right choice of life." For many geographers, the sheer pleasure and intellectual interest of maps is a persistent trait, even if many of our maps today are digital rather than printed. The discipline's continuing concern with maps and presenting information visually remains one of its distinguishing marks.

My own interest in maps developed over time and now follows two somewhat interrelated paths. Since my undergraduate days, I have been interested in creating visual texts that combine maps and images to capture the look of a landscape, place, or region. I have done this in books about Cape Breton Island and the colonial British Atlantic world and, more recently, in a historical atlas of Maine. There is nothing especially original in such visual presentation; it has a long and distinguished history in the discipline. But I do think that geographers have a disciplinary responsibility to produce clear, effective maps and to ground their studies visually in particular environmental contexts.

My second interest has been in the history of mapmaking, specifically the topographic mapping done by the British army and navy along the northeastern seaboard of North America in the 1760s and early 1770s. Probably the biggest "big science" project of their day, the surveys were forerunners of the scientific mapping later undertaken by the British Ordnance Survey and Admiralty Hydrographic Office. Most recently, I've turned to studying American pictorial mapping of the mid-twentieth century. In stark contrast to utilitarian scientific maps, American pictorial maps grew out of the vibrancy and creativity of popular culture. Pictorial maps recorded history, memory, landscape, and architecture, all cultural elements that help make up the genius loci, or spirit, of a place. These richly decorative maps challenge us to think about what defines a map. All these various ways of creating and looking at maps are fundamentally about presenting information visually and accessibly and thereby educating people about their world.

the British Isles) as part of the Great British Migration (1815 to 1850). Two of the largest immigrant groups were the Highland Scots and the Irish. The Highland Scots migrated to Canada after the forces of industrialization dispossessed them of their lands due to the increased mechanization of agricultural practices. A sizable number of Irish immigrated to Canada following eviction from their land, high unemployment, and the potato famine from 1845 to 1852. Of the approximately one hundred thousand Irish who arrived in Canada in 1847, roughly thirty-five thousand landed in Toronto, where they quickly overwhelmed the existing population of twenty thousand citizens. Prior to the Great British Migration, French Canadians were clearly the host society, as they significantly outnumbered their English-speaking counterparts. After 1850, however, the British population was much larger and effectively became the host society. Relations between the British- and French-speaking populations have been strained ever since.

In 1864 the Quebec Conference brought together delegates from the English-speaking (upper Canada) and French-speaking (lower Canada) parts of British North America. On July 1, 1867, the union of three British North American colonies led to establishment of the dominion of Canada and effectively ended the colonial era of Anglo North America. Canada became a self-governing state, with Ontario (formerly upper Canada), Quebec (lower Canada), New Brunswick, and Nova Scotia as its first four provinces.

French settlements in colonial North America were distinctly different from those of their Spanish cousins. Instead of seeking to secure their territory against foreign aggression, the French showed more interest in extracting wealth from whatever local resources they could plunder (e.g., fishing and fur trading). Despite laying claim to a vast territory, the French never developed large population centers in the interior of the continent. Instead, their interior settlements tended to be relatively small, extending along trade and transportation routes, while their larger centers served mainly as break-in-bulk sites for shipping goods back to Europe. Clearly, colonial New France did not move far beyond the fixation stage (figure 2.1). As a result, when foreign invaders encroached upon their lands, they were ill equipped to defend themselves.

British North America

Sandwiched between French lands to the north (Nova Scotia to the St. Lawrence River) and Spanish territory to the south (Florida) (figure 2.2), British settlement started in 1607 at Jamestown (Virginia) under the banner of the Virginia Company of London. Poorly situated at the mouth of the Chesapeake Bay (figure 2.6) and plagued with repeated disasters, the fledgling settlement survived in geographic isolation until the Dutch arrived in 1614 and established fur-trading claims along the Hudson River valley (Cronon 1983). A decade later, Virginia became one of Britain's prized possessions because of local farmers' success raising and exporting tobacco (Earle 1977).

In 1620 the settlement pattern of British North America changed dramatically when various groups of Europeans arrived seeking religious tolerance and a new life free of poverty. First to come ashore were the Puritans (Pilgrims) from

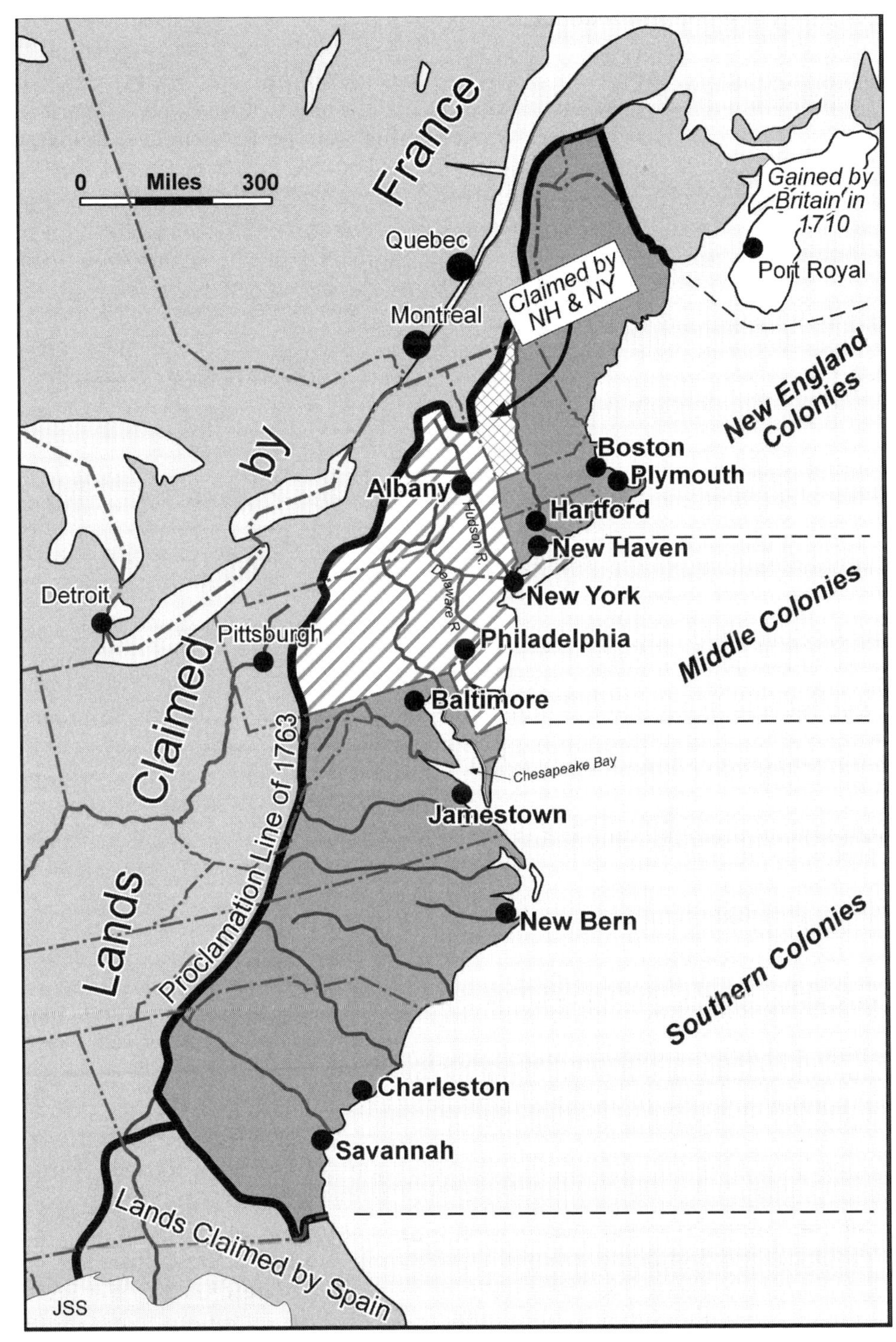

Figure 2.6. Lands claimed by Britain, 1763. U.S. states provided for reference only. Cartography by Jeffrey S. Smith.

Britain and Holland who founded the Plymouth Colony (1620) and Boston's Massachusetts Bay Colony (1628) (figure 2.6). With an economy based on fishing, fur trading, and shipbuilding, the Massachusetts Bay Colony grew to become New England's largest and most important, eventually controlling lands throughout New England as far north as present-day Maine (Harrison and Judd 2011). However, deeming Massachusetts too influential in the New World, King Charles II created New Hampshire as a separate royal colony in 1679. Due to the Puritans' strict lifestyle, dissension was common. Beginning in 1635 a series of groups left the fold and founded other settlements, including Hartford (1635), Rhode Island (1636), and New Haven (1638). In 1662 the Crown joined Hartford and New Haven under the Connecticut charter (Wood 1997).

As early as the 1620s, other Europeans began encroaching upon lands claimed by Britain, particularly in the area later known as the Middle Colonies (figure 2.6). In 1623 John Mason led settlers to the Hudson River, where they purchased the island of Manhattan from local Indians for about $24 and founded New Amsterdam (later New York City). Dutch settlements eventually extended north to Fort Orange (present-day Albany). Between 1638 and 1664, Sweden attempted to secure a foothold along the Atlantic coast by planting two colonies (Fort Christina, 1638, and Fort Gothenburg, 1644) along the Delaware River. Feeling threatened, in 1664 the Dutch seized the Swedish settlements and absorbed the settlers into New Netherland society. Later that same year British forces expelled the Dutch intruders and created the charter colony of New York.

After Quakers had suffered years of persecution in Europe, the British crown granted William Penn (son of a noble, English aristocrat) and his brethren title to land on the Delaware River. When they arrived in 1681 to establish the community of Philadelphia, they found Dutch, Swedish, and Welsh squatters who had fled other colonies. Because the colony emphasized the principles of peace, tolerance, and equality, it attracted farmers and skilled craftsmen from diverse parts of Europe, including Germans (later known as the Pennsylvania Dutch) and the Scotch-Irish from northern Ireland, who escaped years of persecution and trade restrictions in Europe to become accomplished Indian fighters and laborers. Two years after its founding, Philadelphia's population had grown to twenty-five hundred people, and by the turn of the eighteenth century, only Virginia and Massachusetts surpassed it in wealth and population size. Small Quaker settlements grew up adjacent to Pennsylvania in New Jersey (founded in 1664) (Lemon 2001).

In 1634 Lord Baltimore (son of a wealthy Englishman) founded the first of the Southern colonies in Maryland (figure 2.6). Its primary goal was to provide a handsome return for the colony's investors. Much like in Virginia, the success of the Maryland colony hinged upon the cultivation and export of tobacco. Farther south, in 1670 King Charles II granted land to English aristocrats who would provide foodstuffs to support the British sugar plantations in the Caribbean. The Crown saw little connection between Carolina and the other colonies to the north. The British government created Savannah, Georgia (1733), the last of the thirteen original colonies, as a buffer to protect the Carolinas from Spanish and French incursions from the south and west. Both Charleston and Savannah became diverse communities that attracted a wide variety of Europeans, including Germans and Highland Scots.

Within British North America there were three types of colonies: corporate, proprietary, and royal. A corporate colony operated under a charter from the king but was accountable to its stockholders, who sought to turn a profit. Individuals controlled the proprietary colonies after the king issued the land grant. The Crown directly administered all royal colonies. The British founded all thirteen colonies as either corporate or proprietary. By the end of the colonial era (1775), three colonies were still proprietary (Pennsylvania, Delaware, and Maryland), two were corporate (Connecticut and Rhode Island), and the king had assumed direct control over the remaining eight (New Hampshire, Massachusetts, New York, New Jersey, Virginia, North Carolina, South Carolina, and Georgia).

By the mid-seventeenth century the population along the Atlantic coast had grown to just over forty-five thousand. Restricted by the British Proclamation (1763), most colonists lived east of the Appalachian Mountains (figure 2.6). Prior to 1700, living conditions were difficult, and life expectancy was short. Therefore, most population growth was attributed to successive waves of immigrants arriving from Europe. After 1700, European immigration continued, but the colonies had a lower death rate than Europe and a birthrate of nearly 5.5; families began to grow in size. On the eve of the American Revolution (1775), the population of the British colonies stood at 2.5 million people, with about 90 percent of the total population living in rural areas. In contrast to the settlement patterns in French- and Spanish-held lands, the British colonies expanded well beyond principal trade and transportation routes and gained a strong foothold in the interior (figure 2.1).

By 1775, four cities had grown in importance because of their role in trade, transportation, and manufacturing: Philadelphia (approximately forty thousand people), New York City (twenty-five thousand), Boston (sixteen thousand), and Charleston (twelve thousand). Philadelphia became the leading port of entry for newly arriving European immigrants, resulting in higher population densities (as high as forty people per square mile). This also meant that the hinterland serving Philadelphia saw an ever-increasing number of immigrants fan out into the back country, where land was more readily available and less expensive.

Although most of the colonists came from Britain, tens of thousands of other northern Europeans (e.g., Dutch, Germans, Scots, Swiss, Swedes, Finns, Danes) played a key role in settling British North America. As the population grew, notable ethnic enclaves developed throughout the Atlantic coast (figure 2.7). For example, the Dutch settled along the Hudson River, whereas German and Swiss immigrants became concentrated in the greater Delaware River area. In North Carolina, South Carolina, and southern Georgia, a sizable Highland Scots enclave formed. Finally, due in large part to their late arrival and superb fighting skills, the Scotch-Irish settled on the western frontier. When combined, these various populations created the tapestry that formed the foundation of Anglo America's host society. Only by looking at colonial European settlement patterns from a historical geography perspective do we truly come to appreciate the complexity of North American society today.

No mention of HBC!

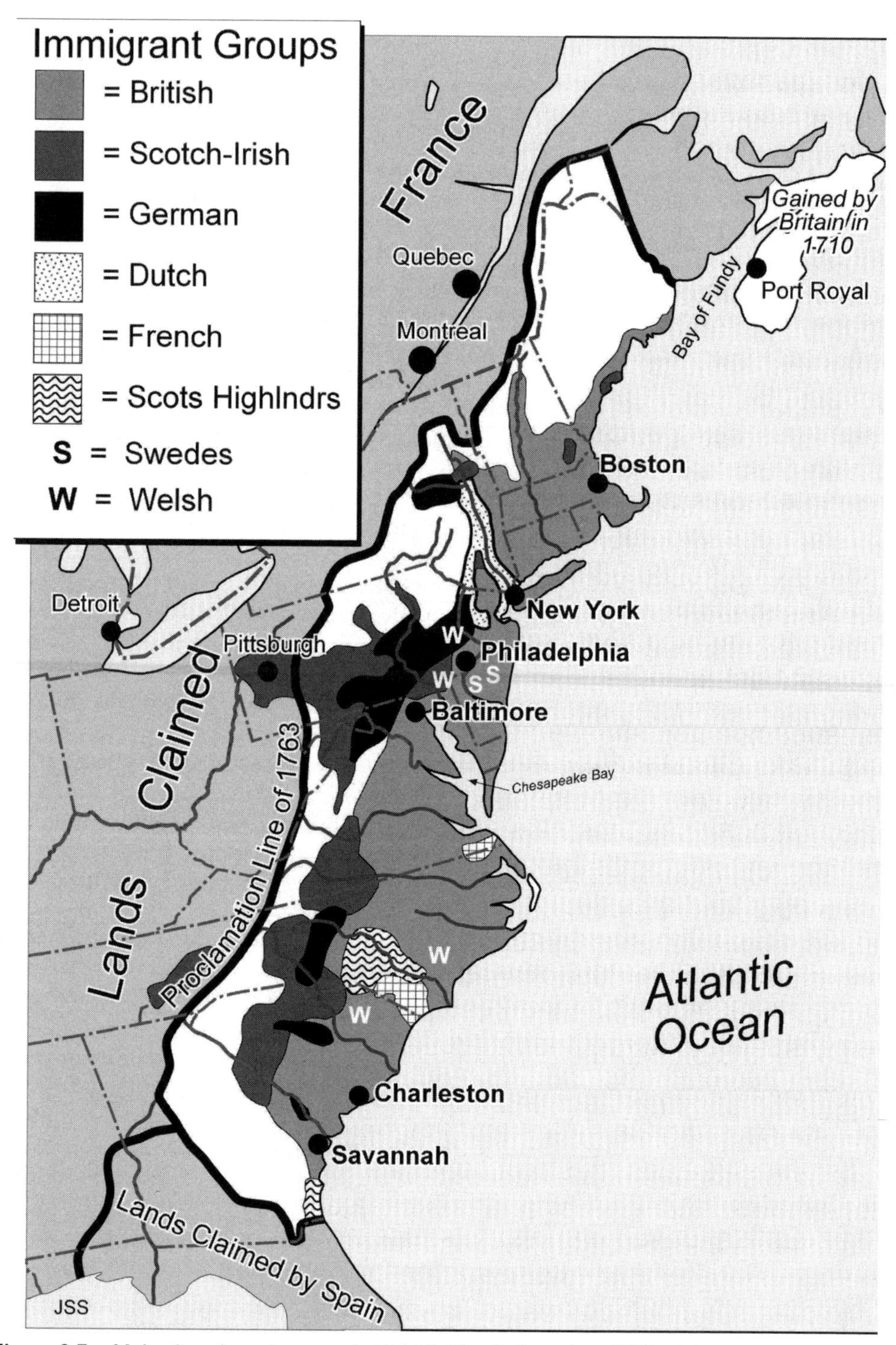

Figure 2.7. Major immigrant groups in British North America, 1775. U.S. states provided for reference only. Cartography by Jeffrey S. Smith.

CONCLUSION

The age of globalization is commonly thought to have started in the 1990s. Affordable long-distance travel and rapid communication via computer have accelerated the exchange of people, goods, and ideas across the globe. However, the first age of globalization began five centuries ago when Europeans began exploring distant lands. Anglo North America, with its huge, relatively uninhabited land, offered European common folk a life free of religious and political persecution and an opportunity to escape entrenched poverty. Today, the United States' and Canada's political, social, and cultural fabric stems from those European group(s) that first settled the land in the late sixteenth and seventeenth centuries. Moreover, these groups created a host society into which subsequent people would integrate. We must keep in mind, however, the differences among the Spanish, French, and British colonial settlement systems. These had a bearing on how lasting their imprints were in Anglo North America.

Instead of encouraging its Spanish and mestizo citizens to relocate, Spain's main strategy in settling its northern frontier involved converting the indigenous population into Spanish citizens (Blake and Smith 2000). As a result, religious missions were Spain's most common settlement type. Concentrated within these religious communities, the Spanish clergy instructed the local Indians on what they considered proper living and the tenants of Christianity. As figure 2.1 shows, this led to a linear, or ribbon, settlement pattern strung out along the principal routes of transportation and communication (e.g., Camino Real). The Spanish crown hoped that eventually the "civilized" Indians would join the ranks of the small but growing Spanish population living in civil settlements around a central plaza. In the 256 years after the founding of St. Augustine, Spain converted relatively few Indians to Christianity. Moreover, with the exception of San Jose, Los Angeles, Santa Fe, Albuquerque, and San Antonio, most of the civil settlements did not grow in size. Spain held a very loose grip on its far-flung northern lands. When Mexico gained its independence in 1821, Spain's direct presence in Anglo North America came to an end.

By comparison, France's chief interest in the New World was the extraction of wealth. No other colonial power was more successful in penetrating the interior of Anglo North America than the French in their pursuit of beaver pelts. They established strings of outposts anchored by settlements placed in strategic geographic locations (e.g., Quebec, Montreal, Detroit, New Orleans). At its height in 1750, France laid claim to over half of North America (from Hudson Bay in the north to the Gulf of Mexico in the south and as far west as the Continental Divide). Yet France's hold on the land was tenuous at best. When the British began carving up French territory in 1713, the small French population was helpless in defending itself against the aggression. As a result, France's zone of influence steadily collapsed to the St. Lawrence Seaway (present-day province of Quebec). By 1800, permanent French settlements were confined to the eastern seaboard in the maritime area (Nova Scotia, Newfoundland, Prince Edward Island, New Brunswick), the St. Lawrence River (Quebec and Montreal), and the northern shores of Lake Ontario and Lake Erie; rural-dwelling Acadians augmented a remnant Creole population in Louisiana. Because France was more committed to acquiring wealth than establishing permanent settlements, it had a fleeting impact on the landscape outside the St. Lawrence River area. Like that of the Spanish, the French settlement structure tended to be linear, this time along waterways that served as their main trade and transportation routes (figure 2.1). The French culture's most enduring legacy was in the province of Quebec. Elsewhere, other northern Europeans (including the British, Highland Scots, and Irish) became dominant.

At first glance, when compared to the vast territories claimed by the Spanish and French, England's colonies along the Atlantic seaboard from present-day Maine to coastal Georgia seemed paltry. Moreover, at the beginning of the eighteenth century, England counted no more than a quarter million settlers sparsely distributed within fifty miles of the coast. Yet a closer examination reveals that the British colonies had a more lasting impact on the landscape and more effectively laid the social, cultural, and political foundation for American society than their French and Spanish contemporaries. Adapting to an environment both harsh and unfamiliar, the British colonial population laid deep roots. Their success rested in large part on their main objective to transplant many aspects of British society to a new land and establish permanent settlements. They introduced institutions (political, religious, and cultural) and provided a stronger, more secure stock population into which all other European immigrant groups integrated. Unlike in the Spanish and French colonies, British settlers came from all walks of life and intended to establish permanent homes in the New World. Furthermore, each of the thirteen colonies was fairly autonomous, entertained diverse ideological and/or business plans, and housed eclectic European populations. This complex society engendered less reliance on the British crown for decision making, more interaction among the colonial populations, and communities with strong economic foundations. The result was a denser, more deeply entrenched population distributed among various nodal settlements (e.g., Boston, New York, Philadelphia, Charleston) (figure 2.1). When the British crown tried to subvert the local autonomy, the colonists were better tooled to resist, leading to the American Revolution and the end of British colonial rule.

This chapter explains the role European immigration played in shaping North America's population dynamics. As illustrated, immigration to Anglo North America was diverse, but during the colonial era people from northern and western Europe predominated overwhelmingly among settlers. By the mid-twentieth century, this trend had changed. As chapters 5 and 6 illustrate, other Europeans, as well as people from Latin America and Asia, have become prominent in parts of the United States and Canada.

NOTES

1. Fellmann et al. (2010) define "host society" as the established and dominant component of a society within which immigrant groups seek accommodation. The mainstream component establishes the cultural norms, customs, and practices (e.g., language, religion, system of government) of a population. To various degrees, new immigrant groups interact with the established cultural foundations of the host society.

2. As the previous chapter so appropriately explains, the Europeans who arrived in the New World were not entering an uninhabited land. It was because of the indigenous populations and their assistance that the Europeans succeeded in settling the lands and amassing great wealth.

3. Mercantilism: a political economic system prevailing in postfeudal Europe based on the principles of accumulating bullion, creating a merchant marine, establishing colonies, and exploiting natural resources to attain a favorable balance of trade.

4. Entrepôt: a commercial center where goods are received for distribution, transshipment, or repackaging (aka break-in-bulk center).

5. Columbian Exchange: both intentional and unintentional exchange of animals, plants, microorganisms, people, and culture between the Eastern and Western Hemispheres.

6. Within Spanish-held lands, the word "mestizo" refers to members of the "mixed blood" population with both Indian and European parentage.

7. Splinter diffusion: the spread of a population whereby migrants splinter from a larger population and establish a new settlement with similar cultural traits. Commonly the process involves overcoming a physical barrier (e.g., mountain chain or river).

REFERENCES

Arreola, Daniel D. 2002. *Tejano South Texas: A Mexican American Cultural Province.* Austin: University of Texas Press.

Barrett, Elinore M. 2012. *The Spanish Colonial Settlement Landscapes of New Mexico, 1598–1680.* Albuquerque: University of New Mexico Press.

Blake, Kevin S., and Jeffrey S. Smith. 2000. Pueblo Mission Churches as Symbols of Permanence and Identity. *Geographical Review* 90, no. 3: 359–80.

Boal Frederick W., and Stephen A. Royle. 1999. *North America: A Geographical Mosaic.* London: Arnold Press.

Bolton, Herbert E. 1921. *The Spanish Borderlands: A Chronicle of Old Florida and the Southwest.* New Haven, CT: Yale University Press.

Brittingham, Angela, and G. Patricia de la Cruz. 2004. "Ancestry 2000." U.S. Bureau of the Census. June 2004. http://www.census.gov/prod/2004pubs/c2kbr-35.pdf.

Cronon, William. 1983. *Changes in the Land: Indians, Colonists, and the Ecology of New England.* New York: Hill and Wang.

Crosby, Alfred W., Jr. 1972. *The Columbian Exchange: Biological and Cultural Consequences of 1492.* Westport, CT: Greenwood Press.

Earle, Carville V. 1977. The First English Towns of North America. *Geographical Review* 67, no. 1: 34–50.

Fellmann, Jerome D., Mark D. Bjelland, Arthur Getis, and Judith Getis. 2010. *Human Geography: Landscapes of Human Activities.* New York: McGraw-Hill.

Finlay, John L., and Douglas N. Sprague. 1999. *The Structure of Canadian History.* Toronto: Pearson Education Canada.

Gentilcore, R. Louis. 1961. Missions and Mission Lands of Alta California. *Annals of the Association of American Geographers* 51, no. 1: 46–72.

Harrison, Blake, and Richard W. Judd, eds. 2011. *A Landscape History of New England.* Cambridge, MA: MIT Press.

Lemon, James T. 2001. Colonial America in the 18th Century. In *North America: The Historical Geography of a Changing Continent,* edited by T. F. McIlwraith and E. K. Muller, 119–39. 2nd ed. Lanham, MD: Rowman & Littlefield.

Meinig, Donald W. 1969. *Imperial Texas: An Interpretive Essay in Cultural Geography.* Austin: University of Texas Press.

———. 1971. *Southwest: Three Peoples in Geographical Change, 1600–1970*. New York: Oxford University Press.

———. 1986. *The Shaping of America: A Geographical Perspective on 500 Years of History*. Vol. 1: *Atlantic America, 1492–1800*. New Haven, CT: Yale University Press.

Nostrand, Richard L. 1992. *The Hispano Homeland*. Norman: University of Oklahoma Press.

Sauer, Carl O. 1966. *The Early Spanish Main*. Berkeley: University of California Press.

Smith, Jeffrey S. 1999. Anglo Intrusion on the Old Sangre de Cristo Land Grant. *Professional Geographer* 51, no. 2: 170–83.

Spicer, Edward H. 1962. *Cycles of Conquest: The Impact of Spain, Mexico, and the United States on the Indians of the Southwest, 1533–1960*. Tucson: University of Arizona Press.

Statcan. 2007. Table 13.3, Selected Ethnic Origins, 2001. In *Canada Year Book 2007*. Statistics Canada. http://www.statcan.gc.ca/pub/11-402-x/2007000/pdf/5219988-eng.pdf.

Stoddard, Elwynn R., Richard L. Nostrand, and Jonathan P. West, eds. 1983. *Borderlands Sourcebook: A Guide to the Literature on Northern Mexico and the American Southwest*. Norman: University of Oklahoma Press.

Trudel, Marcel. 1973. *The Beginnings of New France, 1524–1663*. Toronto: McClelland and Stewart.

Vance, James E., Jr. 1970. *The Merchant's World: The Geography of Wholesaling*. Englewood Cliffs, NJ: Prentice Hall.

Warkentin, R. Cole, and John Harris. 1991. *Canada before Confederation: A Study in Historical Geography*. New York: Oxford University Press.

Weber, David J. 1992. *The Spanish Frontier in North America*. New Haven, CT: Yale University Press.

Wood, Joseph S. 1997. *The New England Village*. Baltimore: Johns Hopkins University Press.

3

African Arrivals and Transformations

Andrew Sluyter

Recent research has overturned the conventional wisdom that long portrayed people of African descent as uncreative laborers in the making of the North American landscape.[1] According to that orthodoxy, enslaved blacks provided the brawn while Europeans, especially white men, provided the brains. Slavers seized some 12.5 million Africans between 1501 and 1866, selling them into slavery to work, often to their deaths, for plantation owners, miners, ranchers, and others in the Americas (figure 3.1).[2] Of the estimated 389,000 or so enslaved Africans who survived the infamous Middle Passage to disembark in North American ports, approximately 15,000 came in the seventeenth century, nearly 296,000 over the eighteenth, and another 78,000 in the nineteenth, mainly before U.S. and British acts of 1807 rendered the transatlantic slave trade illegal (Lachance et al. n.d.). The vast majority, about 211,000, disembarked in Charleston and Savannah, destined for rice and cotton plantations (Eltis, Morgan, and Richardson 2007, figure 11). Another some 129,000 went to the ports of Chesapeake Bay, with many sold to tobacco planters. Northern ports such as New York and Boston received another nearly twenty-seven thousand. And gulf ports, principally New Orleans and Biloxi, disembarked about twenty-two thousand, who mainly ended up on sugar and cotton plantations.

Decades ago a few iconoclastic historians began countering the belief that blacks had provided only labor with evidence that blacks actually played creative roles in the colonial emergence of novel types of places in North America, such as the landscape of tidewater rice plantations in the South Carolina Low Country during the eighteenth century (Wood 1974; Littlefield 1981). Because they relied on archival documents alone, however, those pioneer revisionists had little impact on the conventional wisdom. Racially biased whites, after all, had created most of that documentation; they emphasized their own roles and provided little direct evidence of black ideas and creativity. Moreover, most scholars demanded exactly that—namely, direct evidence—to overturn their indurated assumptions that useful knowledge generally had originated in Europe and diffused to the

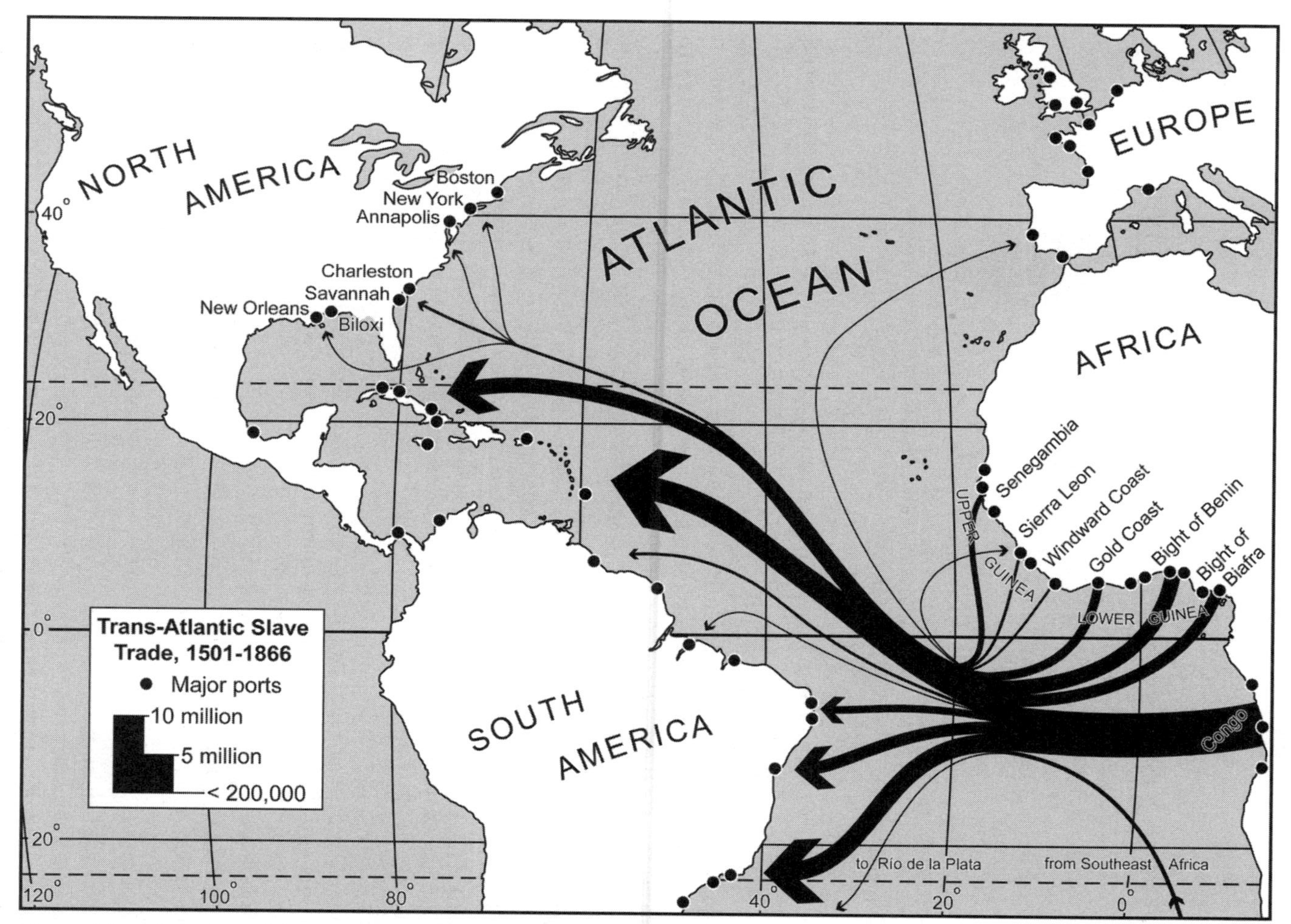

Figure 3.1. Overview of the transatlantic slave trade, 1501 to 1866, showing general flows and selected ports, with an emphasis on North America.

colonies, that slavery so disempowered people that enslaved blacks had played passive social roles, and that whites had therefore dominated in terms of initiative and creativity (Blaut 1993; Sluyter 2002).

Geographers have recently been able to advance the revisionist case, however, convincingly demonstrating that blacks actively contributed to the transformation of at least some places. Use of diverse primary sources—such as landscape vestiges, oral histories, and material culture—that complement archival documents has proven essential to that success (Carney 2002; Carney and Rosomoff 2009; Sluyter 2012). The emergence of the digital humanities has also contributed greatly, especially databases that facilitate analysis of the regional and ethnic origins of enslaved blacks and therefore of the types of African ideas and skills they might have carried across the Atlantic: for example, the Trans-Atlantic Slave Trade Database (Lachance et al. n.d.) and the Afro-Louisiana History and Genealogy database (Hall n.d.). Conceptually, the advent of Atlantic history has opened up scholarly debate on how actors of African, European, Native American, and mixed origins jointly participated in a hemispheric mobilization and hybridization of knowledge and materials through which distinctly North American places emerged (Eltis, Morgan, and Richardson 2007; Eltis et al. 2010).

The two case studies that follow exemplify how geographers have contributed to that major revision of our understanding of the past.[3] The first case treats an aspect of the open-range cattle ranches of the West—namely, lassoing cattle from horseback—from their earliest beginnings south of the Rio Grande during the sixteenth century through a brief florescence on the Great Plains in the nineteenth century, before barbed wire closed the range (Sluyter 2012). The second case involves the establishment of rice plantations along the southern Atlantic seaboard during the eighteenth century (Carney 2002). Jointly, the two case studies span several centuries and much of the continent. They illustrate a spectrum of complementary primary sources. And they demonstrate that blacks played significant creative roles in establishing production systems so fundamental to the environmental and social relations of the colonies that their consequences persist through to the present.

OPEN-RANGE CATTLE RANCHING

A large body of scholarship explicates the general process through which open-range cattle ranching became established in the Americas but largely ignores any active role for blacks (figure 3.2). The cattle from the Canary Islands that Christopher Columbus disembarked on the Caribbean island of Hispaniola in 1493 during his second voyage multiplied as rapidly as the population of native people declined, the herds expanding across an open range of tropical savanna and moribund agricultural fields (Sauer 1966; Crosby 1972). Over the next four centuries, their offspring, together with subsequent introductions, went on to graze other ranching frontiers throughout the Americas (Crosby 1986; Jordan 1993). In North America, cattle and herders from the Caribbean reached the Gulf coast of New Spain, in what is now Mexico, in the 1520s. From that beachhead they moved

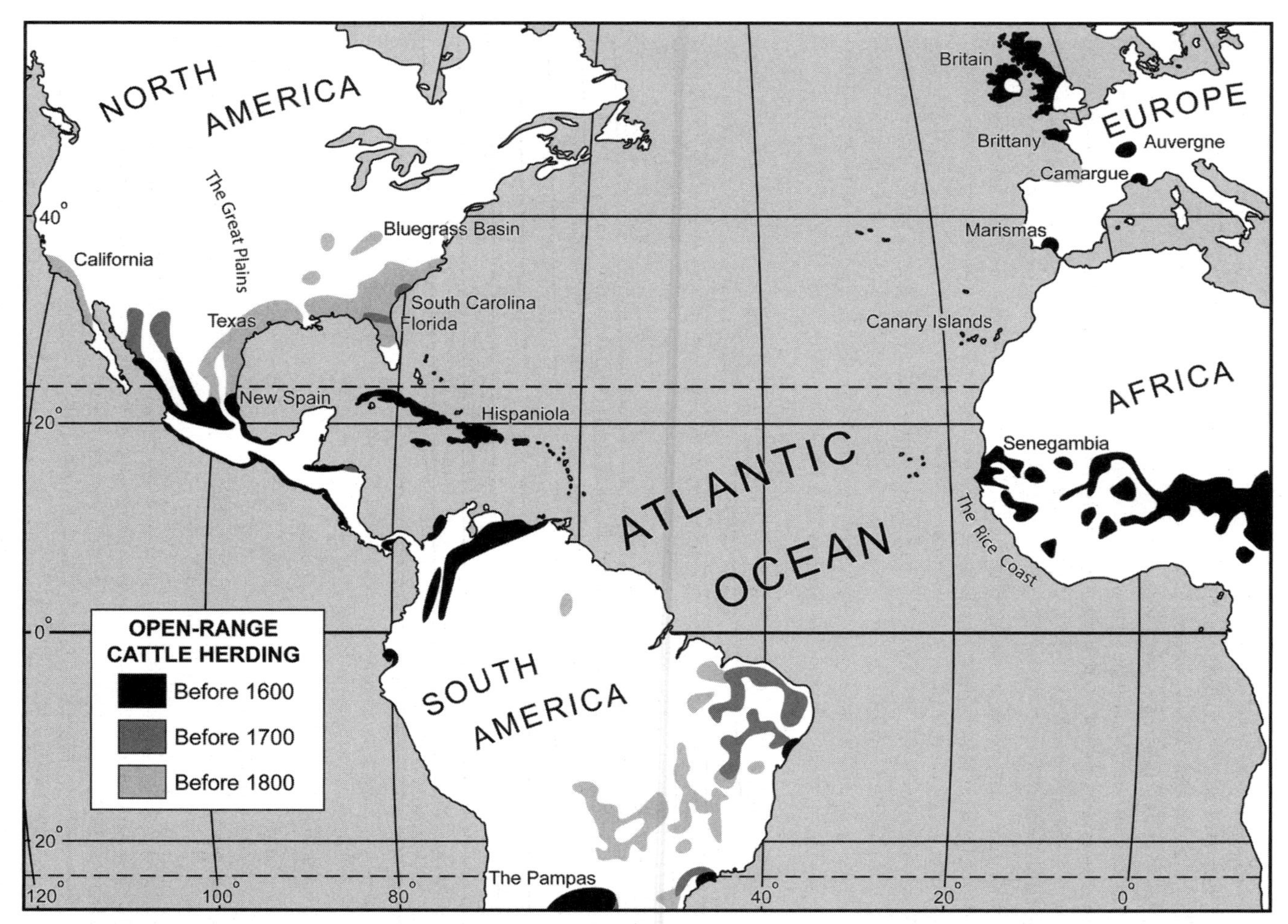

Figure 3.2. Relevant places and areas of open-range cattle herding in the Atlantic world over the sixteenth, seventeenth, and eighteenth centuries.

inland and northward until ranching had become well established along the colony's northern frontier, stretching from Texas to California, during the eighteenth century. Cattle from the Spanish Caribbean reached Florida in the sixteenth century, but ranching only became established in the seventeenth. As other European countries also colonized Caribbean islands and enclaves along the North American coasts, cattle ranching reached British South Carolina late in the seventeenth century and French Louisiana early in the eighteenth. The South Carolinians drove their herds southward into northern Florida, westward along the Gulf coast toward the Texas-Louisiana borderlands, and across the Appalachian Mountains into the Bluegrass Basin of Kentucky. Such ranching frontiers proliferated through the nineteenth century before a major retreat in the twentieth due to an expansion of cropland and intensification of beef production.

Each of those frontiers differed in particular ways, but they shared the general characteristics of open-range cattle ranching (Slatta 1997). All emphasized raising large herds of cattle for beef, hides, and tallow to the virtual exclusion of crops. All privileged cattle ownership over land ownership. All had an open range, sometimes held as common property and sometimes not but always undivided by fences. Ranchers sometimes kept other livestock, such as sheep and pigs, but cattle dominated. Brands rather than fences differentiated ownership of the mobile property. As the herds roamed over the open range for much of the year without human contact, control of breeding, or castration, they became feral and grew imposing horns to protect themselves against predators and herders alike. At roundup time, the cowboys had to ride horses to chase down and manage those wild cattle.

While those general processes, patterns, and characteristics seem clear enough, the role of blacks does not. The conventional wisdom has long maintained that "slavery and ranching did not mix" because it "was obviously impractical" to allow slaves to herd cattle without close, constant supervision by whites (Strickon 1965, 242–43). Even those who recognized that blacks had labored as cowboys argued that no evidence existed "of meaningful African influence in the cultures and adaptive systems of the various American cattle frontiers" (Jordan 1993, 311). The pioneering research of Philip Durham and Everett Jones on the Great Plains certainly demonstrated the active roles of many blacks on that frontier; yet that frontier emerged nearly four centuries after the one on Hispaniola, rendering their conclusion quite parochial: "Thus the story of the Negro cowboys *began* in Texas and the Indian Nations before the Civil War. There thousands of Negroes, most slaves, some free, learned to ride and rope and brand" (1965, 19; emphasis added). No doubt, many blacks did learn to rope on that frontier; so did many whites. That practice, however, involving a cowboy mounted on a horse casting a rope with a running noose around the heads or legs of cattle, did not begin in Texas, even though it became iconic of that frontier. Other cattle herders invented lassoing from horseback on an earlier frontier, someplace and sometime between Hispaniola in 1493 and the Great Plains in the nineteenth century.

Because the practice of lassoing from horseback did not exist in Europe or Africa during the colonial period, cattle herders must have developed it in the Americas. In the Atlantic fringe of Europe, pedestrian herders characterized most of the regions of open-range cattle herding, such as the highlands of Britain and

Ireland, Brittany, and the Auverge. Only the herders of the Marismas in Spain and the Camargue in France managed cattle from horseback; however, they used pike poles rather than lassos to control the herds. They did use lassos while dismounted, for example, to free cattle from mudholes by placing the running noose around the trapped animal's horns, tying the other end to their horse's tail to absorb the strain, and then leading the horse forward. In Senegambia, where the cattle-herding belt that stretches across Africa just south of the Sahara meets the Atlantic, herders used lassos to restrain rebellious bulls but did not manage cattle from horseback at all. They cast their lassos while standing or running and allowed a heavy piece of wood tied to the tail end of the lasso to tire the bull until they could approach to subdue it.

Neither did the herders of the earliest ranching frontiers of the Americas, on the islands of the Caribbean, lasso cattle from horseback. Those vaqueros, or cowboys, chased down the feral herds with dogs and the *desjarretadera*, a pike pole tipped with a crescent hocking knife, for their hides and tallow (figure 3.3).[4] The mounted herders would pursue an animal until able to sever its hamstrings, drop the animal in its tracks remote from any settlement, take the hide and perhaps the tallow and some meat, and leave the bulk of the carcass for the dogs.

On the mainland, herders initially continued to rely on the *desjarretadera* but ultimately abandoned it for less lethal means of catching feral cattle. On the Pampas of South America, gauchos developed two methods to manage the herds from horseback; both derived from the precolonial hunting practices of native peoples. The primary method employed bolas, three stone balls connected by cords, whirled over the head, and thrown at the legs of fleeing cattle in order to

Figure 3.3. Use of the *desjarretadera* in the sixteenth-century Caribbean. Reproduced courtesy of Rare Books and Special Collections, Princeton University Library.

entangle them. The lasso became a secondary method, its tail end secured to an iron ring low on the light gaucho saddle. In order to prevent the jolt of stopping a large bull from breaking the rope or tearing the saddle off the horse, gauchos had to work in pairs, one throwing the lasso around the horns and the other around the hind legs to distribute the force between the two horses. In contrast, the vaqueros of New Spain and later the cowboys of Texas and the Great Plains lacked bolas but used a stiffer, heavier saddle with a horn on the pommel to cinch the tail end of the lasso in order that a single horse and rider could absorb the jolt of roping cattle (figures 3.4 and 3.5).[5]

That distinctive saddle and its use to lasso cattle from horseback emerged in New Spain sometime between the mid-seventeenth and mid-eighteenth century. The earliest evidence that vaqueros were developing the technique comes from

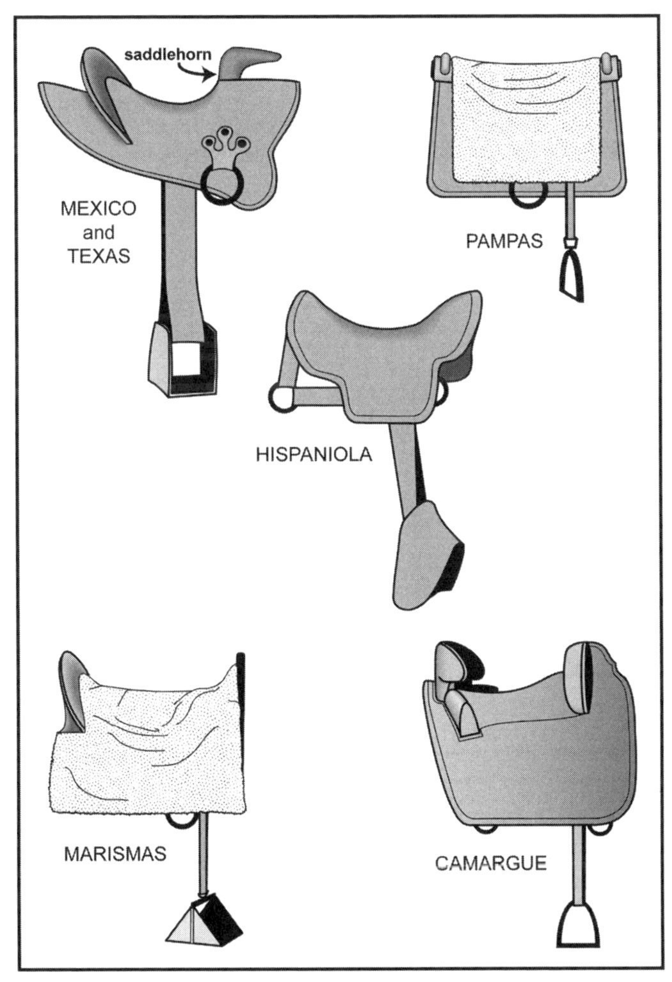

Figure 3.4. Historic saddles used for cattle herding in the Camargue, Mexico and Texas, the Pampas, the Marismas, and Hispaniola.

Figure 3.5. Use of the lasso in nineteenth-century New Spain.

an engraving and description of an equestrian show in Madrid in the 1640s (figure 3.6).[6] The image portrays a vaquero from the Americas demonstrating an innovative lassoing technique. Similarly to the Marismas, the rider tied the tail end of the lasso to the tail of the horse but, dissimilarly, remained mounted while using a pole to place the running noose over the horns. By the mid-eighteenth century, travelers from throughout New Spain, including the northern frontier that stretched from California to Texas, were describing saddles with horns and lassoing from horseback as a fully developed and common practice.

The text associated with the illustration of the lassoing demonstration in seventeenth-century Madrid provides some direct evidence that black vaqueros played a major role in that process of invention and refinement. Although the image portrays the rider with pale skin, its caption reads, "Some creole slaves from the Americas demonstrated the next skill" (Tapia y Salzedo, caption for plate 11).

The ordinances of the Mesta, the association that regulated cattle ranching and sheep herding in New Spain, reveal some circumstances that explain why blacks took the lead role in transforming the lasso from little more than a rope with a running noose into a highly efficient method of rounding up feral cattle from horseback. The municipal council of Mexico City founded the Mesta in 1537 to regulate conflicts among livestock herders and others with a code of seventeen ordinances, preserved in Mexico City's Archivo Histórico del Distrito Federal and published in Dusenberry (1963). In 1574, Viceroy Martín Enríquez de Almanza promulgated a much expanded code of eighty-three ordinances that applied to all of New Spain, preserved in Mexico's Archivo General de la Nación

Figure 3.6. A Creole slave from the Americas demonstrating how to lasso a bull in Madrid in the mid-seventeenth century. Reproduced courtesy of Rare Books and Special Collections, Princeton University Library.

and published in Ventura Beleña ([1787] 1991, vol. 1, pt. 2, 27–64). The viceroy hoped that the new code would reverse the decrease in the cattle population caused by the silver-mining boom of the sixteenth century. The expanding mines, as well as the growing urban population, so increased the demand for hides, tallow, and veal that their prices rapidly inflated and the ranchers began to slaughter not only their excess males but their female calves and cows. With the reduction in the breeding stock, rates of herd growth slowed, supply decreased relative to demand, and prices continued to rise. With a market bust ever imminent, ranchers had great incentive to increase cull rates while high prices lasted, and the indiscriminate slaughter of females by ranchers and rustlers continued to escalate. As a consequence, the 1574 Mesta code prohibited both the slaughter of female cattle and the use of the *desjarretadera*. Instead, vaqueros had to round all cattle up on the hoof and drive them to licensed slaughter yards for inspection of each animal's age, sex, and brand to ensure ranchers did not kill their female calves and cows.

The racially biased penalties that the Mesta imposed for violations of its ordinances provided a strong motive for nonwhite vaqueros to develop lassoing from horseback as an alternative to the *desjarretadera*. Although the ordinances banned its use generally, only nonwhites were fined or punished simply for possessing one: "That there be no desjarretaderas, nor any hocked livestock . . . any native, mulatto, black, or mestizo . . . cannot carry or possess a lance or desjarretadera for any reason, under penalty of twenty pesos, . . . and he who incurs the said penalty and does not have the means to pay will be given a hundred lashes in public" (Ventura Beleña [1787] 1991, vol. 1, pt. 2, 41–43). Given that enslaved vaqueros did not receive wages, the severe public lashing would have been the default penalty. Even free black and mulatto vaqueros received such low wages that twenty *pesos de oro de minas* equaled a year's salary. Whereas white vaqueros could continue to use the *desjarretadera* without fear of a ruinous fine or a brutal public lashing if caught, the 1574 ordinances compelled black vaqueros to develop an alternate technique to catch feral stock.

Blacks had not only that powerful motive but ample opportunity to innovate with the lasso. Many vaqueros in New Spain were of African origin—for example, the two hundred enslaved blacks working the herds of a cattle baron named Hernán Ruiz de Córdoba in the 1570s. Another ordinance of the 1574 Mesta code reveals that, preferring free and enslaved blacks over whites as majordomos because they were "genuine and trustworthy," ranchers allowed them to direct daily ranch operations and gave them thus the freedom to experiment with herding practices (Ventura Beleña [1787] 1991, vol. 1, pt. 2, 43). Some ranchers were themselves free blacks, such as Benito el Negro and Juan el Negro, with even greater latitude to introduce and refine new practices such as lassoing from horseback.

Significantly, many of the black vaqueros came from Senegambia, where the African open-range cattle-herding belt meets the Atlantic between the mouths of the Senegal and Gambia Rivers. The Trans-Atlantic Slave Trade Database records that 35,430 Senegambians disembarked between 1531 and 1650 in Spanish Central America, about 17 percent of the total number of enslaved Africans to arrive during that period (Eltis and Richardson 2010). As the volume of the slave trade increased, so did the number of Senegambians: from 1,607 over 1531 to 1550 (about 85 per year), to 9,704 over 1551 to 1600 (some 198 per year), to 24,119 over 1601 to 1650 (about 494 per year). The proportion of Senegambians among the total arrivals decreased just as steadily—from 85 percent for 1531 to 1550, to 20 percent for 1551 to 1600, to 15 percent for 1601 to 1650—as the focus of the slave trade shifted southward. Nonetheless, hundreds of the black vaqueros of New Spain would have been experts in Senegambian open-range cattle-herding practices and quite capable of introducing those African ideas as well as innovating to suit the new context. They would certainly not have been novices who needed Spanish ranchers to "teach them the ropes."

One idea those Senegambian vaqueros brought to New Spain involved the saddle horn. While Senegambians and other West Africans did not use horses to herd livestock, the military and social elite did ride using saddles with horns that served as a rest for the rein hand and as a hanger for bags (Law 1980). Twentieth-century ethnographers and nineteenth-century explorers report such saddles as early as the 1820s, and they likely have a much greater antiquity (figure 3.7).[7] They also bear a striking resemblance to those developed by the vaqueros of colonial New Spain. In contrast, the Spanish vaqueros of New Spain, even those who had herded cattle from horseback in the Marismas or on Hispaniola, definitely had no such antecedent knowledge of the saddle horn.

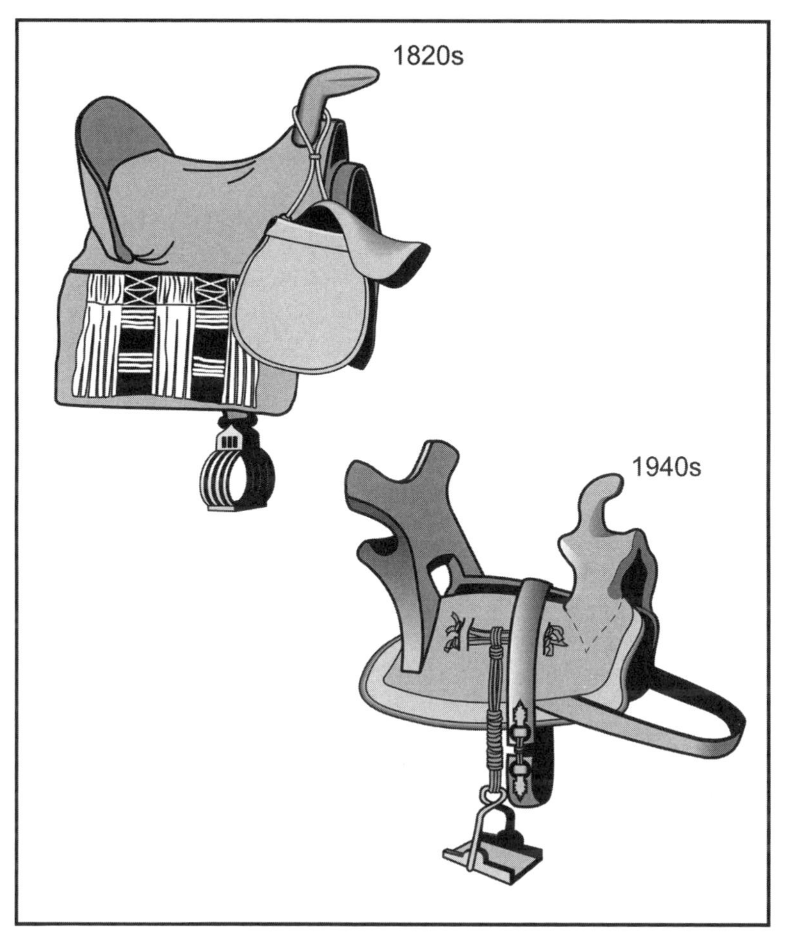

Figure 3.7. Two historic West African saddles with horns, dating from the nineteenth and twentieth centuries.

Blacks had antecedent knowledge of saddle horns, lassos, and open-range cattle herding; they had a substantial presence on ranches in New Spain, sometimes as majordomos and owners with the consequent latitude to innovate; and they had a strong motivation for inventing and refining a nonlethal alternative to the *desjarretadera* to avoid the racially biased sanctions of the Mesta ordinances of the late sixteenth century. No wonder, then, that in Madrid in the mid-seventeenth century, enslaved black vaqueros staged the demonstration of the earliest phase in the process of transforming the lasso from a rope with a running noose into a technique for rounding up feral cattle from horseback. Blacks would continue to develop that technique until the saddle horn allowed them to reliably catch cattle from horseback and sort them by age, sex, and brand before driving the males to the slaughter yard. By the late eighteenth century, the *desjarretadera* had become an anachronism; the lasso had become the preferred technique that all vaqueros, black and otherwise, used to round up cattle as far north as Texas,

California, and other places along the northern frontier of New Spain that in the mid-nineteenth century would become part of the United States.

RICE CULTIVATION

The case for a significant black role in establishing the landscapes of rice plantations along the Atlantic seaboard similarly rests on a combination of complementary primary sources. The conventional wisdom long maintained that British planters introduced rice from Asia soon after founding the South Carolina colony in 1670 and, by the early eighteenth century, had developed techniques to produce it successfully as a commodity on large plantations using unskilled, enslaved African laborers. By the eve of the Revolutionary War, rice plantations extended along the coast from the Cape Fear River in the north to the St. Johns River in the south, and the South Carolina colony was exporting 60 million pounds of rice per year. By the eve of the Civil War, some one hundred thousand enslaved blacks cultivated about 175,000 acres of rice, annual exports had doubled to 120 million pounds, and Charleston had become one of the wealthiest cities in North America. The conventional wisdom also maintained that the Portuguese had introduced rice from Asia to the African Rice Coast and taught blacks to cultivate it in a primitive manner to provision the Middle Passage of the slave trade.

The evidence assembled by Judith A. Carney (2002), however, has overturned both aspects of the conventional wisdom, beginning by demonstrating that rice had been a staple in West Africa since long before the Portuguese arrived in the fifteenth century. Africans domesticated a species of rice (*Oryza glaberrima*) distinct from Asian rice (*Oryza sativa*) at least two thousand years ago. Along with millet and sorghum, rice became a staple in West Africa, with dozens of precisely bred varieties with different tastes and cooking properties attuned to the varied soil moisture and acidity, water depth and salinity, growth period and season, and other conditions across several environmental zones. Farmers typically used hoes to till their fields, whether saline estuaries along the coast, freshwater wetlands inland, riverine floodplains, or hill lands. Coastal rice fields in river estuaries were the most intensive system, requiring the largest labor investment in return for the highest yield. Farmers cleared the mangroves and built systems of embankments, canals, and sluices to reduce the salinity of the fertile estuarine soils. During the dry season, they opened the sluice gates to admit brackish water that also deposited sediments rich in nutrients. As the rains returned, they closed the sluice gates to allow the fields to flood with freshwater that leached the salt out of the soil. After opening the sluice gates at low tide to drain the fields, they transplanted rice seedlings from seedbeds into the fertile, desalinized soil. Farmers used the same infrastructure to regulate the depth of accumulated rainwater in the field in order to control weeds and irrigate the crop over the growing season.

This highly productive rice agriculture supported the densely settled population that attracted European slavers. The slave trade devastated the societies of the Rice Coast, population declined, and rice production contracted and became less labor-intensive. The infrastructure of embankments, canals, and sluice gates deteriorated until the visual evidence of the moribund landscape supported the belief that Africans cultivated Asian rice introduced by the Portuguese with primitive, unproductive methods.

Although no direct evidence exists that blacks first established rice cultivation in South Carolina, the substantial number of Africans enslaved along the Rice Coast who disembarked in Charleston brought with them the accumulated expertise of many generations of rice farmers. The Trans-Atlantic Slave Trade Database estimates that 187,000 enslaved blacks arrived in South Carolina directly from Africa between 1701 and 1808, an astounding figure even if a mere 1.5 percent of the total 12.5 million Africans who endured the Middle Passage (Eltis and Richardson 2010). Moreover, about 40 percent of those who disembarked in Charleston over the eighteenth century had embarked along the Rice Coast (figure 3.8).[8] Rather than being the unskilled laborers of the conventional wisdom, they knew how to grow many different varieties of rice in diverse environments; make and use a range of implements to cultivate, harvest, and mill it; and modify landscapes with embankments, canals, sluices, and other features to regulate soil moisture, salinity, and fertility. The European planters of the colony, in contrast, had little if any experience with rice cultivation.

Many aspects of rice cultivation in South Carolina resembled that of the Rice Coast. The tidewater plantations, for example, that developed after 1750 were the most productive and dominated rice exports until the Civil War. They were located in estuaries, where freshwater river discharge meets the saltwater of the Atlantic, and employed a system of embankments, canals, and sluices to regulate the salinity and depth of water in the fields (figure 3.9).[9] Enslaved blacks would open sluice gates during the flood tide to admit freshwater, which is less dense and floats on top of the saltwater, then close them as salinity increased. When

TO BE SOLD on board the Ship *Bance-Yland*, on tueſday the 6th of *May* next, at *Aſhley-Ferry*; a choice cargo of about 250 fine healthy

NEGROES,

juſt arrived from the Windward & Rice Coaſt. —The utmoſt care has already been taken, and ſhall be continued, to keep them free from the leaſt danger of being infected with the SMALL-POX, no boat having been on board, and all other communication with people from *Charles-Town* prevented.

Auſtin, Laurens, & Appleby.

N. B. Full one Half of the above Negroes have had the SMALL-POX in their own Country.

Figure 3.8. Newspaper advertisement for an auction of 250 enslaved Africans, including some from the Rice Coast, in Charleston in the mid-eighteenth century. Reproduced courtesy of the Prints and Photographs Division, Library of Congress.

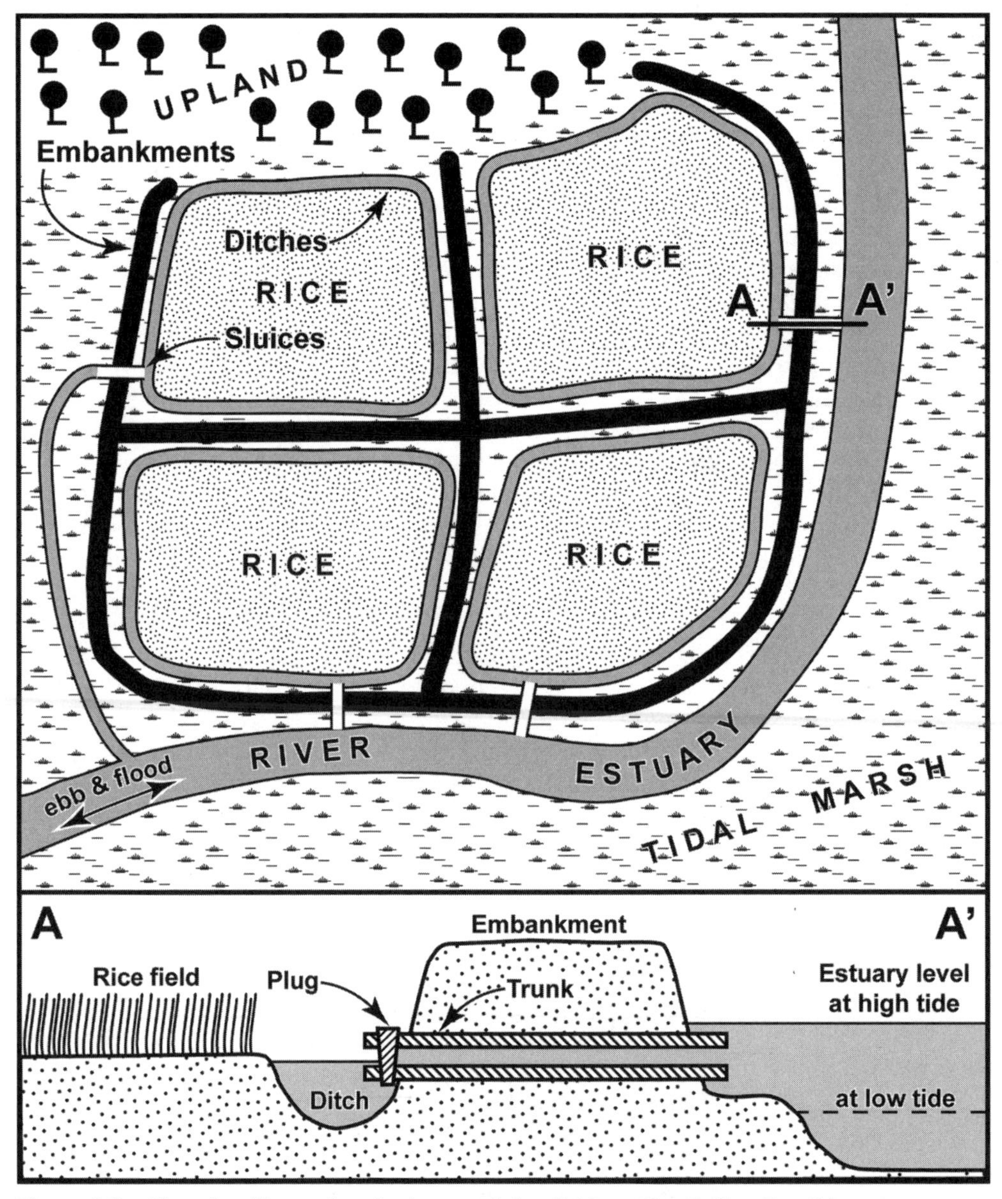

Figure 3.9. Plan view illustrating the layout of rice fields on South Carolina tidewater plantations, with areas of former tidal marsh between the river channel and upland enclosed by ditches and embankments pierced by sluices. The cross section through a sluice shows how a hollow tree trunk with a plug in one end functioned to regulate the flow of water into and out of the field.

the rice had been submerged for the requisite period, they opened the sluice gates at low tide to drain the fields. Not only was the entire system similar to that used in the estuarine fields of the Rice Coast, so were specific elements, such as the sluices called "plug trunks." Although replaced by more elaborate "hanging trunks" over the eighteenth century, the early sluices consisted of hollowed-out cypress logs similar to the hollowed-out palm logs used along the Rice Coast. The sluice gates consisted of a wooden plug fitted into a hole drilled across the axis of the trunk, which "acted on the same principle as a wooden spigot to a beer keg" (Doar [1936] 1970, 12). Agricultural implements such as the hoes used for tilling and the fanner baskets used for winnowing also echoed those employed in the Rice Coast (figure 3.10).[10]

The evidence of a long history of rice cultivation in Africa, the number of blacks enslaved along the Rice Coast who disembarked in Charleston, the probability that some of them were experienced rice farmers, the relative lack of similar experience among the white planters, and the similarities between the

Figure 3.10. Hoeing rice in South Carolina, ca. 1900. Reproduced courtesy of the Prints and Photographs Division, Library of Congress.

systems of rice cultivation on both sides of the Atlantic, as well as between specific elements, all counter the conventional wisdom. Blacks provided both the brawn and the brains that founded the tidewater plantations of South Carolina.

CONCLUSION

Such research expands our historical understanding of North American places well beyond an acknowledgment of the role of blacks in the history of musical genres such as jazz. Rice plantations and open-range cattle ranches established patterns of land and life so fundamental to the colonial economies and ecologies of North America that their material effects linger to the present in the landscapes and societies of the South Carolina Low Country and the West. The discursive effects also persist, albeit more insidiously, such as in the political rhetoric asserting that life for African Americans was better before the Civil War than now: supposedly, puerile blacks lived peacefully and labored passively under the wise tutelage of beneficent masters. A related area of research also has begun to counter that discourse, deconstructing how museums represent the historical roles of North Americans of African origin (see chapter 15).

People of African origin have lived in many parts of what became the United States and, to a much lesser degree, Canada since the sixteenth century. By one measure, the greatest potential for research on their roles in creating the places of North America seems to pertain to those regions dominated by slave-based economies, especially the South. After all, just three years before President Abraham Lincoln issued the Emancipation Proclamation in 1863, 98 percent of the 3,953,761 enslaved Americans, out of a total population of about 31 million enumerated by the 1860 federal census, lived in the thirteen states that would secede to form the Confederacy (NHGIS n.d.). Nonetheless, regions and places that did not have large populations of African origin might nonetheless yield equally significant revisions to our understanding of the North American past. So while the part played by blacks in establishing cattle ranching in South Carolina certainly demands further research, so does their role on the ranches of the coastal valleys of California.

NOTES

I thank Judy Carney for her thoughtful feedback on a draft of this chapter.

1. For examples of that conventional wisdom, see Conzen (1990), McIlwraith and Muller (2001), and the publications cited therein.

2. The figure is based on Eltis, Morgan, and Richardson (2007, figures 6 and 11).

3. The mandated brevity of this chapter dictates that the following sections economize on facts, examples, and citations to the secondary literature and primary sources; for much fuller presentations of the cases and citations beyond the principal literature and sources of illustrations and direct quotes, see the monographic treatments of Carney (2002) and Sluyter (2012).

4. The figure comes from a copy of Molina (1582, pt. 2, bk. 1, ch. 37) in the Laurence Roberts Carton Hunting Collection, Rare Books and Special Collections, Princeton University Library.

5. Figure 3.4 is based on sketches made in rural museums as well as on field observations and illustrations in such sources as Diderot and Le Rond d'Alembert (1751–1772, vol. 25, plate 22). Figure 3.5 comes from a copy of Sartorius (1859, plate following 181) in the author's collection.

6. The figure comes from a copy of Tapia y Salzedo (1643, plate 11) in the Laurence Roberts Carton Hunting Collection, Rare Books and Special Collections, Princeton University Library.

7. The figure is based on illustrations in Denham and Clapperton (1826, plate following 269) and Boyer (1953, figure 21).

8. The figure comes from the Library of Congress, Prints and Photographs Division, Reproduction number LC-USZ62–10293.

9. The figure is based on a description and figures in Carney (2002, 95 and figures 3.3 and 3.4).

10. The figure comes from the Library of Congress, Prints and Photographs Division, Reproduction number LC-USZ62–26232.

REFERENCES

Blaut, James M. 1993. *The Colonizer's Model of the World: Geographical Diffusionism and Eurocentric History*. New York: Guilford.

Boyer, G. 1953. *Un peuple de l'Ouest soudanais: les Diawara*. Dakar: Institut Français d'Afrique Noire.

Carney, Judith A. 2002. *Black Rice: The African Origins of Rice Cultivation in the Americas*. Cambridge, MA: Harvard University Press.

Carney, Judith A., and Richard N. Rosomoff. 2009. *In the Shadow of Slavery: Africa's Botanical Legacy in the Atlantic World*. Berkeley: University of California Press.

Conzen, Michael P., ed. 1990. *The Making of the American Landscape*. New York: Routledge.

Crosby, Alfred W. 1972. *The Columbian Exchange: Biological and Cultural Consequences of 1492*. Westport, CT: Greenwood Press.

———. 1986. *Ecological Imperialism: The Biological Expansion of Europe, 900–1900*. Cambridge: Cambridge University Press.

Denham, Dixon, and Hugh Clapperton. 1826. *Narrative of Travels and Discoveries in Northern and Central Africa in the Years 1822, 1823, and 1824*. London: John Murray.

Diderot, Denis, and Jean le Rond d'Alembert, eds. 1751–1772. *Encyclopédie ou dictionnaire raisonné des sciences des arts et des métiers*. 28 vols. Paris: Briasson, David, Le Breton, and Durand.

Doar, David. [1936] 1970. *Rice and Rice Planting in the South Carolina Low Country*. Charleston, SC: Charleston Museum.

Durham, Philip, and Everett L. Jones. 1965. *The Negro Cowboys*. Lincoln: University of Nebraska Press.

Dusenberry, William H. 1963. *The Mexican Mesta: The Administration of Ranching in Colonial Mexico*. Urbana: University of Illinois Press.

Eltis, David, and David Richardson. 2010. *Atlas of the Transatlantic Slave Trade*. New Haven, CT: Yale University Press.

Eltis, David, Philip Morgan, and David Richardson. 2007. Agency and Diaspora in Atlantic History: Reassessing the African Contribution to Rice Cultivation in the Americas. *American Historical Review* 112: 1329–58.

Eltis, David, Philip Morgan, David Richardson, S. Max Edelson, Gwendolyn Midlo Hall, and Walter Hawthorne. 2010. AHR Exchange: The Question of "Black Rice." *American Historical Review* 115: 123–71.

Hall, Gwendolyn Midlo. n.d. Afro-Louisiana History and Genealogy: 1719–1820. ibiblio. http://www.ibiblio.org/laslave.

Jordan, Terry G. 1993. *North American Cattle-Ranching Frontiers: Origins, Diffusion, and Differentiation*. Albuquerque: University of New Mexico Press.

Lachance, Paul, Manuel Barcia Paz, Steve Behrendt, David Eltis, Manolo Florentino, Antonio Mendes, David Richardson, and Jelmer Vos. n.d. Voyages: The Trans-Atlantic Slave Trade Database. http://www.slavevoyages.org.

Law, Robin. 1980. *The Horse in West African History: The Role of the Horse in the Societies of Pre-colonial West Africa*. Oxford: Oxford University Press.

Littlefield, David C. 1981. *Rice and Slaves: Ethnicity and the Slave Trade in Colonial South Carolina*. Baton Rouge: Louisiana State University Press.

McIlwraith, Thomas F., and Edward K. Muller, eds. 2001. *North America: The Historical Geography of a Changing Continent*. 2nd ed. Lanham, MD: Rowman & Littlefield.

Molina, Gonzalo Argote de. 1582. *Libro de la montería*. Seville: Andrea Pescioni.

National Historical Geographic Information System (NHGIS). n.d. NHGIS. http://www.nhgis.org.

Sartorius, Carl. 1859. *Mexico: Landscapes and Popular Sketches*. Translated by Thomas Gaspey. London: Trübner.

Sauer, Carl O. 1966. *The Early Spanish Main*. Berkeley: University of California Press.

Slatta, Richard W. 1997. *Comparing Cowboys and Frontiers*. Norman: University of Oklahoma Press.

Sluyter, Andrew. 2002. *Colonialism and Landscape: Postcolonial Theory and Applications*. Lanham, MD: Rowman & Littlefield.

———. 2012. *Black Ranching Frontiers: African Cattle Herders of the Atlantic World, 1500–1900*. New Haven, CT: Yale University Press.

Strickon, Arnold. 1965. The Euro-American Ranching Complex. In *Man, Culture, and Animals: The Role of Animals in Human Ecological Adjustments*, edited by Anthony Leeds and Andrew P. Vayda, 229–58. Washington, D.C.: American Association for the Advancement of Science.

Tapia y Salzedo, Gregorio de. 1643. *Ejercicios de la gineta al Príncipe Nuestro Señor D. Carlos Baltasar*. Madrid: Diego Díaz.

Ventura Beleña, Eusebio. [1787] 1991. *Recopilación sumaria de todos los autos acordados de la real audiencia y sala del crimen de esta Nueva España*. 2 vols. Mexico City: Universidad Autónoma de México.

Wood, Peter H. 1974. *Black Majority: Negroes in Colonial South Carolina from 1670 through the Stono Rebellion*. New York: Alfred A. Knopf.

II

REMAKING SOCIETY

4

Reordering the Geography of Indian Country

Historical Geographies of Removal, Reservations, and Assimilation

Steven Silvern

Historical geographers and allied researchers are engaged in describing and developing explanations for the past geographies of native North America. Most have abandoned deterministic explanatory narratives such as the Turnerian frontier thesis—a simplistic story of "primitive" native peoples naturally and inevitably giving way to an advancing and "superior" Euro-American civilization. The historical geography of Native Americans is intertwined with the material and imaginative geographies of European-American settler colonialism. Settler colonialism reshaped the geographies and lives of both native peoples and Euro-American settlers. But unlike in Turner's simplistic historical narrative of frontier expansion, native peoples in North America, scholars now recognize, were not passive victims of colonialism. In myriad ways, conditioned by global and local conditions, they resisted it and found creative means to maintain their lifeways. Nonetheless, native people were unable to fully resist the multiple, often violent, and geographically altering dimensions of colonialism. We are learning that native peoples were active agents in shaping and reshaping the conditions they encountered and experienced, but they faced limitations as to what they could do in the face of multifaceted and rapid demographic, economic, and environmental changes. Recent scholarship has demonstrated the complexity of this story and the difficulty of portraying and understanding intercultural contact, asymmetrical economic and political relations, forces of domination and patterns of resistance, and the dynamics of accommodation in the historical geography of native North America.[1]

Despite a number of recent studies on native historical geographies, the field remains relatively underdeveloped. It is still accurate to say, as James Taylor

Carson did ten years ago, that there is a "relative dearth of geographical work on native America" (2002, 770).[2] This situation provides both opportunities and challenges for geographers interested in American Indians. In this chapter, I examine changes in native geographies during the nineteenth century, perhaps the period of the most dramatic geographical change and territorial reordering in native North America. I highlight how spatial imaginations, along with material economic interests and cultural biases, shaped American geographical expansionism. American expansionism was premised on social and spatial assumptions of how native people ought to fit into the political, cultural, and economic geography of the United States. Spatial concepts and strategies for domination and resistance were crucial to the reterritorializing of native peoples. Despite radical changes in their geographies—displacement and loss of access to their homelands and natural resources—native peoples resisted, survived, and maintained their distinct cultural and geographical identities.

REMOVAL: DISPLACEMENT AND THE RETERRITORIALIZATION OF INDIAN COUNTRY

In the first three decades of the nineteenth century, the zone of spatial contact and the intensity of interactions between Indians and non-Indians expanded and heightened as Euro-American settlement spilled across the Appalachians into Indian territories east of the Mississippi River. Euro-American farmers, miners, and land speculators intruded into this "Indian Country" and, seeking to remove "eastern" Indians and make their territories available to non-Indians, put pressure on the American government to assert its jurisdiction over native space. Europeans imagined Indians as "uncivilized" nomadic hunter-gatherers and viewed them as an impediment to the "march of civilization" and the rightful and inevitable expansion of American territorial sovereignty. They considered Indians' common-property organization and diverse land-use practices inferior and less efficient than the individualized land-ownership and agricultural practices of European-Americans. This imaginary persisted despite the reality that many Indian tribes were sedentary agriculturalists or practiced a mixed economy that integrated seasonal harvesting (hunting, fishing, and gathering) with agriculture. Occupying and utilizing lands coveted by Euro-Americans, Indians endured portrayals as obstacles to "progress" and "proper" resource development; native peoples were deemed a "problem" (Meinig 1993; Prucha 1995).

The Louisiana Purchase provided a temporary geographical solution to this so-called Indian problem. Government officials regarded lands west of the Mississippi River, although occupied by numerous Indian tribes, as a geographical outlet for the displacement of eastern Indian tribes. A peaceful and legal relocation of eastern tribes to these western territories fit into the American political ideal of territorial "expansion with honor" and served various economic interests pressing the government to clear eastern lands of native occupants. Thomas Jefferson was the first of many American presidents in the first half of the nineteenth century to advocate for the removal of eastern Indians to western lands.

Separated and removed from contact and potential conflict with non-Indian settlers, "uncivilized" Indian tribes would acculturate and assimilate to American cultural ideals of agrarianism, fee simple land ownership, individualism, Christianity, and citizenship (Meinig 1993; Prucha 1995).

As non-Indian settlers shifted into the Ohio valley, the Great Lakes region, and the Southeast in the 1820s and 1830s, authorities pressured Indian tribes in these regions to cede or sell their land rights to the United States and remove to western lands. In 1830, Congress made such "removal" the official government policy when it passed the Indian Removal Act authorizing the president to negotiate treaties with tribes for the voluntary exchange of their eastern homelands for "unsettled" western lands. Treaties became the legal and political instrument used by the United States to acquire Indian homelands located between the Appalachians and the Mississippi River. With their "veil of legality," treaties were an "important device for avoiding open warfare" and "were thus used extensively as Americans expanded the boundaries of the nation westward" (Cleland et al. 2011, 10; also see Calloway 2013).

The British created the legal and political precedent for negotiating treaties with Indians to establish "peace and friendship" and acquire title to Indian lands. The United States continued this practice and negotiated (and ratified) 364 treaties with tribal leaders before terminating Indian treaty making in 1871. According to C. E. Cleland et al. (2011, 14), the U.S. government negotiated ninety-nine Indian treaties during the removal period (1830–1849). From a western legal perspective, treaties were agreements between sovereign nations and assumed a degree of political equality. In reality, treaties between the United States and Indian tribes were negotiated in a field of political, economic, and demographic inequality. Tribes almost always negotiated from a position of relative weakness. As Cleland et al. note, government representatives pressured Indians, subjecting them to "intimidation and threats" (2011, 9). Indians "agreed to treaties because they were forced to do so by the simple exercise of power, both covert and overt" (Cleland et al. 2011, 10; also see Pearce 2004). Although, on the surface, the Removal Act called for the voluntary removal of tribes from their homelands, in fact most tribes found it difficult to resist American pressures to cede their homelands and remove west.

The treaty negotiation process favored the United States, placing tribes at a disadvantage. The government initiated negotiations at times and locations of its determination, conducted the discussions in English, and selected and paid interpreters. Treaty language itself was formal, legalistic, and foreign to most tribes' linguistic practices and cultural understandings of land and social relations. There was ample room for miscommunication and misunderstanding of treaty provisions. Lawsuits over the meaning of Indian treaties, especially hunting and fishing rights in the Great Lakes and Pacific Northwest, stem from such linguistic and cultural misunderstandings (Satz 1991; Cohen, La France, and Bowden 1986; Prucha 1994).

Removal treaties, albeit specific to individual tribes, contained a number of typical provisions. Treaties often specified the boundaries of tribal homelands being ceded and the boundaries of the western lands where Indians would remove. Tribes received cash payments for their lands, including payment for improvements made to the land. They received these payments as an annual annuity, with the period differing from treaty to treaty. The government also compensated tribes through the provision of good and services. Goods might include guns, ammunition, clothing, fish nets and traps, and metal goods, which tribal negotiators requested in order for the tribe to maintain economic practices such as fishing, hunting, and gathering. On the other hand, "services" included in the treaties, such as schooling, blacksmithing, carpentry, and farming, were part of the government's efforts to include a "civilizing" component in Indian removal (Prucha 1994; Cleland et al. 2011).[3]

Tribes often differed internally in their response to American removal pressures and requests for treaty negotiations. Some members supported treaty negotiations, feeling it was in their best interests to cede their lands, separate themselves from non-Indians, and relocate west or, where possible, to Canada. For example, several thousand members of the Potawatomi, who lived across southern Wisconsin, northern Illinois, Michigan, and Indiana, removed themselves to Iowa and Kansas and upper Canada (Clifton 1977, 283). In most instances, however, a majority of tribal members were unwilling to cede their homelands and move west to unfamiliar environments. Antiremoval or antitreaty factions found it difficult, however, to resist government removal efforts. The government often employed divide-and-conquer tactics to overcome tribal resistance to removal, identifying pro-treaty leaders to negotiate with and excluding tribal leaders who opposed removal. In a number of cases, such as the tragic and well-known removal of the Cherokee from their southeastern homeland (the "Trail of Tears"), the government employed the military to force tribal members to move west.[4]

Similar in many ways to the Indian removal experience in the Southeast was the displacement of native people living east of the Mississippi River in the "Old Northwest," the region north of the Ohio River and bordering the Great Lakes. By the late 1840s, removal had ousted most, though not all, the native peoples in this region. Non-Indian settlers wanted the rich agricultural lands of Indiana, Illinois, southern Michigan, and Wisconsin. Others sought access to the lead deposits of southwestern Wisconsin and the pine forests and copper deposits of the Michigan and Wisconsin Northwoods. Tribes such as the Miami, Sauk and Fox, Potawatomi, and Ho-Chunk (Winnebago) resisted as best they could, but the majority ultimately felt compelled to cede their homelands and move west.

The Ho-Chunk, for example, signed a number of land-cession treaties between 1829 and 1837 that led to their removal from southwestern and south-central Wisconsin. This process splintered the Ho-Chunk into a treaty-abiding faction, which deemed removal to be in their best interests, and the Disaffected Bands, a nontreaty faction opposed to removal (Lurie 1980, 690, 699). The treaty-abiding group suffered a series of removals (to Iowa, Minnesota, and South Dakota) before signing a treaty purchasing part of the Omaha reservation in northeastern Nebraska in 1865 (Loew 2001). The nontreaty Ho-Chunk were determined to remain in their homeland and tried to avoid removal by living in "small enclaves" in the forests and pine barrens of central Wisconsin (Lurie 1980, 703). They returned to Wisconsin after being "periodically rounded up" and removed to the western reservation (Prucha 1995, 261). The last forced removal of the Ho-Chunk to Nebraska took place in 1874; over the next year, almost two-thirds returned to Wisconsin (Loew 2001, 48). By the late 1870s federal removal efforts had halted, and Ho-Chunk members obtained individual homesteads of forty acres through the Homestead Act of 1862. Further federal legislation in 1881 provided an opportunity to apply for eighty-acre homesteads that would be tax-free for twenty-five years (Bieder 1995, 171). These homesteads were spread out over ten central Wisconsin counties.

The Ojibwe of northern Wisconsin were more successful than other eastern tribes in resisting removal and securing a permanent land base, or reservation, in their homeland. The Ojibwe, spread across northern Michigan, Wisconsin, and Minnesota, lived a seminomadic life centered on the seasonal availability of fish, game, and wild plants and the harvest from small gardens in multifamily summer villages. The first land-cession treaty the United States negotiated with the Wisconsin Ojibwe was the Treaty of St. Peters in 1837. Pressure for Ojibwe lands came from non-Indians who wanted the pine timber of north-central Wisconsin. In exchange for the southern portion of their Wisconsin homeland, the Ojibwe received cash, goods, and services. This included farm implements to promote the "civilization" of the Ojibwe. Throughout the treaty negotiations, the Ojibwe demanded retention of their customary usufructuary rights—hunting, fishing, and gathering rights—to the ceded lands. Article 5 of the 1837 treaty states the "privilege" of hunting and fishing and gathering in the ceded territory was "guarantied [*sic*] to the Indians during the pleasure of the President of the United States." The Ojibwe believed the Americans only wanted pine trees, not other forest resources or the land itself. Scholars note that nothing in the record of the treaty negotiations or in the text of the treaty itself indicates it was intended as a removal treaty (Cleland et al. 2011; Satz 1991). Historian Ronald Satz (1991) argues that the Ojibwe demand for usufructuary rights to the ceded lands makes sense only if they understood the treaty allowed them to remain permanently in the ceded territory and continue their mixed land-based economy.

In an 1842 land-cession treaty, American negotiators sought Ojibwe lands along the south shore of Lake Superior for their copper deposits. Documentary evidence and Ojibwe oral history tell us that the Ojibwe hesitated to negotiate a new treaty unless assured they could remain in their homeland and maintain access to the natural resources needed for their economic and cultural survival. Government negotiator Robert Stuart assured Ojibwe leaders that they would not be asked to leave the ceded territories. According to Satz, the Ojibwe believed they could remain in the territory as long as they maintained a peaceful relationship with the United States. They thought that American demand for copper would not diminish their access to the natural resources of the ceded territory. Reflecting the Ojibwe geographical imagination of the ceded lands as a shared territory, Chief Martin, from the Lac Courte Oreilles Ojibwe community, said, "We have no objection to the white mans [*sic*] working the mines, & the timber & making farms. But we reserve the Birch bark & Ceder [*sic*], for canoes, and Rice & the Sugar tree and the privledge [*sic*] of hunting without being disturbed by whites" (Satz 1991, 44). Article 2 of the 1842 treaty reserved Ojibwe usufruct rights to the ceded territory.

HUMANISTIC PERSPECTIVES ON NATIVE AMERICANS
Chie Sakakibara

To a girl growing up in Japan, America was a distant place. A movie called *Dances with Wolves*, however, changed my relationship with the country for good. I remember how my eyes busily chased the subtitles as my mind became enchanted by the beauty of the land, the people, and the sound of the Lakota language projected upon the silver screen. Delicately entangled with my own subtle yet indigenous (native Ryukyuan) background, it was a moment of falling in love with native North America. Six years later, when I was twenty-one, I found myself under the big blue sky of Oklahoma, also known as "Native America," as a junior student in Native American studies at the University of Oklahoma.

Oklahoma became the home of my heart, while my soul remained in Japan. Walking in the two worlds and constantly being torn between them, I chose to stay in the United States to pursue a PhD in cultural geography at the University of Oklahoma. My doctoral advisor insisted that I immerse myself in a literature of humanistic geography. Throughout the endeavor, I learned how geographers have written about the relationship between space, place, and home and also about a sense of place as a product of these phenomena. I was intrigued by how a humanistic perspective could shed light upon cultural identities during periods of rapid environmental change and uncertain futures.

Lying between Japan and Oklahoma, Alaska became a symbolic place for me that connects my heart and soul. As a humanistic geographer in training, I left for Barrow in 2004—the northernmost place in Alaska—for ethnographic fieldwork to examine how the Iñupiat perceive and culturally respond to environmental changes incurred by climate variability. I specifically investigated the socioecological sustainability of traditional practices and the meaning of these practices in sustaining social life. I found that the relationship between bowhead whaling and a seasonally conditioned set of social activities provide the foundation for an Iñupiat identity as the People of the Whales. Their integrity with the whale is the cornerstone of social life from which practices of cultural resilience emerge.

Throughout my time in the field, the people of Barrow warmly embraced me, welcoming me into their community, and I was adopted by several whaling families. In the process, Alaska became another home in my life. As a geographer, I cannot imagine a happier scenario than my own experience.

In the late 1840s, pressures to remove the Ojibwe to a colony, or large reserve, in Minnesota grew. Territorial officials in Minnesota wanted the economic benefit associated with Ojibwe annuity payments and sought to move the tribe to east-central Minnesota. In 1850, President Zachary Taylor revoked the Ojibwe usufructuary rights and ordered the tribe's removal to unceded Ojibwe lands in the territory. Given their understanding of the treaty negotiations of 1837 and 1842, the Ojibwe protested the removal order as unjustified and illegal. The Wisconsin legislature, local missionaries, and local non-Indians supported them in their efforts. Minnesota officials conspired to remove the Ojibwe, transferring the location of the annual annuity payment three hundred miles west to Sandy Lake, Minnesota, in 1850. The delay of the annuity payment into late autumn, inadequate and poor food supplies, and the spread of infectious disease in the Ojibwe camps at Sandy Lake resulted in the tragic death of some four hundred Ojibwe. The tragedy at Sandy Lake, along with the antiremoval efforts of the Ojibwe and their non-Indian allies, resulted in suspension of the government's campaign. In 1854, as part of treaty negotiations over mineral lands in northeastern Minnesota, the Wisconsin Ojibwe received four permanent reservations located in their northern Wisconsin homelands (Satz 1991; Clifton 1987).

By the 1850s, the U.S. government's removal policy had fundamentally altered the geography of Indian Country in the eastern United States. Even though native geographies were radically transformed and diminished, the story is not one of an absolute geographical displacement of tribes from this region. Some eastern Indian tribes held on to small reserves or scattered homesteads and persist today as culturally and politically autonomous Indian communities. Native communities that successfully resisted removal were often located on the peripheries of non-Indian agricultural and urban settlement. Non-Indians no longer saw them as a threat or as competing for natural or land resources. Remnants of tribes, like the Ho-Chunk and Potawatomi in Wisconsin and the Cherokee in the Smoky Mountains, held on to small portions of their homelands because they were "away from the press of American settlement and held out until the pressure of removal diminished" (Clifton 1977, 280). Others, such as the Ojibwe, managed to garner support for their antiremoval efforts because of their social and economic integration into the non-Indian rural community. Pressures for Indian removal had diminished by the early 1850s, and a new geographical strategy of concentrating Indians in their homelands—on reservations—replaced removal as the U.S. government's Indian policy.

REORDERING THE GEOGRAPHY OF WESTERN INDIAN COUNTRY: RESERVATIONS AS SPATIAL FIX

In the late 1840s, Euro-American settlement expansion in the American West created a new set of geographical challenges for tribes and federal policy makers. Settlement in Texas, California, Oregon, and the eastern plains exhausted the "empty" spaces beyond the settlement frontier. During President Franklin Pierce's administration (1853–1857), a policy of spatial concentration of Indian communities onto reservations replaced the policy of Indian removal, or spatial separation. George Moneypenny, commissioner of Indian affairs at the time, described removal as a "fatal policy" and said that without a "reservation of land," the Indian would "be blotted out of existence" (ARCIA 1856, 231). Moneypenny argued that, to be "domesticated, improved and elevated," Indians "must have a home; a fixed, settled and permanent home" (ARCIA 1855, 18). He emphasized the need for a set location, saying, "How could the Indian become a cultivator of the soil without a permanent and fixed home and habitation" (ARCIA 1855, 17). Moneypenny's successor, Charles Mix, wrote, "We have no longer distant and extensive sections of the country which we can assign them." It was, he said, necessary to pursue a "policy of concentrating the Indians on small reservations of land" and to create a home "where they can be controlled and domesticated" (ARCIA 1858, 9). Through spatial confinement on a reservation, Indians would give up their "nomadic" subsistence culture and economy and become sedentary, Americanized farmers. Reservations were not, however, intended only to promote the spatial and social integration of Indian communities. They also served the economic interests of non-Indians, making the tribes' homelands available for railroads, farms, settlements, speculation, and timber and mineral development.

Treaties, executive orders, and acts of Congress were the tools used to implement the reservation policy of clearing Indian legal title from much of the West and carving reservations out of tribal homelands (Frantz 1999).[5] For example, in the 1850s, treaty negotiations led by Governor Joel Palmer of Oregon and Governor Isaac Stevens of Washington resulted in large land cessions and the creation of Indian reservations in western Oregon and much of what is now Washington State (Richards 2005). In the 1860s, treaty making with Plains and other western Indian tribes led to a number of land-cession treaties and the creation of reservations. The Treaty of Fort Laramie in 1868, for example, resulted in the creation of the Great Sioux Reservation in South Dakota west of the Missouri River. Some western tribes, such as the Apache (Arreola 2012; Perry 1993) and the Nez Perce, resisted confinement within the fixed borders of reservations, and the government resorted to military force to place and keep them on reservations.[6] Not all tribes retained a reservation in their traditional homelands. Government negotiators "induced" some southern Plains tribes to accept reservations in Indian Territory as part of the government's effort to consolidate Indians spatially for the purpose of creating a regime of efficient military and social control of Indian tribes (figure 4.1).

The reservation system aimed to expedite the social, economic, and spatial integration of American Indian communities. Spatial control was a key to social control and social change. Only restricted mobility that enabled authorities to observe individuals and impose a new "disciplinary" logic could accomplish the transformation of "nomadic" and mobile Indian tribes into sedentary, Americanized farmers. Restrictions on mobility would end native land-extensive hunting, fishing, and gathering practices and force native peoples to take up farming and become "civilized." In his study of the creation of Indian reservations in British Columbia, historical geographer Cole Harris identifies restricted mobility as key to the colonial administration of native people, noting that for native peoples who "once moved freely and widely within tribal territories . . . the management of movement associated with property rights was the most essential discipline imposed on them" (2002b, 18). Reserves and Euro-American property rights imposed a new, fixed, and rigid spatial system, "a reconfigured geography" and a "compartmentalized world" (Harris 2002b, 18). In his historical geographical

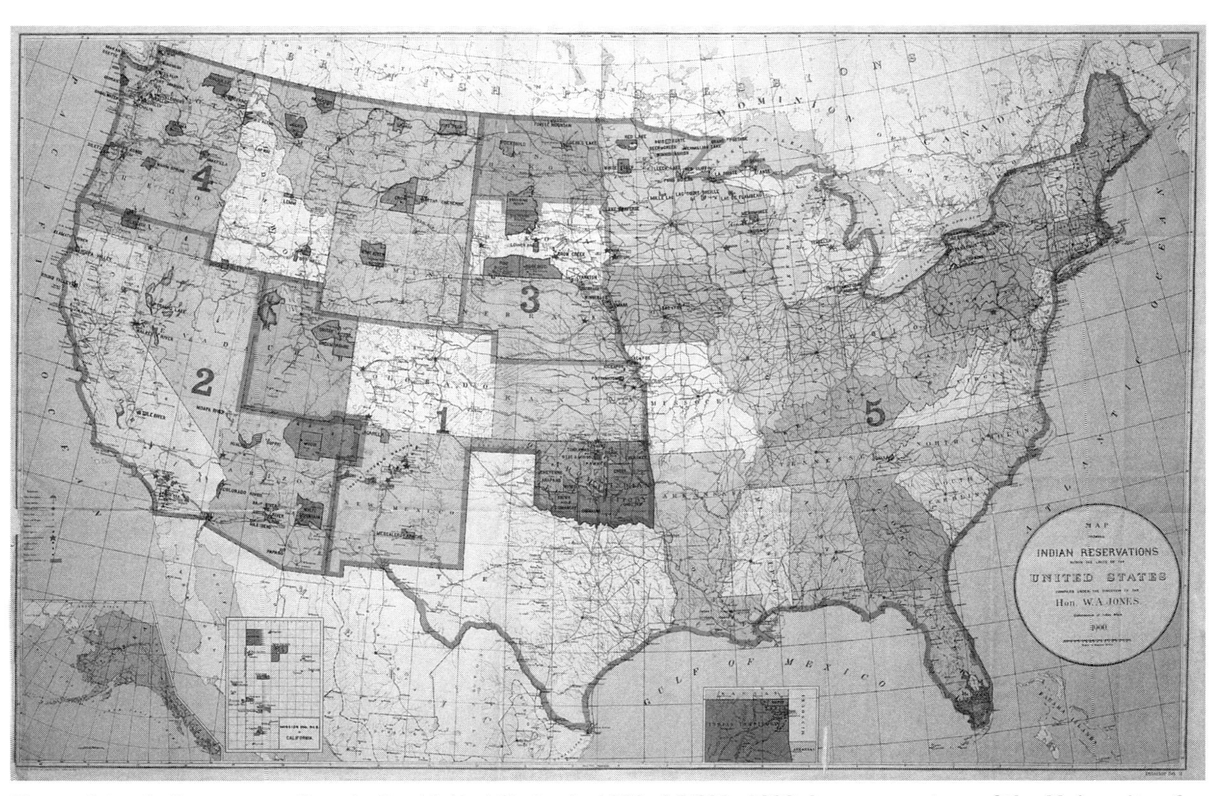

Figure 4.1. Indian reservations in the United States in 1900. ARCIA, 1900. Image courtesy of the University of Wisconsin Digital Collections Center.

study of space and social control of the Oglala Lakota on the Great Sioux Reservation, Matthew Hannah similarly identifies the use of spatial fixation and surveillance to enhance efforts to discipline, control, and "civilize" Indian behavior. "Spatial restriction and fixation," Hannah asserts, allowed for improved surveillance and the policing of unwanted behaviors, providing an adjustment necessary for "any effective system of normalizing social control, [namely] the ability to punish transgressions" (1993, 414, 421).

Reservations, however, did not necessarily become the confined space of assimilation the government intended. Instead, they became places where tribes maintained their communities, identities, and survival as distinct peoples. Within reservations Indians developed "strategies for coping with reservation life that enabled them to either resist or adapt to the 'civilization' programs thrust upon them by the federal government" (Edmunds, Hoxie, and Salisbury 2007, 320). Hannah notes how tribes countered the government's efforts at spatial fixation and surveillance through continued mobility, invisibility, and other "spatial forms of resistance" (2001, 120). According to Hannah, the Oglala Lakota used various forms of mobility, or "scattering," to avoid the government's efforts to "fix them in place" (2002, 123, 120).

Resisting spatial fixation within the reservation and maintaining mobility makes sense when one takes into account tribal spatial perspectives, which viewed reservation borders as permeable rather than rigid and confining. Tribal members crisscrossed reservation borders, traveling to the off-reservation territories historically used for hunting, fishing, and gathering and for ceremonial purposes. Many western tribes reserved treaty rights to off-reservation hunting, fishing, and gathering territories when they ceded their homelands in "exchange" for reservations. In Washington Territory, the Stevens treaties negotiated with Indian tribes along Puget Sound and the Columbia River in 1854–1855 contained clauses reserving hunting, gathering, and fishing rights in the ceded territories at "all usual and accustomed places" and "in common with the citizens of the Territory" (Kappler 1904, 699). Hunting and gathering rights were reserved on "open and unclaimed land" (Cohen, La France, and Bowden 1986). Other tribes held similar spatial perspectives on both treaty-reserved and inherent tribal hunting and fishing rights on off-reserve ceded territories (e.g., Shoshone-Bannock) in the West.

REORDERING RESERVATION SPACE: ALLOTMENT, DETRIBALIZATION, AND NATIVE RESISTANCE

Government policy makers and non-Indian reformers in the post–Civil War period predicated Indian "survival" on abandonment of "nomadic" subsistence practices and adoption of Euro-American farming. With localization of Indian communities on reservations came an effort to speed up detribalization through a policy based on the reordering of reservation space. By eliminating Indian common-property regimes and instituting individualized landholding or allotment in severalty, policy makers and reformers believed they could replace tribal community identities with an individualized, agrarian Euro-American identity.

Allotment, as a spatial strategy designed to promote the assimilation and integration of Indians into Euro-American society, was not a new idea in the 1870s and 1880s. Some Indian treaties had included it beginning in the 1830s. But in 1887, Congress passed the General Allotment Act, or Dawes Act, which made allotment a national strategy applicable to almost all Indian reservations in the United States. Under the Dawes Act, Congress authorized the president to survey reservations, after which tribal members chose their allotments. According to the act, heads of household received allotments of 160 acres, adults over eighteen received 80 acres, and children under eighteen received 40 acres. The government would hold allotments in trust and could not sell or lease them for twenty-five years. Additionally, allotments were exempt from state and local taxes. At the end of the trust period, Indians received fee simple title to their allotments and became U.S. citizens. At this time, their allotments became subject to state and local taxes (Prucha 1995). The goal of the allotment system was "to make Indians spatially like Euro-Americans" (Greenwald 2002, 7). Its framers hoped Indians would mimic the non-Indian settlement pattern of dispersed and individualized farmsteads when selecting their allotments, disregarding the quality of the land, availability of water, and native cultural values and environmental traditions.

The government purchased unallotted, or so-called surplus, lands and then resold them to non-Indians. While promoted as a spatial strategy for Indian assimilation, allotment served the economic interests of non-Indians who sought Indian mineral resources and grazing and agricultural lands. The sale of surplus lands opened up reservations for the first time to non-Indian ownership and settlement. Amendments to the Dawes Act later allowed Indians to lease their allotments and shortened or removed the trust period. This led to increasing amounts of land passing out of Indian control and ownership due to sales of allotments to non-Indians, defaults on mortgages, and government seizure due to property tax delinquency. The result was a checkerboard pattern of Indian and non-Indian land ownership on reservations, with much of the fertile, well-watered, and valuable land ending up in non-Indian hands, which would result in future state-tribal jurisdictional problems (figure 4.2). By the 1930s, when the Indian Reorganization Act ended allotment, reservations were territorially and politically integrated into the United States.[7]

Allotment succeeded in reducing the size of the native estate. From 1881 to 1933, overall native landholdings declined by 103 million acres from 155 million acres (1881) to 52 million acres (1933). The sale of unallotted surplus lands and allotted lands accounted for 26.5 million acres of this reduction (Greenwald 2002, 146; Carlson 1983, 39). The remainder of this substantial loss of Indian lands stemmed from seven large reservation land cessions between 1880 and 1895 (Hoxie 1984, 44).

Allotment did not affect reservations in the Southwest. It did, however, affect most reservations in the northern plains, the Rocky Mountain states, western Oklahoma (and eventually all of Indian Territory), the Pacific Northwest, and the western Great Lakes region. The Wisconsin Oneida, located near Green Bay in northeastern Wisconsin, are an example of a native community that lost much of its land when its allotments became subject to property taxation (Bieder 1995,

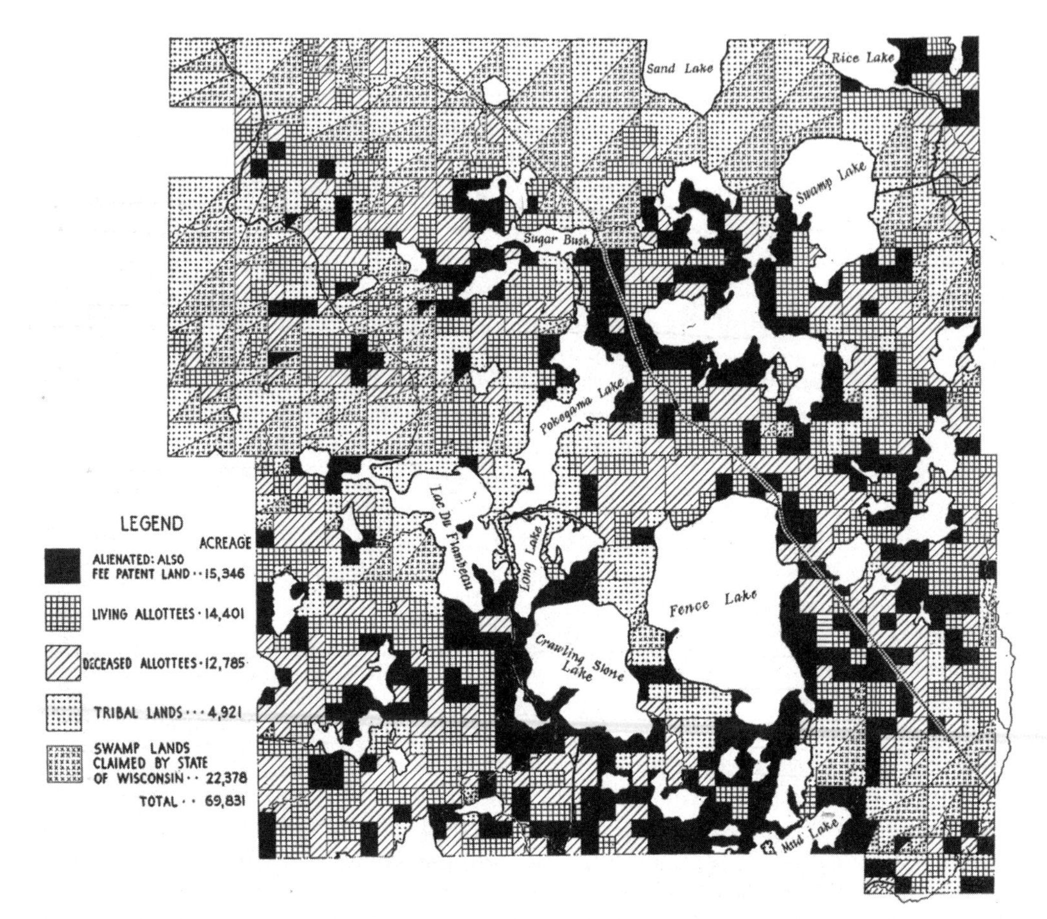

Figure 4.2. Allotment and the "checkerboard" on the Lac du Flambeau Reservation, Wisconsin. United States, 1935.

164). By 1924, foreclosures and tax sales resulted in only 200 acres of the 65,400-acre reservation remaining under tribal ownership (Hill-Kelly 2007). On the Wisconsin Ojibwe reservations, lumbering interests and resort developers acquired allotments when they became available for sale (Danziger 1979). By the time allotment ended in 1934, the Ojibwe land base had declined from 271,653 to 160,561 acres (Loew 2001, 65). Leasing also diminished Indian use of allotments. The Omaha and Winnebago of Nebraska, for example, leased 112,000 acres out of 140,000 acres on their two reservations by 1898 (Prucha 1995, 673).

And yet, the federal government's efforts at spatially reorganizing reservation geographies did not lead to the erosion of native identities. The government did not account for how native people might resist and adapt allotment to suit their own needs and fit it into their own "spatial system." Emily Greenwald's study of allotment on the Nez Perce and Jicarilla Apache reservations demonstrates how tribes adapted allotment to serve their "traditional environmental and cultural practices" (2002, 8). Rather than select dispersed, individual allotments, they "clustered allotments according to environmental features or social structures . . . thwarting the atomization that government officials hoped to achieve" (Greenwald 2002, 8). The Nez Perce and Jicarilla clustered their allotments to maintain access to what they viewed as valued lands, keep extended families together, promote economic cooperation, and maintain group identities. Greenwald maps Nez Perce allotments in better-watered bottom and canyon lands in accordance with traditional subsistence use of these areas and their holding culturally significant sites such as graves. Contrary to the hopes of government officials and advocates of allotment, "Indians used their allotment selections to remake themselves as Indian in the context of a policy that sought to destroy Indianness" (Greenwald 2002, 145). Though the Dawes Act may have not resulted in an elimination of tribal identities, it did open up reservations to non-Indian settlement and spatially integrate reservations into the national (and state) political geography.

OFF-RESERVATION HUNTING AND FISHING TREATY RIGHTS

Spatial reordering of Indian homelands and reservations was a key aspect of the assimilation strategy of the federal government during the nineteenth century. Officials assumed that spatial confinement and the individualized property regime of allotment would transform "nomadic" hunter-gatherer Indians into "civilized" farmers. Traditional hunting, fishing, and gathering activities, in particular, were incompatible with efforts to civilize Indians and convert them into sedentary agriculturalists. Efforts to prevent Indians from venturing to off-reservation traditional resource territories for seasonal hunting, gathering, and fishing were part of the government's spatial assimilationist Indian policies.

For native people, on the other hand, hunting, fishing, and gathering constituted an important means of subsistence and income from the sale of meat, fish, hides, and berries to non-Indians. These culturally significant activities also reflected and reproduced native identities. As such, they were transgressive; they challenged assimilationist efforts to make Indians conform to an American agrarian identity. Many Indian treaties contained explicit provisions guaranteeing access to off-reservation hunting, fishing, and gathering sites either in common with other citizens or as long as such locations were "unclaimed," "unoccupied," or not visibly settled (Spence 1999, 31–32). Native people believed they would share the resources of the ceded territories with non-Indian settlers; it would be a shared topography. They believed their treaty rights were enduring and permanent.

Indian off-reservation hunting, fishing, and gathering rights also ran counter to legal-geographical definitions of state power, non-Indian economic interests (e.g., commercial fishing, tourism), and the romanticized ideal of uninhabited wilderness and national parks. Such ideologies and interests viewed Indian off-reservation subsistence and commercial harvesting as immoral and illegal. In the 1870s and 1880s, state governments enforced conservation laws regarding the locations, timing (seasons), size of hunting territory, and methods of hunting and fishing (Clow 2001; Silvern 2001). Non-Indians complained that Indians were coming off-reservation and "slaughtering" and "wasting" fish and game. Numerous federal investigations found such reports lacking in evidence and instead lay the blame on non-Indians. Regardless of the inaccuracy of accusations against Indian hunters and fishers, state conservation officials sought expanded powers to regulate and control natural resources, especially in western states where federal lands constituted large areas of the public domain. Defining and defending states' rights, they harassed and arrested Indians found hunting and fishing off-reservation (Clow 2001; Spence 1999; Silvern 2001).

In the 1890s, as tensions built in Wyoming, Colorado, Washington, and a number of other states over the question of off-reservation treaty rights, federal and state officials initiated a legal test case to bring clarity to the issue. In 1895, the Bannock Indians consented to the test case, and state game wardens arrested Race Horse, a Bannock leader, for killing seven elk off reservation lands. The Shoshone and Bannock Indians of the Fort Hall Reservation in southeast Idaho reserved a right to "hunt on the unoccupied lands of the U.S." in the 1868 land-cession treaty that created their reservation (Kappler 1904, 1021). After becoming a state in 1890, Wyoming sought to apply conservation laws to Bannock Indians found hunting elk on ceded lands in the state. The Bannock claimed state laws did not apply to their treaty rights and that the lands in question were unoccupied and open for their hunting. As they and other tribes claiming such off-reserve treaty rights understood them, their hunting rights were permanent, though limited to lands not occupied or settled.

Wyoming successfully argued before the U.S. Supreme Court that the act of creating the state essentially occupied the landscape and that state laws should apply homogenously throughout the state to both Indian and non-Indian alike. In its decision in *Ward v. Race Horse* (163 U.S. 504 [1896]), the Court found that the treaty right was a temporary "privilege" and that government treaty negotiators never anticipated that such a "privilege" would remain after statehood and thereby diminish the states' rights. This notion of the impermanence of Indian treaty rights fit with the prevailing assimilationist attitude toward native hunting and fishing as uncivilized practices that agriculture should replace (Silvern 2008).[8]

Ward v. Race Horse became the legal-geographical rationale for states to restrict and regulate Indian off-reservation hunting and fishing treaty rights. In Wisconsin and Michigan, conservation officials cited *Race Horse* when arguing that Ojibwe off-reservation hunting and fishing treaty rights were temporary and that the state had the right to regulate its territory and natural resources. Similar arguments were made in the western states and the Pacific Northwest. The legal-geographical rationale elevating state's rights over Indian off-reservation treaty rights articulated in the *Race Horse* decision coincided with government support of non-Indian commercialization of fisheries in the Pacific Northwest and Great Lakes region,[9] emerging nature tourism and recreation, and sport hunting and fishing interests.

Historian Mark David Spence explores how "wilderness preservation" and the creation of American national parks "went hand in hand with native dispossession" in the last quarter of the nineteenth century (1999, 3; also see Keller and

Turek 1998). Wilderness, conceived of as an "uninhabited Eden," required the removal of any sign of human activity. Many areas that became national parks, such as Yellowstone, had a long and continuous history of native occupation and use, which included hunting and gathering, burning to modify landscapes, and ceremonial activities. For national parks to become uninhabited Edens "set aside for the benefit and pleasure of vacationing Americans" (Spence 1999, 4), native people had to be removed and denied their customary use of the area. Wilderness, constructed as a "natural" and not a humanized landscape, was no place for Indians, who should be kept on their reservations, where they could be "civilized," and not allowed to violate the "sacred," monumental, and nationalist landscapes associated with "national" parks. Native subsistence and ceremonial use of national parks was inconsistent with the norm of the romanticized and recreational experience of wilderness.

At the time of its creation as the nation's first national park in 1872, Yellowstone was the seasonal home to Shoshone, Bannock, and Crow Indians. In 1868 these tribes ceded the territory that made up the park in the Fort Bridger and Fort Laramie treaties, reserving hunting rights on the "unoccupied" lands of the cession. The tribes considered Yellowstone "unoccupied" and continued to hunt, fish, and gather there as part of their seasonal subsistence round. In the late 1870s, the government removed the last native inhabitants of the park and struggled to prevent Indians from entering for subsistence activities (Spence 1999, 58). These initial efforts failed as Indians traveled to "remote" regions of Yellowstone on a seasonal basis, avoiding the main tourist area and the military garrison headquartered in the park (Spence 1999, 60). By the mid-1880s, park officials perceived Indians as a threat to wildlife in Yellowstone and incompatible with its preservation. The military officers who took over management of the park in 1886 viewed Indian hunting as an "unmitigated evil" (Captain Moses A. Harris, quoted in Spence 1999, 63). *Ward v. Race Horse* provided them with the legal rationale for ending native hunting and fishing in the park. According to Spence, "No superintendent had ever questioned his legal authority to obstruct or prevent native use of the national park, but *Ward v. Race Horse* now obligated various state and federal agencies, including the Bureau of Indian Affairs, to keep native hunters away from Yellowstone and safely confined to their reservations" (1999, 68).

With the creation of national parks, Indian tribes confronted another reconfiguration of their homeland geographies. They were now considered trespassers and poachers in parks once part of their traditional seasonal subsistence round. Similar reconfigurations occurred in other regions of the country. For example, local and state governments, railroads, and tourism interests in northern Wisconsin promoted the Ojibwe homeland as a wilderness and natural landscape for non-Indian tourism and recreation. The vision of the Wisconsin Northwoods as a natural playground required the Ojibwe to conform to state laws and Euro-American norms for sport hunting and fishing; those customary subsistence hunting, fishing, and gathering practices that did not were criminalized. The Ojibwe, however, believed they were exercising a treaty right to hunt, fish, and gather on- and off-reservation. Despite arrests by state wardens, Ojibwe continued to claim a moral and legal right to exercise their off-reservation treaty rights (Silvern 1995). Favorable court decisions at the end of the twentieth century recognizing treaty rights turned aside the confluence of socioeconomic forces, legal decisions, and ideologies that worked in tandem to limit native spatial mobility and to exclude native people from their off-reserve ceded resource territories for over one hundred years.

NOTES

1. Historians and historical geographers studying American Indians are using and discussing the lens or framework of settler colonialism and postcolonialism. This also involves placing the American historical experience in a global, comparative perspective—a postexceptionalist view of American history—to shed new light on indigenous peoples in North America. This perspective has allowed for more complex understandings of native agency, adaptation, and resistance and highlighted the importance of space and territoriality in the production of settler colonialism. See Meinig (1993); Limerick (2001); Harris (2002b); Ostler (2004); Whaley (2005); Hoxie (2008); Blackhawk (2011); Calloway ([2008] 2011); Kramer (2011).

2. Also see Colten et al. (2003, 154) who wrote that "much remains to be done" on the historical geography of Native Americans. This is not to suggest that geographers have not made important contributions to understanding the historical geographies of native peoples. See Hilliard (1971, 1972); Kay (1979); Ross and Moore (1987); Meinig (1993, 1998); Wishart (1994); Frantz (1999); Bays (1998); Fouberg (2000); special issue of *Historical Geography* edited by Deur (2002); Kilpinen (2004); Hurt (2003, 2005). For historical geographers using settler colonialism and postcolonial to frame their approach, see C. Harris (2002b); Olund (2002); Morin (2002).

3. For the full text of Indian treaties, see Kappler (1904).

4. The Cherokee were, by 1832, divided into pro- and antitreaty factions. The minority pro-treaty faction negotiated a removal treaty with the United States in 1835 at New Echota, ceding Cherokee lands in exchange for land in Indian Territory (now Oklahoma), and agreed to relocate within two years of the ratification of the treaty by the U.S. Senate. The antitreaty faction, representing the majority of the Cherokee, argued that the pro-treaty faction had no authority to negotiate a treaty and that the removal treaty was invalid. Refusing to leave their homeland, they petitioned Congress not to honor what they deemed a fraudulent document. The approximately thirteen thousand Cherokee forced to emigrate in the fall and winter of 1839 suffered much hardship, and an estimated two to four thousand died on the "Trail of Tears" to Indian Territory (Prucha 1995; Perdue 2012; Perdue and Green 2007).

5. Negotiated treaties continued, until 1871, to be the legal tool for reducing tribal domains and creating reservations. In 1871 Congress ended Indian treaty making. All future reservations, Indian land cessions, and other changes to Indian lands resulted from presidential executive orders, agreements, and acts (statutes) of Congress.

6. Jacoby (2008) and Blackhawk (2006) draw our attention to the need to take into account and understand the role of violence in the history and historical geography of settler colonialism and the diverse responses of native peoples to and involvement in such violence.

7. The Dawes Act excluded from allotment the Five Civilized Tribes (Osage, Miami, Peoria, Sac, and Foxes) in Indian Territory, the Senecas of New York, and Sioux Lands in Nebraska.

8. The Court did not employ the canons of construction or rules it created for interpreting Indian treaties. These rules are in place to remind the Court to take into account Indian understandings of the treaty, liberally construe the treaties in favor of Indians, and "resolve" ambiguities in favor of Indians (Royster and Blumm 2008). The Court failed to do this when it did not consider the Bannocks spatial and temporal understandings of the treaty.

9. For studies of the commercialization of fish and game, the promotion of sport hunting and fishing, and native exclusion from these resources, see D. C. Harris (2008), Doherty (1990), and Warren (1997).

REFERENCES

ARCIA (*Annual Report of the Commissioner of Indian Affairs*), United States. Office of Indian Affairs, Washington, D.C.: Government Printing Office. http://digital.library.wisc.edu/1711.dl/HISTORY.COMMREP (last accessed 24 June 2013).

Arreola, D. D. 2012. Chiricahua Apache Homeland in the Borderland Southwest. *Geographical Review* 102, no. 1: 111–31.

Bays, B. 1998. *Townsite Settlement and Dispossession in the Cherokee Nation, 1866–1907*. New York: Garland.

Bieder, R. E. 1995. *Native American Communities in Wisconsin, 1600–1960: A Study of Tradition and Change.* Madison: University of Wisconsin Press.

Blackhawk, N. 2006. *Violence over the Land: Indians and Empires in the Early American West.* Cambridge, MA: Harvard University Press.

———. 2011. Currents in North American Indian Historiography. *Western Historical Quarterly* 42, no. 3: 319–24.

Calloway, C. G. 1998. *New Worlds for All: Indians, Europeans, and the Remaking of Early America.* Baltimore: Johns Hopkins University Press.

———. [2008] 2011. Presidential Address: Indian History from the End of the Alphabet; and What Now? *Ethnohistory* 58, no. 2: 197–211.

———. 2013. *Pen and Ink Witchcraft: Treaties and Treaty Making in American Indian History.* Oxford: Oxford University Press.

Carlson, L. A. 1983. Federal Policy and Indian Land: Economic Interests and the Sale of Indian Allotments, 1900–1934. *Agricultural History* 57, no. 1: 33–45.

Carson, J. T. 2002. Ethnogeography and the Native American Past. *Ethnohistory* 49, no. 4: 769–88.

Cleland, C. E., with B. R. Greene, M. Slonim, N. N. Cleland, K. L. Tierney, S. Durocher, and B. Pierson. 2011. *Faith in Paper: The Ethnohistory and Litigation of Upper Great Lakes Indian Treaties.* Ann Arbor: University of Michigan Press.

Clifton, J. A. 1977. *The Prairie People: Continuity and Change in Potawatomi Indian Culture, 1665–1965.* Lawrence: Regents Press of Kansas.

———. 1987. Wisconsin Death March: Explaining the Extremes in Old Northwest Indian Removal. *Transactions of the Wisconsin Academy of Sciences, Arts and Letters* 75: 1–40.

Clow, R. L. 2001. Colorado Game Laws and the Dispossession of the Inherent Hunting Right of the White River and Umcompahgre Utes. In *Trusteeship in Change: Toward Tribal Autonomy in Resource Management,* edited by I. Sutton and R. L. Clow, 15–33. Boulder, CO: University Press of Colorado.

Cohen, F. G., J. La France, and V. L. Bowden. 1986. *Treaties on Trial: The Continuing Controversy over Northwest Indian Fishing Rights.* Seattle: University of Washington Press.

Colten, C. E., P. J. Hugill, T. Young, and K. M. Morin. 2003. Historical Geography. In *Geography in America at the Dawn of the 21st Century*, edited by G. L. Gaile and C. J. Willmott, 149–63. Oxford: Oxford University Press.

Danziger, E. J. 1979. *The Chippewas of Lake Superior.* Norman: University of Oklahoma Press.

Deur, D. E., ed. 2002. Indigenous Peoples: Contested Lands, Contested Identities. *Historical Geography* 30.

Doherty, R. 1990. *Disputed Waters: Native Americans and the Great Lakes Fishery.* Lexington: University Press of Kentucky.

Edmunds, R. D., F. E. Hoxie, and N. Salisbury. 2007. *The People: A History of Native America.* Boston: Houghton Mifflin Co.

Fouberg, E. H. 2000. *Tribal Territory, Sovereignty, and Governance: A Study of the Cheyenne River and Lake Traverse Indian Reservations.* New York: Garland Publishing.

Frantz, K. 1999. *Indian Reservations in the United States: Territory, Sovereignty, and Socioeconomic Change.* Chicago: University of Chicago Press.

Greenwald, E. 2002. *Reconfiguring the Reservation: The Nez Perces, Jicarilla Apaches, and the Dawes Act.* Albuquerque: University of New Mexico Press.

Hannah, M. G. 1993. Space and Social Control in the Administration of Oglala Lakota ("Sioux"), 1871–1879. *Journal of Historical Geography* 19, no. 4: 412–32.

———. 2002. Varieties of Oglala Lakota Resistance to Displacement and Control. In *Geographical Identities of Ethnic America: Race, Space, and Place*, edited by K. A. Berry and M. L. Henderson, 116–29. Reno: University of Nevada Press.

Harris, C. 2002a. Native Lands and Livelihoods in British Columbia. *Historical Geography* 30: 15–32.

———. 2002b. *Making Native Space: Colonialism, Resistance, and Reserves in British Columbia.* Vancouver: University of British Columbia Press.

Harris, D. C. 2008. *Landing Native Fisheries: Indian Reserves and Fishing Rights in British Columbia, 1849–1925.* Vancouver: University of British Columbia Press.

Hill-Kelly, J. 2007. Restoring the Reservation, Sustaining the Oneida. *Natural Resources and the Environment* 21, no. 3: 21–23, 75.

Hilliard, S. B. 1971. Indian Land Cessions West of the Mississippi. *Journal of the West* 10, no. 3: 493–510.

———. 1972. Indian Land Cessions (Map Supplement Number 16). *Annals of the Association of American Geographers* 62, no. 2: 374.

Hoxie, F. E. 1984. *A Final Promise: The Campaign to Assimilate the Indians, 1880–1920.* Lincoln, NE: University of Nebraska Press.

———. 2008. Retrieving the Red Continent: Settler Colonialism and the History of American Indians in the U.S. *Ethnic and Racial Studies* 31, no. 6: 1153–67.

Hurt, D. A. 2003. Defining American Homelands: A Creek Nation Example, 1828–1907. *Journal of Cultural Geography* 21, no. 1: 19–43.

———. 2005. "The Indian Home Is Undone": Anglo Intrusion, Colonization, and the Creek Nation, 1867–1907. *Chronicles of Oklahoma* 83: 194–217.

Jacoby, K. 2008. "The Broad Platform of Extermination": Nature and Violence in the Nineteenth Century North American Borderlands. *Journal of Genocide Research* 10, no. 2: 249–67.

Kappler, C. J. 1904. *Indian Affairs: Laws and Treaties, V. 2.* Washington, D.C.: Government Printing Office.

Kay, J. 1979. Wisconsin Indian Hunting Patterns, 1634–1836. *Annals of the Association of American Geographers* 69: 402–18.

Keller, R. H, and M. F. Turek. 1998. *American Indians and National Parks.* Tucson: University of Arizona Press.

Kilpinen, J. T. 2004. The Supreme Court's Role in Choctaw and Chickasaw Dispossession. *Geographical Review* 94, no. 4: 484–501.
Kramer P. A. 2011. Power and Connection: Imperial Histories of the United States in the World. *American Historical Review* 116, no. 5: 1348–92.
Limerick, P. N. 2001. Going West and Ending Up Global. *Western Historical Quarterly* 32, no. 1: 4–23.
Locke, Alain. 1925. *The New Negro: An Interpretation*. New York: Albert & Charles Boni.
Loew, P. 2001. *Indian Nations of Wisconsin: Histories of Endurance and Renewal*. Madison: Wisconsin Historical Society Press.
Lurie, N. O. 1980. *Wisconsin Indians*. Madison: State Historical Society of Wisconsin.
Meinig, D. W. 1993. *The Shaping of America: A Geographical Perspective on 500 Years of History*. Vol. 2: *Continental America, 1800–1867*. New Haven, CT: Yale University Press.
———. 1998. *The Shaping of America: A Geographical Perspective on 500 Years of History*. Vol. 3: *Transcontinental America, 1850–1915*. New Haven, CT: Yale University Press.
Morin, K. 2002. Postcolonialism and Native American Geographies: The Letters of Rosalie La Flesche Farley, 1896–1899. *Cultural Geographies* 9, no. 2: 158–80.
Olund, E. 2002. From Savage Space to Governable Space: The Extension of United States Judicial Sovereignty over Indian Country in the Nineteenth Century. *Cultural Geographies* 9, no. 2: 129–157.
Ostler, J. 2004. *The Plains Sioux and U.S. Colonialism from Lewis and Clark to Wounded Knee*. Cambridge: Cambridge University Press.
Pearce, M. 2004. The Holes in the Grid: Reservation Surveys in Lower Michigan. *Michigan Historical Review* 30, no. 2: 135–66.
Perdue, T. 2012. The Legacy of Indian Removal. *Journal of Southern History* 78, no. 1: 3–36.
Perdue, T., and M. D. Green. 2007. *The Cherokee Nation and the Trail of Tears*. New York: Viking.
Perry, R. J. 1993. *Apache Reservation: Indigenous Peoples and the American State*. Austin: University of Texas Press.
Prucha, F. P. 1994. *American Indian Treaties: The History of a Political Anomaly*. Berkeley: University of California Press.
———. 1995. *The Great Father: The United States Government and the American Indians*. 1st Bison Books ed. Lincoln: University of Nebraska Press.
Richards, K. 2005. The Stevens Treaties of 1854–55. *Oregon Historical Quarterly* 106, no. 3: 342–50.
Ross, T., and T. G. Moore. 1987. *A Cultural Geography of North American Indians*. Boulder, CO: Westview Press.
Royster, J. V., and M. C. Blumm. 2008. *Native American Natural Resources Law: Cases and Materials*. 2nd ed. Durham, NC: Carolina Academic Press.
Satz, R. N. 1991. *Chippewa Treaty Rights: The Reserved Rights of Wisconsin's Chippewa Indians in Historical Perspective*. Madison: Wisconsin Academy of Sciences, Arts and Letters.
Silvern, S. E. 1995. Nature, Territory and Identity in the Wisconsin Treaty Rights Controversy. *Ecumene* 2: 267–92.
———. 2001. Reclaiming the Reservation: The Geopolitics of Wisconsin Anishinaabe Resource Rights. *American Indian Culture and Research Journal* 24, no. 3: 131–53.
———. 2008. State-Centrism, the Equal Footing Doctrine, and the Historical Legal-Geographies of American Indian Treaty Rights. *Historical Geography* 30: 33–58.

Spence, M. D. 1999. *Dispossessing the Wilderness: Indian Removal and the Making of the National Parks.* Oxford: Oxford University Press.
US National Resources Board, Land Planning Committee. 1935. *Report on Land Planning.* Vol. 10: *Indian Land Tenure, Economic Status, and Population Trends.* Washington, D.C.: U.S. Government Printing Office.
Warren, L. S. 1997. *The Hunter's Game: Poachers and Conservationists in Twentieth-Century America.* New Haven, CT: Yale University Press.
Whaley, G. H. 2005. Oregon, Illahee, and the Empire Republic: A Case Study of American Colonialism, 1843–1858. *Western Historical Quarterly* 36, no. 2: 157–78.
Wishart, D. J. 1994. *An Unspeakable Sadness: The Dispossession of the Nebraska Indians.* Lincoln: University of Nebraska Press.
Witgen, M. 2012. The Native New World and Western North America. *Western Historical Quarterly* 43, no. 3: 292–99.

5

Labor and New Community Formation in the Twentieth Century

Ines M. Miyares

Significant eras of interrelated economic and social change characterized the twentieth century in the United States and influenced the geography of American communities. The people who established and transformed these communities reflect these processes. In this chapter, I develop the theme of labor-related immigration and the communities it formed. Although several historical geographers have contributed to this theme, much of the work in his area has been done by ethnic geographers and sociologists who use a historical geography methodology.

Immigration laws provide a framework for labor immigration in the twentieth century. Prior to World War II, immigration law became increasingly restrictive due to fears of people who were culturally different and of laborers willing to work for lower wages than native-born Americans. By 1924, it was difficult for laborers from eastern or southern Europe to immigrate to the United States and impossible for workers from Asia, other than the American-controlled Philippines, to enter. The 1924 Johnson-Reed National Origins Act established the Border Patrol, primarily to police the border with Mexico and inhibit undocumented laborers from entering the country; otherwise, there were no restrictions on Latin American immigration until 1952.

The historical geographies of labor coincide with the transformation of the United States from a commercial agrarian society with a rapidly growing manufacturing sector, into a manufacturing powerhouse with a declining agricultural sector, into a growing services- and telecommunications-based economy with a declining manufacturing sector. Also, in part because of social and economic changes brought about by World War II and in part due to the Cold War, change came in the form of the 1952 McCarran-Walter Immigration and Nationality Act. This legislation reframed immigration law, linking it to economic and scientific competition with the Soviet Union, changing the character of both immigrant labor and new immigrants' communities by creating categories of highly trained professionals who could qualify for immigrant visas. This law also introduced the concept of family reunification, allowing spouses and minor children of naturalized citizens to receive immigrant visas without having to qualify for one of the newly defined labor visa categories. This further changed the face of the country since two-thirds of all new immigrants between 1952 and 1965 entered on family reunification visas. The 1965 Immigration Reform Act took this law one step further, reinforcing the labor categories and expanding the family categories to include extended family members not listed in the 1952 law.

The 1952 Immigration and Nationality Act opened the door to highly skilled Asian immigrants, and the 1965 Immigration Reform Act eliminated the remaining national-origin quotas enacted in 1917 and 1924, which had been preferential to northern and western Europeans and prohibited Asian immigration. Early in the century, labor migrants tended to be less skilled, working in agriculture or industry and typically living in older, poorer urban neighborhoods. In the latter half of the century, immigrants were more likely to be educated professionals settling in middle- or upper-class neighborhoods or in the suburbs and maintaining community networks in very different ways.

Labor migrants settling in cities have formed several different types of communities. In some cases, immigrants of like backgrounds settle in the same neighborhood but work elsewhere, never developing a secondary economy that serves coethnics. While these immigrants establish ethnic neighborhoods, they do not necessarily form ethnic enclaves. Alejandro Portes and Robert L. Bach (1985) define the term "ethnic enclave" as an ethnic community with an entrepreneurial class that has developed an internal economy that both serves and employs coethnics. Some of the immigrant groups discussed in this chapter formed ethnic neighborhoods but worked in mainstream labor jobs such as light and heavy industry and agriculture. If a wave of labor migrants also included entrepreneurs with the human and cultural capital to establish an enclave economy, immigrants had the option of entering the mainstream economy or the secondary enclave economy.

Most research on ethnic neighborhoods and enclaves has examined them as freestanding, distinct communities with possible transnational ties to the home country. However, historical geographer Michael Conzen (1990, 1993) introduced the concept of the ethnic archipelago, a model more representative of a number of twentieth-century settlement patterns. In studying the Lithuanian community in the Midwest, Conzen found that its members maintained a network of settlements, a series of ethnic islands interconnected through a variety of cultural networks. This model has found effective application, primarily in urban and suburban settings, to both Cubans (McHugh, Miyares, and Skop 1997) and the Hmong nationally (Miyares 1997), to Flemish Belgians in the Midwest (Hume 2003), and to the Samoans in Southern California (Koletty 2001).

After 1952, new immigrants from Asian countries such as India and China, countries from which restrictive immigration laws had previously prohibited entry, did not have immediate family members already in the United States and did not qualify for family reunification visas right away. The could only enter legally by qualifying for visas designated for educated professionals and other highly skilled laborers. Instead of settling in poorer neighborhoods abandoned by previous waves of migrants, like their predecessors earlier in the twentieth century, these immigrants settled in middle- and upper-class urban neighborhoods, suburban areas, or "ethnoburbs" (Li 1998), displaying what Wilbur Zelinsky and Barrett A. Lee (1998) have called heterolocalism, a pattern of dispersed settlement by immigrants who maintain a strong sense of community through networks such as churches and the Internet.

EUROPEAN IMMIGRANT NEW COMMUNITY FORMATION

Influenced by the writings of environmental determinist geographer Ellen Churchill Semple, sociologist Robert Park (1928) argued that certain new labor migrants to cities would have such significant social differences that they would never truly assimilate and would remain marginalized populations within the urban social order. He specifically mentioned Japanese and Southern African Americans who were migrating to cities to pursue new labor opportunities. His writings, as well as those of University of Chicago colleague and collaborator Ernest Burgess, led to the development of the Chicago School of Urban Ecology, a school of thought that influenced many ethnic geographers and sociologists studying the communities formed by these pre–World War II labor migrants. Burgess (1928) developed one of the most influential models of labor settlement for both sociologists and geographers (figure 5.1). He argued that in the core of a city, that is, the central business district, there would be very little residential settlement, with the exception of possibly a Chinatown. Patterns of settlement moved out in a radial pattern from this core in relation to how assimilated the laborer community was. Factories would be located near the core of the nineteenth-century city, affecting housing quality proximate to industrial zones. Housing nearest the factories would be of the lowest quality and cost and would attract the most recent migrants—both African American recent urban migrants and recent immigrants—resulting in black ghettos and ethnic communities concentrated in tenements and other forms of low-income housing. Those immigrants able to assimilate over time into higher levels of the urban social order would be found farther out in the Zone of Workingmen's Housing. This zone would also have working-class higher-density housing near newer industrial districts and serve as a steppingstone to the Residential Zone, where one would find single-family homes. The Commuter Zone represented the emerging suburbs, populated by the white middle and upper classes, which could afford to commute to jobs in the central business district.

Richard Harris and Robert Lewis (1998, 2001) have shown that Burgess's model so oversimplifies urban economic zones and ethnic and racial settlement patterns that it fails to represent the urban spatial patterns of the day, even in Chicago, the city on which the model was based. Industrial jobs that attracted less-skilled laborers and recent immigrants could be found in multiple urban areas, including suburbs. They discovered that African Americans commonly lived in the lower-quality housing in the urban core because restrictive covenants and other, then legal race-based real estate practices, prevented them from

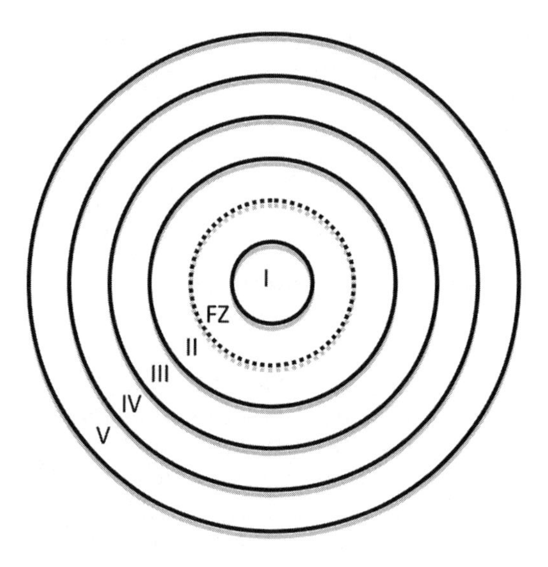

I. Loop (Central Business District)
Factory Zone
II. Zone in Transition
III. Zone of Workingmen's Homes
IV. Residential Zone
V. Commuters Zone

Figure 5.1. Urban zones in the growth of the city. After Burgess (1928).

accessing housing in other areas. Even in the early twentieth century, however, immigrant communities formed in suburbs where industrial jobs were available. Nonetheless, because of the Chicago School's prestige, research on immigrant labor communities of the early twentieth century adopted this faulty conceptual framework, contributing incremental modifications. David Ward, for example, reviewed the settlement patterns of a number of late-nineteenth-century labor immigrant groups, noting that they tended to settle in clusters in close proximity to the specific industries in which they were employed, adding more complexity to Burgess's radial model. They tended to live in older tenements that predated emerging codes that improved housing quality. With lower incomes, recent immigrants found it difficult to afford neighborhoods with higher-quality housing. Over time, the earlier immigrants, the Irish and Germans, were able to move to better housing, and the next waves of immigrants, Italians and Jews, settled in the tenements. These patterns of residential succession continued until developers replaced the dilapidated housing, often with high-density housing of only marginally better quality (Ward 1968).

In her 2006 analysis of the formation of "Little Italies" in various North American cities, Donna R. Gabaccia acknowledges that Burgess's model does apply but was influenced by social processes and the determinist perspective Burgess laid out. She argues that old-stock European Americans saw Italians as culturally distinct and restricted them to segregated neighborhoods, resulting in the formation of residential clusters where they spoke Italian in homes, businesses, and churches and perpetuated Italian culture. Rather than the Italians themselves, however, outsiders who observed the cultural landscape created by the residents dubbed the neighborhoods "Little Italies." "Italo-phobia" was not solely an American phenomenon affecting settlement. Michael Buzzelli (2001) found that Italian settlement in Toronto in the early twentieth century followed similar patterns as a result of sociocultural fears that led to residential segregation by ethnic origin. Italians settled in the older St. Clair neighborhood, which British-descent residents were leaving (Buzzelli 2001). Robert Orsi (1992) explains that "Italo-phobia" arose in a society accustomed to northern and western European "whiteness" and African American "blackness," with no place for olive-skinned "inbetweenness." Thus, Italian immigrants settled in either marginal spaces abandoned by earlier settlers or proximate to African Americans, such as in New York's Harlem (Orsi 1992).

Stavros Constantinou (2007) describes a similar pattern among Greeks in Akron, Ohio, albeit one with different causes. Reconstructing the evolution of the Greek community using historical church records, Constantinou argues that the community formed through patterns of chain migration, as young men followed previous successful migrants and communities formed around traditional Greek social spaces such as coffeehouses. The organization of a Greek Orthodox parish solidified such communities (Constantinou 2007). Chain migration and church membership also played a key role in the creation of early Polish communities, but in a very different way than for Greeks. Thomas Monzell writes that the Roman Catholic parish served as an Americanizing agent since, unlike Greeks, Catholic immigrants came from multiple countries. Once there was a concentration of Poles, there might be a Polish-language parish or service, as well as Polish-language community services through the local church, giving Poles the option of engaging in either English- or Polish-language cultural life (Monzell 1969).

LATIN AMERICAN IMMIGRANT NEW COMMUNITY FORMATION

The Latin American community in the United States is currently the largest non-European population in the country; it is also the fourth-largest Latin American population in the world. It is now quite diverse, but that diversity has developed in recent decades. Prior to World War II, with the exception of Puerto Ricans, as citizens of an American territory, the two largest Latin American immigrant communities were Mexicans and Cubans. Their geographies and settlement experiences were quite different, particularly because they initially came to the United States to fill very different labor niches. Mexicans primarily worked in agriculture in the Southwest and West; Cubans worked in cigar factories in Florida, New Jersey, and New York and in publishing in New York.

Historical cultural geographers have designated distinct Hispanic cultural regions in the Southwest based on settlement patterns set prior to the transfer of territories after the Mexican-American War. Richard Nostrand (1980) and Alvar Carlson (1990) have designated the upper Rio Grande region of north-central New Mexico near Taos and Santa Fe as the Hispano Homeland. Santa Fe is the oldest continually inhabited European-origin civilian settlement in the United States, originally founded by Spain in 1606. The Hispano Homeland designated by Nostrand and Carlson refers to a region that still holds many of the historical linguistic and other cultural markers that predate Mexican independence. Descendants of the Hispanic colonists refer to themselves as Spanish Americans, not Mexican Americans, and with the number of people who cling to this identity after four centuries of settlement, New Mexico has the highest percentage of Hispanics in its population.

Daniel Arreola (1993, 2002) contrasts this territory with the Tejano Homeland in South Texas. The Tejanos, or Texas Mexicans who predate the Anglo takeover of the state and region, settled along the north side of the lower Rio Grande. Whereas the more northern Hispano Homeland has maintained its historic and increasingly relic landscape, Arreola shows that Mexican towns that grew up along the border during the bracero program (1942–1964) and the maquiladora program (1964 to present) maintain the Mexican character and population of the region, which are further strengthened by documented and undocumented migration and family connections across the border.

Mexicans represent an unusual case. Prior to 1848, the American Southwest was Mexican territory. Americans in the region were there as immigrants, often either holding Spanish land grants or working for those who did (Nostrand 1987). Thus, the first "Mexican Americans" became U.S. citizens as a result of the 1848 territorial cessions after the Mexican-American War. Most Mexicans in the newly acquired American territories lived in coastal and Southern California, southern Arizona, the upper Rio Grande area of New Mexico, and the lower Rio Grande area of Texas. Prior to and during World War II, a large proportion of the Mexican community in the United States worked in agriculture in these regions, reinforcing historical settlement patterns.

The Census Bureau has made continual changes to its enumeration methods for the Latin American community in the United States, complicating attempts to represent this group's historical geography accurately. Prior to 1930, census enumerators may have recorded lighter-skinned Mexicans as white and darker-skinned individuals as "Other Colored," since nineteenth- and early-twentieth-century censuses included very few racial and ethnic categories. In 1930, the census tallied only those born in Mexico or whose parents were born in Mexico as Mexican, unless they appeared to the enumerator to be white; thus, the count omitted all whose families had been in the United States more than two generations (Samora and Vandel Simon 1977). In 1940, the census did not include a category for Mexican identity. Instead, it asked about the language spoken in the home, missing any multigeneration Mexican or other Hispanic households in which English was spoken.

In 1950 and 1960, the Census Bureau developed a list of several thousand Spanish surnames in order to identify the Mexican population. The enumerators only asked those who resided in the five southwestern states of California, Texas, Arizona, New Mexico, and Nevada if they were Mexican. A significant number of Mexicans had migrated to Chicago during World War II to fill factory jobs vacated by those serving in the military. Thus the tabulation missed many Mexicans who did not live in these five states, making reconstruction of this group's historical geography more challenging.

Coinciding with the emergence of ethnic self-identification, the 1970 census was the first to enumerate the Hispanic community nationally, but it did so only on the census long form (Samora and Vandel Simon 1977). The 1980 census introduced Hispanic origin as an option on the short form, with the follow-up option of specifying Spanish-origin population (Mexican, Puerto Rican, Cuban, Central or South American, or other Spanish origin). The census continued this practice in 1990, and the national-origin options expanded in each of the 2000 and 2010 censuses, as the Latin American origin population continued to diversify.

World War II was a defining moment for the Mexican-origin population in the United States. Prior to the war, Mexican communities in the United States were primarily a rural and small-town phenomenon. During the postwar period, attracted by the prospect of higher incomes and often displaced by the growing mechanization of agriculture, thousands of Mexicans migrated to cities seeking jobs in the expanding industrial economy (Nelson and Tienda 1985). Today, over 90 percent of the Mexican-origin population in the United States resides in cities, but the fastest-growing regions are outside the Southwest. Many of the new communities have formed as transnational networks with very different settlement geographies than those found in the older Mexican American settlement regions.

Terrance Haverluk (2007) presents a 150-year view of the historical geography of Hispanic settlement, which shows the expansion from the Southwest in the nineteenth century to the communities in the Northeast and the South by 1990. Although an important contribution to the historical ethnic geography of Hispanics in the United States, his work has two significant weaknesses. The changing definitions and geographies of enumeration limit the interpretation of his research since he includes all states, even those where Hispanics were not enumerated prior to 1970. Additionally, he uses the broader census category "Hispanic," masking the geographies of the Puerto Ricans, Cubans, and other Latin Americans who began coming to the United States in large numbers in the 1950s.

In the early decades of the twentieth century, Mexicans began migrating north of the border region in large numbers, taking advantage of labor opportunities in agriculture in areas such as California's San Joaquin valley and parts of Wyoming, Colorado, Nebraska, and Kansas. Additionally, approximately thirty thousand Mexican laborers sought industrial opportunities in Chicago, Illinois, and Gary, Indiana (Haverluk 2007). Emily Skop, Brian Gratton, and Myron Guttman (2006) review the expanding patterns of settlement from the Southwest to the West during and after World War II, when labor recruiters delivered Mexican agricultural laborers to fill jobs left opened by native-born farmworkers serving in the military. The bracero program, whose name derives from the Spanish word *brazo* (arm), continued to augment the flow of Mexican farm laborers after the war until 1964. This laid the foundation for a national geography of Mexicans linked to labor opportunities.

In the later decades of the twentieth century, this geography extended to the Northeast and the South, regions not historically known for concentrations of Mexican labor migrants. Mexican communities grew very rapidly in New York City in the 1980s and 1990s (Mendez and Miyares 2001; Miyares 2004a). At the end of the twentieth century, the most rapidly growing Mexican regions were in North Carolina and Georgia as a result of Mexican labor migrants working in agriculture, food processing, and construction. By the 2000 census, there were only six counties in the entire United States without Mexicans.

Although a much smaller population, Cubans have also been coming to the United States since the nineteenth century. Cubans came to work in the cigar industry in New York City, neighboring communities in New Jersey, and the Tampa Bay and Key West areas of Florida, as well as in the sugar industry in Louisiana and in publishing in New York City. As Thomas Boswell and Terry-Ann Jones (2007) and Kevin E. McHugh, Ines Miyares, and Emily Skop (1997) discuss, the Miami community did not develop until the 1930s, when exiles fled the revolution against Gerardo Machado.

Although Cuban labor migrants continued to come in small numbers, the Cuban Revolution in 1959 triggered the growth of Miami's Cuban population. Unlike labor migrants, the early Cuban refugees were well educated and received federal assistance to establish themselves economically (Boswell and Curtis 1984). However, later waves had more of the characteristics of working-class labor migrants. Federal refugee resettlement programs dispersed them across the United States, but Miami became a "homeland in absentia," a perceived tie to the Cuba that predated the revolution (Boswell 1993). Much of the growth of Miami's Cuban population between 1985 and 1990 involved working-class Cubans who were both more recent arrivals and less skilled (McHugh, Miyares, and Skop 1997). Despite the size of the Miami community, the second-largest concentrations are still in the New Jersey communities that drew Cubans to work in cigar factories in the late nineteenth and early twentieth centuries. After the revolution, thousands of working-class Cubans, particularly those not from Havana, settled in New Jersey, maintaining the vitality of that community.

Despite the growth of the Mexican population in New York, the Hispanic labor migrants have historically been, and continue to be, primarily Caribbean in origin. Puerto Ricans, displaced by the declining sugar industry, began migrating to New York in large numbers to work in the garment industry and other light industries in the city. This population grew rapidly after World War II, when daily commercial flights between San Juan and New York became affordable for the working class. As American citizens, they were free to migrate to the mainland to pursue these labor opportunities without the visa restrictions placed on so many other immigrant groups (Miyares 2004b). Although most mainland Puerto Ricans reside in the New York metropolitan area, they also migrated to other industrial centers in the Midwest and Florida seeking better jobs (Benedict and Kent 2004; Boswell and Jones 2007). Puerto Ricans also went to unexpected parts of the United States, such as Hawaii following the San Ciriaco hurricane of 1899.

Puerto Ricans have continued to migrate to Honolulu, both for labor opportunities and military assignments (Miyares 2008).

Starting in 1965, Dominicans began receiving visas to the United States to escape the political turmoil in their homeland. Since then, waves of both working-class and highly skilled migrants, primarily settling in New York City, have formed a strong enclave economy. Daily flights to Santo Domingo and Puerto Plata from New York–area airports keep this community strongly connected to the Dominican Republic, with many holding dual citizenship and dual voting rights (Miyares 2004b).

Another late-twentieth-century sending region is South America. Andean South American communities have developed nationally and in the Washington, D.C., area (Price 2007). As with the Dominicans, the initial waves fled political turmoil, often bringing human and financial capital to succeed in the American economy. Later waves have been heavily working-class, with variations among the different South American source countries. Like the Dominicans in New York, South American labor immigrants also maintain strong transnational ties.

ASIAN IMMIGRANT NEW COMMUNITY FORMATION

Asian communities in the United States fall into two categories based on the timing of their formation. There are the historic Chinese, Japanese, and other Asian communities that formed prior to progressively more restrictive legislation that closed the door to Asian labor migrants in 1917 and those that formed after the 1952 and 1965 immigration acts. The older communities tend to be in urban cores, and the residents are clustered because of restrictive urban planning codes. Commonly these immigrants developed internal secondary economies employing coethnics and evolved into ethnic enclaves. In contrast, the newer communities are often in suburban areas, and coethnics may not even live in close proximity to one another.

Boston's Chinatown exemplifies the historical geographic processes contributing to these communities' formation in two ways (Murphey 1952). First, the community resulted from migration of Chinese laborers from California in the late nineteenth century. Chinese laborers settled in older, somewhat segregated housing formerly occupied by upwardly mobile second-generation Irish laborers, a process known as sequent occupance. Second, the flow of Chinese laborers before the reopening of the U.S. borders to Asians contributes to the present-day distributions. In 1950, men alone, whether single or with wives in China, dominated Boston's Chinatown, and there was a small number of women and children. Few men attended school in the United States, inhibiting acculturation or even basic acquisition of English-language skills. Cultural fear and prejudice maintained the boundaries of this community, and most Chinese lacked the language skills and other human and cultural capital to move out of the ethnic neighborhood (Murphey 1952).

The history of San Francisco's Chinatown further elucidates the culture of fear that dominated cities with emergent Chinese laborer communities. San

Francisco passed public health laws to protect the city from health risks the Chinese were perceived to pose, and it was the first city to pass zoning laws under the guise of public health ordinances in order to keep the Chinese segregated from the rest of the city (Shah 2001). Rather than just places with high concentrations of Chinese labor migrants, Chinatowns became the only places these migrants could settle (Anderson 1987).

Even in 2000, San Francisco's Asian community was still one of the most segregated urban populations in the United States, following patterns set in the late nineteenth century. Although San Francisco has middle- and upper-class Chinese neighborhoods, much of the older historic Chinatown remains locked in these long-standing geographies of segregation and fear (Pamuk 2004).

These patterns are not solely an American phenomenon. Despite developing a very different cultural history of plurality, Canadian Chinatowns followed very similar patterns. Unlike many other labor migrant communities, Chinatowns are best understood as externally socially constructed within a racial framework defined by the dominant white European population. The white elite viewed concentrations of Chinese as problematic, inspiring cities such as San Francisco to pass public health laws that justified the segregation of Chinese populations (Anderson 1987).

The 1882 Chinese Exclusion Act specifically denied entry to Chinese laborers. Thus, as in the Boston example, Chinatowns resulted from the migration of Chinese already in the United States. Although the act originally only specified a ten-year ban, Congress renewed it every ten years until 1943, when it finally rescinded the law to convince China to ally with the United States during World War II (Miyares and Airriess 2007). This sixty-one-year gap in Chinese labor immigration established a dualistic Chinese society in the United States. Chinese immigration resumed as a trickle in 1943, expanded slightly in 1952, and resumed on a large scale in 1965 when the law allowed the awarding of up to twenty thousand visas to any one country without restrictions on any particular nationality. However, as discussed earlier, the 1965 Immigration Reform Act required immigrants to have immediate family in the United States to qualify for family reunification visas, which had no numerical limits, but the considerable gap made it unlikely for Chinese desiring to immigrate to be able to meet this requirement. To qualify for visas, new immigrants had to be highly skilled. This requirement resulted in very different patterns of settlement and new forms of Chinese communities—urban, educated professionals who preferred middle-class neighborhoods and suburbs and maintained active transnational connections with home communities in China, Taiwan, and Hong Kong. This group contrasted sharply with the rural and small-town unskilled laborers who emigrated from China in the late nineteenth and early twentieth centuries.

Los Angeles's Chinese communities also exhibit significant socioeconomic differences between Chinese in the historic downtown Chinatown and those clustered in other areas of the city (Li 1998). The new clusters are more recent arrivals with higher levels of human capital living in middle-class and affluent areas of the city. The term "ethnoburb"—a suburban cluster of residential and business districts inhabited by a particular ethnic community—distinguishes between the traditional ethnic enclave of Los Angeles's downtown Chinatown and the suburban Monterey Park neighborhood. The suburban community typically does not represent a majority population but is large enough to support a suburban business district. A number of multiethnic ethnoburbs, in which affluent Chinese are a significant residential and economic presence, exist across the United States. In some suburban contexts, such as Chandler, Arizona, affluent Chinese suburbanites have formed heterolocal communities, maintaining social connections through professional and cultural networks not necessarily represented on the landscape (Li 2007).

Japanese labor migrants experienced a similar break in community formation. Early in the twentieth century, most Japanese in the territorial United States were agricultural laborers and farmers in Hawaii (Miyares 2008), with additional significant working-class populations in California, Washington, Oregon, and Montana (Miyares, Paine, and Nishi 2000). Cessation of the influx of new Chinese laborers in 1882 had opened the door for increasing numbers of Japanese. However, by late 1907, fear of the Japanese as culturally distinct, coupled with a Japanese government seeking to curb emigration, led to the signing of the Gentlemen's Agreement between the United States and Japan, restricted new labor immigration. Unlike the Chinese, Japanese already in the United States could send for their relatives, resulting in the immigration of a large number of "picture brides," women whose marriages to Japanese already in the United States were arranged by brokers in home villages. Thus, unlike Chinese men, who tended to be single and dominated early Chinatowns, Japanese labor migrants were able to establish families. This practice stopped in 1924, when the National Origins Act prohibited entry of "aliens ineligible for citizenship," a category imposed by the 1917 Immigration Act on all Asians.

Fear of the Japanese as possible terrorists during World War II led to their forced resettlement away from the Pacific coastal regions where they had lived for several decades. Executive Order 9066 in 1942, ordering their relocation to internment camps, had a profound impact on the historical geography of Japanese settlement following the war (Miyares, Paine, and Nishi 2000). Although many Japanese returned to California from interment camps, ultimately forming the largest Japanese population by state, followed closely by Hawaii, a number of postwar Japanese communities emerged in eastern and Midwestern cities, where former internees were able to find work and establish new lives.

As with the Chinese, the break in immigration between 1924 and 1965 led to a change in the character of Japanese labor migrants. Additionally, with the globalization of the Japanese economy and the growing number of Japanese firms in the United States, many late-twentieth-century labor migrants from Japan were corporate executives and managers, who were heterolocal in their settlement and community formation but maintained strong social and cultural networks.

The 1965 Immigration Reform Act also opened the door to professional labor migrants whose coethnics were either absent or present in very small numbers before that date. One late-twentieth-century highly skilled immigrant community arrived from India. Where group members have settled in cities, such as New York, they have established affluent professional neighborhoods and economies (Miyares 2004b). Referred to as "saffron suburbs," these affluent areas have drawn high-tech industries and employ significant numbers of South Asian professionals (Skop and Li 2005).

Arab immigrants who began coming to the Detroit metropolitan area in the early twentieth century, attracted by opportunities in the nascent automobile industry, constitute another new ethnic community. Political events in the Middle East in the 1960s led to a growth in the Detroit area Arab community and subsequent expansion of Arab and other Muslim communities in other cities across the United States and Canada. Post-1965 Muslim labor immigrants had to qualify for professional visas, resulting in middle-class urban and suburban community formation. Like the Greeks who came earlier in the century, religion plays a key role in their identity, resulting in the establishment of mosques. The mosques serve as both houses of worship and community centers that assist in the adjustment to American culture and help hold the community together (Chacko 2007).

CONCLUSION

Toward the end of the twentieth century, the American economy continued to change, air travel became more affordable, and the Internet transformed business transactions. Consequently, labor migrant communities no longer resembled those of the early decades of the century. Early in the century, labor migrants tended to be working-class and unskilled or less skilled and to settle in older neighborhoods that had formerly housed earlier waves of labor migrants. By the end of the century, new labor immigrants were more likely to be well educated and wealthier and to settle in suburbs and more dispersed patterns, representing the late-twentieth-century professional labor market.

REFERENCES

Anderson, K. J. 1987. The Idea of Chinatown: The Power of Place and Institutional Practice in the Making of a Racial Category. *Annals of the Association of American Geographers* 77, no. 4: 580–98.

Arreola, D. D. 1993. The Texas-Mexican Homeland. *Journal of Cultural Geography* 13, no. 2: 61–74.

———. 2002. *Tejano South Texas: A Mexican American Cultural Province.* Austin: University of Texas Press.

Benedict, A., and R. B. Kent. 2004. The Cultural Landscape of a Puerto Rican Neighborhood in Cleveland, Ohio. In *Hispanic Spaces, Latino Places: Community and Cultural Diversity in Contemporary America,* edited by D. D. Arreola, 187–206. Austin: University of Texas Press.

Boswell, T. D. 1993. The Cuban-American Homeland in Miami. *Journal of Cultural Geography* 13, no. 2: 133–48.

Boswell, T. D., and J. R. Curtis. 1984. *The Cuban-American Experience: Culture, Images, and Perspectives.* Totowa, NJ: Rowman & Allanheld Publishers.

Boswell, T. D., and T. A. Jones. 2007. Caribbean Hispanics: Puerto Ricans, Cubans, and Dominicans. In *Contemporary Ethnic Geographies in America,* edited by I. M. Miyares and C. A. Airriess, 123–50. Lanham, MD: Rowman & Littlefield.

Burgess, E. W. 1928. Residential Segregation in American Cities. *Annals of the American Academy of Political and Social Science* 140: 105–15.

Buzzelli, M. 2001. From Little Britain to Little Italy: An Urban Ethnic Landscape Study in Toronto. *Journal of Historical Geography* 27, no. 4: 573–87.

Carlson, A. W. 1990. *The Spanish-American Homeland: Four Centuries in New Mexico's Rio Arriba*. Baltimore: Johns Hopkins University Press.

Chacko, E. 2007. Immigrants from the Muslim World: Lebanese and Iranians. In *Contemporary Ethnic Geographies in America*, edited by I. M. Miyares and C. A. Airriess, 313–30. Lanham, MD: Rowman & Littlefield.

Constantinou, S. 2007. Ethnic Residential Shifts: The Greek Population of Akron, Ohio, 1930–2005. *GeoJournal* 68, no. 2–3: 253–65.

Conzen, M. P., ed. 1990. *The Making of the American Landscape*. Boston: Unwin Hyman.

———. 1993. Culture Regions, Homelands, and Ethnic Archipelagos in the United States: Methodological Considerations. *Journal of Cultural Geography* 13, no. 2: 13–29.

Gabaccia, D. R. 2006. Global Geography of "Little Italy": Italian Neighbourhoods in Comparative Perspective. *Modern Italy* 11, no. 1: 9–24.

Harris, R., and R. Lewis. 1998. Constructing a Fault(y) Zone: Misrepresentations of American Cities and Suburbs, 1900–1950. *Annals of the Association of American Geographers* 88, no. 4: 622–39.

———. 2001. The Geography of North American Cities and Suburbs, 1900–1950: A New Synthesis. *Journal of Urban History* 27, no. 3: 262–92.

Haverluk, T. 2007. The Changing Geography of U.S. Hispanics, 1850–1990. *Journal of Geography* 96, no. 3: 134–45.

Hernandez-Leo, R., and V. Zuñiga. 2002. Mexican Immigrant Communities in the South and Social Capital: The Case of Dalton, Georgia. Working Papers, Center for Comparative Immigration Studies, University of California, San Diego. eScholarship. http://escholarship.org/uc/item/9r5749mm.

Hume, S. E. 2003. Belgian Settlement and Society in the Indiana Rust Belt. *Geographical Review* 93, no. 1: 30–50.

Kandel, W., and E. A. Parrado. 2004. Hispanics in the American South and the Transformation of the Poultry Industry. In *Hispanic Spaces, Latino Places: Community and Cultural Diversity in Contemporary America*, edited by D. D. Arreola, 255–76. Austin: University of Texas Press.

Koletty, S. R. 2001. The Samoan Archipelago in Urban America. In *Geographical Identities of Ethnic America: Race, Space, and Place*, edited by K. A. Berry and M. L. Henderson, 130–48. Reno: University of Nevada Press.

Li, W. 1998. Anatomy of a New Ethnic Settlement: The Chinese Ethnoburb in Lost Angeles. *Urban Studies* 35, no. 3: 479–501.

———. 2007. Chinese Americans: Community Formation in Time and Space. In *Contemporary Ethnic Geographies in America*, edited by I. M. Miyares and C. A. Airriess, 213–32. Lanham, MD: Rowman & Littlefield.

McHugh, K. E., I. M. Miyares, and E. H. Skop. 1997. The Magnetism of Miami: Segmented Paths in Cuban Migration. *Geographical Review* 87, no. 4: 504–19.

Mendez, N., and I. M. Miyares. 2001. Changing Landscapes and Immigration: The "Mexicanization" of Sunset Park, Brooklyn Migration. In *From the Hudson to the Hamptons: Snapshots of the New York Metropolitan Area*, edited by Ines M. Miyares, Marianna Pavlovskaya, and Gregory Pope, 102–7. Washington, D.C.: Association of American Geographers.

Miyares, I. M. 1997. Changing Perceptions of Space and Place as Measures of Hmong Acculturation. *Professional Geographer* 49, no. 2: 214–24.

———. 2004a. Changing Latinization of New York City. In *Hispanic Spaces, Latino Places: Community and Cultural Diversity in Contemporary America*, edited by D. D. Arreola, 145–66. Austin: University of Texas Press.
———. 2004b. From Exclusionary Covenant to Ethnic Hyperdiversity in Jackson Heights, Queens. *Geographical Review* 94, no. 4: 462–83.
———. 2008. Expressing "Local Culture" in Hawai'i. *Geographical Review* 98, no. 4: 513–31.
Miyares, I. M., and C. A. Airriess. 2007. Creating Contemporary Ethnic Geographies—a Review of Immigration Law. In *Contemporary Ethnic Geographies in America*, edited by I. M. Miyares and C. A. Airriess, 27–50. Lanham, MD: Rowman & Littlefield.
Miyares, I. M., J. A. Paine, and M. Nishi. 2000. The Japanese in America. In *Ethnicity in Contemporary America: A Geographical Appraisal*, edited by J. O. McKee, 263–82. Lanham, MD: Rowman & Littlefield.
Mohl, R. A. 2003. Globalization, Latinization, and the Nuevo New South. *Journal of American Ethnic History* 22, no. 4: 31–66.
Monzell, T. I. 1969. The Catholic Church and the Americanization of the Polish Immigrant. *Polish American Studies* 26, no. 1: 1–15.
Murphey, R. 1952. Boston's Chinatown. *Economic Geography* 28, no. 3: 244–55.
Nelson, C., and M. Tienda. 1985. The Structuring of Hispanic Ethnicity: Historical and Contemporary Perspectives. *Ethnic and Racial Studies* 8, no. 1: 49–74.
Nostrand, R. L. 1980. The Hispano Homeland in 1900. *Annals of the Association of American Geographers* 70, no. 3: 382–96.
———. 1987. The Spanish Borderlands. In *North America: The Historical Geography of a Changing Continent*, edited by R. D. Mitchell and P. A. Groves, 48–64. Totowa, NJ: Rowman & Littlefield.
Orsi, R. 1992. The Religious Boundaries of an Inbetween People: Street *Feste* and the Problem of the Dark-Skinned Other in Italian Harlem, 1920–1990. *American Quarterly* 44, no. 3: 313–47.
Pamuk, A. 2004. Geography of Immigrant Clusters in Global Cities: A Case Study of San Francisco, 2000. *International Journal of Urban and Regional Research* 28, no. 2: 287–307.
Park, R. E. 1928. Human Migration and the Marginal Man. *American Journal of Sociology* 33, no. 6: 881–93.
Portes, A., and R. L. Bach. 1985. *Latin Journey: Cuban and Mexican Immigrants in the United States.* Berkeley and Los Angeles: University of California Press.
Price, M. 2007. Andean South Americans and Cultural Networks. In *Contemporary Ethnic Geographies in America*, edited by I. M. Miyares and C. A. Airriess, 191–212. Lanham, MD: Rowman & Littlefield.
Samora, J., and P. Vandel Simon. 1977. *A History of the Mexican-American People.* Notre Dame, IN: University of Notre Dame Press.
Shah, N. 2001. *Contagious Divides: Epidemics and Race in San Francisco's Chinatown.* Berkeley and Los Angeles: University of California Press.
Skop, E. H., and W. Li. 2005. Asians in America's Suburbs: Patterns and Consequences of Settlement. *Geographical Review* 95, no. 2: 167–88.
Skop, E., B. Gratton, and M. P. Guttman. 2006. La Frontera and Beyond: Geography and Demography in Mexican American History. *Professional Geographer* 58, no. 1: 78–98.
Ward, D. 1968. The Emergence of Central Immigrant Ghettoes in American Cities: 1840–1920. *Annals of the Association of American Geographers* 58, no. 2: 343–59.
Winders, J. 2005. Changing Politics of Race and Region: Latino Migration to the U.S. South. *Progress in Human Geography* 29, no. 6: 683–99.
Zelinsky, W., and B. A. Lee. 1998. Heterolocalism: An Alternative Model of the Sociospatial Behaviour of Immigrant Ethnic Communities. *International Journal of Population Geography* 4, no. 4: 281–98.

6

The Great Migration

Joshua Inwood

In the first decades of the twentieth century, barely two generations removed from slavery—a time when African Americans were regularly lynched, sharecropping dominated southern agricultural practices, and segregationist policies denied freedom to millions—the idea that one could simply pick up and move was revolutionary. The movement of black people from the largely rural South to the urbanized North constitutes one of the significant migratory events in North American history. Isabel Wilkerson (2010) argues that the Great Migration remade the very fabric of urban America, affecting everything from the music we listen to, to our politics, to the economic development of the United States.

Between 1910 and 1940, over 1.75 million black people left a largely rural and subsistence existence for the urbanized North, causing the black population outside the South to nearly double (Hine, Hine, and Harold 2010, 435). Driven by the cataclysmic events of devastated cotton harvests and unmitigated white supremacist violence, as well as by the promise of a better life and jobs in the North and West, African Americans fundamentally changed the geography of the United States by remaking the political and cultural geographies of urban centers in North America. The voluntary movement of black bodies created new cultural and political meanings that ultimately laid the groundwork for the broader civil rights struggle in the United States. As the shifting demographics of the Great Migration gave rise to the Harlem Renaissance, Chicago blues, and the politics of Marcus Garvey and then Malcolm X, African Americans reinvented and reimagined the great cities of the industrial North (Boyd 2011). In the process, new and important black identities emerged that fundamentally challenged notions of U.S. racism, urbanism, and perhaps more significant, the ways geographers have come to understand the black experience in the United States. To understand contemporary racial formation in the United States, one must also acknowledge that in recent decades the Great Migration has reversed, and for the first time since slavery, more black people are moving into the South than are leaving for other regions of the United States (Frey 2004). More than anything, this trend speaks to broader changes in U.S. society, opens up new avenues for research in the field of geography, and holds the promise of illuminating contemporary economic, social, and political processes.

GEOGRAPHIES OF MOBILITY AND THE AFRICAN AMERICAN EXPERIENCE

Racial formation in the United States has long involved a black/white binary predicated on the spatial division of the races (Delaney 1998). The processes involved in creating and maintaining racial separation are complicated, and for the most part, geographers have focused on the dialectical interplay between the production of space and the creation of racialized identity (Inwood and Martin 2008). While this work represents an important academic engagement with broader understandings of the processes shaping U.S. racial geographies, I suggest that notions of mobility play an underexamined role in geographic understandings of race and place in North America (Alderman, Kingsbury, and Dwyer 2013). Mobility in this sense is more than mere movement; it is movement "invested with meaning." Derek Alderman, Paul Kingsbury, and Owen Dwyer write that "people's movements take on social meaning and mobility can be constructed in ways that either control or empower historically marginalized individuals and groups" (2013, 5).

Not surprisingly, as slavery developed in North America, the relationship between white supremacy and efforts to restrict black mobility became intertwined, and these policies focused on policing and regulating the movement of African American bodies (DuBois 1935). At their most basic level, plantations were designed in such a way that "slaveholders [were] able to manipulate the spatial organization of plantations . . . in an effort to control the actions of enslaved workers" (Singleton 2001, 98). Additionally, colonial and later U.S. law linked the "right of mobility" to notions of citizenship that limited the movement of black people (Hauge 2010). In addition to mounting slave patrols, perpetrating sexual violence and beatings, and enacting laws that severely limited with whom black people could socialize, white society invested vast amounts of time and resources in keeping track of the movement of African Americans across the North American continent. Opposing the white supremacist planter class's efforts is an equally long history of African American resistance that often took the form of movement. I argue that we should see the idea of mobility within African American culture as countering white supremacy.

African Americans exercised mobility as a form of resistance through escape and use of the Underground Railroad. But perhaps the greatest example of the role mobility played in overcoming white supremacy occurred in the weeks and months after the Civil War. As the plantation aristocracy collapsed, tens of thousands of former slaves left their places of bondage throughout the South, exercising newfound freedoms of mobility most had never known (Litwack 1998). The ability to travel, locate relatives who had been sold, leave the spaces of slavery, and simply experience freedom drove many African Americans to the road. For whites the prospect of African Americans exercising this newfound freedom was cataclysmic. The South was devastated financially and physically from four years of war, and the plantations that had dominated southern life were, for the most part, ruined (Vann Woodward 2002). Additionally, many whites believed in the patriarchal benevolence of the southern slave aristocracy and were shocked to discover that, at the first moment, former slaves would abandon "the family" and head for an uncertain horizon (Litwack 1998).

Consequently, in the years after the Civil War, particularly after "Southern Redemption" ended the reconstruction of the South, the system of regulating African American movement changed. During the Jim Crow era, dominant in the South from the mid-1870s until the early 1960s, local governments and landowners took several measures to limit the mobility of black people (Vann Woodward 2002). Of critical importance were the ways these policies connected to a broader economic system of agricultural production known as sharecropping. Under the sharecropping system, laborers (former slaves and poor whites) worked land owned by others. The laborers agreed to pay the landowner back at the end of the season for seed, tools, fertilizer, and work animals provided at the beginning of the growing season. Theoretically this system benefited both the laborer and the landowner; in reality it was deeply exploitative. Richard Morrill and Fred Donaldson explain, "A kind of serfdom emerged—former slaves leased land, usually very little, from the plantation owner for a rent of from one-third to one-half of the crop. Very quickly, most sharecroppers became permanently indebted to the owner, and were legally forbidden to move from the owner's holding. Not only was the sharecropper kept in abject poverty, but the system was so inefficient that the owners, too, were much worse off than before the war" (1972, 10). In a landmark anthropological study Hortense Powdermaker (1939) found that only 25 percent of sharecroppers got a fair deal from the landowner. Incredibly, only about 17 percent were able to clear a profit at the end of the year, and most of those folks walked away with less than $30 after the growing season. Even more despicable were the strikingly exploitative conditions in which most sharecroppers lived. High rates of illiteracy, inadequate housing with little or no heat and plumbing, and contracts that limited the movement of sharecroppers had a deleterious effect on the lives of poor and mostly black farm laborers at this time.

In addition, violence against black people in the South, most often in the form of lynching, was common. While violence has always dominated race relations in the United States, scholars note that the Jim Crow period was particularly brutal (Litwack 1998). As slavery gave way to the era of segregation, the limited protections granted to slaves as a function of their status as "private property" disappeared throughout the South (Payne 2007). Although statistics vary and many lynchings went unreported, at least 6,660 African Americans died at the hands of lynch mobs between 1882 and 1969. The practice of lynching reached its fevered pitch in the late nineteenth and early twentieth centuries (Patterson 1998, 177).

Taken as a whole, the varied apparatuses of white supremacy that dominated during the Jim Crow period can be generalized as a transition from slavery to segregation "predicated on various practices of spatialized violence that targeted black bodies and profited from erasing a black sense of place" (McKittrick 2011, 948). White supremacist attempts to ground black identity in particular places in a process that limited and constrained mobility are of special importance to this chapter. Consequently, in order to place the Great Migration in context, we must understand how the movement of black bodies from the rural South to the urbanized North countered white supremacy and economic exploitation (Creswell 1993). Key to this understanding is the emergence of black identity in the Americas—an identity predicated on struggle and how African Americans utilized geographies of white supremacy to inform resistance. Thus, as black people took to the roads at the end of the Civil War, they enacted everyday practices of family and kinship and also rewrote the geography of blackness and black identity.

By taking to the road, black people were, for the first time, able to exercise a freedom of movement and a mobility that had cultural, political, and economic ramifications. In a similar vein, as African Americans moved out of the South to the North and West and to the great industrial centers of the Midwest and West Coast, they created new understandings of a black sense of place that links the Great Migration to broader themes of resistance. This understanding of the Great Migration adds depth and presence to the experience of black mobility and also enhances the theoretical and geographical possibilities for reconceptualizing black mobility. As a result it is necessary to see mobility as central to the construction of black resistance and an identity that stands in opposition to the lynching and exploitation that characterizes so much of our understanding of the black experience during the time of Jim Crow segregation. Thus, the Great Migration is part of a larger transatlantic movement that "is necessarily complex and is characterized by elements of exploitation and subjugation as well as resistance" (Inwood 2009, 489).

THE GREAT MIGRATION AND THE REMAKING OF URBAN AMERICA

In a landmark study on the migration patterns of the U.S. African American population, John Cromartie and Carol Stack (1989) argue that several underlying factors precipitated movement out of the South. While violence and the denial of basic citizenship rights were obvious drivers, several factors in the North helped to turn an initial trickle of out-migrants into a flood. First, with the onset of World War I, federal policy curtailed the European immigration that had served as the backbone of the U.S. Industrial Revolution (Lemann 1992). As the United States became an important player in the international arms trade, and as U.S. factories began to turn out thousands of tons of war-related materials, migrating African Americans replaced those workers. Consequently thousands of labor recruiters traveled throughout the South luring black workers out of the cotton kingdom and into the factories of Chicago, Detroit, and Cleveland (figure 6.1).

In addition, during the late 1920s and early 1930s the global cotton market crashed, and cotton farming became less profitable. The amount of acreage planted in cotton peaked in 1929 and steadily declined during the 1930s and 1940s (Hart 1977, 307). This was due to several factors, including the spread of the boll weevil, which decimated cotton production, as well as the increased mechanization of cotton farming and New Deal–era programs that encouraged

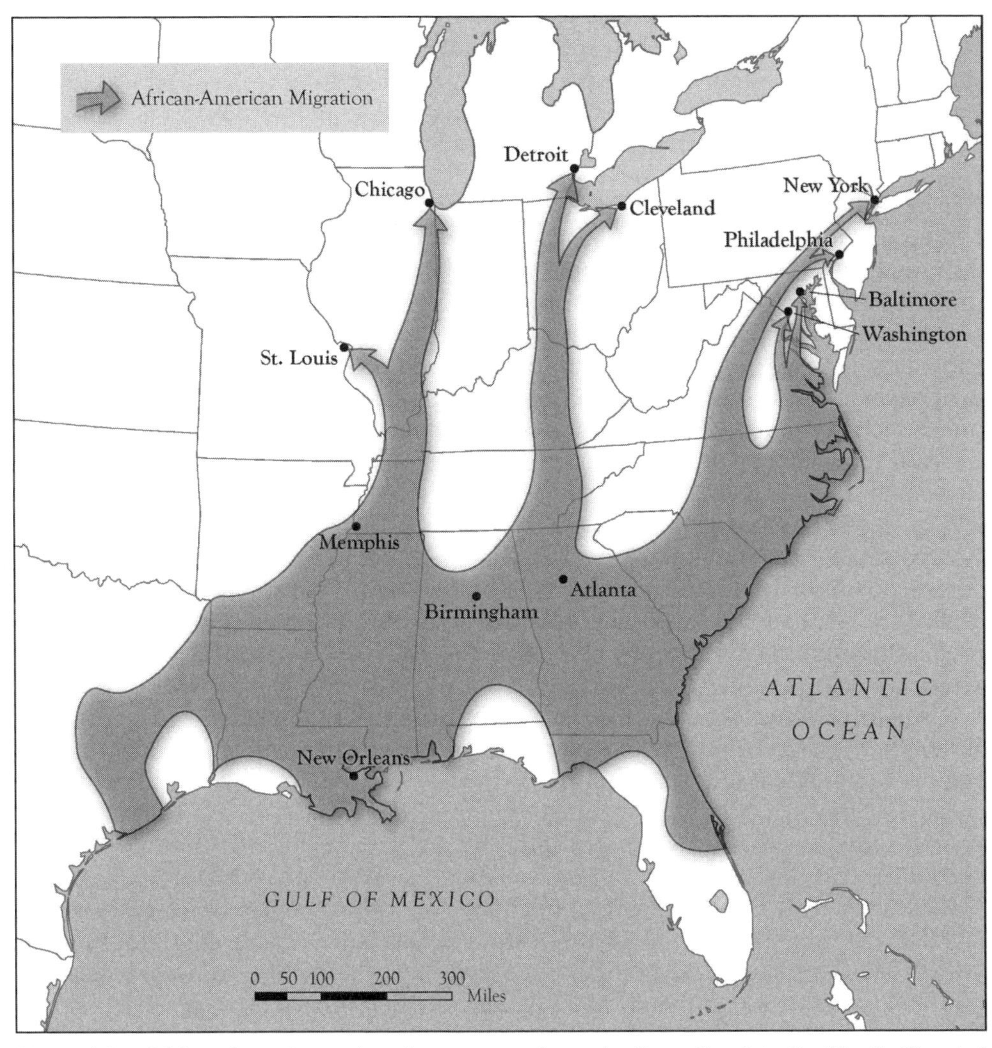

Figure 6.1. African American migration patterns from the Deep South to the North. Created by the University of Tennessee Cartography Lab.

cotton farmers to turn some of their land over to forest production and to other crops that brought higher prices. Initial efforts to recruit black people to the North met with resistance from white southerners, who needed blacks to produce the cotton crop (Payne 2007). It was not unheard of for white mobs to meet incoming labor recruiters at the train station and encourage them to move on to the next town; other tactics to discourage black out-migration included imposing large fines on those departing. However, by the 1930s white plantation owners were actively encouraging black people to move off the cotton farms and beginning to limit their sharecropping contracts. Unsurprisingly, with the demise of the cotton kingdom, incidents of violence and lynching in the South dramatically decreased with the declining need for black labor (Payne 2007).

These changes culminated in the mass out-migration of southern blacks. From 1910 until 1940, the black population in the South fell, and for the first time in the history of the United States, a northern state, New York, had the largest African American population (Morrill and Donaldson 1972, 14). This burgeoning African American urban population changed the geography of U.S. cities. Newly arrived African Americans found that they had traded the de jure segregation of the South for the de facto segregation of the North. As Richard Morrill and Fred Donaldson note, the Great Migration ushered in a new wave of policies designed to restrict African American mobility in the North. These policies included "legal restrictions against housing integration, enforced by the [Federal Housing Administration] itself until 1949; refusal by the real estate industry to show or sell housing to blacks in white areas, and by banks and insurance companies to finance such sales; white and black mutual fear of being alone within the others' territory; lack of information about opportunities; building freeways and renewal projects, which serve as barriers to expansion; white protective organizations that perpetrated violence against blacks who attempt to enter white areas" (1972, 16). The resulting policies severely limited the housing options for African Americans in northern cities or, in the case of "sundown towns" where African Americans feared remaining after dark, made sure African Americans were not allowed to live in the town at all (Loewen 2005). Across the North, sundown towns proliferated and increasingly displaced and discouraged African American settlement.

It is interesting to note, however, that northern ghettos were not necessarily slums. James Grossman (2000) suggests that segregation in itself did not cause a decline in house values or neighborhood quality; rather, it meant that newcomers could not move beyond the tight geographic boundaries of specific neighborhoods. This placed a tremendous strain on the physical infrastructure of neighborhoods, and city services often broke down under these conditions. The strain placed on African American neighborhoods was also economic. Blockbusting, racial fears, and the actions of real estate speculators meant that tremendous profits could be made by flipping homes sold by fearful whites; at the same time, this created a series of housing bubbles in northern cities as African American home owners, unable to shop throughout the city, often purchased homes at inflated prices. As a consequence, "in some cases this left homeowners without enough [resources] to maintain their houses adequately. Despite the continuing presence of middle-class African-American neighborhoods, invisible to whites who blithely equated slum with ghetto, the trend was downward" (Grossman 2000, 112–13). Additionally, white and black landlords quickly realized that you could squeeze more profit out of the limited space in the burgeoning ghettos of the North by subdividing single-family houses into smaller and smaller units. This had the effect of squeezing more and more people into limited spaces and led to an overall deterioration of the housing stock in these neighborhoods. Thus, even though African American geographies were shifting, white supremacy and the interlocking systems of race and the construction of place continued to limit the mobility of black people in the United States.

This process is illustrated perhaps nowhere more vividly than in Chicago. In 1949 the U.S. Congress passed the Federal Housing Act, providing funds for the creation of hundreds of thousands of new public housing developments. Almost immediately Chicago's city council passed a series of laws that would lead to widespread segregation in the city. First, Chicago used most of its urban renewal money to "buy up some of the more promisingly located neighborhoods and turn them over to private companies at bargain prices for demolition and commercial redevelopment, while the former residents were forced to move" (Lemann 1992, 73). Additionally, the Chicago Housing Authority aimed to "build all-black housing projects inside already black (and usually also poor) neighborhoods. The Chicago Housing Authority's role in responding to the great migration from the South would be to try to keep as many of the migrants as possible apart from white Chicago" (Lemann 1992, 73).

The efforts of northern politicians limited the mobility of African Americans and concentrated black people into densely packed urban neighborhoods. Unlike in the South, however, the concentration of African Americans into tightly bounded urban geographies led to an explosion of cultural and political expressions that represent the flowering of some of the most profound art, music, and politics the United States has ever seen. This geographically transformed northern cities and contributed to the eventual growth of powerful coalitions of labor and civil rights organizations that provided financial backing for the U.S. civil rights struggle (Gregory 2005). These settlement patterns have geographic implications central to understanding the development of the urban geography of North America (e.g., Drake and Cayton 1945).

A chief difference in the experiences of African Americans in the South and those who left the region was that, for the most part, blacks who moved north and west concentrated in a half dozen cities, including Chicago, Cleveland, Detroit, Los Angeles, New York, and Washington, D.C., which were at the height of their political, cultural, and economic fortunes (Gregory 2005, 11). This created conditions in which African Americans were able to concentrate political and economic power that shaped the geography of North America. As the United States continued to industrialize throughout the first half of the twentieth century, African Americans enjoyed opportunities they never could have in the South. For example, despite differences in wages between white and black workers in the auto and steel industries, blacks' wages were three to four times those earned in the best years in the South. This led to the growth of an economically viable African American middle class with the time and resources to invest in political and social activities. Additionally, "The brain-drain segment of the Great Migration included men and women with money and entrepreneurial skills and others with educational credentials and specialized occupational training, including a significant number of attorneys, writers, teachers, and social workers" (Gregory 2005, 11).

The high concentration of the African American population, as well as the growth of the middle and professional classes, led to an explosion of the African American counterpublic in these cities (Fraser 1990). The formation of alternative spheres of public engagement in the mid-twentieth century was foundational to the development of African American identity at this time. As Nancy Fraser (1990) shows, the development of the black counterpublic in the first part of the twentieth century stemmed from processes of migration, newfound political freedoms, and the burgeoning African American middle classes. This precipitated the growth of myriad political and social movements in the northern cities (e.g., the National Association for the Advancement of Colored People, the Universal Negro Improvement Association, and the Nation of Islam), as well as the birth of entertainment and cultural icons. Melissa Harris-Lacewell argues that "the heart of the Black Counterpublic is public space, specifically those spaces where African Americans come together in a relatively safe environment free from white society's gaze" (2004, 2). According to Harris-Lacewell (2004, 8) the most important aspect of these public spaces is the belief among African Americans that they are exclusively in the presence of other black people. A major factor in creating the conditions of black counterpublics was the high concentration of black people. Whereas in the South the black population was largely rural and spread out across many miles (some important exceptions include Atlanta, Georgia, and New Orleans, Louisiana), in the North the African American population was densely packed. The resulting urban geographies meant that advantages of "mutual protection . . . the convenience and preferences for black churches, clubs, businesses and especially friends and relatives, and the possibility of political power through spatial concentration . . . proved an important basis for growth of political power and activism in the more recent past" (Morrill and Donaldson 1972, 16).

Historically, the most important "spaces" of the black counterpublic included black churches, the African American press, and popular music. James Gregory (2005) explains that the move to the North expanded the extent and scope of black politics in ways almost unfathomable to black southerners accustomed to the restrictions placed on blacks in the South. The right to vote, along with the ability to build alliances between progressive organizations and the capacity to protest publicly, made for a new kind of politics that allowed black people to exercise an increasing political influence in the cities of the North. The ability to debate, strategize responses to white racism, and enact the multiple identities that exist in African American communities in a place relatively free from the influence of whites was paramount.

The growth of the counterpublic led to the proliferation of clubs and organizations dedicated to improving the lot of new migrants to the North. Organizations like the Urban League developed programs that dispensed advice about proper work habits, housekeeping, and dealing with landlords and city officials (Grossman 2000, 116). These organizations eased the integration of newly arriving migrants into the community and began the process of raising the political consciousness of migrants to the new realities of urban life. James Grossman argues that this process created in black, urban America a sense that African Americans were "entitled to the full rewards of American life[, and this] combined with the ambition and excitement of the Great Migration to form the heart of what came to be called the 'New Negro' movement" (2000, 75).

Most closely associated with Harlem, the "New Negro movement" was in reality a much larger undertaking coined by Howard University professor Alain Locke, who published an edited book titled *The New Negro,* in which he wrote that he aimed to "document the New Negro culturally and socially, to register the transformations of the inner and outer life of the Negro in America that have so significantly taken place in the last few years" (1925, xxv). Of critical importance is Locke's identification of the twin ideas of self-respect and belief in the "ideals of American institutions and democracy" (Grossman 2000, 122). The movement took on added significance as it progressed into social activism, politics, and the arts and literature. At its heart, the New Negro movement was about the empowerment of black people and expressions of humanity in the face of three hundred years of state-sanctioned neglect and murder. Perhaps most interestingly, the New Negro movement facilitated increased interactions among whites and blacks as white folks flocked to Harlem, Chicago's South Side, and East Cleveland to hear jazz and the blues.

Born in New Orleans and tempered by the experiences of black people in the cotton kingdoms of the Deep South, jazz music moved north and by the early 1920s was a national rage. As jazz became more popular, it paid dividends to African American communities throughout the North. The growth of nightclubs, often several dozen in most major cities, provided employment for hundreds of dancers, comedians, and musicians. Although Harlem's was the best known, other cities developed thriving entertainment centers. For example, "Chicago's South Side with more than 1,000 actors, dancers, and musicians, had more professional entertainers than the combined states of Louisiana, Mississippi and Tennessee where the blues and jazz were supposedly invented. Other cities were also involved. St. Louis and Kansas City had more clubs and musicians than New Orleans and Memphis. Detroit, Philadelphia, and Cleveland each had thriving jazz quarters. . . . Black communities were centers for a set of interactions that were remaking American music and other institutions of popular culture" (Gregory 2005, 136).

The popularity of jazz helped fuel the growth of an upwardly mobile black middle class that used its resources to fund civil and social rights organizations. Additionally, northern cities provided a base of support for entertainers from the South who would travel to Chicago and New York to record songs and play in the clubs. As they returned to play on the segregated Chitlin Circuit in Atlanta, Birmingham, New Orleans, and Memphis, an important information exchange took place as musicians told stories, gossiped, and thereby expanded the black counterpublic's reach and extent. In short, "these circulations had all sorts of implications, not only for musical development but also for other aspects of black cultural life" (Gregory 2005, 140).

While white society was working to limit the mobility of black folk, black entertainers were able to break free of the bounds of more formalized segregationist policies and to exercise a kind of mobility that vastly expanded the scope and extent of the growing southern diaspora and presented an image of African Americans that destroyed stereotypes. The success of black artists would be one of several crucial factors in sustaining the U.S. civil rights struggle in the mid-twentieth century, as Harry Belafonte and others gave concerts and donated money at crucial times to sustain the movement. This would not have been possible if two generations of black artists and entertainers had not already broken through the color barrier to find success outside the African American entertainment centers of New York, Harlem, and Detroit. Within geography, these networks of information exchange remain understudied in the literature; furthermore, black entertainers' mobility as resistance to white supremacy remains underdeveloped and is one of several fruitful avenues of research concerning the Great Migration for historical geographers.

CONCLUSION

In 2011 the *New York Times* reported that, for the first time in half a century, the largest growth of the African American population in the United States occurred in the South (Tavernise and Gebeloff 2011). This trend reversed, for the first time in one hundred years, the flood of out-migrants from Dixie. The movements of black bodies out of the North are part of larger trends that show African Americans have been leaving the inner city for the suburbs and are in the process of once again remaking the urban geographies of American metropolitan areas. As a consequence of these changes, the political coalition of the white and African American working class that dominated northern cities for the past half century is withering under the weight of economic downsizing and changing demographics (Frey 2011). However, as the African American population has shifted south, cities like Atlanta and Dallas have seen the opposite effect. New and diverse expressions of African American culture and political power have increasingly influenced these cities and thus the birth of the New South. Cicely Bland, who recently moved from New Jersey to Atlanta, explained, "The business and political opportunities are here. You have a lot of African Americans with a lot of influence, and they're in my immediate networks" (quoted in Tavernise and Gebeloff 2011, A1). Her words crystallize the changing demographics that are remaking southern cities and regions. Recently, the population has shifted again as African American in-migrants to the South have begun to settle in areas with traditionally small African American populations. The challenges that come with this change present a rich story field for geographers to explore the South and ways that the black population is remaking and reimagining traditionally white communities. As a consequence geographers have a chance to explore new and diverse research trajectories that focus on race, place, and mobility in twenty-first-century U.S. society.

REFERENCES

Alderman, Derek, Paul Kingsbury, and Owen Dwyer. 2013. Reexamining the Montgomery Bus Boycott: Toward an Empathetic Pedagogy of the Civil Rights Movement. *Professional Geographer* 65, no. 1: 171–86.

Blackmon, Douglas. 2008. *Slavery by Another Name: The Re-enslavement of Black Americans from the Civil War to World War II.* New York: Anchor Books.

Boyd, Robert. 2011. The Northern "Black Metropolis" of the Early Twentieth Century: A Reappraisal. *Sociological Inquiry* 81: 88–109.

Cresswell, Tim. 1993. Mobility as Resistance: A Geographical Reading of Kerouac's "On the Road." *Transactions of the Institute of British Geographers* 18: 249–62.

———. 2011. Mobilities I: Catching Up. *Progress in Human Geography* 35: 550–58.

Cromartie, John, and Carol Stack. 1989. Reinterpretation of Black Return and Nonreturn Migration to the South, 1975–1980. *Geographical Review* 79: 297–310.
Delaney, David. 1998. *Race, Place and the Law, 1936–1948.* Austin: University of Texas Press.
Drake, St. Clair, and Horrace Cayton. 1945. *Black Metropolis: A Study of Negro Life in a Northern City.* Chicago: University of Chicago Press.
DuBois, W. E. B. 1935. *Black Reconstruction in America, 1860–1880.* New York: Free Press.
Fraser, Nancy. 1990. Rethinking the Public Sphere: A Contribution to the Critique of Actually Existing Democracy. *Social Text* 25: 56–80.
Frey, William. 2004. The New Great Migration: Black Americans' Return to the South, 1965–2000. *Center on Urban and Metropolitan Policy.* Washington, D.C.: Brookings Institute.
———. 2011. Melting Pot Cities and Suburbs: Racial and Ethnic Change in Metro America in the 2000s. *Center on Urban and Metropolitan Policy.* Washington, D.C.: Brookings Institute.
Gregory, James. 2005. *The Southern Diaspora: How the Great Migrations of Black and White Southerners Transformed America.* Chapel Hill: University of North Carolina Press.
Gregory, Steven. 1995. Race, Identity, and Political Activism: The Shifting Contours of the African American Public Sphere. In *The Black Public Sphere,* edited by Black Public Sphere Collective, 151–68. Chicago: University of Chicago Press.
Grossman, James. 2000. A Chance to Make Good: 1900–1929. In *To Make Our World Anew: A History of African Americans from 1880,* edited by Robin Kelley and Earl Lewis, 67–131. Oxford: Oxford University Press.
Harris-Lacewell, Melissa. 2004. *Barbershops, Bibles, and BET: Everyday Talk and Black Political Thought.* Princeton, NJ: Princeton University Press.
Hart, John Fraser. 1960. The Changing Distribution of the American Negro. *Annals of the Association of American Geographers* 50: 242–66.
———. 1977. The Demise of King Cotton. *Annals of the Association of American Geographers* 67, no. 3: 307–22.
Hauge, Euan. 2010. The Rights to Enter Every Other State—the Supreme Court and African American Mobility in the United States. *Mobilities* 5: 331–47.
Hine, Darlene, William Hine, and Stanley Harold. 2010. *African American History.* 2nd ed. New York: Pearson.
Inwood, Joshua. 2009. "Searching for the Promised Land: Examining Dr. Martin Luther King's Concept of the Beloved Community." *Antipode* 41: 487–508.
Inwood, Joshua, and Deborah G. Martin. 2008. Whitewash: White Privilege and Racialized Landscapes at the University of Georgia. *Social and Cultural Geography* 9, no. 4 (June): 373–94.
Lemann, Nicholas. 1992. *The Promised Land: The Great Black Migration and How It Changed America.* New York: Vintage Books.
Litwack, Leon. 1998. *Trouble in Mind: Black Southerners in the Age of Jim Crow.* New York: Vintage Books.
Loewen, James. 2005. *Sundown Towns: A Hidden Dimension of American Racism.* New York: Touchstone Books.
McKittrick, Katherine. 2011. On Plantations, Prisons, and a Black Sense of Place. *Social and Cultural Geography* 12: 947–63.
Morrill, Richard, and Fred Donaldson. 1972. Geographical Perspectives on the History of Black America. *Economic Geography* 48: 1–23.

Patterson, Orlando. 1998. Rituals of Blood: Consequences of Slavery in Two American Centuries. New York: Basic Books.

Payne, Charles. 2007. *I've Got the Light of Freedom: The Organizing Tradition and the Mississippi Freedom Struggle.* Berkeley: University of California Press.

Powdermaker, Hortense. 1939. *After Freedom: A Cultural Study in the Deep South.* New York: Viking Press.

Singleton, Theresa. 2001. Slavery and Spatial Dialectics on Cuban Coffee Plantations. *World Archaeology* 33: 98–114.

Tavernise, Sabrina, and Robert Gebeloff. 2011. Many U.S. Blacks Moving to South, Reversing Trend. *New York Times*, March 24, 14.

Vann Woodward, C. 2002. *The Strange Career of Jim Crow: A Commemorative Edition.* Oxford: Oxford University Press.

Wilkerson, Isabel. 2010. *The Warmth of Other Suns: The Epic Story of America's Great Migration.* New York: Random House.

III

TRANSFORMING THE LAND

7

Making Connections via Roads, Rivers, Canals, and Rails

Karl Raitz

In 1807, Secretary of the Treasury Albert Gallatin submitted to Congress a report on the importance of building transportation infrastructure, especially roads and canals, together with his recommendations for specific projects that would link eastern seaboard towns and, in turn, connect coastal settlements to the interior lands of the trans-Appalachian West. Gallatin argued, "Good roads and canals will shorten distances; facilitate commercial and personal intercourse; and unite, by a still more intimate community of interests, the most remote quarters of the United States" (1816, 8). Implied in Gallatin's report is the need to recognize that human mobility was, and is, the key to economic, social, and intellectual vigor, be it at the scale of the individual, town, state, or nation.

CREATING TRANSPORT ROUTES

Mobility, whether overland or via water, linked emigrants to frontier lands, children to schools, farmers to market towns, and port city merchants to foreign suppliers and domestic customers. Local, regional, and national development required mobility—of people, ideas, and goods—an imperative that most everyone understood. Geographer James E. Vance (1986, 605–23) has argued that if we learn to read the morphology of evolving transport systems as they expand, we can learn much more about the spatial structure and cyclical process of system development than by simply recording the temporal sequence of transport-related events. Therefore, it is important to identify the legal, political, economic, and technological concerns that weighed upon decisions relating to the construction and maintenance of the infrastructure that permitted mobility, such as coastal ports, wagon roads, and inland canals in Gallatin's time; steam-powered riverboats and railroads by mid-nineteenth century; and hard-surfaced roads carrying automobiles and trucks powered by internal combustion engines by the second decade of the twentieth century (Vance 1986, 117).

The 1800 federal census recorded America's population at 5.3 million. By 1830 the count stood at 12.9 million, an increase of 2.4 times over three decades. The most rapid population growth rate was not in the Atlantic coast states, however, but west of the Appalachians. There the populations of Indiana, Kentucky, Ohio, and Tennessee, for example, increased more than twelve times during the same three decades—from 211,000 in 1800 to 2.65 million in 1830 (U.S. Bureau of the Census 1975, 7, 24–36). As the national government and frontier settlers gained control of Indian lands in the West, migrants from coastal states and immigrants from Europe moved onto them. Some walked Indian trails or primitive tracks, such as the Wilderness Road through southwestern Virginia and Cumberland Gap to central Kentucky (Dunbar 1915, 1:19–20). Others followed old military tracks such as Braddocks Road through Pennsylvania to reach the Ohio River near Pittsburgh (figure 7.1). Migrants from New England and New York followed the Mohawk River valley across upstate New York to northern Ohio and Michigan, skirting the northern flank of the Allegheny Mountains by following the Yankee Gangplank, the narrow band of glacial lake benches on the south side of Lake Erie from Buffalo to Cleveland.[1]

In East Coast cities, merchants, speculators, and others eager to expand established trade networks acknowledged the need to improve transportation and associated facilities such as waterfront wharfs and bridges. Furthermore, transport infrastructure had to account for pragmatic concerns that pathways trend in the desired direction, cover the shortest distance, and follow the lowest gradient to lower costs, whether measured in time and effort expended or wear and tear on equipment (Raitz, Levy, and Gilbreath 2010, 315).

TRAVEL ROUTES AND TOPOGRAPHY

Until the availability of steam engines to power earthmoving equipment in the nineteenth century, establishing low-cost routes required careful consideration of natural advantages provided by physical geography: coastal harbors with sheltered deep water for safe anchorage and a minimal tidal range to simplify dockage; overland routes with favorable topographic surfaces and low gradients.

People moved inland from America's East Coast by following creeks and navigable rivers. At rapids or falls they transferred from boats to wagons for travel overland (Vance 1995, 17). Sites where freight transferred from one mode of travel to another are break-in-bulk points, and many such sites employed people in cargo handling and in-transit processing businesses. Towns often grew up at these locations, including Richmond, Virginia; Raleigh, North Carolina; and Columbia, South Carolina.

Mountain ranges such as the Blue Ridge presented major obstacles to movement inland. Travelers focused at passes through the ridge such as the Potomac River Gap at Harpers Ferry. Paralleling the Blue Ridge, the Great Valley aligns northeast to southwest, and in the eighteenth century, the Great Valley Road

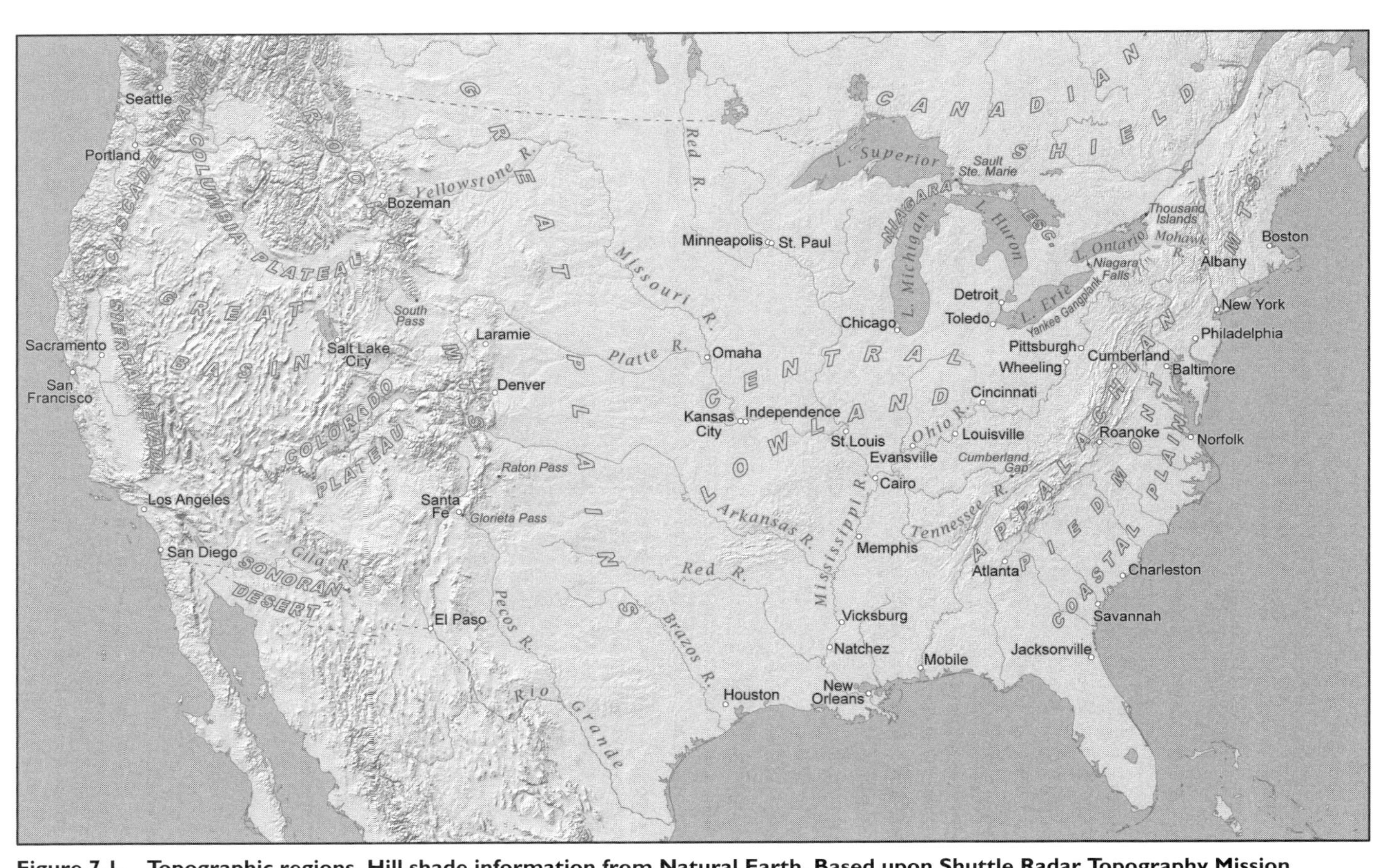

Figure 7.1. Topographic regions. Hill shade information from Natural Earth. Based upon Shuttle Radar Topography Mission (SRTM) data.

followed this lowland from Philadelphia south to Roanoke, Virginia, and Knoxville, Tennessee.

West of the Great Valley lay the Ridge and Valley country, an expansive tract of parallel sandstone ridges and limestone valleys. The Susquehanna and Potomac Rivers and their tributaries cut water gaps through some ridges, but falls and rapids made riverboat travel dangerous. The ridges end abruptly at the Appalachian Front, which presents a wall cresting five hundred to fifteen hundred feet above the adjacent valleys. A valley crosscutting the front at Cumberland, Maryland, permitted passage west, and there, in 1811, laborers began construction on America's first federally funded highway, the National Road. The road reached Wheeling, West Virginia, on the Ohio River in 1818. Once west of the front, the National Road and other trails tracked across the Appalachian Plateau toward the Ohio or Tennessee River valleys. The plateau extends from New York State to northern Alabama. Plateau streams flow westward toward the extensive Central Lowland, which is drained by the Mississippi-Missouri River system. Indian trails followed the larger valleys across the plateau in Tennessee, Kentucky, and West Virginia, tracks that pioneers often adopted to move pack animals and wagons. In New York, the Mohawk River valley provides a low-gradient route between the plateau to the south and the Adirondack Mountains to the north. Engineers completed the Erie Canal, connecting the Hudson River to Lake Erie along this route, in 1825 (Bernstein 2005). Railroads followed this route beginning in the 1830s.

Migrants seeking access to the interior from the West Coast confronted topography substantially different from that of the East Coast. Mountains rise abruptly from the Pacific, restricting access to the interior to a few places where rivers, such as the Columbia River near Portland, Oregon, and the Sacramento River at San Francisco, California, cut water-level gaps through the coastal ranges. To move farther into the interior from the West Coast, routes had to cross the Cascade Mountains to the north and the Sierra Nevada in California.

The extensive Rocky Mountain cordillera occupies much of the western continental interior, and its ranges extend from British Columbia south to Mexico. In breadth, the region extends from central Colorado and Wyoming west to Utah and Idaho. Only a few passes allowed overland wagon transportation for settlers and miners moving west. South Pass in southwestern Wyoming provides a low-gradient passage through the northern Rockies. The Oregon, California, and Mormon Trails all focused at South Pass before continuing west toward their destinations. In the south, Glorieta Pass allowed passage of wagon trains following the Santa Fe Trail across the Sangre de Cristo range of the Rocky Mountains to northern New Mexico.

West of the Appalachian Plateau and east of the Rocky Mountains is the vast Central Lowland. In the north, people could reach the lowland via the St. Lawrence River–Great Lakes system if they could navigate major obstacles, including the St. Lawrence River's La Chine Rapids in southern Quebec, the Niagara Escarpment at Niagara Falls, and the rapids at Sault Ste. Marie, where waters from Lake Superior flow eastward into Lake Huron.

The Great Lakes' deep penetration into the continental interior permitted early exploitation of the region's resources: copper in upper Michigan, iron ore in

Minnesota, Wisconsin, and Michigan, and limestone on Michigan's Lake Huron shore. Industrial cities grew up at lake harbors, including Hamilton, Ontario, and Buffalo, Cleveland, Toledo, Detroit, Chicago, and Green Bay (Lezius 1936, 197–98). Interior industrial cities developed near bituminous coal deposits; in one such city, Pittsburgh, iron ore and limestone from the Great Lakes hinterland arrived via boats and railroads, forging one of the nation's foremost iron and steel manufacturing centers.

The Ohio River begins at the confluence of the Allegheny and Monongahela Rivers at Pittsburgh and flows 981 miles to Cairo, Illinois, where it joins the Mississippi. In the late eighteenth and early nineteenth centuries, travelers moved along the river by flatboats drifting with the current. The Falls of the Ohio required cargo portage, and several towns grew up beside the falls, including Louisville. In Minnesota, St. Paul grew up at a Mississippi River access point. This site became the origin-terminus point for overland oxcart trails that led northwest to Red River valley trading posts and railroads that linked St. Paul to the Pacific Northwest (Jackson 1964, 48–49). At St. Anthony Falls, the Mississippi's head of navigation, Minneapolis became an early milling center. America's early pathfinders by necessity chose routes that provided the best topographic advantage. Improvement and upgrading of those routes awaited financial support, political will, and technological advances.

AMERICA'S EVOLVING TRANSPORTATION SYSTEM

The term "transportation system" implies that transport routes link to one another and adhere to some coherent regional or national plan. Roads that simply connected rural countryside to a local county seat, for example, and lacked connections to adjoining towns, to larger long-distance roads, or to navigable rivers could not be deemed important elements in a system of roads and were of little value to teamsters driving freight wagons to distant destinations. Harbors without road or river connections inland would not become thriving ports. But developing large-scale transportation systems was an expensive proposition because harbors required facilities such as lighthouses, breakwaters, and wharves; navigable streams required channels of predictable depth and cleared of snags and overhanging trees; and roads required bridges rather than fords, as well as low gradients and hard surfaces if overland transportation was to be both reliable and economical. Politicians used the term "internal improvements" to describe such transport-related enhancements.

After the War of 1812, British manufacturers flooded American markets with cheap goods. John Quincy Adams, Henry Clay, and other politicians advocated imposition of steep import taxes or tariffs designed to accomplish two objectives: first, strengthen established American manufacturers situated predominantly in New England, New York, and New Jersey; second, use the funds generated for transportation-related internal improvements. This trade policy, put in place by tariff legislation in 1816 and the 1820s, became known as the American System and was largely supported by the North but strongly opposed by the South, where domestic manufacturing was embryonic and the region depended on imported goods. Until the onset of the Civil War in 1861, the tariff was the largest source of revenue for the federal government (Paskoff 2007, 44–45, 111).

Three primary concerns tempered federal underwriting of internal improvements: constitutionality, regional self-interest, and a lack of information about those places and route ways where funds might be best spent. Initially, internal improvements were popular with presidents and other political leaders. George Washington, John Adams, and Thomas Jefferson supported internal improvement projects whatever their scale. James Madison, James Monroe, and many subsequent presidents, however, were concerned that the Constitution did not permit federal support for improvement projects that would serve local concerns rather than national interests. States and regions supported federal expenditures for transportation projects that would benefit them but strongly opposed projects that would benefit rival areas. New England and the South, for example, opposed federally funded road and canal projects that would benefit primarily New York, Pennsylvania, and the trans-Appalachian West (Phillips 1905, 446; Taylor 1964, 21). Strategic route planning could not proceed without reliable information, a problem addressed by the General Survey Act passed by Congress in 1824. The act permitted the president to use the U.S. Army Corps of Engineers and Topographical Bureau and civilian engineers to conduct surveys for projects deemed of national importance, including the Chesapeake and Ohio Canal and the Baltimore and Ohio Railroad (Calhoun 1960, 38–39).

The lowest-cost transportation modes in the eighteenth and early nineteenth centuries were by water, especially for low-value, bulky commodities such as grain and coal. Overland transport by wagon or coach was difficult and expensive. From 1800 to 1820, freight charges could top fifteen cents per ton-mile on the best roads. Consequently, farmers rarely shipped staple products such as wheat more than one hundred miles. Beyond that distance freight charges could exceed the obtainable market price. By 1830, some overland roads were stone-surfaced turnpikes or toll roads, but the cost of moving freight by wagon remained expensive. Moving a ton of grain by wagon five miles from a farmer's granary to a steamboat wharf, for example, cost roughly same as moving the same ton by ship from an Atlantic coastal port such as Philadelphia to England's Liverpool (U.S. Department of Agriculture 1902, 57). Nevertheless, as borne out by geographer Carville Earle's research on locational and ecological factors as the principal determinants of historic urban development, transport via water or overland supported businesses such as provisioning, repairs, and lodging, which in turn stimulated urban growth at locationally advantaged sites (Earle 1987, 175; 1992, 112–14).

Building and maintaining quality roads that would carry heavy traffic and lower shipping costs was costly and often undertaken with some combination of corporate, local, and state funding. Turnpike tolls paid road upkeep costs, toll gatekeepers' salaries, and dividends to shareholders. Road construction costs varied as topographic conditions changed. The turnpike from Philadelphia to Lancaster, Pennsylvania, in use in 1795 and one of the nation's first hard-surfaced macadam roads, cost $7,500 per mile, whereas the National Road from Cumberland across the Appalachians to Wheeling, West Virginia, two decades later cost $13,000 per mile (Taylor 1964, 30; Raitz and O'Malley 2007, 4). Canals were much more expensive to build than roads, though they provided cheaper transportation—half a cent to two cents per ton-mile (Taylor 1964, 442; Shaw 1990, 188). The Pennsylvania Main Line Canal, completed from Philadelphia to Pittsburgh in 1834, was 395 miles long and cost more than $25,000 per mile. States, cities, and investment banks provided much of the funding for canal construction.

TRANSPORTATION AND TECHNOLOGY EPOCHS

From 1790 to the 1970s, American economic growth resulted in part from collecting, processing, and distributing raw materials and producing manufactured goods, activities enabled by transportation (Borchert 1967, 303–4). But resource endowment differed from region to region, and as transportation technology advanced and one mode of transport replaced another, rural and urban economic development became geographically differentiated. The completion of new railroad systems across the Midwest by the 1880s, for example, left many small Ohio and Mississippi River port towns in anachronistic locations if the railroad bypassed them (figure 7.2).

Geographer John Borchert (1967, 307) contributed to our understanding of the macro-level processes involved in transportation-system evolution by identifying four major historical epochs during which particular technologies have dominated American transportation with formative influence on regional and national economies: (1) Sail-Wagon, 1790–1830; (2) Iron Horse, 1830–1870; (3) Steel Rail,

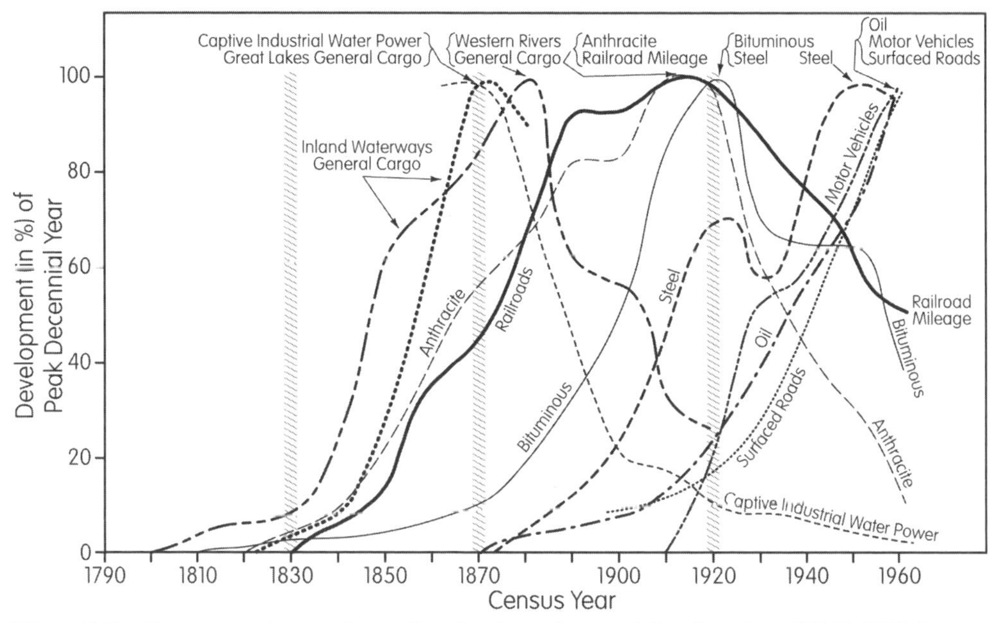

Figure 7.2. Transportation modes and technology change. After Borchert (1967, 302). By permission of the American Geographical Society and the *Geographical Review.*

1870–1920; and (4) Auto-Air-Amenity, 1920–1970. Each epoch's title evokes the transportation modes that came to dominance during its respective period, and technological innovations define epoch boundaries. These epochs include shorter periods with their own characteristics, such as the canal era from the 1810s to the 1840s and the interurban railway period from the 1900s to the 1930s (Borchert 1967, 308).

Forerunners

Prior to the 1790s and the Sail-Wagon epoch, transport centered on coastwise and transatlantic shipping and focused on selected East Coast harbor settlements such as Boston, New York, Baltimore, Philadelphia, Norfolk, Charleston, and Savannah. Several colonial harbor towns became shipbuilding centers. By 1700, New England shipwrights had built more than one thousand vessels, and Salem, Massachusetts, had become the region's shipbuilding center. By the eve of the American Revolution, Philadelphia had developed a major ship-construction industry, having built roughly half of the ships registered in the colonies. During this same period, overland wagon freight service developed between New York and Philadelphia, and by 1750 a stagecoach line operated between New York and Boston (Oliver 1956, 50, 57). Travel inland from important coastal harbors prior to 1790 was along navigable streams or one of many overland trails (Dunbar 1915, 1:152–53).

The Sail-Wagon Epoch: 1790–1830

During the Sail-Wagon period, private companies and state and national governments created improved roads. After 1790, turnpike construction expanded rapidly in the Atlantic coast states. Early on, Pennsylvania and New York had the most miles of toll road, followed by Maryland and Connecticut (Oliver 1956, 175; Taylor 1964, 22). In 1811, construction began on the National Road from Cumberland, Maryland, to St. Louis (Wood 1996, 113–14). Turnpike construction west of the Appalachians began in the 1820s and 1830s. Ohio promoted turnpike construction, and Kentucky chartered more than fourteen hundred turnpikes between 1830 and 1890, most of which served local communities (Raitz and O'Malley 2007) (figure 7.3).

America's canal era began in the 1790s with the construction of several short canals at portage points near the Atlantic coast (Shaw 1990, 3) (figures 7.4 and 7.5). Grander-scale canals linked the Atlantic coast states with the Great Lakes and Ohio River valley. Construction began in 1817 on the 350-mile-long Erie Canal linking the Hudson River near Albany with Lake Erie. The canal opened in 1825. Active trade developed along the route as farm products moved east and manufactured goods moved west, stimulating the creation of towns in a "lakes alignment" along the canal from Albany to Buffalo (Wyckoff 1988, 101). The Erie's dramatic financial success prompted Philadelphia and Baltimore to build competing canals west toward the Ohio valley. The Pennsylvania Portage Canal or Main Line Canal linking Philadelphia and Pittsburgh was completed in 1835 (Oliver 1956, 180; Taylor 1964, 33–36; McGreevy 2009, 11–17). Canals in the

Figure 7.3. Toll gate on Bay Shell Road, Mobile, Alabama, ca. 1901. Laborers often surfaced early roads with local materials, be it sand and gravel, broken rock (macadam), or broken seashells. The toll gatekeeper often lived in the toll house, seen here in the middle distance. Detroit Publishing Co. Collection, Prints and Photographs Division, Library of Congress. Reproduction number LC-D4–13515.

Midwest connected the Great Lakes with the Ohio and Mississippi River system by way of three major north-south trunk lines: the 308-mile Ohio and Erie connected Portsmouth and Cleveland; the 301-mile Miami and Erie linked Cincinnati and Toledo; and the 450-mile Wabash and Erie ran from Evansville, Indiana, to Toledo. Shorter branch canals cross-linked the trucklines, and each stimulated local road construction and town development at road-canal junctions.

The Iron Horse Epoch: 1830–1870

The Iron Horse epoch marks the application of steam engines to water and land transportation and rapidly expanding iron production in southwestern Pennsylvania (Borchert 1967, 303) (figure 7.2). The first steamboat, designed by Robert Fulton, navigated the Ohio and Mississippi Rivers from Pittsburgh to New Orleans in 1811. Flat-bottomed steamboats designed by Henry Shreve and propelled by rear-mounted paddlewheels were in use on the inland river systems by 1830. Given their speed and capacity, the Shreve boats lowered freight rates on

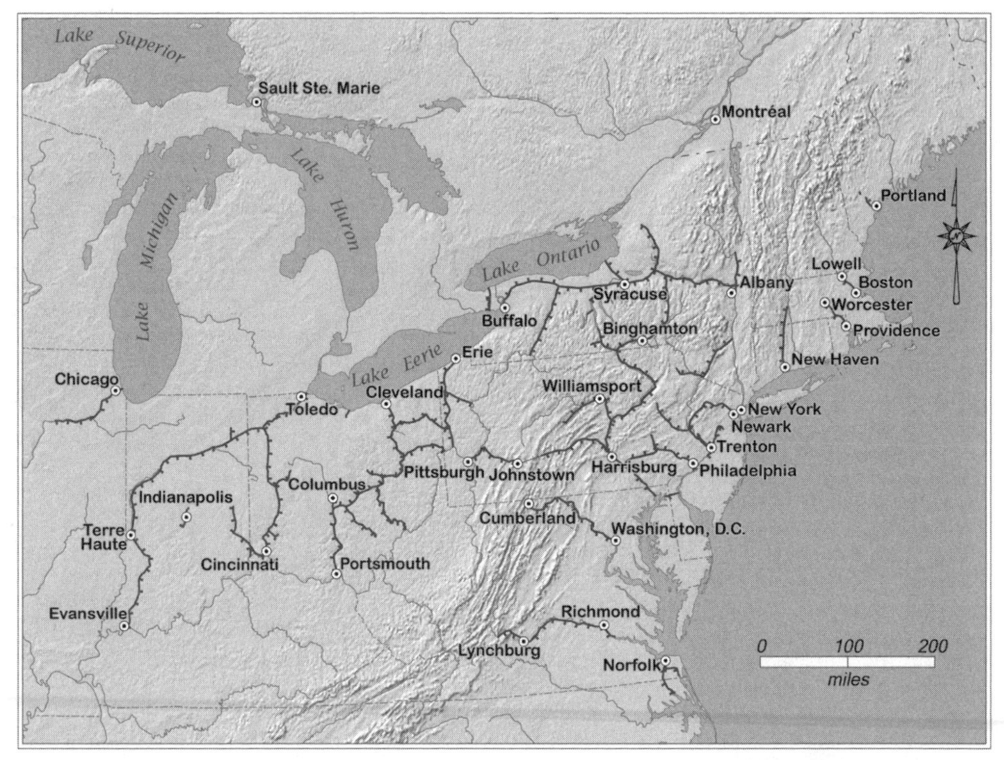

Figure 7.4. Selected northeastern canal routes, ca. 1860. After Paullin (1932, plate 138) and SRTM data.

inland rivers by half (Oliver 1956, 192–93). River towns grew up at superior boat-landing sites—especially where large meander curves intersected a bluff—that also provided ready access to a canal or road leading to interior farmlands, as at Evansville on the Ohio and Memphis, Vicksburg, and Natchez on the lower Mississippi (Burghardt 1959) (figure 7.6).

Steam-powered railroads of this epoch featured wood- or coal-fueled iron locomotives that ran on iron tracks. Three coastal cities—Boston, Baltimore, and Charleston—sought railroad development by the late 1820s and early 1830s, in large part because they were without access to the interior via river or canal. The largest of these rail systems, the Baltimore and Ohio Railroad, was under construction by 1830, reaching Wheeling, West Virginia, on the Ohio in 1853. The nation's rail track totaled 73 miles in 1830, increasing to 30,636 by the Civil War; 75 percent of the track network was in the northeastern and Midwestern states (Taylor 1964, 79) (figure 7.7). New England railroads adopted the standard English track gauge, or distance between the wheels, of 4 feet, 8.5 inches; other gauges prevailed elsewhere: 6 feet in New York and 5 feet in much of the South. Before the Civil War, railroads in the eastern states ran on eleven different railroad gauges (Taylor 1964, 82). Railroads operating on three different gauges provided connections to New York, Cincinnati, and St. Louis, for

Figure 7.5. Chesapeake and Ohio (C&O) Canal at Williamsport, Maryland, ca. 1900 to 1906. Built beside the Potomac River, shown here to the left, the C&O Canal opened in 1831 and operated until 1924, linking Washington, D.C., to Cumberland, Maryland. The canal's primary cargo was Appalachian coal from the Cumberland area. A canal boat is moored in the turning basin, the canal branches to the right, and it crosses Conococheague Creek via a stone aqueduct in the middle distance. Detroit Publishing Co. Collection, Prints and Photographs Division, Library of Congress. Reproduction number LC-D4–16564.

example (Vance 1995, 114). A change in railroad gauge required trains to stop and off-load freight onto railcars of the appropriate gauge, interruptions that reinforced the tradition of the short haul, which characterized the nation's iron railroad systems.

The Illinois Central Railroad (IC), linking Chicago and the Great Lakes to the Gulf coast at Mobile, was an important stimulus to regional development in the central Midwest. In 1850 the IC became the first large railroad system to receive grants of federal land along the main route, more than 3.7 million acres, to underwrite railroad construction (Gates 1934, 41–42; Taylor 1964, 96). To encourage land settlement, hence company profits from hauling farm supplies and commodities, the IC established a company to develop some thirty-three town sites along the tracks, many with standardized plats, block and lot sizes, and street names (Gates, 1934 124–30). The grants set a precedent for granting federal land to several other railroad companies, including the major transcontinental lines that ran

Figure 7.6. The Mississippi River steamboat landing at Vicksburg, Mississippi, ca. 1910 to 1920. Mules pulling two-wheeled carts bring cotton bales to the Vicksburg riverfront for loading onto Shreve-type steamboats. Henry Shreve placed the steam engine on the deck, allowing shallow draft boat configurations that could accommodate low water and comparatively small streams. Detroit Publishing Co. Collection, Prints and Photographs Division, Library of Congress. Reproduction number LC-D4–73472.

from the Midwest to the West Coast (Hudson 1982, 43–44). Indeed, the Pacific Railway Acts of 1862 and 1864 granted western railroad companies 12,800 acres of land for each mile of track built, among other financial subsidies (White 2011, 22–25) (figure 7.8).

Travel across the Great Plains and the West early in this epoch was primarily by trail. The most important trails originated in Independence, Missouri, and Kansas City, Kansas (figure 7.9). In 1821 the Santa Fe Trail initiated trade with Mexico by way of central Kansas and Raton Pass in what today is northeastern New Mexico. Movement of explorers, fur traders, and migrants was active on the Oregon Trail by the 1830s and continued through 1869, when the first transcontinental railroad, the Union Pacific–Central Pacific, opened from Omaha to Sacramento. Auxiliary trails such as the California, Bozeman, and Mormon Trails followed the eastern section of the Oregon Trail before splitting off toward their respective destinations.

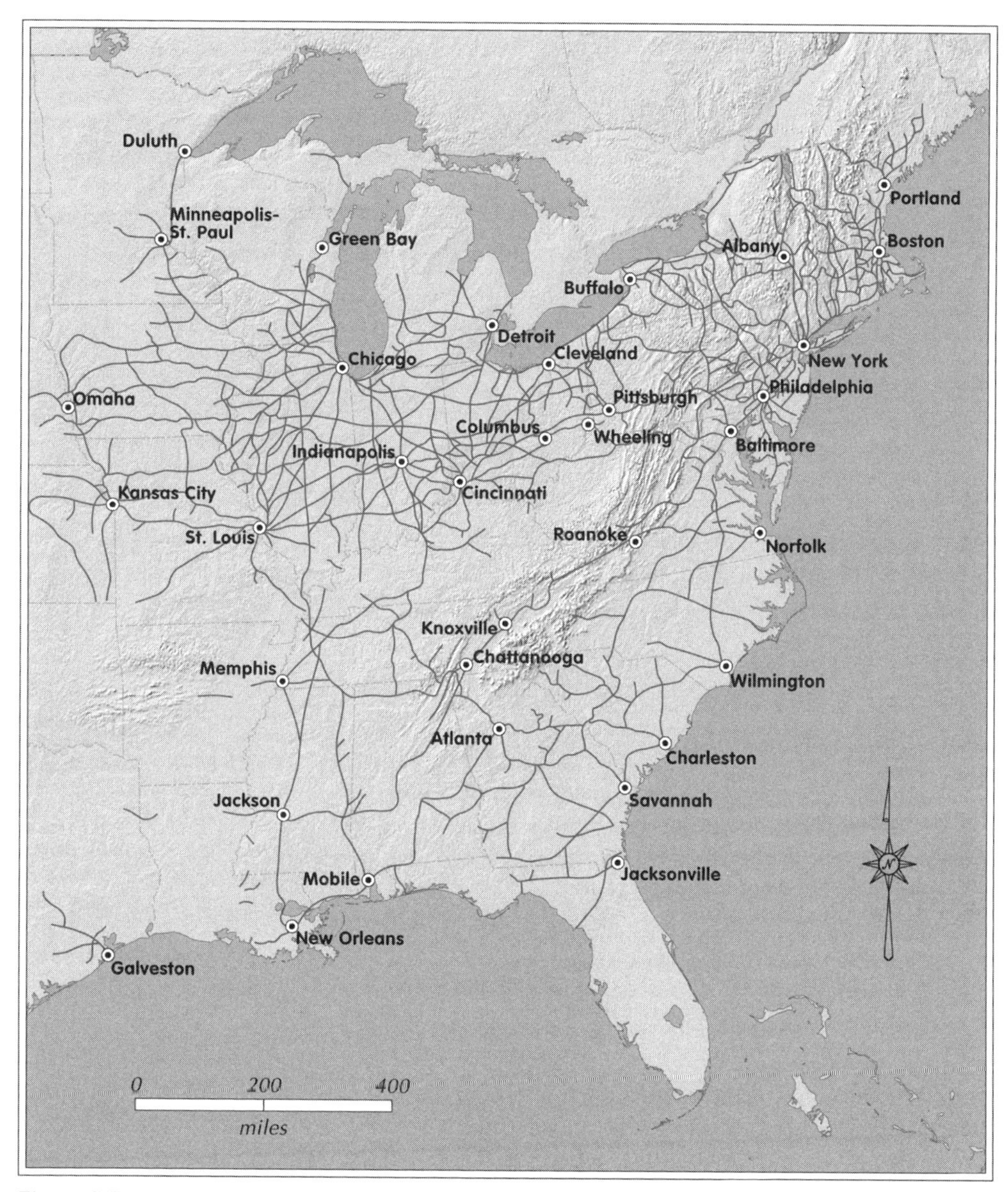

Figure 7.7. Selected railroads in the eastern United States, ca. 1870. After Cram (1892, various plates), Modelski (1984, various plates), Paullin (1932, plate 140), and SRTM data.

The Steel Rail Epoch: 1870–1920

A second major innovation, the Bessemer steel process, enabled this third epoch by bringing revolutionary change to transport equipment. Patented in England in 1855, the Bessemer process produced affordable, high-quality steel. By the 1860s American steel production centered in Pennsylvania at Johnstown and Pittsburgh. Railroads converted from iron to steel rails, locomotives, and rolling stock

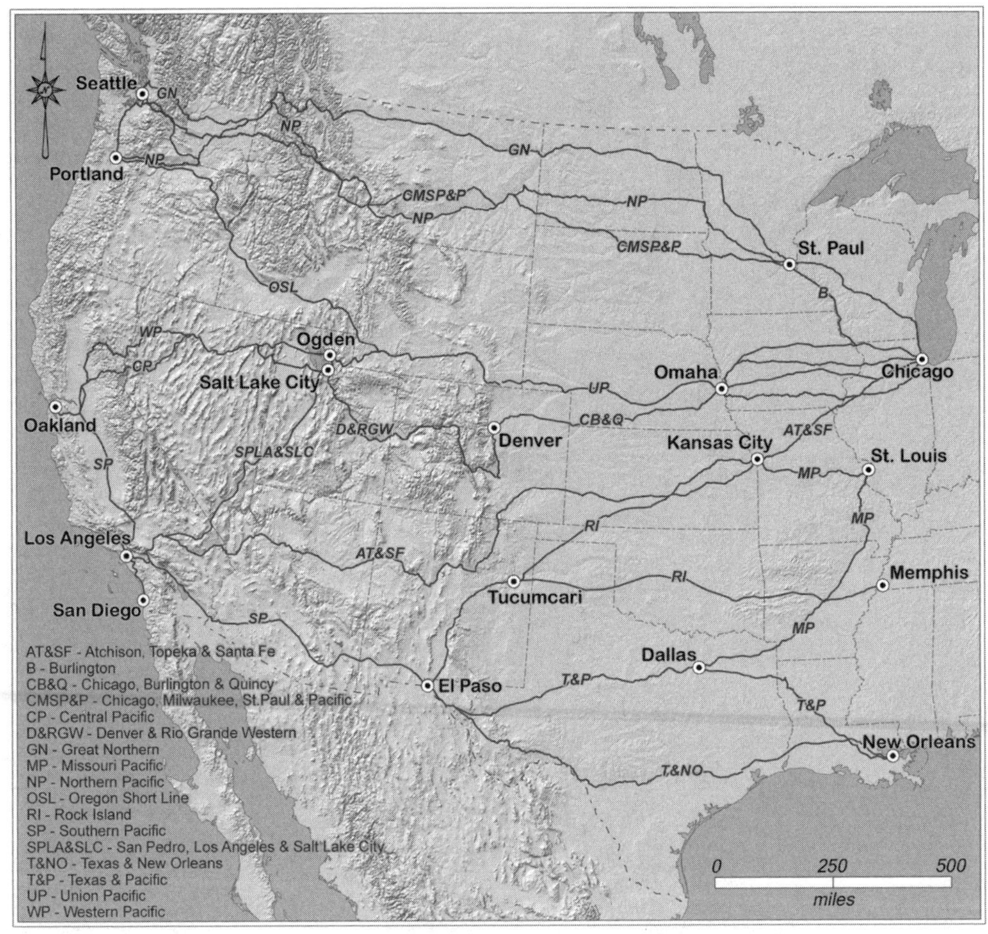

Figure 7.8. Selected railroads in the western United States, ca. 1910. After Modelski (1984, various plates), Paullin (1932, plate 141), and SRTM data.

to remarkable effect. Manufacturers built larger and more powerful steel locomotives and higher-capacity freight cars (White 2011, 153). Bulk cargo could be hauled in greater quantity, and with the standardization of rail gauges, the long-distance haul became commonplace, with significant savings in freight rates. Railroads pushed into the central Appalachian coalfields, from which coal could be economically shipped to coastal ports or steel mills. Refrigerated railcars permitted long-distance shipment of cut meat to large urban markets and helped revolutionize the Midwest and Great Plains livestock-production system. Chicago became a major rail hub, and its Union Stockyards, established in 1865, became one of the nation's largest livestock-processing centers. The railroad's capacity advantage crippled most freight and passenger movement on the nation's turnpikes and rivers (Borchert 1967, 304–5) (figure 7.10). Most canal systems could not compete with the steel railroads. Freight shipments on most

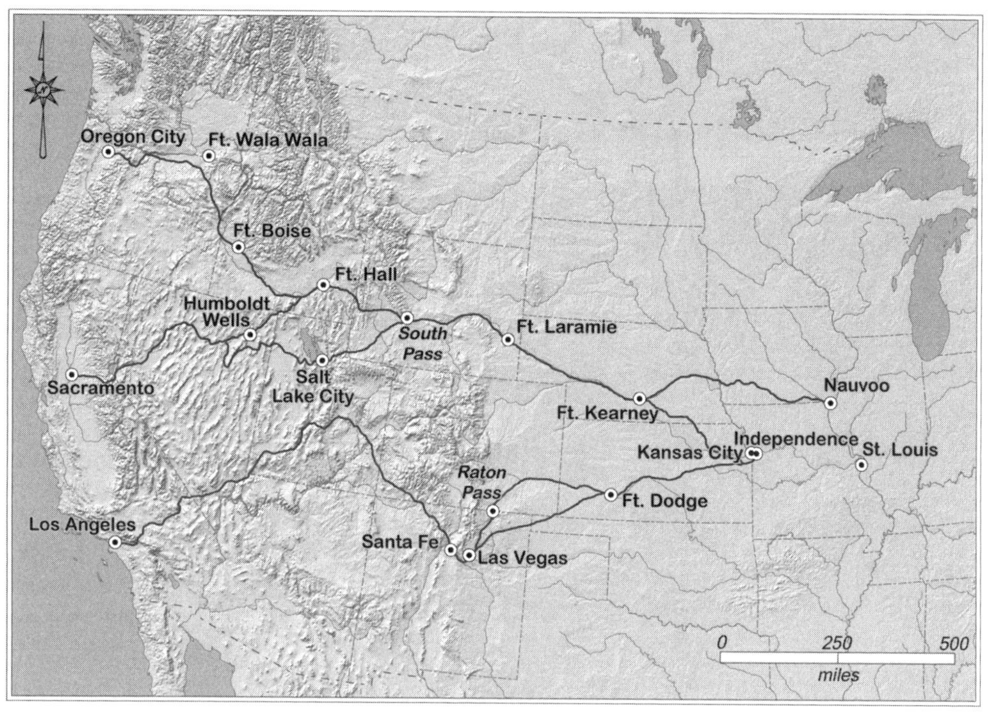

Figure 7.9. Selected western trails, ca. 1820s to 1860s. After National Park Service (n.d.) and SRTM data.

canals, except the Erie, dropped as railroad track mileage increased, and by the 1860s, the canal era had effectively come to an end (figure 7.2). Canal towns that failed to gain a railroad connection stagnated. The railroad also radically altered the financial fortunes of steamboat-dependent river cities. In 1848, St. Louis was a major Mississippi River transport and industrial center located a short distance downstream from the junction of the Illinois and Missouri Rivers. Regarded as the "Gateway to the West," the city was home port to 122 steamboats and 68 freight barges and hosted 3,468 boat landings that year (Lass 2001, 3; Paskoff 2007, 14–15). When engineer James Eads completed the first railroad bridge across the Mississippi at St. Louis in 1874, the event offered tangible evidence that steam-powered river transport had been dealt a substantial blow.

Public transport within America's cities advanced from omnibuses and horse-pulled passenger cars to electrified cars in 1888 when Frank Sprague installed the nation's first viable trolley car system powered by central station electric power in Richmond, Virginia (figure 7.11). By 1890, more than two hundred trolley systems were in operation or under construction in America's cities (Vance 1986, 381–86). The trolleys were economical to ride and provided impetus for suburban development along tracks that could be readily extended from city center to countryside. City trolley lines often connected to electric interurban rail lines that ran from town to town. Total electric railway trackage peaked at

Figure 7.10. A steam train crosses Kentucky's High Bridge in 1907. In 1876, engineers completed the cantilevered truss bridge across the Kentucky River gorge between Lexington and Danville. At 275 feet above the river, it was the highest bridge above navigable water in the nation. Log rafts, tied to the river's east bank, may be headed to downstream sawmills in Frankfort. Detroit Publishing Co. Collection, Prints and Photographs Division, Library of Congress. Reproduction number LC-D4–19977.

more than forty thousand miles in 1917. Thereafter electric car system ridership gradually decreased with increasing competition from automobiles and buses. By the 1950s few urban trolley systems remained in business (Vance 1986, 391–92).

The Auto-Air-Amenity Epoch: 1920–1970

The adaptation of the internal combustion engine to the automobile, truck, and tractor delimits this epoch. European automobiles were available in limited numbers to wealthy Americans prior to 1900; not until Henry Ford's moderately priced Model T was offered for sale in 1908 could middle-class folk afford a car (Flink 1988, 114; Raitz 1998, 372) (figure 7.12). That same year there were only about 650 miles of stone-surfaced macadam road in the United States (Davidson 1951, 280). Several states initiated improved road construction programs as part of the Good Roads Movement, and by 1914 the nation had more than 257,000 miles of surfaced roads (Hugill 1982, 339) (figure 7.2). Until the Federal Aid Road Act of 1916 provided federal matching funding, localities and states bore the responsibility for road construction. This initiative was followed by the Federal

Figure 7.11. Trolley cars on Market Street in Philadelphia, ca. 1904. Detroit Publishing Co. Collection, Prints and Photographs Division, Library of Congress. Reproduction number LC-D4–17516.

Aid Road Act of 1921, which created a Bureau of Public Roads, a plan for a national highway system, and expanded federal funding (Federal Highway Administration 1976, 86–87, 108). In 1925, Congress approved a national gasoline tax to help pay for new highway construction, and the following year the American Association of State Highway Officials approved road sign standardization and a uniform numbering system for the nation's highways. East-west highways received even numbers (the National Road became U.S. 40), whereas north-south roads got odd numbers (the Great Valley Road in Virginia's Shenandoah valley became U.S. 11). Nationwide automobile registrations exceeded 20 million for the first time in 1926 (Raitz 1996, 290). Motor buses provided regional and transcontinental passenger service in direct competition with railroads by 1925; by the early 1950s, buses carried more than one-third of the nation's intercity passengers (Davidson 1951, 290).

By 1910, city retailers, bakers, and dairies were using delivery trucks, and the post office was using trucks to collect mail. During World War I, short-haul trucking increased rapidly, and manufacturers increased production, building three hundred thousand trucks in 1917. After the war, farmers began using trucks

Figure 7.12. Detroit street traffic, ca. 1920 to 1925. Automobiles negotiate an early traffic-control tower positioned in the middle of an intersection. In the early 1920s, Detroit became one of the nation's first cities to install traffic lights, depicted here at eye level and atop the tower. Detroit Publishing Co. Collection, Prints and Photographs Division, Library of Congress. Reproduction number LC-D420–2706.

to ship their produce to market. Unlike trains, trucks were limited by neither track location nor rigid schedules. Trucking companies could make pickups and deliveries at any time and at most any place connected to a road. By the early 1950s, trucks were carrying 75 percent of the nation's freight at some point in its transit between producer and consumer (Oliver 1956, 483–84, 564). During the 1950s, intercity freight carried by trucks, measured in billions of ton-miles, increased from 16 to 22.5 percent of the national total, whereas the railroad's freight traffic share fell from 56 to 43.5 percent (Rae 1965, 190). A large share of truck freight was general cargo or freight shipped in boxes or crates, whereas railroads increasingly concentrated on shipping bulk cargo commodities such as coal (figure 7.2). The development of the standardized shipping container in the 1950s and 1960s brought truck and railroad shippers together, and railroads gradually developed a specialty in long-distance general freight shipping to supplement their bulk cargo business.

As the number of motor vehicles on America's developing roadway system increased, so did concerns about accidents and traffic congestion (Seely 1987, 144, 152). Large metropolitan areas began experiencing traffic jams in the 1920s, and engineers sought solutions in road reconfiguration. Three highway projects served as early demonstrations of traffic control through multiple lanes, controlled access, long radius curves, and other innovative engineering practices. The

Merritt Parkway, constructed in Fairfield County, Connecticut, northeast of New York City in 1938, was the nation's first modern toll road (Vance 1986, 517). The Pennsylvania Turnpike, a 160-mile controlled-access, multilane, all-weather toll road, opened in 1940, becoming the first modern long-distance highway in the United States (Oliver 1956, 568–69; Vance 1986, 517–18). The six-lane Arroyo Seco Parkway, completed in Los Angeles in 1940, was the nation's first freeway.

President Dwight Eisenhower signed into law the Interstate and Defense Highways Act in 1956. The original program authorized $25 billion for construction of forty-one thousand miles of interstate freeways to be financed by fuel taxes. The act obligated the federal government to defray 90 percent of construction costs and the states 10 percent (Seely 1987, 217). Interstate highways largely ran parallel to existing U.S. highways, along which many cities had been established. Controlled-access interstates bypassed smaller cities, though interchanges gave residents access and allowed travelers to exit the highway in search of food, fuel, and lodging. Thereafter, city expansion was often in the direction of the interstate interchange rather than along the old U.S. highway, radically altering established urban morphologies (Schein 1996, 332–37). Parallel interstates often syphoned through-traffic from established roads, and roadside business locations along U.S. highways were devalued and often abandoned in favor of new sites near the interstate interchanges (Raitz 2010, 280–89).

Although railroad-oriented suburbs had emerged in some cities by the early 1850s and were supported by trollies and then automobiles, large-scale, auto-dependent suburban residential development began after World War II with the rapid extension of high-capacity highways and interstates. By the 1970s, large suburban "downtowns" with regional malls, office employment, commercial service provision, and light manufacturing were concentrating in strategic locations, especially near international airports, where arterial highways and circumferential interstates intersected (Baerwald 1978, 308–9; Muller 1997, 46).

CONCLUSION

Laborers and engineers constructed America's transportation systems according to changing technologies and at scales that shift from local to regional to national. Each transport mode also reflects complex interrelationships among economic motivation, engineering expertise, financial wherewithal, and political will. Once completed and in use, road, canal, and railroad systems reduce the friction of distance and convert distance into time.

Innovative technologies such as the steam engine and Bessemer steel manufacturing, while not directly developed for transportation applications, nevertheless had substantial impacts on system improvements. Early transport modes improved the movement of people, mail, and farm produce. City development and growth depended upon transportation access. Technical improvements enabled the economical transport of farm products to market cities and further enhanced passenger travel. Distant mineral deposits became resources once roads or railroads made them accessible. Distant prairies became producers of cattle and grain as high-capacity rail transport moved west. Transportation enabled large-scale human migration from farm to city and from region to region. Places bypassed by new transportation systems tended to stagnate, as growth slowed and then stopped. Places that became transportation hubs and remained so over time also became the nation's major cities. Transportation technologies, be they associated with the ways traveled or the vehicles used, have been in continual flux and change. Transportation-facilities construction and maintenance claim an increasingly large volume of local, state, and national capital, a priority with few detractors. Albert Gallatin's admonition that transportation infrastructure was required to join the country's regions has come to fruition—at a scale and cost that he likely did not imagine.

NOTE

1. The term "Yankee Gangplank" can be attributed to Professor Leslie Hewes, Department of Geography, University of Nebraska, although he apparently never used the term in print.

REFERENCES

Baerwald, T. J. 1978. The Emergence of a New "Downtown." *Geographical Review* 68, no. 3: 308–18.

Bernstein, P. L. 2005. *Wedding of the Waters: The Erie Canal and the Making of a Great Nation.* New York: W. W. Norton.

Borchert, J. R. 1967. American Metropolitan Evolution. *Geographical Review* 57, no. 3: 301–32.

Burghardt, A. F. 1959. The Location of River Towns in the Central Lowland of the United States. *Annals of the Association of American Geographers* 49, no. 3: 305–23.

Calhoun, D. H. 1960. *The American Civil Engineer: Origins and Conflict.* Cambridge, MA: MIT, Technology Press.

Cram, George F. 1892. *Cram's Standard American Railway System Atlas.* Chicago: G. F. Cram.

Davidson, M. B. 1951. *Life in America.* Vol. 2. Boston: Houghton Mifflin Co.

Dunbar, S. 1915. *A History of Travel in America.* Vol. 1. Indianapolis: Bobbs-Merrill.

Earle, C. 1987. Regional Economic Development West of the Appalachians, 1815–1860. In *North America: The Historical Geography of a Changing Continent,* edited by R. Mitchell and P. Groves, 172–97. Totowa, NJ: Rowman & Littlefield.

———. 1992. *Geographical Inquiry and American Historical Problems.* Stanford, CA: Stanford University Press.

Federal Highway Administration. 1976. *America's Highways—1776–1976: A History of the Federal-Aid Program.* Washington, D.C.: Government Printing Office.

Flink, J. J. 1988. *The Automobile Age.* Cambridge, MA: MIT Press.

Gallatin, A. 1816. *Report of the Secretary of the Treasury, on the Subject of Public Roads and Canals, 1807.* Washington, D.C.: William A. Davis.

Gates, P. W. 1934. *The Illinois Central Railroad and Its Colonization Work.* Cambridge, MA: Harvard University Press.

Hudson, J. C. 1982. Towns of the Western Railroads. *Great Plains Quarterly* 2, no. 1: 41–54.

Hugill, P. J. 1982. Good Roads and the Automobile in the United States, 1880–1929. *Geographical Review* 72, no. 3: 327–49.

Jackson, W. T. 1964. *Wagon Roads West: A Study of the Federal Road Surveys and Construction in the Trans-Mississippi West, 1846–1869*. Lincoln, NE: University of Nebraska Press.

Lass, W. E. 2001. The Fate of Steamboats: A Case Study of the 1848 St. Louis Fleet. *Missouri Historical Review* 96, no. 1: 2–15.

Lezius, W. G. 1936. The Lake Port at Toledo. *Economic Geography* 12, no. 2: 197–204.

McGreevy, P. 2009. *Stairway to Empire: Lockport, the Erie Canal, and the Shaping of America*. Albany, NY: State University of New York Press.

Modelski, Andrew M. 1984. *Railroad Maps of North America: The First Hundred Years*. Washington, D.C.: Library of Congress.

Muller, P. O. 1997. The Suburban Transformation of the Globalizing American City. *Annals of the American Academy of Political and Social Science* 551 (May): 44–58.

National Park Service (NPS). n.d. National Trails System Map and Guide. NPS. http://www.nps.gov/hfc/carto/nps-trails.cfm.

Oliver, John William. 1956. *History of American Technology*. New York: Ronald Press Company.

Paskoff, P. F. 2007. *Troubled Waters: Steamboat Disasters, River Improvements, and American Public Policy, 1821–1860*. Baton Rouge: Louisiana State University Press.

Paullin, Charles. 1932. *Atlas of the Historical Geography of the United States*. New York and Washington, D.C.: American Geographical Society and Carnegie Institute.

Phillips, U. B. 1905. Transportation in the Antebellum South: An Economic Analysis. *Quarterly Journal of Economics* 19, no. 3: 434–51.

Rae, J. B. 1965. *The American Automobile: A Brief History*. Chicago: University of Chicago Press.

Raitz, K. 1996. The US 40 Roadside. In *The National Road*, edited by Karl Raitz, 285–318. Baltimore: Johns Hopkins University Press.

———. 1998. American Roads, Roadside America. *Geographical Review* 88, no. 3: 363–87.

———. 2010. U.S. 11 and a Modern Geography of Culture and Connection. In *The Great Valley Road of Virginia: Shenandoah Landscapes from Prehistory to the Present*, edited by W. R. Hofstra and K. Raitz, 239–96. Charlottesville: University of Virginia Press.

Raitz, K., and N. O'Malley. 2007. Local-Scale Turnpike Roads in Nineteenth-Century Kentucky. *Journal of Historical Geography* 33, no. 1: 1–23.

Raitz, K. B., J. E. Levy, and R. A. Gilbreath. 2010. Mapping Kentucky's Frontier Trails through Geographical Information and Cartographic Applications. *Geographical Review* 100, no. 3: 312–35.

Schein, Richard H. 1996. The Interstate 70 Landscape. In *The National Road*, edited by K. Raitz, 319–47. Baltimore: Johns Hopkins University Press.

Seely, B. E. 1987. *Building the American Highway System: Engineers as Policy Makers*. Philadelphia: Temple University Press.

Shaw, R. E. 1990. *Canals for a Nation: The Canal Era in the United States, 1790–1860*. Lexington: University Press of Kentucky.

Taylor, G. R. 1964. *The Transportation Revolution, 1815–1860*. New York: Holt, Rinehart and Winston.

U.S. Bureau of the Census. 1975. *Historical Statistics of the United States, Colonial Times to 1970*. Part 1. Bicentennial ed. Washington, D.C.: Government Printing Office.

U.S. Department of Agriculture. 1902. *Proceedings of the Jefferson Memorial and Interstate Good Roads Convention*, Charlottesville, Virginia, April 2–4. Bulletin no. 25. Washington, D.C.: Office of Public Road Inquiries.

Vance, J. 1986. *Capturing the Horizon: The Historical Geography of Transportation since the Transportation Revolution of the Sixteenth Century.* New York: Harper & Row.

———. 1995. *The North American Railroad: Its Origin, Evolution, and Geography.* Baltimore: Johns Hopkins University Press.

White, R. 2011. *Railroaded: The Transcontinentals and the Making of Modern America.* New York: W. W. Norton.

Wood, J. S. 1996. The Idea of a National Road. In *The National Road,* edited by K. Raitz, 93–122. Baltimore: Johns Hopkins University Press.

Wyckoff, W. 1988. *The Developer's Frontier: The Making of the Western New York Landscape.* New Haven, CT: Yale University Press.

8

Extracting Wealth from the Earth and Forest

Geoffrey L. Buckley

Two decades have now passed since the 1992 publication of *The American Environment: Interpretations of Past Geographies*, edited by Lary Dilsaver and Craig Colten. In the intervening years, a small but growing cadre of historical geographers has followed Dilsaver and Colten down the "road not taken," exploring the environmental impacts of past human activities. Perhaps more important, they have forged links with scholars in other fields engaged in similar work—namely, environmental historians. This cross-fertilization has not only enhanced our collective ability to interpret the past but opened the door to collaborative efforts that transcend disciplinary boundaries, resulting in more geographically informed studies of past environments.

That much of this environmental research focuses on North America should come as no surprise. As Stanley Trimble states in the opening chapter to Michael Conzen's *The Making of the American Landscape*, "North America has had its physical environment transformed more rapidly at the hands of people than any other large area of the world. Generally, within less than 200 years, near-primeval-land has sprouted farms and cities, forests have been removed or changed, and severe hydrologic and geomorphic disruptions have sometimes ensued" (1990, 9). While one may question Trimble's characterization of the environment as "near-primeval," given what we know today about the land-use practices of Native American peoples, his point is well-taken. For geographers, historians, sociologists, and others interested in the study of past environments, North America has proven fertile ground for historical research because many of the changes that have taken place occurred recently enough to ensure that a broad range of historical data sets are available for use.

In this chapter I consider the many and varied ways that logging and mining shaped and reshaped North America's physical environment during the nineteenth and twentieth centuries. Focusing primarily on the United States, I begin by discussing the role that the federal government played in encouraging the development of the nation's resources. Next, I turn to the country's forest resources, recounting their destruction at the hands of settlers, the technological innovations that drove industrial logging, and the Progressive Era conservation measures aimed at forest recovery. I then direct my attention to the mining industry, especially the increase in demand for fuel and nonfuel minerals, changes in mining practices, and the environmental costs of mineral extraction. Throughout the narrative, I emphasize Appalachia, a section of the country that fueled America's Industrial Revolution and whose economy, even today, remains largely dependent on the extraction of raw materials. Perhaps no other section of the United States has experienced the swing of the axe or the blow of the pick to the degree that this region has over the past century and a half.

"GET RID OF IT QUICK"

In his recent volume on sustainability titled *Treading Softly: Paths to Ecological Order*, Thomas Princen explains how Americans justified the extraordinary consumption of natural resources that occurred during the nineteenth and twentieth centuries: "A great nation had to be built, an industrial economy created, foes of democracy defeated. Resources—timber, minerals, oil, water, soil—were virtually unlimited, and waste sinks—where the residues and runoff and combustion gases went—an alien concept" (2010, vii). Although private landowners and corporate entities did the dirty work of extracting most of these resources, the federal government did not sit idly by. Indeed, the U.S. government was complicit in the transformation, offering incentives to landowners and corporations to "cash in" on the nation's natural resources. Or as Gifford Pinchot, the first chief of the U.S. Forest Service put it in a 1947 memoir, "Get timber by hook or by crook, get it quick and cut it quick—that was the rule of the citizen. Get rid of it quick—that was the rule of the Government for the vast timberlands it still controlled. And it has been got rid of both by the Government and by private owners with amazing efficiency and startling speed" (1947, 23).

The best known of the extractive incentives was the Homestead Act. Passed in 1862, this act permitted any head of household or anyone over twenty-one years old to acquire 160 acres of land for free as long as the new owner settled on it for five years and made "improvements." A similar law, the Dominion Lands Act, was passed in Canada a decade later (Wynn 2007). Whereas these two acts aimed to encourage development of the continent's agricultural resources, other acts promoted mining and logging. The Mining Law of 1872, for example, allowed parties to extract mineral resources on the U.S. public domain without paying royalties to the federal government. (After passage of the Mineral Lands Leasing Act of 1920, coal, oil, and natural gas were treated separately.) With respect to forest resources, the Free Timber Act of 1878 offered settlers the opportunity to remove timber from lands reserved for mineral use. Also passed in 1878, the Timber and Stone Act made land "valuable for minerals and stone as well as timber" available to prospective buyers (Merchant 2002, 125). According to Carolyn Merchant, these last two acts "were bonanzas for timber companies, who hired people to stake claims to forest lands and then turn the lands over to the lumber company" (2002, 125). Of course, the federal government encouraged development further by providing land grants to railroad companies building transcontinental lines. By the end of the nineteenth century, three factors—a growing demand for consumer goods, the application of new technologies, and a lax regulatory environment—combined to greatly reduce forest cover across the United States and Canada and to open up public and private lands for the extraction of fuel and nonfuel mineral resources (figure 8.1).

"A SCENE OF AWFUL DESOLATION"

In his seminal volume *Americans and Their Forests: A Historical Geography* (1989), Michael Williams reminds us how dependent residents of the United States once were on this versatile resource. Its wide range of uses prompted James Hall, writing in 1836, to remark, "Well may ours be called a wooden country; not merely from the extent of its forests, but because in common use wood has been substituted for a number of most necessary and common articles—such as stone, iron, and even leather" (quoted in Williams 1989, 5). In addition to being used for construction purposes, wood and wood-derived products, such as pitch and turpentine, were essential to the shipbuilding and naval stores industries. Enormous quantities of timber were cut and manufactured into railroad crossties, fences, and mine props. Wood was used as a fuel, stoking the fires of steamboats and steam locomotives. Converted to charcoal it was burned in iron furnaces. Before the shift to coal, it was America's most important domestic fuel source. All told, wood met about 90 percent of the country's energy needs in 1850 (Olson 1971; Cronon 1983; Williams 1989).

The sheer abundance of forest resources in North America delayed the adoption of new technologies and energy sources. By 1810, for example, Great Britain had moved exclusively to coal- or coke-fired furnaces; in the United States, there were no coke furnaces. Not until the 1830s would Americans begin to experiment with coke as an alternative fuel source. Technology did not lag in the development of more efficient wood-burning stoves, however. Ironically, shortages of fuel wood were not uncommon in the eighteenth century in major cities like New York, Philadelphia, and Boston, all of which boasted populations of one hundred thousand or greater. During the winter months, when rivers froze, it was difficult to transport sufficient quantities of wood from the countryside, where it was plentiful, to the city, where demand was high. Between 1790 and 1845, over eight hundred patents were taken out for stoves, evidence that, generations ago, Americans had to contend with their own "energy crises" (Williams 1989).

To early settlers intent on clearing land for agriculture, the forests of eastern North America must have seemed inexhaustible. Undaunted, they felled the forests of the East in relatively short order. Writing about cultural and ecological change in New England during the colonial period, William Cronon asserts that "deforestation was one of the most sweeping transformations wrought by European settlement" (1983, 126). To these early agriculturalists, trees were obstacles to remove, not resources to manage carefully, a point not lost on visitors touring America during the early national period. In 1794, one such traveler, William

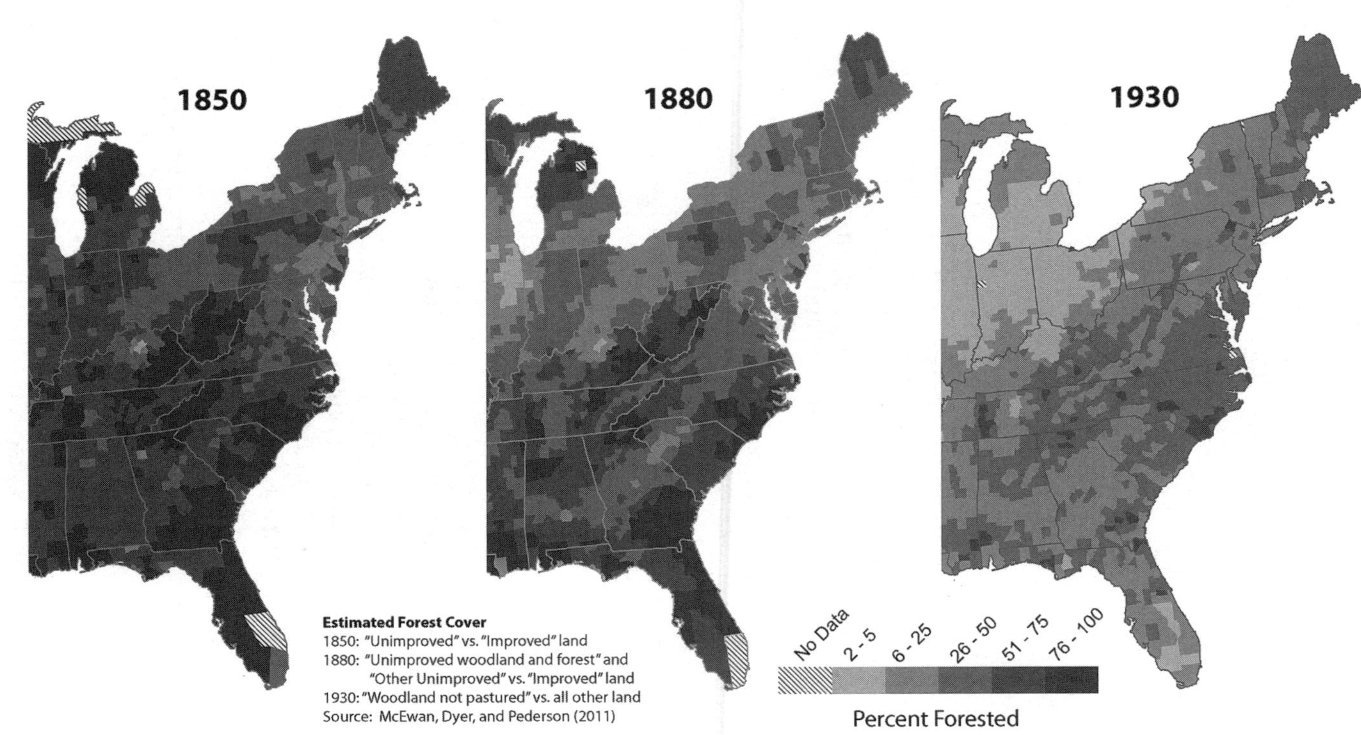

Figure 8.1. Forest cover change in the eastern United States. Wood met 90 percent of the country's energy needs in 1850. It also served a wide variety of domestic, commercial, and industrial purposes.

Strickland of England, observed that all Americans "agree in this; that trees are a nuisance and ought to be destroyed by any, and every means" (quoted in Taylor 1998, 302). Another English traveler, Isaac Weld, marveled that Americans hated trees and "cut away all before them without mercy; not one is spared; all share . . . in the general havoc" (quoted in Taylor 1998, 302).

By 1850 in the United States, settlers had already cleared some 113.74 million acres of land for agriculture, most of it in the eastern half of the nation. Taking advantage of government incentives, settlers pressed on, penetrating the grasslands and plains of the West. Ironically, settlement of nonforested sections of the country stimulated further cutting and the emergence of a trade and transportation network to increase supplies of this scarce commodity for construction and other purposes. Between 1850 and 1859, settlers cleared another 39.705 million acres, a figure roughly equivalent to one-third of all wood cut during the preceding two hundred years. Although the amount of timber cut declined during the Civil War years, the pace accelerated in the ensuing decade, with approximately 49.37 million acres cut between 1870 and 1879 (Williams 1982).

Although cutting for industrial and other purposes occurred at the same time across much of the United States, a distinct geographic pattern emerged in the years leading up to the Civil War. Whereas in 1839 the Northeast accounted for about two-thirds of total production, by 1859 this figure had dropped to about one-third as the timber industry shifted its attention to the forests of Michigan, Wisconsin, and Minnesota. Then, with production figures on the decline in the 1880s and 1890s, the industry began its massive assault on the forests of the American South. As a new century dawned, the industry relocated again, this time to the forests of the Pacific Northwest (Williams 1989; Robbins 1997). In Canada, a similar pattern played out. Prior to 1806, when Napoleon's continental blockade forced Great Britain to look west to meets its burgeoning demand for wood, Canada's fledgling timber industry had merely "nibbled at some of [the] edges" of the country's forests (Harris 2008, 176). Beginning in New Brunswick and lower Canada, then expanding into upper Canada and, later, British Columbia, the industry grew by leaps and bounds. By the middle of the century, the voracious demands of both British and American consumers had converted large expanses of trees into timber (Wynn 2007; Harris 2008).

Advances in cutting technology aided forest destruction. In the old days, two able-bodied men might be able to cut one hundred feet of plank per day using a seven-foot whipsaw. The advent of the water-powered sash saw, then the muley mill, increased this amount to one thousand board feet per day. The introduction of portable steam-powered circular and band saws, in particular, had a tremendous impact on the forest, the latter capable of cutting sixty to eighty thousand feet per day (Williams 1989; Robbins 1997). Along with narrow-gauge railroads and gas-powered chain saws, these innovations left large stretches of land—heretofore inaccessible—practically devoid of trees (figures 8.2 and 8.3). With regard to West Virginia's forest resources, Ronald Lewis identifies 1880 to 1920 as the period during which the state's ancient old-growth forests underwent "industrial conquest." As late as 1880, Lewis estimates, "virgin forest" still covered two-thirds of the state. By 1920, 30 billion board feet had been removed, and it was almost entirely gone. Ronald Eller (1982), Timothy Silver (2003), and

Figure 8.2. Logging, lower Columbia, ca. 1905. Note the whipsaw and axe in the foreground. At the beginning of the twentieth century, these were the most important tools of the trade. J. F. Ford photo, Negative No.: OrHi 37858. Courtesy of the Oregon Historical Society.

Kathryn Newfont (2012) offer similar accounts of the impacts of industrial logging in Kentucky and North Carolina. As Donald Edward Davis (2000) points out, however, an introduced blight—not the woodsman's saw—led to the devastating loss of the American chestnut.

Wasteful cutting practices and carelessness meant that forest fires often followed in the wake of logging operations (Pyne 1997). According to Douglas MacCleery (1993), forest fires claimed anywhere between 20 and 50 million acres per year in around 1900. With no roots to hold the soil in place, deforested and burned-over lands were particularly vulnerable to floods and droughts, resulting in soil erosion, stream siltation, and loss of wildlife. One editorialist, writing about West Virginia's forests for an eastern newspaper in 1904, remarked, "A few

Figure 8.3. Logging with a chain saw. Technological innovations such as the gas-powered chain saw accelerated the pace of forest clearance. Negative No.: OrHi 21156. Courtesy of the Oregon Historical Society.

years ago there were sawmills scattered all along this road from Piedmont to Thomas, but now many of these have disappeared, leaving as evidence of their work miles and miles of country upon which there is left scarcely one living tree. The ground is covered with stumps and condemned, or discarded logs, while hundreds of decayed dead, bare trees make a scene of awful desolation" (*Cumberland Alleganian*, December 22, 1904). The comment could have applied just about anywhere in the eastern United States during the preceding century.

Of course, one way to deal with a diminishing supply of timber is to plant trees. Although planting trees in our urban areas is a long-standing tradition, as Henry Lawrence has shown in his comprehensive volume *City Trees: A Historical Geography from the Renaissance through the Nineteenth Century* (2006), large-scale reforestation of rural lands has no such history—at least not prior to the Civil War. Nevertheless, nearly two decades before the federal government established the country's first national forest reserve, Americans began to plant trees. In 1872, on the occasion of the nation's first Arbor Day, Nebraskans planted more than 1 million trees, earning that state the nickname "The Tree Planters State." Enthusiasm soon spread to other parts of the country, and Arbor Day turned into an annual celebration (Gumprecht 2001; Lawrence 2006). One year later, the federal government passed the Timber Culture Act, which gave settlers 160 acres of land on the condition that they plant 40 acres of it with trees. Widely abused, the act was later amended so that only ten acres had to be planted with trees. As many disillusioned homesteaders learned the hard way, planting trees on the Great Plains or, even more challenging, in the parched desert lands of the Far West would not stem the tide of forest loss (Olson 1971; Merchant 2002).

"THE DUTY OF GOVERNMENTS"

Perhaps the shock of seeing mile after mile of cutover land, or maybe fear of an impending "timber famine," first ignited concern among Americans. Either way, the need for government action to curb the destruction became clear. In 1873, Dr. Franklin B. Hough suggested as much when he presented a paper titled "The Duty of Governments in Preservation of Forests" at a meeting of the American Association for the Advancement of Science. Six months later, Congress created the Division of Forestry in the U.S. Department of Agriculture (USDA) to study the problem. Despite the efforts of Bernhard Fernow, a professionally trained forester appointed to head the Division of Forestry in 1886, little substantive progress was made on the issue of America's disappearing forests. Not only were no Americans trained in the precepts of scientific forest management at this time—Fernow was born in Germany—but there were no forestry schools. The establishment of such schools at Cornell University in 1898 and Yale University in 1900 would soon address this critical need. In the meantime, forest conservation began to take root at the state level. Indeed, one could argue that states like New York and Pennsylvania truly pioneered the conservation of forest resources (Pisani 1997; Steen 1997; Miller 2001; Buckley 2010).

After determining that at least some of the public domain in the American West should remain in federal hands to protect forest resources, President Benjamin Harrison, in 1891, created the country's first national forest reserve on land adjacent to Yellowstone National Park. Together, Harrison and his successor, Grover Cleveland, set aside 40 million acres of forest reserves. Establishing forest reserves was easy enough; deciding how to manage them and for what purpose proved more difficult. Finally, in 1897, President William McKinley signed the Organic Act, which spelled out the purpose of the new reserves: "to ensure predictable supplies of water and timber" (Steen 1997, 50). During President Theodore Roosevelt's tenure in office, the country's system of forest reserves flourished. In 1905, management of the reserves moved from the Department of the Interior to the newly created Forest Service in the USDA, an indication that trees were to be managed as crops. Under the direction of Chief Forester Gifford Pinchot, the first scientifically trained forester from the United States, the number of acres in forest reserves—soon to be renamed national forests—quadrupled, totaling some 150 million acres by 1906 (Williams 1989).

Despite the impressive total land acreage in forest reserves, there remained one problem: all of the national forests were located west of the Mississippi River, where the federal government could create them easily from lands it already controlled. Passage of the Weeks Act in 1911 opened the door for the federal government to begin the process of building national forests in the East, where most land had fallen into private ownership. Essentially, the Weeks Act permitted federal officials to seek permission from individual state legislatures to acquire private property, either through direct purchase or eminent domain, to establish national forests in the East. While many smaller states, like Maryland, rejected the federal overture, arguing that the establishment of a national forest would negatively affect state forestry efforts, others, such as Vermont, opened the door to federal ownership. Although federal ownership of forestland remains heavily weighted to the west, the Weeks Act did achieve an important goal: extending the influence of the Forest Service to a section of the country where it had been largely unknown (Williams 1989; Buckley 2010; Gregg 2010).

In his now classic *Conservation and the Gospel of Efficiency*, Samuel P. Hays reminds us that Progressive Era conservationists were less interested in preserving resources than in promoting their "rational" use "with a focus on efficiency, planning for future use, and the application of expertise to broad national problems" (1969, n.p.). To utilitarian conservationists like Pinchot, nature was a storehouse of resources that need to be used efficiently (Hays 1969). His approach to forest conservation was straightforward: he aimed "to promote the idea of wise use—the greatest good for the greatest number through scientific management" (Rothman 1997, 109). In general, Americans placed a great deal of faith in these resource "experts"—professionally trained engineers, foresters, and soil scientists—who saw it as their job to tackle difficult conservation problems for the public good and free from politics. That faith remained largely unshaken until the latter half of the twentieth century.

Numerous acts passed in the post–World War II era have affected the way the USDA Forest Service manages its holdings and carries out its mission. The Multiple-Use Sustained-Yield Act of 1960, for instance, directed the Forest Service to place timber and range management on equal footing with management of water, recreation, and wildlife resources. The Wilderness Act, signed into law by President Lyndon Johnson in 1964, offered a statutory definition of "wilderness" and required the Forest Service to identify and preserve areas that met this standard. Perhaps most important of all were the National Environmental Policy Act of 1969 and the National Forest Management Act of 1976, which opened the door to public comment and participation in management decisions (Merchant 2002). As Paul Hirt clearly demonstrates in *A Conspiracy of Optimism: Management of the National Forests since World War Two* (1994), balancing contradictory aspects of its mission—from clear-cutting to wilderness preservation—has proved difficult for the Forest Service over the last several decades.

AMERICAN MINING LANDSCAPES

According to Richard Francaviglia, mining—"the process by which treasures locked in the earth are 'won' by man"—creates some of the "most stark and dramatic landscapes on earth" (1992, 89, 92). For many Americans, unfamiliar with the mining process and unaware that so many of our material possessions have components we must procure from the earth, the preceding statement may sound like pure hyperbole. As the following figures bear out, however, the dimensions of many of these sites are staggering. Located in Minnesota's Iron Ranges, the largest iron mine in the United States stretches across thirteen thousand acres and is four hundred feet deep. Three-quarters of a mile down and two and a half miles across, Bingham Canyon in Utah is the world's largest open-pit copper mine. In Appalachia, a controversial practice known as mountaintop removal mining has already leveled hundreds of mountains (Francaviglia 1992; Black 2011). One must view these landscapes from the seat of an airplane to truly appreciate them (figures 8.4 and 8.5).

Starting in the late eighteenth century, miners used hand tools and farm implements to work seams located at or near the surface. As demand for minerals of all kinds rose during the first half of the nineteenth century, miners and engineers developed more sophisticated techniques for extracting these resources. In the post–Civil War years, business consolidation and improved transportation, mostly in the form of railroads, helped to lower production costs and achieve economies of scale. By the 1890s, numerous inventions, from cutting machines

Figure 8.4. Mountain-top-removal coal mining in southern West Virginia. Hundreds of mountains in Appalachia have been leveled in this manner to produce "cheap" coal. Photo by Vivian Stockman/http://www.ohvec.org; flyover courtesy of SouthWings.org.

Figure 8.5. Lavender Pit copper mine near Bisbee, Arizona. Today it takes four hundred tons of host rock to produce just one ton of copper. Photo by William Wyckoff.

and power drills to air pumps and explosives, permitted removal of greater and greater amounts of material from underground and surface mines. Continued mechanization of the industry, adoption of more effective means of chemical treatment that permitted mining of lower grades of ore, and a shift from underground to surface mining—driven by the use of steam-powered and electric shovels after World War II—allowed the mining industry to maintain high levels of production. These developments also increased the scale of mining, further damaging air, water, and forest resources and obviating the need for a large labor force.

Of particular importance during the Industrial Revolution were fuel minerals like coal and oil. U.S. production figures for the nineteenth century clearly reflect the importance of coal, valued for its ability to generate steam. While production grew steadily between 1800 and 1860, from roughly 100,000 to 20 million tons, it soared in the decades that followed the Civil War. By 1885, annual production had increased fivefold. By 1900, production exceeded 243 million tons, making the United States the world's leading producer. Prior to World War II, virtually all of this coal came from Appalachia. As late as the early 1960s, Appalachia still provided 80 percent of the coal consumed in the United States. Today, more than half of the nation's coal is mined west of the Mississippi River, and Wyoming, not Pennsylvania, is the nation's leading coal-producing state. Production in Canada, which focused initially on rich deposits in Cape Breton and Nova Scotia, followed a similar, albeit more modest, trajectory.

How can we account for such rapid growth? Although it did not entirely replace wood as an energy source, coal was now being used increasingly to fuel steamships and steam locomotives. It was also gaining ground as a domestic fuel and as a feedstock for America's nascent steel industry. Of course, coal was not the only fuel buried just below the surface of the earth. By the 1860s, oil production was becoming commercially significant. Originally used in the manufacture of kerosene, oil would prove invaluable to the transportation sector in the decades to come. After the 1940s, natural gas, uranium, and eventually oil shale and tar sands would also be prized for their capacity to generate heat (Black 2000; Buckley 2004b).

As the United States and Canada industrialized, nonfuel minerals, valued for their physical properties, including strength, malleability, corrosion resistance, electrical conductivity, and insulating and sealing capacity, began to attract the attention of industrialists and mine operators. During the nineteenth century, copper, gold, iron, lead, silver, and zinc were the most important nonfuel minerals extracted by the mining industry. According to Duane A. Smith, without these minerals, the United States "could not have emerged as a world power by the turn of the century, nor could it have successfully launched its international career of the twentieth century" (1993, 2). Perhaps none was more important—or challenging to work with—than iron ore (Knowles 2013). As new technologies evolved in the twentieth century, uses emerged for other minerals, including bauxite, bentonite, magnesium, molybdenum, titanium, tungsten, and vanadium (Goin and Raymond 2004). Today, residents of North America depend more than ever on minerals extracted from the earth's crust, be it coal from Wyoming, tar sands from Alberta, or rare earth minerals from the California desert. We also rely on international trade to meet our growing demand for minerals because whatever we cannot produce domestically, we must import from abroad.

An important feature of the historic mining landscape is the company town. In remote sections of the country where labor was in short supply, mining companies had to recruit workers and supply them with housing. In some cases, they also constructed churches, schools, recreation buildings, and stores. This was particularly true in "model" towns, which offered amenities that other towns did not, often in an effort to attract and maintain a loyal workforce—preferably one that would ignore any and all propositions from union organizers (Shifflett 1991; Mosher 1995; Buckley 2004a; Alanen 2007). Companies laid these carefully planned settlements out with one goal in mind—to facilitate the mining process. Although town layouts varied from one region to the next, they often exhibited similar characteristics, including an economy of construction, socioeconomic stratification, and racial and ethnic segregation (Shifflett 1991; Alexander 2002; Buckley 2004a; Hoagland 2010). Although most company towns declined or disappeared once miners gained access to automobiles, some industries, such as copper and uranium, provided housing at more isolated locations well into the second half of the twentieth century (Melzer 1980; Marsh 1987; Amundsen 1995).

In other cases, settlements were established with little thought for their design, reflecting the ephemeral nature of mining activity in a given location (Alanen 1982; Francaviglia 1991). The discovery of gold, for instance, could transform a sleepy valley into a bustling hub of activity almost overnight, but because the "rush" was often short-lived, the "towns" that developed tended to be poorly planned and hastily constructed. While prospectors found gold in many places throughout North America, "gold fever" struck most famously in places like Sutter's Mill in California and the Klondike and Fraser River in Canada (Wynn 2007; Harris 2008). Decades after their works were abandoned, many of these mines and mine towns have become tourist attractions, offering entertainment to visitors and challenges to cultural resource managers (Francaviglia 1991; DeLyser 1999; Goin and Raymond 2004).

"A HOLE IN THE GROUND AND A DUMP FOR WASTE ROCK"

If the mining process has one ineluctable aspect, it is that we always end up removing more material from the ground than we need. Or as geologist Charles Park states in John McPhee's classic *Encounters with the Archdruid*, "When you create a mine, there are two things you can't avoid: a hole in the ground and a dump for waste rock. Those are two things you can't avoid" (1971, 26). As Park suggests, the topographic features of a mining landscape fall into two broad categories: subtractive and additive. Subtractive features include open pits, tunnels, and shafts, whereas additive features include debris piles of various kinds, from simple dumps to waste piles that result from chemical concentrating and intense heating (Francaviglia 1991).

Over time, the dimensions of additive and subtractive features have grown dramatically. Here, the copper industry serves as a good example. Whereas in the late 1800s, miners tapped deposits that were 25 percent pure, by the late twentieth century the ores they worked with were less than 1 percent pure (Francaviglia 1992). Today, it takes about four hundred tons of host rock to produce one ton of copper. This means that for every one ton of copper produced, the mining industry must discard 399 tons of waste material. Due to the nature of the smelting process, which separates the mineral from the host rock, much of this waste is toxic. According to Gavin Bridge, "At least one industry analyst has observed that, since the conventional technologies of mining necessarily produce large amounts of waste material, mining should be considered primarily a waste-disposal business" (2000, 242). It should come as no surprise, then, to learn that mining's increased scale stems not only from increased demand and advanced technology but also from a decline in the grade of ores. This helps to account for the tremendous growth of Montana's Berkeley Pit during the twentieth century, when the expanding copper mine swallowed up even parts of nearby Butte. Today, Berkeley Pit measures 1.5 miles wide and 1,780 feet deep, a hole big enough to completely bury the Empire State Building (Wyckoff 1995).

In a 1970 article titled "The Natural History of a Mine," Homer Aschmann identified what he regarded as the four stages in the life of a mine. During the prospecting and exploration stage, surveyors and geologists evaluate the size and value of a deposit, and a decision is made regarding the acquisition of mineral rights. The investment and development stage involves establishing the infrastructure needed to extract minerals—starting with the highest-grade deposits—and deliver them to market. Technological advancements allow removal of lower-grade deposits during the stable operation stage. In the final stage, decline occurs when either the vein has been exhausted or the cost of production climbs too high. Aschmann neglects to mention that environmental alteration accompanies each of these stages.

"In mining country," writes Richard Francaviglia, "aggressive industrial forces have been unleashed on the land, but not without very high costs" (1991, 4). We can assess the costs of mining in human terms—loss of life and damage to health—or in terms of environmental degradation. In addition to the geomorphological changes brought about by large-scale mining, there is damage to air, water, and vegetation (Rohe 1986). Despite the good intentions of the Clean Air, Clean Water, and Surface Mining Control and Reclamation Acts, there is no escaping the fact that mineral extraction exacts an environmental price. As Christopher Huggard (1994), Katherine Aiken (1999), and David Stiller (2000) have shown, for example, copper smelting has been a source of air pollution for well over a century. Although typically associated with the American West today, as M. L. Quinn (1993) notes, the mining and smelting of copper had its start in the East, in places like Ducktown, Tennessee, in the Appalachian Copper Basin. Then there is gold. During the brief thirty-two-year period when hydraulic mining was permitted in the United States, gold miners blasted away entire hillsides in their frantic quest for mineral wealth, destroying topsoil and filling mountain streams with sediment and debris. The hard-rock mining methods employed after "hydraulicking" was banned in 1884 resulted in the discharge of mercury into local streams (Merchant 2002). Gold mining in Canada's Klondike and Fraser River valley was conducted in much the same way (Wynn 2007; Harris 2008). In his recent *Hard as the Rock Itself: Place and Identity in the American Mining Town*, David Robertson points out that one of the very worst hazardous waste sites in the United States is an abandoned lead and zinc operation: "Few historic mining towns in the United States are plagued by more severe environmental problems than Picher, Oklahoma. In fact, when the Environmental Protection Agency (EPA) compiled its initial list of Superfund sites in 1983, the community was designated as one of the agency's highest priority cleanup areas. . . . Named after the stream that runs through the Picher area, the Tar Creek Superfund Site extends over forty square miles. It is one of the oldest and most costly Superfund sites in the nation" (2006, 121). Robertson goes on to say that mining in Picher "has ravaged the environment and left poverty in its wake" and that the area's "dilapidated, chat-covered landscape produces a kind of 'scorched-earth' reaction in most first-time visitors" (2006, 122). Of course, the coal and oil industries have also left their imprint on the land—one that decades of restoration efforts have been unable to efface completely (Buckley 1998; Black 2011).

LEGACIES

Although sections of the country that were once cleared have become forested again—including agricultural land in New England and the Midwest—and many of our historic mining sites have been reclaimed or repurposed in some way, evidence of past extractive activity remains. In some cases it is obvious: the acid mine drainage that flows from abandoned drift mines in Pennsylvania, the giant open pits that pockmark the Mesabi Iron Range in Minnesota, the tailings left behind by decades of hard-rock mining in Colorado, and the hundreds of thousands of miles of logging and "fire" roads that crisscross our state and national forests. In other cases, the trail is more difficult to follow: invisible radioactivity from uranium mining and milling in Texas or altered species composition on a forested parcel in central Appalachia. As our demand for consumer goods grows, we would be wise to consider the true cost of our consumption, remembering that our material wealth is deeply rooted in the forest and earth. Just as we must contend with the resource decisions that people living in the past made, so too will future generations have to come to terms with ours.

REFERENCES

Aiken, Katherine. 1999. Western Smelters and the Problem of Smelter Smoke. In *Northwest Lands, Northwest Peoples: Readings in Environmental History*, edited by D. D. Goble and P. W. Hirt, 502–22. Seattle: University of Washington Press.

Alanen, Arnold R. 1982. The "Locations": Company Communities on Minnesota's Iron Ranges. *Minnesota History* 48, no. 3: 94–107.

———. 2007. *Morgan Park: Duluth, U.S. Steel, and the Forging of a Company Town.* Minneapolis: University of Minnesota Press.

Alexander, Toni. 2002. The Deceptive Landscape: A Study in Ethnicity in Hornitos, California, 1860–1900. *California Geographer* 42: 41–59.

Amundson, Michael A. 1995. Home on the Range No More: The Boom and Bust of a Wyoming Uranium Mining Town, 1957–1988. *Western Historical Quarterly* 26, no. 4: 483–505.

Aschmann, Homer. 1970. The Natural History of a Mine. *Economic Geography* 46, no. 2: 171–90.

Black, Brian. 2000. *Petrolia: The Landscape of America's First Oil Boom.* Baltimore: Johns Hopkins University Press.

———. 2011. A Legacy of Extraction: Ethics in the Energy Landscape of Appalachia. In *Mountains of Injustice: Social and Environmental Justice in Appalachia*, edited by Michele Morrone and Geoffrey L. Buckley, 32–49. Athens: Ohio University Press.

Bridge, Gavin. 2000. The Social Regulation of Resource Access and Environmental Impact: Production, Nature and Contradiction in the Copper Industry. *Geoforum* 31: 237–56.

Buckley, Geoffrey L. 1998. The Environmental Transformation of an Appalachian Valley, 1850–1906. *Geographical Review* 88, no. 2: 175–98.

———. 2004a. *Extracting Appalachia: Images of the Consolidation Coal Company, 1910–1945.* Athens: Ohio University Press.

———. 2004b. History of Coal Mining in Appalachia. In *Encyclopedia of Energy*, edited by Robert U. Ayres, Robert Costanza, Jose Goldemberg, Marija D. Ilic, Eberhard Jochem, Robert Kaufmann, Amory B. Lovins, Mohan Munasinghe, R. K Pachauri, Claudia Sheinbaum Pardo, Per Peterson, Lee Schipper, Margaret Slade, Vaclav Smil, Ernst Worrell, and Cutler J. Cleveland, 1:495–505. San Diego, CA: Elsevier.

———. 2010. *America's Conservation Impulse: A Century of Saving Trees in the Old Line State.* Chicago: Center for American Places.

Cronon, William. 1983. *Changes in the Land: Indians, Colonists, and the Ecology of New England*. New York: Farrar, Straus, and Giroux.
Davis, Donald Edward. 2000. *Where There Are Mountains: An Environmental History of the Southern Appalachians*. Athens: University of Georgia Press.
DeLyser, Dydia. 1999. Authenticity on the Ground: Engaging the Past in a California Ghost Town. *Annals of the Association of American Geographers* 89, no. 4: 602–32.
Dilsaver, Lary M., and Craig E. Colten, eds. 1992. *The American Environment: Interpretations of Past Geographies*. Lanham, MD: Rowman & Littlefield.
Eller, Ronald D. 1982. *Miners, Millhands, and Mountaineers: Industrialization of the Appalachian South, 1880–1030*. Knoxville: University of Tennessee Press.
Francaviglia, Richard V. 1991. *Hard Places: Reading the Landscape of America's Historic Mining Districts*. Iowa City: University of Iowa Press.
———. 1992. Mining and Landscape Transformation. In *The American Environment: Interpretations of Past Geographies*, edited by Lary M. Dilsaver and Craig E. Colten, 89–114. Lanham, MD: Rowman & Littlefield.
Goin, Peter, and C. Elizabeth Raymond. 2004. *Changing Mines in America*. Santa Fe: Center for American Places.
Gregg, Sara. 2010. *Managing the Mountains: Land Use Planning, the New Deal, and the Creation of a Federal Landscape in Appalachia*. New Haven, CT: Yale University Press.
Gumprecht, Blake. 2001. Transforming the Prairie: Early Tree Planting in an Oklahoma Town. *Historical Geography* 29: 112–34.
Harris, Cole. 2008. *The Reluctant Land: Society, Space, and Environment in Canada before Confederation*. Vancouver: University of British Columbia Press.
Hays, Samuel P. 1969. *Conservation and the Gospel of Efficiency: The Progressive Conservation Movement, 1890–1920*. New York: Atheneum.
Hirt, Paul W. 1994. *A Conspiracy of Optimism: Management of the National Forests since World War Two*. Lincoln: University of Nebraska Press.
Hoagland, Alison K. 2010. *Mine Towns: Buildings for Workers in Michigan's Copper Country*. Minneapolis: University of Minnesota Press.
Huggard, Christopher J. 1994. Mining and the Environment: The Clean Air Issue in New Mexico, 1960–1980. *New Mexico Historical Review* 69, no. 4: 369–88.
Knowles, Anne Kelly. 2013. *Mastering Iron: The Struggle to Modernize an American Industry*. Chicago: University of Chicago Press.
Lawrence, Henry W. 2006. *City Trees: A Historical Geography from the Renaissance through the Nineteenth Century*. Charlottesville: University of Virginia Press.
Lewis, Ronald L. 1998. *Transforming the Appalachian Countryside: Railroads, Deforestation, and Social Change in West Virginia, 1880–1920*. Chapel Hill: University of North Carolina Press.
MacCleery, Douglas W. 1993. *American Forests: A History of Resiliency and Recovery*. Durham, NC: U.S. Department of Agriculture, Forest Service, in cooperation with the Forest History Society.
Marsh, Ben. 1987. Continuity and Decline in the Anthracite Towns of Pennsylvania. *Annals of the Association of American Geographers* 77, no. 3: 337–52.
McPhee, John. 1971. *Encounters with the Archdruid*. New York: Farrar, Straus, and Giroux.
Melzer, Richard. 1980. A Death in Dawson: The Demise of a Southwestern Company Town. *New Mexico Historical Review* 55, no. 4: 309–30.
Merchant, Carolyn. 2002. *The Columbia Guide to American Environmental History*. New York: Columbia University Press.

Miller, Char. 2001. *Gifford Pinchot and the Making of Modern Environmentalism.* Washington, D.C.: Island Press.
Mosher, Anne E. 1995. Something Better Than the Best: Industrial Restructuring, George McMurtry and the Creation of the Model Industrial Town of Vandergrift, Pennsylvania, 1883–1901. *Annals of the Association of American Geographers* 85, no. 1: 84–107.
Newfont, Kathryn. 2012. *Blue Ridge Commons: Environmental Activism and Forest History in Western North Carolina.* Athens: University of Georgia Press.
Olson, Sherry. 1971. *The Depletion Myth: A History of Railroad Use of Timber.* Cambridge, MA: Harvard University Press.
Pinchot, Gifford. 1947. *Breaking New Ground.* New York: Harcourt, Brace.
Pisani, Donald J. 1997. Forests and Conservation, 1865–1890. In *American Forests: Nature, Culture, and Politics,* edited by Char Miller, 15–34. Lawrence: University Press of Kansas.
Princen, Thomas. 2010. *Treading Softly: Paths to Ecological Order.* Cambridge, MA: MIT Press.
Pyne, Stephen J. 1997. *Fire in America: A Cultural History of Wildland and Rural Fire.* Seattle: University of Washington Press.
Quinn, M.-L. 1993. Industry and Environment in the Appalachian Copper Basin, 1890–1930. *Technology and Culture* 34 (July): 575–612.
Robbins, William G. 1997. *Landscapes of Promise: The Oregon Story, 1800–1940.* Seattle: University of Washington Press.
Robertson, David. 2006. *Hard as the Rock Itself: Place and Identity in the American Mining Town.* Boulder: University Press of Colorado.
Rohe, Randall. 1986. Man and the Land: Mining's Impact in the Far West. *Arizona and the West* 28: 299–338.
Rothman, Hal K. 1997. "A Regular Ding-Dong Fight": The Dynamics of Park Service–Forest Service Controversy during the 1920s and 1930s. In *American Forests: Nature, Culture, and Politics,* edited by Char Miller, 109–24. Lawrence: University Press of Kansas.
Shifflett, Crandall A. 1991. *Coal Towns: Life, Work, and Culture in Company Towns of Southern Appalachia, 1880–1960.* Knoxville: University of Tennessee Press.
Silver, Timothy. 2003. *Mount Mitchell and the Black Mountains: An Environmental History of the Highest Peaks in Eastern America.* Chapel Hill: University of North Carolina Press.
Smith, Duane A. 1993. *Mining America: The Industry and the Environment, 1800–1980.* Boulder: University Press of Colorado.
Steen, Harold K. 1997. The Beginning of the National Forest System. In *American Forests: Nature, Culture, and Politics,* edited by Char Miller, 49–68. Lawrence: University Press of Kansas.
Stiller, David. 2000. *Wounding the West: Montana, Mining and the Environment.* Lincoln: Nebraska Press.
Taylor, Alan. 1998. "Wasty Ways": Stories of American Settlement. *Environmental History* 3, no. 3: 291–310.
Trimble, Stanley. 1990. Nature's Continent. In *The Making of the American Landscape,* edited by Michael P. Conzen, 9–26. Boston: Unwin Hyman.
Williams, Michael. 1982. Clearing the United States Forests: Pivotal Years, 1810–1860. *Journal of Historical Geography* 8, no. 1: 12–28.
———. 1989. *Americans and Their Forests: A Historical Geography.* Cambridge: Cambridge University Press.
Wyckoff, William. 1995. Postindustrial Butte. *Geographical Review* 85, no. 4: 478–96.
Wynn, Graeme. 2007. *Canada and Arctic North America: An Environmental History.* Santa Barbara, CA: ABC-CLIO.

9

Redirecting Water

Transforming Waterways

Craig E. Colten

Indigenous North Americans relied on waterways to enable extensive riparian trading networks that delivered valued goods over great distances. Consequently, streams, bayous, and lakes provided the lineaments for natives' geosophy and framed their understanding of space. In the humid eastern forests, fish and pearls obtained from fluvial environments were vital ingredients of diet and wealth, whereas in arid regions water itself was the precious resource, used sparingly to moisten crops. And river waters played a powerful role in religion and custom. Beyond modest stone and wooden weirs and irrigation diversions, native populations did little to modify stream flow. Nonetheless, their settlements and society were tightly affixed to water (see chapter 1).

Europeans arrived via transoceanic craft and immediately began assessing the freshwater resources of the newly discovered continent. French explorers and traders opportunistically penetrated deep into the interior along the St. Lawrence and its tributaries, portaging from the Great Lakes into the Mississippi River basin to establish an extensive riparian settlement system by the 1700s. England, among other nations, encountered many small "entryways" along the eastern seaboard and sized them up for safe harbors, drinking water, hydropower, and fish supplies (Meinig 1986,119). The Fall Zone, however, frustrated inland navigation along most of the eastern seaboard. Spanish in Texas and California, finding few navigable waterways, relied on overland travel routes and applied their techniques to already irrigated lands.

The vast differences presented by water resources, the distinct traditions transported across the Atlantic, and the variations in topography and climate contributed to a complex geography of water use. Diversity continues to characterize how societies in different regions used and managed water. This chapter examines expectations for water in emerging American societies and the steps taken to transform the fluvial landscape of the continent. It considers the role of water in transportation and mechanical power and as a fluid requiring capture or expulsion.

REDIRECTING AND IMPROVING ROUTES

Gravity propelled early European commerce in interior North America. Indigenous and later French traders and trappers paddled downstream off the Canadian Shield, across the Great Lakes to the St. Lawrence, and down the tributaries of the Mississippi. They followed routes long used by indigenous Americans to deliver furs destined for European markets. These trade networks relied on large canoes, perfected by Native Americans, that paddlers could either maneuver through rapids or portage around them. Between 1600 and 1750, French and increasingly English traders interacted with various Indian groups relying on the Ottawa River and the Great Lakes. From Hudson Bay to what is now central Illinois, they collected valuable pelts. Trading posts hugged the waterways, and incipient towns grew at strategic intersections such as Fort Frontenac, Detroit, Kaskaskia, Vincennes, and Fort Kaministquia. Canadian fur trade was unidirectional and flowed from "native space" by canoe to Montreal and from there to Europe, although *coureurs de bois* paddled trade goods deep into the interior to initiate the transatlantic exchange (figure 9.1). Fur trade produced numerous ripple environmental impacts. As native trappers focused on beaver and marten, they seriously thinned the population of these mammals. Also, diseases accompanied European traders along the waterways and decimated native populations (Harris 2008, 105–14) . So vital was the St. Lawrence–Great Lakes waterway in Canada's early history that it came to define the national character (Creighton 1937; Robert 2012).

The Mississippi River provided another gravity-powered route for exports during the colonial period (figure 9.1). French furs coursed downriver to New Orleans, as did wheat, once French farmers settled at Cahokia. During the latter stages of the colonial enterprise, American farmers floated corn, pork, and whiskey to the Creole city. Initially they relied on unwieldy flat boats that transported cargo and then, following disassembly, entered the lumber trade in New Orleans. Keel boats offered a reusable craft but required an exceptional effort to pole or cordell (tow) back upstream. Gravity provided much of the power, and river boatmen did little to alter the river's hydrology.

A diverse set of European societies explored the eastern waterways. Deepwater navigation up the Hudson linked New York City to the Mohawk valley and inland resources and solidified its commercial position. Fur, timber, and eventually agricultural exports from the Delaware River helped establish Philadelphia by the early 1700s (Meinig 1986). Trade in the Chesapeake relied on marine vessels and was largely confined to territory below the Fall Zone through 1700. English efforts to dislodge Indian middlemen and to control trade routes to the interior proved unsuccessful during the 1600s, and British geographical knowledge remained largely coastal. The persistence of indigenous names for many rivers denotes European reliance on native geosophy (Hatfield 2004, 37). As the tobacco economy took root in the Chesapeake, British fleets arrived each

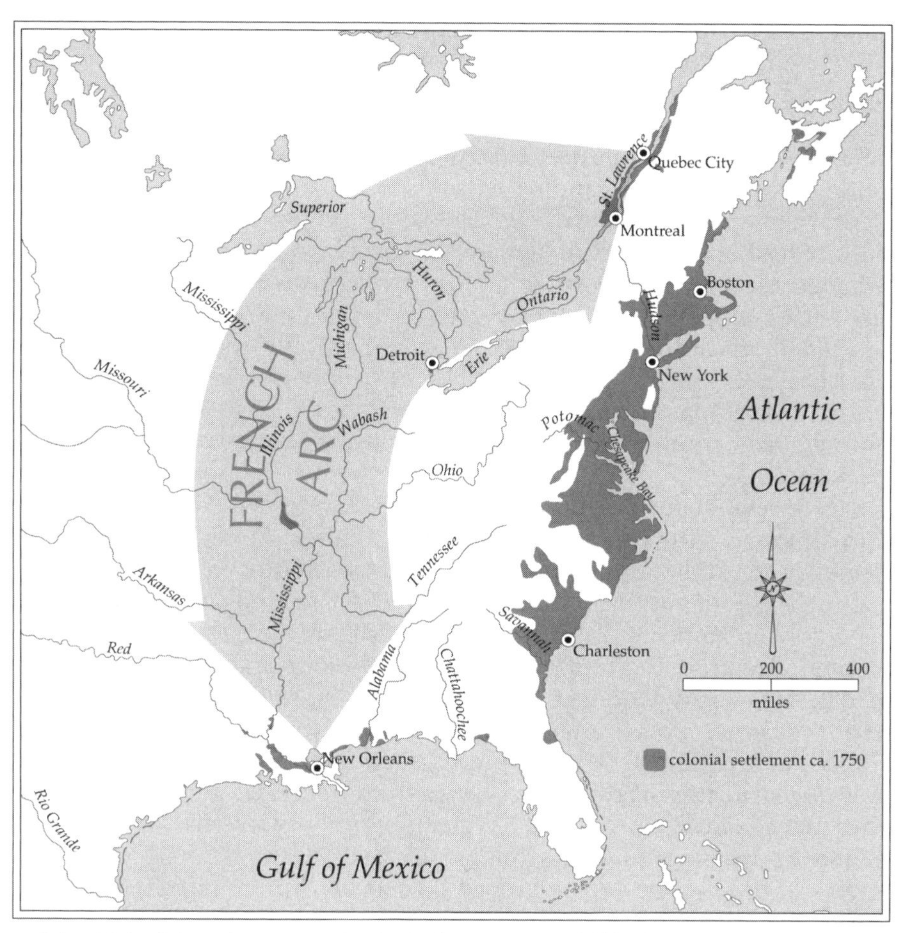

Figure 9.1. Colonial settlement and principal waterways, 1750. Cartography by Richard Gilbreath.

fall to purchase the harvest. Planters delivered their cargo to the fleet in stages. Small "flats" brought the cargo down the smallest rivers to a point where the hogsheads could be assembled and loaded onto larger "druggers," or sloops, for transshipment to the marine vessels (Earle 1975,165–66). Even small rivers played a vital role in this transit.

Numerous small rivers carried furs and naval stores coastward from the Piedmont to colonial ports in the Carolinas and Georgia, and English common law maintained navigation as a priority, thereby inhibiting obstructions on public waterways (Merrens 1964; Meinig 1986; Colten 2010). At the Fall Zone, which formed a natural impediment to navigation, land routes in the interior were more important than waterways in many locations (Ernst and Merrens 1973; Mitchell and Hofstra 1995; Merrens 1964,171–72).

As the cotton economy extended across the South in the nineteenth century, many smaller rivers carried this staple. From the Carolinas to Texas, planters shipped bales to ports for passage to England. With forest removal and crop planting, southern rains produced erosion. Removal of topsoil created gullies and lessened the viability of some farmland, while sediment collected in low areas, creating wetlands that harbored disease-bearing mosquitos (Trimble 1974). Sediment also clogged rivers and contributed to shoaling, which impeded transportation. Ironically, an expanding cotton economy produced undesirable environmental changes for planters.

Following Robert Fulton's successful launch of steamboat service on the Hudson River in 1807, the new technology spread across the Appalachians. With the first steam-propelled delivery of cotton bales at New Orleans in 1812, a new era of inland navigation commenced. Tonnage carried by southern steamboats rose dramatically, from nothing in 1810 to over 1 million tons in 1840, and crested at 3.7 million tons in 1860 (Gudmestad 2011, 167). As steamboats came to dominate river commerce, expectations arose for making the rivers more navigable and reliable.

Henry Shreve, superintendent of western rivers, guided the initial federal program to "improve" the rivers and inadvertently alter the region's ecology (Gudmestad 2011, 118). Beginning in 1829, his crews removed snags, dug cutoffs, blasted rocks throughout the Mississippi River basin, and contributed greatly to the success of steamboats (Paskoff 2007). James Eads's jetties at the mouth of the Mississippi also greatly altered the river's hydrology and navigability (Kelman 2003). The U.S. Army Corps of Engineers modified the channel and eventually erected levees intended to maintain channel depth (Shallat 1994). Numerous unintended consequences flowed from navigation efforts. With steamboats consuming vast quantities of timber harvested from riversides and intentional deforestation carried out by Shreve and his crews, slumping riverbanks foiled some of the deliberate attempts to manage an unruly river (Kelman 2000).

Rivers in their natural state proved inadequate for an emerging commercial empire; nor did they always go to desired destinations. Artificial rivers provided a complementary transportation system to natural waterways (Sheriff 1996). New York State embarked on an ambitious undertaking to connect Lake Erie with the Hudson River beginning in 1817. The project's leaders envisioned the canal as a vital device to overcome nature's deficiencies. It would provide a shorter route than the Great Lakes, avoid the rapids on the Mohawk, and penetrate the lowest point in the Appalachian chain. For eight years engineers guided canal construction that would allow barges to climb and descend across the region's uneven topography. They built reservoirs to store water for the locks and aqueducts to divert streams around the canals. Dozens of feeder canals stretched the environmental alterations across the state of New York. These efforts fundamentally rearranged the region's hydrology. The canal's opening in 1825 allowed substantial trade to flow across the region and fulfilled proponents' hopes that it would enhance New York's commercial position. Following the success of the Erie Canal, other seaboard and Midwestern states tried, without comparable success, to overcome topographic barriers with their own artificial rivers (Scheiber 1969; Meinig 1993; Sheriff 1996). The Rideau Canal represents a comparable effort to enhance inland navigation in Canada (Legget 1955). Each produced localized urban and commercial development, without equaling the Erie Canal in impact.

AN ODYSSEY AMONG DESERTS

K. Maria D. Lane

When I started a project in graduate school on the history of Mars cartography, I had no idea that my whimsical interest in the Mediterranean place names of Mars would soon become an obsession that would prevent continuation of my planned dissertation research on the land conservation movement in Texas. Sadly, the obsession could not be cured; happily, it eventually led to a dissertation and later a book about the first modern scientific understandings of Martian surface geography.

In the course of that study, I discovered that the circulation of nineteenth-century scientific ideas about Mars's landscape functioned to incubate colonial perspectives on deserts and how they should be opened for agricultural settlement through scientific management of water resources. To make sense of these early geographies of Mars, I unexpectedly ended up studying the histories of colonialism, irrigation, and hydrology, among other topics.

Imagine my surprise, then, to find myself moving after graduation into the desert Southwest to take a job in the Geography Department at the University of New Mexico. In my new Albuquerque home, I experienced the urban results of American colonial efforts to enable settlement in arid lands via irrigation development. Since many of the ideals that had guided American settlement in the Southwest had also appeared in nineteenth-century astronomers' accounts of Mars (and its presumed irrigation-based civilization), my move to New Mexico brought me into daily contact with landscapes that I considered intellectually familiar and engaging.

At the same time, this move prompted me to consider that the historical trajectories of cultural and environmental change in New Mexico were not mere geographical imaginations like those I had encountered in the Mars-related archives; they were the messy and specific results of colonial actions and interactions in specific places. I soon realized that any historical research I might conduct on the introduction of science-based resource management to New Mexico would need to grapple with the realities of how management principles were actually enacted across the highly variable and culturally fragmented landscapes of the Rio Grande valley, which indigenous agriculturalists and Spanish colonial settlers had occupied for hundreds of years before the area came under American territorial control in 1848.

In my current book project, therefore, I am digging into local and state archives to explore the unevenness of water-policy implementation in New Mexico during the American territorial (colonial) period. Unlike what happened in the same period with the "blank slate" of Mars, scientific thinking about water and settlement couldn't simply be projected onto the landscape in New Mexico; it had to be enacted in specific practical forms. Attention to these practices has thus sharpened my own approach to historical understandings of early science-based resource management.

Canal boosters in the United States envisioned them as internal improvements for particular states, not as a national navigation system. With a broader mission, the U.S. Army Corps of Engineers worked toward a more comprehensive system. Following the Civil War, the corps worked to reopen southern waterways blocked by the Union Navy. From Jamestown, Virginia, to Savannah, Georgia, they assessed the status of rivers and reported that most prewar "improvements" had failed due to lack of maintenance and the unrelenting powers of nature to undo society's flimsy hydrologic tinkering.

The corps directed major federal projects to replumb the upper Mississippi and Ohio Rivers beginning in the 1870s. As the nation industrialized, navigation interests demanded more dependable waterways, synchronizing the rivers with an industrial society (Scarpino 1985). This meant reengineering the waterways to ensure adequate river depths year round. Despite improvements, railroads in the late nineteenth century were wresting cargo from the steamboats, and shipping interests demanded an even more regulated waterway. At the behest of navigation boosters and in keeping with the Progressive Era "multiple-use" rationale, Congress authorized the construction of a series of hydroelectric dams with navigational locks on the upper Mississippi and the Ohio River (Afinson 2003; Johnson 1991). This approach spread up the Illinois River and other smaller rivers, such as the Chattahoochee in Georgia. The Tennessee and Columbia Rivers host the ultimate examples of this multiuse navigation-power approach (Droze 1965; White 1995).

Canada also responded to the synchronization impulse but encountered substantial challenges. Accommodating large, deep-draft ships on the St. Lawrence required substantial locks around Niagara Falls. Over the years, the Canadians, often in collaboration with American interests, built canals to bypass the falls—most notably the Welland Canal. Also, locks and dams on the river between Lake Ontario and Montreal enable dependable passage of large ships. As the capacity of ships grew, older canals and locks became obsolete. The current configuration stems from a mid-1950s agreement between the United States and Canada to enlarge the waterway, which opened in 1959 (Jenish 2009).

As governments altered the natural regimen of rivers, they introduced massive environmental change. Capturing water and sediment behind dams on the upper Mississippi effectively destroyed the habitat of freshwater mussels that supported a thriving button industry in the early twentieth century (Scarpino 1985). Likewise dams on the western rivers inhibited migration of salmon and greatly reduced the numbers of this highly desirable commercial fish (McEvoy 1990; White 1995; Evenden 2004). At the time these projects moved forward, however, navigation and other uses of waterways trumped the interests of lowly fisherfolk. Single-purpose river-modification projects have consistently produced unintended impacts on aquatic communities.

REDIRECTING HYDROLOGICAL ENERGY

Tapping rivers to power machinery altered the regime of more streams than navigational improvements and pushed far inland from the coastal plain. In New

England and across the southern Piedmont, mill dam construction unleashed conflict. As entrepreneurs erected dams to hold back water for power, they inadvertently flooded upstream farmland or interfered with fish migration. In the mid-eighteenth century, Massachusetts courts commonly compensated farmers when mill dams flooded their land. In addition, legislatures in Massachusetts and Virginia required mill owners to construct fishways to enable the migration of fish (Hardin 1992; Cumbler 2001, 26–27).

During the nineteenth century, Massachusetts legislators encouraged industrial water use by granting greater privileges to mill owners. This policy adjustment unleashed a dramatic ecological transformation of the region (Steinberg 1991). Growth of a textile industry accentuated the need for steady, year-round power, and more of it. Expanding demands required a far-reaching system of multiple and larger dams, reservoirs, and canals to deliver water to large mill complexes. The growing hydrologic system flooded more farmland and further impeded fish migrations. State legislatures and courts tended to favor the dams and the nuisances they produced over other traditional river uses in the 1800s (Steinberg 1991; Rosen 1998).

Using waterwheels to power machinery ties industrial activity to the location of the power source, and New England's industrialization stretched that situation to its limits. Constructing a complex system of reservoirs and canals, mill owners concentrated water power in sizable industrial complexes like Lowell. The mill village, with a couple of small mills, expanded into an industrial city where hundreds of workers lived and earned wages. To an extent, the hydrological manipulation of the Merrimack and Connecticut Rivers lessened the tyranny of topography. Lowell and Holyoke, Massachusetts, and Manchester, New Hampshire, exemplified the success of water-powered industry. Entrepreneurs attempted to replicate this model southward along the Fall Zone and across the Midwest, with less success and fewer environmental impacts (Hunter 1949, esp. ch. 3; Swain 1885).

Despite the technological feats involved in moving water to where it could serve industry, there were limits to the mechanical transfer of power from river to machine. Steam power and, later, electricity freed industry from steam-side locations. And electricity exemplified the next era of hydropower. Hydroelectric generating plants could capture energy, even in remote locations, and transmission lines could transport it to urban centers and industrial complexes. No place rivaled Niagara Falls in capturing the imagination of hydroelectric boosters. Entrepreneurs rushed to exploit the huge falls, and by the early twentieth century, several operations in the United States and Canada were generating electricity to supply a growing electrochemical industry and for use in nearby cities (McGreevy 1994, 110–14). Wonderfully optimistic visions of the future accompanied the hydroelectric power grab. Electric company officials argued that by tapping nature, society could rise above it and create a new and more humane future (McGreevy 1994, 119). At the same time the industrialization of Niagara Falls contributed to the calamitous dumping of chemicals in the infamous Love Canal (Colten and Skinner 1995; Blum 2011), similar visions of social transformation tied to water power occurred elsewhere.

Perhaps the largest examples of hydrological manipulation are the Tennessee River Authority (TVA) and the conversion of the Columbia River into an "organic machine." Authorized by Congress in 1933, the TVA strove to transform a "problem" region. Through a replumbing of the Tennessee and its tributaries, the authority would improve navigation and reduce flooding—its two primary aims—and lift the impoverished Appalachian region out of its economic doldrums (Droze 1965, 34). High-water dams would generate electricity to fuel new industries, which would create a demand for increased navigation (figure 9.2). This enterprise represented multipurpose development on its grandest scale and largely took form during the Great Depression, when New Deal planners were able to secure support for centrally planned projects. By the twenty-first century, the authority was operating twenty-nine hydroelectric power plants, along with conventional and nuclear power plants. Despite criticism on numerous fronts, the TVA stands as a rare example of federal planning to impose a national agenda on a river basin (Droze 1965). With the arrival of industry to the Tennessee valley, water and air pollution became more prominent problems with lasting consequences (Foresta 1984).

The Columbia River offered a western counterpart to the Tennessee. The Corps of Engineers had noted the great hydroelectric power of the basin, and in the midst of the Great Depression, regional boosters touted hydropower as a

Figure 9.2. Wilson Dam on the Tennessee River, 1927. This dam preceded the TVA but serves as a part of the regional system of water management. Courtesy of the Library of Congress.

means to transform society (White 1995, 55). To fulfill that vision, the Corps of Engineers and the Bureau of Reclamation erected a series of dams as part of the Columbia Basin Project. Demand for the power grew with the installation of nuclear research facilities, shipyards, airplane manufacturers, and aluminum plants during World War II. After the war, the Bonneville Power Administration continued to add generating power through the 1950s, and by the 1970s twenty-six federal dams distributed power throughout the region. These dams impeded the migration of salmon and have prompted massive investments in hatcheries, fish ladders, salmon-barging operations, and other measures to try to sustain this species. And as in the Tennessee valley, polluting industries have fouled the air and water, adding another ripple to the impacts of the organic machine.

While hydropower was utilized across the margins of the Canadian Shield in the nineteenth and early twentieth century, the grandest example has been Hydro-Quebec. During the 1960s, provincial leaders pushed to nationalize the electrical utility and to expand the network of dams and generating stations. Over the next several decades, it constructed an expansive system, including nine hydroelectric-power-generating stations that tapped remote rivers draining into James Bay. In 1997, international agreements opened the U.S. market to Hydro-Quebec, and the large demand from the southern market helps sustain the provincial power giant (Hydro-Quebec 2012). Release of organic mercury into the environment and into the food chain was a primary environmental concern following the construction of dams and reservoirs. Flooding of forest lands and changes to the regime of rivers feeding James Bay were among the other impacts produced by this ambitious project. Although often touted as a green energy source, hydropower can produce lasting impacts on the places where it is captured.

REDIRECTING SCARCE MOISTURE

For those tilling the soil, rain does not always fall when or where desired. To offset inadequate and variable precipitation, Native Americans practiced irrigated agriculture. They redirected streams across floodplains to water wild vegetation that provided food or crops in what is now New Mexico, Arizona, and California. Estimates suggest that the precontact Hohokam civilization had as many as 250,000 acres under irrigation (Dudley 2001, 28; Doolittle 2000). Beyond this one civilization, terraces, diversion ditches, and other subtle and ingenious means enabled indigenous farmers to tap precious water supplies for their crops (Doolittle 2000 and chapter 1 in this volume).

When Spanish settlers arrived in the Southwest, they disrupted indigenous agriculture, introduced Iberian practices to the region, and ultimately expanded irrigation up the Rio Grande valley, across southern Arizona, into southern California and south Texas. By diverting water across floodplains, the Spanish expanded agriculture to sustain several emerging population centers. Irrigation was a fundamental part of settlement on the upper Rio Grande beginning in the early 1600s and remains a rooted element of Hispanic agricultural practices there today (Carlson 1990; Nostrand 1992). In Texas, *aquecias*, or irrigation canals, delivered water from the dependable springs issuing from the face of the Edwards Plateau and provided a fluid foundation for the missions at San Antonio. Spanish pioneers in Arizona and southern California relied on irrigation, but the irregular flow of rivers there prompted dam construction to hold water for use during the dry summer months. Through irrigation, the pueblo at Los Angeles achieved self-sufficiency by 1786 (Gumprecht 1999, 42–46; Oberle and Arreola 2008). These labor-intensive irrigation projects commonly relied on communal efforts to reroute local water to nearby fields and, in so doing, augmented the success of modest population centers into the nineteenth century.

In the later half of the nineteenth century, settlers in Utah pushed irrigation across the basins of Utah and Idaho, propelling the creation of the Mormon cultural core (Meinig 1965). Even though their expansion was more aggressive than the creation of the Hispano Homeland on the upper Rio Grande, the Mormons also relied on communal efforts to install the irrigation works that remained local in impact while transforming a sizable homeland. By 1890, Mormon farmers had over 260,000 acres under irrigation (Worster 1985, 77). But they aimed to establish a religious sanctuary, not transform a region's hydrology (Worster 1985, 131–45; Hirt, Gustafson, and Larson 2008).

Other groups had more ambitious visions, and Congress created the Bureau of Reclamation in 1902 to extend western water reallocation and land reclamation. The agency launched thirty dam projects in its first five years of existence. The irrigation projects proved costly and did not abide by the original legislative intent to foster small family farms. Instead, large operations took advantage of the captured water flow (Worster 1985, 171–74). Ultimately, these government projects irrigated only 1.2 million acres out of a total of 20 million irrigated acres in the West—the vast majority paid for with private funds (Worster 1985, 178).

Federal projects continued nonetheless. In 1928, Congress authorized the much larger budget for Hoover Dam, which included hydroelectric-power-generating facilities. During the Great Depression, as federal dollars flowed into navigation projects elsewhere, the West received substantial appropriations for reclamation projects that continued until the end of the major dam-building era in the 1960s. By the 1970s, the Bureau of Reclamation operated over three hundred storage reservoirs and thousands of miles of irrigation canals across the West. Its technology had "remade completely the western river landscape" (Worster 1982, 506) (figure 9.3).

With no expansive deserts, Canada has the image of a well-watered country. But its southern plains are a semiarid grassland that required irrigation for conventional agricultural settlement. Following a survey by government employees, the Canadian Pacific Railroad (CPR) launched an ambitious early-twentieth-century irrigation project to spur land sales and increase traffic on its lines. A series of dams and reservoirs built by the CPR on the Bow River were to provide water to irrigate over eight hundred thousand acres of prairie land. With the infrastructure in place, the CPR marketed the potentially rich farmlands in the 1920s. Farmers encountered numerous challenges such as rodents and the accumulation of salt on irrigated land; then, the economic depression of the 1930s challenged the survival of irrigation agriculture. Only with government assistance, which

Figure 9.3. Gage Irrigation Canal in Riverside County, California, which helped expand agriculture. Courtesy of the Library of Congress.

largely replaced private-sector funding, did irrigated cultivation persist amid a host of environmental complications (Armstrong, Eveden, and Nelles 2009).

Despite the overwhelming initiative of the irrigators, the massive replumbing of the West did not destroy nature. Nature persists in precipitation patterns, the flow of water via gravity, and the migration of fish in rivers—natural or human modified. The humanized landscapes still must contend with natural processes and are not permanent fixtures (White 1995; Fiege 1999).

Rerouting water served not just agriculture. The thirst of western urban centers, most notably in Southern California, prompted massive plumbing projects that directed water from the Colorado and San Joaquin Rivers. Beginning in 1908 Los Angeles, in highly contentious moves, began constructing a series of aqueducts to transfer water from the Owens valley. Meanwhile, a group of western states signed the 1922 Colorado River Compact, apportioning the flow of that waterway among several western states but largely ignoring Mexico. The allocation exceeds the flow during dry years and creates a deficit in terms of the water available to the various states relying on the precious flow. Modified numerous times over the years, including an after-the-fact provision for Mexico in 1944, this arrangement has thoroughly reconfigured the Colorado. A series of dams along the Colorado store the precious water for use by cities and farmers (Reisner 1986; Fradkin 1996). Spectacular urban growth in the Southwest has been possible only with diversion of water from rural areas to cities, and there is increasing competition between agricultural users and urban consumers.

Water rights in western states are based on the principle of "first in time, first in right," or prior appropriation. In recent decades, Native American legal claims based on prior appropriation have challenged diversion of water to serve Anglo farmers and boom cities of the West. Courts have granted water rights to indigenous claimants; in so doing, they have provided important sources of income to tribal groups and enabled them to expand irrigated agriculture on reservation lands (Newell 2001; Hirt, Gustafson, and Larson 2008).

REDIRECTING "EXCESS" WATER

Reclamation in the American West refers to salvaging the agricultural potential of arid lands by rerouting river water that otherwise would be wasted as it flowed to the sea. In the humid east, reclamation means draining water from wet prairies, marshes, and swamps. Europeans arriving on this continent were familiar with drainage and set to work expanding agricultural potential with dikes, pumps, and other engineered solutions.

French settlers in Acadie (Nova Scotia) introduced *aboiteau* to drain salt marshes in the early 1600s. This system expanded during the second half of the century and accelerated after 1710. The Acadians, and later the British who adopted their technology, built dikes with one-way sluice gates to allow run off to drain to the sea while preventing the intrusion of high tides. Given their scale, the sizable and complex drainage works required either extended family collaboration or communal effort for completion (Butzer 2002). In South Carolina, Africans introduced planters to land-reclamation practices, which gave rise to lucrative rice cultivation. Dikes built by centrally administered slave labor in the late 1600s provided a means to transform the coastal wetlands into colonial wealth (Carney 2001). These two independent transatlantic introductions enabled Old World settlers to gain a foothold along the Atlantic seaboard and illustrate contrasting systems of social organization and productivity built on comparable environmental transformations.

Farmers encountered extensive wet prairies in northern Ohio, Indiana, and Illinois and initially avoided them while allowing cattle to graze on their rich grasses. By the mid-1800s railroads traversing Illinois and Iowa promoted the development of the wet prairies they owned, and speculators assembled large tracts of land along the rail lines. Only with the introduction of drainage were farmers able to remove excess water and commence cultivation. Beginning in the Black Swamp of Ohio and the Wabash valley in Indiana, drainage had expanded into Michigan, Illinois, Iowa, and Wisconsin by the 1850s. Major drainage advances took place in the 1870s as farmers buried tiles to accelerate water movement from their fields. In Illinois alone, farmers installed over one hundred thousand miles of drainage tile between 1880 and 1895. Drainage spread across the Midwest, enabling expansion of corn cultivation and helping reduce the risk of mosquito-borne illness such as malaria (Prince 1997). Farmers seeking to de-water Manitoba's prairies relied chiefly on surface ditches and struggled with the complexities presented by administrative units that followed a geometric grid pattern that largely ignored local topography (Bower 2011).

Drainage of the Midwestern prairie was tied to railroad development and land speculation, and transforming southern wetlands for agriculture had a similar stimulus. The classic example is the Florida Everglades. Visions of tropical agriculture replacing the massive wetland followed federal transfer of wetlands to the states in 1850. Florida gained title to some 20 million acres! Before the Civil War, it granted sizable tracts of land to railroads and canal companies in exchange for promises of new transportation systems. Large-scale drainage followed infrastructure construction. Early-twentieth-century boosters claimed that redirecting water flowing from Lake Okeechobee into the Everglades would enable the reclamation of thousands of acres as small farms with all costs paid for by drainage taxes on resident farmers. Yet hurricane-induced flooding, along with subsidence, peat fires, and saltwater intrusion, inhibited successful implementation of small-scale farms. Following World War II, consolidation of land in the hands of large sugar and vegetable growers finally transformed this former wetland into a rich agricultural location. In recent years, new efforts have gotten underway to restore the flow of water to the Everglades, but decades of diversion, urban demands on the water system, and agricultural development greatly complicate that new vision (McCally 1999).

From the Everglades to the Okefenokee, the Atchaflalaya, and California's Central Valley, engineers have experimented with reclaiming vast wetlands (Reuss 1998; Nelson 2005; Wilson 2010). Compared to the wet prairies of the Midwest, the marshes and swamps of the South and West proved more problematic. Myriad complications bogged down progress on projects in the southern wetlands. And recognition of the "environmental services" provided by wetlands, together with federal legislation to protect them in the late twentieth century, has inspired efforts to restore wetlands (Williams 1991).

Flooding presented the other major challenge in terms of excess water. Across North America river floods prompted human adjustments. During the eighteenth and nineteenth centuries in the humid East, avoidance characterized flood management. As cities grew near major waterways, cargo handling, not permanent structures, dominated waterfronts. In many cities, marginally flood-prone areas housed lower-income residents who could not afford to acquire land on higher ground. They maintained a readiness to move belongings to a second story or temporarily evacuate when spring floods arrived (Castonguay 2007).

On the lower Mississippi River, with virtually no high ground, French colonists erected flood barriers, or levees. Structures did not eliminate flooding but encouraged encroachment on flood-prone locations. Perpetual levee heightening ensued and increased the cost of levee construction. During the nineteenth century, Louisiana and Mississippi lobbied for federal assistance to cope with rising costs. In 1879, Congress created the Mississippi River Commission, tasked with responsibility for levees along the lower river—for navigation purposes. Over time, alliances with California legislators and upper Midwest politicians expanded federal responsibility for levees, and the agency's mission shifted to flood control. The particularly extreme flood of 1927 and subsequent floods in the Ohio River basin in the 1930s further expanded federal provision of structural protection across the country (O'Neill 2006) (figures 9.4 and 9.5).

In the 1940s, geographers pointed out that despite increased investment in structural protection, riparian areas were suffering increasing amounts of damage. They made the case that levees provided a false sense of security and prompted development in flood-prone areas (White 1945; White et al. 1958). In Canada, industries in urban floodplains demanded greater flood protection to lessen the impacts of extreme floods that exceeded the design limits of flood-protection barriers. Living behind barriers, residents lost the resilience they had maintained when flooding was regular and suffered greater losses in the less frequent but more extreme floods (Castonguay 2007). Structural protection has contributed to greater urban losses. Rural flood control in Manitoba reflects a complex interaction among local, provincial, and federal authorities that clouds the question of who is responsible (Bower 2010). Nonetheless, as with the management of rivers for power and navigation, nature is never vanquished and continues to play a role in calamities (Bower 2011).

Figure 9.4. African Americans moving soil to hold back the 1927 flood along the Mississippi River. Courtesy of the State Library of Louisiana.

Figure 9.5. Mississippi River levee holding back high water in 1961. Courtesy of the State Library of Louisiana.

CONCLUSION

Human transformation of North America's riparian environments has brought about manifold changes. Colonial societies wrought few direct impacts and indeed relied heavily on native geosophy and maintained many of the indigenous names of the water bodies of the continent. In many respects their modest impacts were comparable to that of their predecessors. The French relied on gravity to propel fur exports and its empire building and fundamentally realigned the flow of commerce across the northern regions of the continent. English colonists tapped the small eastern seaboard rivers to harness mechanical power, float timber and naval stores, put fish on their tables, and move some staple crops to the coast. Meanwhile in the Southwest, Spanish settlers diverted water to irrigate their crops. Over time, changes in scale, environmental impacts, and social adaptations ensued.

In considerations of transportation, hydropower, irrigation, and drainage, the drive to expand the scale of activities is a common feature. Small local canals inspired larger canal systems, and snag removal led to channel straightening and expansive locks and dams. Oceangoing ships now move up the St. Lawrence to the Great Lakes and barge traffic plies the Mississippi from New Orleans to Minneapolis and from Portland to Lewiston on the Columbia. National and international designs on a system of inland waterways have contributed to projects that grew from small river segments to entire basins. Likewise with hydropower, from the small mill dams of New England to the Tennessee River Authority and Hydro-Quebec, a scalar transformation has been the cornerstone of the reworking of river basins. And lastly, in terms of irrigation and controlling excess water, there has been a comparable shift from local- to regional-scale works. Such change generally demands government investment, and that this has been forthcoming reflects a social commitment to grand enterprise.

Critics suggest that environmental manipulation has destroyed nature. But accounts of individual waterways suggest that even large-scale works do not expunge nature; they merely transform portions of it. Indeed, the notion of the organic machine underscores the persistence of nature whether in terms of navigation, hydropower, or irrigation and drainage.

Also obvious is that one change begets subsequent adjustments. Small mill dams gave way to systems of dams and reservoirs in New England as industry grew dependent on water power, and the courts backed the shift. Levees on the lower Mississippi fixed the river course, and engineers have constantly had to raise the levee heights to sustain an effective barrier as the riverbed has adjusted upward. Congressional support and legal adjustments made these technical modifications possible. Social adaptations also reflect this pattern. Irrigation projects underwent adjustments from small operations to corporate enterprises, and western water law accommodated the shifting expectations. Environmental laws in the late twentieth century reflect shifting social attitudes toward the impacts of projects embedded in older policy.

Demands on water have become more intense, and future adjustments will be made to existing fluvial systems. The technical systems erected during the last few centuries and the public policy apparatus put in place to guide water management will frame any alterations. So, just as nature continues to operate in an organic machine, our water past will continue to intrude on our water future.

REFERENCES

Afinson, John O. 2003. *The River We Have Wrought: A History of the Upper Mississippi.* Minneapolis: University of Minnesota Press.

Armstrong, Christopher, Matthew Eveden, and H. V. Nelles. 2009. *The River Returns: An Environmental History of the Bow.* Kingston: McGill-Queen's University Press.

Blum, Elizabeth D. 2011. *Love Canal Revisited: Race, Class, and Gender in Environmental Activism.* Lawrence: University of Kansas Press.

Bower, Shannon S. 2010. Natural and Unnatural Complexities: Flood Control along Manitoba's Assiniboine River. *Journal of Historical Geography* 36, no. 1: 57–67.

———. 2011. *Wet Prairie: People, Land and Water in Agricultural Manitoba.* Vancouver: University of British Columbia Press.

Butzer, Karl. 2002. French Wetland Agriculture in Atlantic Canada and Its European Roots: Different Avenues to Historical Diffusion. *Annals of the Association of American Geographers* 92, no. 3: 451–70.

Carlson, Alvar W. 1990. *The Spanish American Homeland: Four Centuries in New Mexico's Rio Arriba.* Baltimore: Johns Hopkins University Press.

Carney, Judith A. 2001. *Black Rice: The African Origins of Rice Cultivation in the Americas*. Cambridge, MA: Harvard University Press.
Castonguay, Stéphane. 2007. The Production of Flood as Natural Catastrophe: Extreme Events and the Construction of Vulnerability in the Drainage Basin of the St. Francis River (Quebec), Mid-nineteenth to Mid-twentieth Century. *Environmental History* 12, no. 4: 820–44.
Colten, Craig E. 2010. Navigable Waters: A Different Course in the American South. *Water History* 2: 3–17.
Colten, Craig E., and Peter N. Skinner. 1995. *The Road to Love Canal: Managing Industrial Waste before EPA*. Austin: University of Texas Press.
Creighton, Donald G. 1937. *The Empire of the St. Lawrence*. Toronto: Macmillan.
Cumbler, John. 2001. *Reasonable Use: The People, the Environment, and the State, New England, 1790–1930*. New York: Oxford University Press.
Doolittle, William E. 2000. *Cultivated Landscapes of Native North America*. Oxford: Oxford University Press.
Downey, Tom. 2006. *Planting a Capitalist South: Masters, Merchants, and Manufacturers in the Southern Interior, 1790–1860*. Baton Rouge: Louisiana State University Press.
Droze, Wilmon H. 1965. *High Dams and Slack Water: TVA Rebuilds a River*. Baton Rouge: Louisiana State University Press.
Dudley, Shelly C. 2001. Water, the Gila River Pimas, and the Arrival of the Spanish. In *Fluid Arguments: Five Centuries of Western Water Conflict*, edited by Char Miller, 27–39. Tucson: University of Arizona Press.
Earle, Carville V. 1975. *The Evolution of a Tidewater Settlement System: All Hallow's Parish, Maryland, 1650–1783*. Department of Geography Research Paper 170. Chicago: University of Chicago.
Ernst, Joseph A., and H. Roy Merrens. 1973. "Camden's Turrets Pierce the Skies": The Urban Process in the Southern Colonies during the Eighteenth Century. *William and Mary Quarterly*, 3rd Series, 30, no. 4: 550–74.
Evenden, Matthew. 2004. *Fish versus Power: An Environmental History of the Fraser River*. New York: Cambridge University Press.
Fiege, Mark. 1999. *Irrigated Eden: The Making of an Agricultural Landscape in the American West*. Seattle: University of Washington Press.
Foresta, Ronald A. 1984. *America's National Parks and Their Keepers*. Washington, D.C.: Resources for the Future Press.
Fradkin, Philip. 1996. *A River No More: The Colorado River and the West*. Berkeley: University of California Press.
Gudmestad, Robert. 2011. *Steamboats and the Rise of the Cotton Kingdom*. Baton Rouge: Louisiana State University Press.
Gumprecht, Blake. 1999. *The Los Angeles River: Its Life, Death, and Possible Rebirth*. Baltimore: Johns Hopkins University Press.
Hardin, David S. 1992. Laws of Nature: Wildlife Management Legislation in Colonial Virginia. In *The American Environment: Interpretations of Past Geographies*, edited by Lary M. Dilsaver and Craig E. Colten, 137–62. Lanham, MD: Rowman & Littlefield.
Harris, Cole. 2008. *The Reluctant Land: Society, Space, and Environment in Canada before Confederation*. Vancouver: University of British Columbia Press.
Hatfield, April L. 2004. *Atlantic Virginia: Intercolonial Relations in the Seventeenth Century*. Philadelphia: University of Pennsylvania Press.
Hirt, Paul, Annie Gustafson, and Kelli Larson. 2008. The Mirage in the Valley of the Sun. *Environmental History* 13, no. 3: 482–514.
Hofstra, Warren R. 2004. *The Planting of New Virginia: Settlement and Landscape in the Shenandoah Valley*. Baltimore: Johns Hopkins University Press.

Hunter, Louis C. 1949. *Steamboats on the Western Rivers: An Economic and Technological History.* Cambridge, MA: Harvard University Press.

Hydro-Quebec. 2012. History of Electricity in Quebec: Chronology: 1960–1979. Hydro-Quebec. http://www.hydroquebec.com/learning/histoire/periode-1960–1979.html (accessed August 12, 2012).

Jenish, D'Arcy. 2009. *The Saint Lawrence Seaway: Fifty Years and Counting.* Manotick, Ontario: Penumbra.

Johnson, Leland. 1991. Engineering the Ohio. In *Always a River: The Ohio River and the American Experience,* edited by Robert L. Reid, 180–209. Bloomington: University of Indiana Press.

Kelman, Ari. 2000. Forests and Other River Perils. In *Transforming New Orleans and Its Environs,* edited by Craig E. Colten, 45–63. Pittsburgh, PA: University of Pittsburgh Press.

———. 2003. *A River and Its City: The Nature of Landscape in New Orleans.* Berkeley: University of California Press.

Legget, Robert. 1955. *Rideau Waterway.* Toronto: University of Toronto Press.

Mahoney, Timothy R. 1985. Urban History in Regional Context: River Towns on the Upper Mississippi, 1840–1860. *Journal of American History* 72, no. 2: 318–39.

McCally, David. 1999. *The Everglades: An Environmental History.* Gainesville: University of Florida Press.

McEvoy, Arthur F. 1990. *The Fisherman's Problem: Ecology and Law in the California Fisheries, 1850–1980.* New York: Cambridge University Press.

McGreevy, Patrick V. 1994. *Imagining Niagara: The Meaning and Making of Niagara Falls.* Amherst: University of Massachusetts Press.

Meinig, Donald W. 1965. The Mormon Culture Region: Strategies and Patterns in the Geography of the American West, 1847–1964. *Annals of the Association of American Geographers* 55, no. 2: 191–220.

———. 1986. *The Shaping of America: A Geographical Perspective on 500 Years of History.* Vol. 1: *Atlantic America, 1492–1800.* New Haven, CT: Yale University Press.

———. 1993. *The Shaping of America: A Geographical Perspective on 500 Years of History.* Vol. 2: *Continental America, 1800–1867.* New Haven, CT: Yale University Press.

Merrens, Harry R. 1964. *Colonial North Carolina in the Eighteenth Century.* Chapel Hill: University of North Carolina Press.

Mitchell, Robert D., and Warren R. Hofstra. 1995. How Do Settlement Systems Evolve? The Virginia Backcountry during the Eighteenth Century. *Journal of Historical Geography* 21, no. 2: 123–47.

Muller, Edward K. 1977. Regional Urbanization and the Selective Growth of Towns in North American Regions. *Journal of Historical Geography* 3, no. 1: 21–39.

Nelson, Megan K. 2005. Trembling Earth: A Cultural History of the Okefenokee Swamp. Athens: University of Georgia Press.

Newell, Alan S. 2001. First in Time: Tribal Reserved Water Rights and General Adjudications in New Mexico. In *Fluid Arguments: Five Centuries of Western Water Conflict,* edited by Char Miller, 95–119. Tucson: University of Arizona Press.

Nostrand, Richard L. 1992. *The Hispano Homeland.* Norman: University of Oklahoma Press.

O'Neill, Karen. 2006. *Rivers by Design: State Power and the Origins of U.S. Flood Control.* Durham, NC: Duke University Press.

Oberle, Alex P., and Daniel D. Arreola. 2008. Resurgent Mexican Phoenix. *Geographical Review* 98, no. 2: 171–96.

Paskoff, Paul F. 2007. *Troubled Waters: Steamboat Disasters, River Improvements, and American Public Policy, 1821–1860.* Baton Rouge: Louisiana State University Press.

Prince, Hugh. 1997. *Wetlands of the American Midwest: A Historical Geography of Changing Attitudes*. Chicago: University of Chicago Press.
Reisner, Marc. 1986. *Cadillac Desert: The American West and Its Disappearing Water*. New York: Penguin.
Reuss, Martin. 1998. *Designing the Bayous: The Control of Water in the Atchafalalya Basin*. Alexandria, VA: U.S. Army Corps of Engineers, History Office.
Robert, Jean-Claude. 2012. The St. Lawrence and Montreal's Spatial Development in the Seventeenth through the Twentieth Century. In *Urban Rivers: Remaking Rivers, Cities, and Space in Europe and North America*, edited by Stéphane Castonguay and Matthew Evenden, 145–59. Pittsburgh, PA: University of Pittsburgh Press.
Rosen, Christine. 1998. Costs and Benefits of Pollution Control in Pennsylvania, New York, and New Jersey, 1840–1906. *Geographical Review* 88: 219–42.
Scarpino, Philip. 1985. *Great River: An Environmental History of the Upper Mississippi, 1890–1950*. Columbia: University of Missouri Press.
Scheiber, Harry. 1969. *Ohio Canal Era: A Case Study of Government and the Economy, 1820–1861*. Athens: Ohio University Press.
Shallat, Todd. 1994. *Structures in the Stream: Water, Science, and the Rise of the U.S. Army Corps of Engineers*. Austin: University of Texas Press.
Sheriff, Carol. 1996. *The Artificial River: The Erie Canal and the Paradox of Progress, 1817–1862*. New York: Hill and Wang.
Steinberg, Theodore. 1991. *Nature Incorporated: Industrialization and the Waters of New England*. Amherst: University of Massachusetts Press.
Swain, George. 1885. General Introduction. In *Reports on the Water-Power of the United States, Part 1*. Washington, D.C.: U.S. Department of the Interior, Census Office.
Trimble, Stanley W. 1974. *Man-Induced Soil Erosion on the Southern Piedmont*. Ankeny, IA: Soil and Water Conservation Society.
Walsh, Margaret. 1978. The Spatial Evolution of the Mid-western Pork Industry, 1835–1875. *Journal of Historical Geography* 4, no. 1: 1–22.
White, Gilbert. 1945. *Human Adjustment to Floods: A Geographical Approach to the Flood Problem in the United States*. Research Paper 29. Chicago: University of Chicago, Department of Geography.
White, Gilbert F., Wesley C. Calef, James W. Hudson, Harold M. Mayer, John R. Sheaffer, and Donald J. Volk. 1958. *Changes in Urban Occupance of Flood Plains in the United States*. Research Paper 57. Chicago: University of Chicago, Department of Geography.
White, Richard. 1995. *The Organic Machine: The Remaking of the Columbia River*. New York: Hill and Wang.
Williams, Michael. 1991. The Human Use of Wetlands. *Progress in Human Geography* 15, no. 1: 1–22.
Wilson, Robert. 2010. *Seeking Refuge: Birds and Landscapes of the Pacific Flyway*. Seattle: University of Washington Press.
Worster, Donald. 1982. Hydraulic Society in California: An Ecological Interpretation. *Agricultural History* 56, no. 3: 503–15.
———. 1985. *Rivers of Empire: Water, Aridity, and the Growth of the American West*. New York: Pantheon.

10

Preserving Lands for Future Generations

The U.S. Experience

Lary M. Dilsaver

The terms "conservation" and "preservation" are often used as synonyms, although they are not. They spring from different motivations and different groups that arose in nineteenth-century America.[1] Conservation typically refers to the careful and hopefully sustainable use of natural resources. It arose from a concern among scientists and others over the wasting of America's forests. Preservation, on the other hand, means the protection of places, both relatively pristine ecosystems and significant historical sites, keeping them as unaltered as possible. Artists, literati, and early environmentalists gave rise to this movement. Policy on protected lands fosters limited forms of recreation and prohibits consumptive resource uses. This chapter summarizes the evolution of preserved areas in the United States, focusing particularly on the two largest systems, the national parks and legally designated wilderness areas.

In February 2012 the Congressional Research Service reported that the national park system contains 397 units comprising nearly 85 million acres. The national wilderness system consists of 759 areas and nearly 110 million acres. Many of these units overlap, as some national parks contain wilderness areas. The U.S. Forest Service, the Bureau of Land Management, and the U.S. Fish and Wildlife Service manage 66 million wilderness acres. Not included in these figures are more than sixty-six hundred state parks totaling 13 million acres and thousands of regional, county, and city parks (NASPD 2012). The federal and state governments together control 38 percent of the land in the United States not including tribal territories. One-fifth of that land is part of the nation's preservation heritage.

WHY PRESERVATION?

Nineteenth-century America seemed an unlikely place for a preservation movement to begin. The General Land Office had one job: to disperse its land to private individuals in order to settle the country, raise funds, and pursue the Jeffersonian agrarian ideal. American citizens, immigrants, and Congress supported this goal wholeheartedly. Yet a preservation ideology arose, took hold, and created a model that much of the rest of the world has copied but often modified. National parks and wilderness areas ideally maintain land in its least humanized form for the benefit of future generations. They differ from private preserves and other national forest lands in that they are open to the public and eschew consumptive uses. Although no lands are immune to human influence, these parcels are supposed to come closest to unfettered natural processes.

The earliest preservation lands became part of the national park system. Six factors led to the transformation of America's materialistic and pragmatic culture into one that, at least among the wealthier, educated classes, supported the first preserved parklands. First was an evolving appreciation of nature and wild places that originated in Europe. By the late eighteenth century, a fascination with landscapes described as "sublime"—still somewhat frightening but also wild and beautiful—had replaced the medieval fear of mountains and forests (figure 10.1). Landscape architects brought tamed examples to the great estates of Britain and later America, while artists, poets, and authors celebrated wild landscapes through such movements as the Hudson River School of painting. Many scholars

Figure 10.1. Sierra Club hikers head for the wilderness high country in Sequoia National Park. Photograph courtesy of the National Park Service, Sequoia National Park.

have suggested that this reappraisal of wild country arose in response to industrialization (Nash 2001).

Another outcome of vigorous industrial expansion in the United States was the rise of the Progressive movement, especially its concern for providing open space and recreation for the laboring masses in the cities. Wealthy classes feared unrest and believed that exposure to the natural beauty found in—and higher thoughts inspired by—wild places would blunt it (Hays 1959). Coincident with this belief was a third factor worrying some Americans: the closure of the frontier, as proclaimed by the U.S. Census Bureau in 1890. Although several parks existed by that time, uneasiness about the frontier's closing accelerated the creation of parks and monuments dramatically after the turn of the century.

Two more factors that shaped the budding preservation movement were a sensitivity to European criticism and the tawdry private exploitation of the scenic wonders in the country's East. Blistering criticism by respected visitors like Charles Dickens, coupled with the country's lack of history and accompanying landmarks, forced embarrassed Americans to look to the land's environmental wonders for identity and bragging rights. The glorious terms with which American writers extolled Niagara Falls plainly demonstrated a national inferiority complex. Unfortunately, private land claims locked the viewing sites into a dismal complex of shabby and overpriced tourist traps satirized by Mark Twain and disdained by most well-bred citizens. Surely, they felt, America could do better with such extraordinary scenic wonders as Yosemite Valley (Foresta 1984, 9–16; Runte 1997, 11–32).

The final factor that led the United States to invent the national park was the support of the country's biggest business: the railroads. The Northern Pacific at Yellowstone National Park, the Great Northern at Glacier National Park, and the Atchison, Topeka, and Santa Fe at the Grand Canyon actively supported the establishment of parks, in many cases building visitor infrastructure and widely advertising them to the public. Their motive was simple: passengers visiting remote places salvaged profit from otherwise unsupportable lines. Railroad companies formed a critical lobby at a time when Congress doubted the propriety of removing land from the public domain for no apparent commercial reason (Runte 2011).

EARLY HISTORY OF THE NATIONAL PARKS

Yellowstone National Park was technically the first national park in the world. However, several antecedents are now part of the U.S. national park system. The earliest units are associated with the design and construction of Washington, D.C. Congress authorized the National Mall and the White House in the 1790s and then transferred them to the National Park Service (NPS) in 1933. On April 20, 1832, President Andrew Jackson signed a bill giving federal protection to the Arkansas Territory's popular thermal springs. The Hot Springs Reservation, as it was known, became a national park on March 4, 1921 (NPS 2005a, 2005b). Yosemite Valley and a nearby grove of giant sequoias were the most important antecedent to Yellowstone when Congress removed them from the public domain in 1864 and gave them to California as a park, with the stipulation that they be preserved for the enjoyment of future generations. The state hired eminent landscape architect Frederick Law Olmsted Sr. to inspect the park and make recommendations for its management. Olmsted's 1865 report became the blueprint for the policies of the NPS when it was established fifty-one years later (Olmsted 1994; Huntley 2011, 107–44). Finally, on March 1, 1872, Congress established Yellowstone, calling it a national park because it lay within a territory rather than a state. Legislators faced considerable confusion as they fielded requests for forest reserves, national parks, and national monuments during the rest of the nineteenth century. However, they did protect four more national parks, four military parks, and the Casa Grande archaeological site, which would be redesignated as a national monument in 1918 (NPS 2005b).

The early twentieth century brought increased activity by Congress to create both utilitarian conservation reserves (national forests) and preservation units (parks and monuments). President Theodore Roosevelt extensively used the 1906 Antiquities Act (Public Law 59–209) to unilaterally proclaim national monuments on federal land. Later this act would become a vital tool for saving areas from development while a disinterested or recalcitrant Congress refused to hurry a national park bill (Harmon, McManamon, and Pitcaithley 2006, 1–12). At the same time, legislators established a number of new national parks, including Crater Lake and Glacier. After the intrusion by San Francisco water interests into Yosemite's Hetch Hetchy valley, attention focused on the need for a bureau to run all the parks and monuments hitherto under the disorganized supervision of the Department of the Interior. When Congress established the NPS in 1916, the system it would manage included fourteen national parks and twenty-one national monuments, as well as the Hot Springs and Casa Grande Ruins Reservations (NPS 2005b).

ENLARGING THE PARK SYSTEM

Stephen Mather, the first director of the NPS, and his assistant and successor, Horace Albright, faced a huge task as they contemplated the future of the park system. They needed to expand and popularize the system in the face of very real threats from the U.S. Forest Service to usurp control of the parks and subsume them under its "greatest use for the greatest number of people" mission. Mather and Albright embarked on a vigorous publicity campaign, using the railroads, newspapers, and the National Geographic Society as allies and venues. More important, they sought to extend the system into the eastern states, where most Americans lived (Runte 1997, 82–137). The NPS became an aggressive colonizer, going after lands managed by other federal agencies and occasionally some under private ownership. In so doing they incurred the wrath of the Forest Service and many citizens whose ways of life were disrupted when large tracts of land suddenly became off limits to most uses. Although the Park Service did not widely seize private holdings by eminent domain until the 1950s, farmers in the Appalachians knew who was behind the state condemnation of their lands for the Shenandoah and Great Smoky Mountains National Parks (Brown 2000, 87–103).

Although the Park Service aggressively sought new units, it maintained standards contained in the nebulous phrase "of national significance." The public response to Mather's publicity campaign brought hundreds of letters nominating places to become national parks, most of them of dubious quality. Mather responded by cohosting the first meeting of the state park agencies in order to support their development and to detour lower-caliber suggestions to those systems (Landrum 2004, 74–89).

The onset of the Great Depression and the election of President Franklin Roosevelt in 1932 heralded a great surge in NPS prestige and activities. Three processes began. First, the agency directed the work of the Civilian Conservation Corps, planning its projects and becoming the lead recreation organization in the country for all levels of parks. Second, on August 10, 1933, a federal executive branch reorganization added to the park system forty-nine units consisting of battlefields, forts, cemeteries, and memorials from the War Department and national monuments from the Forest Service. This brought the park system to 112 units. Third, increased funding allowed the Park Service to expand its planning for a more complete system (Unrau and Williss 1983). Park personnel developed a plan for natural resource areas based on the geological and botanical diversity of the country cross-listed with geographer Nevin Fenneman's physiographic divisions of the United States (NPS 1990). Genesis of a plan for historic areas came from a model study done by the War Department to identify battlefields for preservation and from the urgent need for units in the eastern part of the country. Congress established the first two historic units, George Washington Birthplace National Monument and Colonial National Historical Park, in 1930 (NPS 2005b).

The national park system today contains five types of units: parks, monuments, battlefields, historic sites, and recreation areas. The last of these categories includes units called national recreation areas, as well as national rivers, trails, parkways, seashores, and lakeshores. Creation of recreation areas began during the 1930s as park planners surveyed river basins, reservoirs, and mountain roads looking for worthy additions to the system. Congress authorized the Blue Ridge Parkway as the first recreation unit in 1933. Three years later legislators transferred two small recreation demonstration areas, Catoctin Mountain Park and Prince William Forest Park, to the Park Service from the Resettlement Administration. Also in 1936, the Park Service began co-management of Lake Mead, another reservoir recreation area, with the Bureau of Reclamation. This presaged a variety of recreation demonstration areas where the Park Service managed the recreation on reservoirs administered by other agencies. Most of these would eventually be dropped, but several, like Lake Roosevelt, later became full units of the park system (Wirth 1980, 166–200; Unrau and Williss 1983, 129–43).

On the eve of World War II, the park system included 149 units. The war and preoccupation with other matters slowed its expansion and retarded its funding until the mid-1950s. NPS director Conrad Wirth convinced President Dwight Eisenhower and Congress to fund a special program to rehabilitate and expand the park system for the agency's fiftieth anniversary. Mission 66 is most noted for its commitment to building housing and visitor infrastructure in the parks, but it also significantly increased planning by the agency and boosted its drive for more units (Carr 2007, 28–30). With concomitant national interest in the country's recreation needs spurred by the Outdoor Recreation Resources Review Commission studies, the NPS developed a series of wish lists for "filling out" the system. It also encouraged Congress to create national wild and scenic rivers, trails, parkways, and urban recreation units in cities like New York and San Francisco. The latter in particular precipitated a crisis within the agency as old-time rangers questioned whether urban areas qualified for addition to a system of spectacular natural wonders.

Through the 1960s and 1970s, the park system expanded almost as fast as in the 1930s. Congress added dozens of new historic sites in the eastern half of the country, broadening the system's geographical extent. Although two criteria besides national significance existed—feasibility (whether a unit is affordable and manageable) and suitability (whether a unit duplicates resources already in the system and whether the proposed site is the best of its resource type)—the Park Service rejected most proposed parks on their quality (NPS 1971). With the elaborate matrices for natural and historical resources, however, many places could still qualify. The end of this bonanza of national park making came as President Jimmy Carter prepared to leave office. On December 2, 1980, he signed the Alaska National Interest Lands Conservation Act (ANILCA) (Public Law 96–487), cementing the status of a large collection of Alaskan parks that he had protected with the Antiquities Act two years earlier. ANILCA more than doubled the acreage of the park system and increased the number of units to 330 (Williss 1985).

Since the 1970s, the pace of park making has slowed despite the addition of nearly seventy more units. Most of these are very small historic parks reflecting the changes in American attitudes toward minorities, women, and hitherto unrepresented social and labor movements. The small size of most historical units makes them more acceptable to a cost-conscious Congress that has restricted the Park Service's ability to study new areas and questioned whether proposed sites might be managed adequately by some nonfederal entity. At the same time, three other processes are underway that would surprise early agency rangers. First, President Carter's 1978 withdrawal of lands from other units to be made into parks also created two national monuments on U.S. Forest Service land in Tongass National Forest. Since that time both the Forest Service and the Bureau of Land Management have gained national monuments and national recreation areas. Second, those sister agencies have developed more nuanced management prescriptions and now include national scenic areas, areas of critical environmental concern, and other designations that demand enhanced resource protection. Finally, the NPS now has units that it co-manages with other government and private organizations. Indeed, a few units within the park system have no federally owned land at all (NPS 2005a; Vale 2005, 61–159).

MANAGING THE NATIONAL PARKS

The most complex and controversial issue facing the NPS has been the evolving management of those treasured places. Initially, protection of resources in the national parks suffered from a lack of scientific knowledge and a legally powerless administration. Establishment of the NPS in 1916 led to more coherent policies that nevertheless evolved over time. Congress supplied the basic policy statement in the act creating the agency: "The fundamental purpose of the said parks, monuments, and reservations . . . is to conserve the scenery and the natural and historic objects and the wildlife therein and to provide for the enjoyment of the same in such manner and by such means as will leave them unimpaired for the enjoyment of future generations" (39 Stat. 535).

National park management must answer four questions: (1) Who should dictate how the parks will be managed? (2) How much land should the government control in each park unit? (3) What exactly does preservation "unimpaired" mean? (4) What level and types of public uses are appropriate? Over the last century, American society, science, and environmental awareness have changed, and these questions have generated hot debate. For a number of years the NPS alone managed its units, although it sought advice from specialists and experts. However, challenges to some policies, especially construction of roads and other infrastructure, appeared by the mid-1930s. After the building boom of Mission 66 and the failure of the Park Service to pay adequate attention to advances in ecology, an increasingly powerful environmental movement sought to end government closed-door planning. In 1969 Congress approved the National Environmental Policy Act (83 Stat. 852), which mandates public participation in federal land management.

The Park Service has always preferred to hold fee simple title to all land in a national park unit. In fact this is quite rare. Settlement preceded the establishment of most parks, especially in the east. In many cases private "inholdings" remain, and the threat of incompatible development on them worries park managers. The agency will condemn lands if necessary, but local antagonism and political connections can make this approach infeasible. In Glacier National Park, well-connected families own seventy-one parcels of land abutting Lake McDonald. The political power of this group makes government acquisition of these lands impossible (Dilsaver and Wyckoff 2005). Government legislation may also allow persistence of incompatible uses in order to placate locals. The 1976 Mining in the National Parks Act (90 Stat. 1342) has made the industry difficult and expensive in parklands but has not stopped it in Death Valley National Park, Mojave National Preserve, and several parks in Alaska. Even more difficult to control are popular public uses that national park status should terminate. At Cape Hatteras National Seashore, continued dredging keeps Oregon Inlet open for boaters, despite the flow of sediment that would block it if left to nature (USACE 2012).

The size and boundaries of a park also affect land control. Congress established most early parks with simple geometric boundaries and of sufficient size to encompass only the most desirable natural features. It did not take long to recognize the deficiencies of these approaches. Lines derived from the rectangular land division system rarely matched natural divisions on the ground, such as ridgelines and watershed boundaries. Hence activities outside their borders often threatened early parks. Not only were segments of vegetation communities left unprotected, but animals wandered in and out of the parks at will. Congress has passed hundreds of boundary changes over the last century in order to include ecosystems and wildlife ranges within the parks (NPS 2005a). Nevertheless, most natural units do not contain adequate territory to fully protect biotic resources. Yellowstone National Park encompasses more than 2 million acres; yet its rangers are unable to stop bison, wolves, and bears from crossing onto surrounding private lands. Neighboring ranchers fear that bison will pass brucellosis to their cattle and wolves will kill their sheep. Surrounding states have authorized the destruction of these "trespassing" park animals if they threaten agricultural livelihoods (Patten 1991; Wright 1996).

THE MEANING OF PRESERVATION "UNIMPAIRED"

Beginning with Frederick Law Olmsted's (1994) recommendations in 1865 for Yosemite Valley, resource managers have understood that parks are to be maintained in relatively pristine condition for future generations. Standard policy forbids logging, hunting, clearing vegetation, agricultural development, and major water diversions. However, that does not mean that the working policies for preservation have remained constant throughout the history of the national parks. The first parks saw little protection until the U.S. Army began patrolling them. Soldiers prevented burning, timber cutting, and poaching; they also evicted shepherds and their flocks, stopped tourists from breaking off tree limbs for firewood, and built fences around giant sequoias so souvenir hunters could not remove their bark. However, some actions reflected the limited understanding of ecology. Early civilian rangers eliminated predators like grizzly bears and mountain lions in order to increase the numbers of deer, which were popular with the visiting public. The mentality running through all these actions was that specific resources—individual trees, meadows, and animals—were to be protected by what might be called "object preservation." Few park superintendents understood or carried out more holistic management (Sellars 1997, 11–27).

The second phase of management began with the new NPS. Mather and Albright had strong opinions about what parks should look like, and they employed a number of landscape architects to implement their ideas. Early concessioners built large lodges in some of the parks to house visitors. New agency landscape architects argued for building less obtrusive structures to avoid detracting from the natural scenes. Hence Sequoia National Park saw the construction of several hundred small cabins in the primary sequoia grove instead of a single large lodge like those in Yellowstone and Glacier National Parks. This widespread construction did visually subsume cabins under the big trees but also impacted the shallow roots of this endangered species over a much wider area (Dilsaver and Tweed 1990, 139–53). Many images that people have of the parks arose out of this "atmosphere preservation." The Going-to-the-Sun Road in Glacier is a work of art, with its tunnels and revetments of local stone. Yet this form of preservation was inherently human oriented. The purpose came to be preservation of the appearance of naturalness, not necessarily the natural state's actual protection. Ultimately, atmosphere preservation became an obsession with some park superintendents. John White (1994) of Sequoia National Park offered a summary of this view in 1936, railing against electrification, golf courses, dance halls, bars, and anything else he thought more appropriate to an urban or private resort setting.

The science of ecology matured through the 1930s, and soon the Park Service employed park biologists to help plan and manage its parks and wildlife. The

OLD FAITHFUL'S CULTURAL LANDSCAPE
Karl Byrand

As a child growing up in southwestern Pennsylvania, I never once visited a national park. My father, a mill worker, would take our family car camping and fishing at state and county parks, but aside from some brief summer visits to my mother's childhood home in maritime Canada, we rarely ventured more than a couple hundred miles from Pittsburgh. I became nominally acquainted with western national park landscapes through shows such as *Mutual of Omaha's Wild Kingdom*. Thus, I saw Yellowstone National Park and its star feature, Old Faithful, for the first time on the television. From the moment I watched that geyser's eruption, I was hooked on the idea of exploring a subterranean landscape alive with fire, water, wonder, and danger—one considerably more exciting than the tectonically dead hills of western Appalachia that I called home.

Summer after summer, I pestered my parents to take the family on a vacation out west so we could view Old Faithful's eruption, but they had no interest in venturing beyond the ninety-eighth meridian. I wanted so much to go that I daydreamed about a trip, relying on my best recollection of the TV special I had watched. I saw the geyser as an isolated thermal feature in the vast wilderness of northwestern Wyoming. I imagined that my parents and I would drive to a small, remote gravel parking area where we would access a trailhead and then engage in a long hike through wilderness that would terminate in a clearing with Old Faithful's thermal cone at its center. Here, surrounded by trees, we would view the geyser's miraculous eruption in the splendor of isolation.

Not until I attended Montana State University in Bozeman did I finally have the opportunity to visit Yellowstone. As I drove through the park and exited the loop road to the Upper Geyser Basin, I was struck by a panorama that completely countered my childhood notions. Instead of remote wilds, I found a humanized landscape full of roads, parking lots, and buildings. But rather than being disappointed, I became fascinated. I had to discover how and understand why this unique and revered physical landscape came to be developed on such a large scale, and I had to determine how the changes of the evolving cultural landscape affected the way visitors experienced it during different times in the park's history. The product of my curiosity was a three-hundred-page master's thesis and subsequently a book on Yellowstone's cultural-landscape evolution.

leading proponent was George Wright, a wealthy young man trained at the University of California. He established the biology division of the agency and even used his own funds to support other scientists who worked with him. Slowly they began to have an effect, leading to policies that ended bear feeding, extirpation of predators, and stocking of waterbodies with exotic fish. Unfortunately George Wright died in 1936, and with him went much of park biologists' influence in determining overall policy and planning in the parks (Sellars 1997, 126–49).

Wright's death delayed the last phase of resource management until the beginning of the 1960s. Excessive browsing by elk in Yellowstone led to a special committee that sought the causes and a solution to the problem. A panel of scientists appointed by Secretary of the Interior Stewart Udall concluded that the elimination of predators had allowed elk to overpopulate their range. The panel grabbed this opportunity to severely criticize the Park Service for ignoring science in its resource management. Secretary Udall agreed with the findings and ordered the agency to manage for ecological protection henceforth (Dilsaver 1994, 237–52). Soon the parks fielded teams of scientists and natural resource management specialists. Close cooperation with university scientists kept management up to date with new data and a deeper understanding of biological and geological systems. Many policies abruptly changed to allow natural environmental processes to proceed even if they diminished the visual attractiveness of a scene. Hence Mirror Lake in Yosemite Valley, a beautiful pond that reflected looming Half Dome, has been allowed to progress through succession to a meadow.

Fire management has been even more controversial. As early as the 1950s, the Park Service began experimenting with burning at Everglades National Park in order to foster new vegetation growth. Later a series of studies showed that no new sequoias had grown since absolute fire prevention began in Yosemite and Sequoia. Experiments with controlled burns began shortly and quickly proved scientists correct as hundreds of new seedlings sprouted in areas where fire had charred the soil and eliminated competing species (Dilsaver and Tweed 1990, 263–65). In 1988 a huge fire that affected more than a third of Yellowstone set back fire management, but the scientific evidence of its benefits soon reestablished this proactive policy. Today naturally ignited fires are allowed to burn if they do not threaten rare resources, areas outside the parks, or human structures. If no fires have occurred, the Park Service can carefully set prescribed fires to reduce the fuel loads of its forests (Sellars 1997, 255–58, 275–76). In this instance, however, there is a clash between these preservation philosophies. Fire has improved the giant sequoia's prospects for survival as a species, but it also chars the bark on the trees and can even burn heartwood, leaving an aspect of desolation in the short term. Some in the public have challenged this apparent desecration, which damages the object and atmosphere preservation of the parks.

PUBLIC USE OF THE PARKS

Since 1916 the central conundrum for park managers has been the dual mission of public use and preservation. Within the agency itself, there is no agreement as to how many people parks should admit or what recreational activities they should forbid. The Park Service has recognized overcrowding as a major problem since the early 1920s, even though only a fraction of the land in most parks is devoted to visitor infrastructure and popular attractions. Park rangers prefer to use "indirect" controls, such as limits on lodging capacity, campsites, and parking slots to surreptitiously curb overcrowding. The placement of downed trees and large rocks can curb off-trail wandering and vehicle parking. Most visitors do not stop to think that the boulders alongside campsite parking spots are there on purpose, even though the Park Service had to determine the minimum size in order to keep campers from moving them to get their cars closer to their tents. As popular parks became crowded, park personnel developed other public-use areas, encouraged off-season use, and installed free public transportation. In many areas, such as Yosemite Valley, none of these tactics have worked. Cars are now delayed on holiday weekends at the entrances to the valley when enough have entered to take every available parking place (YNP 2012, 14). Ironically, many of the parks, either through disinterest or distance, remain lightly visited. But generations of writers have worried that the famous and accessible parks are being "loved to death."

Another issue in the parks arises from the presence of private concessions. Stephen Mather set the policy whereby these companies typically enjoy a monopoly within each park. He reasoned that the distance of the early parks from urban areas meant that these companies faced seasonal closures and limited access, so they deserved advantageous arrangements. Long after some parks became well attended or even overcrowded, their concession companies used this rationale to push for more development. At the same time, neighboring communities joined them in calling for more road construction to and through the parks (Everhart 1983,107–121).

Perhaps the most contentious issue in many national parks concerns the types of recreation permitted and, more specifically, the toys allowed. Across the system the old idea that parks should not try to duplicate commercial resort activities still prevails. Nevertheless, some parks, particularly urban recreation units, have golf courses and swimming pools. Many parks inherited these facilities from earlier land users. Motorized access to the parks causes more controversy. The post–World War II boom in jet skis, snowmobiles, and all-terrain vehicles has seriously challenged park resource management. Controversial proposals to ban speedboats in Voyageurs National Park and snowmobiles in Yellowstone have led to threats of violence. Most national seashores and lakeshores have banned jet skis, although trespass is common and largely uncontrollable.

THE WILDERNESS SYSTEM

The national park system is the oldest and best known of the preservation lands in the United States, but the wilderness system has more units and more land. The word "wilderness" has a long history in Western civilization, denoting a dangerous and preferably avoidable place. However, the same forces that led to national parks transformed the term into one indicating a desirable place of nature and renewal (Nash 2001, 8–66). Three factors led to the origin and development of this widespread system, which encompasses nearly 5 percent of the nation's land area: (1) the desire of the U.S. Forest Service and the public to include recreation in that agency's multiple-use mission; (2) competition between the Forest Service and the Park Service for territory, funding, and influence; and (3) the advocacy of several key preservation individuals, including Aldo Leopold, Bob Marshall, and Howard Zahniser. Today all four of the major land-management agencies of the federal government include designated wilderness areas among their territories (Roth 1988, 1–36).

With the Forest Service's establishment in 1905, its leaders saw their primary mission as management of consumptive activities like timbering, mining, grazing, and water use. At the same time, they recognized recreation as desirable. A decade later foresters discussed zoning some areas in the national forests specifically for recreation. The appearance of the NPS, however, immediately challenged the Forest Service's land-management leadership, especially in terms of recreation. A rivalry developed between the agencies as Congress carved many parks out of Forest Service land while that agency's leaders protested that they should run the parks. Later campaigns, such as those at Olympic and Kings Canyon National Parks, demonstrated the two agencies' conflicting missions and intense mutual dislike. The Park Service's noisy promotion of itself as the only agency saving wild areas led foresters to answer with their own prescription for primitive land management (Roth 1988, 1–4; NPS 1992, 34–84).

One of the earliest advocates for wilderness preservation was Aldo Leopold, whose *A Sand County Almanac* (1949) is a classic in environmental literature. He grew up in the East and enjoyed the primitive areas of New Mexico's Carson National Forest, where he was forest supervisor. As early as 1913, he voiced support for the idea of saving wilderness as part of the Forest Service's mandate. He suggested protected areas be at least five hundred thousand acres in size. In 1924 Forest Service leaders designated the Gila Wilderness in New Mexico with restrictive policies aimed at maintaining its roadless and undeveloped character. It became the model for later legislation and wilderness designation. Subsequently Leopold and Arthur Carhart, a Forest Service landscape architect, convinced senior officials to abandon plans for new roads and recreation cabins in several other national forests. Although both men left the Forest Service in the early 1920s, their legacy continued, as roadless, primitive areas became a category in national forest-management zoning (Roth 1988, 2–3; Sutter 1998).

A key individual was Robert "Bob" Marshall, another easterner who craved wilderness experiences and sought to preserve the diminishing sections of the country where they could take place. Initially employed by the Department of the Interior, he first tried to ensure legal wilderness protection in the national parks but met resistance from the Park Service and the National Parks Association. Park Service leaders resisted external controls on their management options, while association members worried about the fate of the developed parts of the parks. In 1937 Marshall joined the Forest Service, where he established regulations for primitive/wilderness areas that prohibited timbering and road construction and required permits for building recreation structures. In this effort he received aid from a new organization, the Wilderness Society, which he, Aldo Leopold, and several others founded in 1935 (Sutter 2007).

Despite the new regulations, the decentralized structure of the Forest Service allowed individual forest supervisors to continue altering the remaining wild sections of the national forests. The Wilderness Society, especially its executive director, Howard Zahniser, began searching for ways to legally remove these tracts from development threats. Zahniser enlisted cooperation from a coalition of preservationists who had blocked construction of a dam in Dinosaur National Monument. In early 1956 he drafted the legislation that would become the Wilderness Act (78 Stat. 890) eight years later. The 1964 act defined wilderness as a place "where the earth and its community of life are untrammeled by man, where man himself is a visitor who does not remain." It specifically prohibited roads, motor vehicles, motorized equipment, aircraft, structures or installations, and any "form of mechanical transport." The act also immediately designated fifty-four wilderness areas totaling 9.1 million acres, all on Forest Service land. Later Congress passed another law, popularly called the Eastern Wilderness Areas Act of 1975 (88 Stat. 2096), which enjoined the land agencies to accept formerly settled and farmed areas and maintain them until they could evolve into primeval-looking places undergoing natural processes (Roth 1988, 6–45).

Between the Wilderness Act and August 2012, Congress designated more than seven hundred additional areas comprising another 100 million acres. As is the case with the national parks, more than half the wilderness acreage lies in Alaska, and most of the rest is in the eleven western states. Yet forty-four states and Puerto Rico have some designated wilderness. The 1964 law mandated that wilderness areas must be at least five thousand acres in size, but subsequent Congresses have ignored that stipulation in a few cases. Among the agencies, the Forest Service has the greatest number of areas with more than 450, covering nearly 37 million acres. The NPS manages the largest amount of wilderness land with more than 44 million acres in only sixty areas; most of that acreage lies in the Alaskan parks (Wilderness Institute n.d.). In addition the land-management agencies also manage wilderness study areas, which are treated as wilderness until a determination can be made about their suitability for addition to the system.

Subsequent legislation and numerous court cases have shaped the management of wilderness areas. Policies prohibit all new construction, restrict maintenance of existing structures to minimum, nonmotorized tools, and ban all mechanized vehicles, including bicycles. Visitors may use wheelchairs, but there is no infrastructure to facilitate their use. Caveats to the wilderness law's application exist, particularly for preexisting settlement and land uses. Grazing can continue, and ranchers may use vehicles if they can show a practical need. Emergency crews may use helicopters in human-rescue situations. Some unimproved roads continue to allow access to private property within wilderness areas. Nevertheless wilderness designation has taken decision making out of the hands of federal land managers. As long as Congress does not vote for its elimination, a wilderness area has the most stringent preservation mandate of any American lands (Dawson and Hendee 2009).

CHALLENGES TO THE PARKS AND WILDERNESS AREAS

Despite considerable popular support, both the national park system and the wilderness areas face some opposition. Support for the parks has waned as the generation that produced the environmental era of the 1960s and 1970s has aged and younger people focus on other forms of entertainment and competing tourist destinations. Also, in this era of growing opposition to big government, many legislators would prefer to see the park system reduced in size or turned over to private companies to be managed for self-sufficiency or profit. Some park officials worry that future generations may not defend the park system from legislative threats as their predecessors have (NPS 2007).

The wilderness system also faces public and legislative constituencies that either oppose its existence because of access or use restrictions or simply do not care about it. Another challenge comes from scholars who question the wisdom of setting aside areas to remain natural as if they were part of another realm of existence. Historian William Cronon and others posit that this allows society to blithely treat cities and other areas with less environmental care. Far better, they suggest, for humans to realize that they must inhabit and work all the earth in a sustainable and ecologically responsible way (Cronon 1995). Yet this raises a question asked earlier in this chapter: Why preservation? Wilderness areas and national parks are legal entities set aside for future generations to experience and enjoy. For thousands of years, Native Americans and, later, Euro-Americans have humanized most of them. Nevertheless, they remain relatively less altered from their natural conditions, and they can tell us much about our past.

CONCLUSION

A number of forces and ideas coalesced in the last part of the nineteenth century that called for preservation of lands in the United States in as natural a condition as possible. To early policy makers, that meant stopping consumptive uses and wanton destruction of natural resources. Soon Congress began establishing national parks and monuments, followed by an agency to manage them. The NPS's early leaders aggressively expanded the system while diversifying its topical and geographic coverage. At the same time, the U.S. Forest Service countered with its own recreation plans. Competition between the two agencies helped amass more units and more acreage but disappointed those who wanted vestiges of pristine wilderness left for future generations. Eventually this crystallized into the Wilderness Act, which converted huge portions of federal land under all four land-management agencies into legally protected natural enclaves. Proliferation of both the national park and wilderness systems has enabled them to encompass almost 7 percent of the country's land, more than half of it in Alaska. Special areas with preservation regulations outside the park system, as well as state and local parks, national heritage areas, and natural and historic landmark sites, further the preservation impulse in twenty-first-century America. These treasured places have enhanced settlement, real estate values, and local economies around them (Rothman 2000). Questions of management priorities and the future of preservation itself remain debatable, but the national park idea, an American invention, has spread around the world. The wilderness concept has met much more international resistance. Still, both have removed large tracts of land from the myriad processes that continue to alter the nation's geography.

NOTE

1. The Canadian national park experience began with the establishment of Banff National Park in 1885, the third such reserve in the world. The Canadian parliament created five more parks before 1911, four of them in the Rocky Mountains. That year legislators established the world's first agency to manage a system of parks, today called Parks Canada. Early managers followed a multiple-use policy, but through time it evolved into one that preserves ecological heritage and diversity for present and future generations. In 1970 Parks Canada shifted to a policy that seeks to represent each of the country's thirty-nine ecological regions with at least one park. In 2012 the system included forty-two parks or preserves representing twenty-eight regions. Some sources list up to forty-four parks because the agency has acquired land that will be included in parks not yet developed. In addition the agency manages 167 historic sites and four marine conservation areas. Along with the land for future units the system contains 301,000 square kilometers (approximately 75 million acres) of territory. That figure does not include hundreds of provincial parks and other historic sites. Throughout their decades of coexistence, the American and Canadian agencies have benefited from frequent consultation and exchanges of ideas and research. Nevertheless differences are evident, especially in the way the two organizations cope with settlement inside their parks. For more information about Parks Canada, begin by exploring the many reports and data sources on its website (http://www.pc.gc.ca). Another fruitful resource is the preserved-area journal, called the *George Wright Forum*. Volume 27, number 2, published in 2010, has eleven articles totaling more than one hundred pages on many aspects of Parks Canada management. Three other excellent sources are Kopas (2007), Campbell (2011), and Parks Canada (2011).

REFERENCES

Brown, Margaret Lynn. 2000. *The Wild East: A Biography of the Smoky Mountains*. Gainesville: University Press of Florida.

Campbell, Claire E. 2011. *Century of Parks Canada, 1911–2011*. Calgary, Alberta: University of Calgary Press.

Carr, Ethan. 2007. *Mission 66: Modernism and the National Park Dilemma*. Amherst: University of Massachusetts Press.

Congressional Research Service (CRS). 2012. Federal Land Ownership: Overview and Data. Federation of American Scientist. February 8. http://www.fas.org/sgp/crs/misc/R42346.pdf.

Cronon, William. 1995. The Trouble with Wilderness; or, Getting Back to the Wrong Nature. In *Uncommon Ground: Toward Reinventing Nature*, edited by William Cronon, 69–90. New York: W. W. Norton.

Dawson, Chad P., and John C. Hendee. 2009. *Wilderness Management: Stewardship and Protection of Resources and Values*. 4th ed. Golden, CO: Fulcrum Publishing.

Dilsaver, Lary M. 1994. *America's National Park System: The Critical Documents*. Lanham, MD: Rowman & Littlefield.

Dilsaver, Lary M., and William Tweed. 1990. *Challenge of the Big Trees: A Resource History of Sequoia and Kings Canyon National Parks*. Three Rivers, CA: Sequoia Natural History Association.

Dilsaver, Lary M., and William Wyckoff. 2005. The Political Geography of National Parks. *Pacific Historical Review* 74, no. 2: 237–66.

Everhart, William C. 1983. *The National Park Service*. Boulder, CO: Westview Press.

Foresta, Ronald A. 1984. *America's National Parks and Their Keepers*. Washington, D.C.: Resources for the Future Press.

Glass, James A. 1990. *The Beginnings of a New National Historic Preservation Program, 1957–1969*. Nashville, TN: American Association for State and Local History.

Harmon, David, F. McManamon, and D. Pitcaithley. 2006. Introduction: The Importance of the Antiquities Act. In *The Antiquities Act: A Century of American Archaeology, Historic Preservation, and Nature Conservation*, edited by D. Harmon, F. McManamon, and D. Pitcaithley, 1–12. Tucson: University of Arizona Press.

Hays, Samuel P. 1959. *Conservation and the Gospel of Efficiency: The Progressive Conservation Movement, 1890–1920*. Cambridge, MA: Harvard University Press.

Huntley, Jen A. 2011. *The Making of Yosemite: James Mason Hutchings and the Origin of America's Most Popular National Park*. Lawrence: University Press of Kansas.

Kopas, Paul. 2007. *Taking the Air: Ideas and Change in Canada's National Park*. Vancouver: University of British Columbia Press.

Landrum, Ney C. 2004. *The State Park Movement in America: A Critical Review*. Columbia: University of Missouri Press.

Leopold, Aldo. 1949. *A Sand County Almanac, and Sketches Here and There*. New York: Oxford University Press.

Nash, Roderick. 2001. *Wilderness and the American Mind*. 4th ed. New Haven, CT: Yale University Press.

National Association of State Park Directors (NASPD). 2012. State Park Facts. http://www.naspd1.org/dotnetnuke/Portals/0/NASPD/ASP-flyer.pdf.

National Park Service (NPS). 1971. *Criteria for Parklands*. Washington, D.C.: Office of Planning, Files of the Chief of Planning.

———. 1990. *Natural History in the National Park System and on the National Registry of Natural Landmarks*. Natural Resource Report NPS/NR/NRTR-90–03.

———. 1992. *Administrative History: Olympic National Park*. Seattle, WA: NPS Northwest Regional Office.

———. 2005a. *The National Parks: Index 2005–2007*. Washington, D.C.: NPS.

———. 2005b. *The National Parks: Shaping the System*. Washington, D.C.: NPS.

National Park Service, U.S. Department of the Interior. 2007. National Park Visitation Continues Downward Trend. American Trails. March 14. http://www.americantrails.org/resources/fedland/npsvisit07.html.

Olmsted, Frederick Law. 1994. The Yosemite Valley and the Mariposa Big Tree Grove. In *America's National Park System: The Critical Documents*, edited by L. M. Dilsaver, 12–27. Lanham, MD: Rowman & Littlefield.

Parks Canada. 2011. "State of Canada's Natural and Historic Places 2011." Catalog No: R61–63/2011E-PDF. http://www.pc.gc.ca/eng/docs/pc/rpts/elnhc-scnhp/2011/index.aspx.

Patten, Duncan T. 1991. Defining the Greater Yellowstone Ecosystem. In *The Greater Yellowstone Ecosystem: Redefining America's Wilderness Heritage*, edited by Robert B. Keiter and Mark S. Boyce, 19–26. New Haven, CT: Yale University Press.

Roth, Dennis M. 1988. *The Wilderness Movement and the National Forests*. College Station, TX: Intaglio Press.

Rothman, Hal K. 2000. A History of U.S. National Parks and Economic Development. In *National Parks and Rural Development: Practice and Policy in the United States*, edited by Gary E. Machlis and Donald R. Field, 51–66. Washington, D.C.: Island Press.

Runte, Alfred. 1990. *Yosemite: The Embattled Wilderness*. Lincoln: University of Nebraska Press.

———. 1997. *National Parks: The American Experience*. 3rd. ed. Lincoln: University of Nebraska Press.

———. 2011. *Trains of Discovery: Railroads and the Legacy of Our National Parks*. 5th ed. Lanham, MD: Roberts Rinehart Publishers.

Sellars, Richard W. 1997. *Preserving Nature in the National Parks: A History*. New Haven, CT: Yale University Press.

Sutter, Paul S. 1998. "A Blank Spot on the Map": Aldo Leopold, Wilderness, and the U.S. Forest Service Recreation Policy, 1909–1924. *Western Historical Quarterly* 29, no. 2: 187–214.

———. 2007. Putting Wilderness in Context: The Interwar Origins of the Modern Wilderness Idea. In *American Wilderness: A New History*, edited by Michael Lewis, 167–85. New York: Oxford University Press.

Unrau, Harlan D., and G. Frank Williss. 1983. *Administrative History: Expansion of the National Park Service in the 1930s*. Washington, D.C.: National Park Service.

US Army Corps of Engineers (USACE). 2012. Oregon Inlet. USACE Field Research Facility. http://www.frf.usace.army.mil/oregoninlet/oregoninlet.stm.

Vale, Thomas R. 2005. *The American Wilderness: Reflections on Nature Protection in the United States*. Charlottesville: University of Virginia Press.

White, John R. 1994. Atmosphere in the National Parks. In *America's National Park System: The Critical Documents*, edited by Lary M. Dilsaver, 142–48. Lanham, MD: Rowman & Littlefield.

Wilderness Institute. n.d. Wilderness Data Search. Wilderness Institute. http://www.wilderness.net/NWPS/advSearch.

Wilderness Society. n.d. Why Wilderness? Wilderness Society. http://www.wilderness.org/why.

Williss, G. Frank. 1985. *Administrative History: The National Park Service and the Alaska National Interest Lands Conservation Act of 1980*. Washington, D.C.: National Park Service.

Wirth, Conrad L. 1980. *Parks, Politics, and the People*. Norman: University of Oklahoma Press.

Wright, R. Gerald. 1996. *National Parks and Protected Areas: Their Role in Environmental Protection*. Cambridge, MA: Blackwell Science.

Yosemite National Park (YNP). 2013. Superintendent's Compendium. National Park Service. http://www.nps.gov/yose/parkmgmt/upload/compendium.pdf.

11

Animals and the American Landscape

Robert Wilson

Picture two American homes, one in 1814, the other in 2014. The first house is a farm in central New York, an area recently settled by Euro-Americans. The second is in the same region but part of a modern American suburb. The nineteenth- and twenty-first-century families not only differ culturally but also have vastly different technologies at their disposal. These families also differ in their relationship with animals.

On the early American farm, a wide array of animals would have lived on the property: cattle, chickens, mostly likely some pigs. The family might also hunt wild animals such as deer—although by the 1810s, deer were becoming scarce in upstate New York. In the spring, migrating ducks and geese passed overhead, as did passenger pigeons, a now extinct species that once numbered in the tens of millions. The family would have eaten meat mostly from animals they raised themselves or bought from neighbors. They likely had few books, if any, in the house. And those they did have likely did not depict animals. However, the family was likely conversant in a rich body of folklore, some of it about animals.

Now peer into the twenty-first-century American suburban household. There are no domestic farm animals on the property, even though the family probably eats beef, poultry, or pork (and perhaps all three) on a daily basis. Indeed, it is quite possible that no one in the family has ever seen an animal that ended up on the dining room table before the creature was slaughtered. Such killing occurs at slaughterhouses hundreds of miles away. The cattle were most likely fattened on a feed lot in Colorado or Nebraska before being butchered; the chickens were probably raised in the southern United States in giant sheds and killed in massive poultry-processing plants. The living animals in the suburban home might include a dog or a cat, the two most common pets in America. Most likely, the family adopted these animals from an animal shelter or purchased them at a pet store in a shopping mall. Although the family only encounters a small number of dead and living animals on a daily basis, wildlife abounds on the television set, either in fictional, animated Disney movies or on dozens of documentary animal programs. If they want to see wild animals in person, they can take an afternoon excursion to the local zoo or a longer trip to view wildlife in a national park or refuge or perhaps to see killer whales, dolphins, and other megafauna at a marine theme park. Then there are the "unloved" animals, such as rats or other vermin. Even the deer, which Indians and early Americans hunted, are now considered a pest in the suburbs, trampling flowers and eating garden plants.

These descriptions not only illustrate different relationships with animals but suggest different geographies. On the early-nineteenth-century farm, encounters with animals were immediate, everyday affairs. Horses, mules, and oxen were used for power: to plow fields, transport crops, or carry riders. It was a local world. In contrast, in the twenty-first-century suburban home, encounters with animals are, for the most part, highly mediated. The family buys the meat it eats from a grocery store, which in turn gets it from one of the handful of meatpacking companies in America. The dogs and cats in the living room and the wildlife the family views at a zoo or theme park constitute what historian Richard White (1994) calls animals of leisure: animals valued not as food but primarily for companionship or entertainment.

This chapter examines the historical geography of animals in the United States over the past few hundred years.[1] The vast period covered and brief available space necessitate a broad-brush treatment. Yet, through it, one can trace the basic outlines of how Americans' relationship with animals radically changed from the experience of a family on a rural farm to that of the suburban American family. Animals transformed the American landscape: it was modified by animals and altered for animals. Early Euro-American settlers cleared forests to make pastures for livestock and eradicated wolves and other predators to protect their domestic animals. In the nineteenth and twentieth centuries, they created industrial spaces such as feed lots and slaughterhouses to raise and kill animals. But they also designated spaces for people to view animals: zoos in cities and national parks and refuges in the countryside. The shifting connections between Americans and animals led to changes in the geography of animals, both wild and domestic.

ANIMALS OF CONQUEST AND RESISTANCE

Animals accompanied the Europeans exploring and settling North America. Indeed, they were absolutely essential to European colonization, becoming, in the words of historian Virginia de John Anderson (2004), "creatures of empire." For Alfred Crosby (1986), a leading environmental historian, livestock such as cattle, chickens, hogs, and horses proved vital tools for dispossessing native peoples of their lands and developing agriculture (see also Diamond 1997). When settling North America, Europeans drew on a long tradition of mixed husbandry, to which animals were essential. Incorporating animals into their farming and settlement systems entailed substantial transformations to the landscape. Livestock needed the grasses found in pastures, and such pastures were often in short supply in heavily forested landscapes. Farmers spent many of the early years of settlement cutting trees to clear lands for planting but also to create pasturelands.

In riparian areas, marsh grasses proved invaluable fodder for animals, especially in winter, as the cut grasses nourished livestock through the long, frigid months. Colonists left other livestock to search for their own sustenance. Hogs roamed northeastern forests, feasting on acorns and native plants. Requiring little direct oversight and able to eat a variety of foods, hogs converted wild plants and other organisms into the pork eaten by settlers (Cronon 1983; Anderson 2004).

Livestock did not range across a land devoid of people. Indeed, colonists often lived in close proximity to Native Americans. In the Massachusetts Bay Colony, for instance, colonial and Indian villages sometimes existed side by side. Under such conditions, roaming livestock were bound to cause conflicts between the two groups. Indians did not fence the crops they raised, such as maize, squash, or beans. These plants proved irresistible to hogs. More than just a nuisance, such depredations of native foods threatened Indian survival. Destruction of their crops by hogs left them vulnerable to starvation in the winter months when wild foods, both plants and animals, became scarce (Anderson 2004).

Other conflicts between Indians and colonists arose due to their fundamentally different understandings of animals. Prior to European colonization, Indians had little experience with domestic animals other than the dog. Native peoples had far more experience with wild animals, which they saw as nonhuman persons. From our twenty-first-century vantage, it is difficult to understand this way of relating to animals. Indians believed they had spiritual qualities, or *Manitou*, as well as emotions and desires. Incorrect behaviors by Indians could offend the animal spirits, leading them not to return in later years, thereby depriving Indians of game to hunt. It is easy to oversentimentalize this relationship. Understanding animals as nonhuman persons did not prevent Indians from using them; they killed and slaughtered animals. Yet their relationship with animals was fundamentally social, entailing, like any relationship, responsibilities and decorous practices (White 1994; Anderson 2004).

Colonists, on the other hand, tended to see their animals in far more utilitarian terms, as "beasts of burden" to be worked or eaten. This does not mean they were unnecessarily cruel to their animals. Rather, humans ranked above animals in a clear hierarchy, enshrined in Christian doctrine—which granted humans dominion over all other living creatures—as well as custom and day-to-day practice. Most important, colonists saw their livestock as property. They owned these animals not only when they died and became mere meat but also while they lived and breathed. Colonists displayed this ownership through marks on the very bodies of animals, perhaps a notch made in a hog's ear or, in later decades, a brand on a cow's hide. In this way, animals evidenced the radical transformation of the North American environment as the natural resources of the continent became property.

When an Indian killed a stray cow or hog, he destroyed somebody's property and faced the displeasure—sometimes the wrath—of the colonist who had lost his beast. Colonists sought redress in English colonial courts, forcing Indians to provide reparations. By the 1670s in colonial New England, Indians' loss of crops to, and killing of, colonials' marauding livestock served as an important factor contributing to King Philip's War, a bloody confrontation between colonists and Indians that left thousands dead. Indians assaulted not only colonial villagers but their domestic animals. Indians clearly understood the cows and hogs as, in some ways, creatures of conquest encroaching on their territories and undermining their livelihoods (Anderson 2004). Colonists also waged campaigns against animal "varmints," such as wolves, which they saw as vicious marauders killing their defenseless livestock (Emel 1998; Coleman 2004).

Such histories can lead to very simple stories of Indians succumbing to Europeans' conquests due not only to the latter's growing population and military might but to the very animals that accompanied them. European animals were creatures of conquest; however, they were also creatures of resistance. Indians did not passively watch as colonists appropriated native land and resources. Rather, they often resisted these encroachments by incorporating into their lifeways the animals that Europeans had brought to the continent, sometimes supplementing preexisting means of using resources and moving across the landscape. In a few cases these adaptations radically altered Indian ways of living, opening up once unimaginable possibilities but also new vulnerabilities.

The Comanches provide the most telling example of the effects of incorporating domesticated animals into native worlds. An Indian nation made famous by countless western novels and films in the nineteenth and twentieth centuries, the Comanches in the late 1600s were a small band of Indians and rather inconsequential players among the other Indian groups and the Spanish on the southern Great Plains. Like other Indian nations, however, they began using horses, which enabled them to venture farther in the grasslands of the plains and hunt bison and other game. Although not alone in adopting this powerful new creature, they proved among the best horsemen, shrewdest diplomats, and most skillful warriors. By the late 1700s and early 1800s, the Comanches had created an empire on the southern plains, keeping other native groups at bay, as well as slowing or outright stopping Spanish and, later, Mexican encroachments. Only after the American Civil War, with the arrival of the industrialized armies of the U.S. military, were the Comanches subdued and confined to reservations. Until then, they radically reworked and influenced the political geography of the southern plains by holding off various Indian nations and European powers. Only adoption of the horse made this possible (Hämäläinen 2010).

Elsewhere in North America, cattle served as agents of conquest. The roots of ranching in the United States lie in Britain, Spain, and the African Sahel, and the characteristics of these ranching cultures were exported overseas. British herders moved through eastern South Carolina and then, in the eighteenth and nineteenth centuries, to the Ohio valley and Midwest. At the same time, Spanish ranching traditions moved through the Caribbean into Mexico. By the mid-nineteenth century, Anglo Texas and Midwestern cattle systems had developed in their respective regions, and contrary to popular myth, the Texas system did not prevail over much of the western United States, the region most associated today with ranching. Rather, Midwestern ranchers, who paid more attention to the welfare of their animals by providing them with feed and protection during the harsh winter months in the U.S. interior, predominated (Jordan 1993).

ANIMALS IN INDUSTRIAL AMERICA

The colonial story of animals as creatures of conquest, resistance, and accommodation continued even after the United States became a nation and enlarged its domain through territorial acquisitions and annexation. But as the nineteenth century progressed, cities grew to a scale vastly larger and more complex than their eighteenth-century predecessors. As Americans sought to adapt to new circumstances in the nation's cities, they brought animals with them. Thus, animals played a role in shaping the North American city, as they had the colonial landscape, and Americans created spaces, purposely and unwittingly, for animals to survive in metropolitan landscapes.

The horse proved invaluable to this process, even in industrial cities that were becoming more dependent on fossil-fuel power. Machines are commonly understood to have replaced human and animal labor during the Industrial Revolution. And to a certain extent, they did. Certainly, steam engines enabled the development of larger factories, whether for producing textiles or forging steel. And in transportation, the railroad revolutionized the movement of people and goods between cities and regions. Despite all these changes, the number of horses increased in the nineteenth century, even in cities where the changes wrought by industrialization were most visible. Although railroads carried goods into and out of the city, horses and wagons still had to transport those goods to warehouses, shops, and homes (McShane and Tarr 2007; Greene 2008).

Horses were not the only animals in the nineteenth-century American city. Today, our cities and rural areas are segregated in terms of animals: food animals (chickens, pigs, and cattle) reside in the country, whereas the city is mostly a place for pets and other companion species. In the nineteenth century, Americans not only had far fewer pets but often kept livestock within the city limits. As during the colonial era, pigs were useful for converting vegetation and other unusable items into meat fit for human consumption. In the colonial era, these pigs would have roamed the commons—or what Europeans saw as the commons, that is, an area where people used and had access to natural resources that were not privately owned—beyond their settlements. In the city, these commons were the streets, where pigs feasted on the organic garbage left by city residents. This was an era largely before the development of modern urban sanitation and trash disposal. While some saw the pigs as filthy and their owners as undesirable, urban pigs played a vital role in clearing away waste. For their owners, pigs ultimately proved an essential way to supplement their diets (Steinberg 2009).

In the name of cleanliness and efficiency, municipal governments had banned free-roaming pigs from most American cities by the late 1800s. The largely poor city residents who controlled them lost an inexpensive way to put meat on the table. But the mid- to late nineteenth century saw the return of pigs and cattle into some parts of the city—not as free-roaming animals but as livestock shipped in for slaughter in meatpacking districts. At the largest and most famous of these, the Union Stock Yard in Chicago, millions of pigs and cows met their end in the massive slaughterhouses. This was animal processing on a new, industrial scale. Such slaughterhouses pioneered the "disassembly line": workers killed animals and took them apart as the carcasses moved along a line. Each worker severed a leg or carved off a side of meat. The modern industrial slaughterhouse routinized and streamlined the butchering process. Whereas some critics recoiled in horror, others considered such stockyards and slaughterhouses a way to mass-produce meat and deliver it cheaply to American tables (Cronon 1991).

Collectively, banishing pigs and the development of large, centralized slaughtering facilities formed part of the historical geography of modernizing America. A central aspect of modernity was the perceived severing of man from nature. This was always a fiction, but as Americans removed animals from the city, it became easier for them to imagine they had no relation to nature except as tourists visiting parks or rural forests for a leisurely hike. Horses soon followed the pig as Americans deported them to the countryside. New forms of transportation replaced horses and horse-drawn omnibuses, such as the electric streetcar, then the automobile and the truck. Many urban residents were happy to see them go: horses produced massive amounts of manure, one of the nineteenth century's chief pollution problems. Yet, even as these animals left the cities, others were coming in. Increasingly, urban Americans valued animals less for food or labor and more for leisure and pleasure. In this way, animals became part of another force reshaping the American mosaic: the development of a consumer society.

MANAGING WILDLIFE

The growth of America's cities and the increasing demands of industry took a toll on animal habitats. Yet this same era of expansion in the late nineteenth and early twentieth centuries also witnessed the growing influence of a conservation movement aimed first at curtailing the destruction of forests and then curbing the wanton slaughter of the nation's wildlife. Americans' voracious demand for farmland and natural resources to feed the country's industries threatened the abundance of wild animals so often remarked on by early North American explorers. Wildlife conservation was more than a response to the massive changes occurring in the country's landscape. It would also alter the country's geography through creation of new spaces designated fully or in part for the welfare of wild animals—namely, national parks and wildlife refuges (Stradling 2004).

The drastic diminishment of two species—the bison and the passenger pigeon—became emblematic of the loss. Bison were the iconic animal of the Great Plains. Numbering perhaps 27 to 30 million, they were a crucial part of the lifeways of Plains Indians, serving not only as an essential source of food and raw materials for blankets and tepees but also as key figures in native cosmology. Between 1800 and the 1860, both Indian and non-Indian hunters began killing and processing bison for markets. Yet, not until after the Civil War did bison numbers begin to spiral rapidly downward. The intrusion of the railroad onto the Great Plains hastened their demise by enabling more hunters to reach the area while also providing the means to take their hides and bones back east. There, manufacturers turned the bison hides into leather for industrial belts used in the nation's factories and ground the bones for fertilizer. Competition with cattle for valuable forage and infection with the diseases they carried (such as brucellosis) also took a toll on the bison. The result was their astonishing collapse. By the 1880s, there were only a few thousand left in the United States, most of them confined to Yellowstone National Park (Isenberg 2000).

The passenger pigeon, one of the most abundant birds in eastern North America in the early nineteenth century, met a swift decline too. As with the bison, population estimates for the passenger pigeon are merely a best guess. Regardless of their exact numbers, passenger pigeons, by the sheer size of their flocks, were well known even among Americans who cared little about wildlife. Hunters killed the animals by the tens of thousands, some for market, others to supplement their diets on frontier settlements. In the mid-nineteenth century, passenger pigeons became targets for recreational shooters who released the birds from traps to be shot from the sky. Although their destruction serves as an example of human avarice, their fate did not stem simply from careless hunting. The harvesting in the upper Midwest of mature hardwood trees, which served as their nesting sites, also contributed to the birds' demise. Together, overhunting and habitat loss led to their extinction. Martha, the last known passenger pigeon, died at the Cincinnati Zoo in 1914 (Price 1999).

For some late-nineteenth-century Americans, the extinction of the passenger pigeon and the near eradication of the bison provided further evidence of the failures of unregulated natural resource use and the need for state management. Others, such as George Perkins Marsh, a diplomat and author of *Man and Nature* (1864), had called earlier for the state to step in. Using examples from antiquity, Marsh argued that massive deforestation and soil erosion had brought about the demise of ancient civilizations. A similar fate might befall the United States. Sound management of the nation's forests by trained experts would solve this problem. Conservationists, as they came to be called, took up this challenge late in the nineteenth century by creating national forests in the western United States and establishing forestry schools to train those who would manage them. One of the first of these institutions, the Yale School of Forestry, was created by forester Gifford Pinchot, who received his training in European forestry schools. Foresters with conservation training were far more concerned with forests as a source of timber than as habitat for wild animals. Yet the approach to managing nature championed there and at other schools like it would become the model for managing wild animals.

The late nineteenth and early twentieth centuries saw not only the advent of new types of knowledge and institutions for managing wild animals but also the establishment of new spaces for wildlife, such as national parks and wildlife refuges. Just as zoos became designated areas within cities for wild animals, parks and refuges became areas allotted within the larger rural landscape for wildlife. Yellowstone National Park was the first of these sorts of spaces, established by Congress in 1872 (Sellars 1997). Although primarily set aside for its geological wonders, such as hot springs and geysers, it served as a de facto wildlife refuge for bison, antelope, and elk. President Theodore Roosevelt created the first areas expressly for wildlife when he established the Pelican Island Bird Reservation in 1903. Over the next few years, President Roosevelt created other refuges. Most of them were quite small—some with only a few hundred acres to protect nesting birds (Wilson 2010).

One could easily cast the establishment of parks and refuges and the development of institutions to manage them as a story of a benevolent government saving wildlife and their habitat from rapacious hunters and careless developers. Such a perspective overlooks the effect of state management on local people who depended on wildlife for subsistence. Locals regarded one of the first protected areas, Adirondack State Park in upstate New York, as an imposition. Many had used the forests and wildlife within them as a commons. The creation of the park and the imposition of hunting regulations effectively redefined many rural people who sought to harvest wildlife in traditional ways as poachers. Locals often resisted such new forms of governance by ignoring the new regulations as best they could or destroying the property of park managers; in rare cases, they assaulted or killed game wardens. Such opposition reoccurred throughout the country as state management of wildlife arrived in the countryside (Jacoby 2001).

The management of wildlife had common elements, regardless of the species or habitat officials sought to manage. First, wildlife managers regulated the harvesting of wildlife by imposing bag limits and requiring hunting permits. Second, they developed methods to assess wildlife populations and their movements. Wildlife managers and scientists went into the field to count deer; in the case of migratory birds, they climbed into airplanes to survey birds resting on the ground and did their best to estimate their numbers. Fishery scientists tagged fish and collected tags back from fishermen who harvested the fish. Ornithologists banded migratory birds with metal rings inscribed with an identification number. Before releasing the birds, scientists noted the time and place. Later, when hunters shot these birds, they noted where and when and sent this information to scientists. Although relatively crude methods, tagging and banding gave scientists a rough sense of the movements of organisms. In the last third of the twentieth century, scientists and wildlife managers began to employ radio transmitters and, more recently, satellite transmitters, to track wildlife in real time. Collectively, these techniques offered wildlife management agencies tools for understanding the geography of wildlife movement (Evenden 2004; Wilson 2010; Benson 2010).

At the heart of this sort of environmental governance was an effort to make wildlife legible and more amenable to state management. The term "legibility," from political scientist and anthropologist James Scott (1998), reflects the state's needs for information about the resources it manages (in this case, wildlife). Schools of salmon, herds of elk, and flocks of geese were reduced to populations—aggregates of individual members. Along with this more in-depth knowledge of wildlife populations came a narrowing of vision. Wildlife managers concerned themselves not with all animals using the national parks or refuges they managed. Rather, they became highly interested in the species most valued by fishermen or hunters—often to the detriment of other species. For instance, on wildlife refuges, managers sought to increase the number of ducks and geese using the lands and marshes under their care by raising barley, rice, and other crops these birds ate. Yet, the pesticides used to kill insects and weeds that threatened these crops flowed into the waters, where they poisoned other species, such as fish, which were in turn eaten by fish-eating birds such as grebes and bald eagles. Ironically, then, the attempt to conserve birds prized by hunters—namely, ducks and geese—led to the contamination of fish and other species of birds (Wilson 2010).

ANIMALS OF LEISURE

Although the animals they ate—and eventually rode and used to transport their products—disappeared from cities, Americans never lost their interest in animals. They were selective about the species they incorporated into their urban lives, choosing those they enjoyed viewing or that offered companionship. Zoo animals and pets became a more central and permanent feature of American cities, and in many ways, these animals became Americans' primary direct contact with living animals.

Zoos were a key part of this transformation. For centuries, aristocrats in Europe had kept wild animals for their amusement. These menageries showcased "exotic" species, typically from Africa or Asia. The collection and display of such creatures from different corners of the globe served as a powerful symbol of European dominance—over not just other animals but other peoples and territories. In the mid-nineteenth century, such animals moved from the privileged estates of the wealthy into public zoos in the cities. London established the first zoo in 1828; Philadelphia followed suit with the first American zoo in 1874. Philadelphia's zoo proved the template for future nineteenth-century zoos, which were open to the public and located in large, urban parks. They were unlike the private menageries in other ways. While zoos displayed exotic animals, they also had an educational role. Zoos further distinguished themselves from their menagerie forebearers by displaying animals scientifically (Hanson 2002).

Americans also brought animals into their homes. Dogs and cats had long been part of American lives, although largely as workers rather than as friends and companions. People had kept cats before the late nineteenth century but primarily to control mice in the home or on the farm. Dogs were used for hunting and, if kept in the home, ate table scraps or scavenged items rather than their own special dog food. With the growth of the urban middle class through the early decades of the twentieth century, Americans increasingly saw dogs and cats as members of the family, valuable companions, and essential elements of domestic life. Historian Katherine Grier (2006) shows how at this time a domestic ethic of kindness emerged wherein middle- and upper-class men were expected to exhibit kindness, restraint, and mercy toward those in their family, including pets. Such traits became associated with humane behavior; those who mistreated their animals became seen as uncivilized. As the middle class came to view animals such as dogs strictly as pets, they branded those who continued with practices like dog fighting as barbaric. Thus, the redefinition of dogs and cats as pets led to a redefinition among the classes of who was genteel and who was not.

In mid-twentieth century America, one of the most conspicuous places to find animals was the television set. As TVs became commonplace in American homes, wildlife programs became a staple of the new medium. The most influential of these was Marlin Perkins's *Zoo Parade* and later *Wild Kingdom*. On *Zoo Parade*, Perkins brought animals, typically infants or juveniles, from the zoos to a nearby TV studio to share fun facts about the creatures. By the time *Wild Kingdom* aired, the format had evolved, allowing Perkins and various assistants to film animals in their natural habitats. Typical of such programs was a focus on "charismatic megafauna"—large mammals, often predators—hunting and chasing prey. Such exciting portrayals of animals were vital for keeping viewers' interest (Bouse 2003; Mitman 2009). Walt Disney, founder of the Disney theme parks and entertainment empire and creator of the popular animal cartoon *Bambi* (1942), also played a pivotal role in the development of wildlife programing. His *True-Life Adventures* series told exciting and amusing stories about animals in the wild. Other wildlife filmmakers widely duplicated this basic format, which persists in many wildlife programs to this day.

CONCLUSION

Animals were not bit players in the North American past. They were, in the words of historian Thomas Andrews, "our constant companions and ceaseless victims" (2010, 139). In the colonial era, animals proved indispensible tools in colonizing the Americas. But they also proved a threat to many Native Americans, who quickly understood animals' role in helping colonists dispossess them of their ancestral territories. Yet, by adopting animals such as the horse or sheep, Indians showed their ability to adapt to new circumstances and use these new creatures for their own ends. In the rapidly urbanizing and industrializing America of the nineteenth century, animals persisted. They towed boats on the Erie Canal, transported goods through city streets, carried soldiers to battle, and provided entertainment for Americans in zoos. Even as they continued as part of Americans' lives, other animals disappeared from view. By the early twentieth century, most Americans were far removed from the animals they ate. Pigs no longer roamed the streets of the nation's cities, and cattle met their end in vast stockyards and slaughterhouses in cities such as Chicago. For the meatpackers and those who consumed the meat they produced, "it was easy not to remember that eating was a moral act inextricably bound to killing" (Cronon 1991, 256).

Whether one sees these animals as "victims," to use Andrews's term, depends on whether one thinks animals have rights. In early-twenty-first-century America, animals were certainly companions and, for many, friends and family. Americans lavished an array of custom dog or cat food, toys, and bedding on their pets. The pet industry generated $38 billon a year; in suburban shopping complexes, big-box stores like PetSmart and Petco sold every imaginable item for pets (Nast 2006, 895). Such expenditures and stores vividly displayed Americans' affections for their pets. But there was a dark side to the story. Animal shelters euthanized 4 million dogs and cats a year, a small number compared to the billions of animals in the country slaughtered for food but still a staggering reflection of the amount of unwanted dogs and cats in the United States. As with the animals killed and processed in slaughterhouses, the deaths of these companion animals occurred largely out of sight. Animal control services cleared the streets of unwanted dogs and cats, and shelters placed them up for adoption. If no one took them home, a shelter worker injected them with a lethal drug or gassed them in a steel box.

Pets in animal shelters, dogs in living rooms, wildlife in refuges, and livestock in slaughterhouses may seem far removed from the early-American farm where this chapter began. Yet they are part of the changing historical geography of people and animals in the United States. By the early twenty-first century, Americans had largely segregated animals they loved and cherished, which resided in homes, zoos, national parks, and refuges, from those they ate, which lived much of their lives in confined feeding operations and met their ends in slaughterhouses. If Americans considered themselves more humane than their distant ancestors, perhaps it was because so many of the unsavory aspects of their relations with animals now occurred out of sight (Pachirat 2011).

NOTE

1. This chapter does not address animals elsewhere in North America, such as Canada. The historical geographies of animals in the United States and Canada are similar in many ways. Canadians, like Americans, once lived in close proximity to many types of animals and now experience animals in limited, highly mediated ways. For the history of animals in Canada, see Gillespie 2007, Loo 2006, Piper and Sandlos 2007, and Sandlos 2007.

REFERENCES

Anderson, V. 2004. *Creatures of Empire: How Domestic Animals Transformed Early America*. New York: Oxford University Press.

Andrews, T. 2010. Contemplating Animal Histories: Pedagogy and Politics across Borders. *Radical History Review* 107: 139–65.

Benson, E. 2010. *Wired Wilderness: Technologies of Tracking and the Making of Modern Wildlife*. Baltimore: Johns Hopkins University Press.

Bouse, D. 2003. *Wildlife Films*. Philadelphia: University of Pennsylvania Press.

Coleman, J. 2004. *Vicious: Wolves and Men in America*. New Haven, CT: Yale University Press.

Cronon, William. 1991. *Nature's Metropolis: Chicago and the Great West*. New York: Norton.

———. 1993. *Changes in the Land*. New York: Hill and Wang.

Crosby, Alfred W. 1986. *Ecological Imperialism: The Biological Expansion of Europe, 900–1900*. Cambridge: Cambridge University Press.

Davis, Susan G. 1997. *Spectacular Nature: Corporate Culture and the Sea World Experience*. Berkeley: University of California Press.

Diamond, J. 1997. *Guns, Germs, and Steel: The Fates of Human Societies*. New York: W. W. Norton and Co.

Emel, J. 1998. Are You Mean Enough, Big and Bad Enough? Wolf Eradication in the U.S. In *Animal Geographies: Place, Politics, and Identity in the Nature-Culture Borderlands*, edited by J. Wolch and J. Emel, 91–117. New York: Routledge.

Evenden, M. 2004. *Fish versus Power: An Environmental History of the Fraser River*. New York: Cambridge University Press.

Gillespie, G. 2007. *Hunting for Empire: Narratives of Sport in Rupert's Land, 1840–70*. Vancouver: University of British Columbia Press.

Greene, A. N. 2008. *Horses at Work: Harnessing Power in Industrial America*. Cambridge, MA: Harvard University Press.

Grier, K. C. 2006. *Pets in America: A History*. Chapel Hill: University of North Carolina Press.

Hämäläinen, P. 2010. The Politics of Grass: European Expansion, Ecological Change, and Indigenous Power in the Southwest Borderlands. *William and Mary Quarterly* 67, no. 2: 173–208.

Hanson, E. 2002. *Animal Attractions: Nature on Display in American Zoos*. Princeton, NJ: Princeton University Press.

Isenberg, A. C. 2000. *The Destruction of the Bison: An Environmental History, 1750–1920*. Cambridge: Cambridge University Press.

Jacoby, K. 2001. *Crimes against Nature: Squatters, Poachers, Thieves, and the Hidden History of American Conservation*. Berkeley: University of California Press.

Jordan, T. G. 1993. *North American Cattle-Ranching Frontiers: Origins, Diffusion, and Differentiation*. Albuquerque: University of New Mexico Press.

Loo, T. 2006. *States of Nature: Conserving Canada's Wildlife in the Twentieth Century*. Vancouver: University of British Columbia Press.

Marsh, George P. 1864. *Man and Nature, or, Physical Geography as Modified by Human Action*. New York: C. Scribner.

McShane, C., and J. A. Tarr. 2007. *The Horse in the City: Living Machines in the Nineteenth Century*. Baltimore: Johns Hopkins University Press.

Mitman, G. 2009. *Reel Nature: America's Romance with Wildlife on Film*. Seattle: University of Washington Press.

Nast, Heidi. 2006. Critical Pet Studies? *Antipode* 38, no. 5: 894–906.

Pachirat, T. 2011. *Every Twelve Seconds: Industrialized Slaughter and the Politics of Sight*. New Haven, CT: Yale University Press.

Piper, L., and J. Sandlos. 2007. A Broken Frontier: Ecological Imperialism in the Canadian North. *Environmental History* 12, no. 4: 769–95.

Price, J. 1999. *Flight Maps: Adventures with Nature in Modern America*. New York: Basic Books.

Sandlos, J. 2007. *Hunters at the Margin: Native People and Wildlife Conservation in the Northwest Territories*. Vancouver: University of British Columbia Press.

Scott, J. 1998. *Seeing Like a State: How Certain Schemes to Improve the Human Condition Have Failed*. New Haven, CT: Yale University Press.

Sellars, R. W. 1997. *Preserving Nature in the National Parks: A History*. New Haven, CT: Yale University Press.

Steinberg, T. 2009. *Down to Earth: Nature's Role in American History*. 2nd ed. New York: Oxford University Press.

Stradling, D. 2004. *Conservation in the Progressive Era: Classic Texts*. Seattle: University of Washington Press.

Weisiger, M. 2009. *Dreaming of Sheep in Navajo Country*. Seattle: University of Washington Press.

White, R. 1994. Animals and Enterprise. In *The Oxford History of the American West*, edited by Clyde A. Milner II, Carol A. O'Connor, and Martha A. Sandweiss, 236–73. New York: Oxford University Press.

Wilson, R. 2010. *Seeking Refuge: Birds and Landscapes of the Pacific Flyway*. Seattle: University of Washington Press.

IV

SHAPING THE LANDSCAPE

12

"Dividing the Land"

Timothy G. Anderson

Settlers arriving in eastern North America from Europe during the colonial period brought with them a variety of land tenure and subdivision traditions, methods, and laws that varied from region to region. In North America, however, certain social, economic, and environmental pressures favored some traditions at the expense of others, creating new attitudes about land ownership that engendered altogether new land tenure and subdivision methods. Two large-scale processes seem to have been at work in determining which traditions survived across the Atlantic and which did not. First, the earliest colonization of the eastern seaboard was highly selective with respect to regional origins and social class. That is, certain "fragments" of European societies, each distinguished by region of origin, class, and cultural traditions, settled in separate eastern seaboard locations, implanting their particular traits and traditions (Harz 1964, 1–6; Mitchell 1978, 67). The initial settlers of nuclear New England, for example, represented a particular fragment of English society, driven to emigration by political pressures and their Puritan religious ideologies, bringing with them cultural traditions typical of East Anglia, the primary source region for many of the earliest settlers.

Second, traditions of land tenure and social stratification in eastern North America came to be highly restructured over time compared to those in Europe. In much of Europe at the time of the initial colonization of North America, vestiges of the ancient feudal system of land tenure, characterized by a highly uneven distribution of land and wealth, remained codified in law and practice. In such a socioeconomic system, land was expensive and in short supply, whereas labor was plentiful and cheap. From the beginning of European settlement in North America, however, Europeans viewed land as a commercial commodity to be bought and sold; as such, access to land—the source of wealth in a preindustrial agricultural economy—was open to a much larger share of the population. This contrasted fundamentally with the age-old system of land tenure in which the aristocracy, the state, and the church held and controlled land and access to land ownership. When Europeans, especially those from the landless underclasses, encountered a socioeconomic system in which land was inexpensive (even free) and markets were poorly defined, many of the complexities regarding land tenure, class, and social relations of production characteristic of Europe were "simplified" (Harris 1977, 469). Many of the regional differences so common in Europe also disappeared with the emergence of national-scale policies and trends resulting from the mixing together of a large variety of social customs and material culture traditions.

This central difference—the commercialization of land—was the basis for new attitudes and rules concerning land tenure and subdivision that developed in North America, manifested in the basic American pattern of private land subdivision in discretely occupied property units. Coupled with European tenets concerning the central social role of the nuclear family and the strong desire for private land ownership, this ultimately produced rather egalitarian and autonomous rural societies of farmers built around the ideal of the nuclear family along the eastern seaboard during the colonial era (Harris 1977, 469–75; Mitchell 1978, 66–70). Europeans tended to equate land ownership with independence. For those from the landless underclasses, this meant independence not from king or state but, rather, from strict subject bonds as tenants or laborers within feudal social relations of production (Hofstra 2004, 144). By the federal period (roughly 1790–1850), population growth, territorial limitations, and the development of clearly articulated market structures in interior regions had led to rising land prices, generating increased social stratification and leading to the control of larger and larger tracts of land by a rising bourgeoisie of wealthy farmers, companies, and syndicates at the expense of smaller-scale farmers holding smaller pieces of land (Harris 1977, 474–75). In the Southwest borderlands, Spanish colonists introduced similar ideals regarding the primacy of the nuclear family and the desire for land ownership. However, the distinctive agropastoral subsistence economy based on Iberian antecedents that developed there was not as easily transformed into a commercial farming enterprise, at least compared to Anglo American farming systems as they developed in the East (Van Ness 1987, 205).

SPANISH AND MEXICAN LAND SUBDIVISION IN THE SOUTHWEST BORDERLANDS

The formal colonization of the American Southwest by Spain began in 1598 with the colonization of New Mexico under the leadership of soldier-settler Juan de Oñate (Nostrand 1992, 26–32; Kornwolf 2002, 102). Although Spanish political and "cultural" control of the borderlands advanced in a rather uneven fashion, characterized by small numbers of colonists and serious mistreatment of native populations, the Spanish were nevertheless the first effective European settlers in the region (Zelinsky 1992, 13–14). This resulted in a cultural landscape impress, including distinctive land tenure and subdivision methods, that persisted in the region beyond Mexican independence (1821) and annexation by the United States (1846–1848) and continues to set the region apart even today.

New Mexico

With regard to the shaping of rural land tenure patterns and land subdivision techniques, the most significant Spanish colonial institution was the practice of granting relinquished Crown lands (*mercedes*) to individuals and groups of colonists, a policy continued in modified form by the Mexican government after independence. Before 1680, most *merced* grants were in the form of *encomiendas*, large grants of land to individuals (often soldier-settlers) in return for services rendered to the Crown for the purpose of extracting tribute from Indian populations in the form of labor and surplus agricultural production (especially corn and livestock) on sometimes substantial and prosperous haciendas. After 1692, however, Spanish authorities altered this policy in favor of a land tenure system designed to attract more settlers to the region in order to more effectively occupy this northern frontier zone. This new policy manifested itself in the form of *ejidos*, large tracts of land granted to groups of settler families who formally petitioned the Crown for the grant. About sixty of these colony/community grants were awarded in the upper Rio Grande valley in the eighteenth and early nineteenth centuries alone. Spanish authorities expected settlers on such tracts to engage in farming and stock raising and to establish self-sufficient communities. Colony grants generally included irrigable bottomland, upland, and woodland, and each settler had access to each type of land. By 1750 this system became the most common method for settling Spain's northern frontier lands and the basis for establishing hundreds of small agricultural villages. As such, from about 1700 until the end of the Spanish period in 1821, loose agglomerations of small farmsteads (*ranchos*) strung out along arable river bottomlands, rather than large haciendas, became the characteristic unit of colonization in New Mexico, and the Mexican government continued this policy essentially unchanged after 1821 (Simmons 1969, 11; Carlson 1975, 49–50; Van Ness 1987, 159–61; Nostrand 1992, 70–75; Starrs 1998, 94–95; Gonzales 2003, 296).

As a result of these land tenure policies, such colony grants with individual *rancho* settlements, grouped around a *villa* with a central open plaza containing a church, came to characterize the rural settlement landscape of Hispano northern New Mexico. The layout of the village of Anton Chico and its associated agricultural fields in Guadalupe County illustrates this characteristic pattern (figure 12.1). The village is located within the Anton Chico colony grant, some thirty miles south of Las Vegas, awarded to Manuel Rivera and thirty six other petitioners in 1822 (Bowden 2012). According to Spanish and Mexican policy, each family involved in the colony grant received a lot in the village (*propios*) and a privately held agricultural allotment (*suerte*). All of the settlers held the majority of the grant parcel in common for the purposes of grazing (mostly sheep) and obtaining resources such as firewood and building materials. Given the subhumid nature of the natural environment, each settler obtained legal access to water from the main irrigation ditch (*acequia madre*), constructed to service agricultural lots with river water diverted from behind a dam upriver from the village. Individual villagers typically divided their bottomland agricultural holdings into long, narrow strips (long-lots) with frontage on the irrigation ditch. The custom of partible inheritance (equal division of property among heirs) led to the further division of these lots into smaller strips over successive generations. This system placed ownership of the land and responsibility for local

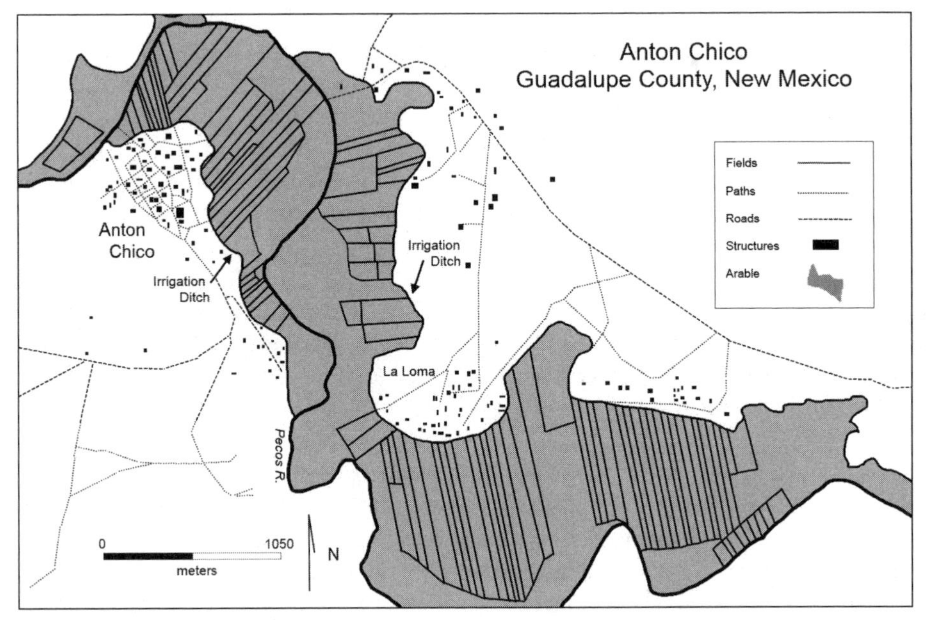

Figure 12.1. Cadastral patterns at Anton Chico, New Mexico. Google; USDA Farm Service Agency. Map by author.

governmental organization in the hands of the villagers and created well-defined social relationships and tight-knit community identities resulting from communal use of grazing lands, each household's participation in irrigation ditch maintenance, and strong religious and linguistic group identity (Church 2002, 226; Gonzales 2003, 296–98).

The subdivision of individually held irrigated bottomland fields into long-lot strips persists to this day, even though New Mexico was surveyed under the U.S. Public Land Survey System (PLSS) in 1855. Each *suerte* field allotment fronts the irrigation ditch and is laid out at right angles to the ditch across the floodplain. Thus, each parcel can be irrigated with water from the ditch, which flows down through the field and drains into the river. Spanish government officials apparently developed this field pattern, ubiquitous throughout the upper Rio Grande basin, in the mid-eighteenth century to service the needs of settlers in the colony grants. A leading authority on Spanish land tenure in New Mexico argues persuasively that the long-lot field pattern was adopted as a practical measure to balance local environmental conditions (a semiarid climate and limited water and land resources) with the need to equitably partition irrigable land with frontage on an irrigation ditch among a fairly large number of colonists (Carlson 1975, 55). Later researchers support this supposition, contending that the distinctive settlement morphology of Hispano villages in New Mexico resulted from the practices of local officials and settlers in colonizing a region with a particular physical environment within the context of Spanish/Mexican settlement goals and policies (Wright and Campbell 2008, 553).

Texas

Although Spanish explorers had ventured north of the Rio Grande into what is now Texas in the sixteenth and seventeenth centuries, effective settlement of the region did not begin until 1690 when Spanish authorities established a mission in eastern Texas in response to the French claim to Louisiana. In addition, as a response to French incursions the Spanish built ten presidios in Texas between 1701 and 1780, the most in any of the Spanish territories in what is now the United States (Jordan 1993, 147; Kornwolf 2002, 125–26). As in New Mexico, the effects of Spanish and Mexican land tenure and subdivision policies remain visible in the cultural landscape today. In South Texas, this is especially true with respect to present-day cadastral boundaries and rural settlement patterns.

Spanish colonists initially settled the area of present-day South Texas between the Nueces and the lower Rio Grande as a part of the two colonial provinces of Nuevo Santander and Coahuila. Mirroring the land tenure schemes employed in the upper Rio Grande valley in New Mexico, the granting of land to individuals and groups of colonists by the Crown (and later the Mexican government) was central to Spanish colonization efforts in the lower Rio Grande valley. Among the earliest land grants in Texas were long-lot *suerte* town lots with irrigation ditch frontage in San Antonio, allocated to colonists from the Canary Islands in 1731 in a process similar to that for Hispano *rancho* settlements in northern New Mexico. By mid-century, however, much larger grants for open-range livestock (mainly cattle) ranching purposes were being made farther south, along the Nueces and the lower Rio Grande in a region of subtropical savannah grasslands and grassy salt marshes (Miller 1972, 5–8; Jordan 1974, 71; Arreola 1992, 57–58; Lang and Long 2012).

Due to the semiarid nature of the local environment and the need for livestock to have access to water, authorities fashioned the mid-eighteenth-century land grants along the lower Rio Grande in long-lot form—long, narrow strips, each with frontage on the river to provide drinking water. Known as *porciónes*, these long-lots were much larger than those associated with *villa* or *rancho* settlements in San Antonio or northern New Mexico, mainly because the lands in southern and southeastern Texas were considered nonirrigable and better suited to dry farming and grazing; most measured about one kilometer in width and sixteen or more kilometers in length and averaged nearly sixty-five hundred acres in area. Most of these original *porcion* grants came to be subdivided into smaller units over successive generations due to partible inheritance customs, but this distinctive Spanish land subdivision practice has had a lasting and profound effect on the region's cultural landscape, especially with regard to transportation (road) and cadastral patterns (Jordan 1974, 74, 84–86; Price 1995, 306–8; Lang and Long 2012) (figure 12.2).

As a result of its unique and intricate settlement history, Texas has without a doubt the greatest variety of land survey systems found in the United States. At least four primary survey methods are found in the state (figure 12.3). Dating from the Spanish era, long-lot surveys are chiefly concentrated along rivers and streams. The majority of the Texas long-lot surveys date from the Mexican era, but the method continued to be utilized well into the Republic of Texas era as well (Jordan 1974, 71, 74–76). In much of the eastern half of Texas, both irregular rectangular and irregular metes and bounds surveys were employed to subdivide

Figure 12.2. Cadastral patterns in a portion of Starr County, Texas. Google; Texas Orthoimagery Program; INEGI. Map by author.

public lands. Under the irregular rectangular survey method, property boundaries followed straight survey lines oriented to compass directions, but unlike the U.S. rectangular Public Land Survey System (discussed below), the rectangular surveys in this part of Texas were more "abstract" in that settlers selected the parcel they wished to occupy before the survey was made. After receiving a land grant (called a "headright"), the holder chose a particular tract of land and then requested that a survey of the tract be made. This produced gaps of unsurveyed land among the tracts of surveyed land, creating an "irregular" rectilinear system of land survey (Epping 1997, 13–14). In the case of irregular metes and bounds surveys, also common in much of the United States east of the Appalachians, topographical features such as water courses and physical landmarks delineate property boundaries; such surveys in eastern Texas predate the headright system. Texas did not participate in the U.S. federal Public Land Survey System when annexed by the United States in 1845. However, the state of Texas employed a similar "rigid" rectangular survey system based on units of square miles in the disposition of public lands settled after statehood, primarily in the panhandle and high plains regions settled by farmers and stockmen from the Midwest during the late nineteenth and early twentieth centuries (Price 1995, 321–26).

LAND SUBDIVISION SYSTEMS IN THE EAST

To understand the fundamental differences between land tenure and subdivision in the American Southwest and the East, it is useful to reflect upon distinctions

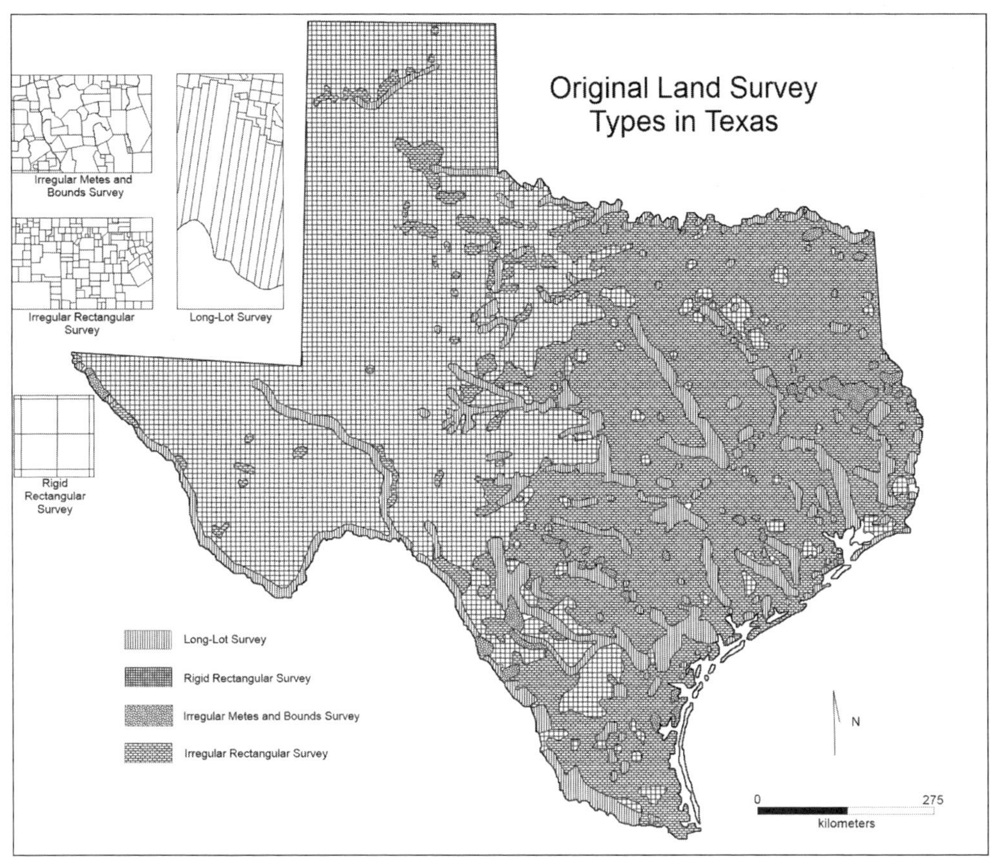

Figure 12.3. Original land survey types in Texas. Jordan (1974, 72); adapted from Arbingast et al. (1976, 41). Map by author.

regarding the settlement of the two regions with respect to the primary impetus behind colonial settlement ventures and the regional origins of early settlers. The Southwest borderlands region was a northern frontier zone of New Spain, an extension from its base in the central highlands of Mexico, itself the center of an Iberian outreach across the Atlantic from southwestern Europe. This outreach was organized within the context of a highly formalized system of conquest, with significant "top-down" control over settlement processes and land tenure practices. In contrast, the settlement of the North American East was part and parcel of an Atlantic outreach from northwestern Europe, characterized by societies increasingly dominated and controlled, by the sixteenth century, by merchant capitalist interests led by individuals, families, societies, guilds, and syndicates rather than by the royalty and an aristocracy, as was the case in Iberian Europe. As a result, English and French colonial efforts in North America were much more experimental, diverse, and uncertain in nature (Meinig 1986, 50–51).

The Chesapeake Tidewater and Greater Virginia

As in New Spain, the practice of issuing patents (grants) of land to private individuals emerged as the primary method for alienating relinquished Crown lands in Tidewater Virginia and Maryland during the colonial period. Unlike in the Spanish borderlands, however, the survey of private landholdings employing an irregular metes and bounds system that drew on English antecedents, coupled with a discrete physical environment and colonial economy, resulted in a starkly different rural settlement landscape.

The earliest colonists in the Tidewater region of Virginia and Maryland comprised two discrete fragments of English society—a landless underclass and a landed gentry elite—that hailed from the south of England between London and Bristol, a region of large manors controlled by wealthy aristocratic families and farmed by landless tenants. This migration introduced into the Tidewater, at least initially, a tradition of land tenure and control that was inherently unequal in nature (Fischer 1989, 31–49, 236–46).

At the outset, the settlement of Virginia was a commercial and speculative enterprise. The first land tenure system formulated to encourage settlement was the headright system, appearing as early as 1617. This scheme entitled anyone paying his own passage to Virginia to fifty acres of land, with an additional fifty acres for each family member or servant whose passage he paid. Under this system persons with wealth were able to acquire extensive landholdings by employing indentured labor; by the mid-seventeenth century, land patents of over six hundred acres were not uncommon. As a consequence of the headright system, landholding in Virginia came to be distributed among a rather diverse range of individuals with regard to wealth and size of holdings. A headright entailed not a grant for a specific piece of land but rather the right to claim any piece of land the headright owner wished, provided another had not already claimed it. Further complicating matters was the absence of a universal system of land survey. Colonial surveyors employed irregular metes and bounds survey methods, used for centuries in England as an element of English common law, to demarcate headright and plantation boundaries. In such surveys, the surveyor described the property boundaries using natural geographic features, such as water courses and other topographical features ("metes"), as demarcation points, joined together by lines ("bounds"). This resulted in an often chaotic settlement process that proceeded in piecemeal fashion without much oversight. Moreover, rather unsophisticated surveying techniques employing compasses and chains often resulted in overlapping surveys that led to legal disputes in later years. Today, the irregular metes and bounds survey system remains evident in the landscape of Virginia and in most other regions of the country settled prior to the adoption of the federal Public Land Survey System (Meinig 1986, 146–47; Price 1995, 90–98; Kornwolf 2002, 530–31) (figure 12.4).

Early in the eighteenth century, a system of land grants meant to encourage more extensive settlement in interior regions beyond the immediate Tidewater zone began to replace the headright system. This property distribution system was accomplished largely through the creation of a number of small subsidiary companies granted large tracts of land within which grantees were expected to

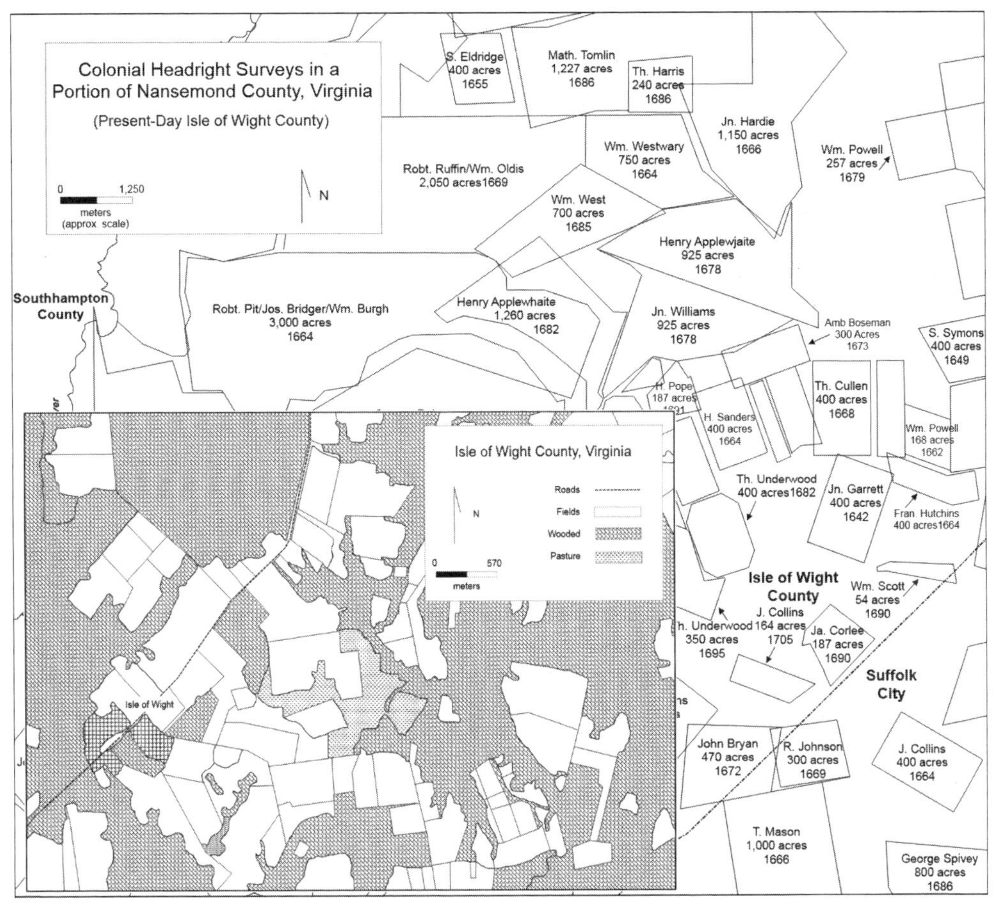

Figure 12.4. Colonial headright surveys and present-day field patterns in a portion of Isle of Wight County, Virginia. Adapted from http://andersonnc.files.wordpress.com/2010/07/deeds_for-web.jpg; Commonwealth of Virginia; Google. Map by author.

develop towns and agricultural enterprises. The Crown granted the earliest and largest of these tracts to those with aristocratic backgrounds or political and social ties to royalty (Thomas, Lord Fairfax's grant totaled 6 million acres, but most were much smaller). During the first half of the eighteenth century, an increasing number of such grants (often referred to as "hundreds"), spaced about ten miles apart on "necks" of land occupying relatively higher ground between creeks and rivers, came under the control of individual wealthy families, and this basic pattern became the model for the Tidewater plantation (Meinig 1986, 146; Farmer 1993, 49–62).

New England

Whereas the plantation represented a settlement ideal in the Chesapeake Tidewater and Greater Virginia, the town epitomized a similar spatial ideal in colonial

New England, the term itself imbued with particular meaning and significance. For New Englanders, the town was a discrete, bounded geographical entity of a few square miles carved out of the wilderness, a place that both literally and figuratively represented a refuge from the surrounding wastelands. Together with the nucleated village at its center, towns later became the basis for the formation of the first counties. After the initial establishment of settlements along the Massachusetts coast, the planting of a large number of new towns in the interior occurred in quick succession as groups of settlers sought new land for husbandry. The process for establishing new towns was rather uniform: a group wishing to settle a new town would choose a number of men from their own (selectmen) to petition the colony's general court for permission to seek out a location to establish a new settlement. After locating a suitable site, they received a grant of land for that location from the court and returned to lay out house lots, planting fields, and common fields. As soon as possible, they also recruited a clergyman, erected a meeting house, and set aside a plot of land nearby for a burial ground. An open area designated as the common or green near the center of each settlement served as a space devoted to outdoor religious assemblies, livestock collection, and the mustering of the local militia. Together, these features formed the nucleus of the New England village (Stilgoe 1982, 46–49; Wood and Steinitz 1992; Wood 1997, 66–67, 165).

The New England town also represented an East Anglian social and spatial ideal in which individuals worked the land in a nucleated settlement in pursuit of the common good; as such, the town emerged as a material embodiment of a corporate-community attitude that shaped New England's geographical space and social structure. The Old World antecedent of the New England town was likely the rural English parish before the enclosure of open fields in the seventeenth century: farmers living in a cluster of houses near a church, farming noncontiguous strips of land in common fields. Although initially transplanted across the Atlantic, the ideal of the parish (town) was rarely fully enacted as a settlement ideal in New England due to altogether different circumstances regarding the commercialization of land and weakly defined markets in North America. Despite the corporate-community model, land and rights were rarely allocated equally, the availability of new land engendered speculation, and economic development led to greater social stratification. With regard to land subdivision, a standard scheme was never applied to the layout of towns and villages. Some towns were rectilinear in shape, but most were irregular tracts shaped more than anything else by the peculiarities of the local topography. Village greens appeared in a large variety of shapes: some were circular, some were square, and still others were rectangular. As such, local economic, social, and environmental conditions, to which New Englanders were keen to adapt, stymied the nucleated settlement ideal in New England (Stilgoe 1982, 44–45; Meinig 1986, 104–5; Price 1995, 32–48, 49–55; Wood 1997, 44–45).

Greater Pennsylvania

William Penn, founder and proprietor of Pennsylvania, also believed that colonial settlers should live in nucleated villages. Bequeathed an enormous tract of land in North America by King Charles II in 1681 as repayment for a debt owed to his father, Penn proposed a settlement pattern in which farmers, craftsmen, and merchants would live in small villages set within an orderly arrangement of townships, bound together by a regular and methodical cadastral pattern and road network to be surveyed prior to settlement. As in New England, however, local conditions and circumstances thwarted many of Penn's plans for the development of a neat and systematic settlement landscape. In order to "control" the speed and extent of settlement north and west of Philadelphia, in the earliest years Penn and his agents granted land to individuals, groups of settlers, and companies in collections of contiguous tracts called "townships" or "manors," warrants of land that were granted and then subsequently surveyed by a Board of Property.

By the first decades of the eighteenth century, however, increasing demand for land that was cheap and readily available resulted in the development of a booming land speculation business that challenged the plan for orderly and contiguous settlements. Furthermore, an increasing number of settlers resorted to "squatting" on tracts of land before attaining legal warrants for the land; that is, settlement preceded survey. In time, most squatters eventually attained warrants for their land and arranged for surveys, but their boundaries were more often than not described using metes and bounds, and this method continued to be employed in later years, resulting in a highly irregular cadastral pattern of dispersed farmsteads still visible in the landscape of much of southeastern Pennsylvania today. Local factors regarding the choice of sites for farming also discouraged Penn's plan for the spread of settlement in an orderly fashion. In the ethnically plural society that set Pennsylvania apart, many settlers pursued and obtained holdings in close proximity to those they had immigrated with or to those of like ethnicity or theological belief (this was particularly true of the so-called Pennsylvania Germans, who included groups such as the Amish and Mennonites). Other factors, such as soil quality, the availability of land, access to markets, and immigrants' time of arrival, to say nothing of the actions of proprietors and land speculators, also influenced where colonists chose to settle (Price 1995, 257–72; Lemon 2002, 50–51, 69, 98–99, 102).

French Land Subdivision in Canada and the Interior

The effective settlement of French Canada began as a commercial fur-trading endeavor along the St. Lawrence River, but with time it expanded into the interior via the Great Lakes, to the Illinois Country along the lower Ohio and its tributaries, and eventually down the Mississippi to Louisiana. Eventually, the French created a rather fragile inland empire comprising an arc of trading posts, missions, forts, and small agricultural settlements anchored by two large rivers—the St. Lawrence and the Mississippi—that provided access to claimed territory in the North American interior (Meinig 1986, 109–10; Fischer 2008, 227–53, 401–26).

Distinctive land tenure and subdivision patterns in New France resulted largely from the implementation of a seigneurial system, a "vestige" of the French feudal system of land tenure in which the Crown granted seigneurs (manorial lords under the feudal system) large blocks of land (seigneuries, or fiefs), in return for the promise to pay for the immigration of habitants (tenant farmers) to whom they would grant portions of their fief for agricultural purposes. About ten thousand immigrants (mostly indentured servants, released soldiers, and exiled prisoners) came to New France under this system. Different social, economic, and environmental conditions in New France, however, precluded the full implementation of the system as it appeared back home in France. Because there were so few settlers and so much available land, and because the initial markets for agricultural products were rather weakly articulated, lord-fief relationships never became very firm. Since the incomes from their lands were rather small, most seigneurs chose to live in Quebec or Montreal and became, in effect, absentee landlords who simply collected annual dues from their habitants, otherwise leaving them much to their own devices. With time, the middle and lower St. Lawrence valley under the French regime became a region dominated by small subsistence farmers on individually farmed tracts of land (Meinig 1986, 109–17; Harris 1977, 476–77; Harris 1984, xvii, 7–8).

Despite this, cadastral patterns and road networks in much of southern Quebec and parts of the United States first effectively settled by French colonists still reflect the legacy of land tenure practices under the seigneurial system (figure 12.5). With regard to land subdivision, the most iconic element of the system was the practice of subdividing seigneuries into individual farms in long-lot fashion: long, thin strips of land were cleared from the forest, each with

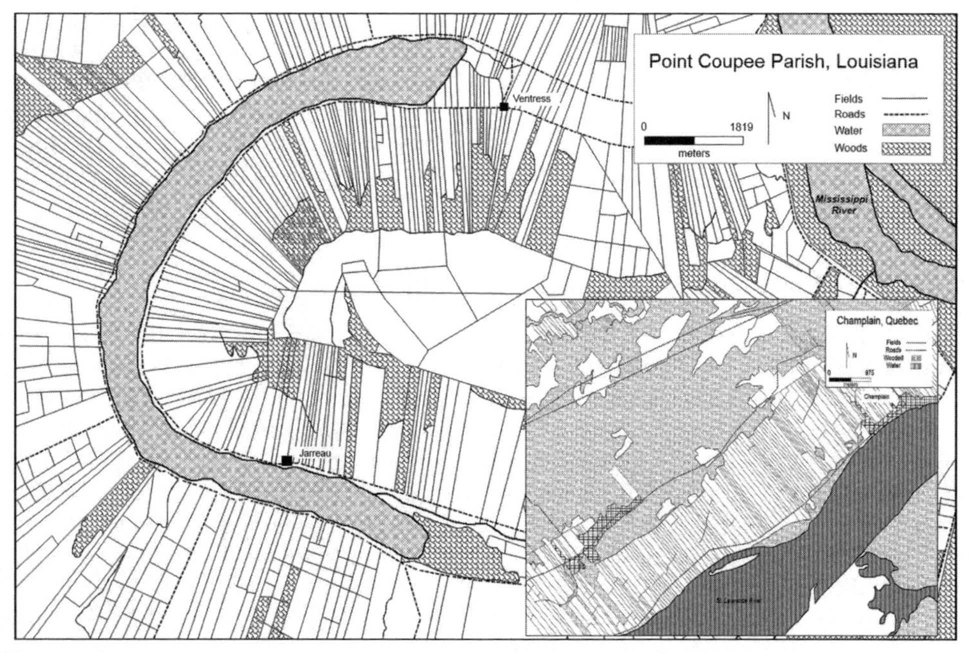

Figure 12.5. Long-lot cadastral patterns in Louisiana and the St. Lawrence valley. GeoEye; Google; Digital Globe; USDA Farm Service Agency. Map by author.

frontage on the St. Lawrence. In some instances, these long-lot strips were only a few meters wide but up to a kilometer or more in length. When all available land with shoreline frontage in a seigneury had been taken, another *rang* (range) of long-lots appeared behind the shoreline range of lots, and over time partible inheritance patterns resulted in even narrower strips as land became subdivided among heirs. French colonists repeated the custom of laying out individual fields in long-lot form in interior locations. In some locales where the French established small communities of settlers associated with trading posts, missions, and forts, the practice had a permanent impact on local cadastral patterns and road patterns that were incorporated into later cadastral surveys. Examples occur at Detroit, Michigan (1701), Kaskaskia, Illinois (1703), Vincennes, Indiana (1733), and most pervasively in the lower Mississippi river valley (Gentilcore 1957, 285–89, 293; Johnson 1976, 21–24; Price 1995, 289–300).

Experts debate the origin of the long-lot tradition in New France and whether it stemmed from European antecedents. It is highly likely that the long-lot pattern emerged as a "logical" adjustment to local social, economic, and environmental conditions rather than as a tradition imported from Europe. This appears to be the case in northern New Mexico and southern Texas as well (Harris 1984, 119–21).

THE U.S. PUBLIC LAND SURVEY SYSTEM

Seen from an airplane or from space, a large part of the western two-thirds of the United States (and much of western Canada) resembles a continental-scale checkerboard, a vast "regular" pattern of squares fashioned upon the landscape stemming from the rigid geometry laid down with the implementation of the U.S. Public Land Survey System. Conceived in the late eighteenth century and implemented during the nineteenth, this survey (also known as the "Township/ Range" system) had a profound and lasting impact on the American cultural landscape in much of the country west of the Appalachians, especially with regard to cadastral patterns and road networks. The public land surveys are built around the grid of latitude and longitude lines, imparting a strong north-south-east-west orientation to the landscape (figure 12.6). Although the system is not without Old World antecedents (the Roman system of centuriation, for example), it nevertheless represents a distinctive approach to a particularly "American" problem—the alienation of a substantial amount of territory in the public domain into the hands of private individuals. The solution to this problem ultimately resulted in a regular cadastral survey pattern whose omnipresence and scale is unequaled anywhere else in the world.

In 1783 the new federal government faced a variety of complex issues relating to the dispossession of vast tracts of territory (roughly between the Appalachians and the Mississippi River) that it had acquired as a result of the Treaty of Paris that ended the Revolutionary War. The addition of even more territory as a consequence of the Louisiana Purchase (1803) and then of much of the present-day Southwest after the Mexican-American War (1846–1848) compounded these issues. First, the government had to address the issue of claims to territory on the

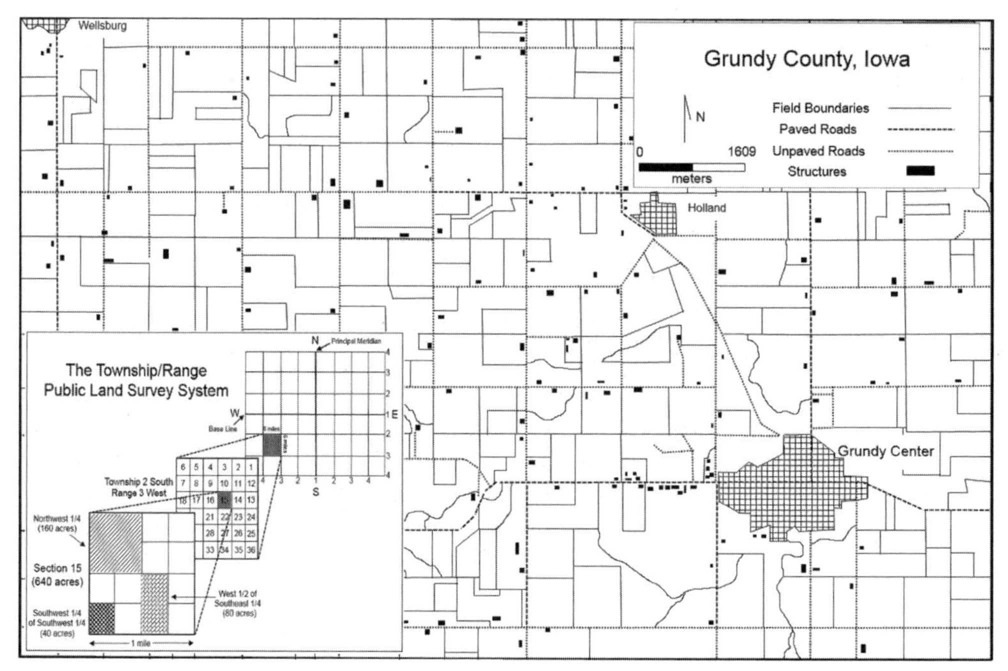

Figure 12.6. Cadastral boundaries and road networks in a portion of Grundy County, Iowa. Google. Map by author.

part of hundreds of different Native American tribal groups. Second, Congress had to manage conflicting claims to territory west of the Appalachians by several eastern states dating from some of the earliest "sea-to-sea" colonial charters. Finally, it had to devise an orderly and practical method for alienating millions of acres of public lands (also referred to as "Congress lands" and the "public domain") into the hands of private individuals.

With regard to Native American claims, Congress essentially continued the former British policy of "excluding" Indians from their territorial homelands through a series of military ventures and quasi-legal treaties that eventually resulted in the cession of virtually all claimed ancestral territories (Meinig 1986, 212–13). Next, in a complex and at times contentious sequence of negotiations, Congress successfully won the concession of virtually all territory claimed by eastern states in the interior (largely in return for federal assumption of the states' war debts), upon which these territories became part of the public domain. There were some exceptions: Both Connecticut and Virginia negotiated the "reservation" of territory in the Northwest Territory, in what is now Ohio, for the purposes of satisfying land warrants issued to militiamen and war veterans. The Virginia Military District (1784) encompassed some 4.2 million acres in southern Ohio between the Scioto and Little Miami Rivers, and the Connecticut Western Reserve (1786) amounted to about 3.5 million acres in northern and eastern Ohio. The federal government also reserved a "military district" (1796) of about 2.5 million acres in the central part of Ohio to satisfy land warrants issued to soldiers who had fought in the Revolutionary War. Although the numbering system of townships differs in each, in the Western Reserve and the U.S. Military District privately hired surveyors subdivided both tracts, employing a rectilinear system of twenty-five-square-mile townships, completed largely before settlement. In the Virginia Military District, surveyors utilized the irregular metes and bounds survey system, in which settlement largely preceded survey. As a result of this distinctive settlement history, Ohio (with the important exception of Texas) has the largest variety of land subdivision and survey systems of any state (Sherman 1925, 12–37, 79–88, 89–94; Thrower 1966; Hubbard 2009, 308).

The federal government's view of the value and utility of its public domain lands has shifted over time and space, but in the beginning it chiefly viewed the public domain as a source of revenue to be sold to individual settlers and investors in order to replenish the treasury. The government experimented with the concept of selling large tracts to private companies and investors, especially in western New York and Ohio, but few of these ventures were economically successful, and these schemes ultimately failed to provide the amount of revenue that officials anticipated. Congress eventually opted for a system under which the federal government could sell the public domain to private individuals. In 1784 a committee headed by Thomas Jefferson drafted a plan for the survey of public domain lands into one-hundred-square-mile tracts, further subdivided into one-square-mile lots, for later sale at public auction at the price of $1 per acre. Dissention among members of Congress regarding this system, especially the ideal size of lots, ultimately resulted in a system that was not based on decimal measures of land (basic grids of seven and eventually six miles square were eventually adopted) but retained the fundamental characteristics of Jefferson's system: a rectilinear survey grid and square subdivisions of land (White 1983, 9–16).

Congress adopted the system as the Land Ordinance of 1785, and its basic tenets remain part of the PLSS today. The ordinance called for the survey of public domain lands into thirty-six-square mile townships. Each survey comprised a grid built around a beginning north-south line (the "principal meridian") and a beginning east-west line (the "base line"). Federal surveyors constructed the grid around north-south lines (township lines) and east-west lines (range lines) every six miles from the "initial point" where the principal meridian and base line intersected. The basic unit of land became the one-square-mile "section" (640 acres), which could be further subdivided into half sections (320 acres) and "quarters" (160 acres). The system for numbering townships went through a series of revisions, but a 1796 act of Congress established a permanent system that remains in place today. The PLSS as adopted in the Land Ordinance of 1785 was first applied in the so-called Seven Ranges in present-day eastern Ohio and later implemented throughout the country in thirty-seven different surveys undertaken as new territories and states were added (figure 12.7).

The PLSS is the legal standard basis for land tenure and subdivision in all regions of the United States, except areas settled prior to 1785 under other survey systems: the original thirteen states; Kentucky, Tennessee, and West Virginia; Hawaii; parts of New Mexico and Texas initially settled under Spanish rule; parts of Louisiana, Wisconsin, and Michigan originally settled under French rule; and the Virginia Military District in Ohio. In addition, similar nonfederal (i.e., not

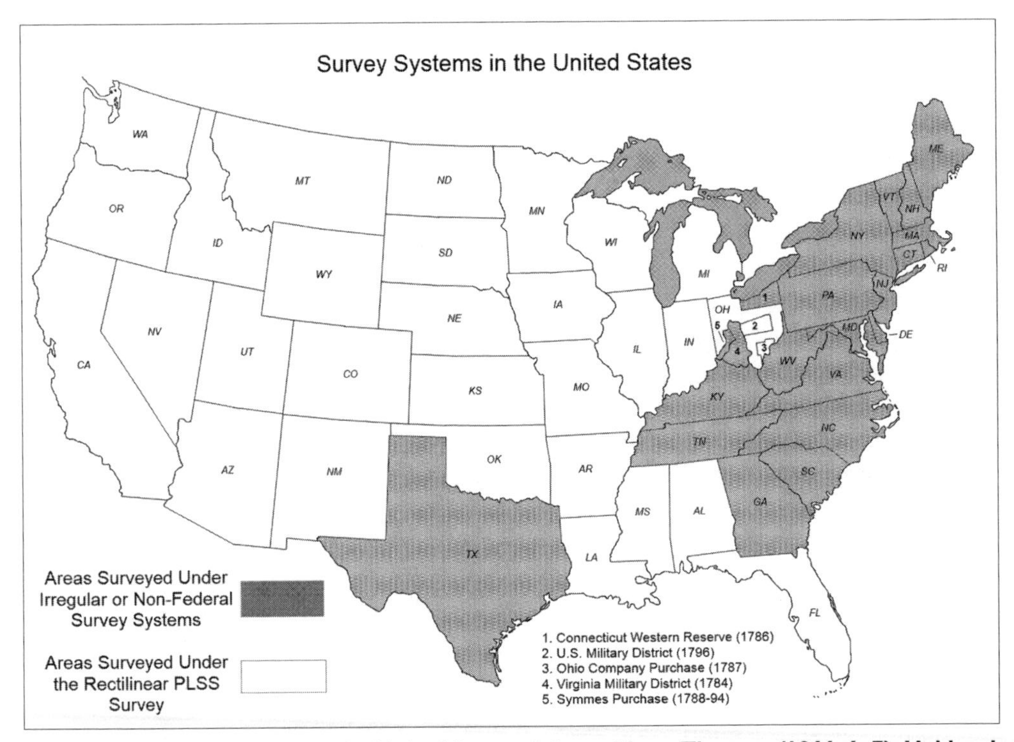

Figure 12.7. Survey systems in the United States. Adapted from Thrower (1966, 6–7); Hubbard (2009, 309). Map by author.

part of the PLSS) rectilinear surveys appear in certain areas as a result of unique settlement circumstances. Examples include the Holland Land Company's purchase in western New York (Wyckoff 1986), much of western and northwestern Texas (the state of Texas adopted its own rectangular survey system), and the Connecticut Western Reserve in northeastern Ohio. Canada also adopted the U.S. PLSS for the survey of "dominion lands" in its western territories. The Canadian survey uses the thirty-six-section township of the American system, but instead of multiple surveys it begins at a principal meridian (ninety-eight degrees west longitude) and then "restarts" at meridians spaced four degrees east and west of this meridian (Hubbard 2009, 347).

In analyses of the genesis and implementation of the systematic rectilinear system of survey employed in the PLSS, some scholars have argued that the system represents a distinctly American expression of abstract principles such as "Newtonian rationalism" or "republican individualism" in the nation's cultural landscape. Modern detailed studies of the history of the PLSS and other locales where "regular" (rectilinear) cadastral survey systems exist reveal that their design and implementation were largely the result of a "fusion" of various land subdivision methods of the time. Wherever they occur in the North American landscape, rectilinear cadastral surveys, including the PLSS, represent, more often than not, "practical and functional" solutions to complex problems with respect to the management and control of large tracts of land (Wyckoff 1986, 142, 144, 158). As such, the PLSS recalls a familiar overarching process with regard to the settlement of North America by Old World peoples—namely, the "reconfiguration" of Old World customs, traditions, and ideals in the face of new social, economic, and environmental realities (Mitchell 1978, 66–67).

NOTE

The title for this chapter is adopted from Edward T. Price's (1995) seminal monograph on North American land survey and subdivision systems.

REFERENCES

Arbingast, S. A., L. G. Kennamer, R. H. Ryan, J. R. Buchanan, W. L. Hezlep, L. T. Ellis, T. G. Jordan, C. T. Granger, and C. P. Zlatkovich. 1976. *Atlas of Texas*. Austin: University of Texas, Bureau of Business Research.

Arreola, D. D. 1992. Plaza Towns of South Texas. *Geographical Review* 82, no. 1: 56–73.

Bowden, J. J. 2012. Anton Chico Grant. New Mexico Office of the State Historian. http://admin.newmexicohistory.org/filedetails/php?fileID=24814 (accessed November 27, 2012).

Carlson, A. W. 1975. Long-Lots in the Rio Arriba. *Annals of the Association of American Geographers* 65, no. 1: 48–57.

Church, M. C. 2002. The Grant and the Grid. *Journal of Social Archaeology* 2, no. 2: 220–44.

Epping, P. G. 1997. Community Contours: The Enduring Consequence of the Rectangular Land Survey System and Texas Abstract Survey System. PhD diss., University of Texas, Arlington.

Farmer, C. J. 1993. *In the Absence of Towns: Settlement and Country Trade in Southside Virginia, 1730–1800*. Lanham, MD: Rowman & Littlefield.

Fischer, D. H. 1989. *Albion's Seed: Four British Folkways in America*. New York: Oxford University Press.

———. 2008. *Champlain's Dream*. New York: Simon & Schuster.

Gentilcore, R. L. 1957. Vincennes and French Settlement in the Old Northwest. *Annals of the Association of American Geographers* 47, no. 3: 285–97.

Gonzales, P. B. 2003. Struggle for Survival: The Hispanic Land Grants of New Mexico, 1848–2001. *Agricultural History* 77, no. 2: 293–324.

Harris, R. C. 1977. The Simplification of Europe Overseas. *Annals of the Association of American Geographers* 67, no. 4: 469–83.

———. 1984. *The Seigneurial System in Early Canada: A Geographical Study, with a New Preface*. Kingston: McGill-Queen's University Press.

Harz, L. 1964. *The Founding of New Societies*. New York: Harcourt Brace.

Hofstra, W. R. 2004. *The Planting of New Virginia: Settlement and Landscape in the Shenandoah Valley*. Baltimore: Johns Hopkins University Press.

Hubbard, R., Jr. 2009. *American Boundaries: The Nation, the States, and the Rectangular Survey*. Chicago: University of Chicago Press.

Johnson, H. B. 1976. *Order upon the Land: The U.S. Rectangular Land Survey and the Upper Mississippi Country*. New York: Oxford University Press.

Jordan, T. G. 1974. Antecedents of the Long-Lot in Texas. *Annals of the Association of American Geographers* 64, no. 1: 70–86.

———. 1993. *North American Cattle-Ranching Frontiers: Origins, Diffusion, and Differentiation*. Albuquerque: University of New Mexico Press.

Kornwolf, J. D. 2002. *Architecture and Town Planning in Colonial America*. 3 vols. Baltimore: Johns Hopkins University Press.

Lang, A. S., and C. Long. 2012. Land Grants. Handbook of Texas Online. Texas State Historical Association. http://www.tshaonline.org/handbook/online/articles/mpl01 (accessed September 3, 2012).

Lemon, J. T. 2002. *The Best Poor Man's Country: Early Southeastern Pennsylvania*. Rev. ed. Baltimore: Johns Hopkins University Press.

Mauro, G. 1988. *Guide to Spanish and Mexican Land Grants in South Texas*. Austin: Texas General Land Office.

Meinig, D. W. 1986. *The Shaping of America: A Geographical Perspective on 500 Years of History*. Vol. 1: *Atlantic America, 1492–1800*. New Haven, CT: Yale University Press.

Miller, T. L. 1972. *The Public Lands of Texas, 1519–1970*. Norman: University of Oklahoma Press.

Mitchell, R. D. 1978. The Formation of Early American Culture Regions: An Interpretation. In *European Settlement and Development in North America*, edited by J. R. Gibson, 66–90. Toronto: University of Toronto Press.

Nostrand, R. L. 1992. *The Hispano Homeland*. Norman: University of Oklahoma Press.

Price, E. T. 1995. *Dividing the Land: Early American Beginnings of Our Private Property Mosaic*. Chicago: University of Chicago Press.

Sherman, C. E. 1925. *Original Ohio Land Subdivisions*. Columbus: Ohio Department of Natural Resources, Division of Geological Survey.

Simmons, M. 1969. Settlement Patterns and Village Plans in Colonial New Mexico. *Journal of the West* 8: 7–21.

Starrs, P. F. 1998. *Let the Cowboy Ride: Cattle Ranching in the American West*. Baltimore: Johns Hopkins University Press.

Stilgoe, J. R. 1982. *Common Landscape of America, 1580 to 1845*. New Haven, CT: Yale University Press.

Thrower, N. J. W. 1966. *Original Survey and Land Subdivision: A Comparative Study of the Form and Effect of Contrasting Cadastral Surveys*. Chicago: Association of American Geographers.

Van Ness, J. R. 1987. Hispanic Land Grants: Ecology and Subsistence in the Uplands of Northern New Mexico and Southern Colorado. In *Land, Water, and Culture: New Perspectives on Hispanic Land Grants*, edited by C. L. Briggs and J. R. Van Ness, 141–214. Albuquerque: University of New Mexico Press.

White, C. A. 1983. *A History of the Rectangular Survey System*. Washington, D.C.: U.S. Government Printing Office.

Wood, J. S. 1997. *The New England Village*. Baltimore: Johns Hopkins University Press.

Wood, J. S., and M. Steinitz. 1992. A World We Have Gained: House, Common, and Village in New England. *Journal of Historical Geography* 18, no. 1: 105–20.

Wright, J. B., and C. L. Campbell. 2008. Landscape Change in Hispano and Chicano Villages of New Mexico. *Geographical Review* 98, no. 4: 551–65.

Wyckoff, W. 1986. Land Subdivision on the Holland Purchase in Western New York State, 1797–1820. *Journal of Historical Geography* 12, no. 2: 142–61.

Zelinsky, W. 1992. *The Cultural Geography of the United States*. Rev. ed. Englewood Cliffs, NJ: Prentice Hall.

13

Science and Sentiment

The Work of Photography in Nineteenth-Century North America

Joan M. Schwartz

> The image of a place is always formed by a multitude of cultural mediations where photographs play a crucial and unquestionable role.
>
> —Susana Martins (2010, 85)

IMAGES AND IMAGININGS

In his essay "Forging a Canadian Nation," Graeme Wynn explains that for much of the nineteenth century, Canada was an artificial geographical expression, a political projection on the natural landscape: "The country began, quite simply, as an idea" (1987, 373); "science and sentiment" overcame the natural north-south grain of the North American continent. This idea that Canada was a "projection"—or, as Suzanne Zeller (1987) has argued, "an invention of Victorian science"—resonates with Benedict Anderson's (1991) concept of a nation as an "imagined community" and with Edward Said's contention that "the struggle over geography . . . is complex and interesting because it is not only about soldiers and cannons but also about ideas, about forms, about images and imaginings" (1993, 7). Indeed, such struggles unfolded across North America.

There were, of course, soldiers and cannons—the Mexican-American War, the American Civil War, the Indian Wars—that had an indelible impact on the physical and human landscape. Soldiers—and engineers (in the U.S. Army Corps of Engineers and the Royal Engineers)—also helped to safeguard territory, build roads, and clear the land of real and perceived impediments to the "progress" of civilization—including native peoples. But the struggles to overcome vast distances, physical obstacles, and human conflict also proceeded under the watchful eye of the camera.

From the discovery of Mayan ruins in the Yucatán in the early 1840s to the discovery of gold in the Yukon in the late 1890s, military explorers and scientific travelers, gold seekers and government departments, land speculators and armchair tourists created, commissioned, and collected photographs (Wyckoff and Dilsaver 1997; Hoelscher 1998, 2008a, 2008b; Sandweiss 2002; Kelsey 2007; Schwartz 2003a, 2003b). Photographs conveyed facts and stirred feelings, acted as filters and served up fantasies—about the nature of the past, the state of the present, and the prospects for the future. As visual arguments, rooted in both science and sentiment, they were created and conscripted to preserve natural wonders and exploit natural resources, survey boundaries and settle diplomatic disputes, study ancient civilizations and subjugate native peoples, justify Manifest Destiny and celebrate empire.

With a research focus on form and function, intention and impact, this chapter looks at examples of photographs that had very public lives. It offers a brief and necessarily selective look at the ways in which photography played a role in the struggle over North American geography in the nineteenth century. It also suggests that, in the nascent New World nations of nineteenth-century North America, photographic images and the imaginings that they both embodied and emboldened fashioned and furthered ideas about place and identity.

"WORKING OBJECTS IN THEIR OWN TIME"

Photography became an integral part of the geographical encounter with new lands and new peoples in nineteenth-century North America. Critics hailed it as a way of "annihilating space" and bringing the world to "tarry-at-home" travelers. Through photographs, photographically based engravings in books, and such pictorial weeklies as the *Illustrated London News* and *Frank Leslie's Illustrated Newspaper*, Europe came to know North America, just as North Americans learned about the continent beyond their doorstep. Photography became a visual means of gathering data for scientific study. For example, Louis Agassiz at Harvard University used daguerreotypes of African American slaves in South Carolina to support his theory of "separate creation" (polygenesis), while Thomas Henry Huxley in London collected photographs of Vancouver Island "native types" to study "races of the British Empire" and argue in favor of Darwin's theory of evolution (Wallis 1995; Edwards 2001). But photographic facts also served more complex purposes. As tools of decision making and instruments of nation building, photographs were spaces where government lawmakers and corporate financiers, eager immigrants and enterprising citizens, merchant princes and railroad barons conjured visions of North America upon which individual and collective futures were built.

As selective visual records of past landscapes, photographs offer valuable facts about outward appearances. In them, we can discern sizes, shapes, textures, similarities, dimensions, proximities. Their content suggests what people at the time deemed worthy of recording, remembering, and reporting. However, to consider them simply windows onto a vanished past would do them a disservice. As John Berger has cautioned, "The simplicity with which we usually treat the experience [of looking at a photograph] is wasteful and confusing. We think of photographs as works of art, as evidence of a particular truth, as likenesses, as news items. Every photograph is in fact a means of testing, confirming and constructing a total view of reality" (Berger [1974] 1980, 294). Equally, it is misguided to judge nineteenth-century photographs solely against the aesthetic yardstick by which images and image makers now enter the canon of art history or the white-walled spaces of the museum. Photographs, as Abigail Solomon-Godeau has observed, "do not, of course, become works of art the way caterpillars become butterflies; rather, they are deemed works of art through the complex and interconnected needs and desires of the culture which is apprehending and consuming them" (1991, 26). How, then, are photographs imbricated in the historical geographies of North America?

However scientific or "truthful" or "accurate" they may have appeared to contemporary viewers, photographs were never neutral or objective or value-free (Tucker 2006). Rather, their makers invested them with meaning(s), and the images generated meaning(s) in their viewers. If both science and sentiment shaped those meanings, form and function also configured them. Available camera technology and prevailing chemical processes shaped physical form and material makeup; in turn, these shaped how photographs looked, circulated, and reached viewers. Popular in the 1840s and into the 1850s, daguerreotypes were unique images on highly polished silver-coated copperplates. From the 1850s into the 1870s, glass-plate negatives could yield paper prints in multiple copies and a variety of formats. These early photographs were physical objects, the product of cumbersome equipment and refractory processes. Slow emulsions required long exposures and could not stop motion, record moving objects, or register subjects in low light. The need to transport hundreds of pounds of photographic paraphernalia—large and heavy cameras, tripods, plates and plate holders, portable darkrooms, copious chemicals, and even water—burdened work in the field. Heat, cold, rain, wind, sand, and insects only added to the difficulties of outdoor work. And, of course, although early processes were capable of producing finely detailed images, they could not record color.

In view of the lengths to which travelers and explorers, surveyors and scientists went to produce and publish photographs, the very existence of the photographs discussed in this chapter is, in many ways, remarkable. This realization—of the difficulties, time, cost, and effort that went into the production of photographs in the mid-nineteenth century—shifts scholarly attention beyond immediate content and focuses it on "needs and desires," purpose and impact. Returned to the "action" in which they participated, interrogated against the changing contexts in which they were conceived and created, circulated and viewed, used and preserved, photographs can furnish insights into the intentions, aspirations, and values invested in them, the influence they wielded, and the impact they had. Photographs were, as Michel Frizot has observed, "working objects in their own time" (1998, 12). Studied as "objects" that performed "work" in "their own time," the examples that follow represent a few of the ways in which photographs both expressed and shaped responses to past, present, and future landscapes in nineteenth-century North America.

PICTURING THE PAST: LANDSCAPES OF THE MAYA

Yucatán, arguably the southernmost area of North America, was a mecca for early travelers and explorers inspired by the writings of Alexander von Humboldt and rumors of fantastic ruins of an ancient civilization. Naturalists drawn to the region's exotic flora and fauna were additionally rewarded with archaeological finds, reports of which further piqued European curiosity. Travelers' accounts of truly astonishing ruins often appeared marvelous, and readers were eager for visual records of "simple truth and precision" to substantiate seemingly wild descriptions (Schwartz [2000] 2006). Austrian, American, Hungarian, and French explorer-travelers who adopted the camera as a tool of field work in their mapping of the geography and archaeology of Yucatán summoned the photograph's "radically new authenticity" to support the claims of archaeological discovery (Davis 1981).

Virtually immediately after the advent of the new medium, photography became an integral part of the discovery and documentation of the past landscapes of the Maya. The first daguerreotype outfit arrived in Yucatán in 1840 in the baggage of Baron Emanuel von Friedrichsthal, an Austrian traveler, naturalist, diplomat, and amateur archaeologist, who first recorded the monuments at Chichen Itza and Uxmal (Palmquist and Kailbourn 2000; Fischer-Westhauser 2007). According to an account in the *New York Journal of Commerce* on August 24, 1841, von Friedrichsthal set up as a daguerreotypist during his short residence in Campeche in the spring of 1841, before returning to Europe via New York, where he displayed his daguerreotypes to public acclaim (Fischer-Westhauser 2007). In London, he exhibited "twenty-five or thirty" of his daguerreotypes at a meeting of the senior staff of the British Museum, and in Paris his daguerreotypes met the scholarly gaze of members of the Académie Royale des Inscriptions et Belles-Lettres, where he delivered a lecture orchestrated by Humboldt ("Les monuments de l'Yucatan," 1841). Von Friedrichsthal's photographic show-and-tell carried news of his discoveries to learned audiences at a time when prevailing photographic and printing technology made it impossible to mass-produce photographs or publish original photographs directly alongside letterpress text. In March 1842, shortly after his return to Vienna, von Friedrichsthal died before he could publish a report or illustrations of his archaeological research.

Von Friedrichsthal went to the jungles of Yucatán armed with news of John Lloyd Stephens and Frederick Catherwood's first visit to Central America in 1839–1840. When Stephens, an American lawyer, traveler, and writer, and Catherwood, an English architect and illustrator, assisted by Dr. Samuel Cabot of Boston, returned to Yucatán in 1841–1842, they brought along a daguerreotype apparatus, which they used to record the overgrown pyramids, carved stelae, and wall ornamentation of the Maya at "forty-four ruined cities, or places in which remains or vestiges of ancient population were found" (Stephens 1843, iii). Stephens employed the exquisitely detailed daguerreotype plates, in concert with Catherwood's meticulous camera lucida drawings, to produce 120 illustrations for his popular two-volume narrative, *Incidents of Travel in Yucatan*, first published by Murray in London and by Harper and Brothers in New York in 1843. The following year, Catherwood published, at his own expense, *Views of Ancient*

"DECISIVE PLACES"
Steven Hoelscher

Like a good photograph (at least the kind I most admire), historical geography is a unique blend of time and space. Henri Cartier-Bresson may be most famous for conceiving photography as a "decisive moment," or the "simultaneous recognition, in a fraction of a second, of the significance of an event." But the French photographer also recognized the essential spatial component of his medium. "The discovery of oneself is made concurrently with the discovery of the world around us which can mold us, but which can also be affected by us," he wrote in 1952. "As the result of a constant reciprocal process, both these worlds come to form a single one. And it is this world that we must communicate."

Today, more than six decades after Cartier-Bresson articulated his uniquely geographical understanding of visual culture, I am increasingly drawn to the art form that he mastered—not as a photographer myself, per se, but as a historical geographer influenced by the medium that has so profoundly shaped both our discipline and also our understanding of the world. It hardly seems coincidental that both photography and academic geography came of age at the same time. To be sure, so successfully has the camera visualized a slice of the world that, as one of my graduate school mentors, Yi-Fu Tuan, once observed, "In the classroom, a geography lecture without slides is as anomalous as an anatomy lecture without bones."

And yet, only rather recently have historical geographers chosen to study photographs themselves as objects of inquiry—as primary sources—and not simply as illustrations to make a larger point about vegetation change, urban morphology, or settlement patterns. I am indebted to historical geographers for the study of photography: I'm thinking specifically of Denis Cosgrove, who first opened geography's doors to visual culture studies; Gillian Rose, who persuasively reminds me to combine both theoretical rigor and empirical depth; and Joan Schwartz, who brought an archivist's attention to a photograph's materiality. But I also read well beyond the borders of geography since so much of the most important writing on photography comes from American studies scholars like Alan Trachtenberg, historians like Martha Sandweiss, curators like John Szarkowski, critics like Susan Sontag, theorists like Walter Benjamin, photo editors like Fred Ritchin, and photographers like Cartier-Bresson. Decisive places belong to the realm of historical geography, to be sure, but more important, they belong to the world that is our work—indeed, our responsibility and privilege—to communicate.

Monuments in Central America, Chiapas and Yucatán (1844), which consisted of twenty-five folio, hand-colored lithographs with accompanying text, in an edition of three hundred copies.

Taken between October 1841 and June 1842 on "the most extensive journey ever made by a stranger in that peninsula" (Stephens 1843, iii), the daguerreotypes launched the serious use of photography in Mayan archaeology. In the preface to the first volume of *Incidents of Travel in Yucatan*, Stephens assured readers that the illustrations were based on "daguerreotype views and drawings taken on the spot by Mr. Catherwood, and the engravings were executed under his personal superintendence" (1843, iv). Here a closely supervised process of production further guaranteed the geographical concern for on-the-spot observation and the public faith in camera-made images, leaving no doubt about the existence of the great monuments and the veracity of their visual representations. Whereas Catherwood's original daguerreotype plates were destroyed in a fire and his folio was an expensive, limited edition publication, Stephens's *Incidents of Travel in Yucatan* has gone through seventy editions in English and Spanish since it first appeared in 1843 and is credited with drawing others to Yucatán.

Inspired by Humboldt, Hungarian naturalist Paul de Rosti (or Rosti Pál, in Hungarian), embarked on his American travels in early August 1856, after studying photography in France with noted photographer Gustave Le Gray. De Rosti toured the United States from New York to Wisconsin, then sailed from New Orleans to Havana, visiting Venezuela and the islands of the Caribbean before finally arriving in Mexico. There, he retraced Humboldt's 1803 journey, photographing cities, architecture, Aztec ruins, natural wonders, and local vegetation (Palmquist and Kailbourn 2000). De Rosti presented an album of his photographs (now in the Agfa-Ludwig Museum, Köln) to Humboldt on his return to Europe in 1857 and, in 1861, published *Uti Emlékezetek Americkából*, a book about his travels illustrated with lithographs, the majority of which were based on his original photographs. In the preface, de Rosti declared, "I believe there is no more effective device for the spreading of geographical knowledge than providing clear images about the places, cities, buildings, plants, etc. of various climates by characteristic faithful drawings. Therefore, I consider the major goal of my journey to create such images by means of light drawing [photography]" (Sloan 2013). Originally written in Hungarian, de Rosti's book has had limited circulation and has made neither de Rosti nor the visual record of his travels widely known in the English-speaking world.

Another traveler caught up in the zeitgeist of early Mayan archaeological exploration was French traveler, writer, and photographer Claude-Joseph Désiré Charnay, who first encountered the work of John Lloyd Stephens in his early twenties while working in New Orleans. Prompted to visit the "equinoctial region" made known by Humboldt and the Mayan ruins made famous by Stephens, Charnay quit his teaching post and returned to his native France, where he secured financial backing for a round-the-world "artistic mission" to produce an *Album Universel*. In April 1857, Charnay left France and, with two colleagues, first set up shop for one month in Quebec City in late June, before continuing up the St. Lawrence River, visiting Niagara Falls, and then traveling down the Mississippi to New Orleans and on to Yucatán. According to Keith Davis, his "systematic use of photography as a tool in Mexican Archaeology . . . set the scientific standard for all later researchers" (1981, 104). Charnay collaborated with a Mexico City bookseller and publisher to produce the first photography book in Mexico, *Album fotográfico mexicano*, which included four views taken at Quebec and Niagara and also presented the plazas, buildings, and a panorama of modern Mexico City (Charnay and Barthe 2007, 40). Charnay's views of Mitla (figure 13.1), Chichen Itza, Uxmal, and other sites were published in *Cités et ruines américaines, Mitla, Palenqué, Izamal, Chichen-Itza, Uxmal*, a lavish and costly folio volume of forty-seven original prints and two photolithographs published in 1862; a companion volume of text, with an essay by noted French architect and theorist Eugène Viollet-le-Duc, was published the following year. Charnay's photographs of Meso-American archaeological sites purportedly have had "an extraordinary impact due to their timing, extent, and quality" (American Philosophical Society 2013).

PICTURING THE PRESENT: LANDSCAPES OF WAR

Soon after the invention of the medium, the federal government used photographs to muster topographical facts in support of U.S. territorial claims in the wake of the Aroostook War of 1838–1839, a bloodless conflict over the northeastern boundary between the state of Maine and the British colony of New Brunswick. According to an early account of photography in the United States, published by Marcus Aurelius Root in Philadelphia in 1864, Edward Anthony, a civil engineer, accompanied the British and American commissioners to the

Figure 13.1. As François Brunet has noted, the findings and images of Stephens and Catherwood were widely and quickly disseminated and served as a reference and model for Charnay, many of whose photographs, especially those of Uxmal, are strongly reminiscent of illustrations in *Incidents of Travel in Yucatan*. In addition to photographing the ruins and landscapes of the Maya, Charnay also produced a visual record of the plazas and buildings of modern Mexico City. Claude-Joseph Désiré Charnay (1828–1915), Palais de Mitla, albumen print (32.3 × 80.7 centimeters), on card mount (51.9 × 92.2 centimeters). Musée du Quai Branly Inv. Iconotheque: PP0154722 © 2013 Musée du Quai Branly/Scala, Florence.

Aroostook territory where the location of the border was under dispute. Having learned photography from Samuel Morse, who introduced Louis Daguerre's process to the United States in 1839, Anthony took daguerreotype views of the "highlands"—the height of land that constituted the international boundary established by the Treaty of Paris. Root claimed, "These views are preserved in the national archives, and, so far as we know, this was the first recourse ever had, by any government, to the services of the sun-painting art" (1864, 361). While Anthony's daguerreotypes have yet to be found, both historical and contemporary sources contend that they "influenced the final decision of the commission" and "proved invaluable in the eventual settlement" that led to the Webster-Ashburton Treaty of 1842 (Root 1864, 361; Taft [1938] 1964, 52). That these photographs of historical and geographical significance have not survived does not diminish our ability to study their role in "picturing the present" "in their own time."

The earliest photographs of war on the North American continent are rare daguerreotypes showing the people and places of the Mexican-American War (1846–1848), from Chief of Artillery Major Washington to volunteers leaving Exeter, New Hampshire, for Mexico, from a street scene in Durango to the burial site of the son of Henry Clay (Sandweiss, Stewart, and Huseman 1989; Sandweiss 2002). Now preserved in the Beineke Rare Book and Manuscript Library at Yale University and the Amon Carter Museum in Fort Worth, Texas, these daguerreotypes stand witness to an armed conflict that determined the fate of Texas, established the Rio Grande as an international border, and "helped give final definition to the geography of the American nation" (Sandweiss 2002, 21). They show us the "soldiers and cannons" caught up in the struggle over the annexation of Texas, but they do not record the "movement and chaos of battle"; nor do they "convey the causes or consequences of warfare" (Sandweiss 2002). As daguerreotypes, they were unique images. They could not be produced in numbers or published except as woodcuts, lithographs, or engravings in books or the pictorial press. With limited circulation, they can be ascribed little political agency or emotional impact "in their own time." Today, easily reproduced and widely disseminated, these images are freighted with political significance and patriotic sentiment.

Civil War photographs taken fifteen years later possess a very different social biography. Taken with the wet-collodion process and printed on albumen paper, photographs of the landscapes and horrors of the War between the States were mass-produced for sale to the public and widely circulated to diverse audiences in a variety of forms. Taken in peril for viewing in safety, they brought the grim realities of the battlefront to audiences on the home front. Two exhibitions of Civil War photographs, mounted 150 years apart, demonstrate how photographs served up both information and emotion, simultaneously and not always in equal measure, and how they continue to do so today.

The Battle of Antietam was fought on September 16 to 18, 1862. On October 6, 1862, the *New York Times* drew the attention of its readers to an exhibition of Civil War photographs under the heading "Antietam Reproduced":

> —If our readers wish to know the horrors of the battle-field, let them go to BRADY's Gallery, and see the fearful reproductions which he has on exhibition,

> and for sale. In all the literal repulsiveness of nature, lie the naked corpses of our dead soldiers side by side in the quiet impassiveness of rest. Blackened faces, distorted features, expressions most agonizing, and details of absolute verity, teach us a lesson which it is well for us to learn. . . . The pictures, of a size convenient for albums, can be seen and bought at the National Gallery, corner of Broadway and Tenth-street.

Two weeks later, on October 20, 1862, the *Times* reviewed the exhibition under the heading "BRADY'S PHOTOGRAPHS.; Pictures of the Dead at Antietam."

> We recognize the battle-field as a reality, but it stands as a remote one. . . . Mr. BRADY has done something to bring home to us the terrible reality and earnestness of war. If he has not brought bodies and laid them in our dooryards and along the streets, he has done something very like it. At the door of his gallery hangs a little placard, "The Dead of Antietam." Crowds of people are constantly going up the stairs; follow them, and you find them bending over photographic views of that fearful battlefield, taken immediately after the action.

Brady's Washington studio operator, Alexander Gardner, had taken the photographs on display in New York City two days after the battle. Captured before the dead were buried, the images showed the public the human toll of the turmoil. "These pictures have a terrible distinctness," the *Times* declared; "broken hearts cannot be photographed." The "repulsiveness" of the scenes held a lurid attraction for nineteenth-century viewers who flocked to Brady's studio. But, note: the photographs were "on exhibition and for sale." Printed in "a size convenient for albums," they were there not just to be seen but to be purchased, collected, and compiled into personal albums. Their visual facts wielded affective power. Science guaranteed their "absolute veracity"; sentiment secured their sale.

The Battle of Gettysburg was fought on July 1 to 3, 1863. To commemorate the landmark battle 150 years later, the Metropolitan Museum of Art, across Manhattan from Brady's old studio, displayed in a major exhibition of Civil War photography many of the same photographs that captivated New Yorkers in 1862. Gardner's photographs of Antietam took their place alongside Timothy O'Sullivan's now infamous print *A Harvest of Death* (figure 13.2) and George Barnard's documentation of the siege of Atlanta. The exhibition also included studio portraits by a host of small-town photographers who thrived on the public's desire to have a likeness of loved ones going to war and the soldier's fervent wish to carry a memento of family and friends left behind. With museumgoers primed by Ken Burns's 1990 PBS documentary on the Civil War and the patriotic call of the sesquicentennial of a defining moment in the nation's history, the exhibition was a tourist attraction, a veritable pilgrimage site; it also exemplified the commodification of American history.

On view in a temple of fine art and available for purchase only as postcards or in the accompanying publication, the photographs once sold by Brady have now achieved canonical status. Revered as art and collected by art connoisseurs, on the one hand, and Civil War aficionados, on the other, they fetch astronomical prices on the auction market. But the landscape photographs of war, on view in 1862 in Brady's studio on Tenth Street and in 2013 at the Met on Fifth Avenue,

Figure 13.2. ***A Harvest of Death*, taken by Timothy H. O'Sullivan at Gettysburg, Pennsylvania, July 4, 1863, is now a canonical image by a celebrated photographer. However, in its own time, it circulated as an original photograph in Alexander Gardner's two-volume *Photographic Sketch Book of the War.* The accompanying letterpress text concluded, "Such a picture conveys a useful moral: It shows the blank horror and reality of war, in opposition to its pageantry. Here are the dreadful details! Let them aid in preventing another such calamity falling upon the nation." Albumen print and accompanying text, plate 36, *Gardner's Photographic Sketch Book of the War,* Vol. 1, 1865. J. Paul Getty Museum, 84.XO.1232.1.36. Digital image courtesy of the Getty's Open Content Program.**

have also been "working documents" in their own time as well as in ours. Through careful analysis of the changing contexts of their creation, circulation, reception, preservation, ongoing use, and abiding power to inform and affect viewers, they emerge as a tool by which generations of Americans have come to comprehend the nature and consequences of the War between the States, to construct notions of place, identity, the Confederate South, the Union North, freedom, slavery, and civil rights, and to celebrate the Civil War as the "crucible of American history" (Rosenheim 2013).

PICTURING THE FUTURE: LANDSCAPES OF THE WEST

While early photographic technology was ponderous, unreliable, and costly, by the late 1850s, official photographers or surveyors trained in photography joined topographical artists on military, scientific, and geographical expeditions sent by the Canadian and American governments to map territory, assess natural resources, and establish routes to open up new lands. The first to attempt photography in explorations of the American West was John Charles Frémont. On his first two expeditions to the West in 1842 and 1843–1844, Frémont took along a daguerreotype apparatus and a small number of plates to "record scenes of particular aesthetic, geologic, or historic importance," but his embrace of photography in the field was unsuccessful: "At best it was a supplement to the work of artists while at worst it was a total failure" (Shlaer 2000, 21). Frémont abandoned photography on his next two expeditions; however, in 1853, on his fifth and final expedition to the West, Frémont recruited Solomon Nunes Carvalho as artist and daguerreotypist, along with Baron Frederick Wilhelm von Egloffstein as topographer, to carry out a systematic visual documentation of the terrain he projected for a railway to the Pacific. Whereas Egloffstein's later (1857–1858) shaded relief map of the Grand Canyon has drawn the attention and praise of geographers as a "spectacular new way of depicting, seeing, and understanding landscape" (Krygier 1997, 27; Demhardt 2012), and while Carvalho's *Incidents of Travel and Adventure in the Far West with Colonel Fremont's Last Expedition across the Rocky Mountains* (1858) provides the only detailed account of Frémont's fifth expedition, Carvalho's daguerreotypes and the steel engravings made from them for Frémont's *Memoirs of My Life* ([1886] 1887) have escaped scholarly investigation as a similarly "spectacular new way of depicting, seeing, and understanding landscape."

Within just a few years, the daguerreotype process used by Carvalho in 1853 gave way to the equally refractory wet-collodion, or "wet-plate," process, which had the advantage of being able to produce many paper prints from a single glass-plate negative. Humphrey Lloyd Hime first employed it in Canada on the Assiniboine and Saskatchewan Exploring Expedition under the command of Henry Youle Hind (Huyda 1975; Schwartz 2003a). Sent to the Great Northwest by the Canadian government in 1858, Hime was tasked with furnishing "a series of Collodion Negatives for the full illustration of all objects of interest susceptible of photographic delineation, from which any number of copies can be taken to illustrate a narrative of the Expedition and a report on its results" (Hind 1859). Here, the government specified the choice of subject matter loosely but clearly anticipated the use of negatives. However, Hime's photographs more than accompanied the official report and Hind's popular two-volume *Narrative of the Canadian Red River Exploring Expedition of 1857 and of the Assiniboine and Saskatchewan Exploring Expedition of 1858* (1860); when exhibited at the Provincial Exhibition in Kingston, used as the basis of engravings in the *Illustrated London News*, and circulated as a separate portfolio of albumen prints published by Hogarth in London, they also furnished scientific facts and fueled expansionist sentiment among socially and geographically diverse audiences (figure 13.3).

South of the border, photographs of pristine natural landscapes of the American West, now credited with contributing directly to U.S. federal government legislation to set aside Yosemite as a wilderness preserve (and, later, to establish Yellowstone as a national park), carried a vision for the future. In 1861, Carleton Watkins, one of the great American photographers of the mid-nineteenth century, ventured into the Yosemite Valley with his mammoth (18 × 22 inch) glass-plate

Figure 13.3. Humphrey Lloyd Hime's *The Prairie, on the Banks of Red River, Looking South* presents a quintessential image of prairie topography, one that has become an enduring image of regional identity. This stark image was included in the landmark 1981 Museum of Modern Art (MOMA) exhibition "Before Photography: Painting and the Invention of Photography." In the accompanying book, MOMA curator of photography Peter Galassi wrote, "Radical formal simplicity is such an important element of modern art that one almost instinctively views Hime's photograph as a bold, adventurous work. The picture, however, is probably best understood as a competent description of an intractably empty landscape" (1981, 139). This differential assessment of modern art or competent description typifies contemporary approaches to the photograph but fails to recognize the function and power of this image "in its own time" to stir economic hopes and fuel political dreams among Canadian expansionists and British imperialists. Albumen print, Library and Archives Canada, C-18694.

view camera, portable darkroom, and hundreds of pounds of equipment and supplies and emerged with the first photographs of El Capitan, Half Dome, the Mariposa Trail, and Vernal Falls (figure 13.4). In December 1862, his Yosemite views went on public display at the New York branch gallery of Goupil et Cie, the leading art dealership in France. According to Peter Palmquist and Thomas Kailbourn, Joseph Roos and Albert Wunderlich, San Francisco dealers in photographs and art supplies who acted as a "depot" for Goupil's fine art prints, arranged the "landmark exhibition" (2000, 460). Seen in this prestigious New York space, Watkins's California views gave East Coast viewers their first impressions of the famed valley and raised public awareness of Yosemite as an area of outstanding natural beauty (Palmquist 1983; Nickel 1999; Naef and Hult-Lewis 2011). A review, under the heading "Fine Arts," in the December 12, 1862, issue of the *New York Times* declared, "Nothing in the way of landscape can be more impressive or picturesque."

Figure 13.4. ***River View—Down the Valley—Yo Semite*** **was one of thirty photographs taken with a mammoth (18 × 22 inch) camera by Carleton Watkins in 1861. The glass-plate negative for a single mammoth-plate view weighed about four pounds. It is estimated that to produce his first series of Yosemite views, Watkins relied on mules, horses, and assistants to haul nearly a ton of gear from the village of Mariposa to the Yosemite Valley, up steep paths and along rough wilderness trails (Naef 2008, 5). Mount Watkins, the peak seen in views of Mirror Lake, was named "as a compliment to the photographer who has done so much to attract attention to this region" (Whitney 1871, 61) J. Paul Getty Museum, 85.XM.361.13. Digital image courtesy of the Getty's Open Content Program.**

Scholars hold up Watkins's Yosemite views as an example of how photographs have influenced public opinion and shaped public policy. Although the link between Watkins's photographs and the passage of the 1864 act of Congress that protected Yosemite from private mining and logging interests and established it as a wilderness preserve remains more conjectural than conclusive, the *Times* praised Watkins's photographs as "indescribably unique and beautiful" views of "lofty mountains, of gigantic trees, of falls of water which seem to descend from heights in the heavens and break into mists before they reach the ground" ("Fine Arts," December 12, 1862). Thus, they served as a way for others to see, and by extension to experience vicariously, a distant landscape and to secure its future as an area of outstanding natural beauty. Appropriated by preservationists with their own agenda, the Yosemite views possessed persuasive powers that lay in the transparency of photographic representation and the sublime feelings that their subject matter aroused. Sent east, Watkins's landscape photographs were read "in their own time" as an Arcadian vision that connected the western frontier to prevailing ideas about nature, wilderness, God's bounty, and the future of America as a nation.

PICTURING PROGRESS: LANDSCAPES OF URBAN DEVELOPMENT

Perhaps nowhere was the progress of Western "civilization across the North American continent more obvious or impressive than in photographs which documented the meteoric rise of cities—legislative seats, mercantile cities, manufacturing centres, railway hubs" (Hales 1984). Urban development assumed different configurations, and photographers used different formats to highlight site and situation. The panorama, for example, offered a wide-angle view of a city, often from a height or across a waterfront. Its multiple-plate format utilized contiguous exposures on separate sheets of glass to produce two or more negatives that, when printed and aligned, conveyed the sweep of the landscape more effectively than a single view could achieve. In 1848, Charles Fontayne and William Porter took eight whole-plate (6.5 × 8.5 inch) daguerreotypes that offered a panoramic view of some two miles of Cincinnati's waterfront. Five years later, William Shew produced a spectacular five-part daguerreotype panorama of San Francisco's harbor. Contemporaries understood such visual productions in the context of the prevailing popular appeal of larger artistic and theatrical panoramic illusions that drew crowds to rotunda paintings and moving panoramas.

Similarly, from the invention of the medium, photographers carried their cameras (and portable darkrooms) to the tops of hills and tall buildings to record expansive landscape vistas. On October 13, 1860, two years after French photographer Nadar first attempted true aerial photography in a tethered balloon over Paris, James Black (1825–1896) took an aerial view of Boston from the basket of Samuel King's hot air balloon *Queen of the Air*. Seeing familiar landmarks in this first aerial view of an American city moved Oliver Wendell Holmes to exclaim, "Boston, as the eagle and the wild goose see it, is a very different object from the same place as the solid citizen looks up at its eaves and chimneys" (1863, 12). It was, indeed, a very different way to see the world, to situate oneself on the face of the earth, and to represent and understand urban form. Black's photograph shows curving narrow streets lined with five- and six-story buildings, a jumble of facades and rooftops, and a bewildering array of windows and chimneys, skylights and dormers, with the church spire of the Old South Meeting House in the foreground and the waterfront piers of the harbor in the distance. This view of Boston, "as the eagle and the wild goose see it," furnished visual facts about the physical layout and cultural fabric of the city. More important, it gave a spiritual dimension to the view from "on high," allowing viewers not just to "read" the city but to rise above their earth-bound existence and partake of a "God's-eye" view of the earth, associated with authority and omniscience (Cosgrove and Fox 2010; Amad 2012).

In 1856, George Fardon published *San Francisco Album: Photographs of the Most Beautiful Views and Public Buildings of San Francisco.* Considered the earliest published photographic record of an American city, it used a carefully crafted combination of word and image to generate a visual narrative popular with nineteenth-century audiences. The format would later serve as a model for a genre of promotional city-view books (Fardon 1856; Fardon 1999; Schwartz 1999). Like Timothy O'Sullivan's survey photographs of the American West (Kelsey 2007), Fardon's photographs were "never meant to stand as independent works of art" (Sandweiss 2002, 184); rather, they required explication in terms of presentational form, order, accompanying text, and related documents. Similarly, stereoscopic views issued in series, when read collectively, carried impressions of place. "America in the Stereoscope," the first series of "New World views" published by the London Stereoscopic Co., allowed "hundreds of thousands in Great Britain who are continually hearing of the grandeur and beauty of scenery in the United States and Canada . . . a chance of examining its peculiar marvels and graces" (1860, 221). Cataloged and numbered, labeled on the recto and with letterpress descriptions on the verso (figure 13.5), the views, read as a series, conjured an Edenic vision of the New World (Schwartz 2011). In July 1860, a review published in the *Art-Journal* (London) boldly claimed,

> The photograph, however, cannot deceive; in nothing can it extenuate; there is no power in this marvelous machine either to add to or take from; we know that what we see *must* be TRUE. So guided, therefore, we can travel over all the countries of the world, without moving a yard from our own firesides. . . . The series of stereoscopic views recently brought under our notice by the London Stereoscopic Co.—taken in various parts of Canada and the United States—bring us, as far as they go, into closer and safer acquaintance with the New World than all the books that have been written on the subject. . . . It is indeed impossible to over-rate the debt we owe for so much of pleasure and of information. ("America in the Stereoscope" 1860, 221)

The review made the role of photographs abundantly clear: they offered the vicarious experience of place. As a source of both information and pleasure, they provided facts but also aroused emotions. Functioning as both education and entertainment, the London Stereoscopic Co.'s series did not simply show—more important, it constructed—ideas about North American reality.

Through this variety of visual discourses—the panoramic discourse of the multiple-plate wide-angle view, the panoptic discourse of the aerial view, the narrative discourse of the photographic album or series of stereoscopic views—photographs performed their work, documenting and promoting, confirming and celebrating urban development, public architecture, and city streetscapes. Each had its own appeal and rhetorical effect; each possessed a particular strength for conveying factual information, on the one hand, and for generating emotional response, on the other.

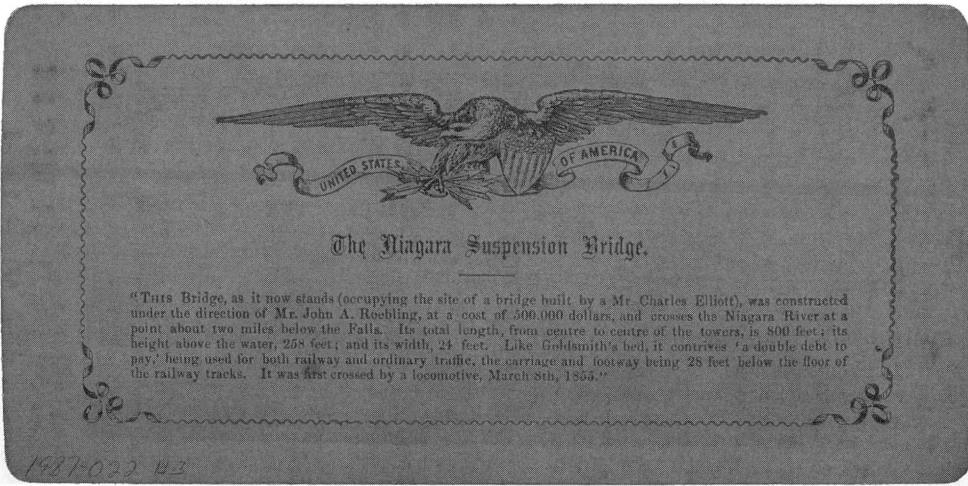

UNITED STATES OF AMERICA

The Niagara Suspension Bridge.

"This Bridge, as it now stands (occupying the site of a bridge built by a Mr. Charles Elliott), was constructed under the direction of Mr. John A. Roebling, at a cost of 500.000 dollars, and crosses the Niagara River at a point about two miles below the Falls. Its total length, from centre to centre of the towers, is 800 feet; its height above the water, 258 feet; and its width, 24 feet. Like Goldsmith's bed, it contrives 'a double debt to pay,' being used for both railway and ordinary traffic, the carriage and footway being 28 feet below the floor of the railway tracks. It was first crossed by a locomotive, March 8th, 1855."

Figure 13.5. Each view in "America in the Stereoscope" was accompanied by "a brief but carefully written description, giving such particulars as are requisite for a complete comprehension of the theme, in its grandeur, or its beauty, or its combination of both" (from the letterpress text on the back of the card mount of #18). *The Niagara Suspension Bridge* framed how the individual scene was to be viewed and understood—through reference to the great engineer who designed it, its considerable cost, geographical location, physical dimensions, and twofold utilitarian service, and the relative recency of its inaugural use. However, situated within the context of the company's promotional catalog, other images, and verso texts, this view contributed to an overall narrative about the New World. Albumen prints on cardboard mount, PA-200389 (recto); PA-200390 (verso). Digital image courtesy of Library and Archives Canada.

PHOTOGRAPHIC ODYSSEYS: PICTURING NINETEENTH-CENTURY NORTH AMERICA

In nineteenth-century North America, photographs served as purveyors of information. They were gathered and used as proof of opportunities to pursue or obstacles to avoid. They generated raw, incontrovertible facts upon which to make informed decisions—about boundary placement, territorial expansion, resource extraction, rail routes, settlement, and land use. But photographic images also aroused emotions, fueled arguments, stirred controversies, bolstered resolve, and shaped and reshaped attitudes to landscape and notions of place.

In the process of "picturing North America," photographers were complicit in government and corporate efforts to gloss over the long history of human presence in the Yosemite Valley, around Yellowstone, and throughout the lands of the American Southwest (Sandweiss 2002). Used to picture and confirm the erasure, both visual and physical, of Native Americans from the lands of the trans-Mississippi, the photographic record they created mirrors the interwoven stories of the advance of white civilization and the decline of native populations, which nurtured the myth of the virgin land and the vanishing race and sustained the metaphor of the West as frontier and future. From Timothy O'Sullivan's *Ancient Ruins in the Cañon de Chelly, New Mexico* (figure 13.6), to a group photograph of Navajo on the Long Walk of 1864, to views of the Lakota dead at Wounded Knee, images presented indigenous peoples as long gone or soon to disappear. Collectible mass-produced carte-de-visite likenesses of "native types," portraits of the vanquished of the Indian Wars, souvenirs of Wild West show performers, and Edward Sheriff Curtis's (1907–1930) "North American Indian" project portrayed Native Americans, often simultaneously, as primitive and noble, savage and dangerous, docile and quaint. Beyond recording costumes and customs, such photographs formed part of how North America's past, present, and future landscapes were explained and envisioned, pictured and narrated. Indeed, the myriad ways in which the colonialist gaze objectified and subjugated the indigenous peoples of North America constitute a rich, important, and painful topic, far broader and more complex than this chapter can address.

Careful study of nineteenth-century photographic images and the geographical imaginings they expressed and generated "in their own time" has much to add to historical geographies of North America. The examples presented in this chapter are, as noted at the outset, highly selective. Chosen primarily to pique curiosity, they stem from the first decades of photography, the years of the daguerreotype and wet-plate processes when photography was anything but a casual or spontaneous undertaking. Clearly, a number of topics are conspicuous by their absence here. I have not touched upon the spatial glue and social significance of portrait photography during this period of massive immigration and westward migration; nor have I introduced the geographical consequences of tourist photography at a time of improved transportation and increased global and transcontinental travel. Also left unexamined are the extensive photographic archives of the surveys, construction, and completion of the Union Pacific, Central Pacific, Canadian Pacific, and other railways. Even within the examples noted here, there are many more issues to pursue from a geographical perspective,

Figure 13.6. Timothy O'Sullivan's *Ancient Ruins in the Cañon de Chelly, New Mexico, in a Niche 50 Feet above Present Cañon Bed, 1873* is another icon of nineteenth-century American photography, but we must not conflate aesthetic quality and public meaning. Read against repeated discussion of "numerous and interesting ruins of habitations of extinct tribes" in Wheeler's survey reports and descriptive legends in albums issued under the imprint of the War Department, U.S. Army Corps of Engineers, O'Sullivan's view of the abandoned cliff dwellings of the Anasazi played an integral role in a government narrative about a landscape rich in resources, emptied of indigenous peoples, and awaiting prospective settlers and westward expansion. Library of Congress, LC-DIG-ppmsca-10055 (full mount). Digital image courtesy of the Library of Congress.

notably the relationship between survey photographers and landscape artists (Goldfarb 2009; Jackson 1989), between photographic and other forms of graphic representation (Cosgrove 2008; Kelsey 2007; Harley 2001), and between word and image. Distinct changes in photographic production, physical form, and social function with the improved photographic technology of the dry-plate process of the 1870s and widespread distribution of photographs that came with the advent of photomechanical reproduction in the late 1880s only serve to complicate the picture further.

This discussion also suggests that, just as photography is an integral part of the historical geographies of North America, a historical geography of nineteenth-century photography in North America remains unwritten. Writing it would entail tracing three interwoven geographical odysseys: one would follow the creation and circulation of photographic images; another would focus on the wanderings of pioneer photographers; a third would track the spread of photographic technology and practice. These odysseys are key to understanding the influence visual images once wielded and how we now value them. Created in one place, nineteenth-century photographs have passed through many hands, circulated alone or in close physical proximity to words or maps or other visual images, and ultimately come to rest in a public institution or private collection in another part of the country or the world. The odyssey of their makers also unfolds as a complex story of social and geographical mobility. Some photographers were itinerant portrait and view takers, traveling with portable darkrooms or in specially outfitted railcars with all the equipment and paraphernalia of the wet-collodion era. Others, equally burdened, covered thousands of miles on horseback, by canoe, by covered wagon or Red River cart, or by foot with government exploring expeditions, boundary commissions, and geological surveys. Similarly, the odyssey of photographic image-making technologies, processes, and practices was intimately linked to the state of transportation and communication, the spread of print culture, the demographics of demand, and the accessibility of know-how, equipment, and supplies.

These odysseys help us to understand how, in nineteenth-century North America, photographers and their clients employed images in historically significant ways and with geographically significant consequences. Enlisted in support of scientific investigations, artistic endeavors, international diplomacy, government administration, political ends, economic initiatives, and social change, photographs functioned in two distinct but allied ways. As visual information gathered through optical-chemical means, they commanded the authority of "on-the-spot" observation; as such, viewers embraced them as trustworthy and as furnishing purportedly objective facts. Simultaneously, photographic facts were invested with meaning, carried symbolic weight, and aroused strong emotions; their content was freighted with time-bound implications, and the technological means of production, circulation, viewing, use, and reuse circumscribed their impact. These odysseys—of photographic images, photographic image makers, and photographic image-making technologies—are, quite clearly, closely related. Retrieved from the outer edges of scholarly enterprise, their narratives of spatial and temporal displacement furnish the larger contexts for interrogating the contribution of photographic "images and imaginings" to the growth of "imagined communities" and of "science and sentiment" to the production of geographical knowledge, to the perception of space, the construction of place, and the experience of landscape in nineteenth-century North America.

REFERENCES

Amad, Paula. 2012. From God's-Eye to Camera-Eye: Aerial Photography's Post-humanist and Neo-humanist Visions of the World. *History of Photography* 36, no. 1: 66–86.

America in the Stereoscope. 1860. *Art-Journal* (July): 221.

American Philosophical Society. 2013. Abbot-Charnay Photograph Collection, 1859–1882. American Philosophical Society. http://www.amphilsoc.org/mole/view?docId=ead/Mss.913.72.Ab23-ea d.xml (accessed May 24, 2013).

Anderson, Benedict. 1991. *Imagined Communities: Reflections on the Origin and Spread of Nationalism*. Rev. ext. ed. London: Verso.

Antietam Reproduced. 1862. *New York Times*, October 6.

Berger, John. [1974] 1980. Understanding a Photograph. In *The Look of Things: Selected Essays and Articles*. New York: Viking Press; reprinted in *Classic Essays on Photography*, edited by Alan Trachtenberg, 291–94. New Haven, CT: Leete's Island Books.

Brady's Photographs; Pictures of the Dead at Antietam. 1862. *New York Times*, October 20.

Brunet, François. 2007. L'Entreprise américaine de Désiré Charnay. In *"Le Yucatán est ailleurs": expéditions photographiques (1857–1886) de Désiré Charnay*, edited by Désiré Charnay and Christine Barthe, 10–23. Paris: Actes Sud.

Carvalho, Solomon Nunes. [1858] 2004. *Incidents of Travel and Adventure in the Far West with Colonel Fremont's Last Expedition across the Rocky Mountains: Including Three Months' Residence in Utah, and a Perilous Trip across the Great American Desert to the Pacific*. New York: Derby and Jackson; rpt. ed., Lincoln: University of Nebraska Press.

Catherwood, Frederick. 1844. *Views of Ancient Monuments in Central America, Chiapas and Yucatán*, by F. Catherwood. London: F. Catherwood.

Charnay, Claude-Joseph Désiré. 1862–1863. *Cités et ruines américaines: Mitla, Palenqué, Izamal, Chichen-Itza, Uxmal*. Paris: Gide.

Charnay, Claude-Joseph Désiré, and Christine Barthe. 2007. *"Le Yucatán est ailleurs": expéditions photographiques (1857–1886) de Désiré Charnay*. Paris: Actes Sud.

Cosgrove, Denis E. 2008. *Geography and Vision*. London: IB Tauris.

Cosgrove, Denis E., and William L. Fox. 2010. *Photography and Flight*. London: Reaktion.

Curtis, Edward Sheriff. 1907–1930. *The North American Indian: Being a Series of Volumes Picturing and Describing the Indians of the United States, and Alaska/Written, Illustrated, and Published by Edward S. Curtis; Edited by Frederick Webb Hodge, Foreword by Theodore Roosevelt; Field Research Conducted under the Patronage of J. Pierpont Morgan*. Seattle, WA, and Cambridge, MA: E. S. Curtis and University Press.

Davis, Keith F. 1981. *Désiré Charnay: Expeditionary Photographer*. Albuquerque: University of New Mexico Press.

Demhardt, Imre Josef. 2012. An Approximation to a Bird's Eye View, and Is Intelligible to Every Eye [. . .] Friedrich Wilhelm von Egloffstein, the Exploration of the American West, and Its First Relief Shaded Maps. In *History of Cartography: International Symposium of the ICA Commission, 2010*, no. 6: 57–74.

Edwards, Elizabeth. 2001. Professor Huxley's "Well Considered Plan." In *Raw Histories: Photographs, Anthropology and Museums*, 131–56. Oxford: Berg.

Fardon, George Robinson. 1856. *San Francisco Album: Photographs of the Most Beautiful Views and Public Buildings of San Francisco*. San Francisco: Herre and Bauer.

———. 1999. *San Francisco Album: Photographs 1854–1856*. San Francisco: Chronicle Books/Fraenkel Gallery.

Fine Arts. 1862. *New York Times*, December 12.

Fischer-Westhauser, Ulla. 2007. Emanuel von Friedrichsthal: The First Daguerreotypist in Yucatán. *Photoresearcher* 10 (August): 9–16.

Frémont, John Charles. [1886] 1887. *Memoirs of My Life: Including in the Narrative Five Journeys of Western Exploration during the Years 1842, 1843–4, 1845–6–7, 1848–9, 1853–4.* Chicago and New York: Belford, Clark and Co.

Frizot, Michel, ed. 1998. *A New History of Photography.* Köln: Konemann.

Galassi, Peter. 1981. *Before Photography: Painting and the Invention of Photography.* New York: Museum of Modern Art.

Goldfarb, Hilliard T., ed. 2009. *Expanding Horizons: Painting and Photography of American and Canadian Landscape, 1860–1918.* Montreal: Montreal Museum of Fine Arts.

Hales, Peter Bacon. 1984. *Silver Cities: The Photography of American Urbanization, 1839–1915.* Philadelphia: Temple University Press.

Harley, J. B. 2001. *The New Nature of Maps: Essays in the History of Cartography,* edited by Paul Laxton. Baltimore: Johns Hopkins University Press.

Hind, Henry Youle. 1859. *North-West Territory: Reports of Progress, Together with a Preliminary and General Report on the Assiniboine and Saskatchewan Exploring Expedition, Made under Instructions from the Provincial Secretary, Canada.* Toronto: Printed by John Lovell.

———. 1860. *Narrative of the Canadian Red River Exploring Expedition of 1857 and of the Assiniboine and Saskatchewan Exploring Expedition of 1858.* 2 vols. London: Longman, Green, Longman and Roberts.

Hoelscher, Steven. 1998. The Photographic Construction of Tourist Space in Victorian America. *Geographical Review* 88, no. 4 (October): 548–70.

———. 2008a. *Picturing Indians: Photographic Encounters and Tourist Fantasies in H. H. Bennett's Wisconsin Dells.* Studies in American Thought and Culture Series. Madison: University of Wisconsin Press.

———. 2008b. Viewing the Gilded Age River: Photography and Tourism along the Wisconsin Dells. In *Rivers in History: Perspectives on Waterways in Europe and North America,* edited by Christof Mauch and Thomas Zeller, 149–71. Pittsburgh, PA: University of Pittsburgh Press.

Holmes, Oliver Wendell. 1863. Doings of the Sunbeam. *Atlantic Monthly* 12 (July). http://www.gutenberg.org/files/15016/15016-h/15016-h.htm#sunbeam.

Huyda, Richard J. 1975. *Camera in the Interior, 1858: H. L. Hime, Photographer. The Assiniboine and Saskatchewan Exploring Expedition.* Toronto: Coach House Press.

Jackson, Christopher E. 1989. *With Lens and Brush: Images of the Western Canadian Landscape, 1845–1890.* Calgary: Glenbow Museum.

Kelsey, Robin. 2007. *Archive Style: Photographs and Illustrations for U.S. Surveys, 1850–1890.* Berkeley: University of California Press.

Krygier, J. B. 1997. Envisioning the American West: Maps, the Representational Barrage of 19th Century Expedition Reports, and the Production of Scientific Knowledge. *Cartography and Geographic Information Systems* 24, no. 1: 27–50.

Les monuments de l'Yucatan, par M. le Chevalier Emmanuel de Friederichsthal. 1841. *Nouvelles Annales des Voyages et des Sciences Géographiques* 92: 291–314.

Lyden, Anne M. 2003. *Railroad Vision: Photography, Travel, and Perception.* Los Angeles, CA: J. Paul Getty Museum.

Martins, Susana S. 2010. Between Present and Past: Photographic Portugal of the 1950s. In *Time and Photography,* edited by Jan Baetens, Alexander Streitberger, and Hilde Van Gelder, 85–101. Leuven, Belgium: Leuven University Press.

Naef, Weston. 2008. *Carleton Watkins in Yosemite.* Los Angeles, CA: J. Paul Getty Museum.

Naef, Weston, and Christine Hult-Lewis. 2011. *Carleton Watkins: The Complete Mammoth Photographs.* Los Angeles, CA: J. Paul Getty Museum.
Nickel, Douglas R. 1999. *Carleton Watkins: The Art of Perception.* San Francisco: San Francisco Museum of Modern Art.
Palmquist, Peter E. 1983. *Carleton E. Watkins: Photographer of the American West.* Albuquerque: University of New Mexico Press.
Palmquist, Peter E., and Thomas R. Kailbourn. 2000. *Pioneer Photographers of the Far West: A Biographical Dictionary, 1840–1865.* Stanford, CA: Stanford University Press.
Root, Marcus Aurelius. 1864. *The Camera and the Pencil: Or the Heliographic Art, Its Theory and Practice in All Its Various Branches; e.g. Daguerreotypy, Photography, &c.; Together with Its History in the United States and in Europe; Being At Once a Theoretical and Practical Treatise, and Designed Alike, as a Text-Book and a Hand-Book.* Philadelphia: M. A. Root and J. B. Lippincott.
Rosenheim, Jeff. 2013. *Photography and the American Civil War.* New Haven, CT: Yale University Press.
Rosti, Pál. 1861. *Uti Emlékezetek Americkából.* Pest: Kiadja Gusztáv Hekcenast.
Said, Edward W. 1993. *Culture and Imperialism.* New York: Vintage.
Sandweiss, Martha A. 2002. *Print the Legend: Photography and the American West.* New Haven, CT: Yale University Press.
Sandweiss, Martha A., Rick Stewart, and Ben W. Huseman. 1989. *Eyewitness to War: Prints and Daguerreotypes of the Mexican War, 1846–1848.* Washington, D.C., and Fort Worth, TX: Smithsonian Institution Press and Amon Carter Museum.
Schwartz, Joan M. 1999. Narrative and Illusion: Harnessing the Visual Imagination. In *San Francisco Album: Photographs 1854–1856,* edited by George Robinson Fardon. San Francisco: Chronicle Books/Fraenkel Gallery.
———. [2000] 2006. "Records of Simple Truth and Precision": Photography, Archives, and the Illusion of Control. *Archivaria* 50 (Fall): 1–40; reprinted in *Archives, Documentation, and Institutions of Social Memory: Essays from the Sawyer Seminar,* edited by Francis X. Blouin and William G. Rosenberg, 61–80. Ann Arbor: University of Michigan Press.
———. 2003a. More Than "Competent Description of an Intractably Empty Landscape": A Strategy for Critical Engagement with Historical Photographs. *Historical Geography* 31: 105–30.
———. 2003b. Photographs from the Edge of Empire. In *Cultural Geography in Practice,* edited by Alison Blunt, Pyrs Gruffudd, Jon May, Miles Ogborn, and David Pinder, 154–71. London: Arnold, 2003.
———. 2007. Photographic Reflections: Nature, Landscape, and Environment. *Environmental History* 12, no. 4 (October): 966–93.
———. 2011. The Archival Garden: Photographic Plantings, Interpretive Choices, and Alternative Narratives. In *Controlling the Past: Documenting Society and Institutions: Essays in Honor of Helen Willa Samuels,* edited by Terry Cook, 69–110. Chicago: Society of American Archivists.
Shlaer, Robert. 2000. *Sights Once Seen: Daguerreotyping Frémont's Last Expedition through the Rockies.* Santa Fe: Museum of New Mexico Press.
Sloan, Dorothy. 2013. "Lot 515. ROSTI, Pál. *Uti Emlékezetek Americkából.* Pest: Kiadja Gusztáv Heckenast, 1861." Dorothy Sloan Books, Auction 23. http://www.dsloan.com/Auctions/A23/item-rosti-uti_emlekezetek-1861.html (accessed May 24, 2013).
Solomon-Godeau, Abigail. 1991. *Photography at the Dock: Essays on Photographic History, Institutions, and Practices.* Minneapolis: University of Minnesota Press.
Stephens, John Lloyd. 1843. *Incidents of Travel in Yucatan.* 2 vols. London and New York: John Murray and Harper and Brothers.

Taft, Robert. [1938] 1964. *Photography and the American Scene: A Social History, 1838–1889*. New York: Macmillan; rpt. ed., New York: Dover.

Tucker, Jennifer. 2006. *Nature Exposed: Photography as Eye Witness in Victorian Science*. Baltimore: Johns Hopkins University Press.

Wallis, Brian. 1995. Black Bodies, White Science: Louis Agassiz's Slave Daguerreotypes. *American Art* 9, no. 2: 38–61.

Wheeler, George Montague. 1875a. *Photographs Showing Landscapes, Geological, and Other Features of Portions of the Western Territory of the United States, Obtained in Connection with Geographical and Geological Explorations and Surveys West of the 100th Meridian, Seasons of 1871, 1872, and 1873*. Washington, D.C.: War Department, Corps of Engineers, U.S. Army.

———. 1875b. *Report upon Geographical and Geological Explorations and Surveys West of the One Hundredth Meridian in Charge of First Lieut. Geo. M. Wheeler . . . under the Direction of the Chief of Engineers, U.S. Army. Published by Authority of . . . the Secretary of War in Accordance with Acts of Congress of June 23, 1874, and February 15, 1875. In Six Volumes, Accompanied by One Topographical and One Geological Atlas*. Vol. 3: *Geology*. Washington, D.C.: Engineer Department, U.S. Army.

———. 1879. *Report upon United States Geographical Surveys West of the One Hundredth Meridian in Charge of First Lieut. Geo. M. Wheeler . . . under the Direction of the Chief of Engineers, U.S. Army. Published by Authority of . . . the Secretary of War in Accordance with Acts of Congress of June 23, 1874, and February 15, 1875. In Seven Volumes, Accompanied by One Topographical and One Geological Atlas*. Vol. 7: *Archaeology*. Washington, D.C.: Engineer Department, U.S. Army.

Whitney, Josiah D. 1871. *The Yosemite Guide-Book: A Description of the Yosemite Valley and the Adjacent Region of the Sierra Nevada, and of the Big Trees of California, with Two Maps*. Cambridge, MA: University Press.

Wyckoff, William, and Lary M. Dilsaver. 1997. Promotional Imagery of Glacier National Park. *Geographical Review* 87, no. 1: 1–26.

Wynn, Graeme. 1987. Forging a Canadian Nation. In *North America: The Historical Geography of a Changing Continent*, edited by Robert D. Mitchell and Paul A. Groves, 373–409. Lanham, MD: Rowman & Littlefield.

Zeller, Suzanne. 1987. *Inventing Canada: Early Victorian Science and the Idea of a Transcontinental Nation.* Toronto: University of Toronto Press.

14

Making Mythic Landscapes

Kevin Blake

North America has always occupied a special place in the geographical imagination. For the indigenous peoples who have lived here for thousands of years, the homeland is a mythic landscape, elemental to a worldview and symbolically represented by natural landmarks (Jett 1995; Blake 2001a; Lane [1988] 2002). For European adventurers and explorers, the promise of a northwest passage (Tuan 1977; Quinn 1997) or a Garden of Eden (Denevan 1992; Cronon 1996) assumed mythic proportions. After European settlement, myths continued on the land, whether in the vision of America as home to rugged, individualistic pioneers (Mitchell 2001) or Canada's legend of virginal forest (Samuels 1979). Of course, some dominant myths proved stunningly false—most notably, the idea that the land, prior to European contact, had been largely uninhabited and ecologically pristine (J. B. Wright 2003).

What is a "mythic landscape"? The study of these landscapes began in historical geography with John K. Wright's 1947 essay describing the lure of the unknown and coining the term "geosophy" to refer to the study of the world as people imagine it. Stephen Daniels and Denis Cosgrove define landscape as "a cultural image, a pictorial way of representing, structuring, or symbolizing surroundings" (1988, 1). They argue that we see landscapes but also imagine them through paintings and poetry, for example. A mythic landscape is a type of imagined landscape, a symbolic landscape imprinted in the mind as much as on the ground (Meinig 1979a). Myths are amorphous and may be difficult to articulate; thus a landscape may be mythic without a person being able to describe exactly what makes it so. It may be a feeling, a belief just outside the mind's grasp, buried deep within the cultural subconscious that transforms a landscape into something mythic. Indeed, "in the most basic sense, myth that is understood is no longer myth" (Lane [1988] 2002, 24). J. B. Wright captures the problematic nature of myth: "Myths are things that never were but always are. . . . Myths arise whenever needed" (2003, 86). One might add that they arise wherever needed as well.

Two basic types of mythic landscapes arise from the true-false dialectic of myth. With the assertion that a myth is false, a mythic landscape becomes "a fuzzy area of defective knowledge," only loosely tied to the realities of historical geography (Tuan 1977, 86; Pringle 1988). Conversely, we may perceive myths not as falsehoods but rather as "stories drawn from history, that have acquired through usage over many generations a symbolizing function that is central to the cultural functioning of the society that produces them" (Slotkin 1985, 16). Conceptualizing myths as stories leaves undiminished their significance for understanding landscape in Native American communities (Kelley and Francis 1994; Francaviglia 2003; Reinhardt 2003). With this outlook, a mythic landscape is a powerful spatial construct, very much alive and real to its believers, with deep cultural meaning (Blake 1999).

Consider, for example, the mythic landscape of Monument Valley along the Arizona-Utah border (figure 14.1). Monumental landforms often become enduring places that speak to humanity (Tuan 1977). According to Robert Riley, Monument Valley extends a merely visible landscape into one that is visceral and "richer and more personal . . . the mythic setting for Native Americans and cowboys—and the Marlboro Man" (1997, 207). Monument Valley also illustrates

Figure 14.1. West Mitten Butte is the most iconic landform of the mythic Monument Valley landscape along the Arizona-Utah state line. Already mythic in Navajo nation lore, the area garnered worldwide fame through Hollywood films, beginning with *The Vanishing American* in 1925 (based on the Zane Grey book of the same name) and then the John Ford and John Wayne westerns, such as *Stagecoach* (1939) and *She Wore a Yellow Ribbon* (1949). Photo by the author, June 2007.

the ebb and flow of myth and reality. A person who has seen this place only in film could easily envision it with defective knowledge; for instance, the name Monument Valley might generate the assumption that the area is a low point instead of having an average elevation of five thousand feet above sea level. Whether seen in person or in film, this same landscape evokes the longest-lived and most dominant of American myths: that of the frontier (Slotkin 1985; Vale 2005). Furthermore, this mesa-and-butte landscape is such a familiar backdrop in the westerns of film and fiction that it represents the quintessential West (Blake 1995).

At the same time, however, Monument Valley is a spiritual mythic landscape in the worldview of the Navajo, the people who administer the tribal park that encompasses the iconic landforms. Mythic landscapes often spring from religion because they provide a context for interpretations of our existence, for our perception of reality (Olmanson 2007). In a Native American context, the sacred story of creation reinforces the mythic power of certain landscapes (Blake 2001b; Farmer 2008). Myth is central to the making of a sacred landscape like Monument Valley because it brings people closer to their spiritual understanding by evoking supernatural beings (Jett 1995; Lane [1988] 2002).

Thus, the concept of a mythic landscape is neither new nor unique to North America, but it may endure over many centuries and through great upheaval (della Dora 2011). Myths manifest and perpetuate themselves in many cultures through the landscape, an arena that is witness to "continued and even renewed fascination with myth" (Cosgrove 1994, 394). The tentacles of myth reach deep into the land; even in the face of meticulous scientific rationalism, myths remain as rooted as religion (Stegner 1954).

To assess and illustrate the significance of mythic landscapes, this chapter explores the processes and ideologies that contribute to their making. What gives them form and meaning? How do time and space shape them? Where are some of the most powerful or enduring mythic landscapes in North America? I include examples from various regions but forego attempts to be all-inclusive due to the cultural and temporal fluidity of the mythic landscape concept. I focus on the United States since American identity intertwines with national mythology much more so there than in Canada (Brown 1997). Canada also lacks the myth of occupying a bountiful land, which is a pervasive component of the national myth of the United States (Shortridge 1989; Wynn 2001). Within the United States, though, I draw most of the examples from the American West, arguably a mythic region beyond compare (Smith 1950; Athearn 1986).

SHAPING MYTHIC LANDSCAPES

Though mythic landscapes are a particular type of landscape, landscapes are not equal in their ability to evoke myth. A mythic landscape is not just an imaginary construct projected onto earth; it is a place transformed into myth (Schama 1995). Natural places, or those perceived as naturalistic, are at the core of many mythic landscapes. The Arcadian myth that emphasizes nature's spiritual over its economic value and laments the loss of human connection to nature in the modern world is a staple of the American landscape (Schmitt 1969). Nature is the primary source of mythic awe, in part due to the incomparable power of storms and floods that reduce human activities and structures to comparatively inconsequential "scratching on the skins of Mother Earth" (Meinig 1979b, 34). Nature myths have an indelible quality because natural elements, such as rock, soil, water, and wood, imbue the stories with a sense of permanence that is central to a landscape of myth (Schama 1995; della Dora 2011) (figure 14.2). This permanence comes from how we metaphorically talk about natural landscapes, using phrases like "rock of ages" and "everlasting hills," and from how we build structures of permanence with rock, soil, and wood (Meinig 1979b; Blake and Smith 2000).

A built environment may be mythic as well, be it a skyscraper, suburb, or the Statue of Liberty (Domosh 1994; Duncan and Duncan 2001; Hoskins 2006). Las Vegas, Nevada, for instance, is intentionally the most mythic of American cities (Raento 2003). Mythic landscapes are more common, however, in wild landscapes like the Grand Canyon that we perceive as both a natural and a cultural resource, a duality that is "intimately bound up with the American

Figure 14.2. Natural elements, such as rock, soil, water, and wood, capture the human imagination and are central to the concept of mythic landscapes. At Redwood National Park, California, where the tallest trees in the world soar more than three hundred feet overhead, nature is at its most awesome. Photo by the author, June 2010.

creation myth and American exceptionalism and the human stewardship of nature everywhere'' (Pyne 1998, 154). Indeed, any vestiges of civilization can be problematic to the conception of a mythic landscape, as witnessed by the adage, ''Where the pavement ends, the West begins'' (Goin and Starrs 2005, 12). Wild animals contribute to mythic landscapes too. What would the Alaskan wilderness be without grizzlies, the Northwoods without wolves, the Great Plains without buffalo (figure 14.3), or the Everglades without alligators and crocodiles (McPhee 1977; Lopez 1978; Goetzmann and Goetzmann 1986; Grunwald 2006)?

Authenticity is also necessary in mythic landscapes. Interpretations sponsored by governmental authorities help trigger authenticity even in contrived landscapes, such as Bodie, California, or Santa Fe, New Mexico, thus opening the door to other values (DeLyser 1999; Wilson 1997). Western cinema aspires to historical authenticity and utilizes mythic landscapes for filming locations to that end (Hausladen 2003). Conversely, at Denali National Park the park service utilizes inauthenticity to achieve cultural hegemony and legitimacy with respect to visitor interactions and experiences (Palka 2000).

Mythic landscapes and memory go hand in hand, with myth organizing social memory into a concept that teaches society about itself (Sopher 1979; Slotkin 1985; DeLyser 2005). Race, ethnicity, and gender, however, expose the lie of a mythic landscape with universal meaning (Schein 2006). Myths perpetuate memories that a dominant culture may document, monumentalize, or otherwise commemorate; yet, the imprint of myth in landscapes results in an often contested

Figure 14.3. A buffalo bull (American bison) grazing on the shortgrass prairie completes the image of a mythic Great Plains landscape at Theodore Roosevelt National Park, North Dakota. Photo by the author, June 2003.

reality (Harvey 1979; Foote 1997; Olsen 2012). Consider the sharply divided cultural contrasts in the resonance of these iconic American landscapes: Plymouth Rock, the Alamo, Little Bighorn, Pearl Harbor, Mount Rushmore, Manzanar, Selma, and Wounded Knee. Racist stereotypes, such as the noble savage, vanishing American, and mystical shaman, fuel some mythic landscapes (Reinhardt 2003). The exploits of women who challenged the myth of mountaineering as a purely male pursuit contribute to the meaning of Longs Peak, Colorado, as a mythic landscape (Morin 2003). Mythic landscapes may be culturally inclusive, such as memorials on the National Mall, but others may be exclusive, such as the western landscape as constructed by cinematic myth that left women, Mexicans, Native Americans, and Mormons out of the "pantheon of heroes" (Hausladen 2003, 300).

It is not necessary to touch a landscape in order to believe it mythic, but people must represent and disseminate the myth in some symbolic form tied to a place, such as with art, photography, or literature. Even though a mythic landscape is a cultural phenomenon, an individual has the power to shape one through envisioning, designing, articulating, or expressing an ideal (Samuels 1979). Visual imagery is particularly potent in expressing and reinforcing mythic landscapes. The use of nature as the subject of the landscape paintings by American artists of the Hudson River School, for example, guaranteed originality compared to European subjects and helped cast nature as the central element in national identity (Schuyler 1995). These paintings taught a nation what a mythic landscape should be. Painters Albert Bierstadt and Thomas Moran popularized the myths of the American West with sweeping canvases depicting the region as an unspoiled Arcadian wonderland that reduces people to insignificant foreground features revering nature's magnificence (Goetzmann and Goetzmann 1986; Blake 1995). Thomas Moran's iconic triptych of *Grand Canyon of the Yellowstone* (1872), *Chasm of the Colorado* (1874), and *Mountain of the Holy Cross* (1875) idealized rather than replicated nature, rearranging features to express a transcendental truth within the context of national identity (Pyne 1998; Blake 2008) (figure 14.4). Additional examples of visual imagery shaping mythic landscapes include how film director John Sayles demythologized the Mexican American borderland in *Lone Star* (Arreola 2005) and how Frida Kahlo juxtaposed tension and harmony in the same mythic landscape with her painting *Self-Portrait on the Border Line between Mexico and the United States* (Pankl and Blake 2012).

Photographs add a sense of realism and immediacy to landscapes, imbuing place with a cultural code for understanding landscape (Schwartz 2007). The common and idealized views of picture postcards are among the most powerful photographs in terms of shaping place imagery (Arreola 2001; Jakle 2003; DeBres and Sowers 2009). Postcards and other visual representations have the ability to miniaturize and harmonize scenery, conveying landscapes in visual totality. The postcard image is mobile and thus may shape geographical imaginations far from the source, magnifying its iconicity (della Dora 2011). Postcards, though, are not "innocent documents or perfect facsimiles of the environment" (Youngs 2011,

Figure 14.4. Mount of the Holy Cross, Colorado, was made mythic in part by the visual representations of the peak in William Henry Jackson's photographs, Thomas Moran's paintings, and thousands of postcards, such as this one manufactured by the Detroit Photographic Co. Though the copyright date indicates 1898, this lithographic postcard with an undivided back was likely produced in 1901 based on the stock number. Moran's 1875 oil painting *Mountain of the Holy Cross*, itself a fanciful view of the mountain landscape, is cropped for this postcard image. From the author's collection.

138). They are the product of a complex production process that not only manipulates the image to achieve an idealized landscape but also mythologizes nature for a wide audience (Youngs 2012).

Mythic landscapes also take shape from the words used to describe them, including place names (toponyms) and evocative metaphors, such as "river of grass" in the Everglades or "buffalo commons" in the Great Plains (Douglas 1947; Popper and Popper 1999; Lopez and Gwartney 2006). Literature thus provides context for the form and process of making mythic landscapes and, most important, for their cultural meaning (Salter and Lloyd 1977). The concept of the place-defining novel, a work by a popular novelist employing lively and memorable prose that defines how Americans imagine landscapes, illustrates the power of fiction to shape mythic landscapes. Examples of novels with mythic landscape overtones include Margaret Mitchell's *Gone with the Wind*, Sinclair Lewis's *Main Street*, William Faulkner's *Absalom, Absalom!*, Erskine Caldwell's *Tobacco Road*, Gene Stratton-Porter's *Freckles*, John Steinbeck's *The Grapes of Wrath*, and Zane Grey's *Riders of the Purple Sage* (Aiken 1977; Shortridge 1991; Blake 1995) (figure 14.5).

REGIONAL EXAMPLES OF MYTHIC LANDSCAPES

Mythic landscapes in the American geographical imagination are arrhythmic, developing and subsiding with uneven rates and patterns over time and space. Region, therefore, is more than a useful organizing concept for understanding mythic landscapes; it provides an essential and illuminating structural cohesion to an otherwise amorphous subject. Devising a comprehensive list of American mythic landscapes is impossible, due in part to the complexity and diversity of culture, ethnicity, and landscape; yet historians and geographers provide some distinctive regional examples from the past and present (Wyckoff 2003).

One of the strongest examples of a mythic landscape in eastern North America is Niagara Falls on the New York–Ontario border (figure 14.6). This natural landscape has been an icon of the mythic sublime since word of the falls reached Europe in the late 1600s. The falls have represented much more, however: an alluring tourism landscape imagined from afar, a metaphor for death, a place to realize the industrial myth and futuristic dream of technological might in the East (Shortridge 1989; McGreevy 1994). With so many layers of meaning, the falls attracted waves of sightseers and an astonishing array of human accumulations. The promotion in postcard views of all the falls have to offer further reinforced the making of a mythic landscape that persists to this day (Saunders 1995).

Elsewhere in the eastern United States, the New England village represents an invented tradition of a contrived colonial-revival landscape, with large, white wood-frame houses, town commons, and nodal villages with a soaring church steeple. With the popular celebration and academic acceptance of the village ideal, the landscape not only objectified but also validated the myth of tradition. This is an example of a mythic landscape that eventually became a regional image (Wood 1997; Meinig 1979a).

Mountain landscapes and cultures have also shaped ideas about mythic landscapes east of the Mississippi. The writings of Emerson and Thoreau, as well as the burning of area forests to eradicate wolves, transformed New Hampshire's Mount Monadnock in the northern Appalachians into a mythic landscape (Doty 1995). The high point of New Hampshire, Mount Washington, is a mythic landscape of weather extremes and seemingly easy, yet potentially deadly, summit attempts. Yet the most famous mythic landscape of rock in the Granite State is

Figure 14.5. ***Riders of the Purple Sage*, Zane Grey's most famous western romance novel, first published in 1912 by Harpers, exemplifies the place-defining novel. Through his fifty-five westerns, Grey popularized the mythic West among millions of readers. This dust jacket is from a Grosset and Dunlap reprint edition published within a decade or so of the first edition. Wendell Galloway is the illustrator. From the author's collection.**

the Old Man of the Mountain, whose 2003 collapse illustrates the reshaping of myth. Farther south, the stereotype of mountain culture as homogenous and backward imbues the vast deciduous forests of Appalachia with mythic qualities (Rehder 2004; Lutts 2009).

Gone with the Wind in literature (1936) and film (1939) enshrined the grand white-pillared plantation mansion of the antebellum era as the American South's dominant mythic landscape (P. Lewis 1994). Southern elites first invented the myth, complete with the paternalistic slave owner, in the post-Reconstruction era, with Natchez as its culture hearth (Hoelscher 2006). Cotton endured in regional myths when those who sought to change southern agriculture postulated

Figure 14.6. The mythic landscape of Niagara Falls: the three major waterfalls are American Falls in the left foreground; the much smaller Bridal Veil Falls, just beyond American Falls on the same side of the Niagara River; and Canada's Horseshoe Falls, the largest and most powerful of the three, in the distant center of this view. Some of the tens of millions of annual tourists walk along the New York side of the river in the foreground to access a closer view of American Falls. The famous Maid of the Mist boat tour heads upstream toward Horseshoe Falls. The skyline of Niagara Falls, Ontario, is in the distant right of the image, complete with high-rise hotels and observation towers. Photo by the author, June 2001.

the boll weevil as the destroyer of the cotton culture (Giesen 2011). Race also continues as a prominent theme in mythic landscapes of the South, such as in the racially contested landscape of the myth of the lost cause along Richmond, Virginia's Monument Avenue (Leib 2006). Susan Wiley Hardwick (2002), meanwhile, demystifies the supposed racial, ethnic, and socioeconomic harmony in historic Galveston, Texas, along with the myth of abundance and an ideal climate.

Like the South, the Midwest is both a repository for myths that express a broad cultural consciousness and a region with specific mythic landscapes. On the one hand, the myth of pastoralism and agrarianism has dominated the region, contributing the yeoman farmer and traditional values such as wholesomeness, integrity, and nostalgia to the national identity (Schmitt 1969; Shortridge 1989, 1997). Off the farms and in the small towns, mid-America is home to the myth of an idyllic Main Street with tidy linear business blocks and a courthouse square

(Meinig 1979a). *Main Street* by Sinclair Lewis, however, portrays the small-town landscape in fictional Gopher Prairie, Minnesota, as suffocating rather than idyllic, and the book's publication in 1920 contributed to a negative sea change in the regional image of the Midwest (Shortridge 1989; Lane [1988] 2002). Other mythic landscapes in the mid-continent may include the Northwoods of Paul Bunyan (Harty 2007) or the Mississippi River, whether seen as Mark Twain's highway to adventure or as the mythic Garden of Eden (Lane [1988] 2002). Lake Superior serves as a mythic landscape where geographical imaginations have shaped the interplay between nature and human ideals for centuries (Olmanson 2007). Gordon Lightfoot's 1976 ballad "The Wreck of the Edmund Fitzgerald" memorializes this inland sea, also a mythic landscape for the Ojibwe, as the scene of maritime tragedy.

Alaska and Canada's Far North is a mythic landscape of unspoiled frontier and limitless resources, an image fostered by John Muir's travel accounts and furthered by James Oliver Curwood and Jack London. John McPhee (1977) and Barry Lopez (1986) attempted a reality check for this myth by placing wilderness adventures in the context of political economy and the global realities of the oil industry. The last frontier myth persists, however, as witnessed by the Big Oil argument that development is compatible with environmental protection in such a changeless, wild land. In addition to problematizing ideologies of environmentalism, the myth of the last frontier collides with indigenous land rights (Kollin 2001). The mythic landscape of Denali National Park also symbolizes Alaska as pristine wilderness and last frontier (Palka 2000).

THE MYTHIC WEST

More than for any other section of the continent, myth is at the heart of the American West (Hausladen 2003). This region is arguably the most mythic ever created by a nation from its past (Murdoch 2001). Many of the myths once associated with the entire continent, as well as other myths still dominant in American identity, are firmly entrenched in the western landscape (Meinig 1972; Vale and Vale 1989). For example, the myth of America as an agrarian utopia, a virgin land as the garden of the world, moved westward across the continent to the plains and beyond (Smith 1950). The legend endured, even in the face of John Wesley Powell's myth-busting report in 1879, which drove home the point that the agricultural practices of the well-watered East could not be sustained in the more arid West (Stegner 1954; Starrs 1998). The West also offers the clearest expression of the myth of American exceptionalism, the notion that this region's (and by extension, America's) history, landscape, and values are special and that the western process of Manifest Destiny and the myth of the frontier created a unique region and nation (Kollin 2001; Hausladen 2003). Ultimately, the romantic sublimity in western landscapes—stunning vistas, challenging terrain, and a dramatic frontier—supplanted all else in the national myth (Blake 1995; Vale 2005).

The West is also a valuable case study for mythic landscapes because its scholars and residents have challenged its regional myths. Though the plains of the West produced the most mythic characters ever known to America, including the cowboy, the buffalo hunter, and the Plains Indian, revisionist histories deromanticize these heroic western characters and instead focus upon environmental limits (Shortridge 1985; Wrobel and Steiner 1997). Managing these environmental realities still proves problematic, however, since western mythic landscapes provide the venue for a ritualistic acting out of myth (Sopher 1979). The power of myth is manifest in frequent land-use contestations, such as "sagebrush rebellions" whereby local forces attempt to gain control of federal public lands to enhance resource extraction and development (Graf 1990). Myths have a continued value, though, because they remain central to our interpretations of western wilderness; it does no more good to throw out the myth of Turnerian progression, for example, than to rely solely upon it to understand the meaning of wilderness (Vale 2005).

Within the West, subregions have their own mythic identities. The vast grasslands of the Great Plains, for example, have seen remarkable swings between myth and reality. To Euro-Americans in the early 1800s, the plains were the Great American Desert. By the late 1800s, a series of wet years and the emergence of the promotional myth that "rain follows the plow" launched a settlement rush. Global political and economic forces combined with high winds and prolonged drought to turn the mythic plains into the Dust Bowl by the 1930s (Stegner 1954). Even an ecological crisis like the Dust Bowl launched its own unique set of mythic characters, from "dustbowl desperadoes" like Pretty Boy Floyd to the Okie of John Steinbeck's imagination (J. R. Allen 2006). In the mythology of *The Grapes of Wrath*, the wanton cruelty of the Dust Bowl rips the Okie farmer from the land and thrusts him on the capricious road to the promised land of California. In reality, however, most Okies were not from Oklahoma or even from the area affected by the Dust Bowl, and most were not farmers. Moreover, farm failure was not the primary cause of the migration (Worster 1979). Even so, the settlement myth of expectations for rising prosperity still holds sway in the plains counties of the "waning West" (Wyckoff 2002).

Overland exploration and migration created other mythic landscapes on the plains, such as the Lewis and Clark, Santa Fe, Mormon, California, and Oregon Trails (Olsen 2012). The mapping by Lewis and Clark, for example, promulgated myth, but commemorations along the trail have evoked the epic national myth of the frontier to the occasional exclusion of Plains Indians (Stegner 1954; Blake 2004; W. G. Lewis 2010). To Native Americans, the plains endure as a mythic landscape of spiritual encounters in the homeland (Schnell 2000; Farmer 2008).

West of the Great Plains, the vast continental interior landscape of mountains, plateaus, and deserts constitutes the heart of the mythic West. National parks form the foundation for many of the mythic landscapes here: Yellowstone, Grand Canyon, Crater Lake (figure 14.7), Redwood, Glacier, Yosemite, Mount Rainier, Rocky Mountain, Arches, Zion—the list goes on (Saunders 1995; Wyckoff and Dilsaver 1997; Deur 2002; Dilsaver 2003). Some of these landscapes were mythic long before national park designation, such as the Grand Canyon, home to the Havasupai nation and the location of the *sipapu*, or point of emergence for the Hopi people. Spiritual meaning is not limited to Native Americans or parklands, however, as illustrated by the mythic Mormon settlement landscape (Meinig 1965; Francaviglia 2003; Jackson 2003; Farmer 2008). In addition, mysticism extends

Figure 14.7. A mythic landscape to the Klamath Tribes of southern Oregon since time immemorial, Crater Lake became a national park in 1902. At the right side of this view is Wizard Island, a cinder cone. It is the largest of the lake's two islands and the most photographed scenic wonder in the park. Photo by the author, July 2006.

beyond spirituality, whether in California's ghost towns or its Ramona myth of an aristocratic Mexican hacienda landscape (DeLyser 2001, 2005).

Latino American, Native American, and Anglo American identities contribute to the Southwest region, "where mystery and myth are as factual and everyday as any other aspect of contemporary life in the United States" (Meinig 1971; P. G. Allen 1997, 343). These ethnicities, for example, contributed to Santa Fe, New Mexico's architectural history, which illustrates the multiplicity of myth. A half-truth of invented tradition and tri-cultural harmony arose here but also became a unifying force promoting a shared vision for the community (Wilson 1997). Native American sacred mountains punctuate the region with mythic qualities and link it together in a system of intervisibilities and correlated meanings (Blake 1999, 2001a, 2001b).

THE FUTURE OF MYTHIC LANDSCAPES

Though history informs and shapes our views of mythic landscapes incalculably, the fluidity of time with respect to mysticism warrants a look ahead at what may come for mythic landscapes in America. National parks, famously dubbed America's "best idea" by Wallace Stegner (1983, 5), generate a passion few mythic landscapes match. In a nation with deep political divisions, the parks unite more than divide; places like Longs Peak in Rocky Mountain National Park serve as a mythic dreamscape for western tourists of all stripes (figure 14.8). Efforts by the National Park Service to represent cultural and ethnic diversity in the parks more completely will encourage greater numbers Americans to visit and better understand these mythic landscapes (Dilsaver 2003). With Asian Americans now the fastest-growing ethnic group and Latino Americans currently numbering more than 50 million in the United States—more than double the number in 1990 (Arreola 2004)—more of the nation's mythic park landscapes are sure to represent these people. As native people in North America's indigenous landscapes continue to reconcile a history and geography not all of their own making with traditional beliefs, nonnatives, for their part, will be more likely to recognize these lands as mythic and worthy of protection (Arreola 2012).

Figure 14.8. Rocky Mountain National Park and its crown jewel, Longs Peak, offer a mythic dreamscape for over 3 million annual visitors. Longs Peak, rising to over fourteen thousand feet in elevation, is the northernmost of the famous Colorado Fourteeners. Colorado residents and visitors often name Longs Peak, a mythic climbing challenge, as their favorite mountain. The Keyboard of the Winds defines the ridge to the right of Longs Peak in this view from the Flattop Mountain Trail. Photo by the author, August 2008.

Idealized wild nature, whether in parks or other public lands, shows no sign of lessening as a source for mythic landscapes in America. The Colorado Fourteeners, mountains rising over fourteen thousand feet above sea level, are examples of increasingly popular mythic landscapes (Blake 2002). Pikes Peak, for example, became a symbol of the mythic West with its sighting by Zebulon Pike in 1806 and the myth of a strike-it-rich-quick gold rush in 1859 (Farmer 2008). The peak has become more than a regional symbol, however: it is America's most famous mountain. *America the Beautiful*, penned by Katherine Lee Bates after a trip to the summit in 1893, helped popularize the peak, and the moniker "America's Mountain" became firmly associated with it by the mid-1900s. Whether by foot, burro, automobile, or cog railway, access to the summit shapes this mythic mountain landscape, celebrated in postcards primarily for the aesthetics of a pristine and wild nature (figure 14.9). The process of achieving a connection to and representing mythic landscapes like the Colorado Fourteeners will likely continue to shift to Internet media in future years. There, in the virtual world, Americans will continue their quest to make mythic landscapes.

Figure 14.9. With the opening in 1915 of the automobile highway to the summit of Pikes Peak, tourists gained a more comfortable access to the views of wild nature that imagery has portrayed in an idealized way for "America's Mountain." The highway, now entirely paved, nearly circumnavigates the mountain on its way to the Summit House, where food and gifts are for sale at 14,115 feet. The annual summer Pikes Peak International Hill Climb features racecar drivers who cover over twelve miles of the highway to the summit in less than ten minutes. Curt Teich Co. of Chicago manufactured this postcard in 1916 based on a photographic image made in 1915. The Hyde Paper Co. in Pueblo, Colorado, published the postcard, and the message on the reverse (mailed in 1918) says, "It is grand and cool out here, and we are having a fine time." From the author's collection.

REFERENCES

Aiken, C. S. 1977. Faulkner's Yoknapatawpha County: Geographical Fact into Fiction. *Geographical Review* 67, no. 1: 1–21.

Allen, J. R. 2006. Dust Bowl. In *Home Ground: Language for an American Landscape,* edited by B. Lopez and D. Gwartney, 118. San Antonio: Trinity University Press.

Allen, P. G. 1997. Cuentos de la Tierra Encantada: Magic and Realism in the Southwest Borderlands. In *Many Wests: Place, Culture, and Regional Identity,* edited by D. M. Wrobel and M. C. Steiner, 342–65. Lawrence: University Press of Kansas.

Arreola, D. D. 2001. La Cerca y las Garitas de Ambos Nogales: A Postcard Landscape Exploration. *Journal of the Southwest* 43, no. 4: 505–41.

———, ed. 2004. *Hispanic Spaces, Latino Places: Community and Cultural Diversity in Contemporary America.* Austin: University of Texas Press.

———. 2005. Forget the Alamo: The Border as Place in John Sayles' *Lone Star. Journal of Cultural Geography* 23, no. 1: 23–42.

———. 2012. Chiricahua Apache Homeland in the Borderland Southwest. *Geographical Review* 102, no. 1: 111–31.

Athearn, R. G. 1986. *The Mythic West in Twentieth-Century America.* Lawrence: University Press of Kansas.

Blake, K. S. 1995. Zane Grey and Images of the American West. *Geographical Review* 85, no. 2: 202–16.

———. 1999. Sacred and Secular Landscape Symbolism at Mount Taylor, New Mexico. *Journal of the Southwest* 41, no. 4: 487–509.

———. 2001a. Contested Landscapes of Navajo Sacred Mountains. *North American Geographer* 3, no. 1: 29–62.

———. 2001b. In Search of a Navajo Sacred Geography. *Geographical Review* 91, no. 4: 715–24.

———. 2002. Colorado Fourteeners and the Nature of Place Identity. *Geographical Review* 92, no. 2: 155–79.

———. 2004. Great Plains Native American Representations along the Lewis and Clark Trail. *Great Plains Quarterly* 24, no. 4: 263–82.

———. 2008. Imagining Heaven and Earth at Mount of the Holy Cross, Colorado. *Journal of Cultural Geography* 25, no. 1: 1–30.

Blake, K. S., and J. S. Smith. 2000. Pueblo Mission Churches as Symbols of Permanence and Identity. *Geographical Review* 90, no. 3: 359–80.

Brown, R. M. 1997. The Other Northwest: The Regional Identity of a Canadian Province. In *Many Wests: Place, Culture, and Regional Identity,* edited by D. M. Wrobel and M. C. Steiner, 279–314. Lawrence: University Press of Kansas.

Cosgrove, D. E. 1994. Worlds of Meaning: Cultural Geography and the Imagination. In *Rereading Cultural Geography,* edited by K. E. Foote, P. J. Hugill, K. Mathewson, and J. M. Smith, 387–95. Austin: University of Texas Press.

Cronon, W., ed. 1996. *Uncommon Ground: Toward Reinventing Nature.* New York: W. W. Norton.

Daniels, S., and D. Cosgrove. 1988. Introduction: Iconography and Landscape. In *The Iconography of Landscape,* edited by D. Cosgrove and S. Daniels, 1–10. Cambridge: Cambridge University Press.

DeBres, K., and J. Sowers. 2009. The Emergence of Standardized, Idealized, and Placeless Landscapes in Midwestern Main Street Postcards. *Professional Geographer* 61, no. 2: 216–30.

della Dora, V. 2011. *Imagining Mount Athos: Visions of a Holy Place from Homer to World War II.* Charlottesville: University of Virginia Press.

DeLyser, D. 1999. Authenticity on the Ground: Engaging the Past in a California Ghost Town. *Annals of the Association of American Geographers* 89, no. 4: 602–32.
———. 2001. When Less Is More: Absence and Landscape in a California Ghost Town. In *Textures of Place: Exploring Humanistic Geographies*, edited by P. C. Adams, S. Hoelscher, and K. E. Till, 24–40. Minneapolis: University of Minnesota Press.
———. 2005. *Ramona Memories: Tourism and the Shaping of Southern California*. Minneapolis: University of Minnesota Press.
Denevan, W. M. 1992. The Pristine Myth: The Landscape of the Americas in 1492. *Annals of the Association of American Geographers* 82, no. 3: 369–85.
Deur, D. 2002. A Most Sacred Place: The Significance of Crater Lake among the Indians of Southern Oregon. *Oregon Historical Quarterly* 103, no. 1: 18–49.
Dilsaver, L. M. 2003. National Significance: Representation of the West in the National Park System. In *Western Places, American Myths: How We Think about the West*, edited by G. J. Hausladen, 111–32. Reno: University of Nevada Press.
Domosh, M. 1994. The Symbolism of the Skyscraper: Case Studies of New York's First Tall Buildings. In *Re-reading Cultural Geography*, edited by K. E. Foote, P. J. Hugill, K. Mathewson, and J. M. Smith, 48–63. Austin: University of Texas Press.
Doty, R. M. 1995. Monadnock Burning. In *Landscape in America*, edited by G. F. Thompson, 213–22. Austin: University of Texas Press.
Douglas, M. S. 1947. *The Everglades: River of Grass*. New York: Rinehart.
Duncan, J. S., and N. G. Duncan. 2001. Sense of Place as a Positional Good: Locating Bedford in Space and Time. In *Textures of Place: Exploring Humanistic Geographies*, edited by P. C. Adams, S. Hoelscher, and K. E. Till, 41–54. Minneapolis: University of Minnesota Press.
Farmer, J. 2008. *On Zion's Mount: Mormons, Indians, and the American Landscape*. Cambridge, MA: Harvard University Press.
Foote, K. E. 1997. *Shadowed Ground: America's Landscapes of Violence and Tragedy*. Austin: University of Texas Press.
Francaviglia, R. V. 2003. *Believing in Place: A Spiritual Geography of the Great Basin*. Reno: University of Nevada Press.
Giesen, J. C. 2011. *Boll Weevil Blues: Cotton, Myth, and Power in the American South*. Chicago: University of Chicago Press.
Goetzmann, W. H., and W. N. Goetzmann. 1986. *The West of the Imagination*. New York: W. W. Norton and Co.
Goin, P., and P. F. Starrs. 2005. *Black Rock*. Reno: University of Nevada Press.
Graf, W. L. 1990. *Wilderness Preservation and the Sagebrush Rebellions*. Savage, MD: Rowman & Littlefield.
Grunwald, M. 2006. *The Swamp: The Everglades, Florida, and the Politics of Paradise*. New York: Simon & Schuster.
Hardwick, S. W. 2002. *Mythic Galveston: Reinventing America's Third Coast*. Baltimore: Johns Hopkins University Press.
Harty, J. P. 2007. Legendary Landscapes: A Cultural Geography of the Paul Bunyan and Blue Ox Phenomena of the Northwoods. PhD diss., Kansas State University, Manhattan.
Harvey, D. 1979. Monument and Myth. *Annals of the Association of American Geographers* 69, no. 3: 362–81.
Hausladen, G. J., ed. 2003. Where the Cowboy Rides Away: Mythic Places for Western Film. In *Western Places, American Myths: How We Think about the West*, edited by G. J. Hausladen, 296–318. Reno: University of Nevada Press.
Hoelscher, S. 2006. The White-Pillared Past: Landscapes of Memory and Race in the American South. In *Landscape and Race in the United States*, edited by R. H. Schein, 39–72. New York: Routledge.

Hoskins, G. 2006. Poetic Landscapes of Exclusion: Chinese Immigration at Angel Island, San Francisco. In *Landscape and Race in the United States*, edited by R. H. Schein, 95–112. New York: Routledge.

Jackson, R. H. 2003. Mormon Wests: The Creation and Evolution of an American Region. In *Western Places, American Myths: How We Think about the West*, edited by G. J. Hausladen, 135–65. Reno: University of Nevada Press.

Jakle, J. A. 2003. *Postcards of the Night: Views of American Cities*. Santa Fe: Museum of New Mexico Press.

Jett, S. C. 1995. Navajo Sacred Places: Management and Interpretation of Mythic History. *Public Historian* 17, no. 2: 39–47.

Kelley, K. B., and H. Francis. 1994. *Navajo Sacred Places*. Bloomington: Indiana University Press.

Kollin, S. 2001. *Nature's State: Imagining Alaska as the Last Frontier*. Chapel Hill: University of North Carolina Press.

Lane, B. C. [1988] 2002. *Landscapes of the Sacred: Geography and Narrative in American Spirituality*. Exp. ed. Baltimore: Johns Hopkins University Press.

Leib, J. 2006. The Witting Autobiography of Richmond, Virginia: Arthur Ashe, the Civil War, and Monument Avenue's Racialized Landscape. In *Landscape and Race in the United States*, edited by R. H. Schein, 187–212. New York: Routledge.

Lewis, P. 1994. Common Houses, Cultural Spoor. In *Re-reading Cultural Geography*, edited by K. E. Foote, P. J. Hugill, K. Mathewson, and J. M. Smith, 82–110. Austin: University of Texas Press.

Lewis, W. G. 2010. *In the Footsteps of Lewis and Clark: Early Commemorations and the Origins of the National Historic Trail*. Boulder: University Press of Colorado.

Lopez, B. H. 1978. *Of Wolves and Men*. New York: Scribner.

———. 1986. *Arctic Dreams: Imagination and Desire in a Northern Landscape*. New York: Scribner.

Lopez, B. H., and D. Gwartney. 2006. *Home Ground: Language for an American Landscape*. San Antonio: Trinity University Press.

Lutts, R. H. 2009. Like Manna from God: The American Chestnut Trade in Southwestern Virginia. In *Environmental History and the American South: A Reader*, edited by P. S. Sutter and C. J. Manganiello, 247–80. Athens: University of Georgia Press.

McGreevy, P. V. 1994. *Imagining Niagara: The Meaning and Making of Niagara Falls*. Amherst: University of Massachusetts Press.

McPhee, J. 1977. *Coming into the Country*. New York: Farrar, Straus, and Giroux.

Meinig, D. W. 1965. The Mormon Culture Region: Strategies and Patterns in the Geography of the American West, 1847–1964. *Annals of the Association of American Geographers* 55, no. 2: 191–220.

———. 1971. *Southwest: Three Peoples in Geographical Change, 1600–1970*. New York: Oxford University Press.

———. 1972. American Wests: Preface to a Geographical Interpretation. *Annals of the Association of American Geographers* 62, no. 2: 159–84.

———, ed. 1979a. Symbolic Landscapes: Some Idealizations of American Communities. In *The Interpretation of Ordinary Landscapes: Geographical Essays*, 164–92. New York: Oxford University Press.

———, ed. 1979b. The Beholding Eye: Ten Versions of the Same Scene. In *The Interpretation of Ordinary Landscapes: Geographical Essays*, 33–48. New York: Oxford University Press.

Mitchell, R. D. 2001. The Colonial Origins of Anglo-America. In *North America: The Historical Geography of a Changing Continent*, edited by T. F. McIlwraith and E. K. Muller, 89–117. 2nd ed. Lanham, MD: Rowman & Littlefield.

Morin, K. M. 2003. Narrating Imperial Adventure: Isabella Bird's Travels in the Nineteenth-Century American West. In *Western Places, American Myths: How We Think about the West*, edited by G. J. Hausladen, 204–22. Reno: University of Nevada Press.

Murdoch, D. H. 2001. *The American West: The Invention of a Myth*. Reno: University of Nevada Press.

Olmanson, E. D. 2007. *The Future City on the Inland Sea: A History of Imaginative Geographies of Lake Superior*. Athens: Ohio University Press.

Olsen, M. L. 2012. Myth and Memory: The Cultural Heritage of the Santa Fe Trail in the Twentieth Century. *Kansas History: A Journal of the Central Plains* 35, no. 1: 43–60.

Palka, E. J. 2000. *Valued Landscapes of the Far North: A Geographical Journey through Denali National Park*. Lanham, MD: Rowman & Littlefield.

Pankl, L., and K. Blake. 2012. Made in Her Image: Frida Kahlo as Material Culture. *Material Culture* 44, no. 2: 1–20.

Popper, D. E., and F. J. Popper. 1999. The Buffalo Commons: Metaphor as Method. *Geographical Review* 89, no. 4: 491–510.

Powell, J. W. [1879] 1962. *Report on the Lands of the Arid Region of the United States: With a More Detailed Account of the Lands of Utah*. Cambridge, MA: Belknap Press of Harvard University Press.

Pringle, T. R. 1988. The Privation of History: Landseer, Victoria and the Highland Myth. In *The Iconography of Landscape*, edited by D. Cosgrove and S. Daniels, 142–61. Cambridge: Cambridge University Press.

Pyne, S. J. 1998. *How the Canyon Became Grand: A Short History*. New York: Viking.

Quinn, D. B. 1997. The Northwest Passage in Theory and Practice. In *North American Exploration*. Vol. 1: *A New World Disclosed*, edited by J. L. Allen, 292–343. Lincoln: University of Nebraska Press.

Raento, P. 2003. The Return of the One-Armed Bandit: Gambling and the West. In *Western Places, American Myths: How We Think about the West*, edited by G. J. Hausladen, 225–52. Reno: University of Nevada Press.

Rehder, J. B. 2004. *Appalachian Folkways*. Baltimore: Johns Hopkins University Press.

Reinhardt, A. D. 2003. Native America: The Indigenous West. In *Western Places, American Myths: How We Think about the West*, edited by G. J. Hausladen, 184–203. Reno: University of Nevada Press.

Riley, R. B. 1997. The Visible, the Visual, and the Vicarious: Questions about Vision, Landscape, and Experience. In *Understanding Ordinary Landscapes*, edited by P. Groth and T. W. Bressi, 200–209. New Haven, CT: Yale University Press.

Salter, C. L., and W. J. Lloyd. 1977. *Landscape in Literature*. Resource Papers for College Geography 76–3. Washington, D.C.: Association of American Geographers.

Samuels, M. S. 1979. The Biography of Landscape: Cause and Culpability. In *The Interpretation of Ordinary Landscapes: Geographical Essays*, edited by D. W. Meinig, 51–88. New York: Oxford University Press.

Saunders, R. 1995. Graphic Images and Publisher Exploitation of Yellowstone Park in Postcards: "Viewing the Marvelous Scenes in Wonderland." In *Postcards in the Library: Invaluable Visual Resources*, edited by N. D. Stevens, 121–39. New York: Haworth.

Schama, S. 1995. *Landscape and Memory*. London: HarperCollins Publishers.

Schein, R. H. 2006. Race and Landscape in the United States. In *Landscape and Race in the United States*, edited by R. H. Schein, 1–22. New York: Routledge.

Schmitt, P. J. 1969. *Back to Nature: The Arcadian Myth in Urban America*. New York: Oxford University Press.

Schnell, S. M. 2000. The Kiowa Homeland in Oklahoma. *Geographical Review* 90, no. 2: 155–76.

Schuyler, D. 1995. The Sanctified Landscape: The Hudson River Valley, 1820 to 1850. In *Landscape in America*, edited by G. F. Thompson, 93–110. Austin: University of Texas Press.

Schwartz, J. M. 2007. Photographic Reflections: Nature, Landscape, and Environment. *Environmental History* 12, no. 4 (October): 966–93.

Shortridge, J. R. 1985. Cowboy, Yeoman, Pawn, and Hick: Myth and Contradiction in Great Plains Life. *Focus* 31, no. 4: 22–27.

———. 1989. *The Middle West: Its Meaning in American Culture*. Lawrence: University Press of Kansas.

———. 1991. The Concept of the Place-Defining Novel in American Culture. *Professional Geographer* 43, no. 3: 280–91.

———. 1997. The Expectations of Others: Struggles toward a Sense of Place in the Northern Plains. In *Many Wests: Place, Culture, and Regional Identity*, edited by D. M. Wrobel and M. C. Steiner, 114–35. Lawrence: University Press of Kansas.

Slotkin, R. 1985. *The Fatal Environment: The Myth of the Frontier in the Age of Industrialization, 1800–1890*. New York: Atheneum.

Smith, H. N. 1950. *Virgin Land; The American West as Symbol and Myth*. Cambridge, MA: Harvard University Press.

Sopher, D. E. 1979. Landscapes of Home: Myth, Experience, Social Meaning. In *The Interpretation of Ordinary Landscapes: Geographical Essays*, edited by D. W. Meinig, 129–49. New York: Oxford University Press.

Starrs, P. F. 1998. *Let the Cowboy Ride: Cattle Ranching in the American West*. Baltimore: Johns Hopkins University Press.

Stegner, W. 1954. *Beyond the Hundredth Meridian: John Wesley Powell and the Second Opening of the West*. Boston: Houghton, Mifflin.

———. 1983. The Best Idea We Ever Had: An Overview. *Wilderness* 46, no. 160: 4–13.

Tuan, Y. 1977. *Space and Place: The Perspective of Experience*. Minneapolis: University of Minnesota Press.

Vale, T. R. 2005. *The American Wilderness: Reflections on Nature Protection in the United States*. Charlottesville: University of Virginia Press.

Vale, T. R., and G. R. Vale. 1989. *Western Images, Western Landscapes: Travels along U.S. 89*. Tucson: University of Arizona Press.

Wilson, C. 1997. *The Myth of Santa Fe: Creating a Modern Regional Tradition*. Albuquerque: University of New Mexico Press.

Wood, J. S. 1997. *The New England Village*. Baltimore: Johns Hopkins University Press.

Worster, D. 1979. *Dust Bowl: The Southern Plains in the 1930s*. New York: Oxford University Press.

Wright, J. B. 2003. Land Tenure: The Spatial Musculature of the American West. In *Western Places, American Myths: How We Think about the West*, edited by G. J. Hausladen, 85–110. Reno: University of Nevada Press.

Wright, J. K. 1947. Terrae Incognitae: The Place of the Imagination in Geography. *Annals of the Association of American Geographers* 37, no. 1: 1–15.

Wrobel, D. M., and M. C. Steiner, eds. 1997. *Many Wests: Place, Culture, and Regional Identity*. Lawrence: University Press of Kansas.

Wyckoff, W. 2002. Life on the Margin: The Evolution of the Waning West. *Montana: The Magazine of Western History* 52, no. 3: 30–43.

———. 2003. Understanding Western Places: The Historical Geographer's View. In *Western Places, American Myths: How We Think about the West*, edited by G. J. Hausladen, 21–56. Reno: University of Nevada Press.

Wyckoff, W., and L. M. Dilsaver. 1997. Promotional Imagery of Glacier National Park. *Geographical Review* 87, no. 1: 1–26.

Wynn, G. 2001. Realizing the Idea of Canada. In *North America: The Historical Geography of a Changing Continent,* edited by T. F. McIlwraith and E. K. Muller, 357–78. 2nd ed. Lanham, MD: Rowman & Littlefield.
Youngs, Y. 2011. On Grand Canyon Postcards. *Environmental History* 16: 138–47.
———. 2012. Editing Nature in Grand Canyon National Park Postcards. *Geographical Review* 102, no. 4: 486–509.

15

The Historical Geography of Racialized Landscapes

Derek H. Alderman and E. Arnold Modlin Jr.

African Americans did not have a major place in the general geographic literature before the mid-1960s, and, until recently, many published studies have focused on the racial group strictly in terms of social problems, population characteristics, and spatial segregation (Dwyer 1997). We can accuse traditional research in historical geography of even greater neglect of the African American experience. Thomas McIlwraith and Edward Muller's *North America* (2001), for instance, certainly includes African Americans, but we get little feel for the black social experience beyond macro-level discussions of settlement, migration, urbanization, and labor. Such a perspective privileges a description of patterns over an understanding of how America has breathed life into racial divisions and created racist geographies with often painful and even deadly results for African Americans. According to Audrey Kobayashi and Linda Peake, the American landscape is "deeply racialized," and "racism is a product of specific historical geographies" (2000, 392). Strikingly, McIlwraith and Muller devote only a few pages of their classic to discussing the racial discrimination faced by blacks.

Traditionally, historical geographers of the United States tended to pay attention to the theme of ethnicity more than race, often stressing the cultural diffusions and landscape imprints resulting from European immigrant groups (e.g., Conzen 1990). Terry Jordan and Matti Kaups's (1989) tracing of a distinctive American backwoods culture to the influence and frontier advancements of Finns and Swedes exemplifies this type of research. Of course, historical geographers have examined ethnicity in more diverse ways, as is evident in Daniel Arreola's (2002) long-running work on Hispanic place making along the United States–Mexico borderlands. Despite intense academic debate regarding use of the term, cultural and historical geographers have employed the concept of "homeland" to characterize the strong demographic and emotional connection that can develop between ethnic identity and the historical development of places (e.g., Nostrand

and Estaville 2001). Scholars have essayed to identify and discuss a black historical homeland—consider, for example, Charles Aiken's (2001) work on the plantation South—but they cannot so easily subsume race under, and conflate it with, self-defined ethnicity without encountering contradictions. Indeed, Aiken noted that plantation regions "were not 'homelands' to which blacks freely emigrated" (2001, 54).

While early historical geography research did not emphasize African Americans, it did not ignore them either (e.g., Zelinsky 1950). Historical geographers like Sam Hilliard (1972) acknowledged the role of African Americans in creating and expanding U.S. culture, and Judith Carney (2001) built on the work of previous historical geographers by highlighting the roles of blacks, particularly descendants from certain African ethnic groups, in the development of the Sea Island rice culture. Carville Earle (1978) recognized the importance of black labor to North American development and sought to explain the geography of slavery by applying an economic interpretation of labor systems and costs. Charles Aiken (1985, 1987, 1998) focused attention on the movement and settlement morphology of African Americans after emancipation, the evolution of the southern cotton plantation, and white control of formerly enslaved populations through segregation and political disenfranchisement, including municipal exclusion. Bobby Wilson (2010) examined the shift of African Americans from slave to wage laborers and consumers after the Civil War, pointing out that fixed racism during enslavement gave way to a more flexible form that maintained the racial status quo but allowed African Americans to participate in commodity exchange and consumption. Wilson (2000a, 2000b) is also well known for analyzing the historical African American experience in Birmingham, Alabama, in the context of the rise of industrial capitalism and the civil rights movement.

Aiken and Wilson serve as important bridges between traditional and newer historical geographic work on African Americans and race relations in the United States. As their work illustrates, it is not enough simply to include African Americans in analyses. We must also develop a deeper historical geographic understanding of racism and white privilege in the United States. Contemporary historical geographers, because of their engagement with critical race theory and broader debates in human geography, increasingly recognize the socially constructed and politically contestable nature of race and racial identity, including, but certainly not limited to, African American identity. This new scholarship investigates not only the historical role racial prejudice and inequality played in fashioning landscapes but also how these same landscapes worked to sustain or challenge racial hierarchies. In the words of Richard Schein, "Racial processes take place and racial categories get made, in part, through cultural landscapes" (2006, 6). Schein and other scholars have offered the term "racialized landscape" to capture how race and landscape are mutually constructed in consequential and often discriminatory ways. This chapter adopts a "racialized landscape" framework, providing examples from U.S. historical geography to illustrate how the landscape serves as a site for supporting, but also challenging, racist social practices. In addition to documenting the impact of racism on the landscape, our discussion recovers the idea of African Americans as historical agents who sought to make places of resistance and antiracism even as they faced hostile oppression.

ON THE SOCIAL CONSTRUCTION OF RACE

The growing importance of race within historical geographic analysis accompanies a broader rethinking of the definition of race. Traditional definitions of race reflect what we can call an "essentializing" perspective. In other words, they suggest that essential and inherently important biological characteristics such as skin and hair color, bone structure, and other aspects of physical appearance characterize racial groups. Rather than simply accepting race as a biological "fact," historical geographers, along with the wider social science community, increasingly recognize it to be a social construction. A constructionist perspective does not deny that physical differences exist between people but suggests that people construct racial identities when they attach meaning and value to these physical differences. We can more accurately view racial categories considered "natural" as products of social relations and practices that "other," or racialize, certain groups of people and their identities (Inwood and Yarbrough 2010). Racialization, according to Kobayashi and Peake, is "a process by which racialized groups are identified, given stereotypical characteristics, and coerced into specific living conditions, often involving social/spatial segregation" (2000, 393). Important to historical geographers, the concept of racialization places great importance on critical historical and spatial analysis and recognizing how patterns of racial othering develop over time and space to form the assumptions we have about racial difference and identity today. Amy Sumpter (2011, 461) perhaps captures it best: "Because race is a social construction, geographers and other researchers have a pressing interest in determining the *how*, *why*, and *where* of the production of racial identity" (emphasis in the original).

Racial categories and hierarchies are frequently imposed. An important component of a social constructionist argument is that these racial categories and hierarchies are often defined in rather arbitrary and uneven terms. Historically, for example, in some instances the broader American public treated certain ethnic groups in racialized terms, even though ethnicity conventionally refers to a group with a common nationality or culture rather than shared biological traits. The story of the Irish in nineteenth-century America illustrates this dynamic. In the decades leading up to the Civil War, white American Protestant nativists persecuted Irish Catholic immigrants and publicly depicted them as grotesque, physically inferior, and apelike, a practice also applied to the "othering" of African Americans. The efforts of Irish Americans to redefine their negative identity led many of them to support slavery and further distinguish themselves from blacks as occupying the absolute bottom rung of the American social ladder, even though many in Ireland supported abolition (Ignatiev 1996). Early-twentieth-century picture postcard images of housescapes presented a stereotyped view of Mexican Americans as dirty and primitive, reinforcing Anglo anxiety about a so-called Mexican problem (Arreola 2006). This racialization of Hispanics endures, as Jamie Winders (2008) has noted when examining public opposition to Latino migration to the southeastern United States. While not every ethnic group is a racial group, it is important to note that a focus on racialization can assist us in understanding the historically marginalized place of ethnic minority groups within America. As the Irish and Latino cases illustrate, the history of racialization in North America is not simply a white-black binary but a relationally based process of positioning multiple groups, or "racial triangulation" (Lai 2012).

Even for African Americans, the process of racialization varied depending on the social and historical context at hand. The U.S. Census, which has both reflected and defined how the American public views race, is a testament to the inconsistent and politicized racial classification of African Americans. By 1890, the U.S. Census Bureau had devised several identity categories to capture racial mixture among African Americans (negro, mulatto, quadroon, and octoroon), a response to pressures from Congress to consolidate white supremacy after the Civil War (Hochschild and Powell 2008). The idea that one could be racialized even if a small portion of one's ancestry or bloodline included African Americans eventually had landmark legal consequences. In the famous 1896 Supreme Court case *Plessy v. Ferguson*, which established the "separate but equal" principle sanctioning segregated public facilities, plaintiff Homer Plessy was one-eighth black and for all purposes appeared white. Plessy's lawyers used his mixed racial background to represent the absurdity of segregated railcar seating and to challenge, although unsuccessfully, their client's arrest for sitting in a white section. Later, prominent black leaders such as W. E. B. DuBois called on the Census Bureau to abandon the mulatto designation and to tighten the line between white and black so as to build African American political unity, demonstrating how racial categories and identities are not simply imposed externally (Hochschild and Powell 2008).

A racialization perspective calls on historical geographers not only to analyze the experiences and struggles of explicitly racialized minorities but also to recognize how the racial category of whiteness is constructed and to delve into the social and historical geographic processes by which society represents being white as normative or normal (Inwood and Martin 2008). From this perspective, racism is not limited to the "results of direct racial hatred, such as violence, racial slurs, and direct discrimination"; it also "involves the manipulation of power to mark 'white' as a location of social privilege" (Kobayashi and Peake 2000, 393). The use of the word "location" here is figurative, but it is also most assuredly a literal geographic coordinate. A deep analysis of the historical geography of racialized landscapes involves uncovering the historical force of white privilege in shaping the use and identity of space and place and the legacy of this racial control for how we see these geographies in the present.

In some places, it is easy to see how whites employed the landscape to reaffirm their authority, for instance, by posting "white only" signs across the pre–civil rights American landscape. However, in many other places, it can be difficult to see the impact of white supremacy. As Don Mitchell (2000) has argued, landscapes can often hide the social and economic struggles behind their making. Kay Anderson (1987) famously uncovered the fight that created the Chinatown landscape in Vancouver, British Columbia. According to her research, although Chinatowns, in Vancouver and elsewhere, may appear as an organic, voluntary spatial expression of Chinese identity, they were actually the product of exclusionary nineteenth-century urban policies designed to spatially control and segregate the supposedly unsanitary and morally depraved Chinese population. Fierce opposition faced those Chinese who sought to move out of Chinatown. In reality, the Chinatown historical landscape speaks as much to the mindset of European whites as to that of the Chinese.

Other historical geographies reaffirmed the idea that whites belonged while racial minorities did not in subtler but no less important ways. Dianne Harris (2006) found this to be the case when examining the post–World War II boom in suburban home building in America and the inscription of ideas of privacy and security into these structures architecturally. The design of these homes "symbolized security from not just outsiders . . . but also the security of confirmed membership in the white, middle-class, American majority" (Harris 2006, 129). The emphasis on the middle class is important. People often internalize as natural racialized notions of who belongs and where because of differences in socioeconomic status, although racism has long shaped and been shaped by a politics of social class in America. The often unconscious and unquestioned nature of whiteness makes white privilege so powerful and, at times, difficult to study, since it asks the overwhelmingly white field of historical geography to question its own everyday frame of reference.

THE CONCEPT OF RACIALIZED LANDSCAPES

As our brief discussions above of Chinatown and the American suburban home suggests, racialization does not occur simply through the circulation of ideas about the supposed inferiority of racial minorities and the presumed superiority of whiteness. It also requires the construction of landscapes and other spatial expressions of control that materially support white privilege and legitimize racial segregation and inequality. The late Clyde Woods (1998) asserted that the production of racial oppression and black poverty in the Mississippi delta was, at its core, geographically driven and historically traceable to a plantation regime that for generations arrested the development of working-class African Americans by maintaining control of the landscape and social structure of the region.

The "racialized landscape" concept is an increasingly important framework used by historical geographers to analyze the relationship between the social construction of racial identity and the production of place. Racialized landscapes are not simply the outcome of racially based social values, fears, and relations. Because landscapes are ways of ordering the world as well as material things, they participate in promoting and institutionalizing dominant ideas about race and the racial identities of African Americans and other minorities—creating a visual legitimacy for how society ought to be. In other words, racialized landscapes have a normative power and work, through their physicality and permanence, to make racial hierarches and inequalities appear as part of the normal and necessary order of things (Schein 2003). Important here is the recognition that racialized landscapes are produced by (and in turn produce) what Daniel Trudeau has called a "territorialized politics of belonging" (2006, 422), in which places are racially bounded in ways that enforce exclusion and discrimination.

Although this territorialized politics of belonging appeared through the historical geography of the United States, in certain places its presence was especially glaring. For example, Norris, Tennessee, now a suburb of Knoxville, was a planned community built by the Tennessee Valley Authority (TVA) in the 1930s, created first to house laborers working on the nearby Norris Dam and later developed as an experiment in social engineering and, ironically enough, a demonstration of cooperative living. We say "ironically enough" because the TVA planned Norris, from the start, as an all-white community and blatantly excluded African Americans not only from living there but also from participating in Norris Dam–related vocational training in the community during the day. Although the TVA emerged out of a progressive ideology and a desire to radically transform the region, the agency, like many New Deal institutions, advocated a "grassroots" philosophy and acquiesced to (rather than challenged) local southern customs of racial segregation and inequality. African American organizations at the time, some of which vehemently but unsuccessfully protested the TVA's policies, saw Norris as perpetuating and institutionalizing white privilege, its geography loudly communicating the territorial message that African Americans held an inferior social position or simply did not belong. The legacy of this message endures: of the 1,491 people living in Norris according to the 2010 census, only three were African American (Alderman and Brown 2011).

As the historical geography of Norris illustrates, the racialization of landscape has had very real consequences for African Americans. This is perhaps no more apparent than in an examination of the Jim Crow era, which began in the 1870s and continued until the civil rights movement of the 1960s. During Jim Crow, African Americans endured separate (and unequal) schools, transportation, and public accommodations, deprivation of political and economic rights, and a hypersegregated society that criminalized racial mixing. Importantly, violence—from the pervasive lynching (hanging, mutilation, and/or burning) of blacks by the Ku Klux Klan and vigilante mobs to numerous white-on-black race riots in the first half of the twentieth century—also served during this era as a tactic for intimidating and controlling African Americans. In 1919 alone, riots occurred in twenty-five different U.S. cities (Collins 2012). Because of their visibility and public nature, the landscapes employed in injuring and killing African Americans became means to harden racial hierarchies of power, marking in blood and soil the presumed inferiority of victims and the broader black community while also demonstrating the supposed supremacy of whites. One should not underestimate the extent to which these brutal expressions of white power have affected the long-term socialization of African Americans, including their interaction with landscapes. For instance, scholars such as Cassandra Johnson (1998) have argued that African American aversion to certain nature-based recreation and travel is possibly linked to a collective memory of Jim Crow lynching—which often took place in wildland areas.

Every racialized landscape, even the most oppressive, holds the seeds of its undoing and the potential for resisting racism and exclusion (Schein 2003). Indeed, the civil rights movement would later use the tradition of whites inflicting violence against African Americans—captured in national media images of police brutality—to garner sympathy from the federal government and the broader U.S. public. More radical branches of the movement, such as the Black Panther Party, challenged racialized violence with self-defense. Robert F. Williams, an early important advocate of this approach, debated the merits of nonviolence with Martin Luther King Jr. in the 1950s and formed an armed Black Guard in his hometown of Monroe, North Carolina, to defend against local Klan attacks (Tyson 1999).

Landscape resistance is not always direct and confrontational. Through daily practices and performances, African Americans have turned the landscapes created to segregate them into counterpublic spaces, places where black identities and cultural traditions flourished separate from and in opposition to the white-dominated public sphere. Noteworthy sites of historical black counterpublic development include Beale Street (Memphis), Harlem (New York City), Auburn Avenue (Atlanta), and Faubourg Tremé (New Orleans) (Crutcher 2010; Inwood 2011). Consequently, as we analyze the historical geography of racialized landscapes, it is important to analyze not only the use of places to perpetuate racist social relations but also the potential for marginalized groups to claim these same places as their own and use them to contest racialized social hierarchies and enact antiracist goals.

Gareth Hoskins's (2006) research on the Angel Island Immigration Station is instructive about how racialized landscapes extend beyond the African American experience. From 1910 to 1940, the station detained approximately 175,000 Chinese immigrants, severely restricting their entry into the United States as part of the Chinese Exclusion Act of 1882. As a place of racialization, it "worked to defend the nation's borders from a perceived Asian menace and, by association, served to construct the legitimate American public as white" (Hoskins 2006, 96). Today, Angel Island is a state park that retells this uncomfortable history, most vividly through the preservation and interpretation of the poems that detainees inscribed on barrack walls. These inscriptions "communicate how racial exclusion played a role in the building of the United States" and inform ongoing debates about immigration, citizenship, and national identity—debates that call into question the very racial injustices that Angel Island carried out in the early twentieth century.

As Hoskins's work suggests, contemporary historical geographers are not simply concerned with the racialization of landscapes in the past. Rather, they are also interested in the politics of social or collective memory and how landscapes become embroiled in struggles over how to deal with the history of racism in the present and the future, which in turn influences the need for redress. Indeed, a theme of growing importance among historical geographers is the extent to which remembering the past can be highly racialized and the role played by landscapes of memory, including memorials, monuments, museums, preserved historic sites, heritage festivals, and even roadside markers. Southern plantation museums are perhaps ground zero in this struggle over how (or even whether) we should remember past racist practices and landscapes. Museum managers have traditionally ignored or minimized the identities and contributions of the enslaved community, representing slavery, when discussed, as a benign institution of caring masters and faithful servants, perpetuating a racial stereotype of the faithful, happy-go-lucky slave that dates back to the antebellum period (Alderman and Modlin 2008). These misrepresentations of the realities of enslavement, long used by whites not only to promote tourism but also to justify racial inequalities, play a foundational role in race relations (Hoelscher 2003).

Although this erasure of the slave experience takes place on many fronts, the manipulation of the plantation's landscape—its artifacts and architectural spaces and places—plays an especially powerful role in narrating a history of antebellum life in which the absence of a critical discussion of slavery and its moral and social implications seems natural. Indeed, docent-led tours of the southern plantation have tended to emphasize the furnishings, the china, and even the chamber pots owned by the planter class over the details of slave life, thereby subjugating, if not erasing, the identities of African Americans as well as misrepresenting the very real role that slavery played within plantation societies (Modlin 2011) (figure 15.1). While historical geographers have traditionally treated historical objects and relics simply as evidence of the past, the southern plantation landscape offers an example of how elites in a society can employ material legacies and traces, whether strategically or subconsciously, to normalize white privilege and deflect needed discussions of racism and the legacy of slavery (Modlin, Alderman, and Gentry 2011).

Figure 15.1. One- and two-story slave quarters are shown in the foreground, with the plantation mansion in the far background at Somerset Place, Creswell, North Carolina. These structures and a slave hospital were reconstructed in the early 2000s during Dorothy Redford's tenure as site manager, illustrating her efforts to give the enslaved community a material presence and legitimacy within the plantation landscape and providing a counterpoint to historical narratives that have traditionally rendered slavery invisible to tourists. Photography by E. Arnold Modlin Jr., December 2012.

Racist narrations of the past at the southern plantation museum have not gone unchallenged, however. Not all tourists acquiesce to this traditionally dominant reading of the plantation, sometimes openly questioning docents about the racial politics of plantation history. Some African Americans have produced counternarratives that bring the slave struggle front and center within the retelling of the Old South (Hoelscher 2003). The story of Dorothy Redford (1988) exemplifies this geographic and commemorative agency among blacks. Inspired by Alex Haley's *Roots*, Redford began a lifelong project of reconstructing her genealogical connection with the slave community at Somerset Plantation in Creswell, North Carolina, eventually leading to several large family reunions at the plantation and her management of the site as a state park. At Somerset, Redford carried out an excavation, both literal and figurative, of the names, traditions, material artifacts, living and working spaces, and struggles of the enslaved. Her efforts illustrate how the artifact politics of the plantation museum can perhaps be reversed and become a platform for recovering, rather than merely unmaking, an African American sense of place.

A discussion of public commemoration and historical representation prompts us to consider how the racialization of landscapes, while certainly relying on the explicit use of segregation and violence, also involves a deeper cultural and symbolic structuring of space and place around exclusion. Even seemingly insignificant and taken-for-granted aspects of landscapes can become sites for defining, controlling, and possibly resisting racialized identities. Perhaps no better example of the everyday nature of racialization is the history in the United States of place naming, one of the fundamental ways in which people inscribe the landscape with meaning and value and create a physical marker of their collective identity. Over forty years ago, Karl Raitz questioned the validity of the idea of the "American melting pot" and the homogenization of cultural differences and identities, arguing that racial and ethnic communities had used place naming historically to "create a distinctive cultural landscape, a mirror of their beliefs and values" (1973, 31). In particular, he demonstrated that place names, or toponyms, on U.S. Geological Survey topographic maps could be used to identify African American settlements. In addition, some place names in the southern United States, historically believed to be of Native American or European origin, are really of African derivation, specifically retentions from the Bantu language group (Vass 1980). While the diaspora and enslavement were no doubt imposing and brutal, African thought and creativity were not extinguished completely but instead mixed with and affected white, European naming practices.

In emphasizing African American influence on place naming, one should not lose sight of the fact that toponyms have historically reinforced stereotypical racial identities while also normalizing a white perspective on the landscape. Mark Monmonier has examined the impact of racism on U.S. place names, the historical use of racially and ethnically derogatory terms in toponyms, and the slow progress of the federal government in renaming these features. White control of place naming continued even in the wake of the civil rights movement. When U.S. courts ordered schools in Bulloch County, Georgia, to integrate racially in 1971, white authorities responded by changing the names of formerly all-black schools, some of which bore the names of important black leaders. African American students boycotted the first six days of the 1971 school year in protest, but to no avail. By the 1990s, African Americans were clearly using toponyms as a way of resisting the historical racialization of the landscape and as part of a broader campaign to recognize their black leaders' contributions. In 1992, the black-controlled Orleans Parish school board passed a policy prohibiting school names honoring slave owners and other historical purveyors of racial inequality. The names of many white historical figures (including the slaveholding first president of the United States, George Washington) were removed from schools and replaced with others commemorating prominent African Americans, including slain civil rights leader Martin Luther King Jr. (Alderman 2008).

The renaming of public places, most often streets, is arguably the most widespread of African American efforts to use the landscape for antiracist purposes. The naming of streets for King began shortly after his assassination in 1968, and there are now over nine hundred roads named for him, although controversy often accompanies the naming process as white opponents seek to control not just whether King will be honored but where and on which street. Indeed, these opponents have often succeeded in having King's namesakes confined to (or segregated within) black neighborhoods, suggesting that even a landscape seemingly designed to advocate antiracism can become reracialized (figure 15.2). As place-naming patterns suggest, landscapes are not given over entirely to challenging or reinforcing racist practices but clearly serve as "arenas" for debating the meaning of race in American history and culture (Alderman 2008).

LANDSCAPES OF HOSPITALITY, TRAVEL, AND TRANSPORTATION

Although the field of historical geography is increasingly undertaking the study of racialized landscapes, numerous themes that geographers have not examined widely represent avenues for future work. We devote the final section of the chapter to discussing racialization in the context of the landscapes created and used for the purposes of hospitality, travel, and transportation—linking these seemingly unproblematic issues to a larger historical geography of civil rights.

Recognizing travel landscapes as potential sites of racialization requires a critical understanding of hospitality as more than simply the commercial provision of tourist services or a friendly willingness to assist someone. Gestures of hospitality significantly structure social relations and help negotiate the distinction between self and other, shaping the terms of welcoming, belonging, and citizenship. Much of the power of hospitality lies in how it creates and legitimizes social categories and identities. "Host and guest are not innocent terms" (2007, 8), write Jennie Germann Molz and Sarah Gibson. A critical analysis of hospitality poses questions such as "Who gets to be guest, and under what conditions? Who gets to be a host and under what conditions? Who gets to move between these categories? How do these categories authorize some people's right to travel and to be welcomed, while delegitimizing other claims to mobility and

Figure 15.2. Martin Luther King Drive in Greenville, North Carolina, speaks to how the landscape, while seeming to work for antiracism purposes, can reinforce historically entrenched racialized boundaries. Originally African American leaders wanted all of Fifth Street renamed for King, not just part of it, but residents and business owners on the predominantly white eastern end strongly opposed the proposal and subsequent efforts to extend the name. Photography by Derek Alderman, September 2006.

belonging?" (Molz and Gibson 2007, 8). A politics surrounds these questions as hospitality rarely operates in a completely inclusive or open way. Expressions of hospitality target certain groups, whereas others receive less welcoming, if not outright hostile, receptions.

The African American historical experience clearly demonstrates the discriminatory way in which hospitality is extended and how landscapes of travel become sites for reinforcing, as well as possibly resisting, broader racial inequalities. Any meaningful analysis of hospitality must come to terms with the hostile barriers that traditionally limited African American travel and mobility. As Euan Hague notes, "African Americans in the era of slavery were immobilized on plantations and movement from plantation space was illicit, codified as illegal, and required the hidden networks of the Underground Railroad" (2010, 331). The white power structure controlled black mobility even after emancipation through the use of vagrancy laws and other legal sanctions designed to intimidate and exploit black labor (Blackmon 2008). The Jim Crow era extended to African

Americans a highly segregated and unequal geography of hospitality and tourism that restricted them to a limited number of separate parks, beaches, hotels, restaurants, restrooms, and other accommodations (Algeo 2013). They confronted considerable humiliation, harassment, and even violence when traveling. The creation of racially hostile landscapes of travel meant more than limited tourism options for African Americans; it was part of a broader denial of the legitimacy of their identity and right to belong.

The *Negro Travelers' Green Book* (first published as the *Negro Motorist Green Book)* offers valuable insight into the racialization of hospitality and travel in the early and mid-twentieth century, although it has received scant attention from historical geographers (but see Foote 2012). The *Green Book*, published annually from 1936 to 1964 by New York postal employee Victor Green, was a guide identifying hospitable or safe accommodations to help middle-class African Americans avoid discrimination and segregation during their travels. Arranged by state and city, the book included the locations of welcoming lodging, restaurants, barber shops/beauty salons, taverns, and other services. The *Green Book* could assist historical geographers in mapping, both literally and metaphorically, the racialized landscapes of African American travel (figure 15.3). On one hand, the very need to have such a guide speaks loudly to the power of white supremacy in the time before and during the American civil rights movement and the influence

Figure 15.3. The *1949 Negro Motorist Green Book* showed the distribution of cities providing establishments that would welcome African American travelers. This edition of the *Green Book* listed 3,702 establishments located in 527 cities across forty-six states, an alternative landscape of mobility that spoke to both the social control and the resistance that characterized Jim Crow. Cartography by Richard Kennedy.

that racism, realized and anticipated, exerted on many facets of black life, including where and how to travel. While the *Green Book* does not inventory all African American–friendly establishments during segregation, it clearly documents a spatial inequality in the location of these businesses and how easily black families might find themselves with nowhere to eat or spend the night. Hotels and other accommodations were particularly limited for African Americans traveling out west (Foster 1999). A detailed locational mapping of *Green Book* establishments reveals how black travelers were spatially confined to certain parts of the city and how other areas were effectively off limits to them. These patterns of hospitality reflected and reinforced the wider social geography of segregation as well as a racialized urban economy.

On the other hand, the racialized landscape of American hospitality did not shut down all possibilities for black travel and consumption. The *Green Book* also speaks to how black motorists could navigate the obstacle-filled Jim Crow landscape in creative, resistant, and antiracist ways. Thus, a mapping of the book also reveals points of black power and self-determination in the face of white supremacy. In the guide's pages, one could learn about Robbins, Illinois, located outside Chicago and promoted as "a city owned and operated by" African Americans. The *Green Book* would also lead visitors to safe establishments along Pettigrew and Fayetteville Streets in Hayti, North Carolina, now part of Durham, which began as an independent African American community founded after the Civil War. In Denver, *Green Book* establishments were clustered in the city's Five Points area, which became the center of the African American community during the Great Migration (Foote 2012). The businesses highlighted in the travel guide represented places of escape for black travelers and served as early sites for creating the African American tourist we see today. *Green Book* establishments also functioned as information-sharing nodes, providing travelers with advice about hospitable places and routes perhaps not listed in the guide, as well more general political and social news, especially during the civil rights movement. Black-run beauty parlors, frequently listed in the *Green Book*, were important refuges from prying white eyes and ears during the movement.

Recognizing the importance of the *Green Book* requires that we understand its place within the larger historical geography of African American activism, which can refer to formal political protest but also a politics of everyday, informal resistance. For instance, there is a history of what Wilson (2012) calls "commodity activism" within the African American community, that is, instances in which blacks circumvented white-controlled forms and locations of consumerism to avoid discrimination. For instance, he has argued that the popularity of mail-order purchases and the consumption of prepackaged brands among African Americans constituted resistance to poor treatment by white store owners and their practice of cheating black customers when measuring purchased food and goods. Similarly, a larger political value surrounded African American tourist consumption using the *Green Book* as a way to mock Jim Crow and avoid inflated prices, poor service, and inedible food from the few white establishments that would serve them. Moreover, "journeying by auto gave some black motorists a vantage point from which to assess the absurdity and self-defeating characteristics of segregation" (Foster 1999, 141), particularly when they saw white-only businesses with few customers.

The analytical value of the *Green Book* is further established when we recognize that it was just one of many instances in which African Americans resisted oppressive modes of travel and constructed alternative landscapes of transportation and mobility. During the same period of Jim Crow segregation, African Americans carried out the famous Montgomery Bus Boycott of 1955–1956, which became one of the first major victories of the civil rights movement and resulted in a landmark Supreme Court decision (*Browder v. Gayle*) that struck down the constitutionality of bus-segregation laws. As usually retold, the history of this seminal campaign emphasizes the sacrifices of Rosa Parks and Martin Luther King Jr., as well as the collective decision of seventeen thousand boycotters to refuse to ride the city bus line, in the face of intense white opposition and retaliation, for 381 days. But their activism surpassed simply refusing to patronize Montgomery buses. They designed, operated, and financed an insurgent transportation system to ensure that boycotters, especially those without automobiles, could travel to and from work, home, and shops. This alternative landscape of travel included subsidized taxis, a complex network of carpool drop-off and pick-up points, boycotters walking several miles a day, and even a fleet of privately bought station wagons called "rolling churches" (Alderman, Kingsbury, and Dwyer 2013).

Working behind the scenes in orchestrating this reconstruction of African American mobility were members of the Women's Political Council who had spoken out against segregated bus seating long before Rosa Parks's famous defiant stand and who are credited with actually initiating the Alabama boycott. Of particular interest to geographers, one of the major leaders of this council, Thelma Glass, was a professor of geography at Alabama State University. In 1956, Glass lent her perspective on the geographical inequities of the Montgomery bus system when testifying at the conspiracy trial of Martin Luther King Jr., reporting that "bus stops were more closely spaced in white communities than in Black" (George, Monk, and Gaston 2004, 333). Strangely enough, despite a geographer's involvement in resisting and redefining racial conditions in Montgomery, few historical geographers have focused much attention on the famous boycott.

Mobility is about more than making an abstract journey from point A to B, be it to take a vacation or a city bus ride. Landscapes of travel can provide a useful barometer of patterns of hospitality (or hostility), the social and historical conditions under which people are granted mobility, and the power of certain social groups to claim the American landscape on those journeys. We suggest that the broader historical geography of African American travel and transportation represents an important but largely untapped area for studying the landscape as a site for racial identity construction and broader struggles over rights, citizenship, and being welcome in one's own country. Important to the racialization perspective is the ability to use historical patterns of inequality to understand contemporary experiences and perceptions. Without an analysis of racialized hospitality and the discourses of racial control and resistance running through the *Green Book*, how can we adequately understand why some contemporary African Americans continue to use travel strategies that date back to Jim Crow and why black travel decisions remain greatly affected by concerns about racial acceptance (Carter 2008)?

In conclusion, historical geographers increasingly stand in an important position to unravel the role of racist and antiracist social practices in shaping, and being shaped by, the U.S. landscape and to advance a broader understanding of African American life. Doing so requires recognizing the social construction of racial identities and hierarchies, including whiteness and white privilege, in ways that have legacy effects on people, places, and practices. It is also important to understand how the landscape—both as a product of past social processes and as a conduit for remembering in the present—has the power to legitimize and delegitimize racialized categories and power relations. Investigating the historical geography of African Americans and racialization is about exploring racism and antiracism as evocative and highly politicized landscape spectacles but also as subtler, everyday spatial practices and performances. Finally, a focus on racialization will not only lead to better and more critical historical geographic analysis but contribute to the creation of a field that, in the words of George Lipsitz, helps society "disassemble the fatal links that connect race, power, and place" (2007, 10).

REFERENCES

Aiken, C. S. 1985. New Settlement Pattern of Rural Blacks in the American South. *Geographical Review* 75: 383–404.

———. 1987. Race as a Factor in Municipal Underbounding. *Annals of the Association of American Geographers* 77, no. 4: 564–79.

———. 1998. *The Cotton Plantation South since the Civil War*. Baltimore: Johns Hopkins University Press.

———. 2001. Blacks in the Plantation South: A Unique Homeland. In *Homelands: A Geography of Culture and Place across America*, edited by R. L. Nostrand and L. E. Estaville, 53–72. Baltimore: Johns Hopkins University Press.

Alderman, D. H. 2008. Place, Naming, and the Interpretation of Cultural Landscapes. In *The Ashgate Research Companion to Heritage and Identity*, edited by B. Graham and P. Howard, 195–213. Burlington, VT: Ashgate Publishing Co.

Alderman, D. H., and E. A. Modlin Jr. 2008. (In)Visibility of the Enslaved within Online Plantation Tourism Marketing: A Textual Analysis of North Carolina Websites. *Journal of Travel and Tourism Marketing* 25, nos. 3–4: 265–81.

Alderman, D. H., and R. N. Brown. 2011. When a New Deal Is Actually an Old Deal: The Role of TVA in Engineering a Racialized Jim Crow Landscape. In *Engineering Earth: The Impacts of Mega-engineering Projects*, edited by S. Brunn, 3:1901–16. Dordrecht: Springer.

Alderman, D. H., P. Kingsbury, and O. J. Dwyer. 2013. Reexamining the Montgomery Bus Boycott: Toward an Empathetic Pedagogy of the Civil Rights Movement. *Professional Geographer* 65, no. 1: 171–86.

Algeo, K. 2013. Underground Tourists/Tourists Underground: African American Tourism to Mammoth Cave. *Tourism Geographies* 15, no. 3: 380–404.

Anderson, K. J. 1987. The Idea of Chinatown: The Power of Place and Institutional Practice in the Making of a Racial Category. *Annals of the Association of American Geographers* 77, no. 4: 580–98.

Arreola, D. D. 2002. *Tejano South Texas: A Mexican American Cultural Province*. Austin: University of Texas Press.

———. 2006. The Picture Postcard Mexican Housescape: Visual Culture and Domestic Identity. In *Landscape and Race in the United States*, edited by R. H. Schein, 113–26. New York: Routledge.

Blackmon, D. 2008. *Slavery by Another Name: The Re-enslavement of Black Americans from the Civil War to World War II*. New York: Anchor Books.

Carney, J. A. 2001. *Black Rice: The African Origins of Rice Cultivation in the Americas*. Cambridge, MA: Harvard University Press.

Carter, P. 2008. Coloured Places and Pigmented Holidays: Racialized Leisure Travel. *Tourism Geographies* 10: 265–84.

Collins, A. V. 2012. *All Hell Broke Loose: American Race Riots from the Progressive Era through World War II*. Santa Barbara, CA: Praeger.

Conzen, M. P., ed. 1990. *The Making of the American Landscape*. Boston: Unwin Hyman.

Crutcher, M. E. 2010. *Tremé: Race and Place in a New Orleans Neighborhood*. Athens: University of Georgia Press.

Dwyer, O. J. 1997. Geographical Research about African Americans: A Survey of Journals, 1911–1995. *Professional Geographer* 49, no. 4: 441–51.

Earle, C. V. 1978. A Staple Interpretation of Slavery and Free Labor. *Geographical Review* 68, no. 1: 51–65.

Foote, K. 2012. Editing Memory and Automobility and Race: Two Learning Activities Focusing on Contested Heritage and Place. *Southeastern Geographer* 52, no. 4: 384–97.

Foster, M. S. 1999. In the Face of "Jim Crow": Prosperous Blacks and Vacations, Travel and Outdoor Leisure, 1890–1945. *Journal of Negro History* 84, no. 2: 130–49.

George, S., J. Monk, and J. Gaston. 2004. Teachers and Their Times: Thelma Glass and Juanita Gaston. In *The South's Role in the Making of American Geography*, edited by J. O. Wheeler and S. Brunn, 327–42. Columbia, MD: Bellwether Press.

Hague, E. 2010. "The Right to Enter Every Other State"—the Supreme Court and African American Mobility in the United States. *Mobilities* 5: 331–47.

Harris, D. 2006. Race, Class, and Privacy in the Ordinary Postwar House, 1945–1960. In *Landscape and Race in the United States*, edited by R. H. Schein, 127–55. New York: Routledge.

Hilliard, S. 1972. *Hog Meat and Hoecake: Food Supply in the Old South, 1840–1860*. Carbondale: Southern Illinois University Press.

Hochschild, J. L., and B. M. Powell. 2008. Racial Reorganization and the United States Census, 1850–1930: Mulattoes, Half-Breeds, Mixed Parentage, Hindoos, and the Mexican Race. *Studies in American Political Development* 22, no. 1: 59–96.

Hoelscher, S. 2003. Making Place, Making Race: Performances of Whiteness in the Jim Crow South. *Annals of the Association of American Geographers* 93, no. 3: 657–86.

Hoskins, G. 2006. Poetic Landscapes of Exclusion: Chinese Immigration at Angel Island, San Francisco. In *Landscape and Race in the United States*, edited by R. H. Schein, 95–111. New York: Routledge.

Ignatiev, N. 1996. *How the Irish Became White*. New York: Routledge.

Inwood, J. F. J. 2011. Constructing African American Urban Space in Atlanta, Georgia. *Geographical Review* 101: 147–63.

Inwood, J. F. J., and D. G. Martin. 2008. Whitewash: White Privilege and Racialized Landscapes at the University of Georgia. *Social and Cultural Geography* 9, no. 4 (June): 373–95.

Inwood, J. F. J., and R. A. Yarbrough. 2010. Racialized Place, Racialized Bodies. *GeoJournal* 75: 299–301.

Johnson, C. 1998. A Consideration of Collective Memory in African American Attachment to Wildland Recreation Places. *Research in Human Ecology* 5, no. 1: 50–15.

Jordan, T. G., and M. Kaups. 1989. *The American Backwoods Frontier: An Ethnic and Ecological Interpretation*. Baltimore: Johns Hopkins University Press.

Kobayashi, A., and L. Peake. 2000. Racism Out of Place: Thoughts on Whiteness and an Antiracist Geography in the New Millennium. *Annals of the Association of American Geographers* 90, no. 2: 392–403.

Lai, C. 2012. The Racial Triangulation of Space: The Case of Urban Renewal in San Francisco's Fillmore District. *Annals of the Association of American Geographers* 102, no. 1: 151–70.

Lipsitz, G. 2007. The Racialization of Space and the Spatialization of Race: Theorizing the Hidden Architecture of Landscape. *Landscape Journal* 26, no. 1: 10–23.

McIlwraith, T. F., and E. K. Muller, eds. 2001. *North America: The Historical Geography of a Changing Continent*. 2nd ed. Lanham, MD: Rowman & Littlefield.

Mitchell, D. 2000. *Cultural Geography: A Critical Introduction*. Malden, MA: Blackwell Publishing.

Modlin, E. A., Jr. 2011. Representing Slavery at Plantation-House Museums in the U.S. South: A Dynamic Spatial Process. *Historical Geography* 39: 147–73.

Modlin, E. A., Jr., D. H. Alderman, and G. W. Gentry. 2011. Tour Guides as Creators of Empathy: The Role of Affective Inequality in Marginalizing the Enslaved at Plantation House Museums. *Tourist Studies* 11, no. 1: 3–19.

Molz, J., and S. Gibson. 2007. Introduction: Mobilizing and Mooring Hospitality. In *Mobilizing Hospitality: The Ethics of Social Relations in a Mobile World*, edited by J. Molz and S. Gibson, 1–25. Burlington, VT: Ashgate Publishing Co.

Monmonier, M. 2006. *From Squaw Tit to Whorehouse Meadow: How Maps Name, Claim, and Inflame*. Chicago: University of Chicago Press.

Nostrand, R. L., and L. E. Estaville, eds. 2001. *Homelands: A Geography of Culture and Place across America*. Baltimore: Johns Hopkins University Press.

Raitz, K. 1973. Ethnic Settlements on Topographic Maps. *Journal of Geography* 72, no. 8: 29–40.

Redford, D. 1988. *Somerset Homecoming: Recovering a Lost Heritage*. New York: Doubleday.

Schein, R. H. 2003. Normative Dimensions of Landscape. In *Everyday America: Cultural Landscape Studies after J. B. Jackson*, edited by C. Wilson and P. Groth, 199–218. Berkeley: University of California Press.

———. 2006. Race and Landscape in the United States. In *Landscape and Race in the United States*, edited by R. H. Schein, 1–22. New York: Routledge.

Sumpter, A. 2011. Racial Identity, Spatial Mobility, and Labor in the Non-Plantation Rural South, 1880–1940. *Journal of Historical Geography* 37, no. 4. 460–69.

Trudeau, D. 2006. Politics of Belonging in the Construction of Landscapes: Place-Making, Boundary Drawing and Exclusion. *Cultural Geographies* 13: 421–43.

Tyson, T. B. 1999. *Radio Free Dixie: Robert Williams and the Roots of Black Power*. Chapel Hill: University of North Carolina Press.

Vass, W. 1980. *The Bantu Speaking Heritage of the United States*. Los Angeles: University of California, Los Angeles, Center for Afro-American Studies.

Wilson, B. M. 2000a. *America's Johannesburg: Industrialization and Racial Transformation in Birmingham*. Lanham, MD: Rowman & Littlefield.

———. 2000b. *Race and Place in Birmingham: The Civil Rights and Neighborhood Movements*. Lanham, MD: Rowman & Littlefield.

———. 2010. Postbellum Race Relations in Commodity Exchange. *GeoJournal* 75: 273–81.

———. 2012. Commodity Activism in the Jim Crow South. Paper presented at Race, Ethnicity, and Place Conference 6, San Juan, Puerto Rico, October 25.

Winders, J. 2008. An "Incomplete" Picture? Race, Latino Migration, and Urban Politics in Nashville, Tennessee. *Urban Geography* 29, no. 3: 246–63.
Woods, C. 1998. *Development Arrested: Race, Power, and the Blues in the Mississippi Delta*. London: Verso.
Zelinsky, W. 1950. The Population Geography of the Free Negro in Ante-bellum America. *Population Studies* 3: 386–401.

16

Toward a Gendered Historical Geography of North America

Mona Domosh

Some of the most iconic landscapes that have come to symbolize North America are gendered in one way or another: the robed female figure of Libertas—better known as the Statue of Liberty—that has greeted immigrants, visitors, and returning citizens since its dedication in 1886; the urban skyline created through financial capitalism's competitive masculinity; and the suburban single-family home whose "master" bedroom and "family" room are direct expressions of the heteronormative middle-class family. If you look out your window right now or around the classroom or other space where you are reading this, you are seeing at all times arrangements of spaces and places shaped by the many cultures that preceded you, and constituting each of those cultures are varied and variable gendered, racialized, classed, and sexualized relationships of power. In this sense, all landscapes and all places are gendered—that is, shaped by gendered relationships, discourses, and practices (and other topologies of power, including "race," class, and sexuality). In this chapter I draw out the various ways in which the historical geography of North America is fundamentally a gendered geography that we can only adequately understand by paying attention to the relations and representations of power through which it was created and continues to be recreated. Drawing on (predominantly) recent historical geographic research, I discuss the gendering of the North American landscape by focusing on four main periods/spaces: landscapes, frontiers, and European-native encounters; late-nineteenth/early-twentieth-century cities; postwar–Cold War cities and suburbs; and gentrification and late-twentieth-century cities.

LANDSCAPES, FRONTIERS, AND EUROPEAN-NATIVE ENCOUNTERS

The gendering of the North American landscape began much earlier than its European "settlement." Before Europeans and Africans arrived on the shores of

North America, Native American cultures had been shaping the landscape for thousands of years. Settlement types that ranged from urban systems to mobile housing forms give some sense of the diversity of native landscapes (see chapter 1). But it is important to note that gendered relationships and practices were fundamental to shaping these geographies. For example, the Navajo people of the American Southwest believe that the occupation and spatial arrangements of their everyday lives are sacred. Accordingly, their homes, or hogans, are in some senses replications of their cosmic worldview. These structures are circular in form, reiterating the Navajo view of the circular cosmos, with the door facing east, the direction in which the sun rises each day. In addition, in accordance with their belief system, the hogan is symbolically divided into equally important halves, with one side designated as female and the other as male (Nabokov and Easton 1989). In other native cultures, different forms of architectural spaces reflected or symbolized particular gendered societal arrangements, and prescribed gender roles often dictated land-use patterns. The longhouses of the Chippewas—Native Americans who lived in the region surrounding Lakes Superior and Huron—were divided into spaces of women's and men's work, with the central hearth area typically assigned to the men but ceded to the women when the men left for the hunt (Nabokov and Easton 1989).

From the fifteenth century on, the diverse array of Europeans and Africans who landed on the eastern shore of North America and moved westward altered, conquered, and often obliterated native cultures and landscapes. In the contact zone where these different cultures encountered each other (Pratt 1992; Pickles and Rutherdale 2005), gendered bodies, ideals, imaginations, and practices often came into conflict. Literary scholar Annette Kolodny (1975, 83) has argued that even before settling the land, European explorers and colonists imagined North America as virginal and untouched. In 1616, for example, John Smith described the New England seacoast thus: "Her treasures having yet never been opened, nor her originals wasted, consumed, nor abused" (quoted in Kolodny 1975, 12–13). Sixteen years later, Thomas Merton described the area in similar terms: "Like a faire virgin, longing to be sped, And meet her lover in a Nuptial bed" (quoted in Kolodny 1975, 13). The effect of such descriptions was twofold: they naturalized the conquest and consumption of the land by Europeans and totally effaced Native Americans as agents of landscape change. Gendered and sexualized imaginings of North America, in other words, played central roles in legitimizing European settlement, use, and destruction of the continent's natural resources.

Gendered imaginations also served to position Native Americans as different from and inferior to Europeans. From the outset, encounters between Europeans and native peoples were fraught with overlapping and at times conflicting intentions, desires, and needs. In general, European explorers and colonists wanted Native American lands and resources. In order to justify dispossessing native peoples, they imagined them as incapable of participation in the Enlightenment ideals of rights and citizenship. They were, in the parlance of the day, "uncivilized." In the eighteenth and nineteenth centuries, "civilized" societies practiced industrial capitalism, were predominantly white, and were controlled largely by men. With respect to the last of these, "civilized" men were meant to be productive and to participate in the public sphere, while women were meant to be reproductive and to remain in the domestic sphere (Bederman 1995; Newman 1995). Judged according to these criteria, Native Americans were savage, not civilized, and therefore neither capable nor worthy of possessing and cultivating land.

Yet these broad generalizations about how groups of people imagined each other ignore the daily realities of Europeans encounters with native peoples, first on the eastern seaboard and then, as dispossession of native peoples continued, on the various western frontiers. Recent historical scholarship has begun to explore the range of gendered, sexualized, and racialized relationships that characterized contacts between European colonists, visitors, and native peoples—relationships that add complexity and nuance to the binary of civilized or savage. Historian Adele Perry (2005) has documented how nineteenth-century European notions of gender were integral to the Catholic, Methodist, and Anglican mission system established in the mid-nineteenth century in British Columbia. European missionaries used the notion of separate spheres, particularly the "proper" role of women, to judge the relative "civilized" nature of different native peoples and as an ideal toward which to direct mission activities. For example, given that mobile and communal living arrangements were considered signs of primitive societies, Perry shows how many mission activities centered on building permanent settlements of single-family homes for native peoples. The alignment of women with the domestic meant that missionaries focused attention on native women, encouraging them to abandon their previous work and take up their "proper" roles as housekeepers, mothers, and wives. These encounters with native cultures, in which women participated in a diverse range of activities, led many women missionaries to question their own gendered assumptions. As Perry argues, "The variety of ways people organized households gave the lie to the foundational assumption that there was a universal and transhistoric connection between womanhood, the home, and morality" (2005, 114). In other words, for some women missionaries, encountering and living with people whose gender roles and behavior differed quite a bit from their own forced a reevaluation of their own beliefs in "fixed" gender roles.

In a related fashion, geographer Karen Morin (1998, 1999, 2002) has examined how the American West was imagined and shaped through encounters between native peoples, Europeans, and white Americans—encounters that were always in one way or another gendered. The impoverishment of native peoples in the mid- to late nineteenth century—due primarily to dispossession of their lands and ways of life—was evident in many regions of the United States, but a primary site of encounter was at train stations along the newly completed rail lines in the Midwest and Great Plains. Here, in the 1870s and 1880s, some displaced native peoples earned income by begging or entertaining visitors with their skillful "feats." Through an analysis of travelers' accounts of these encounters, Morin discerns how women travelers imagined and understood the American West and Native Americans. Some women wrote about native peoples as aesthetic objects or as noble savages, symbols of America's past. Others emphasized the primitiveness of natives, thereby legitimizing white American conquest. But given women's bourgeois roles as domesticators and "civilizers" in British society,

FOR A PARTICIPATORY HISTORICAL GEOGRAPHY
Dydia DeLyser

As a feminist cultural-historical geographer, I strive in my published research to link rich empirical work with theoretical engagements. But that simple description masks an equally important part of my research endeavors: I also strive to make my research participatory and to forward community agendas as part of efforts to give back to the communities that have contributed in different ways to my research. That's part of a feminist commitment to research that is politically and socially progressive and potentially emancipatory—research that seeks to help overturn decades (or centuries) of multiple forms of discrimination and to empower those most often overlooked or directly disempowered. Understanding historical geography as participatory also makes our research more than just a textual exercise bound up with papers in archives; it highlights the doing of historical geography as an embodied practice.

But how can historical geography be participatory when the people we study are almost always dead? Like all participatory research, participatory historical geography takes thought, time, and effort, and it requires first coming to a careful understanding of the community. In all my historical research, I've made explicit efforts toward participatory historical geographies; here, I present just one example of how I've tried.

I began my research on early women pilots as a woman pilot myself, feeling a connection to the women I studied and interested in the cause they championed (equality for women and recognition for women pilots). Though the women I was studying were deceased, they had established the 99s, an organization of and for women pilots founded by the ninety-nine licensed women pilots flying in 1929, and I was a member. I became the first scholar to use the collections at the 99s Museum of Women Pilots and immediately saw where I could put my academic skills to use: much of the collections were unprocessed, so as I did the research, I volunteered to catalog parts of them. I also supported those collections by buying and donating materials about early 99s. And I ran for international election for a seat on the museum's board—I'm now in my second term serving the museum and its visitors. Because the women I studied had made their goals explicit, and because a museum now represents those interests, I've been able to participate in that community and to forward its goals, even though all the original community members are now gone.

Of course, not all the research we do need be overtly participatory—it may not always be possible or even desirable. And even when research is not overtly participatory, that does not prevent it from having a positive community impact. After all, community members can discover research not designed to be participatory long after it is published and then use it for the benefit of that community. My point is that historical research can be participatory and can be of benefit to a community—even to a community of the dead. And that makes efforts at participatory historical geography worth integrating, where appropriate and possible, into our research practice.

some sympathized with the plight of native peoples, either commenting on ways to "help" native women become more "civilized" or, interestingly, realizing that gender roles indeed differed between cultures. Morin documents how one traveler, Theresa Longworth, writing in 1876, particularly empathized with native culture. Longworth highlighted the various ways that gender roles differed in native cultures and by thus "calling into question an essentialist construction of gender and racial difference . . . foreground[ed] herself in sympathy with both Native women and men" (Morin 1998, 324). Much as Perry did in British Columbia, Morin finds that encountering cultures with different gender relationships forced some European women to question the universality of their own beliefs. This focus on gender and the reciprocity evident in some forms of everyday encounters by no means denies the brute facts of dispossession and conquest (Harris 2004). Nor does it dismiss the powerful economic, political, cultural, and social formations through which white Americans, male and female, dominated and controlled native men and women. But it does draw attention to the construction of North American landscapes not only out of ideological, military, and cultural clashes but also through everyday encounters between peoples who imagined, saw, and judged each other by the gendered norms of their own cultures. Those judgments most often confirmed their own views but, as Perry and Morin have shown, sometimes challenged them.

LATE-NINETEENTH/EARLY-TWENTIETH-CENTURY CITIES

Encounters on the edge of empire tell us much about the gendering of settler colonies as they made themselves into nations, while the gendered landscapes at the heart of those empires—in cities—puts front and center the political and economic underpinnings of those nations. In the late nineteenth century, as the United States was ascendant as a world economic power, some landscapes became symbolic of its newfound power. Monuments like the Statue of Liberty reflected the long-standing trope of nations as homelands/feminine, literally embodying the female form in steel and iron (Johnson 1994, 1995). But other, subtler landscape symbols of economic power could be found within the nation's cities and towns, which, in the late nineteenth and early twentieth centuries, were experiencing the massive changes of large-scale industrialization and immigration. In cities such as New York, Chicago, and Toronto, people of different classes, genders, "races," and ethnicities confronted each other on crowded downtown streets, in high-rise office buildings, on factory floors, and in the leisure spaces of theaters, restaurants, and bars (Domosh 1998; Dennis 2008). And each of these spaces was shaped in and through gendered ideals and practices.

For example, some scholars have argued that the emergence of a distinctive shopping district in downtown New York City related directly to prevailing gendered norms (Abelson 1989; Domosh 1996a, 1996b). According to the ideology of separate spheres, women were in charge of the domestic, reproductive sphere, while men oversaw the productive, public sphere. These separate gendered realms extended into urban space: the home and domestic spaces were seen as feminine, while the downtown streets and places of commerce were viewed as masculine. At the same time, in the late nineteenth century, industrial capitalism was reshaping the ways Americans made and sold products. Mass-production technologies made everyday and even luxury goods far more affordable and, in turn, required high levels of consumption to keep factories running profitably. In other words, the economic system required mass consumption and a new class of consumers. Since men were in charge of the "productive" sphere, women became positioned as consumers. However, to act as the main class of consumers, women had to venture out of the home and onto the city streets, spaces deemed inappropriate for bourgeois women. The spaces of consumption, therefore, had to appear to conform to late-nineteenth-century ideals of femininity, which positioned women within the domestic and cultural realm instead of the productive and commercial one. The large department stores built during this time accommodated these ideals through architectural designs that resembled cultural rather than commercial sites.

The first such department store, Stewart's, opened in 1856, was designed to look like a palace (Domosh 1996a), its facade lined with marble and its interior decorated in traditional European revival styles, all to create an atmosphere resembling an upper-class home. Stewart's second store, opened in 1863 and located farther uptown, had a cast-iron facade; on the inside a series of open arcades created a theatrical space for women to view each other and most of the commodities for sale (figure 16.1). With more and more middle- and upper-class women being drawn downtown, the area was made even more amenable to the ideal of separate spheres. Wide sidewalks and better gas lighting accommodated the movement of women along the streets and into carriages, then later onto streetcars and the elevated railway. By the 1880s the shopping area of New York City had become known as the Ladies' Mile, an area along Fifth and Sixth Avenues between Union and Madison Squares, dotted with ornate department stores, smaller boutiques, tea rooms, and restaurants meant to satisfy the needs of middle-class women (M. C. Boyer 1985). Of course, working-class women also shopped in these areas, just as they worked in the thousands of sweatshops that produced the garments sold in these stores, as well as in many other factory and domestic jobs. The example of the mid- to late-nineteenth-century department store and shopping area, however, points to the ways that gendered ideologies, particularly with regard to bourgeois women, created distinctive landscapes in American cities.

At the same time that retail stores were flourishing, the companies producing the goods sold in them were expanding. In the late nineteenth and early twentieth centuries, the United States became a primary manufacturing center for a range of commodities, selling first to a national and then an international market. Financial growth accompanied this manufacturing success, as American banks and insurance companies accumulated and reinvested capital in national and then global markets. Much of the wealth accumulated by these companies was housed in and expressed through the early skyscrapers that began to dot the New York City skyline (figure 16.2). New York's first skyscrapers housed industries that required large amounts of office space and relied on material expressions of wealth and dominance. And the men who ran these corporations often occupied the offices at the top, with views looking down on and over the city (Domosh

Figure 16.1. Interior, ca. 1880s, of Stewart's Astor Place store, which opened in 1863. The internal design of the store, featuring galleries encircling a large rotunda, afforded women a fairly limitless visual experience, one that was unusual in a time when women's places and spaces were very circumscribed. Courtesy of the New York Historical Society, negative no. 70132.

1988, 1996b). This visual dominance of the city streets reflected the ideal of early-twentieth-century masculinity—a white man in control of the productive activities he oversaw. Occupying many of the cubicles in the stories below, however, were clerical workers, a number of them women. Geographer Kate Boyer (1998, 2003) has examined how women working in clerical positions in downtown Montreal at the turn of the twentieth century presented a challenge to dominant notions about the "place" of women. As corporations grew in size and complexity, they needed more white-collar workers and looked to middle-class women as a cheap labor source. However, women occupying public space in the city and working in commercial settings challenged the notion of separate spheres. Boyer shows how

Figure 16.2. The New York City skyline in the early decades of the twentieth century. The new skylines that came to symbolize turn-of-the-century American cities comprised gendered spaces: men and ideals of masculinity governed some of those spaces, while women and ideals of respectable femininity inhabited others.

this apparent challenge was managed through the notion of respectability, which for women meant corporeal and sexual restraint. "More than a shorthand for class," respectability "was a way of speaking about and organizing gendered, racialised, and sexed bodies" (Boyer 1998, 268). Since corporations wanted to maintain their own public legitimacy, they only hired women who looked and behaved in the very circumscribed and restrained manner that "respectability" allowed. So the new skylines that came to symbolize turn-of-the-century American cities comprised gendered spaces: men and ideals of masculinity governed some of them, while women and ideals of respectable femininity inhabited others.

Boyer's discussion of the challenges engendered by women entering the urban workforce indicates some ways in which the enormous scale of economic, demographic, and social change characteristic of turn-of-the-century North American cities created anxieties for many different groups. The Progressive Era in the United States was defined partly by attempts to control the perceived unjust and unequal effects of these changes. As historians have noted (Deutsch 2000; Spain 2001), middle- and upper-class women often spearheaded urban progressive movements, in effect taking their domestic caregiving and homemaking roles into the public sphere. Jane Addams, for example, led efforts to establish Hull House, a public institution meant to educate and provide opportunities for immigrant women and children in turn-of-the-century Chicago. Other bourgeois women organized clubs and associations that aimed to create safer and more orderly streets and public spaces. Geographer Phillip Mackintosh (2005), for instance, has documented how the Toronto Local Council of Women organized itself into distinct committees to suggest solutions to many of the problems deemed to be plaguing the city of Toronto, including traffic congestion, poor water and sanitation, and faulty construction. The council dispatched women to explore, survey, and document conditions within the city and then report back with possible remedies for perceived negative living and working conditions. Taking their "domestic" roles into the public sphere often meant that their activities contradicted the ideology of separate spheres, but because they were middle- and upper-class members of the bourgeoisie, their activities were tolerated and condoned. As Mackintosh argues, in essence this form of municipal housekeeping indicates how women were directly involved in reshaping the North American city: "Thus it makes sense to see women's engagement in virtually every aspect of reform in the city, from the design and construction of public space and its infrastructure, to the discovery, assessment and correction of housing and social conditions, including factory- and labour-life, to public health, and to the informal reconfiguration of municipal politics . . . as their explicit participation in the embourgeoisment of the city, the creation of a city as parlour" (2005, 32).

In a similar vein, other reform efforts throughout the United States and Canada involved women and the notion of public domesticity, shaping legislation with regard to labor conditions, education, housing, and even agricultural modernization (Hayden 1982, 2002; Gagen 2000, 2004). In the first decades of the twentieth century, federal officials and select corporations developed programs to "modernize" agricultural land use and technologies. They often hired women educated in the new field of home economics to train women in rural areas in how best to care for their farm homes and lands, offering advice and guidance in the new sciences of sanitation, health management, and agriculture (Frankel and Dye 1991; Stage and Vincenti 1997). International Harvester Corp., the largest U.S.-based manufacturer of agricultural implements, established its own agricultural extension outreach service, offering advice to farmers throughout the United States. The company also provided hands-on assistance to farmers, particularly in the American South, where agricultural techniques were thought to be "behind" other areas of the country (Scott 1970). The company sent trained men on long train tours throughout the region, stopping at small towns along the route to give lectures and distribute educational materials about "modern" farming techniques, while women visited farm homes to offer advice on cleaning and arranging yards and interiors (figure 16.3). Similar in some ways to the encounters between British and Native American women on the U.S. frontier, the interactions between white northern women and African American farm women were filtered through dominant racist and gendered ideologies. As we have seen through these examples, the reformist impulse of the Progressive Era reshaped southern agricultural landscapes and northern cities in ways that benefited some—elite white women who gained power by moving their domestic authority into the public, groups who benefited from reform legislation regarding work conditions, and others who gained education about better agricultural and house-management techniques—but did little to alter the oftentimes oppressive gendered, classed, and racialized norms that guided behavior and dictated roles.

Figure 16.3. Women trained in home economics and under the employ of International Harvester visiting a farm family in Seale, Alabama, February 20, 1915. The original caption—which reads, "The brush broom made by tying a bundle of brush together, is used a great deal in the South, as it costs nothing to make and serves well as a broom for rough sweeping around the yard. A custom which most of the Southern people follow"—provides many clues about the ways in which the South and particularly African American farmers were made to seem less than "modern." Courtesy of the International Harvester Co. Collection, Wisconsin Historical Society, Image ID 79982.

POSTWAR–COLD WAR CITIES AND SUBURBS

One of the most dramatic landscape changes following World War II was the shift in the proportion of the U.S. population living in suburban versus urban areas. In the year immediately following the war (1946–1947), the suburbs accounted for at least 62 percent of new home construction, and by 1950 the suburban growth rate was ten times that of the inner city (Jackson 1985, 238). The causes behind this rapid transformation of the metropolitan landscape are diverse, ranging from demographic shifts to federal housing and transportation policies to racism and Cold War anxieties (Jackson 1985; Farish 2005, 2010). As many historians have pointed out, shifting gendered roles were also key to understanding the suburban housing boom (Wright 1983; Hayden 2002; Colomina 2007). During the war, with much of the male labor force overseas, many U.S. factories and defense agencies looked to women as a temporary source of labor. After the war, the return of soldiers to the United States and Canada forced "Rosie the Riveter" and other working women out of their jobs and, under increasing societal pressure, back into the domestic roles deemed most desirable: stay-at-home wife and mother. Real estate developers like William Levitt took advantage of new federal policies making low-interest home mortgages widely available to mass-produce single-family housing on inexpensive farmland on the edges of major cities, constructing new, low-density residential communities seemingly overnight (figure 16.4).

Shaping the material and discursive landscape of these suburbs was a dominant set of beliefs about the meaning of good citizenship in postwar America.

Figure 16.4. The Levey family in front of their home in Levittown, New York, 1950. These early suburban houses and the patriarchal, heteronormative families who lived in them became symbols of postwar America. Courtesy of Bernard Hoffman/Time & Life Pictures/ Getty Images.

Home ownership in the suburbs and membership in a heterosexual nuclear family were interlinked elements that defined and supported America's economic and social order in at least three ways. First, the construction of these new communities and the consumption necessary to fill these new houses with durable goods (e.g., televisions, furniture, appliances) helped keep America's factories running smoothly. Second, the notion of private property that they embodied served as an ideological tool in the Cold War battle against communism. And third, the emphasis on motherhood and child rearing contributed to the reproduction of the labor force. Through a case study of a working-class suburb in Pittsburgh, Pennsylvania, geographer Patrick Vitale (2009) has documented the role of women in creating and maintaining these intertwined identities of class, gender, community, and citizenship in the postwar period. Built between 1949 and 1957, Westwood Hills was a typical postwar suburban community of curvilinear streets lined with small, detached homes. Most of the families living there consisted of husbands working in the nearby mills and factories, women working at home as housewives and mothers, and young children. Through interviews and analyses of the newsletter put out by the Westwood Hills Women's Association (WHWA), Vitale outlines the work of suburban women in creating and recreating this American way of life: "It was women who enacted the edicts of the WHWA: watched over children in the neighborhood, led the Cub Scouts, and created a community library. It was women who scrubbed floors and made meals and took part-time jobs for additional money. While men's wages generally paid for the suburban dream of home ownership and community in Westwood Hills, it was women's work that actualized this dream" (2009, 768). In other words, women, acting out socially prescribed roles, materially and discursively shaped one of the quintessential American landscapes: the postwar suburb. This does not discount the fact many women (and men) found these suburban lives unsatisfactory (think of Betty Friedan's 1963 *The Feminine Mystique*); nor does it preclude the subversive possibilities that women's community organizing could generate (for some, activism against racist practices and in support of environmental movements). But it does point to the importance of understanding the everyday lives of women in order to fully explain the creation of the American landscape.

Though highly segregated by class and race, these communities shared certain assumptions about their inhabitants. As evidenced by their overall design—as detached structures meant for one "nuclear" family, located in a "bedroom" community from which father commuted daily by car into the city, while mother stayed at home raising the kids—suburban single-family homes would house heterosexual couples with children. This assumption was also evident in the actual design of these houses. Cape Cod and ranch houses—the most common postwar styles—contained master bedrooms for parents, family rooms and yard space for children's leisure, a kitchen for women's work, and a garage or basement for men to gather in (Jackson 1985). In the 1960s these styles evolved into the modernist "open-plan" arrangement of living spaces with fewer dividing walls that allowed housewives to survey and interact with children while conducting household chores, which the new class of educational experts deemed necessary for "good" child rearing.

However, the heteronormative assumptions literally built into the new postwar suburbs were never fully or universally realized. Geographers and other scholars have documented the diversity of families that actually inhabited postwar suburbs: single mothers, gay and queer couples, extended families, and so forth (Johnston and Valentine 1995; Dowling 1998). Nonetheless, postwar suburbs became popularly associated in scholarship and the media (think of *Father Knows Best* or *Leave It to Beaver*) with the heterosexual, nuclear family and a domesticated form of masculinity. Meanwhile, in the urban centers, a different form of housing emerged. Concurrently with construction of ranch houses for the ideal nuclear family in American suburbs, modernist high-rise apartment buildings appeared on the skyline, with apartments targeting primarily single men. As scholars have shown (Wagner 1996; Wojcik 2010), the bachelor pad—a one-bedroom apartment outfitted with the latest design technology and surrounded with large windows offering panoramic views of the city—was in some ways the residential equivalent of the office in a corporate skyscraper. These masculine spaces afforded the occupant the pleasure of surveying the city from a vantage of power, affirming masculinity in style as well as location.

GENTRIFICATION AND LATE-TWENTIETH-CENTURY CITIES

The urban bachelor pad and other imagined and real landscapes of the late twentieth century reflected and shaped what became a dominant way of seeing the North American city, as dangerous, sexual, and hypermasculine, while the suburbs became increasingly associated with safety, domesticity, and maternal femininity. This imagined geography resulted from the range of factors that I have already alluded to: racism and white flight from the city, the perceived nuclear threat to urban density, economic support for new housing and additional consumption, increased emphasis on gendered spheres, and a spike in birth rates after the war. By the early 1990s, almost 60 percent of all Americans residing in metropolitan areas had chosen the suburbs (U.S. Department of Commerce 1992, 56). But the pace of suburbanization began to slow during the 1980s, as cities underwent reimagining again, oftentimes as hip environments for emerging new gendered and sexualized identities. Various socioeconomic changes—including a change in the economy from industrialization to the service sector, the maturing of the baby boom generation, shifting social identities due to the antiwar, women's, and civil rights movements, and a relatively large "rent gap" that attracted investors to central cities (Smith 1987; Bondi 1991, 1999)—prompted the phenomenon now known as gentrification.

Given the previous discussion concerning the heteronormativity of suburban neighborhoods, it is not difficult to understand why people living in different types of family arrangements might not find suburban living attractive. Geographers Manuel Castells (1983) and Larry Knopp (1995, 1998) have documented the key role that gay men played in early gentrification in such cities as San Francisco, New York, London, and Sydney. Gay men were involved in the process as these landscapes' producers—as developers, designers, and real estate agents—and as their consumers, often as the first group of homeowners willing to buy property in downtown neighborhoods abandoned by landlords or left in an undesirable condition. These newly gentrified neighborhoods became associated with a gay community not only through home ownership but also because many gay-identified commercial spaces, such as bars, cafes, and community centers, opened there. As Larry Knopp discovered, the processes of space making and the politics of gay empowerment often went hand in hand: "Forms of male gay identity politics are strongly linked to the infiltration by gay men of mainstream economic and political institutions and the related construction and economic development of territorial spaces" (1998, 154). Similarly, Tamar Rothenberg (1995) identified the processes through which an early gentrified neighborhood in Brooklyn, Park Slope, became home to a lesbian community.

Single and professional non-gay-identified women have also been key players in gentrifying markets in particular cities. For example, in the late 1980s Damaris Rose (1989) examined the connections between public-sector jobs in education, health, and social services increasingly being filled by professional women, the rise of single-women and single-mother households, and the gentrification of particular inner-city neighborhoods. Rose found that "changes in women's employment situation, mediated by other aspects of gender relations, may often be *constitutive* of gentrification processes" (1989, 133). Gentrified neighborhoods attracted professional women for a range of reasons already outlined (e.g., cost of housing, lifestyle choices), as well as because the city offered an array of nearby conveniences. In the suburbs, professional and other working women had to drive oftentimes long distances to get to work, drop their children at daycare and school, and do the shopping and other errands. And even though by the mid-1980s household chores and child rearing had become somewhat more equally distributed among men and women, geographers found that women with children still preferred to live closer to work than men did (Hanson and Pratt 1995; McDowell 1997). Through intensive interviews with women working in the financial sector in London, for example, Linda McDowell (1997) found that women with children felt compelled to live close to work in order to meet the demands on their time of both work and home. This held true in American cities as well, and not only for the professional classes. Geographers Susan Hanson and Geraldine Pratt (1995) studied the spatial relationships between work, home, and gender in the predominantly working-class town of Worcester, Massachusetts, in the 1980s and early 1990s. Their findings have done much to complicate geographers' models of commuting behavior, partly because they found that women in the paid labor force almost always chose their home locations based on proximity to their workplace. Like McDowell, they found that women—even those without school-age children—preferred to live close to work.

And it wasn't just gentrifying women who preferred to live close to work. Hanson and Pratt found that women living in the suburbs, many of whom by the late twentieth century were working outside the home, also deemed proximity between work and home of paramount importance. Finding work closer to the suburbs for some of these women became easier, partly because in the late 1980s the suburbs became more diverse sites of not just bedroom communities but also office buildings, large retail areas, and even some light manufacturing. These new "edge cities" (Garreau 1992), located miles from nineteenth-century downtowns, were primarily sites of employment, places people commuted to in the morning and left at night. In addition, the types of families living in suburban areas also became diverse. Geographer Wei Li (1998) coined the term "ethnoburb" to refer to multiethnic residential and commercial suburban areas. This new diversity also pertained to gendered roles and expectations. Even in the postwar period, suburban residents encompassed varying classes and ethnicities, religions and ages, and gender roles and ideals. But the overall social shifts in North American society increased the range of those differences. Robyn Dowling (1998) completed in-depth interviews with women and men living in two middle-class suburbs of Vancouver, British Columbia, in the late 1980s. She found that differences in women's lives stemmed not only from whether they lived with children or worked outside the home but also from their values (religious and otherwise) regarding mothering and caretaking. Instead of the homogeneity oftentimes identified with suburban women, Dowling found "accounts of the multiple gender identities constructed in and through suburban environments and the nuances and complexities embedded in the local context" (1998, 85). Women's identities and the particularities of where they lived, she discovered, were interlinked.

CONCLUSION

I started this chapter listing some iconic North American landscapes, including the postwar suburb, that were gendered in one way or another. Landscape symbols of national identity such as the Statue of Liberty speak to the ways that geographic imaginations are often gendered: nations are imagined as female or feminine (while states are usually considered masculine). In this way, sets of values and ideals, associated at a particular time and place with particular genders, are inscribed literally onto spaces and places. As we have seen, in the seventeenth and eighteenth centuries, Europeans often imagined North America as feminine, a place to conquer, while in the postwar period, the downtown became imagined as masculine and the suburb as feminine. Prescribed gender roles of the time shaped other iconic landscapes, such as the urban skyline: men were in charge of the large corporations that, in the late nineteenth century, relied on agglomerations of commercial and financial activities in city centers and therefore constructed tall office buildings. Women who worked in these buildings often filled clerical positions and had limited access to offices with skyline views. Their presence in the city, however, disrupted prescribed gender roles. In order to maintain their status as bourgeois women, they had to act in a "respectable" manner. And the quintessential postwar suburb was shaped through and embodied a heteronormative ideal of family life, molded both by gendered imaginations of what the city and suburb were meant to be and by assumptions about sexual identities and gendered roles. As we have seen throughout this chapter, understanding and explaining the North American landscape requires analyses of gendered roles, ideals, imaginations, and behaviors. This chapter merely highlights some aspects of the deep entanglements between gender, sexuality, and landscape. Other episodes in this history and geography await discovery.

REFERENCES

Abelson, Elaine. 1989. *When Ladies Go A-Thieving: Middle-Class Shoplifters in the Victorian Department Store.* New York: Oxford University Press.

Bederman, G. 1995. *Manliness and Civilization: A Cultural History of Gender and Race in the United States, 1880–1917.* Chicago: University of Chicago Press.

Bondi, L. 1991. Gender Divisions and Gentrification: A Critique. *Transactions of the Institute of British Geographers* 16, no. 2: 190–98.

———. 1999. Gender, Class, and Gentrification: Enriching the Debate. *Environment and Planning D: Society and Space* 17: 261–82.

Boyer, K. 1998. Place and the Politics of Virtue: Clerical Work, Corporate Anxiety, and Changing Meanings of Public Womanhood in Early Twentieth-Century Montreal. *Gender, Place and Culture: A Journal of Feminist Geography* 5, no. 3: 261–75.

———. 2003. "Neither Forget nor Remember Your Sex": Sexual Politics in the Early Twentieth-Century Canadian Office. *Journal of Historical Geography* 29, no. 2: 212–29.

Boyer, M. C. 1985. *Manhattan Manners: Architecture and Style, 1850–1900.* New York: Rizzoli Press.

Castells, M. 1983. *The City and the Grassroots: A Cross-Cultural Theory of Urban Social Movements.* Berkeley: University of California Press.

Colomina, B. 2007. *Domesticity at War.* Cambridge, MA: MIT Press.

Dennis, R. 2008. *Cities in Modernity: Representations and Productions of Metropolitan Space, 1840–1930.* Cambridge: Cambridge University Press.

Deutsch, S. 2000. *Women and the City: Gender, Space, and Power in Boston, 1870–1940.* New York: Oxford University Press.

Domosh, M. 1988. The Symbolism of the Skyscraper: Case Studies of New York's First Tall Buildings. *Journal of Urban History* 14, no. 3: 320–45.

———. 1996a. The Feminized Retail Landscape: Gender, Ideology and Consumer Culture in Nineteenth-Century New York City. In *Towards the New Retail Geography,* edited by M. Lowe and N. Wrigley, 257–70. New York: Addison Wesley Longman.

———. 1996b. *Invented Cities: The Creation of Landscape in Nineteenth-Century New York and Boston.* New Haven, CT: Yale University Press.

———. 1998. Those "Gorgeous Incongruities": Polite Politics and Public Space on the Streets of Nineteenth-Century New York City. *Annals of the Association of American Geographers* 88, no. 2: 209–26.

Dowling, R. 1998. Suburban Stories, Gendered Lives: Thinking through Difference. In *Cities of Difference,* edited by R. Fincher and J. M. Jacobs, 69–89. New York: Guilford Press.

Farish, M. 2005. Cities in Shade: Urban Geography and the Uses of Noir. *Environment and Planning D: Society and Space* 23: 95–118.

———. 2010. *The Contours of America's Cold War.* Minneapolis: University of Minnesota Press.

Frankel, N., and N. S. Dye, eds. 1991. *Gender, Class, Race, and Reform in the Progressive Era.* Lexington: University Press of Kentucky.

Friedan, B. 1963. *The Feminine Mystique.* New York: Dell Publishing.

Gagen, E. A. 2000. An Example to Us All: Child Development and Identity Construction in Early 20th-Century Playgrounds. *Environment and Planning A* 32, no. 4: 599–616.

———. 2004. Making America Flesh: Physicality and Nationhood in Early Twentieth-Century Physical Education Reform. *Cultural Geographies* 11, no. 4: 417–42.

Garreau, J. 1992. *Edge City: Life on the New Frontier.* New York: Doubleday.

Hanson, S., and G. Pratt. 1995. *Gender, Work, and Space.* New York: Routledge.

Harris, C. 2004. How Did Colonialism Dispossess? Comments from an Edge of Empire. *Annals of the Association of American Geographers* 94, no. 1: 165–82.
Hayden, D. 1982. *The Grand Domestic Revolution: A History of Feminist Designs for American Homes, Neighborhoods and Cities*. Cambridge, MA: MIT Press.
———. 2002. *Redesigning the American Dream: The Future of Housing, Work, and Family Life*. New York: W. W. Norton and Co.
Jackson, K. T. 1985. *Crabgrass Frontier: The Suburbanization of the United States*. New York: Oxford University Press.
Johnson, N. 1994. Sculpting Heroic Histories: Celebrating the Centenary of the 1798 Rebellion in Ireland. *Transactions of the Institute of British Geographers* 19, no. 1: 78–93.
———. 1995. Cast in Stone: Monuments, Geography, and Nationalism. *Environment and Planning D* 13: 51–51.
Johnston, L., and G. Valentine. 1995. Wherever I Lay My Girlfriend, That's My Home. In *Mapping Desire: Geographies of Sexualities*, edited by D. Bell and G. Valentine, 99–113. New York: Routledge.
Knopp, L. 1995. Sexuality and Urban Space: A Framework for Analysis. In *Mapping Desire: Geographies of Sexualities*, edited by D. Bell and G. Valentine, 149–61. New York: Routledge.
———. 1998. Sexuality and Urban Space: Gay Male Identity Politics in the United States, the United Kingdom, and Australia. In *Cities of Difference*, edited by R. Fincher, and J. M. Jacobs, 149–76. New York: Guilford Press.
Kolodny, A. 1975. *The Lay of the Land: Metaphor as Experience and History in American Life and Letters*. Chapel Hill: University of North Carolina Press.
Li, W. 1998. Anatomy of a New Ethnic Settlement: The Chinese Ethnoburb in Los Angeles. *Urban Studies* 35, no. 3: 479–501.
Mackintosh, P. G. 2005. Scrutiny in the Modern City: The Domestic Public and the Toronto Local Council of Women at the Turn of the Twentieth Century. *Gender, Place and Culture: A Journal of Feminist Geography* 12, no. 1: 29–48.
McDowell, L. 1997. *Capital Culture: Gender at Work in the City*. Malden, MA: Blackwell Publishers.
Morin, K. M. 1998. British Women Travellers and Constructions of Racial Difference across the Nineteenth-Century American West. *Transactions of the Institute of British Geographers* 23, no. 3: 311–30.
———. 1999. Peak Practices: Englishwomen's "Heroic" Adventures in the Nineteenth-Century American West. *Annals of the Association of American Geographers* 89, no. 3: 489–514.
———. 2002. Postcolonialism and Native American Geographies: The Letters of Rosalie La Flesche Farley, 1896–1899. *Cultural Geographies* 9, no. 2: 158–80.
Nabokov, P., and R. Easton. 1989. *Native American Architecture*. New York: Oxford University Press.
Newman, L. M. 1995. *White Women's Rights: The Racial Origins of Feminism in the United States*. New York: Oxford University Press.
Perry, A. 2005. Metropolitan Knowledge, Colonial Practice, and Indigenous Womanhood: Missions in Nineteenth-Century British Columbia. In *Contact Zones: Aboriginal and Settler Women in Canada's Colonial Past*, edited by K. Pickles and M. Rutherdale, 109–30. Vancouver: University of British Columbia Press.
Pickles, K., and M. Rutherdale, eds. 2005. *Contact Zones: Aboriginal and Settler Women in Canada's Colonial Past*. Vancouver: University of British Columbia Press.
Pratt, M. L. 1992. *Imperial Eyes: Travel Writing and Transculturation*. New York: Routledge Press.

Rose, D. 1989. A Feminist Perspective of Employment Restructuring and Gentrification: the Case of Montreal. In *The Power of Geography: How Territory Shapes Social Life*, edited by J. Wolch and M. Dear, 118–38. Boston: Unwin Hyman.
Rothenberg, T. 1995. "And She Told Two Friends": Lesbians Creating Urban Social Space. In *Mapping Desire: Geographies of Sexualities*, edited by D. Bell and G. Valentine, 150–65. New York: Routledge.
Scott, R. 1970. *The Reluctant Farmer: The Rise of Agricultural Extension to 1914*. Urbana: University of Illinois Press.
Smith, N. 1987. Gentrification and the Rent Gap. *Annals of the Association of American Geographers* 77, no. 3: 462–65.
Spain, D. 2001. *How Women Saved the City*. Minneapolis: University of Minnesota Press.
Stage, S., and V. B. Vincenti, eds. 1997. *Rethinking Home Economics: Women and the History of a Profession*. Ithaca, NY: Cornell University Press.
Vitale, P. 2009. Learning to Be Suburban: The Production of Community in Westwood Hills, Pennsylvania, 1952–1958. *Journal of Historical Geography* 35, no. 4: 743–68.
Wagner, G. 1996. The Lair of the Bachelor. In *Architecture and Feminism*, edited by D. Coleman, E. Danze, and C. Henderson, 183–220. Princeton, NJ: Princeton Architectural Press.
Wojcik P. R. 2010. *The Apartment Plot: Urban Living in American Film and Popular Culture, 1945–1975*. Durham, NC: Duke University Press.
Wright, G. 1983. *Building the Dream: A Social History of Housing in America*. Cambridge, MA: MIT Press.

17

Shaping Tourism

Yolonda Youngs

Tourism involves more than visiting pretty places, collecting photographs, or recounting the activities of a summer vacation. It is a series of experiences—planned, lived, shared, and remembered—that inform our perceptions of the world around us. To reach their destinations, tourists must embark on physical journeys aboard trains, planes, automobiles, boats, and buses. Each of these modes of transportation requires alteration of the physical environment and the creation of an elaborate infrastructural network. It is an intellectual odyssey as well, challenging tourists' preconceived notions of beauty, leisure, or wilderness. For well over a century, tourists in North America have traveled near and far to see and experience the continent's grand and scenic landscapes. Tracing the historical geography of tourism in North America provides a deeper understanding of leisure and recreation activities of the past and a greater awareness of "modern touristic phenomena" (Meyer-Arendt and Lew 2003, 527).

This chapter explores how changing modes of travel, shifting ideas about leisure and recreation, and evolving environmental perceptions shaped tourism in North America from the 1890s to the present. As K. J. Meyer-Arendt and A. A. Lew remind us, tourism encompasses "distinct place, time, distance and activity patterns" that leave unique landscape signatures in their wake (2003, 524). Historical geographers are well equipped to examine such patterns and have made significant contributions to this highly interdisciplinary field by exploring spatial relationships, regional identities, cultural landscape evolution, the role of iconic images in place making, the centrality of cultural and social issues, and the changing dynamics of human-environment interactions.

SIGHTS OF WONDER

From the 1880s to the 1910s, an increasing number of travelers embarked on journeys across North America for leisure, recreation, and sightseeing (MacCannell 1976). Perhaps inspired by the allure of romanticized experiences in exotic locations, these hardy tourists endured long-distance and fragmentary transportation routes, expensive tickets and services, and a wide variety of hospitality conditions to reach these destinations. These early tourists left lasting cultural, social, and economic imprints on the places they visited. A distinct east-west regional dichotomy emerged as affluent easterners ventured west to see firsthand the national parks, historic sites, and scenic locations distributed throughout the western United States and Canada.

Iconic imagery and place making fueled early tourism in North America, shaping visitors' expectations and perceptions of the places they encountered. Short excerpts from government survey reports, explorers' journals, and tourist accounts circulated widely in popular newspapers and magazines. Oftentimes, illustrations and photographs accompanied these short and evocative descriptions of western lands. The combination of text and imagery spurred a national interest in experiencing these sights in person. Niagara Falls, for example, drew curious visitors to stand on the edge of the chasm and experience the tremendous rush of water and air (figure 17.1). Starting in the 1840s Niagara became one of North America's most famous tourism destinations. It also served as a warning of the environmental and economic costs of commercialization and unplanned development at scenic locations (Runte 1972). The falls offered an odd mixture of ideas, meanings, and activities that went beyond mere sightseeing (McGreevy 1994). It was a place for marriage celebrations and suicides as well as parks, religious shrines, circuses, horror museums, and factories. Using tourist accounts and imagery, as well as the descriptions of popular writers, including Walt Whitman, Henry James, and H. G. Wells, Patrick McGreevy takes a long view of history at Niagara, tracing the popularity of this site and its international acclaim back to the 1830s. Seeing Niagara Falls became an obligation for travelers in both Canada and the United States, especially after the opening of the Erie Canal increased accessibility to the falls. "Niagara Falls became not only a stimulus for reflection but also a metaphor for death, nature, or the future" (McGreevy 1994, 11). McGreevy suggests we must examine imaginings of the falls in popular imagery and literature before we can understand the complex meanings and ideas associated with this landscape.

Visual representations and popular media served as important sources of information for tourists in the late nineteenth and early twentieth centuries. Postcards, advertisements, and magazine photographs of places such as the Wisconsin Dells (Hoelscher 1998b) and the American West (Wyckoff and Nash 1994) informed visitors about the activities, locations, and environments they would encounter on their journeys. In the western United States, romantic ideas of wilderness attached to western locales through novels, newspaper accounts, and other popular press outlets shaped environmental perceptions of and tourism activities at these locations (Allen 1992; Squire 1994). Popular accounts of Yellowstone National Park, for instance, depicted the park as an "exotic rather than pastoral or even picturesque" location (Sears 1989, 165). By traveling to and around Yellowstone, visitors from the eastern United States could experience a landscape that challenged and invigorated their perceptions of the American West as a source of entertainment and exotic landscapes. Part of the fuel for these ideas derived from image making in the twentieth century that drew on ignorance of

Figure 17.1. Horseshoe Falls afforded a popular scenic viewpoint for tourists at Niagara Falls. Standard Scenic Co. (1906).

western environments. Easterners relied on reports and survey records from a handful of individuals who had actually traveled in the West. Through these remote networks, Americans along the eastern seaboard formed often exaggerated ideals and expectations of western landscapes that cumulatively created a mythic West of unrealistic proportions (Athearn 1986).

Even with this picturesque appeal as an inspiration, tourists encountered numerous logistical and financial hurdles to reach their destinations. Railroads, stagecoaches, and horseback riding formed the backbone of leisure and recreational travel modes; however, the uneven distribution of railroad lines and reliable roads in the late nineteenth century hindered cross-continental travel. In the United States, railroad networks connected major eastern and Midwestern cities such as New York, Chicago, and St. Louis to communities and travel destinations in the western United States. These travel networks shifted and enlarged after 1869 with the completion of the transcontinental railroad at Promontory, Utah, where the tracks of the Union Pacific and the Central Pacific Railroads joined together, ushering in a wave of railroad building across the western United States (figure 17.2). By the early twentieth century, the Burlington, Southern Pacific, Great Northern, and Northern Pacific Railroads connected east and west as well as points in between (Beck and Haase 1989). At places such as the Grand Canyon in Arizona, the arrival of the railroad provided direct access to an otherwise remote travel destination. According to Stanley Trimble, "The turn of the twentieth century brought the railroad right to the Grand Canyon Village, and tourists came just to see the place, to revel in this American wonder" (2006, 17).

Early travel was an arduous, expensive, and exclusive experience, enticing only the hardiest and most affluent of travelers. After traveling for days or weeks on railroads, passengers then alighted from the trains to travel along local and regional stagecoach or horseback trails (figure 17.3). The dusty and bumpy stagecoach ride left tourists exhausted, often craving longer stays to recuperate and enjoy their trips. Railroads and stagecoach routes formed important arteries of travel that dictated the speed of movement (slow) and the locations of emerging nodes of visitor services.

Concessionaire activity at tourist destinations during the late nineteenth and early twentieth centuries was fragmented and uneven in quality. Heavy financial

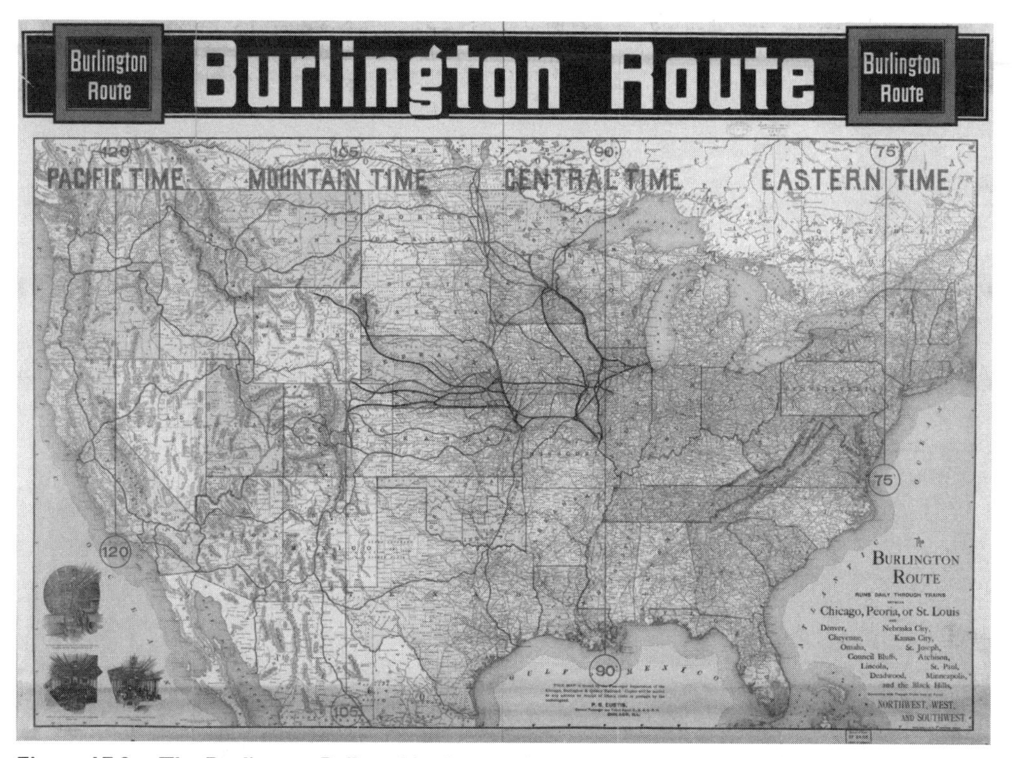

Figure 17.2. The Burlington Railroad had extensive cross-country routes in the United States that offered transcontinental transportation for tourists, connecting eastern audiences with western scenic locations. Burlington and Quincy Railroad Co. (1892).

Figure 17.3. Early tourism relied on group stagecoach tours to transport tourists to their destinations. Here a group of visitors to Yosemite in 1905 pass through the "Wawona tunnel tree" on their route around the upper Mariposa Grove of giant sequoias. Ingersoll View Co. (1905).

investment from the railroads supported the construction of the first permanent overnight accommodations at many tourist sites, especially in western North America. Joint business ventures between transportation companies and nascent concessionaires provided the financial backing and business framework to build and maintain infrastructure, transportation corridors, and hospitality services. During World War I, leisure and recreation travel waned as tourist numbers decreased and facilities closed. After the war ended in 1918, tourism revived, but visitors placed new demands on facilities and travel networks that remained closed or poorly maintained through the war years.

Transportation and popular imagery often worked together to stimulate tourism as railroads launched massive publicity campaigns to promote their rail service and the destinations along their lines (Rothman 1998). Businessmen and boosters encouraged tourists to "See America First" through a publicity movement that welded ideas about national pride to tourism in western American landscapes (Schaffer 1996, 2001). Boosters shaped landscapes through the building and development of tourism infrastructure and services, including hotels, restaurants, and gift shops. David Wrobel (2002) explores this theme in his examination of American boosters' promotion of western lands through a variety of schemes; he pays particular attention to how visual representations informed social memory and encounters with American tourist destinations. Anne Hyde (1990) explores visitor expectations of the western United States through a close examination of the types of hotels, interpretive tours, and recreational experiences available to early-twentieth-century tourists.

Railroad companies were major players in the development and promotion of national parks and protected areas as tourism sites during this pre-automobile era (Rothman 1998; Runte 2010). Lawmakers and park promoters set aside certain federally owned tracts of land, citing their worthlessness for mining or forestry extraction, and created a mandate of preservation for the "benefit and enjoyment of the people" (Hall and Shultis 1991; Dilsaver 1992, 28). Established in 1872, Yellowstone became the world's first national park and soon earned the sobriquet "Wonderland" for its wide variety of exotic geothermal features, dramatic mountain scenery, and western wilderness (Meyer 2003; Smith 2004). Other parcels followed the Yellowstone model as North America's roster came to include a growing list of parks, especially after the establishment of the U.S. National Park Service in 1916 and Parks Canada in 1911 (Figueiredo 2007; Young and Dilsaver 2011).

Late-nineteenth and early-twentieth-century tourism invoked complicated social and cultural relationships. In particular, tourism conflicted with Native American and First Nations peoples' land-use practices, migration patterns, and cultural values. Cultures collided in antagonistic and sometimes violent ways as national park managers' preferences for tourism collided with Native American land claims and uses, creating social, cultural, and political inequities (Morehouse 1996; Spence 1999; Cronin 2011).

Class and gender issues shaped tourism geographies as well. Only wealthy patrons with the financial means and flexible work schedules could afford the expensive train or stagecoach fare, hotel stay, and time away from work to take the extended trips required of late-nineteenth-century travel (Germic 2001). Gender roles shaped how men and women carried out recreation and tourism from camping (Kropp 2009) to living and working in resort settings (Kaufman 1996; Hall and Page 2006). Women participated in a variety of recreation and leisure travel activities ranging from mountaineering (Smith 1989) to touring in the Canadian Rockies (Squire 1995), as well as a number of other pursuits across the American West (Morin 1998, 1999).

Geographers have explored the birth of modern tourism through a variety of case studies that emphasize spatial relationships and regional identities. John Towner focuses his work on North America, Western Europe, and Britain, noting how tourism and recreation have shaped landscapes across these areas. He remarks that East Coast businesses and European firms drove the initial development of transportation networks in North America through "marketing, transport, and accommodation investment, thereby supplying and controlling where visitors went" (1986, 244). For example, railroads promoted day excursions from West Coast population centers, such as Los Angeles and San Diego, along a variety of loop tours, from circular routes to the figure eight "kite-shaped" route connecting Los Angeles to the Bernardino Mountains in the 1890s (Towner 1986, 247). Towner outlines a framework for understanding tourism processes through

THE PASSIONATE GEOGRAPHER
Terence Young

Ci vuole passione in tutte le cose; Se non ce' passione, non si riesce a niente.

—Luisa Pettinelli

The successful scholar typically is self-reflective and employs an incisive theoretical framework, solid data, and an engaging presentation. Of the three, the last rests most heavily on an author's shoulders, demanding that he or she be persuasive. How does one persuade? Many elements contribute, but without passion, it is difficult to succeed.

When I was a new doctoral student at UCLA, my advisor, J. Nicholas Entrikin, and I engaged in a series of discussions about the future direction of my dissertation topic and thesis. As I suspect is typical, we did not initially agree on either. I recall having esoteric notions about exotic subjects, many of which met with similar questions: "Why is this topic important?" "Has any geographer argued for or against this thesis (or mentioned it at all)?" "Where will you obtain the evidence?" Growing frustrated and misunderstanding the purpose of these questions, I asked my advisor if he would recommend a subject and its approach. "Absolutely not," Nick replied. Instead, he encouraged me to find a path by drawing on my life experiences and interests and by interacting with him, the other members of my committee, and the literature. Why? Because, he insisted, a scholar who brings her or his own passion and excitement to a topic is more likely to generate an engaging, persuasive argument than one who is following instructions.

I followed this sage advice to the completion of a dissertation on San Francisco's park system and have applied it in most subsequent research. Unsurprisingly, my current historical-geographic project, camping in America, meets Nick Entrikin's criteria. The subject intrigued me because it offered a novel path for understanding the cultural importance of nature for Americans. Why, I wondered, have tens of millions of Americans annually engaged in this form of recreation? Moreover, I have been an avid and frequent camper since childhood. My experiences have allowed me to know the feelings that a century of travelers have claimed as a consequence of camping vacations in places like Yosemite National Park. At the same time, research has permitted me to understand and explain the origins and significance of those feelings. As a consequence of this intersection, I am enthusiastic about the topic, have worked hard to exhume the lost characters and social forces that shaped its historical geography, and have tried my best to persuade readers of camping's revealing complexity. However my work is ultimately received, its pursuit has been a pleasure, and my dedication to it has never flagged because I have remained passionate.

"visitor generating areas, visitor destination areas, and transportation" links that joined these places, for remaining cognizant of the context of environments that shaped tourism, and for considering the values imposed on certain places seen as pleasure sites (1986, 267).

Tourism is a shared and social practice often experienced through group activities, tours, and transportation options. At the turn of the twentieth century, group travel was de rigueur as tourists boarded trains and stagecoaches and traveled days or weeks with other passengers, sharing meals and experiences. Group transportation services were essential and expected aspects of the journey, linking transcontinental visitors to sights of wonder through local and regional sightseeing stagecoach or horseback tours (Youngs, White, and Woodrich 2008). Once at their destinations, tourists required complete hospitality services, including housing, entertainment, and food. Popular East Coast resort areas offered activities, lodging, and restaurants in scenic locations, such as Bar Harbor (Hornsby 1993) and the Catskill Mountains (Johnson 1990). National park sites aspired to resort standards as well, offering visitors a range of services during their stay. At Yellowstone National Park, an 1897 guidebook noted that the Yellowstone Lake "hotel tends greatly toward making the Yellowstone Lake the resort, par excellence, of the Park. Here everything is so arranged that guests can spend the entire season, if they so desire, making short, easy trips of sightseeing or explorations to all points of the great reserve. . . . To visit any or all of the points circumjacent to this grand mountain lake, vehicles of all kinds, saddle and pack animals, guides, rowboats, and steamers are ever at command" (Guptill 1897).

As attractive as these resort settings may have been, they were often too expensive for middle-class travelers. Camp companies such as Wiley Camps or Shaw and Powell Permanent Camping Co. offered a viable and popular alternative for national park travelers (figure 17.4). The spatially extensive canvas-tent camps acted as stagecoach hubs for organized tours to nearby attractions as well as centralized locations for lodging, entertainment, and dining services.

BETTER ROADS

From the 1910s to the early 1940s, stagecoach and train travel gave way to automobile touring. The growth of dependable, cross-continental road networks, flowering of motorist hospitality services, and expanding list of tourist attractions nurtured this shift in travel modes. As more private automobiles afforded tourists the opportunity to experience travel at their own pace, ideas about leisure and recreation embraced amenities and activities located near established and marked roads. The expanding network of roads also influenced travelers' perceptions of the environments they encountered on their trips. Increased travel speeds and accessibility to previously remote or inaccessible locations allowed tourists to experience rural locations, parks and wilderness areas, and roadside landscapes in new ways.

Auto travel was not an easy proposition during this era of poorly maintained road systems and unreliable traveler information. Federal and state governments

Figure 17.4. Shaw and Powell's organized group camping and stagecoach tours in the early twentieth century opened Yellowstone National Park's Land of Wonders to adventurous and budget-minded middle-class visitors. This brochure features a crowd perilously close to the geyser Old Faithful during an eruption. The image cleverly uses the ascending steam from the geyser to lead viewers' eyes upward to the message that Shaw and Powell offers a modern, right way (their competition must offer the wrong way) to see the iconic geyser and other park sights. Shaw and Powell Permanent Camping Co. n.d.

in the United States responded sluggishly to calls for better roads. Private citizens formed highway associations and "Good Roads" groups to promote, mark, and improve roadways that connected cities and towns to regional and national attractions (Jakle and Sculle 2008, 33–40). Routes such as the National Road, Lincoln Highway, and Dixie Overland; the Lee, Ozark, and Stone Trails; the Pike's Peak Ocean to Ocean Highway; and others created east-west travel corridors across the United States (Raitz 1996; Jakle and Sculle 2008, 43–56). Major north-south routes such as the Meridian Highway, King of Trails, and Jefferson and Pacific Highway connected the United States and Canada. The push for expanded road networks was so popular that highway maps in the early 1920s included "three hundred different named highways" (Jakle and Sculle 2008, 43), although some of these routes were more planned than paved. Loop touring routes emerged as well, linking established roads in circular patterns and connecting popular attractions. For example, the so-called Park-to-Park Highway created a loop tour between western cities and towns and national parks and monuments (Louter 2006, 42–43).

Gradually, paved roads replaced their dirt predecessors. However, the Lincoln Highway, Pacific Highway, Yellowstone Trail, and other established routes did not immediately increase transcontinental traffic. The Great Depression negatively impacted tourism and the expansion of travel corridors as the effects of this widespread economic calamity rippled across North America and the world. State and federal governments possessed limited funds to contribute to road-expansion projects. Private businesses and boosters lacked the capital to expand their tourism infrastructures. Meanwhile, few Americans and Canadians could spare the money or the time to travel far from home.

In the later 1920s and 1930s, amid the economic and social hardships of the Great Depression, auto tourism expanded its reach. Cars became an affordable means of transportation for an increasing number of middle-class travelers as a system of reliable, paved routes and tourist services expanded across the continent. Ancillary businesses flourished with this growing travel network. Auto-touring guidebooks, for example, provided valuable information about travel routes, sights, and distances between services (figure 17.5). The shift from public, group travel via trains and stagecoaches to more independent, single-vehicle travel also called for a new scheme and distribution of tourist service facilities. Campgrounds filled this need by providing inexpensive, overnight lodging for travelers in private autos with their own increasingly specialized equipment (Young 2000, 2010). These camps also provided a less adventuresome but essential aspect of travel: sanitation. Scattered and impromptu camping areas proliferated along popular travel corridors, generating trash and other refuse scattered along the route. Established campgrounds centralized auto camping and lessened the impact of visitor use. In national and theme parks and at other popular tourist attractions, managers established spatially extensive hospitality services (Byrand 2007). In some national parks, free public automobile campgrounds provided centralized services to hundreds of visitors each night (figure 17.6).

Automobile tourism's influence extended beyond physical alterations to road surfaces, structures, and routes. It also shaped popular ideas about leisure and recreation. Railroad timetables, horse-drawn coaches, and limited concessionaire services defined pre-auto tours. Automobile travel shifted the temporal and spatial components of this venture. Cars allowed for increased travel speeds, thereby accelerating visitors' experiences with the places they encountered, the timing of their stays at destinations, and the routes they accessed along the way. Tourist practices also engaged social memory, cultural values, and ideas about the places they encountered (Algeo 2009). In Southern California, for example, tourists embarked on automobile pilgrimages to visit homes, churches, and other landmarks associated with a fictional character named Ramona, the heroine of a popular 1884 novel (DeLyser 2003b, 2005). Although Ramona never lived in any of these California locations, a tourism industry sprouted and flourished, selling this fictional landscape to tourists. In Vermont, rural out-migration from the 1880s to the 1930s inspired state officials, rural residents, and reformers to sell

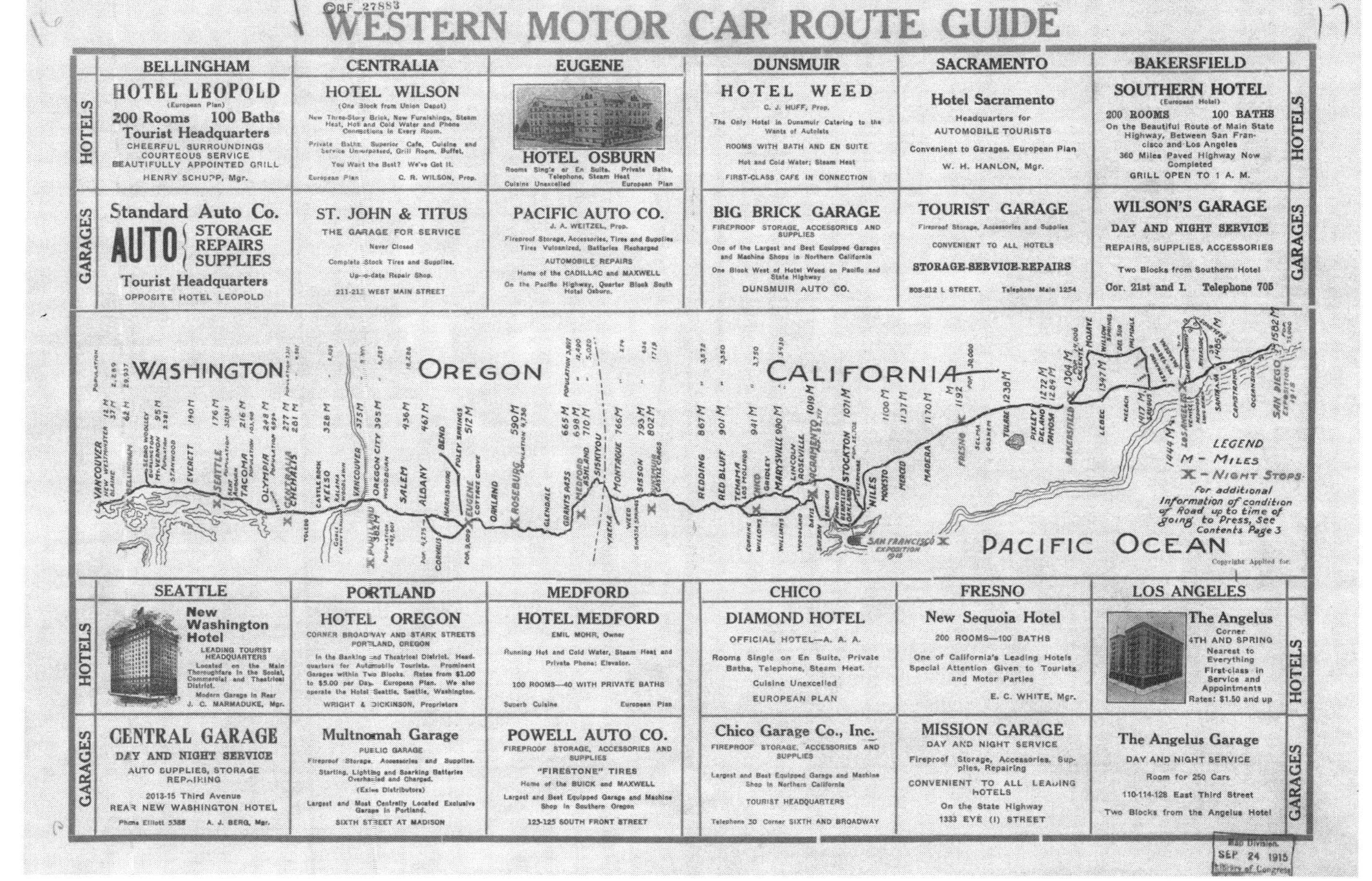

Figure 17.5. Auto-touring guides offered independent motorists efficiently abbreviated and yet detailed sources of information to plan and expedite their travels. This *Western Motor Car Route Guide* combines a table of advertised hotels and garages that can be cross-referenced with a map of towns along the route. The detailed strip map of Washington, Oregon, and California showing a route from Vancouver to San Diego lists towns, mileages, and populations, along with suggestions for "overnight stops" along the way to and from the site of the San Francisco and San Diego expositions of 1915. *Western Motor Car Route Guide* 1915.

Figure 17.6. This oblique aerial photograph shows the Fishing Bridge campground carved out of the thick lodgepole pine forests along Yellowstone Lake's shorelines. This extensive, free, public campground maintained by the National Park Service provided hundreds of tourists an inexpensive and popular overnight lodging option during the short summer season. Its time was short-lived. The NPS built the lakeshore campground in the post–World War II era to meet rising tourism demands but later stripped it from the landscape due to increased human-bear interactions and changing environmental impact and management policies. Fishing Bridge Automobile Campground 1963.

abandoned homes to summer tourists in the hopes of reinvigorating the state's economy (Harrison 2005, 2006). While the plan drew visitors into the state, insider-outsider tensions rose as "persistent fears that a new leisure-based economy and allegedly 'wrong kinds' of visitors would undermine the integrity of the state's traditional rural identity" (Harrison 2005, 478).

Parks and public spaces served as popular sites of local tourism and represented ideals of recreation and leisure. City park planners and advocates in San Francisco, for example, built their park system around the ideas of public health, prosperity, social coherence, and democratic equality, creating a world-renowned system of greenways and public areas (Young 2004). World's Fairs, theme parks, and smaller roadside attractions attracted North American and international visitors (Rydell 1987; Rydell, Findling, and Pelle 2000). Ideas about park management, use, and planning evolved to meet local and regional environmental and cultural contexts. At Mammoth Cave National Park, for instance, "resource extraction, tourism, and environmentalism became the dominant ideology" for managing the park (Algeo 2004).

State parks played an important role in shaping tourism through connections to the national parks movement and state forestry programs. State parks provided outlets for urban residents for recreation and access to open and public spaces that aimed to transcend class lines. In some states, such as Maryland, early state park promoters worked hand in hand with state forestry officials to create parks that drew in tourists from Baltimore and nearby urban centers (Buckley and Grove 2001; Buckley, Bailey, and Grove 2006).

Popular imagery and regional promotional strategies made powerful visual arguments that enticed travelers to hit the road and railway (Blodgett 2007). Tourists made journeys to Grand Canyon National Park, seeking the colorful, dramatic, and scenic views promoted through postcard imagery (Youngs 2012). Executives with the Great Northern Railway promoted Glacier National Park through a nationwide campaign of photographs and imagery that highlighted selective locations and themes in the park (Wyckoff and Dilsaver 1997). Santa Fe Railroad endorsed southwestern tourist attractions along the railroad's route through a highly stylized and artistic visual campaign that connected railroad lines with iconic southwestern imagery (Rothman 1998, 81–112). Richard Francaviglia notes that this promotional strategy drew tourists to the Southwest and "actually created a romanticized landscape to match the stereotypes, reminding us that art and commerce are interconnected in the region" (1994, 29–30).

MASS APPEAL

From the latter 1940s to the 1970s, American and Canadian tourism boomed. The end of World War II brought a surge in recreational and leisure travel as many Americans and Canadians tapped into their affluence, increased leisure time, and curiosity to see more of their home countries. This era invoked a golden age of automobile tourism that transformed landscapes across North America. Indeed, John Jakle argues that "no other technological innovation has so transformed the geography of the United States as the automobile" (2010, 403). National high-speed transportation networks connected North Americans with sights and attractions across the continent. Auto tourism evolved into a distinct culture of its own with signature landscape elements, such as gas stations, roadside motels, local and regional tourist attractions, truck stops, and bus stations (Jakle and Sculle 1994; Jakle, Sculle, and Rogers 1996). Lodging, food services, and entertainment venues lined road networks, drawing in services and attractions in linear spatial patterns similar to railroad-development schemes of previous eras. Transcontinental east-west highways and north-south corridors such as Highway 89 (Vale and Vale 1989), U.S. 40 (Vale 1983), and Route 66 (Krim 2005) shaped regional development and provided tourists with reliable and direct access to towns, cities, parks, and other attractions. Postwar tourism also benefited from increasing air service and flights connecting small airports with larger hub-and-spoke systems of air travel across North America (Schwantes 2003). Advances in flight technology, navigation tools, and plane design from the war effort translated into faster planes and a boom in the commercial air industry. Overall, air travel became more affordable and accessible to a wider range of travelers as regional and national jet service expanded across North America. For the more adventuresome tourist, helicopter tours provided dramatic, up-close views of scenic locations on a local or regional level (figure 17.7).

The mid-century boom in recreation and travel also benefited from another influential, if less obvious, contribution from the wartime effort: innovations in technology and construction materials for outdoor recreational equipment. Prior to the war, rudimentary equipment and the relative inaccessibility of many outdoor activities left many such pursuits to a few bold and specially trained experts. After the war, stronger, lighter, less expensive, and more durable materials replaced bulky components in equipment (Young 2000, 2010).

Figure 17.7. As tourism transportation options diversified after World War II, airline travel connected visitors with their travel destinations. Airplane tours, such as this one advertised for the Grand Canyon of Arizona, are a more recent development that offers visitors dramatic views of the canyon in just a few hours. Grand Canyon Airlines (2006). Advertisement brochure from the author's collection.

Mass manufacturing of recreational equipment decreased consumer prices, making specialized gear more widely available for a growing number of active and adventuresome travelers. For example, canvas tents, hemp climbing rope, and heavy cast-iron cookware—standard equipment in previous eras—gave way to polyethylene sheets for tent sides, kernmantel or core-and-sheath synthetic material ropes (developed by alpinists in Europe and then introduced to the United States in the 1960s), and lightweight aluminum pots and pans. A climbing guidebook praised the advantages of new rope materials compared to the standard laid or twisted ropes, yet also pointed out their disadvantages: "a readiness to kink, a tendency to unwind and spin a free-hanging climber, and greater friction on rock" (Ferber 1974).

Small, lightweight, inexpensive, and reliable kerosene, gasoline, or liquid-butane gas-fueled stoves replaced open fires for cooking meals. Lightweight, durable, and affordable backpacks and tents encouraged an increasing number of active and adventurous travelers to explore backcountry and wilderness trails that formerly required the equipment of an outfitter or a guide service. Indeed, the availability of outdoor gear may have overwhelmed some tourists. "The profusion of designs, sizes, weights, and materials makes choice difficult and requires many hours of poring over mountain shop catalogs" (Ferber 1974). Automobile campers embraced these new technologies as lightweight aluminum trailers complete with beds hit the open road. Inexpensive and accessible car-camping accouterments, from cooking pots to sleeping bags, encouraged tourists to hit the open road and stay at the expanding system of car-friendly campgrounds (figure 17.8).

As new materials and equipment types diversified, so did the range of leisure and recreational activities. Hiking, camping, rock climbing, skiing, whitewater rafting, and mountain biking attracted new practitioners who developed and refined these sports in various adventure recreation hearth areas throughout the western United States. In certain locations, the confluence of postwar affluence, mass tourism, advanced equipment technology, and a growing interest in experiencing the outdoors through adventure recreation defined these hearth areas. We can trace the origins of the modern whitewater rafting industry, for example, to wartime technologies and the innovative use of surplus military equipment in the depths of the Grand Canyon during the 1950s. Using surplus military rafts, ammunition cans, ropes, and other durable and waterproof equipment, individuals such as George White Clark formed rafting companies that offered "share-the-expense" group trips down the Colorado River (Lavender 1985; Westwood 1997, 47–52). The trips transformed sections of the mighty Colorado and other rivers across the United States from places once the domain solely of elite rafters into popular sites of mass tourism that hosted thousands of visitors each year (figure 17.9). Mountain resort towns, such as Jackson, Wyoming, and Ketchum, Idaho, attracted skiers in the winter and hikers and outdoor festival enthusiasts in the summer. These seasonal resorts grew and expanded during the 1960s and 1970s, benefiting from an increasingly mobile and adventuresome population of outdoor recreationalists (Rothman 1998; Coleman 2004; Childers 2012).

Mass tourism flourished on public lands, especially in national forests and parks. While public lands managers struggled to meet the demands of increasing

Figure 17.8. For this family, "Camping in Adventureland" at Lake Powell in Utah afforded many of the pieces of outdoor equipment and conveniences of the late 1960s and early 1970s, such as the tent and car trailers seen in this image. "Guide to Glen Canyon Dam and Lake Powell" (n.d.). Color brochure from the author's collection.

numbers of visitors, they also contended with dilapidated facilities that had suffered from limited use and maintenance during wartime closures. Renovation programs such as Mission 66 (U.S. National Park Service) and Operation Outdoors (U.S. Forest Service) strove to refurbish and expand campgrounds, hotels, dining areas, and other tourist services (Dilsaver 1997; Steen 2004). The rise in automobile tourism during the 1950s and 1960s increased visitors' expectations of a "windshield wilderness," an encounter with nature that they could consume visually and conveniently through the windshields of their cars (Louter 2006). Managers and planners in national parks and protected areas negotiated the terrain of changing visitor use and evolving environmental-management strategies (Smith 2007; Yochim 2007). Not all Americans had equal access to parks and protected areas facilities, however, as Jim Crow laws reinforced racial segregation by enforcing separate access to park tourist facilities in southern U.S. state parks (O'Brien 2007).

In national parks especially, the relationship between cars and nature tourism was complicated, resting both on conceptions of wilderness as nature separate from human-modified landscapes and on expectations for ever more access to wilderness areas via automobile routes. In Yosemite National Park, park managers removed or altered the placement of cultural landscape features such as sewage treatment stations, garbage-collection sites, and water-distribution facilities to hide them from the public viewshed along roads (Colten and Dilsaver

Figure 17.9. With the use of surplus military rafts, ammunition cans, and other equipment and materials developed during World War II, modern whitewater rafting boomed as a popular adventure sport in the United States. In this image, tourists aboard two rafts lashed together with rope experience "adventure in the raw" as they float down the Colorado River through Grand Canyon National Park. "Guide to Glen Canyon Dam and Lake Powell" (n.d.). Color brochure from the author's collection.

2005). This manipulation of the environment reflected visitors' conflicting expectations of a pristine wilderness environment fitted with a range of convenient, comfortable, and affordable hospitality services. In Great Smoky Mountains National Park, park managers and planners altered roads and pullouts, creating a carefully choreographed tour of the park (Young 2002). Their actions guided and controlled the spatial configuration and timing of tourist activities in the park, which in many ways mimicked the experience of traveling through a theme park in a more urban location.

The influence and impact of postwar mass tourism extended beyond rural and wilderness locations as cities became some of the "most important tourist attractions in North America" (Jakle 1985, 284). Many North Americans sought out spatially extensive, urban, consumer landscapes for their leisure and recreational pursuits (Berger 1967). New York and Chicago, urban attractions in their own right, gained additional acclaim as theaters and movie houses expanded to encompass entire city blocks (Conzen 2010, 432–33). Las Vegas expanded and developed into a large-scale gambling center that evolved with vacation and entertainment attractions (Conzen 2010, 441). Mass tourism fed the creation and proliferation of a range of urban leisure and recreation landscapes, including sports stadiums, cruise ships, convention and exposition facilities, megachurches, museums, and large shopping centers (Conzen 2010).

Massive theme parks such as Disneyland Resort in California and its eastern counterpart, Walt Disney World Resort in Florida, drew tourists who contributed economically to the nearby cities of Anaheim and Orlando. These theme parks boasted extensive hotel and resort facilities in addition to rides and amusement centers. These massive urban parks attracted sizable labor forces to serve tourists' needs. Disney World opened in 1971, employing thousands of workers from around the world who settled in Orlando, shaping the economic, cultural, and social landscapes of these areas (Rothman 1998; Conzen 2010). Disney theme parks also exerted a powerful cultural influence through mass-marketing campaigns, attracting millions of tourists each year (Eco 1986; Lippard 1999).

Alongside these postwar developments in recreational equipment, activities, and locations, ideas about the environment shifted to accommodate a growing consciousness regarding the impacts of human behavior and insights gained from ecological theory. As more tourists experienced the outdoors and wilderness areas, many developed newfound affinities for the locations they visited on their journeys (Philpott 2013; Rugh 2010). However, mass media combined with consumer culture to form a powerful and influential force that shaped popular imaginations and tourist landscapes (Berger 1967). The tourism industry of Jasper National Park, for example, commodified the park's landscape through a visual campaign that used photographs, postcards, and advertisements to downplay environmental threats to the park while simultaneously promoting the park's scenic viewpoints and charismatic wildlife (Cronin 2011). Popular media and environmental perceptions shaped visitor experiences in a wide range of locations, creating iconic landscapes that became firmly embedded in the popular imagination. Newspaper reports, postcards, photographs, and other images shaped the place identity of Colorado's Fourteeners and contributed to a building iconography of Mount of the Holy Cross (Blake 2002, 2008). Auto-tourism literature, photographs, music, and a variety of other forms of media captured popular imaginations and promoted Route 66 as an iconic symbol of freedom and individual exploration (Krim 2005).

BEYOND THE TRAIL

Changing modes of travel, shifting ideas about leisure and recreation, and environmental perceptions remain enduring themes in tourism scholarship. While tourists continue to rely on planes, trains, and automobiles to reach their destinations, new media forms available through computers and mobile technology allow for virtual trips to far-away places. Theme parks, hotels, cruise lines, convention and exposition facilities, museums, stadiums and sports facilities, cities, and a variety of other tourist attractions boast websites bursting with promotional information for potential visitors. In some cases, websites have nearly replaced the touring guidebooks popularized during the early auto-tourism age. The U.S. Department of Transportation, for example, hosts the American Byways website, which informs travelers along the Ohio sections of the Lincoln Highway about camping, gasoline availability, lodging, dining options, and other services along the historic route (NSBO 2012). Recognizing that tourism has greatly expanded its reach beyond the trails and roads of turn-of-the-century travelers, some scholars seek new ways to engage with the subject. Lucy Lippard explores tourism "all over the place" as movement from home to places "on and off the map" (1997, 4), paying particular attention to how tourism, art, and place interact through the role of memory, perceptions of nature, and social constructions of landscape. Interdisciplinary approaches that weave together cultural criticism, geography, history, anthropology, and contemporary art inform studies that explore how places are conceived, represented, and transformed as tourism sites (Lippard 1999; Crouch and Lubbren 2003).

Heritage tourism, a subset of contemporary leisure and recreational travel, appeals to visitors seeking historical interpretations of landscapes (Francaviglia 2000). Semiotic discourse analysis and critical social theory permeate many contemporary studies, encouraging a deeper analysis and discussion of the cultural and social values associated with tourism sites. Tourism is an increasingly multicultural activity embedded in a "multicentered society" that draws on a variety of tourist experiences, locations, and marketing campaigns, some of which may be self-referential or contextual (Lippard 1997). Such is the case with heritage tourism at Mount Rushmore National Memorial, Wall Drug Store, and Rapid City Dinosaur Park in South Dakota. Tourism at these sites may be seen as an act of nationalism and a way for visitors to take part in an "imagined community," acting out key aspects of national identity through travel to specific sites associated with key moments or events in U.S. national history (Pretes 2003). Dydia DeLyser (1999) asks what role authenticity plays in contemporary tourist practices at locations that offer a thin line between historical artifact and artificial landscape. At Bodie, California, for example, park staff and managers maintain the crumbling settlement of a ghost town in a suspended state of decay as a source of entertainment for tourists (DeLyser 1999). Theme park landscapes such as Disneyland and Sea World, towns like Gatlinburg, Tennessee, and "Little Switzerland" attractions (Hoelscher 1998a) challenge ideas of authenticity and heritage in tourism practices (figure 17.10).

Recent scholarship also tackles diverse human-environment issues. Historical geographers' contributions to contemporary tourism studies are particularly well represented in national parks and protected areas research. Park management and environmental impacts of tourism are treated in historical geographic studies of Sequoia and Kings Canyon (Dilsaver and Tweed 1990), Cumberland Island National Seashore (Dilsaver 2004), Yosemite National Park (Runte 1990), Yellowstone National Park (Yochim 2005, 2009), Alberta (Bella 1987), Jasper (MacLaren 2007), and Ontario (Killan 1993). Human-environment interactions are a prime theme in this vein of work, as the U.S. National Park Service, Parks Canada, and other federal public lands agencies grapple with changing ecological conditions, wilderness-management priorities, and a greater understanding of visitor impacts (Colten and Dilsaver 1992; Sellars 1997; Pritchard 1999; Vale 2005), sustainability (Meyer 2001), and the political geography of national parks (Dilsaver and Wyckoff 2005, 2009).

Figure 17.10. Town planners and community members revitalized and renovated Helen, Georgia, just a few hours north of Atlanta in the Blue Ridge Mountains, as a replica of an unspecified alpine village. Helen typifies many contemporary tourist attractions that challenge ideas of authenticity and heritage. The town caters to tourists with a range of seasonal festivals and events, including the Bavarian Nights of Summer and Oktoberfest, with numerous open-air beer gardens, shops, and restaurants. Photograph by Yolonda Youngs, 2009.

Although geography is in many respects an inherently interdisciplinary field, historical geographers increasingly call upon scholarship from a variety of fields to address issues of race, class, and gender embedded in tourist identities. Stephen Hanna and Vincent Del Casino (2003) present an edited volume centered on ideas of representation and practices of identity that brings together voices from across the discipline of geography. North American case studies include essays about political tourism and memory in Quebec City (Shields 2003), Alabama's civil rights and the role of memory (Dwyer 2003), ghost towns and tourism maps (DeLyser 2003a), and the politics of representation and environmental protection in Butte, Montana (Curran 2003).

Finally, contemporary tourism research is evolving and integrating applied perspectives, behavioral approaches, and emerging technologies. C. Michael Hall and Stephen Page (2006) explore tourism, recreation, leisure, and mobility in North America and across the globe with a special emphasis on the role of human behavior, supply and demand, and the social-environmental impacts of tourism.

Drawing on the findings of geographers, recreation and tourism specialists, economists, and psychologists, Hall and Page pay close attention to the "spatiality of leisure" found in the "patterns, processes and implications" of tourist activity (2006, 34), including barriers to recreation, the seasonality of some activities, and financial and social constraints that impede tourists' access to certain activities or locations. Tourism sites range from city parks and urban open spaces, to coastal and marine locations, to rural locations in the "pleasure periphery" of wilderness and national parks. Hall and Page (2006, 312–39) also note that the values attached to and demands for these areas vary through time. Evolving technologies within the field of geography such as geographic information science provide valuable insights for scholars interested in tourism planning, resource management, and marketing (Henry and Armstrong 2004; Hall and Page 2006; Algeo, Epperson, and Brunt 2011).

REFERENCES

Algeo, K. 2004. Mammoth Cave and the Making of Place. *Southeastern Geographer* 44, no. 1: 27–47.

———. 2009. Indian for a Night: Sleeping with the "Other" at Wigwam Village Tourist Cabins. *Material Culture* 41, no. 2: 1–17.

Algeo, K., A. Epperson, and M. Brunt. 2011. Historical GIS as a Platform for Public Memory at Mammoth Cave National Park. *International Journal of Applied Geospatial Research* 2, no. 4: 19–36.

Allen, J. L. 1992. Horizons of the Sublime: The Invention of the Romantic West. *Journal of Historical Geography* 18, no. 1: 27–40.

Athearn, R. G. 1986. *The Mythic West in Twentieth-Century America*. Lawrence: University Press of Kansas.

Beck, W. A., and Y. D. Hasse. 1989. *Historical Atlas of the American West*. Norman: University of Oklahoma Press.

Bella, L. 1987. *Parks for Profit*. Montreal: Harvest House.

Berger, A. A. 1967. *Manufacturing Desire: Media, Popular Culture, and Everyday Life*. New Brunswick, NJ: Transaction Publishers.

Blake, K. S. 2002. Colorado Fourteeners and the Nature of Place Identity. *Geographical Review* 92, no. 2: 155–79.

———. 2008. Imagining Heaven and Earth at Mount of the Holy Cross, Colorado. *Journal of Cultural Geography* 25, no. 1: 1–30.

Blodgett, P. 2007. Defining Uncle Sam's Playgrounds: Railroad Advertising and the National Parks, 1917–1941. *Historical Geography* 35: 80–113.

Buckley, G. L., and J. M. Grove. 2001. Sowing the Seeds of Forest Conservation: Fred Besley and the Maryland Story, 1906–1923. *Maryland Historical Magazine* 96 (Fall): 303–27.

Buckley, G. L., R. F. Bailey, and J. M. Grove. 2006. The Patapsco Forest Reserve: Establishing a "City Park" for Baltimore, 1907–1941. *Historical Geography* 34: 87–108.

Burlington and Quincy Railroad Co. 1892. *Burlington Route*. Chicago: Rand McNally and Co. Call number: G3701.P3 1892 .R3 RR 357. Library of Congress Geography and Map Division, Washington, D.C. http://memory.loc.gov/cgi-bin/query/h?ammem/gmd:@field(NUMBER + @band(g3701p + rr003570)).

Byrand, K. 2007. Integrating Preservation and Development at Yellowstone's Upper Geyser Basin, 1915–1940. *Historical Geography* 35: 136–59.

Childers, M. 2012. Colorado Powder Keg: Ski Resorts and the Environmental Movement. Lawrence: University of Kansas Press.

Coleman, A. 2004. *Ski Style: Sport and Culture in the Rockies*. Seattle: University of Washington Press.

Colten, C. E., and L. M. Dilsaver, eds. 1992. *The American Environment: Interpretations of Past Geographies*. Lanham, MD: Rowman & Littlefield.

———. 2005. The Hidden Landscape of Yosemite National Park. *Journal of Cultural Geography* 22, no. 2: 27–50.

Conzen, M. 2010. Developing Large-Scale Consumer Landscapes. In *The Making of the American Landscape*, edited by M. P. Conzen, 423–50. 2nd ed. New York: Routledge.

Cronin, J. K. 2011. *Manufacturing National Park Nature: Photography, Ecology, and the Wilderness Industry of Jasper*. Vancouver: University of British Columbia Press.

Crouch, D., and N. Lubbren. 2003. Introduction. In *Visual Culture and Tourism*, edited by D. Crouch and N. Lubbren, 1–22. Oxford: Berg.

Curran, M. 2003. Dialogues of Difference: Contested Mappings of Tourism and Environmental Protection in Butte, Montana. In *Mapping Tourism*, edited by S. P. Hanna and V. J. Del Casino, 1–27. Minneapolis: University of Minnesota Press.

DeLyser, D. 1999. Authenticity on the Ground: Engaging the Past in a California Ghost Town. *Annals of the Association of American Geographers* 89, no. 4: 602–32.

———. 2003a. "A Walk through Old Bodie": Presenting a Ghost Town in a Tourism Map. In *Mapping Tourism*, edited by S. P. Hanna and V. J. Del Casino, 1–27. Minneapolis: University of Minnesota Press.

———. 2003b. Ramona Memories: Fiction, Tourist Practices, and Placing the Past in Southern California. *Annals of the Association of American Geographers* 93, no. 4: 886–908.

———. 2005. *Ramona Memories: Tourism and the Shaping of Southern California*. Minneapolis: University of Minnesota Press.

Dilsaver, L. 1992. Stemming the Flow: The Evolution of Controls on Visitor Numbers and Impact in National Parks. In *The American Environment: Interpretations of Past Geographies*, edited by L. M. Dilsaver and C. E. Colten, pp. 235–55. Lanham, MD: Rowman & Littlefield.

———. 1997. *America's National Park System: The Critical Documents*. Lanham, MD: Rowman & Littlefield.

———. 2004. *Cumberland Island National Seashore: A History of Conservation Conflict*. Charlottesville: University of Virginia Press.

Dilsaver, L. M., and W. Tweed. 1990. *Challenge of the Big Trees: A Resource History of Sequoia and Kings Canyon National Parks*. Three Rivers, CA: Sequoia Natural History Association.

Dilsaver, L. M., and W. Wyckoff. 2005. The Political Geography of National Parks. *Pacific Historical Review* 74, no. 2: 237–66.

———. 2009. Failed National Parks in the Last Best Place. *Montana: The Magazine of Western History* 59 (Autumn): 3–24.

Dwyer, O. J. 2003. Memory on the Margins: Alabama's Civil Rights Journey as a Memorial Text. In *Mapping Tourism*, edited by S. P. Hanna and V. J. Del Casino, 1–27. Minneapolis: University of Minnesota Press.

Eco, U. 1986. *Travels in Hyperreality*. San Diego, CA: Harcourt.

Ferber, P., ed. 1974. *Mountaineering: The Freedom of the Hills*. 3rd ed. Seattle, WA: Mountaineers Books.

Figueiredo, Y. 2007. Inventing Yosemite Valley: National Parks and the Language of Preservation. *Historical Geography* 35: 12–37.

Fishing Bridge Automobile Campground. 1963. Yellowstone National Park Museum Collections. Call number 27127. http://www.nps.gov/yell/historyculture/museum.htm.

Francaviglia, R. V. 1994. Elusive Land: Changing Geographic Images of the Southwest. In *Essays on the Changing Images of the Southwest*, edited by R. Francaviglia and D. Narrett, 8–39. College Station: Texas A&M Press.

———. 2000. Selling Heritage Landscapes. In *Preserving Cultural Landscapes in America*, edited by A. Alanen and R. Melnick, 44–69. Baltimore: Johns Hopkins University Pres.

Germic, S. 2001. *American Green: Class, Crisis, and the Deployment of Nature in Central Park, Yosemite, and Yellowstone*. Lanham, MD: Lexington Books.

Grand Canyon Airlines. 2006. Advertisement brochure from the author's collection.

"Guide to Glen Canyon Dam and Lake Powell." n.d. Color brochure from the author's collection.

Guptill, A. B. 1897. *Haynes' Guide to Yellowstone Park: A Practical Handbook*. Saint Paul, MN: F. J. Haynes.

Hall, C. M., and S. J. Page, eds. 2006. *The Geography of Tourism and Recreation: Environment, Place, and Space*. 3rd ed. London: Routledge.

Hall, C. M., and J. Shultis. 1991. Railways, Tourism and Worthless Lands: The Establishment of National Parks in Australia, Canada, New Zealand and the United States. *Australian-Canadian Studies: A Journal for the Humanities and Social Sciences* 8, no. 2: 57–74.

Hanna, S. P., and V. J. Del Casino, eds. 2003. *Mapping Tourism*. Minneapolis: University of Minnesota Press.

Harrison, B. 2005. Tourism, Farm Abandonment, and the "Typical" Vermonter, 1880–1930. *Journal of Historical Geography* 31 (July): 478–95.

———. 2006. *The View from Vermont: Tourism and the Making of an American Rural Landscape*. Burlington: University of Vermont Press.

Henry, M., and L. Armstrong, eds. 2004. *Mapping the Future of America's National Parks: Stewardship through Geographic Information Systems*. Redlands, CA: ESRI Press.

Hoelscher, S. 1998a. *Heritage on Stage: The Invention of Ethnic Place in America's Little Switzerland*. Madison: University of Wisconsin Press.

———. 1998b. The Photographic Construction of Tourist Space in Victorian America. *Geographical Review* 88, no. 4 (October): 548–70.

Hornsby, S. J. 1993. The Gilded Age and the Making of Bar Harbor. *Geographical Review* 83, no. 4: 455–68.

Hyde, A. 1990. *An American Vision: Far Western Landscape and National Culture*. New York and London: New York University Press.

Ingersoll View Co. 1905. *Wawona Tunnel Tree, Upper Mariposa Grove, Yosemite, California*. Library of Congress, Prints and Photographs Collection. Call Number: LOT 11958–11. http://www.loc.gov/pictures/collection/stereo/item/89711579.

Jakle, J. A. 1985. *The Tourist: Travel in Twentieth-Century North America*. Lincoln: University of Nebraska Press.

———. 2010. Paving America for the Automobile. In *The Making of the American Landscape*, edited by M. P. Conzen, 403–22. 2nd ed. New York and London: Routledge.

Jakle, J. A., and K. A. Sculle. 1994. *The Gas Station in America*. Baltimore: Johns Hopkins University Press.

———. 2008. *Motoring: The Highway Experience in America*. Athens: University of Georgia Press.

Jakle, J. A., K. A. Sculle, and J. S. Rogers. 1996. *The Motel in America*. Baltimore: Johns Hopkins University Press.

Johnson, K. A. 1990. Origins of Tourism in the Catskill Mountains. *Journal of Cultural Geography* 11, no. 1: 5–16.

Kaufman, P. W. 1996. *National Parks and the Woman's Voice: A History.* Albuquerque: University of New Mexico Press.
Killan, G. 1993. *Protected Places: A History of Ontario's Provincial Park System.* Toronto: Dundurn Press.
Krim, A. 2005. *Route 66: Iconography of the American Highway.* Santa Fe: Center for American Places.
Kropp, P. 2009. Wilderness Wives and Dishwashing Husbands: Comfort and the Domestic Arts of Camping in America, 1880–1910. *Journal of Social History* 43, no. 1: 5–30.
Lavender, D. 1985. *River Runners of the Grand Canyon.* Grand Canyon Village, AZ: Grand Canyon Association.
Lippard, L. R. 1997. *Lure of the Local: Senses of Place in a Multicentered Society.* New York: New Press.
———. 1999. *Tourism, Art, and Place.* New York: New Press.
Louter, D. 2006. *Windshield Wilderness: Cars, Roads, and Nature in Washington's National Parks.* Seattle: University of Washington Press.
MacCannell, D. 1976. *The Tourist: A New Theory of the Leisure Class.* New York: Schocken Books.
MacLaren, I. S., ed. 2007. *Culturing Wilderness in Jasper National Park: Studies in Two Centuries of Human History in the Upper Athabasca River Watershed.* Edmonton: University of Alberta Press.
McGreevy, P. V. 1994. *Imagining Niagara: The Meaning and Making of Niagara Falls.* Amherst: University of Massachusetts Press.
Meyer, J. L. 2001. Withstanding the Test of Time: Yellowstone and Sustainable Tourism. In *Tourism, Recreation, and Sustainability: Linking Culture and the Environment,* edited by S. F. McCool and R. N. Moisey, 142–57. 2nd ed. Oxford, UK: CABI Publishing.
———. 2003. *The Spirit of Yellowstone: The Cultural Evolution of a National Park.* Lanham, MD: Roberts Rinehart Publishers.
Meyer-Arendt, K. J., and A. A. Lew. 2003. Recreation, Tourism, and Sport. In *Geography in America at the Dawn of the 21st Century,* edited by G. L. Gaile and C. J. Willmott, 524–40. Oxford: Oxford University Press.
Morehouse, B. 1996. *A Place Called Grand Canyon: Contested Geographies.* Tucson: University of Arizona Press.
Morin, K. M. 1998. British Women Travellers and Constructions of Racial Differences across the Nineteenth-Century American West. *Transactions of the Institute of British Geographers* 23, no. 3: 311–30.
———. 1999. Peak Practices: Englishwomen's "Heroic" Adventures in the Nineteenth-Century American West. *Annals of the Association of American Geographers* 89, no. 3: 489–514.
National Scenic Byways Online (NSBO), U.S. Department of Transportation (DOT). 2012. American Byways: Ohio Lincoln Highway Historic Byway Visitor Services. Washington, D.C.: U.S. DOT Federal Highway Administration National Scenic Byways Program.
O'Brien, W. 2007. The Strange Career of a Florida State Park: Uncovering a Jim Crow Past. *Historical Geography* 35: 160–84.
Philpott, W. 2013. *Vacationland: Tourism and Environment in the Colorado High Country.* Seattle: University of Washington Press.
Pretes, M. 2003. Tourism and Nationalism. *Annals of Tourism Research* 30, no. 1: 125–42.
Pritchard, J. A. 1999. *Preserving Yellowstone's Natural Conditions: Science and the Perception of Nature.* Lincoln: University of Nebraska Press.
Raitz, K., ed. 1996. *The National Road.* Baltimore: Johns Hopkins University Press.

Rothman, H. 1998. *Devil's Bargains: Tourism in the Twentieth-Century American West*. Lawrence: University Press of Kansas.
Rugh, S. 2010. *Are We There Yet? The Golden Age of American Family Vacations*. Lawrence: University Press of Kansas.
Runte, A. 1972. How Niagara Falls Was Saved: The Beginning of Aesthetic Conservation in the United States. *Conservationist* 25 (April–May): 32–35, 43.
———. 1990. *Yosemite: The Embattled Wilderness*. Lincoln: University of Nebraska Press.
———. 2010. *National Parks: The American Experience*. 4th ed. Lanham, MD: Taylor Trade Publishing.
Rydell, R. 1987. *All the World's a Fair: Visions of Empire at American International Expositions, 1876–1916*. Chicago: University of Chicago Press.
Rydell, R., J. Findling, and K. Pelle. 2000. *Fair America: World's Fairs in the United States*. Washington, D.C.: Smithsonian Institution Press.
Schaffer, M. S. 1996. "See America First": Re-envisioning Nation and Region through Western Tourism. *Pacific Historical Review* 65, no. 4: 559–81.
———. 2001. *See America First: Tourism and National Identity, 1880–1940*. Washington, D.C.: Smithsonian Institution Press.
Schwantes, C. A. 2003. *Going Places: Transportation Redefines the Twentieth-Century West*. Bloomington: Indiana University Press.
Sears, J. F. 1989. *Sacred Places: American Tourist Attractions in the Nineteenth Century*. New York: Oxford University Press.
Sellars, R. W. 1997. *Preserving Nature in the National Parks: A History*. New Haven, CT: Yale University Press.
Shaw and Powell Permanent Camping Co. n.d. *See It Right*. Booklet. Yellowstone National Park Museum Collections. Call number 132051. http://www.nps.gov/yell/historyculture/museum.htm.
Shields, R. 2003. Political Tourism: Mapping Memory and the Future at Quebec City. In *Mapping Tourism*, edited by S. P. Hanna and V. J. Del Casino, 1–27. Minneapolis: University of Minnesota Press.
Smith, C. 1989. *Off the Beaten Track: Women Adventurers and Mountaineers in Western Canada*. Jasper, Alberta: Coyote Books.
Smith, L. 2004. The Contested Landscape of Early Yellowstone. *Journal of Cultural Geography* 22, no. 1: 3–26.
———. 2007. Cape Hatteras: Birth of the National Seashore. *Historical Geography* 35: 38–55.
Spence, M. D. 1999. *Dispossessing the Wilderness: Indian Removal and the Making of the National Parks*. Oxford: Oxford University Press.
Squire, S. J. 1994. The Cultural Values of Literary Tourism. *Annals of Tourism Research* 21, no. 1: 103–20.
———. 1995. In the Steps of Genteel Ladies: Women Tourists in the Canadian Rockies, 1885–1939. *Canadian Geographer* 39, no. 1: 2–15.
Standard Scenic Co. 1906. Horseshoe Falls from Goat Island, Niagara Falls, NY. Library of Congress, Prints and Photographs Collection. Call Number: LOT 11556–19. http://www.loc.gov/pictures/item/93503753.
Steen, H. 2004. *The U.S. Forest Service: A History*. Seattle: University of Washington Press.
Towner, J. 1986. *An Historical Geography of Recreation and Tourism in the Western World, 1540–1940*. Chichester, UK: John Wiley and Sons.
Trimble, S. 2006. *Lasting Light: 125 Years of Grand Canyon Photography*. Flagstaff, AZ: Northland Publishing.

Vale, T. R. 1983. *U.S. 40 Today: Thirty Years of Landscape Change.* Madison: University of Wisconsin Press.
———. 2005. *The American Wilderness: Reflections on Nature Protection in the United States.* Charlottesville: University of Virginia Press.
Vale, T. R., and G. R. Vale. 1989. *Western Images, Western Landscapes: Travels along U.S. 89.* Tucson: University of Arizona Press.
Western Motor Car Route Guide. 1915. Library of Congress Geography and Map Division, Washington, D.C. Call number: G4231.P2 1915 W4 TIL. Library of Congress catalog number: 99446217. http://www.loc.gov/item/99446217.
Westwood, R. 1997. *Woman of the River: Georgie White Clark, Whitewater Pioneer.* Logan: Utah State University Press.
Wrobel, D. M. 2002. *Promised Lands: Promotion, Memory, and the Creation of the American West.* Lawrence: University Press of Kansas.
Wyckoff, W., and L. M. Dilsaver. 1997. Promotional Imagery of Glacier National Park. *Geographical Review* 87, no. 1: 1–26.
Wyckoff, W., and C. Nash. 1994. Geographical Images of the American West: The View from Harper's Monthly, 1850–1900. *Journal of the West* 33, no. 3: 10–24.
Yellowstone National Park Museum Collections (YNPMC). n.d. Photographs and brochures. Yellowstone National Park Museum Collections, Yellowstone National Park, Wyoming.
Yochim, M. J. 2005. Kayaking Playground or Nature Preserve? *Montana: The Magazine of Western History* 55, no. 1: 52–64.
———. 2007. A Water Wilderness: Battles over Values and Motorboats on Yellowstone Lake. *Historical Geography* 35: 185–213.
———. 2009. *Yellowstone and the Snowmobile: Locking Horns over National Park Use.* Lawrence: University Press of Kansas.
Young, T. 2000. Camping Out in America: From 1869 to Present. *Arroyo View* 12, no. 2: 9.
———. 2002. Virtue and Irony in a U.S. National Park. In *Theme Park Landscapes: Antecedents and Variations,* edited by T. Young and R. Riley, 157–81. Washington, D.C.: Dumbarton Oaks Research Library and Collection.
———. 2004. *Building San Francisco's Parks: 1850 to 1930.* Baltimore: Johns Hopkins University Press.
———. 2010. Terence Young on Camping and Its Equipment. *Environmental History* 15 (January): 120–28.
Young, T., and L. M. Dilsaver. 2011. Collecting and Diffusing the "World's Best Thought": International Cooperation by the National Park Service. *George Wright Forum* 28, no. 3: 269–78.
Youngs, Y. 2012. Editing Nature in Grand Canyon National Park Postcards. *Geographical Review* 102, no. 4: 486–509.
Youngs, Y., D. White, and J. Woodrich. 2008. Transportation Systems as Cultural Landscapes in National Parks: A Historical and Interpretive Study of Visitors' Transportation Behavior in Yosemite Valley. *Society and Natural Resources: An International Journal* 21, no. 9: 797–811.

18

Creating Regional Landscapes and Identities

William Wyckoff

Think about some of North America's quintessential regional landscapes. What are some examples of landscapes that symbolize regional identity? In some cases, generic features shape how we see a region. Tidy New England villages, opulent southern plantation houses, Quebec's picturesque French Canadian settlements, the Hispano plaza towns of northern New Mexico, or Southern California's sprawling suburbs might come to mind (Conzen 2010). In other cases, specific landmarks can symbolize larger regional stories. Ponder the powerful social memories linked to the Alamo in Texas, the Mormon Temple in Salt Lake City, or the sacred peaks of identity that Navajos honor across the Southwest (Nostrand and Estaville 2001).

How do these powerful connections between landscapes and regional identity evolve? What processes shape the links between landscape features and how people think about place? Furthermore, how do these social memories shape contemporary perceptions of the landscape and how we continually reinvent the past to serve our modern needs?

Questions that center on the intersection of the visual landscape and regional identity have long fascinated historical geographers (Conzen 1993; Wynn 1993; Baker 2003). This chapter explores the ideas that historical geographers have used to understand these connections. It also samples several regional case studies that illustrate how the process has unfolded in particular settings. Finally, it considers the larger significance of this perspective, particularly for those interested in topics such as historic preservation, landscape interpretation, and regional analysis.

LANDSCAPES AND REGIONAL IDENTITY

How does a landscape become a symbol of regional identity? The process is complex and historical. New England historian Joseph Conforti reminds us that "regional identity is not simply an organic outcome of human interaction with the natural environment of a particular place. Regional identity is both *historically grounded and culturally invented*" (2011, 17; emphasis added).

For example, Conforti and others have explored how the myth of the classic New England village, centered on a nucleated settlement with its white-steepled church and village green, evolved in the popular imagination (Meinig 1979; Wood 1997; Harrison and Judd 2011). That landscape, long an integral part of regional art, literature, and historical narratives, was less a reality of colonial America than a reinterpretation of market towns that evolved in the nineteenth century as the New England economy became more commercial (figure 18.1). As historical geographer Joseph Wood has demonstrated, colonial-era New England settlement was actually quite dispersed, presaging the larger continental pattern of isolated farmers on the rural landscape. But as market towns appeared in the region in the nineteenth century, New Englanders successfully incorporated these landscape features into their myths about the communal and republican virtues of early New England life. Thus, New England's regional identity became enduringly oriented toward a cultural invention that took shape long after the colonial era.

In addition to the key landscape features (either generic or specific) and place-centered meanings linked to a locality, we need to appreciate other variables that define regional identity. We can ask at what scale it operates and then try to identify the varied forces shaping its evolution. One can certainly argue that "regional identity" can include features broadly linked to a large area such as

Figure 18.1. This nineteenth-century town view of Methuen Falls, Massachusetts, captures some of the elements of the quintessential New England village, complete with clustered buildings, church steeples, and a central commons. American Antiquarian Society.

New England, the American South, or the Southwest. But place-based identities can also focus on very specific features associated with smaller areas (an Amish settlement, Ukrainian communities on the Canadian prairies, or even an urban neighborhood such as West Hollywood's gay community or Miami's Little Havana).

We also need to ask about time. How long does it take for a distinctive regional identity to take shape? In the case of western Montana, Salish peoples have occupied the region for centuries, while Vietnamese suburbanization in Southern California's Orange County (Little Saigon) has taken shape only over the past thirty or forty years. Is one set of cultural meanings associated with place more authentic or significant than the other? How much time must pass to create enduring landscape meanings in a place?

We can also ask how and why place-based identities change over time. Kevin Blake (2008), for example, has traced how Colorado's famous Mount of the Holy Cross (a cross-like image is carved in the peak) emerged between 1880 and 1930 to become a regional Christian symbol in the Rocky Mountains, a pilgrimage spot for faith-based healing, and an iconographic signature celebrated in paintings and photographs all the way to the halls of the Vatican. Then, things changed. Key promoters of the pilgrimage died, World War II interrupted visits, and a new postwar outdoor recreation and wilderness aesthetic drew people to the spot simply because it was a high and beautiful peak (it is one of the Colorado Fourteeners). Today most popular interest in the Mount of the Holy Cross has merged with a larger regional identity celebrating the Colorado high country.

We also need to consider the participants in the creation and fostering of regional identity. For example, who invented and sustained the social memories (and associated landscape features) that linked Spanish colonial-style architecture to Southern California? Obviously Spanish colonization of California is a part of the story, but so is the later reinvention and marketing of these traditions in the twentieth century. For example, San Diego's Panama-Pacific Exposition in 1917 helped redefine and popularize the "Spanish Colonial Revival" in the region. Similarly, eight years later, when an earthquake and fire destroyed much of Santa Barbara, city officials and business people saw an opportunity to reimagine and redesign much of the downtown in the Spanish colonial tradition. We can ask who participates in both the creation and consumption of these regional identities and for what purpose. Santa Barbara's case illustrates how an area's elite local population (insiders) reworked landscapes to market (with great success) a regional identity designed to entertain thousands of nonlocal visitors (outsiders).

Historical geographers are well positioned to make several distinctive contributions as we explore these connections between landscapes and regional identity (Meinig 1979). As Wood's detailed work on the reconstruction of colonial New England settlement patterns demonstrates, we can ask what the landscapes that served as the foundation for the symbol were really like. Careful analysis often reveals the gap between reality and myth. We can also explore the social processes that generated the "cultural inventions" Conforti describes. One approach to the task is to assess how stories, oral traditions, art, regional literature, and visual media—everything from school textbooks to mass-marketed films—have portrayed key landscape features. As cultural geographer Dydia DeLyser reminds us, "Much of the meaning we as humans, as cultural beings, make in our lives is triggered by the objects and artifacts around us, by the landscape" (2005, xv). DeLyser adds that people often widely share such meaning grounded in landscape and that its "stability lies not in its veracity but rather in its ability to adapt to present needs" (2005, xiv). Finally, historical geographers can assess the broader cultural significance of these powerful landscape images. What purpose do they serve, and what do these connections between landscape and regional identity tell us? In the examples of New England and Santa Barbara, they suggest persisting linkages between cultural values and place that can offer insight into contemporary phenomena as diverse as political discourse, tourism, and consumer advertising (West 1996; Shaffer 2001; Harrison and Judd 2011).

CHANGING IDEAS ABOUT REGION, LANDSCAPE, AND PLACE IDENTITY

Historical and cultural geographers have long shared an interest in pondering the connections between regional identity and the cultural landscape (Conzen 1993). Earlier ideas are important because they set the context for how we frame these questions today. Varied European traditions shaped how North American geographers thought about regions and landscapes. For example, nineteenth-century German geographer Otto Schlüter argued that if we carefully studied how the natural landscape was transformed into a landscape shaped by people (a *Kulturlandschaft*), we could understand how regions with characteristic features evolved over time (Martin and James 1993; Baker 2003). French geographer Paul Vidal de la Blache explored similar ideas with somewhat different language, suggesting how different homogeneous areas in France developed a character (displayed in the visible landscape of settlement patterns, agricultural practices, and architecture) that reflected the culture and ways of life (or *genre de vie*) of the people living there (Martin and James 1993; Baker 2003). It is important to understand that many of these earlier ideas linking landscapes and regional identity emphasized the belief that the region inherently possessed the characteristics that we see as culturally invented traditions today.

North American geographers moved toward this more nuanced view in the early and mid-twentieth century. Certainly Carl Sauer's fascination with the notions of both cultural landscape and regional personality were early and enduring contributions to our more contemporary ideas about the relationship between landscapes and regional identity (Martin and James 1993; Conzen 1993; Riesenweber 2008). For Sauer and many of his students at Berkeley, historical geography was the study of the evolution of the cultural landscape over time. These cultural landscapes were a function both of the natural setting and of the active agency of people transforming a part of the earth's surface. Furthermore, Sauer argued that these evolving landscape features were essential components of regional definition and identity (Baker 2003). Sauer (and others) often used the term "personality" to describe this close relationship between a regional setting, its characteristic assortment of cultural landscape features, and how both inhabitants and visitors saw the region's identity, typically shaped over a long period (Baker 2003).

Many of Sauer's contemporaries embraced his appreciation for landscape and the language he used to describe regional evolution over time. Derwent Whittlesey, Preston James, and others produced sequent occupance studies reconstructing multiple past landscapes for an area over time as a way to identify key elements of regional character (Conzen 1993). Similarly, in his own way, historical geographer Ralph Brown often focused on settlement patterns and the built environment as he described the historical evolution of North America's major regions (Brown 1948; Conzen 1993; Wyckoff 2003). From a different perspective, John K. Wright examined the role of the human imagination in the creation of geographical knowledge (or geosophy), suggesting that past ideas about regional landscapes, both real and imagined, merited study (Conzen 1993).

A more explicit exploration of how landscape features shaped the social construction of regional identity emerged in North American cultural and historical geography after 1960 (Conzen 1993; R. D. Mitchell 2001a; Riesenweber 2008). These innovative ideas flowered along a broad front of interrelated studies and initiatives. First, there was new and sustained interest in the creation and identification of distinctive North American culture regions, exemplified most enduringly in the work of Donald Meinig and Wilbur Zelinsky (Meinig 1965, 1968, 1971b, 1972; Zelinsky 1973; Wyckoff and Colten 2009, iii–x). Second, sparked by the behavioral turn in human geography, an interest developed in perceptual regions, or regions perceived to exist by their inhabitants (Conzen 1993). Third, there was a growing fascination with the everyday, vernacular North American landscape. J. B. Jackson led this initiative with his thoughtful explorations of ordinary features like commercial strips and trailer parks (Meinig 1979; Conzen 1993; J. B. Jackson 1994, 1997; Groth 1998; Groth and Wilson 2003). As geographer Peirce Lewis (1979) argued, every vernacular landscape reflected important cultural values. Other scholars, such as John Stilgoe, Fred Kniffen, Wilbur Zelinsky, and Henry Glassie, explored everything from North American railroad depots to folk buildings and cemeteries (Kniffen and Glassie 1966; Lewis 1975; Stilgoe 1982, 1983, 2005; Zelinsky 1994, 2011). A related impulse focused on interest in ethnic landscapes and homelands, suggesting that characteristic landscape features (e.g., settlement patterns, place names, architectural styles) can play defining roles in establishing place-based identities for different cultural groups (Noble 1992; Nostrand and Estaville 2001). Finally, a discussion emerged about how North America's key symbolic landscapes, rooted in both fact and fancy, revealed important insights about different notions of community. Specifically, Donald Meinig highlighted the enduring importance of the New England village, Main Street, and suburban California landscapes as "symbolic communities," and this work anticipated the interest in linking regional identity and landscape that developed after 1980 (Meinig 1979).

Broader impulses in human geography and social theory have informed more recent work linking landscapes and regional identity within historical geography (D. Mitchell 2000; Knowles 2001; Adams, Hoelscher, and Till 2001; Harrison and Judd 2011). Critical approaches to landscape since 1980 have suggested how the very act of describing "landscapes" imposes a well-established set of cultural conventions (worthy of closer examination) that frame and limit our analysis. Studying the cultural meanings invested in landscape can tell us a great deal about who created the landscape and for what purpose (Cosgrove 1998; Groth and Wilson 2003; Riesenweber 2008). Others have demonstrated how landscapes powerfully structure and limit our navigation of the everyday world. This view of "landscape as discourse" suggests it makes visible enduring power relationships that shape how regional identity emerges in the first place (Schein 1997, 2009). More generally, a growing interest in linking landscape and labor incorporates that critical economic and political ingredient into our understanding of regional identity, whether in the American South, California's agricultural fields, or New England's tourism industry (Harrison 2006; Schein 2006; D. Mitchell 2010; Harrison and Judd 2011).

SAMPLING LANDSCAPES OF REGIONAL IDENTITY

North America is a rich repository of enduring symbolic landscapes that have helped shape regional identity from eastern Canada to the southwestern deserts. Consider French Canadian Quebec, particularly the narrow, long-established corridor of settlement that lines the St. Lawrence River valley from near Quebec City to Montreal (Harris 2001, 2008, 2010). This was the heart of French colonial settlement in the region, beginning in the early seventeenth century. By 1692, about ten thousand French-speaking settlers lived along the river, mostly on farms or in the principal urban centers of Quebec City and Montreal. While French political control of the region ended in the 1760s with defeat by the British (and with about sixty thousand French-speaking settlers in the area), the St. Lawrence valley retained much of its distinctive cultural character, which was actually an amalgam of diverse French traditions combined with a mix of New World influences and innovations.

Although Quebec City and Montreal both retain distinctive historical landscapes and neighborhoods, the rural settlement landscape lining the St. Lawrence River contains the most enduring and recognizable landscape signatures of persisting French influence and regional identity (figure 18.2). Seen from above, this landscape features long, narrow farm lots originally surveyed in this fashion (a tradition borrowed from Normandy) by local landlords, or seigneurs. These lots maximized access to the water, provided tenants (or habitants) varied lands for mixed farming (with fields allocated for grains, pasture, and garden plots), and offered opportunities to have reasonably close neighbors (farmhouses were three hundred to twelve hundred feet apart) in semidispersed rural neighborhoods along the river. Neat farmhouses (often whitewashed with narrow dormer windows and large chimneys) and a scattering of parish churches completed the picture. Such an enduring rural scene, today much modified by land-use changes, suburban sprawl, and tourism, still captures the imagination of both Quebec natives as well as visitors. This mosaic of landscape features (seen most spectacularly in autumn) has become an integral part of the province's persisting regional

Figure 18.2. The classic French Canadian rural settlement pattern along the St. Lawrence River includes a landscape of long-lots oriented perpendicularly to the shoreline and a string of semiclustered farms and settlements parallel with the river. Author's collection.

identity, along with the larger issues that revolve around language (also visible on the landscape in the form of place names) and political power.

In the northeastern United States, in addition to the mythic New England village, other settings offer enduring landscape signatures that remain integral elements of persisting regional identity. New York's Hudson valley (and select portions of nearby New Jersey), for example, became an outpost of scattered Dutch settlement in the early seventeenth century (Meinig 1977; R. D. Mitchell 2001b; Panetta 2009). About the same time that Samuel de Champlain helped establish settlement colonies along the St. Lawrence River (1608), Henry Hudson, sailing under the Dutch flag, explored the Hudson valley far to the south (1609). While actual Dutch settlement, which began in New Amsterdam (later New York City) in 1624, was miniscule compared to the French presence in the St. Lawrence valley, elements of the Dutch landscape flowered in New Netherlands. The region, even after the British took control in 1664, retained elements of Dutch influence thereafter. The social memory of Dutch culture, minimized right after the British takeover, reemerged in the nineteenth century and is celebrated today. Most obviously, place names like Brooklyn (Breuckelen), Harlem (Haerlem), Schenectady, and the Catskill (Kats Kill) Mountains recall Dutch influence. More broadly, elements of Dutch architecture, mixed farming, rural property subdivision, religion, and law have endured. Today, visitors to the Hudson valley still recognize the region's connections to its Dutch past, seek out surviving examples of Dutch architecture, and perhaps spend the weekend in a "Dutch-style" bed-and-breakfast. Indeed, in 1997, the village of North Tarrytown, New York (a former Dutch settlement made famous in Washington Irving's novel *The Legend of Sleepy Hollow*) changed its legal name to Sleepy Hollow to tap into the ongoing public interest in Dutch regional history.

In nearby Pennsylvania, distinctive colonial settlement produced its own assortment of landscape features that help define regional identity across the Keystone State (Lamme 2001; Pillsbury 2001; Lewis 2010; McMurry and Van Dolsen 2011). Most enduringly, the area west of Philadelphia (centered on the rolling, fertile hills of Lancaster County) attracted Pennsylvania German (or *deutsch*) settlement during the later colonial era. These diverse German immigrants (erroneously called "Pennsylvania Dutch") were attracted by some of eastern North America's best farmland and by the liberal terms of settlement that became a hallmark of William Penn's colony. Between 1727 and 1755, more than fifty thousand German colonists settled in Pennsylvania. In particular, Lancaster County's fame as a distinctive cluster of German settlement, farming practices, and architecture (watch for large, multilevel barns with overhanging forebays) has survived to the present.

Even though the actual settlement history of the region featured substantial mixing with English, Scotch Irish, and other non-Germanic groups, the area's distinctive German heritage has been reinterpreted and reinvented to fulfill the demands of a multi-million-dollar tourist industry, much of which has developed since 1950. The special visibility of the area's Old Order Amish settlements (plain dress, buggies, traditional farming practices) forms a distinctive element in this Germanized landscape, but this group's peculiar identity for many casual tourists blends effortlessly with a broader array of regional landscape experiences (figure 18.3). Some of these are steeped in history (take Amish country tours or visit the Landis Valley Village and Farm Museum), while others are happily invented diversions that nevertheless tap into the region's historical identity (enjoy Dutch Wonderland mini golf in Lancaster or take a tour of the Waltz Vineyards in Mannheim).

The American South is home to other powerful landscape symbols that have shaped the region's identity. The classic antebellum plantation house, perhaps made most famous in the 1939 film *Gone with the Wind*, featured grand Greek columns, sprawling verandas, paternalistic slave owners, and jovial slaves. But like the ideal of the New England village, this regional image represents another invented (and white) tradition that is part history and part fiction (figure 18.4). Certainly plantation houses had become a fixture across the South by the early nineteenth century as the region supported several zones of large-scale commercial agriculture, much of it oriented toward the production of subtropical crops by slave labor (Aiken 1998, 2010). From the Virginia Tidewater and coastal South Carolina to the Alabama Black Belt and the lower Mississippi valley, the plantation landscape featured fields of specialized crop production (including tobacco, sugar cane, rice, and cotton), a central "big house" where the white landowner lived (often near the fields but sometimes in nearby urban areas), quarters for field

Figure 18.3. Local guidebooks to Pennsylvania Dutch country highlight the distinctive German American landscape features associated with Lancaster County in the southeastern portion of the state. Author's collection.

slaves and house laborers, and other barns and outbuildings that served various functions.

After the Civil War, however, many wealthy southern whites actively reimagined their antebellum past. The landscape of the southern plantation house became an active player in the drama. As Steven Hoelscher (2006) describes the process (using Natchez, Mississippi, as an example), between 1880 and 1940 southern white elites created an idealized plantation landscape (what he calls the "white-pillared past"), often focused on a vision of the plantation house as a grand mansion of epic proportions. The mansion embodied a romanticized, idealized white version of antebellum life and helped perpetuate a myth of difference

Figure 18.4. Dunleith Plantation in Natchez, Mississippi, evokes regional images of the white antebellum South and today offers bed-and-breakfast accommodations. Local tours also visit the forty-acre estate. Library of Congress. Prints and Photographs Division, photography by Carol M. Highsmith (LC-HS503-1867).

between the white and black populations. Period artists, novelists, and popular writers celebrated and embraced this imagery. Local white elites "preserved" this past through monuments, museums, house tours, and annual pageants and celebrations. While it offered a powerful regional identity for select white southerners, this imagined landscape entailed fundamental problems. Only a very small percentage of actual plantation houses looked anything like their *Gone with the Wind* re-creations, and then there was the even larger issue of how this reconstructed setting portrayed blacks (or rendered them invisible).

Since the 1960s, however, the southern plantation house has witnessed yet another reincarnation in select regional venues (Hoelscher 2006; Dennis 2006). Reflecting the civil rights movement and the growing cultural and political power of black Americans, the narratives of many historic plantation house landscapes have been rewritten to more fully recognize the role played by the slave populations (and later tenant farmers and sharecroppers) so pivotal in their creation. Federally protected landmarks and historic sites (many managed by the National Park Service) have led these efforts. In the case of Natchez, Hoelscher cites the popularity of *A Southern Road to Freedom*, an annual black gospel performance that began in the 1980s. The tradition offers an effective counternarrative to the celebratory tours of white southern mansions and an annual Confederate pageant that still bring in large numbers of tourists. *A Southern Road to Freedom* celebrates the successful black experience in the region, tells the story of the Civil War very differently, and reimagines the symbolic importance of local plantation houses in ways never anticipated by the town's white elite.

To the north, what iconic landscapes do we associate with the Midwest and Great Plains and what do they say about the regional identity of the heartland? From Ohio and southern Michigan to West Texas and the Dakotas, one of the world's most productive agricultural systems, a heady mix of crops and livestock that sprouted in waves of generally westward-moving settlement between 1800 and 1920, dominates the landscape of the vast continental interior. Two interwoven landscape features remain central elements of this vast agricultural region. Both the unending rectilinear verities of the township-and-range survey system and the predictable order of Main Street in nearby farm towns created landscape features within this region that are rich in cultural meaning, especially for those who live in their midst (Hart 1972; Mather 1972; Meinig 1979; Shortridge 1989; Hudson 2010; Johnson 2010).

Look at the Public Land Survey System and its ubiquitous impact on the region (figure 18.5). With roots tracing to eastern Ohio in the late eighteenth century, the regular geometry of the federal land survey system (as articulated in the Land Ordinance of 1785) created a landscape of cardinally oriented, six-square-mile townships, each containing thirty-six numbered sections of 640 acres, which were further subdivided and sold—all as part of a land-disposal system that helped organize a large portion of the North American interior (a similar system developed in Canada). Today, property lines, field boundaries, and a generally rectangular road system that typically follows section lines reflect the survey landscape. Isolated farmsteads are an integral part of this settlement pattern, suggesting the long-standing American penchant (already obvious in colonial-era New England) for dispersal and independence on the rural scene.

Unlike the contrived legacy of the New England village or the rarefied opulence of the antebellum plantation house, the simple, rational virtues of the survey system and its related patterns of rural settlement have firm historical roots. Deeply, if quietly, etched upon the region's cultural landscape, the system's Euclidean order, some observers have suggested, reflects regional values of efficiency, simplicity, and democracy (J. B. Jackson 1979). Although artists, writers, and schoolteachers occasionally explore its expression as a landscape, we most commonly encounter it in the prosaic, legal language of property identification and location. For the majority of residents and visitors to the region, it is an uncelebrated cultural memory experienced daily in navigating its predictable geometry of fences, section-line roads, regular intersections, and scattered farmsteads.

Main Street and its surrounding townscape complement the rural scene (figure 18.6). Often christened in earlier times by railroad interests and real estate

Figure 18.5. The cardinally oriented roads and fields and the regular, dispersed settlement landscape of rural Iowa are a legacy of the township-and-range survey system visible across much of North America's agricultural heartland. Landsat image.

boosters, Midwest and Great Plains market towns (also on the Canadian prairies) are important centers of local economic and political power, as well as additional repositories of regional cultural identity. These towns (often laid out in their own grid pattern of lots and streets) are home to grain elevators, banks, agricultural equipment dealerships, railroad depots, and local seats of government, important links that connect surrounding farmers and ranchers to the world beyond. Even more, however, their predictable, orderly landscapes of brick buildings, businesses, courthouses, and nearby churches and neighborhoods have created their own symbolic landscapes celebrated in literature, popular culture, and the collective social memories of regional residents.

What values do these ordinary landscapes reflect? Donald Meinig describes these places as "the seat of a business culture of property-minded, law-abiding citizens devoted to 'free enterprise' and 'social morality,' a community of sober, sensible, practical people" (1979, 167). This landscape and community epitomizes Iowa politics, the virtues of "small-town life," and the pragmatic ideals of a practical people leading predictable lives. Although the reality of the complex

Figure 18.6. Main Street's stately two- and three-story commercial buildings give Ottumwa, Iowa, an air of stability and permanence in this turn-of-the-century postcard view. Author's collection.

twenty-first century is not always so accommodating (for example, new immigrant laborers have vastly complicated the cultural geographies of many heartland towns, and what about the long-term impacts of global climate change on nearby farms?), the region's collective social memory remains rooted in these enduring landscape signatures. Both the grid and Main Street remain potent elements of land and life in "Middle America."

Finally, consider some of the landscape images that have shaped our popular understanding of the American West and its regional identity. They typically feature an imaginative mix of generalized environmental characteristics and historical stereotypes (Meinig 1972; Athearn 1988; White 1991; Wyckoff 2003). On the broadest scale (often explored in western art, literature, and films and in mass advertising featuring western localities), the landscapes of the symbolic West are certainly populated by cowboys and Indians, cattle ranches, ghost towns, open space, cloudscapes larger than Delaware, high mountain wilderness, cacti, sagebrush, dry lakes (and a general notion of aridity), good fly-fishing, and plenty of wild animals (figure 18.7). More nuanced attempts to appreciate contemporary human signatures might include an appreciation of public lands, irrigated agriculture (and federal dams and water projects), sprawling suburbs, ski resorts, amenity-oriented exurbs, and even solar farms. In actuality, the West's breathtaking internal diversity, historical complexity, and cultural heterogeneity should discourage us from making too many sweeping generalizations about its overall character in the first place, but the region's enduring potency in the

Figure 18.7. ***The Trail Ahead*, located south of Hobbs, is a four-hundred-foot-long metallic sculpture (completed in 2000) that celebrates southeastern New Mexico's cattle culture. Photo by the author.**

national imagination often minimizes the complex reality one encounters on the ground (Meinig 1972; Wyckoff and Dilsaver 1995).

What about some of the rich variations one encounters within the West? Place identity within the region—especially for residents—is more often rooted locally than in the sweeping pan-regional tropes invented for and consumed by the larger world. For example, the continuing subregional vitality of Mormon Country remains across much of Utah and southeastern Idaho (especially in rural settings) (Meinig 1965; Francaviglia 1979; Bennion and Peters 1987; R. H. Jackson 2003; Starrs 2009). When the Latter Day Saints arrived in the region beginning in 1847, their settlement patterns reflected a shared cultural vision of the world. Today, while non-Mormons fill diverse urban localities such as Salt Lake City, many smaller farm towns and rural settings retain a set of enduring landscape features still associated with Mormon settlement and ideals. Watch for local ward chapels (powerful symbols of community), wide streets (often numbered along a cardinally oriented grid), well-maintained irrigation ditches, and large in-town lots that often contain gardens, unpainted barns, and even livestock (figure 18.8). Certainly, non-Mormon retirees, tourists, and amenity seekers are steadily altering many of these traditional signatures of Mormon regional identity. St. George, Utah, for example, is today a hybrid settlement with Mormon roots but a plethora of suburban California additions. Still, even in diluted form, the Mormon landscape remains a recognizable feature in the western interior.

Figure 18.8. Built in 1902, this Mormon chapel in Spring City, Utah, remains in use today and symbolizes the stability and shared values of the local Latter Day Saints community. Photo by the author.

Although every western state (and Canadian province) remains home to significant numbers of native peoples, the Southwest's Indian Country retains major regional-scale concentrations of Native Americans and some of the continent's largest Indian reservations (the Navajo Reservation contains more than 15 million acres) (Meinig 1971a; Jett 1992, 2001; Francaviglia, Narrett, and Narramore 1994; Butzer 2010; Arreola 2012). These indigenous communities have developed close and long-lived connections with their regional settings and associated cultural landscapes. As a result, residents in these Native American homelands have strong regional identities anchored by the landscape that surrounds and sustains them (figure 18.9). For the Navajo people, for example, part of that identity resides in sacred mountains that border their region, including Tsisnaasjini' (southern Colorado's Mount Blanca), Tsoodzil (New Mexico's Mount Taylor), Doko'oosliid (Arizona's San Francisco Peaks), and Dibé Nitsaa (southern Colorado's Mount Hesperus). For the Navajo, as well as for the Hopi and other Pueblo peoples within the region, traditional place names, settlement patterns, agricultural adaptations, and artwork are also tied powerfully to the region's physical and cultural landscape.

Varied examples of Hispanic settlement and the broader legacy of Spanish colonization in the region have shaped other portions of the Southwest (Nostrand 1992, 2001; Wyckoff 1999) (figure 18.10). For example, northern New Mexico and southern Colorado are the focus of traditional Highland Hispano settlement.

Figure 18.9. Snow-capped even in summer, New Mexico's Mount Taylor (Tsoodzil) is a landmark sacred to the Navajo people. The peak (11,305 feet) is located near Grants, in the western portion of the state. Photo by the author.

Figure 18.10. This mural in downtown Albuquerque (the *Frutos de la expresión*) celebrates the region's Hispanic culture and the liberating impact of the First, Fifteenth, and Nineteenth Amendments on the region's population. Photo by the author.

Dating to the early seventeenth century (Santa Fe was founded in 1610), these settlements (often called plaza towns, or *placitas*) represented the northern edge of Spanish colonization and featured Catholic churches, centralized clusters of earth-toned adobe and brick houses, and surrounding village-controlled pastures and individually farmed strips of irrigated cropland (often laid out in long, narrow lots). For several centuries, this Hispanic population has shaped the Southwest's cultural geography, often blending with Native American and, more recently (the area became part of the United States in the late 1840s), Anglo elements.

Building on the region's rich cultural heritage and its exotic natural environment, later railroad boosters and local leaders successfully reimagined and promoted elements of this landscape in the early twentieth century and marketed it to national and international tourists, a multi-million-dollar initiative that continues today (Francaviglia, Narrett, and Narramore 1994; Weigle and Babcock 1996; Wilson 1997; Rothman 1998; DeLyser 2005; Schwantes and Ronda 2008; Hornbeck 2010). This invented past is often a blend of varied native and Hispanic influences. For example, cultural and business entrepreneur and local politician Edgar Hewitt reworked the Santa Fe landscape between 1900 and 1930, mandated the use of Pueblo-style architecture, attracted regional artists and writers to the scene, and developed a series of enduring annual traditions and cultural institutions that cultivated the region's unique identity. Today, just wander the carefully manicured streets of old Santa Fe and enjoy the mix of southwestern architecture, New Age/New Mexican fusion-style restaurants, and souvenir shops filled with cattle skulls, chili peppers, sculptures of flute-playing Kokopellis, and turquoise jewelry (figure 18.11).

SIGNIFICANCE OF REGIONAL LANDSCAPES

North America's distinctive regional landscapes and the identities they help invent are important for several reasons. First, whether we are looking at New England towns or southwestern architecture, these features and the social memories that give them contemporary meaning reveal a set of dynamic cultural and political processes at work that tell important stories about how places are created and how these ideas evolve over time (Meinig 1979; Lowenthal 1985; Wilson and Groth 2005; Schein 2006; Riesenweber 2008). What key landscape characteristics anchor a region in the popular imagination? What people contributed to their creation and what purposes do these regional identities serve? What media (e.g., oral traditions, commercial advertising, annual festivals, popular movies) shape and sustain these connections between region and landscape? Historical geographers are well positioned to address all of these questions on a variety of scales.

Second, understanding the nature and evolution of these regional identities informs the practice of historical preservation (Lowenthal 1985; Morley 2006; Young 2006; Longstreth 2008). What of the past do we choose to preserve? How do we decide what stories to tell and which stories remain invisible? Since 1980, historic preservation efforts, both by governmental agencies such as the National Park Service and by private nonprofit groups and experts involved in preserving,

Figure 18.11. This Santa Fe alleyway features an assortment of bleached cattle skulls, dried chili peppers, and festive sun ornaments. Nearby shops featuring art, jewelry, and other souvenirs display more regional treasures. Photo by the author.

restoring, and reinterpreting historical features, have gradually integrated the cultural landscape concept. One perennial problem facing many preservation initiatives entails how to frame the landscape features (perhaps a building or an entire neighborhood) or events being highlighted. Creative landscape interpretation helps put places in wider historical contexts and demonstrates how an isolated feature relates to larger-scale processes at work. Seeing the landscape as a great cumulative creation—both of material features and of evolving cultural meanings—helps place it within the fuller flow of time rather than some fixed, unchanging past. People engaged in historical preservation projects also need to see themselves as active creators of regional identity: they both shape and are shaped by the cultural memories we associate with regions and localities.

Finally, exploring connections between cultural landscapes and regional identities can contribute to the larger goal of place appreciation (Meinig 1971a, 1979; Lowenthal 1985; J. B. Jackson 1994, 1997; Cronon 1996). Historical geographers remain superbly positioned to tell stories about places in a language accessible to the general public. We can produce public geographies that creatively connect everyday landscapes with the past and say a great deal about who we are and where we have come from. Cultivating that broad sensibility can lead to a stronger connection between people and the neighborhoods, communities, and regions they call home. Using the language of landscape (both visually and textually) can be a powerful way to make these connections. Thus, by examining regional place identities in fresh ways, historical geographers themselves can serve as active agents in inventing a past that enriches our appreciation of the world we live in today.

REFERENCES

Adams, P. C., S. Hoelscher, and K. E. Till, eds. 2001. *Textures of Place: Exploring Humanist Geographies.* Minneapolis: University of Minnesota Press.

Aiken, C. S. 1998. *The Cotton Plantation South since the Civil War.* Baltimore: Johns Hopkins University Press.

———. 2010. Transforming the Southern Plantation. In *The Making of the American Landscape,* edited by M. P. Conzen, 115–41. New York: Routledge.

Arreola, D. D. 2012. Chiricahua Apache Homeland in the Borderland Southwest. *Geographical Review* 102, no. 1: 111–31.

Athearn, R. G. 1988. *The Mythic West in Twentieth-Century America.* Lawrence: University Press of Kansas.

Baker, A. R. H. 2003. *Geography and History: Bridging the Divide.* Cambridge: Cambridge University Press.

Bennion, L. C., and G. B. Peters. 1987. *Sanpete Scenes: A Guide to Utah's Heart.* Eureka, UT: Basin/Plateau Press.

Blake, Kevin S. 2008. Imagining Heaven and Earth at Mount of the Holy Cross, Colorado. *Journal of Cultural Geography* 25, no. 1: 1–30.

Brown, R. H. 1948. *Historical Geography of the United States.* New York: Harcourt, Brace and Co.

Butzer, K. W. 2010. Retrieving American Indian Landscapes. In *The Making of the American Landscape,* edited by M. P. Conzen, 32–57. New York: Routledge.

Conforti, J. A. 2011. Regional Identity and New England Landscapes. In *A Landscape History of New England,* edited by B. Harrison and R. W. Judd, 17–34. Cambridge, MA: MIT Press.

Conzen, M. P. 1993. The Historical Impulse in Geographical Writing about the United States, 1850–1990. In *A Scholar's Guide to Geographical Writing on the American and Canadian Past,* edited by M. P. Conzen, T. A. Rumney, and G. Wynn, 3–90. Geography Research Paper No. 235. Chicago: University of Chicago Press.

———, ed. 2010. *The Making of the American Landscape.* New York: Routledge.

Cosgrove, D. E. 1998. *Social Formation and Symbolic Landscape.* Madison: University of Wisconsin Press.

Cronon, W. 1996. The Trouble with Wilderness; or, Getting Back to the Wrong Nature. In *Uncommon Ground: Rethinking the Human Place in Nature,* edited by W. Cronon, 69–90. New York: W. W. Norton.

DeLyser, D. 2005. *Ramona Memories: Tourism and the Shaping of Southern California.* Minneapolis: University of Minnesota Press.

Dennis, S. F., Jr. 2006. Seeing Hampton Plantation: Race and Gender in a South Carolina Heritage Landscape. In *Landscape and Race in the United States,* edited by R. H. Schein, 73–94. New York: Routledge.

Francaviglia, R. V. 1979. *The Mormon Landscape.* New York: AMS Press.

Francaviglia, R. V., David Narrett, and Bruce Narramore, eds. 1994. *Essays on the Changing Images of the Southwest.* College Station: Texas A&M University Press.

Groth, P. 1998. J. B. Jackson and Geography. *Geographical Review* 88, no. 4: iii–vi.

Groth, P., and C. Wilson. 2003. The Polyphony of Cultural Landscape Study: An Introduction. In *Everyday America: Cultural Landscape Studies after J. B. Jackson*, edited by C. Wilson and P. Groth, 1–22. Berkeley: University of California Press.

Harris, R. C. 2001. France in North America. In *North America: The Historical Geography of a Changing Continent*, edited by T. F. McIlwraith and E. K. Muller, 65–88. 2nd ed. Lanham, MD: Rowman & Littlefield.

———. 2008. *The Reluctant Land: Society, Space, and Environment in Canada before Confederation.* Vancouver: University of British Columbia Press.

———. 2010. Retracing French Landscapes in North America. In *The Making of the American Landscape*, edited by M. P. Conzen, 73–90. New York: Routledge.

Harrison, B. 2006. *The View from Vermont: Tourism and the Making of an American Rural Landscape.* Burlington: University of Vermont Press.

Harrison, B., and R. W. Judd, eds. 2011. *A Landscape History of New England.* Cambridge, MA: MIT Press.

Hart, J. F. 1972. The Middle West. *Annals of the Association of American Geographers* 62: 258–82.

Hoelscher, S. 2006. The White-Pillared Past: Landscapes of Memory and Race in the American South. In *Landscape and Race in the United States*, edited by R. H. Schein, 39–72. New York: Routledge.

Hornbeck, D. 2010. Refashioning Hispanic Landscapes. In *The Making of the American Landscape*, edited by M. P. Conzen, 58–72. New York: Routledge.

Hudson, J. C. 2010. Remaking the Prairies. In *The Making of the American Landscape*, edited by M. P. Conzen, 188–206. New York: Routledge.

Jackson, J. B. 1979. The Order of a Landscape: Reason and Religion in Newtonian America. In *The Interpretation of Ordinary Landscapes: Geographical Essays*, edited by D. W. Meinig, 153–63. New York: Oxford University Press.

———. 1994. *A Sense of Place, a Sense of Time.* New Haven, CT: Yale University Press.

———. 1997. *Landscape in Sight: Looking at America.* New Haven, CT: Yale University Press.

Jackson, R. H. 2003. Mormon Wests: The Creation and Evolution of an American Region. In *Western Places, American Myths: How We Think about the West*, edited by G. J. Hausladen, 135–65. Reno: University of Nevada Press.

Jett, S. C. 1992. The Navajo in the American Southwest. In *To Build in a New Land: Ethnic Landscapes in North America*, edited by A. G. Noble, 331–44. Baltimore: Johns Hopkins University Press.

———. 2001. The Navajo Homeland. In *Homelands: A Geography of Culture and Place across America*, edited by R. L. Nostrand and L. E. Estaville, 168–83. Baltimore: Johns Hopkins University Press.

Johnson, H. B. 2010. Gridding a National Landscape. In *The Making of the American Landscape*, edited by M. P. Conzen, 142–61. New York: Routledge.

Kniffen, F. B., and H. H. Glassie. 1966. Building in Wood in the Eastern United States: A Time-Place Perspective. *Geographical Review* 56, no. 1: 40–66.

Knowles, A. 2001. Afterword: Historical Geography since 1987. In *North America: The Historical Geography of a Changing Continent*, edited by T. F. McIlwraith and E. K. Muller, 465–70. 2nd ed. Lanham, MD: Rowman & Littlefield.

Lamme, A. J., III. 2001. Old Order Amish Homelands. In *Homelands: A Geography of Culture and Place across America*, edited by R. L. Nostrand and L. E. Estaville, 44–52. Baltimore: Johns Hopkins University Press.

Lewis, P. F. 1975. Common Houses, Cultural Spoor. *Landscape* 19 (January): 1–22.

———. 1979. Axioms for Reading the Landscape: Some Guides to the American Scene. In *The Interpretation of Ordinary Landscapes: Geographical Essays*, edited by D. W. Meinig, 11–32. New York: Oxford University Press.

———. 2010. Americanizing English Landscape Habits. In *The Making of the American Landscape*, edited by M. P. Conzen, 91–114. New York: Routledge.

Longstreth, R., ed. 2008. *Cultural Landscapes: Balancing Nature and Heritage in Preservation Practice*. Minneapolis: University of Minnesota Press.

Lowenthal, D. 1985. *The Past Is a Foreign Country*. Cambridge: Cambridge University Press.

Martin, G. J., and P. E. James. 1993. *All Possible Worlds: A History of Geographical Ideas*. New York: John Wiley and Sons.

Mather, E. C. 1972. The American Great Plains. *Annals of the Association of American Geographers* 62: 237–57.

McMurry, S., and N. Van Dolen, eds. 2011. *Architecture and Landscape of the Pennsylvania Germans, 1720–1920*. Philadelphia: University of Pennsylvania Press.

Meinig, D. W. 1965. The Mormon Culture Region: Strategies and Patterns in the Geography of the American West, 1847–1964. *Annals of the Association of American Geographers* 55, no. 2: 191–220.

———. 1968. *The Great Columbia Plain: A Historical Geography, 1805–1910*. Seattle: University of Washington Press.

———. 1971a. Environmental Appreciation: Localities as a Humane Art. *Western Humanities Review* 25 (Winter): 1–11.

———. 1971b. *Southwest: Three Peoples in Geographical Change, 1600–1970*. New York: Oxford University Press.

———. 1972. American Wests: Preface to a Geographical Interpretation. *Annals of the Association of American Geographers* 62, no. 2: 159–84.

———. 1977. The Colonial Period, 1609–1775. In *Geography of New York State*, edited by J. H. Thompson, 121–39. Syracuse, NY: Syracuse University Press.

———, ed. 1979. *The Interpretation of Ordinary Landscapes: Geographical Essays*. New York: Oxford University Press.

Mitchell, D. 2000. *Cultural Geography: A Critical Introduction*. Malden, MA: Blackwell Publishing.

———. 2010. Battle/fields: Braceros, agribusiness, and the violent reproduction of the California agricultural landscape during World War II. *Journal of Historical Geography* 36: 143–56.

Mitchell, R. D. 2001a. The North American Past: Retrospect and Prospect. In *North America: The Historical Geography of a Changing Continent*, edited by T. F. McIlwraith and E. K. Muller, 3–24. 2nd ed. Lanham, MD: Rowman & Littlefield.

———. 2001b. The Colonial Origins of Anglo-America. In *North America: The Historical Geography of a Changing Continent*, edited by T. F. McIlwraith and E. K. Muller, 89–117. 2nd ed. Lanham, MD: Rowman & Littlefield.

Morley, J. M. 2006. *Historic Preservation and the Imagined West: Albuquerque, Denver, and Seattle*. Lawrence: University Press of Kansas.

Noble, A. G., ed. 1992. *To Build in a New Land: Ethnic Landscapes in North America*. Baltimore: Johns Hopkins University Press.

Nostrand, R. L. 1992. *The Hispano Homeland*. Norman: University of Oklahoma Press.

———. 2001. The Highland-Hispano Homeland. In *Homelands: A Geography of Culture and Place across America*, edited by R. L. Nostrand and L. E. Estaville, 155–67. Baltimore: Johns Hopkins University Press.

Nostrand, R. L., and L. E. Estaville, eds. 2001. *Homelands: A Geography of Culture and Place across America*. Baltimore: Johns Hopkins University Press.

Panetta, R., ed. 2009. *Dutch New York: The Roots of Hudson Valley Culture*. New York: Fordham University Press.

Pillsbury, R. 2001. The Pennsylvanian Homeland. In *Homelands: A Geography of Culture and Place across America*, edited by R. L. Nostrand and L. E. Estaville, 24–43. Baltimore: Johns Hopkins University Press.
Riesenweber, J. 2008. Landscape Preservation and Cultural Geography. In *Cultural Landscapes: Balancing Nature and Heritage in Preservation Practice*, edited by R. Longstreth, 23–34. Minneapolis: University of Minnesota Press.
Rothman, H. 1998. *Devil's Bargains: Tourism in the Twentieth-Century American West*. Lawrence: University Press of Kansas.
Schein, R. H. 1997. The Place of Landscape: A Conceptual Framework for an American Scene. *Annals of the Association of American Geographers* 87, no. 4: 660–80.
———, ed. 2006. *Landscape and Race in the United States*. New York: Routledge.
———. 2009. A Methodological Framework for Interpreting Ordinary Landscapes: Lexington, Kentucky's Courthouse Square. *Geographical Review* 99, no. 3: 377–402.
Schwantes, C., and J. Ronda. 2008. *The West the Railroads Made*. Seattle: University of Washington Press.
Shaffer, Marguerite S. 2001. *See America First: Tourism and National Identity, 1880–1940*. Washington, D.C.: Smithsonian Institution Press.
Shortridge, J. R. 1989. *The Middle West: Its Meaning in American Culture*. Lawrence: University Press of Kansas.
Starrs, P. F. 2009. Meetinghouses in the Mormon Mind: Ideology, Architecture, and Turbulent Streams of an Expanding Church. *Geographical Review* 99, no. 3: 323–55.
Stilgoe, J. R. 1982. *Common Landscape of America, 1580 to 1845*. New Haven, CT: Yale University Press.
———. 1983. *Metropolitan Corridor: Railroads and the American Scene*. New Haven, CT: Yale University Press.
———. 2005. *Landscape and Images*. Charlottesville: University of Virginia Press.
Weigle, M., and B. A. Babcock, eds. 1996. *The Great Southwest of the Fred Harvey Company and the Santa Fe Railway*. Phoenix: Heard Museum.
West, E. 1996. Selling the Myth: Western Images in Advertising. *Montana Magazine* 46, no. 2: 36–49.
White, Richard. 1991. *"It's Your Misfortune and None of My Own": A New History of the American West*. Norman: University of Oklahoma Press.
Wilson, C. 1997. *The Myth of Santa Fe: Creating a Modern Regional Tradition*. Albuquerque: University of New Mexico Press.
Wilson, C., and P. Groth, eds. 2005. *Everyday America: Cultural Landscape Studies after J. B. Jackson*. Berkeley: University of California Press.
Wood, J. S. 1997. *The New England Village*. Baltimore: Johns Hopkins University Press.
Wyckoff, W. K. 1999. *Creating Colorado: The Making of a Western American Landscape*. New Haven, CT: Yale University Press.
———. 2003. Understanding Western Places: A Historical Geographer's View. In *Western Places, American Myths: How We Think about the West*, edited by G. J. Hausladen, 21–56. Reno: University of Nevada Press.
Wyckoff, W. K., and C. E. Colten. 2009. A Tribute to Donald Meinig. *Geographical Review* 99, no. 3: iii–x.
Wyckoff, W. K., and L. M. Dilsaver, eds. 1995. *The Mountainous West: Explorations in Historical Geography*. Lincoln: University of Nebraska Press.
Wynn, G. 1993. Geographical Writing on the Canadian Past. In *A Scholar's Guide to Geographical Writing on the American and Canadian Past*, edited by M. P. Conzen, T. A. Rumney, and G. Wynn, 91–124. Geography Research Paper No. 235. Chicago: University of Chicago Press.

Young, T. 2006. False, Cheap and Degraded: When History, Economy, and Environment Collided at Cades Cove, Great Smoky Mountains National Park. *Journal of Historical Geography* 32, no. 1: 169–89.
Zelinsky, W. 1973. *The Cultural Geography of the United States.* Englewood Cliffs, NJ: Prentice Hall.
———. 1994. *Exploring the Beloved Country: Geographic Forays into American Society and Culture.* Iowa City: University of Iowa Press.
———. 2011. *Not Yet a Placeless Land: Tracking an Evolving American Geography.* Amherst: University of Massachusetts Press.

V

URBANIZING THE LAND

19

Making Urban Wealth

The Primacy of Mercantilism

Michael P. Conzen

It is difficult for the vast majority of contemporary North Americans to imagine their continent without an extensive and complex array of large—and, in many cases, extremely large—cities. Today, the United States and Canada are essentially "urban" nations, in demography and mentality if not in percentage of territorial land use. Even rural areas, with their now well-established patterns of variable population loss or fragile stability, live by largely urban expectations and urban supply of gadgetry and conveniences. Mass consumerism has tied agricultural communities firmly to urban centers, and innovations, technical or cultural, emanate mostly from cities. It requires, therefore, a feat of imagination to visualize and understand how comparatively recent the widespread urbanization of the North American continent has been, what forms it has taken at different points in its development, and what forces have been at work creating those forms. And yet clues to that grand transformative process—the mass urbanization of America—reside in a number of dimensions of American life. Perhaps the most prominent are the antiurban sentiments that underlie numerous attitudes toward urban growth and encroachment, the political dislocations brought about by the growing needs of cities for a greater share of national resources and governmental management, and the peculiarly conflicted American reverence for wilderness as the "other" realm of the environment. These features hint at the long-term changes that have converted the continent from a pair of more or less Jeffersonian rural republics to one of teeming cities controlling the destiny of the whole earthly habitat.

This chapter can present only the barest outlines of this transformation with a necessary economy of topic and geographical coverage. Although the characteristics of Canadian towns and cities that distinguish them and the life lived in them from their southern counterparts in the United States are revealing and deserve attention, those they share in common far outnumber the dissimilarities.

So, the force of the argument offered here pertains especially to the U.S. experience but, by substantial extension, to Canada as well. I offer a profoundly geographical view, however, in that we can best understand the urbanization of the continent and the wealth it has created as an interweaving of historically and spatially variable forces acting upon an environment of seemingly finite dimensions, yet continually redefined by demographic, cultural, and technological prowess.

North American cities in the early twenty-first-century are still adjusting to the radical redefinition of the role of manufacturing (especially heavy manufacturing) in their economies brought about by the current phase of finance-driven globalization of markets and industrial production over the last fifty years. Deindustrialization, at times severe, has been widespread, and while it is revising policies concerned with economic advancement in the short term, at both the level of the system as a whole and that of individual urban agglomerations, it is also changing our perception of the role of industrialism in American urban history over the long term. It is no longer to be seen as an inevitable and permanent addition to the cumulative structures of urban economies; rather, it is possibly a more temporary phase in the global reordering of production. Historico-geographical interpretations of urbanization in North America need therefore to take this into account.

And yet the significant reduction of manufacturing in the United States over the last five decades—and its near disappearance in many towns and cities, particularly in the so-called Rust Belt—has not led to widespread deurbanization. Commercial trade and consumption continue to expand, rural areas and foreign countries continue to give up their young to American cities, and mercantilism thrives as never before. So this is the crux of the argument: huge parts of American heavy manufacturing have come and gone, but commerce remains vibrant, because 350 million people need to be serviced, and American ingenuity has never failed to invent new forms of consumption. Mercantilism indeed remains prime.

How best to conceptualize the broad and deep forces that have transformed American cities since the appearance of recognizably modern towns on the continent? The story is fundamentally one of colonial imposition, nationalization of regional interests (i.e., political independence), continental expansion and subsequent integration, and, ultimately, the supremacy of the urban way of life over the rural. Cities in North America were, for the most part, exclusively European imports. Indigenous cultures had little need of them and rarely created them. The few exceptions, such as Cahokia in Illinois or the Cherokee towns of the southern Appalachians, cannot in any way be said to have determined the course of modern American urban development, either in timing, scale, or character. So we look to the application of European models for the seeds of American urban distribution and form, seen in the context of the overseas expansion of European economic interests from the fifteenth century onward.

Viewed geographically, this calls for examination in two dimensions: distribution and form. At the large-scale (regional, national, continental), American cities have always performed as part of a distributed system, an interlocking network of towns and cities, large and small, servicing the surrounding local areas and at the same time linking them with the global channels of exchange. This "system" grew from zero to several hundred over the course of four centuries. But then, viewed more locally (at the scale of individual sites), cities take up space, and once they have grown to any size, the internal organization of that space becomes ever more critical and problematic to the city's continued capacity to function. As urban communities have developed and needs have changed, so have the forces that allocated urban space. Consequently, spatial patterns have evolved—awkwardly near the center because of the costs of selectively retrofitting occupied ground and profligately at the urban fringe because greenfield extension has always been cheaper. So the historical geography of city distribution serves as the opening topic, and that of internal urban spatial organization follows. This provides a basic framework for understanding the geographical underpinnings of changes in production and consumption at the two spatial scales that matter: regional and local. It also provides a framework for considering their consequences, both for the shape of the national urban system—the winners and losers in capturing growth—and for the choices made in allocating urban space. Both themes call for a chronological approach.

DIFFERENTIATING PHASES OF THE EVOLVING URBAN SYSTEM FROM PHASES OF INTERNAL SPATIAL ORDER

When one considers what has driven fundamental change in the organization of the developing national network of cities, as well as in the evolving spatial structure of urban places, it is apparent that inventions that may be mutually reinforcing in general have not always appeared at the same time. Consequently, what precipitated a new epoch in the development of the national urban system did not always synchronize with what worked at the local scale to change the internal structure of cities. In an attempt to conceptualize this, figure 19.1 offers a generalized scheme by which to compare the two streams of change.

It can be argued, for example, that the American urban system underwent continental expansion before factory industrialism transformed the interiors of many cities. While railroads quickly affected the layout of new cities, they had a delayed impact on established ones. The internal combustion engine brought congestion to towns not designed for it long before the national urban network, as a network, showed any measurable impact of the car and truck. Therefore it is not entirely unexpected that this attempt to identify broad epochs of prevailing organizational logic yields five phases in the case of the urban network but only four in the case of cities' internal arrangement. So the chronologies of city system and city interior followed somewhat distinct paths, and to the extent that there were differences in the economic and social character of individual cities throughout the system and across the full range of specialized roles, one can recognize both epochs of systemic evolution and a proliferation of city types with quite distinct internal geographies.

Both chronologies show a quickening in the pace of change over the four centuries of North American European-led urbanization. A variety of broad socioeconomic drivers best describe the city network chronology, whereas the shifting

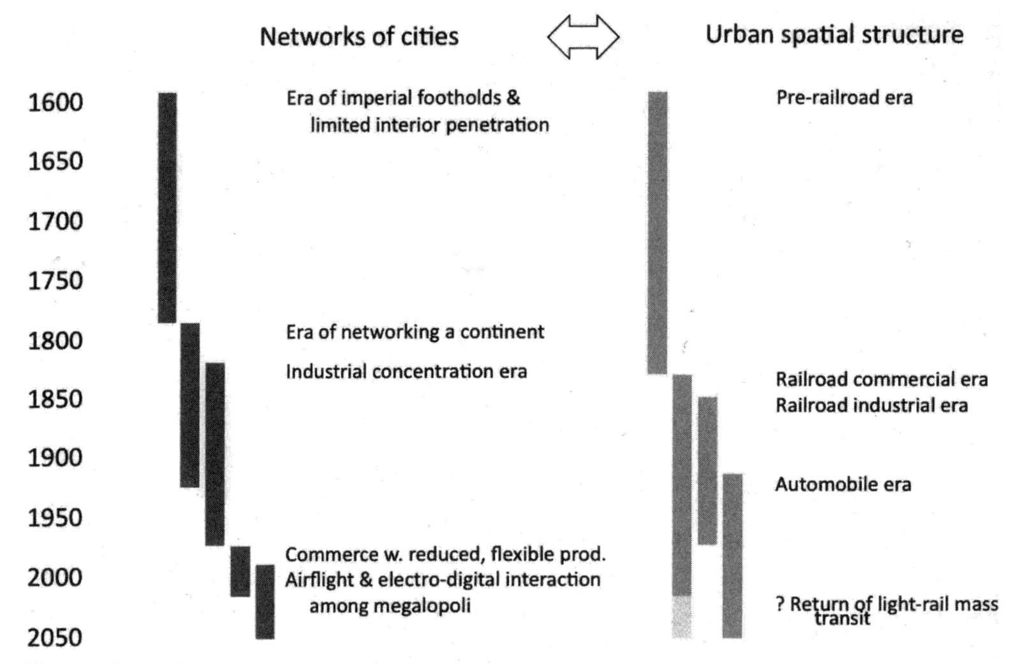

Figure 19.1. Evolutionary logic of the U.S. network of cities and urban spatial structure.

determinants of internal city space are more intimately associated quite simply with transportation indicators. Both scales reveal the emergence by the mid-nineteenth century of multiple "forces" operating to transform urban processes more or less simultaneously. But whereas the city system displayed a clearer pattern of technology sequencing and economic organization over time, city interiors held on to multiple forms of mobility, probably because of the density of activities and infrastructural investments.

EVOLUTIONARY LOGIC OF THE U.S. NETWORK OF CITIES

The American city system can be said to have passed through five historic phases, reflecting (1) points of potamic (i.e., water-linked) colonial attachment, (2) continental absorption, (3) rise of an industrialized core region, (4) commercial resurgence amid selective industrial withdrawal, and (5) consolidation around globally competitive megalopolises (Conzen 1981) (figure 19.2).

Before the emergence of the American republic around 1790, the networks of European-inspired towns on the continent comprised peripheral, coastal strongholds oriented to the major colonial powers of the Old World. The core of Spain's imposed urban network lay in present-day Mexico and South America, so those towns of Spanish origin within the present-day United States (e.g., St. Augustine, 1565; San Diego, 1769) served largely as defensive frontier outposts with quite

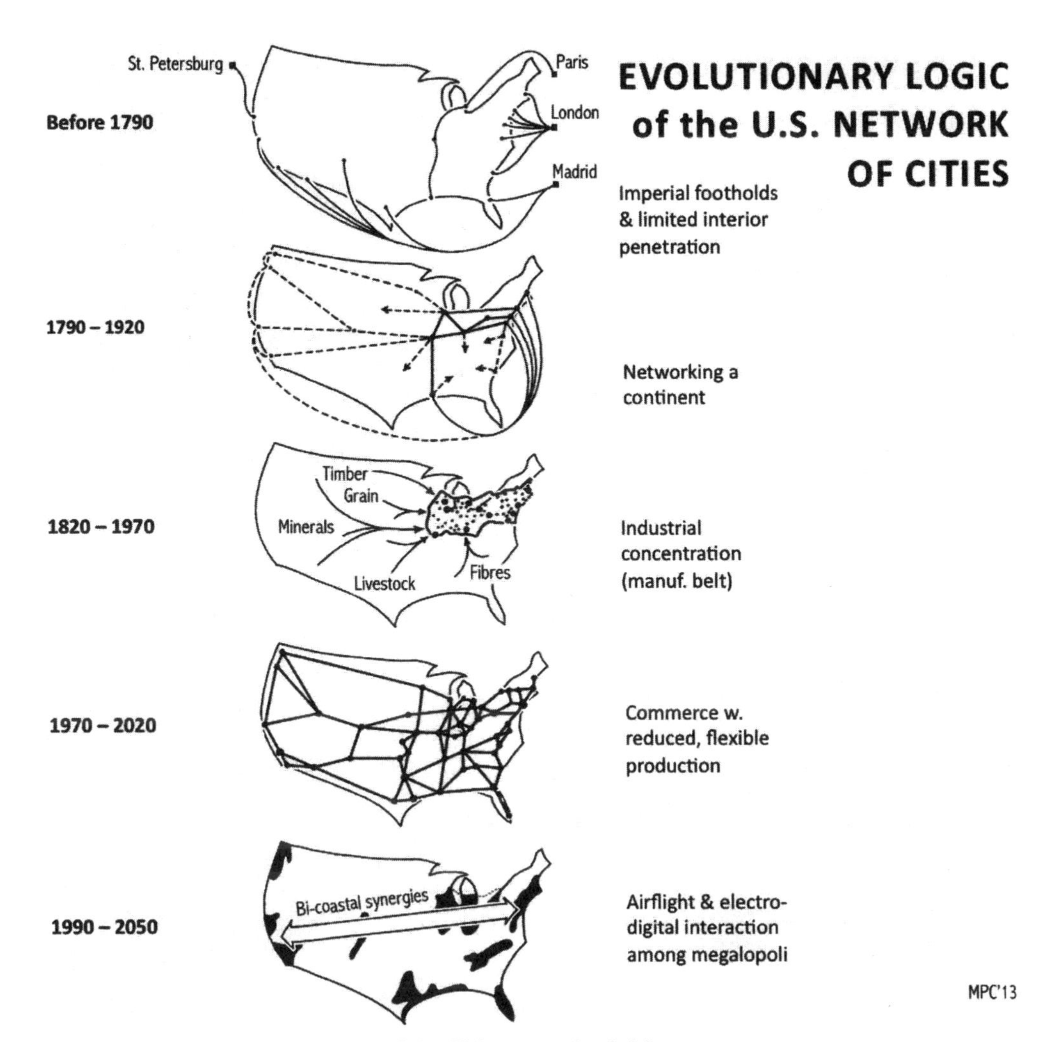

Figure 19.2. Evolutionary logic of the U.S. network of cities.

limited commercial value. Within North America itself, France was more fortunate, because while it also created towns to defend its imperial ambitions (Quebec City, 1608; Montreal, 1642; New Orleans, 1718), these places also functioned as conduits for a highly profitable fur trade. Tardy Russian colonial interests on the Pacific Rim led to the eventual founding of Fort Ross in Northern California in 1812, but it was to little too late to achieve urban status in a vastly overextended Russian empire and quickly faded.

Of greatest consequence were the towns established or absorbed by the British along the eastern seaboard, anchored by their major seventeenth-century waterfront centers: New York (established by the Dutch in 1624 but British by 1664), Boston (1630), and Philadelphia (1682). The Spanish and French towns formed thin chains over vast territory with tiny and widely separated nodes, whereas the British colonies formed a compact region coordinated by significant cities only one or two hundred miles apart from each other. Even though these towns directed most of their commerce to London, the scope this opened up to develop lateral economic linkages and reach inland for added trade—especially following political independence—is plain. North Americans speak English today because Britain from the outset yielded up enough immigrants (and other investments) to stock the colonies with pioneers in rural agriculture and urban trade sufficient to outflank the competition. During the eighteenth century, only a few small towns, such as Pittsburgh (1758) and Lexington (1775), broke the fastness of the trans-Appalachian frontier, but they signaled the appearance of what would develop later into the great wholesaling corridors that crisscrossed the continent (Vance 1970).

The second major epoch in urban network growth was the extraordinary expansion of towns over the remainder of the national territory. Accomplished by ship, wagon, and later railroad, this lasted the whole of the "long" nineteenth century (1790s–1920s). This expansion minted service towns de novo wherever woodland, prairie, and marsh could be made agriculturally profitable and transport-support towns where mountain ranges could be breached or resorts established. The South supported a thinner sprinkling of this "central place" development pattern, but its coastal export centers flourished. Most notable was the role of railroads, which in the more advanced East played catch-up in a vital urban integration that added lines of steel alongside existing turnpikes and canals and laced the territory in between. West of Chicago and Cincinnati, in areas void of prior settlement, railroads became the pioneers themselves, evolving into full-service homesteading and commercial agencies in their own right. Ultimately they would offer through-tickets to migrants from Hamburg and London to the Dakotas and other points west (Hudson 1985). The Gold Rush at mid-century put San Francisco (1776, wrested from Mexico 1848) on the American urban-system map and, there and in other Pacific coast ports, provided the incentive to fulfill the continental dreams of Manifest Destiny long held by eastern politicians and businessmen.

The third epoch overlapped substantially with the second (figure 19.1, left), but it is worth treating as a separate overarching geographical process because the driver of change here—industrial machine technology—operated not so much to disperse its benefits as to concentrate them in what became known as the Manufacturing Belt (Meyer 2003). Large factory districts took shape from the 1820s on in Massachusetts, spread to Philadelphia and New York City, and by the 1850s had permeated the Midwest. This occurred for several reasons. Dense rural and urban populations of the East and the adjacent Great Lakes represented a huge resident market. Basic raw materials (e.g., iron ore, coal, limestone, timber) were readily available in this quadrant of the United States. The mature transport environment eased assembly and distribution. And lastly, the Manufacturing Belt's quite broadly educated population promoted inventiveness and entrepreneurship. At first, industrialization completely bypassed the South with its slave-based plantation economy, but by the middle third of the twentieth century, much mass-market manufacturing had seeped southward, seeking low-wage, pliant labor. Insufficient population densities and local markets ultimately halted the westward spread of the Manufacturing Belt, although in the Far West, Northern California nurtured a small industrial base, supported by Gold Rush wealth, that sheer distance long sheltered from competition.

The fourth epoch of the nation's urban system came with the long-term effects of global recovery from World War II and the challenge to home industry from cheap producer and consumer goods made elsewhere in developing countries (figure 19.1, left). The resulting substantial deindustrialization of many cities, especially in what was now being labeled the Rust Belt, brought crises that placed renewed emphasis on commerce, especially in services and the infrastructure needed to distribute the growing overall abundance of material wealth. The systemic effect was a sort of "equalization" in which the New South gained some manufacturing, while the Rust Belt learned to adjust to light and highly specialized industry and flexible production. Agriculture everywhere industrialized on a vast new scale; advanced services, whether for business or social needs, grew in numerous places; and air travel brought many cities into heightened contact with other regions. The interstate highway system, constructed between 1950 and 1970, precipitated a crisis in railroad management and profitability but cemented an elaborate wholesale distribution system, often in quite new places, thanks to the positioning of freeways.

It is increasingly clear that the urban network has entered a fifth epoch in the twenty-first century. Air travel expanded with deregulation during the 1990s, and what we might think of as the "electro-digital" revolution has matured to the point where industrial innovation, higher education (especially of a technical nature), bioengineering, health care, and entertainment loom large in the portfolio of urban growth dynamics. These trends have favored the emergence of large megalopolitan regions of grown-together proximate cities and engendered in a premium on innovation clusters, referred to by some as "nerdistans." Silicon Valley in California, Routes 128 and 495 in Massachusetts, and the Research Triangle in North Carolina are simply the better-known cases of high-tech zones that every major city development agency has sought to replicate in its jurisdiction. Noticeable in all this has been the rise of a commercial and cultural bicoastalism that has brought with it the drudgery of long-distance "red-eye" travel for critical face-to-face meetings that, despite the electronic revolution, still command business resources.

If this sequence of epochs characterizes, in some skeletal way, the history of the American city network, it remains only to reiterate how regionally varied and temporally calibrated each phase has been. Implicit in this model of the system's evolution is the assumption that a core region developed early that, as it expanded and became more functionally complex, emitted diffusionary waves of change. They spread, first westward and secondarily southward, so that each initially fringe region ultimately shared many of the characteristics of the core, suggesting a partial equalization of urban roles among cities of similar size. And yet, for all the veneer of functional convergence, their forms to some extent retain signs of their particular historical periods of most virile growth. For instance, despite central Boston's possessing all the accouterments of modern living, the built environment of its historic core remains worlds away from the far less complex appearance of central Phoenix.

THE CHANGING LOGIC OF URBAN SPATIAL STRUCTURE

It is an axiom of urban historical geography that the specific circumstances of particular locations forever mediate generic processes of urban formation and the patterns they produce. This is exemplified in the way some urban sites bequeath enduring characteristics in the city's structure that even the most powerful generic reshaping forces cannot erase. Most fundamentally, there is a historical divide between those places that arose as port cities—whether on a coast or simply a navigable river—and those that did not. Those not on major water include any city in which the local river, for most if not all of its history, played no significant commercial role. So essential to understanding port cities' growth and cumulative structure are their historic waterfronts (whether active or defunct) that they justify recognizing for any era a basic distinction between port cities and inland cities (figure 19.3). Waterfronts represent a crucial "fixation line" that, however sinuous, sharply fixes in space a whole series of connected functions and land uses within the total urban area that do not occur in places without them. St. Louis, Missouri (founded 1764), strung out along the west bank of the great Mississippi River, represents a classic case. Although railroads have often played an analogous role, they usually came sufficiently later in any major city's development and multiplied too promiscuously across urban space to have the same localizing effect, as evidenced in Atlanta, Georgia (founded 1837). Therefore the review of each epoch considers this distinction.

As regards dividing the evolution of urban space in U.S. cities into broad periods, the focus turns to transport technology, because the constant growth in

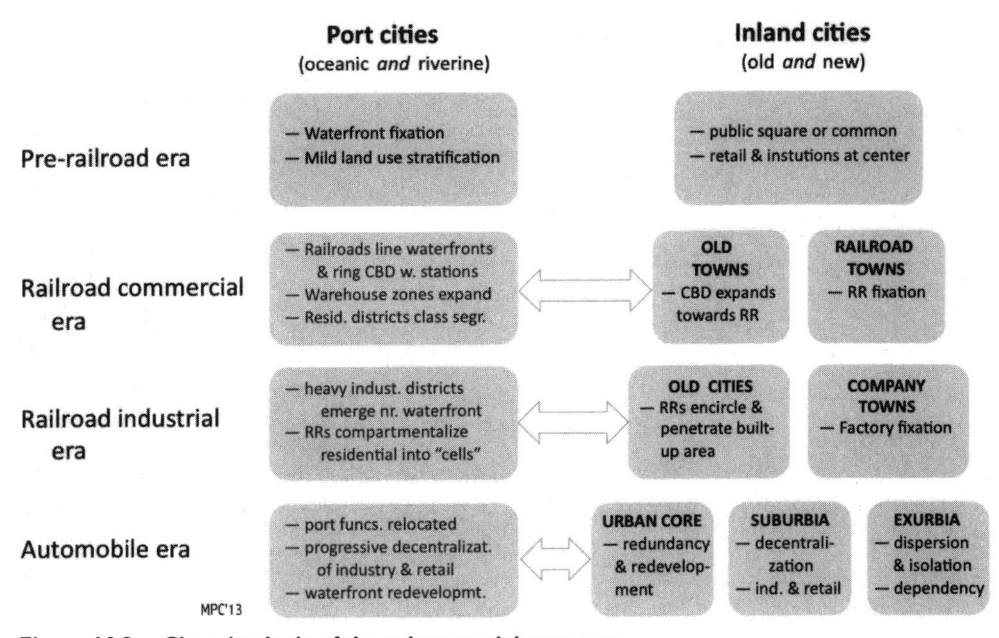

Figure 19.3. Changing logic of the urban spatial structure.

physical extent of all successful cities inevitably eroded local accessibility and forced citizens to battle increased distances, overcrowded arteries of movement, and poorly located facilities. From an internal point of view, three technologies have held sway: foot traffic (people, horses), rails (streetcars, commuter trains), and automobiles (buses, cars, trucks)—not forgetting, though largely disregarding here for simplicity, transitional hybrid types (omnibuses, horsecars, and trolley-buses). However, the three main technologies have predominated in four distinct ways, suggesting four phases tied to different processes: (1) the prerailroad epoch, (2) a passenger railroad regime serving essentially commercial environments, (3) a freight railroad regime serving heavy industry, and (4) the automobile epoch (figure 19.1).

The Prerailroad Era

America's oldest cities are all port cities. Their waterfronts were key: they were not only the gateway to the metropolitan center of the mother country across the ocean (London, in the British case) but also the hinge to the city's resource-rich hinterland (figure 19.3). In the prerailroad era, port city land use was weakly segregated behind the all-important waterfront, although Martyn Bowden has proposed a "colonial replica city" model in which land uses were stratified in narrow bands tapering off from extensive maritime services and commerce close to the waterfront to institutional and residential uses away from it, as demonstrated by Stephen Hornsby for Charleston, South Carolina, in the 1780s (Bowden, cited in Hornsby 2005, 186). In the case of inland towns, the focus instead was often a public square or common, usually centered on a courthouse, surrounded by retail businesses and key institutions, such as hotels, churches, and opera houses. Lancaster, Pennsylvania (founded 1730) is one prototype of this spatial order, so powerful a model that it diffused clear across the nation (Price 1968; Conzen 2006b).

Towns and cities built before the 1830s concentrated status at or near the center, although the scale of building was usually small enough that, at a district level, rich and poor might well be found together. As the commercial center expanded and neighborhoods multiplied, social segregation increased, but within limits, as most colonial and early-republic towns were effectively walkable from end to end. When railroads did make their entrance in established cities in the East and the Ohio valley from the 1840s on, their depots had to settle for initially fringe sites. Both in their town planning and architecture, with their combination of Philadelphia- and New York–inspired grid layouts and comfortable mix of federal-style and Greek Revival building traditions, the newly emerging cities of the Midwest and upper South spread an essentially eastern town type deep toward the line of the Mississippi River (Reps 1965; Ballon 2012).

Distinctions between the Railroad Commercial and Industrial Eras

The historical geography of American cities created two types of urban space attributable to railroads in the nineteenth century, commercial and industrial, depending on internal location and economic specialization. The distinction lies not so much in the character and engineering of rail lines and their equipment, for nearly all companies ran passengers and freight over most lines then, but rather in their localizing effects on land use in different districts and in their timing. In considering commercial impacts, this chapter includes streetcar lines with commuter rail lines because both threaded neighborhoods together in long strings, the former within the older core of large cities, the latter going beyond to the new train-based suburbs. By contrast, many railroad lines fostered intensive concentrations of industry along their margins, especially when they connected with rivers, canals, and lakefronts. The timing of these distinct impacts was also different. They overlap chronologically, but not completely. In cities that developed commuter train service, the commercial-residential impact came first, because commuter trains quickly generated far-flung suburbs, whereas industrial investment in new railroad sites was always more intensive and slower moving. The closings of these eras also differ, in that industrial use of railroads within the tight confines of large cities ended long before most commuter passenger service began.

The Railroad Commercial Era

In the second epoch of urban spatial structure, railroads serving commerce came to dominate the economic and social geography of cities. In all the major ports, railroads colonized the docks along the waterfront and formed a ring of terminal stations around the remaining perimeter of the central business district (CBD). This was more easily done in Chicago, founded in 1830, where the first railroad appeared a mere fourteen years later and land occupation was still fluid, than in Baltimore, a century old by the time the first railroad pierced its commercial core (Olson 1997). The quickening of trade enabled by the spread of railroads nationally between 1850 and 1890 spurred rapid growth among all port cities—along the East Coast, the Great Lakes, the Ohio-Mississippi-Gulf corridors, and the Pacific coast. Great warehouse districts grew up near the docks as railroads reinforced the commercial structure of cities long oriented to their waterfronts. By the late nineteenth century, the CBDs of the port cities were decidedly appendages to the transfer districts of wharves and maritime servicing. Elsewhere in these cities, as commerce and associated manufacturing created vast numbers of jobs, immigrants and rural migrants crowded into near-central neighborhoods that quickly transformed from streets of tradesmens' modest homes to ones lined with tall tenements and apartment blocks. Tradesmen, artisans, and a growing clerical class moved further out to newer neighborhoods made accessible by streetcars and commuter rail lines. In this, they simply followed in the wake of the quickly suburbanizing wealthy. Both types of rail took workers to their jobs, heavily concentrated in and around the city center, and both types stimulated the clustering of retail businesses around their stops. Streetcars created linear shopping districts along their routes because they stopped at every block. The historic crisscross pattern of this phenomenon in Chicago on major streets at mile intervals running north-south and east-west can still be found in relict form today. By all these means, the scale of the largest port cities became thoroughly impersonal, class and ethnic segregation rose, and land use became more chaotic, hastening the regulatory age of municipal land-use zoning, beginning in New York in 1916 (Ward 1989).

Those large cities that matured during the age of railroad dominance have maintained these patterns. The interior spatial organization of the major East Coast cities and some Midwestern ones, such as Chicago, continues to reflect the historic impact of rail networks that served this largely commercial function. Furthermore, as rapid transit modes weakened in the face of rising automobile usage, congestion clogged the circulation of most sizable cities in the late twentieth century to such an extent that "light rail" has made a limited comeback, not just in cities that once had extensive streetcar networks but also in places without historic rapid transit networks (e.g., Phoenix, Houston) (figure 19.1).

In inland cities of any size—those of over one hundred thousand people by 1900—many of these trends were also in full swing during this long era, but without the powerful conditioning element of a waterfront. In a Minneapolis (founded 1839) or a Denver (1858), railroads had more freedom to shape the commercial and industrial pattern, creating compass-rose sectors of associated land use, even if they were somewhat late coming to the city. Further down the urban hierarchy, similar processes sorted urban space, but with less severity. Universal, however, was the tendency of railroad stations to suck retail activity toward them along an often newly busy street leading there from the traditional business core, whether an ancient crossroads center, a courthouse square, or a canal landing. Syracuse, New York, and San Antonio, Texas, serve as examples.

The railroads' role in shaping urban space discussed so far has concerned established towns and cities, but railroad-borne mercantilism also produced a singularly American type of urban space, particularly in the West: the railroad town. In newly settling western territory where the railroad was the very agent of colonization, its influence was direct and regimented. New towns were laid out with simple plats aligned strictly parallel with the train tracks or, alternatively, in conformity with the orthogonal national survey grid. In each case the railroad occupied a reserved strip with ample space for businesses that would generate shipments by rail—grain elevators, lumberyards, stockyards, coal yards, and the like. Often the railroad owned or managed these facilities and, going even further, advertised for investors in and lessees of hotels, banks, and other small-town services (Hudson 1985). Store-sized business lots were platted along a Main Street that would either parallel the tracks or intersect them at right angles (so-called I or T towns). Railroad officials thus implemented the skeletal outlines of such towns; as a result, hundreds of such towns came to dot vast commodity regions like the Great Plains (which produced wheat, corn, and livestock). Some would grow to substantial size—Sioux Falls, South Dakota (incorporated 1876; 2010 population 153,000), for instance—and some remained no more than whistle-stops, but with a claim to urban purpose (Conzen 2010).

The Railroad Industrial Era

In contrast to the wholesale-retail and residential effects of rail transport within large cities, the railroads' industrial impact was different. This became powerful by the 1850s and lasted many decades, but it ended emphatically during the 1960s

WHAT INSPIRED *Mastering Iron*?
Anne Kelly Knowles

The initial inspiration for researching the U.S. iron industry was a question that occurred to me while I was finishing my first book, about Welsh immigrants on Ohio's industrial frontier. Why did it take nearly seventy years for U.S. iron companies to match the scale and productivity of the British iron industry? This question gripped my imagination because it had so many facets—labor, technology, capital, markets, transportation, resources—all the geographical circumstances of industrial production. I had a hunch that the iron industry had played a crucial but virtually unknown role in American industrialization. The possibility of filling a gap in historiography made the research irresistible.

When I began *Mastering Iron*, I was becoming caught up in the exciting development of historical Geographic Information Science (GIS), an interdisciplinary effort to use GIS to study the past in new ways. Although the GIS I built of the antebellum iron industry (with many people's help) was essential to my research, I did not want the mechanics of database construction or data analysis to get in the way of the main story. At the same time, I wanted to show how crucial visual evidence was to my analysis, in the form of maps generated from the GIS and drawings and paintings of iron landscapes and workers that revealed much about the working environments and cultures of iron making. These desires inspired the form of the book, which combines verbal and visual narrative.

Had the research itself not been inspiring, I could not have stayed with the book for the sixteen years it took to complete. Exploring the historical GIS of the industry, I found surprising variations from place to place. Locating ironworks in topographic quadrangles and on historical maps filled my mind with images of iron-making landscapes, tiny industrial outposts, big works on train lines, and the importance of rivers. Manuscript letters were my greatest treasures. One set of letters revealed the enmity between a naively ambitious Welsh artisan and the ignorant American superintendent who obstructed his efforts while driving some of Boston's wealthiest men into bankruptcy. Most precious was a letter written for the illiterate immigrant engineer who built Tredegar, the South's largest ironworks, shortly before he died in a fistfight in Richmond, Virginia. Knowing who he was, I wanted to shout across the years to change his fate. I knew at that moment that the iron industry's story was one I had to tell.

and 1970s. The effects on major cities were extensive, as factories at first clustered into areas of still open and cheap land avoided by residential construction, often on sites convenient to water transportation (Muller and Groves 1979). Sometimes these industrial corridors simply followed major rivers, estuaries, and canals, such as along the Menomonee, Kinnickinnic, and Milwaukee Rivers in

Milwaukee or the Allegheny, Monongahela, and Ohio Rivers in Pittsburgh (Bauman and Muller 2006). But in other cities, such as Chicago, the railroads laced large sectors of the metropolitan area with industrialized rail corridors, cutting urban neighborhood space into "cells" separated by grade crossings or, once grade separation occurred in the early twentieth century, raised railroad embankments and underpasses (Hudson 2006). In old cities, port and inland alike, the industrial impact of railroads was great; huge areas became dedicated to factory complexes, railroad spurs, classification yards, and industrial dumping grounds. Once urban constriction and traffic congestion led many firms to decentralize away from city sites and competition from road transport rendered many tracks redundant, these corridors often became blighted landscapes, only partially redeemable through loft-living gentrification.

As with the spatial character of the classic railroad town in regions usually far from the Manufacturing Belt, there developed quite another prototypical spatial type: the company town. Also creatures of the railroad age, American company towns were usually formed by industrialists eager to exploit mineral resources in remote places, where they had to provide the basic equipment of a town to attract and keep a workforce (Allen 1966), or the towns were built as economic and social experiments with either minimal or carefully controlled facilities. Standardized, regimented housing, a company store, a vast factory, and a rather monotonous, utilitarian environment were the usual results. By far the most celebrated example of a comprehensively planned company town is Pullman, Illinois, established in 1881 (Buder 1967). Not surprisingly, the central principle of company towns was that, in spatial terms, the needs of the factory determined the configuration of the entire community. In historical experience, most company towns had a fixed useful life, and when the factory closed, much in the community's social cohesion and physical environment unraveled (Buckley, Bain, and Swan 2005).

The Automobile Era

It is tempting to suggest that, of all transport technologies, the automobile has been the most transformative force in reshaping the American city. Henry Ford's Model T car, first produced in 1908, began the process on a mass scale, with 15 million sold by 1927. For the first time in history, individuals and families were empowered to travel on their own schedules anywhere suitable roads and streets existed. As cars diffused through society, urban congestion followed, both in terms of traffic flow and parking. So great was the pressure, compared with rapid and mass transit forms, that the car forced the redesign of urban spaces. In new suburbs, street systems changed in scale and geometry, but in existing urban fabrics, vehicles could only fill up willy-nilly available spaces never meant to accommodate them.

In port cities, automobiles in the form of trucks affected waterfronts by adding their bulk and space needs to those of the railroad, encouraging the adaptation of existing piers and warehouses to their scale and ultimately the relocation of transfer facilities to larger premises closer to major highways. More broadly in the automobile era, the congestive impact of cars, trucks, and buses fueled the decentralization not only of commercial and industrial land uses but also of shopping and retail services in general. Port operations often shifted to more remote sites (e.g., Chicago's port famously from the Chicago River south fifteen miles to the Calumet District), and close-in docklands atrophied until ripe for radical redevelopment, as waterfronts slowly turned into leisure and entertainment venues during the second half of the twentieth century. CBDs attracted the fiercest concentrations of automobiles, turning over large amounts of on-and off-street ground to "machine space," with megalithic parking ramps shoehorned between high-rise office towers (Horvath 1974; Jakle and Sculle 2004). The general effect was to hasten the obsolescence and replacement of many older buildings in downtown areas that, absent the automobile, might have survived many more decades. Such transformations occurred, of course, similarly in all inland cities, large and small.

The postindustrial changes that occurred in urban core areas from the 1970s on brought new forms of commerce to revalorize neighborhoods nearby, based in the arts and other creative enterprises. Especially in cities positioned atop the urban hierarchy and most active in expanding their reach in global markets and finance, urban cores have remained vital, attracting high-wage, skilled, white-collar workers who fed the gentrification of these neighborhoods (Lloyd 2005). But in all too many smaller cases, relentless decentralization has stripped American downtowns of their former purpose, leaving eviscerated government facilities as their main tenants.

As the automobile brought arteriosclerosis to much existing urban fabric across the nation, its influence was more sweeping in newly built suburban districts. It revolutionized residential street widths and layouts, made allowance for residential garages, and shaped the location and design of commercial and industrial facilities. The superhighways that pioneered the urban fringes of metropolitan America after the 1950s absorbed ever-larger amounts of land as interchanges multiplied and curves were made more generous to accommodate faster traffic. The general decentralization of many urban functions, including jobs and services, to the periphery not only tipped the nation's "urban" center of gravity toward the suburbs but also urbanized them to some extent. These created what Joel Garreau (1991) termed "edge cities" and thereby divorced vast populations from effective contact with the urban core, with far-reaching political and social consequences of alienation and contest. As twentieth-century suburbs aged, however, many faced the same problems of infrastructure maintenance as central cities, though often without the tax base to cope (especially low-income suburbs). Prototypical of the spread of a suburban ethos during the twentieth century was the rise of Los Angeles. Although its origins trace back to 1781, the metropolis exploded during the age of the automobile, carried on a wave of development fueled by irrigated agriculture, oil, and a global entertainment industry (Keil 1998; Scott 2004).

A final feature in the changing logic of American urban spatial structure demanding mention is the rise of exurbia. Identified as a distinctive phenomenon in the 1950s, exurbs are pseudo-urban settlements dotting the outer reaches of metropolitan fringes, disjointed fragments of urban form in a countryside with which they have little interaction (Lang 2003; Conzen 2006a). Enabled by the ubiquitous automobile, cheap land for subdivision-style development, and a liking for unincorporated territory with low taxes (and often few or no services), exurbs appeal due to their spacious country surroundings, even if shopping and other facilities are miles distant. Eventually, those exurbs closer in become incorporated in the denser sprawl of advancing suburbia, as new exurbs form farther out. Socially and economically diverse, this settlement type depends precariously on the support systems of the nearest towns or metropolis for their existence.

CONCLUSION

American urban environments, of whatever type, have developed and flourished as the optimum means of controlling the creation of wealth across the continent and its extensions in all historical periods. In the earliest days, they were mere speck on the land, usually at the edge of significant bodies of water. Their overriding purpose was trade, supplemented by administration. As the American commonwealth expanded, territorially and in organizational complexity, import substitution by domestic manufacturing became integral to the system, and the United States excelled in light and heavy industrial production. By the late twentieth century, much low-return manufacturing had migrated to cheaper production sites elsewhere in the world, and American cities have compensated for their loss by constant reinvention: elaboration of a service economy, ever-tighter connection to scientific discovery and its commercial applications, and growth of an amusement economy, including urban tourism, city branding, trade conventions, and so on. In the globalization of industrial output, American-based manufacturing has shrunk, specialized, and found geographically dispersed niches in which to remain profitable. Through all of these changes, the nation's urban population has continued to swell, and that "success" has provided continued room for commercial growth to fill the myriad needs of that urban mass.

Yet for all the revolutions in technology, economic imperatives, urban design, and social character of American cities over the last four centuries, as well as the seismic increase in physical scale and functional convergence of the system as reflected in the standardization of urban equipment across the nation as a whole, geographical differences endure. Los Angeles is second in size only to New York City, but the two are radically different places to live. Chicago has dropped to North America's fourth most populous city (if we exclude Mexico City), overtaken by Toronto, and they, too, are very different places. It takes a historical and geographical sensibility to understand the true multiplicity of urban experiences that have evolved in this large region.

REFERENCES

Allen, J. B. 1966. *The Company Town in the American West.* Norman: University of Oklahoma Press.

Ballon, H. 2012. *The Greatest Grid: The Master Plan of Manhattan, 1811–2011.* New York: Columbia University Press.

Bauman, J. F., and E. K. Muller. 2006. *Before Renaissance: Planning in Pittsburgh, 1889–1943.* Pittsburgh, PA: University of Pittsburgh Press.
Buckley, G. L., N. R. Bain, and D. J. Swan. 2005. When the Lights Go Out in Cheshire. *Geographical Review* 94, no. 4: 537–55.
Buder, S. 1967. *Pullman: An Experiment in Industrial Order and Community Planning, 1880–1930.* New York: Oxford University Press.
Campanella, R. 2008. *Bienville's Dilemma: A Historical Geography of New Orleans.* Lafayette: Center for Louisiana Studies, University of Louisiana, Lafayette.
Conzen, M. P. 1981. The American Urban System in the Nineteenth Century. In *Geography and the Urban Environment: Progress in Research and Applications*, edited by D. T. Herbert and R. J. Johnston, 4:295–347. New York and London: John Wiley and Sons.
———. 2006a. Exurbs. In *Encyclopedia of Human Geography*, edited by B. Warf, 148–50. Thousand Oaks, CA: Sage Publications.
———. 2006b. The Non-Pennsylvania Town: Diffusion of Urban Plan Forms in the American West. *Geographical Review* 96, no. 2: 183–211.
———. 2010. Understanding Great Plains Urbanization through the Lens of South Dakota Townscapes. *Journal of Geography* 109, no. 1: 3–17.
Garreau, J. 1991. *Edge City: Life on the New Frontier.* New York: Doubleday.
Hornsby, S. J. 2005. *British Atlantic, American Frontier: Spaces of Power in Early Modern British America.* Hanover, NH: University Press of New England.
Horvath, R. J. 1974. Machine Space. *Geographical Review* 64, no. 2: 167–88.
Hudson, J. C. 1985. *Plains Country Towns.* Minneapolis: University of Minnesota Press.
———. 2006. *Chicago: A Geography of the City and Its Region.* Chicago: University of Chicago Press.
Jakle, J. A., and K. A. Sculle. 2004. *Lots of Parking: Land Use in a Car Culture.* Charlottesville: University of Virginia Press.
Keil, R. 1998. *Los Angeles: Globalization, Urbanization, and Social Struggles.* New York: Wiley.
Lang, R. E. 2003. *Edgeless Cities: Exploring the Elusive Metropolis.* Washington, D.C.: Brookings Institution Press.
Lloyd, R. 2005. *NeoBohemia: Art and Commerce in the Post-industrial City.* New York: Routledge.
Meyer, D. R. 2003. *The Roots of American Industrialization.* Baltimore: Johns Hopkins University Press.
Muller, E. K., and P. A. Groves. 1979. The Emergence of Industrial Districts in Mid-nineteenth Century Baltimore. *Geographical Review* 69, no. 2: 159–78.
Olson, S. H. 1997. *Baltimore: The Building of an American City.* Rev. exp. bicentennial ed. Baltimore: Johns Hopkins University Press.
Price, E. T. 1968. The Central Courthouse Square in the American County Seat. *Geographical Review* 58, no. 1: 29–60.
Reps, J. W. 1965. *The Making of Urban America: A History of Urban Planning in the United States.* Princeton, NJ: Princeton University Press.
Scott, A. J. 2004. *Hollywood: The Growth of the Motion Picture Industry.* Princeton, NJ: Princeton University Press.
Vance, J. E., Jr. 1970. *The Merchant's World: The Geography of Wholesaling.* Englewood Cliffs, NJ: Prentice Hall.
Ward, D. 1989. *Poverty, Ethnicity, and the American City, 1840–1925: Changing Conceptions of the Slum and the Ghetto.* Cambridge: Cambridge University Press.

20

"If Ever a City Needed the Definite Plan"

Planning Spatial Order for American Cities

Edward K. Muller

At the request of civic leaders anxious to improve their industrial city, nationally renowned city-planning advocate Charles Mulford Robinson came to smoky Pittsburgh in 1909 and concluded, "The final word, which has to do with the needs of the whole community, hardly requires saying. It is a plea for comprehensive planning. Surely, if ever a city needed the definite plan . . . it is Pittsburgh" (1909, 818). At the turn of the century, Progressive reformers like Robinson believed that carefully crafted plans could improve the city environment, bring order to chaotic land uses, diminish crippling inefficiencies, and inspire proper citizenship. Cities had grown so rapidly that they struggled with serious social, economic, health, and environmental issues. Their populations, including suburbs, often exceeded 1 million people, forming complex urban regions that fragmented local governance and inhibited metropolitan-wide solutions to problems. During the ensuing decades, planners gained credence as professionals and became institutionalized in municipal government. They and like-minded civic leaders helped to shape the unfolding geography of the metropolis (Scott 1969). Ultimately, however, they failed to create the sort of orderly, safe, healthy, and efficient environments envisioned.

Despite their passion, expertise, and confidence, planning advocates ran headlong into the twin pillars of the American system: capitalism and political democracy. For many Americans, planning meant undesirable governmental intervention in the free market and control over the rights of private property owners. For advocates, planning had to bend to the dictates of elected public officials representing diverse interests and often under the influence of powerful businessmen and political bosses. Ironically, these same special interests admitted that unfettered operation of the market sometimes created consequences that impaired economic growth and a healthy city. Believing their self-interest to be linked to their city's success, they called for and supported specific interventions. Planning functioned in this space between free market imperatives and the need for intervention. It involved professional planners (at first, mostly private consultants and, later, members of government), civic leaders, and activists who, in pursuit of the common good, focused on guiding urban spatial development and improving the design of public and residential spaces. Through land-use regulation, the framework of plans supported by public officials and special interests, and the market place of ideas, planning influenced the evolving geography of the city in significant ways.

PLANNING BEFORE PROFESSIONALIZATION

Until the twentieth century, market forces largely shaped the physical development of cities. The initial platting of street plans, along with additive subdivision plans, provided the spatial framework for development. The gridiron plan—modeled on Philadelphia, adopted by New York in 1811 for expansion on Manhattan Island, and adapted as its use spread across the continent—became the prevalent town layout due to its appealing economic advantages, convenience, orderliness, and transparency (Vance 1990; Conzen 2006; Upton 2008). With minimal governmental oversight, development occurred in a piecemeal fashion, producing a seemingly haphazard mix of land uses. The early concentration of economic activity on the waterfront and the distance decay of land values yielded a bell curve settlement pattern, in effect a town focused on the merchant's world, which began to give way during the rapid growth and initial industrialization of the antebellum years. Dell Upton argues for a republican spatial imagination in this period, which favored a visual equality in building fabric, systematization of needed infrastructure like water supply or street numbering, and monumental structures signaling essential civic institutions (Wright 1981; Upton 2008).

Faced with accelerating growth after mid-century and deteriorating physical conditions, cities pursued what Jon Peterson calls special purpose planning through both public and private agency. Most undertook the construction of sewer, water, and mass transit projects. These large-scale projects required huge amounts of capital, expertise, and centralized planning, all precursors to more comprehensive visions of planning the city (Olson 1980; Peterson 2003). Some cities sought to promote the health and moral welfare of residents by creating open space, following the example of New York's Central Park designed by Frederick Law Olmsted Sr. and Calvert Vaux. A few developers constructed fully designed, upper-income suburban neighborhoods (Schuyler 1986; Tuason 1997; Young 2004; Buckley, Bailey, and Grove 2006).

In order to understand the possibilities for American cities, many engineers, architects, and landscape architects toured European cities that were more advanced in planning and accepted governmental intervention more readily (Rodgers 1998). They encountered public gardens, ensembles of monumental buildings, grand boulevards, spacious plazas, and civic art, all of which inspired them to "civilize" America's cities. Civic improvement societies had long worked to beautify dreary urban landscapes, but they had only succeeded in enhancing small spaces around the urban area. The returning design professionals harbored grander ideas for cities.

PROGRESSIVE PLANNING

Engineers, design professionals, and citizen activists believed that social, economic, and political reforms were essential for American cities to provide healthy, uplifting, and efficient environments. Bringing beauty and order to the environment by controlling land use, banning unsightly nuisances, and remaking neighborhoods and infrastructure would, they argued, improve individual behavior, enhance social stability, and promote progress (Boyer 1983; Gillette 2010). Reform efforts split in different directions and produced mixed results, but they left lasting imprints on the geography of cities and led to the formation of the planning profession.

One planning thrust involved aesthetic betterment as a strategy to morally uplift the city. The immensely successful Chicago World's Fair in 1893, with its architectural ensemble known as the "Court of Honor" and superb site and grounds designed by Frederick Law Olmsted Sr., spurred civic leaders and design professionals to rethink the dreary appearances of their cities. At the turn of the twentieth century, civic-improvement societies opposing billboards and promoting systematic tree planting joined municipal art groups busily erecting patriotic monuments and organizations promulgating landscape improvements through parks, public gardens, and boulevards to advocate beautifying cities in the public interest (Peterson 2003; Buckley and Boone 2011). Directed by architect Daniel Burnham, who oversaw the Chicago World's Fair, the 1902 McMillan Plan for Washington, D.C., presented an unprecedented, comprehensive vision for the capital's public spaces, especially the Mall and an expansive park system (figure 20.1). In Peterson's words, the plan "suggest[ed] a new vision of urban planning for the nation as a whole" (2003, 78).

With the aid of tireless advocates like Charles Mulford Robinson and Horace McFarland, these various organizations coalesced around the idea of a City Beautiful movement for remaking cities in the initial years of the century. Plans materialized for grand boulevards (e.g., Philadelphia's Benjamin Franklin Parkway), landscaped waterfronts (e.g., Harrisburg's Susquehanna riverfront), civic centers of public building ensembles (e.g., Cleveland), and park systems (e.g., Seattle). Several comprehensive city plans followed, notably Burnham's grand visions for San Francisco and Chicago. Bold and fanciful, these plans reimagined public spaces of civic centers and parks on a grand scale and proposed massive reorganization of railroad, transit, and highway networks, which intruded on private property imperatives and exceeded municipal budget capabilities. Although only individual elements of plans were constructed, usually in modified forms, many City Beautiful ideas remained part of the public conversation for decades to come (Wilson 1989; Smith 2006). The aesthetics of this early planning raised the standard for public spaces and aspirations for the built environment writ large; however, by not directly addressing social issues and concerns of massive traffic congestion, most City Beautiful planning failed to attract widespread support.

Figure 20.1. The McMillan Commission's plan for Washington, D.C., 1902. Courtesy of the Frances Loeb Library, Harvard Graduate School of Design.

Social Progressives criticized City Beautiful adherents for ignoring the scabrous slums of American cities, while another segment of planning advocates, led by Frederick Law Olmsted Jr., favored a pragmatic approach that might garner greater influence with businessmen and public officials for the nascent profession. Reformers appalled by severe overcrowding in dilapidated tenements promoted "limited-dividend" model housing and regulatory codes with only marginal success. They believed that governmental intervention in property markets similar to German and British programs was necessary to control land use, diminish property speculation, and lower population density (Lubove 1962). Under the prevailing laissez-faire view of government, such programs were too radical for the pragmatic planners. In 1910 the housing reformers split away from the more conservative planning movement, not to reunite until the 1930s (Peterson 2003).

The split with housing reformers allowed planners to focus on improving the physical city while developing authority through technical competence. Eschewing the soaring rhetoric of the City Beautiful, Olmsted advanced the notion of a master plan based on a continual process of data collection, mapping, and expert analysis as a flexible guideline for development. He and colleagues like John Nolen worked with engineers to make the city more efficient. They recommended widening streets, opening new thoroughfares, separating streetcars from other vehicles, and improving transit and port facilities. They proposed distributing playgrounds equitably about the city, constructing small parklets for respite from the ambient cacophony, and designing larger parks more for organized recreation than the contemplative value of naturalistic spaces popular in the earlier romantic park era. They also suggested grouping public buildings into civic centers and coordinating plans with contiguous suburban communities. Businessmen could support such practical proposals so that many infrastructure projects were completed. The new infrastructure affected the pace, direction, and composition of development, relieved congestion temporarily, and improved a city's functioning. However, politicians refused to abdicate their decision-making power over projects to newly formed planning commissions (Scott 1969; Olson 1980; Bauman and Muller 2006). The relegation of planning commissions to advisory roles frustrated the planners' desire for greater power to effect change, to match accomplishment with aspiration more closely.

Despite the parting of ways, the goals of American planners and Social Progressives overlapped in the town-planning movement spawned by Englishman Ebenezer Howard's garden city scheme. At the turn of the century, Howard ([1898] 1902) proposed combining the advantages of the country and city in the development of new towns, or garden cities, distant from the metropolis. Howard's communities would be autonomous with factories and warehouses, collective in land ownership and provision of public infrastructure, and communitarian in the layout of neighborhoods and houses. Public institutions and shops would be centrally located and grouped around a park, while houses would be arranged in neighborhood units both proximate to common open space and accessible to a greenbelt surrounding the town. The first two English towns, Letchworth and Hampstead Garden, were built as manifestations of garden city principles and designed to encourage neighborliness, interdependence, and commitment to community (Hall 1996; Gillette 2010).

More than Howard's social theories, the design of the initial garden city projects appealed to American Progressives, who saw in them a means to reduce overcrowding, improve housing for workers, and inculcate civic spirit. The newly formed Garden City Association of America advocated corporate-financed garden suburbs for workers, essentially model company towns, but it collapsed from lack of support in the financial panic of 1907. The socially progressive Russell Sage Foundation sought to implement garden city ideas in a master-planned suburb in Queens along the Long Island Railroad only nine miles from Manhattan. Many reformers despaired that speculative suburban development reproduced the monotonous, planless, and disordered built environment of the city. The foundation wanted to demonstrate that comprehensive planning and good design could create a garden-like suburban community and still make a profit. It hoped to set an aesthetic standard for future suburban development. Designed by Frederick Law Olmsted Jr. and architect Grosvenor Atterbury and opened in 1911, Forest Hills Gardens eschewed the relentless New York gridiron for a hierarchy of gently curved, tree-lined streets, infrastructure completed at the outset, a sequence of open spaces, a mix of detached and semidetached houses and apartments (figure 20.2), communal space in the interior of several blocks, and shops and a central plaza, all unified by a master plan (Klaus 2002). Russell Sage did not adopt Howard's social experiment in collective ownership and instead sold lots to individuals. In the end, Forest Hills became a middle-class suburb because workers could not afford the property or the commute. In this sense, it emulated earlier planned residential suburbs from New Jersey's Llewelyn Park (1850s) to Chicago's Riverside (1870s) and Baltimore's Roland Park (1890s).

Forest Hills Gardens rekindled interest in the possibilities of employing well-designed workers' communities to dampen labor militancy and increase commitment to civic life. Poorly planned towns and villages for workers dotted the

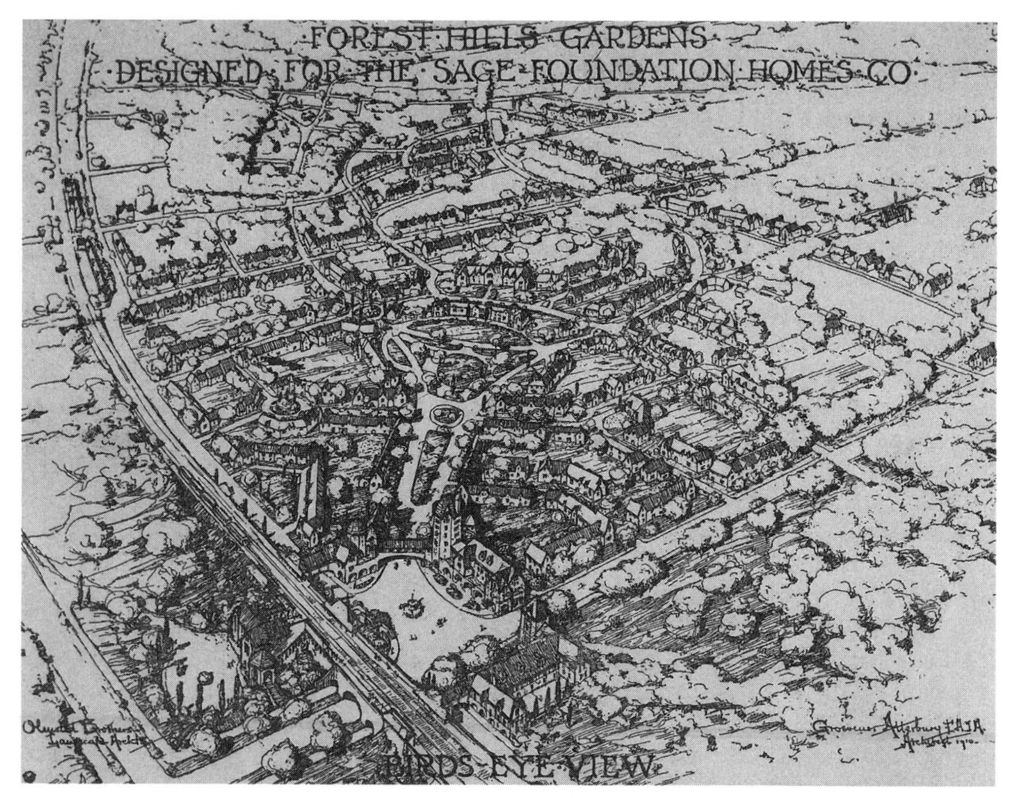

Figure 20.2. Bird's-eye view of Forest Hills Gardens, 1910. Courtesy of the Rockefeller Archive Center.

nineteenth-century landscape, from notorious mining company towns to cheaply built industrial subdivisions near the factory gates. Noteworthy—though not entirely socially successful—exceptions were George Pullman's eponymously named town south of Chicago and Apollo Iron and Steel's Vandergrift near Pittsburgh (Buder 1967; Mosher 2004). After Forest Hills, several planned industrial towns incorporated garden city design elements into master plans, provided infrastructure and public institutions from the outset, fit street plans to site topography, and built modest semidetached and detached Arts and Crafts–style cottages. With the support of industrial sponsors, workers (usually skilled ones) could purchase their homes, a clear indication that Howard's collectivist goals did not conform to America's capitalist economy (Buder 1990; Garner 2000).

The federal government's funding—and at times direct development—of defense workers' housing during World War I expanded the incorporation of garden city elements into planned industrial towns. The housing demand for defense workers was intense by 1917. Even though private enterprise could not meet the need, Congress dithered over governmental participation in the private housing market. Resolving that federally built housing would be sold after the war, Congress authorized work in 1918; twenty-seven communities were completed, mostly after the armistice. At Bridgeport, Connecticut; Wilmington, Delaware; Portsmouth, New Hampshire; and Camden, New Jersey, among other places, two federal agencies employed design professionals to plan, in some instances, entire communities for workers, which intentionally projected a middle-class ideal for living, unlike speculatively built workers' housing (Karolak 2000). The experience convinced some that communities designed along garden city principles held greater potential for social reform than smaller, scattered housing-reform projects (Buder 1990).

Thus, by 1920 planning by engineers, design professionals, planners, and citizen groups had begun to shape cities and their suburbs through large parks and park systems; improved public spaces; water, sewer, and road infrastructure projects; and master-planned garden suburbs and industrial communities. As important, the idea of intervening in the development of cities through planning had entered the civic discourse, and planners had begun to be sought for their technical competence.

PLANNING IN THE NEW AUTOMOBILE AGE

During the 1920s, vigorous growth resumed and exacerbated long-standing urban problems of poverty, overcrowding, substandard workers' housing, pollution, and intense traffic congestion. The following decade of severe economic depression worsened urban conditions and challenged civic leaders to find solutions. Due to the emergence of planning during the prewar years, planners participated in the public conversation about policies and programs to improve cities. At the same time, they joined builders in designing large communities in the suburban periphery. Their advocacy and actions in the decades after World War I not only affected the city around them but also prepared the ground for the significant developments of the long post–World War II era.

America's enthusiastic embrace of the automobile during the Roaring Twenties overwhelmed the nineteenth-century city built around horse-based technologies and pushed suburban development between and beyond electric streetcar lines (Tarr and McShane 2007). Manufacturers learned how to mass-produce and -market automobiles. The public welcomed the liberation from public transit as well as the greater spatial mobility and privacy that automobiles afforded. Political leaders asked planners to help retrofit the built environment for this new technology. Traffic engineers and planners scrambled to propose new and widened streets, tunnels, bridges, and traffic protocols. They faced the unprecedented issue of parking large numbers of automobiles and the intrusion of gasoline stations, repair shops, and new car dealers in residential neighborhoods. Accommodating the automobile consumed enormous amounts of planners' time, diverting them from the comprehensive planning they assigned a higher priority (Bottles 1987; Bauman and Muller 2006; Jakle and Sculle 2008).

The lack of paved roads in the rural periphery of cities posed a different challenge. Both farmers and the motorized public demanded improved roads. While the federal government aided states with the financial challenge, planners predicted that paved highways would spur suburban growth and soon be clogged with through-traffic and commuters. With highway engineers, planners mapped out radial and circumferential highway networks for metropolitan regions. High costs and dysfunctional relationships between city and suburban governments delayed completion of such plans, although New Deal public works programs funded construction of many highway projects (Seely 1987).

Congestion, accidents, and generally unpleasant driving experiences on the new highways led to the innovation of parkways, the forerunners of freeways in design. While in the previous century Olmsted Sr. had planned parkways for horse-drawn carriages to connect parks, the first one designed for automobiles was the Bronx River Parkway. Opened in 1923, it meandered up the Bronx River valley from the Bronx Zoo into Westchester County. The idea was to restore and preserve the valley's natural features, while providing a pleasant, recreational driving experience. Landscape architect Gilmore D. Clarke and his team established a broad right-of-way, or corridor, around the four-lane road, eliminated access from adjacent properties, prohibited commercial traffic, removed unsightly roadside structures, and emphasized the natural landscape. Due to the enthusiastic reception of the parkway, Westchester County decided to build a parkway system, while Robert Moses developed parkways around New York City and on Long Island. Clarke also consulted on the Mount Vernon Memorial Highway along the Potomac River, and Connecticut completed the Merritt Parkway in 1940, which, through the integration of an environmental sensibility with outstanding highway engineering and architecture, seemed the apogee of parkway development (Clarke 1959; Radde 1993; figure 20.3).

However, the aesthetic emphasis of the parkway—the sense of driving through an elongated park—soon encountered the burgeoning demand to accommodate commuters and serve the needs of the modern metropolis. The Depression eliminated funds for what engineers considered landscape embellishments and for broad right-of-way buffers. Even though Moses recognized the need for efficient commuter highways and tried to marry parkway ideals with utilitarian goals, by World War II the shift to aesthetic considerations as afterthoughts rather than integral components of freeway planning was underway. Wartime exigencies hastened the change from parkway principles to the freeway's emphasis on speed, volume, and utility (Brugge and Snow 1959; Leach 1990).

Before and during the war, planners and civic leaders of many cities drew up freeway proposals in order to help counter an anticipated postwar recession by reducing traffic congestion and stimulating urban revitalization. Under intense pressure from federal and state officials and highway industry representatives, Congress approved a national highway plan with the Federal Aid Highway Act of 1944. The act included urban freeways but minimal provision for funding them. It continued existing fund-sharing arrangements between federal and state governments and left construction to state highway agencies. Further, it excluded funding for wider than necessary rights-of-way, which effectively marginalized aesthetic considerations and separated freeway and urban renewal planning. Thus, urban freeway construction after the war would privilege utilitarian attributes over aesthetic features and social consequences (Rose 1979; Ellis 2001).

Figure 20.3. The Merritt Parkway near New Canaan, Connecticut. Courtesy of the Department of Transportation, State of Connecticut.

Many planners viewed the automobile, telephone, and electricity as means to further decentralize both residential and nonresidential activities from the city. By the late nineteenth century, many manufacturers had found the congestion, higher taxes, and verticality of older buildings of the city uneconomical. They sought cheaper sites on the urban periphery, which had access to railroad and/or water transportation. In some cases developers, planners, and railroad companies bought land and prepared it to attract manufacturers into new industrial districts (Muller 2001; Lewis 2008). Simultaneously, mass transit enticed middle-class families to move to subdivisions at increasing distances from the city center, while railroads served growing numbers of upper-class commuters. Motor vehicles significantly expanded the potential sites for industrial and residential development, while electricity facilitated capturing the economies of horizontal mass-production layouts and telephones maintained close contact with downtown administrative and financial services. Without either land-use controls or guiding master plans, the unbridled energy of speculative development threatened to create haphazard and sprawling patterns of land use across local municipalities. This movement to the rapidly expanding periphery formed a complex metropolitan area (McKenzie 1933; Walker and Lewis 2004).

Civic leaders, businessmen, and suburbanites cheered the growth of metropolitan areas and fought political consolidation of municipalities. Enthusiastic support for development on the periphery especially came from real estate interests, contractors, bankers, and developers, who profited from it (Jackson 1985). Reformers and planners also believed decentralization would preserve the viability of downtowns, diminish the overcrowding of tenements, and move workers to better living conditions. Glaring inefficiencies of political fragmentation resulted from inadequately coordinated infrastructure among local municipalities. Despite the success of a few notable exceptions, such as the Boston area's park and sewer commissions, suburban governments rejected consolidation of infrastructure and increasingly fought annexation by the city. Since most states opposed imposing metropolitan-wide governmental structures, planners resorted to cooperating with civic leaders to manage metropolitan development.

There was disagreement over the ideal spatial form of a managed metropolitan area, and that difference in opinion depended on how much land-use control was desirable. A small, vocal group of reformers saw in the new technologies the opportunity to diffuse development in a region in such a way as to preserve downtown's primacy and emphasize ecological and communitarian attributes. Architect Clarence Stein, conservationist Benton MacKaye, cultural critic Lewis Mumford, and several others formed a loose-knit organization in the 1920s that they called the Regional Planning Association of America (RPAA). The RPAA promoted directing development into entire planned communities along the lines of garden cities. Its members wished to preserve land in the larger region for farming, green buffers, parks, and forests. Within the communities, they proposed street, block, and site plans that departed from traditional suburban subdivisions by emphasizing innovations of garden suburbs (Spann 1996).

The RPAA's vision contrasted markedly with that of those who promoted less radical strategies to shape suburban growth. The metropolitan tradition, as historian Robert Fishman describes, accepted the basic form of emerging metropolitan regions but, through coordination and land-use controls, recommended sorting growth more clearly into a downtown center of commerce and entertainment; a middle zone of industry, pleasant workers' neighborhoods, and middle-class subdivisions; and an outer edge reserved for parkland, elite communities, and forest preserves. The multivolume *Regional Plan of New York* (1929) most clearly laid out this vision, in which the centrality of downtown Manhattan would be maintained by land-use zoning controls and an axial commuter transit and highway network. Roughly circumferential freight railroad and highway networks would facilitate the emergence of the industrial zone (Fishman 2000b).

Planners in other metropolitan regions clung to similar conceptions of encouraging decentralization to reduce traffic congestion and lower residential densities, while enhancing downtown as the region's hub. In the 1920s, downtown businesses and real estate interests already feared the growing challenges of outlying commercial centers and debilitating traffic congestion, which would intensify after World War II (Fogelson 2001). Pittsburgh planners, for example, struggled to plan a feasible highway loop around downtown and projected a belt-like highway network through the suburbs that intersected the axial roads coming out from downtown (Bauman and Muller 2006). Like other cities, the

Steel City could only construct pieces of these plans in the face of local governmental fragmentation and then the Depression, which devastated funding capabilities. New Deal highway construction in the periphery and housing policies generally worked against inner-city rehabilitation. By the time extensive infrastructure development resumed after World War II, mass transit in most cities was declining in competition with automobiles and the new visions of high-speed, limited-access freeways. During the war, the federal government's massive support of defense plant construction furthered suburban industrial growth. The idea of managing metropolitan growth, whether in a communitarian manner or in the classic metropolitan tradition, no longer had traction against those profiting from unprecedented suburban expansion (Fishman 2000b).

As the viability of comprehensive planning on a metropolitan or even city scale waned after World War I, housing reformers and their planning allies strove to improve housing and living conditions by controlling land use and implementing garden suburb designs. Excited by the success of planned defense housing communities, reformers such as the RPAA's Stein and Henry Wright searched for financial backing to create garden suburbs and self-contained towns. With the support of the private limited-dividend City Housing Corp., they designed the modest development of Sunnyside Gardens in Queens a few miles from Manhattan, fitting superblocks of town houses into the existing grid in such a manner as to make internal common open space accessible to the houses. As this initial project neared completion in the late 1920s, the reformers undertook the construction of a garden city for thirty thousand people in suburban New Jersey. The financial devastation of the Depression allowed for the construction of only a part of this new town of Radburn. Planning it on a large scale, the designers created a hierarchy of streets to control traffic, separated pedestrians from automobiles with a footpath system using underpasses, laid out superblocks with interior parks and cul-de-sacs, and organized all into neighborhood units (Birch 1983).

As the Depression stymied private ventures in community reform, the New Deal promised a program of working-class greenbelt communities on the edges of cities, which incorporated garden suburb features. In the end, only Greenbelt outside Washington, Greendale on the edge of Milwaukee, and Greenhills near Cincinnati materialized before political opposition to governmental involvement in housing by industry and conservative critics in Congress blocked the rest of the program. The same opposition severely compromised the funding for and design of public housing created by the U.S. Housing Act of 1937 and of wartime defense housing authorized by the Lanham Act (Radford 1996; Szylvian 2000). Although initially embraced by tenants, the resulting uninspired projects signaled housing for the poor and ultimately undermined the Progressives' dreams of publically sponsored housing reform. The housing and community experiments of the interwar years, concluding nearly four decades of reform effort, did not regain momentum after World War II, but they and especially Radburn demonstrated the desirability of many design features, some of which postwar suburban developers adopted in various ways (Birch 1983).

The efforts by reformers to obtain governmental support for nontraditional housing and community plans aroused real estate industry, banking, and political opponents, who intensely disliked governmental involvement in private markets and feared creeping socialism. In the 1920s Secretary of Commerce Herbert Hoover promulgated homeownership as essential to American democracy. He endorsed organizations that advocated a suburban ideal of widespread ownership of single-family houses built on large lots and filled with modern appliances. Business, government, and voluntary organizations such as the Better Homes in America movement cooperated successfully in marketing this vision. Although the Depression ended the suburban boom of the 1920s, New Deal policies to salvage and restart the housing industry through governmental participation in the real estate market embraced the suburban ideal. The Home Owners Loan Corp. blunted the foreclosure crisis by lending money for troubled mortgages, and legislation establishing the Federal Housing Administration provided mortgage insurance to lenders against default and liberalized lending terms. Guidelines for obtaining insurance favored low-density and newer housing areas and discriminated against older, often explicitly African American neighborhoods. This redlining policy reinforced segregation and diminished investment in inner-city areas (Jackson 1985).

Both planners in government and private consulting firms strongly believed in protecting property values and the social composition of residential areas from commercial intrusions and dissimilar peoples deemed undesirable. Narrow nuisance laws prohibiting such ventures as slaughterhouses and later housing codes setting minimum standards had afforded some degree of protection. As a means to control the design and composition of neighborhoods, developers and planners increasingly turned to covenants on property deeds forbidding certain kinds of uses and sales to classes of people identified by national origin, religion, and race. American reformers looked favorably on German land-use regulations that specified uniform zones of use and building standards to lower density, diminish speculation, and require public services. In 1916 New York City passed the first comprehensive zoning law; more cities followed in the 1920s, especially after the Department of Commerce published the Standard Zoning Enabling Act and the Standard City Planning Enabling Act as models for local adoption. When the Supreme Court validated zoning in *Euclid v. Amber* in 1926, ruling that protecting the public's health and safety falls within a municipality's police powers, zoning became a primary tool for shaping urban development, ideally in concert with a comprehensive plan (Burgess 1994).

The scale and design of communities offered another way to affect social composition. The cost of houses could be exclusionary. In the 1920s, with the aid of design professionals and planners, community builders such as J. C. Nichols in Kansas City and Walter Leimert in Los Angeles planned and built suburban developments on large tracts of land, incorporating some physical features advocated by garden suburb planners as well as public spaces, shops, civic institutions, and proximity to employment opportunities. These private developers supported public planners in establishing zoning laws and subdivision regulations that ensured orderly development and protected their investments (Weiss 1987; Hise 1997). Also in the 1920s, Clarence Perry, with the support of the RPAA, proposed building neighborhoods with civic and recreational facilities at the center and protected by keeping commercial services and major roads on the boundaries.

Perry had lived in Forest Hills Gardens and advocated using schools as multifunctional community centers. Like other reformers, he preached that a properly designed neighborhood unit yielded a web of positive social relations that enhanced quality of life and encouraged citizenship (figure 20.4). Although Perry also felt that a homogeneous social composition buttressed the well-designed neighborhood's success, this perspective opened his concept to critics who disliked its inherent exclusionism and argued that the city's heterogeneity and expansive communication technologies were rendering tight-knit neighborhoods increasingly obsolete. Even as planners widely embraced Perry's neighborhood design in the 1930s, concerns over the city's immense scale of blight and slums, the attraction of suburbs, and the congestion plaguing downtowns were turning attention toward sweeping schemes of redevelopment and away from smaller neighborhood visions (Gillette 2010).

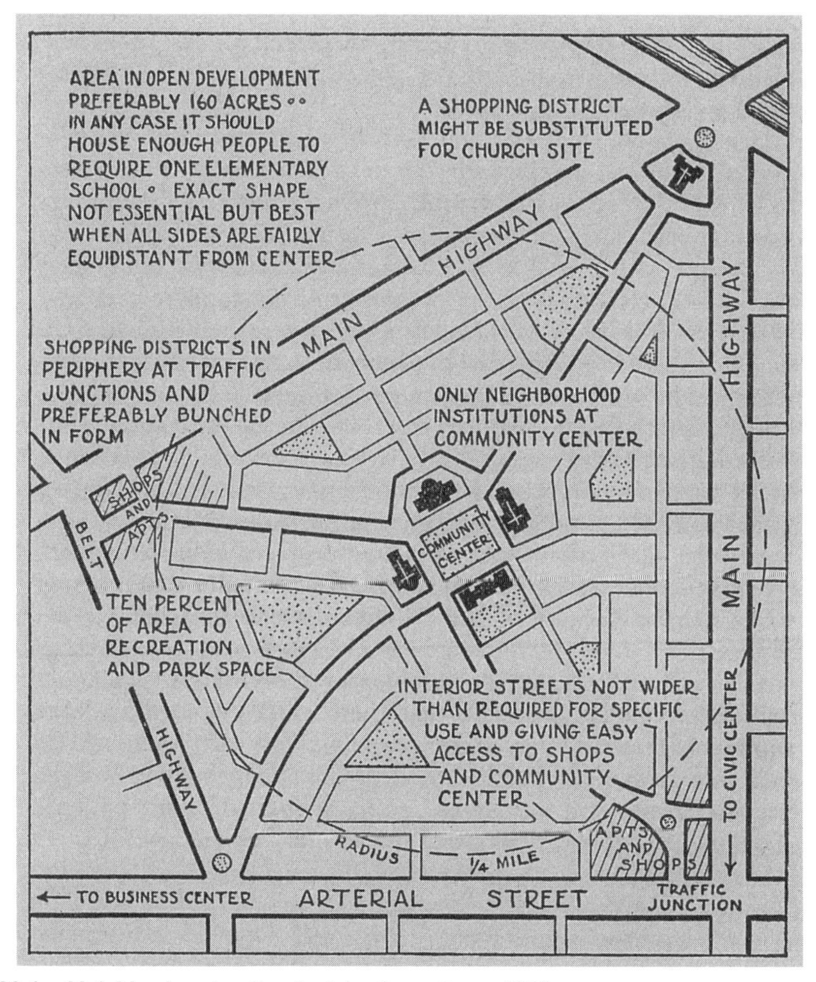

Figure 20.4. Neighborhood-unit principles from Perry, 1929.

While proponents of garden cities and suburbs, neighborhood units, public housing, and planned workers' communities strove to improve America's deplorable housing conditions, other design professionals and private industry leaders embraced a strategy of modernism based on European precedents, new technologies and materials, mass production, and scientific management. Drawing on the earlier work of artists, architects, and writers, a number of architects established the Bauhaus school of design in Germany in the 1920s, where they popularized an emerging international style for buildings that emphasized concrete, glass, and steel materials, angular machinelike lines, and no ornamentation. Their light, functionalist apartment projects suggested the possibilities of mass production. Swiss architect Le Corbusier visualized these functionalist buildings in spacious landscapes of plentiful open grounds surrounding residential towers separated from commercial uses and served by high-speed highways. Meanwhile, modernism attracted American designers and planners, the Harvard School of Design switched to a modernist curriculum in the late 1930s, and leading German proponents such as Walter Gropius and Mies van der Rohe, who fled Hitler, came to America and championed the new style (Relph 1987).

For many, modernism seemed the appropriate vision for redeveloping the inner core of America's tired industrial cities after years of depression. In 1939, at the New York World's Fair, General Motors thrilled visitors with the Futurama exhibit in its Highways and Horizons pavilion, which depicted the orderly modernist city of uncongested multilane highways, pedestrian skyways, skyscrapers clustered at the center, and residential areas zoned free of commercial activities. Everything had its place, and in the eyes of civic leaders, many planners, and designers, the transformation to the modern city required large-scale projects—not block-by-block or even neighborhood-by-neighborhood incremental rehabilitation—that used the public's power of eminent domain to clear slums and assemble land for private business to redevelop. Simultaneously, high-speed freeways would also replace blighted areas and provide efficient access to revitalized cores (Rydell and Schiavo 2010). Several states enacted legislation to facilitate public participation in partnership with private businesses for redevelopment. Finally, after years of wrangling, Congress passed the Housing Act of 1949 that established federal assistance to local agencies for redevelopment projects if they conformed to local entities' comprehensive plans. Thus, by 1950 legislative frameworks for urban freeways and large urban renewal projects were in place. Although housing for residents displaced by slum clearance was to be provided, practice fell short of need (Teaford 1990). Planning for redevelopment and modern living that manifested efficiency had superseded the reformers' earlier focus on physical planning for social ends.

CONCLUSION

Emerging as one strategy among several that Progressive reformers used to address urban problems at the turn of the century, planning struggled to carve out a place among the design professions and bring about a more orderly, inspiring, and humane city. Challenged by rapid growth and society's laissez-faire view of government, fierce defense of private property rights, and aggressive capitalism, planning narrowed its sights from soaring reform rhetoric and social goals to more pragmatic endeavors of well-planned infrastructure, civic and cultural centers, and improved neighborhood and community designs. Planners soon partnered with local governments, civic leaders, and developers rather than battle them over grand schemes. In so doing, they became institutionalized in local government and valued as private consultants. By mid-century their plans and designs were visible in the landscape, their ideas routinely part of the conversation about future development, and their technical expertise and procedures part of the regulatory apparatus. Public spaces, highways and other infrastructure, residential subdivisions, and even entire communities bore the imprint of planners.

Planning's success in becoming a respected profession and part of the public and private development process came at a cost that became evident after mid-century. Social goals of housing and community planning had taken a backseat to physical and aesthetic features more acceptable to private interests. The mantle of technical expertise neglected residents' ideas and desires. Visions and plans for improving the city's commercial and residential environments conveniently ignored the problem of race. When large-scale, modernist projects for renewing the city attracted powerful political and private interests, the habits of top-down, racially blind, and pragmatic physical planning rendered planners and their design colleagues neither intellectually prepared nor politically situated to challenge them. The shift from parkways to freeways reflected this dilemma for planning. The parkways pioneered by landscape architects and embraced by planners gave way to the highway engineers' functionalist freeways, and those planners concerned with the potentially negative impacts on the city's social fabric and built environment did not have the connections to political bodies such as Congress and state governments and to involved industries that the engineers had. The challenge to damaging freeway and urban renewal projects would come most effectively from outside the profession in the 1960s (Kemp 1986; Ellis 1996). Planning had significantly participated in shaping the geography and landscape of American cities, but for some, the impact and influence fell short of the early reformers' lofty goals. Other planners viewed the profession's post–World War II rapid growth optimistically and thrilled at the prospect of remaking the modern city through urban renewal and with freeways.

REFERENCES

Bauman, J. F., and E. K. Muller. 2006. *Before Renaissance: Planning in Pittsburgh, 1889–1943.* Pittsburgh, PA: University of Pittsburgh Press.

Birch, E. L. 1983. Radburn and the American Planning Movement: The Persistence of an Idea. In *Introduction to Planning History in the United States*, edited by D. A. Krueckeberg, 40–57. New Brunswick, NJ: Rutgers University Press.

Bottles, S. L. 1987. *Los Angeles and the Automobile: The Making of the Modern City.* Berkeley: University of California Press.

Boyer, M. C. 1983. *Dreaming the Rational City: The Myth of American City Planning.* Cambridge, MA: MIT Press.

Brugge, W. A., and W. B. Snow. 1959. The Complete Highway. In *The Highway and the Landscape*, edited by W. B. Snow, 3–32. New Brunswick, NJ: Rutgers University Press.
Buckley, G. L., and C. G. Boone. 2011. "To Promote the Material and Moral Welfare of the Community": Neighbourhood Improvement Associations in Baltimore, Maryland, 1900–1945. In *Environmental and Social Justice in the City: Historical Perspectives*, edited by G. Massard-Guilbaud and R. Rodger, 43–65. Cambridge, UK: White Horse Press.
Buckley, G. L., R. F. Bailey, and J. M. Grove. 2006. The Patapsco Forest Reserve: Establishing a "City Park" for Baltimore, 1907–1941. *Historical Geography* 34: 87–108.
Buder, S. 1967. *Pullman: An Experiment in Industrial Order and Community Planning, 1880–1930.* New York: Oxford University Press.
———. 1990. *Visionaries and Planners: The Garden City Movement and the Modern Community.* New York: Oxford University Press.
Burgess, P. 1994. *Planning for the Private Interest: Land Use Controls and Residential Patterns in Columbus, Ohio, 1990–1970.* Columbus: Ohio State University Press.
Clarke, G. D. 1959. The Parkway Idea. In *The Highway and the Landscape*, edited by W. B. Snow, 33–55. New Brunswick, NJ: Rutgers University Press.
Conzen, M. P. 2006. The Non-Pennsylvania Town: Diffusion of Urban Plan Forms in the American West. *Geographical Review* 96, no. 2: 183–211.
Ellis, C. 1996. Professional Conflict over Urban Form: The Case of Urban Freeways, 1930 to 1970. In *Planning the Twentieth-Century American City*, edited by M. C. Sies and C. Silver, 262–79. Baltimore: Johns Hopkins University Press.
———. 2001. Interstate Highways, Regional Planning and the Reshaping of Metropolitan America. *Planning Practice and Research* 16, nos. 3–4: 247–69.
Fishman, R. 2000a. The American Planning Tradition: An Introduction and Interpretation. In *The American Planning Tradition: Culture and Policy*, edited by R. Fishman, 1–29. Washington, D.C.: Woodrow Wilson Center Press.
———. 2000b. The Metropolitan Tradition in American Planning. In *The American Planning Tradition: Culture and Policy*, edited by R. Fishman, 65–85. Washington, D.C.: Woodrow Wilson Center Press.
Fogelson, R. M. 2001. *Downtown: Its Rise and Fall, 1880–1950.* New Haven, CT: Yale University Press.
Garner, J. S. 2000. The Garden City and Planned Industrial Suburbs: Housing and Planning on the Eve of World War I. In *From Tenements to the Taylor Homes: In Search of an Urban Housing Policy in Twentieth-Century America*, edited by J. F. Bauman, R. Biles, and K. M. Szylvian, 43–59. University Park: Pennsylvania State University Press.
Gillette, H. 2010. *Civitas by Design: Building Better Communities, from the Garden City to the New Urbanism.* Philadelphia: University of Pennsylvania Press.
Hall, P. 1996. *Cities of Tomorrow: An Intellectual History of Urban Planning and Design in the Twentieth Century.* Oxford: Blackwell Publishers.
Hise, G. 1997. *Magnetic Los Angeles: Planning the Twentieth-Century Metropolis.* Baltimore: Johns Hopkins University Press.
Howard, E. [1898] 1902. *To-Morrow: A Peaceful Path to Real Reform.* London: Swan Sonnenschein; republished as *Garden Cities of To-Morrow*, edited by F. J. Osborn. Cambridge, MA: MIT Press.
Hutchinson, J. 2000. Shaping Housing and Enhancing Consumption: Hoover's Interwar Housing Policy. In *From Tenements to the Taylor Homes: In Search of an Urban Housing Policy in Twentieth-Century America*, edited by J. F. Bauman, R. Biles, and K. M. Szylvian, 81–101. University Park: Pennsylvania State University Press.
Jackson, K. T. 1985. *Crabgrass Frontier: The Suburbanization of the United States.* New York: Oxford University Press.

Jakle, J. A., and K. A. Sculle. 2008. *Motoring: The Highway Experience in America.* Athens: University of Georgia Press.

Karolak, E. J. 2000. "No Idea of Doing Anything Wonderful": The Labor Crisis Origins of National Housing Policy and the Reconstruction of the Working-Class Community, 1917–1919. In *From Tenements to the Taylor Homes: In Search of an Urban Housing Policy in Twentieth-Century America,* edited by J. F. Bauman, R. Biles, and K. M. Szylvian, 60–80. University Park: Pennsylvania State University Press.

Kemp, L. W. 1986. Aesthetes and Engineers: The Occupational Ideology of Highway Design. *Technology and Culture* 27 (October): 759–97.

Klaus, S. F. 2002. *A Modern Arcadia: Frederick Law Olmsted, Jr. and the Plan for Forest Hills Gardens.* Amherst: University of Massachusetts Press.

Leach, S. A. 1990. Fifty Years of Parkway Construction in and around the Nation's Capital. In *Roadside America: The Automobile in Design and Culture,* edited by J. Jennings, 185–97. Ames: Iowa State University Press.

Lewis, R. 2008. *Chicago Made: Factory Networks in the Industrial Metropolis.* Chicago: University of Chicago Press.

Light, J. S. 2009. *The Nature of Cities: Ecological Visions and the American Urban Professions, 1920–1960.* Baltimore: Johns Hopkins University Press.

Lubove, R. 1962. *The Progressives and the Slums: Tenement House Reform in New York City, 1890–1917.* Pittsburgh, PA: University of Pittsburgh Press.

McKenzie, R. D. 1933. *The Metropolitan Community.* New York: McGraw-Hill.

Mosher, A. E. 2004. *Capital's Utopia: Vandergrift, Pennsylvania, 1855–1916.* Baltimore: Johns Hopkins University Press.

Muller, E. K. 2001. Industrial Suburbs and the Growth of Metropolitan Pittsburgh, 1870–1920. *Journal of Historical Geography* 27, no. 1: 58–73.

Olson, S. H. 1980. *Baltimore: The Building of an American City.* Baltimore: Johns Hopkins University Press.

Perry, Clarence Arthur. *The Neighborhood Unit.* London: Routledge, 1929.

Peterson, J. A. 1983. The City Beautiful Movement: Forgotten Origins and Lost Meanings. In *Introduction to Planning History in the United States,* edited by D. A. Krueckeberg, 40–57. New Brunswick, NJ: Rutgers University Press.

———. 2003. *The Birth of City Planning in the United States, 1840–1917.* Baltimore: Johns Hopkins University Press.

Radde, B. 1993. *The Merritt Parkway.* New Haven, CT: Yale University Press.

Radford, G. 1996. *Modern Housing for America: Policy Struggles in the New Deal Era.* Chicago: University of Chicago Press.

Relph, E. 1987. *The Modern Urban Landscape.* Baltimore: Johns Hopkins University Press.

Robinson, C. M. 1909. Civic Improvement Possibilities of Pittsburgh. *Charities and the Commons* 21, no. 19: 801–26.

Rodgers, D. T. 1998. *Atlantic Crossings: Social Politics in a Progressive Age.* Cambridge, MA: Harvard University Press.

Rose, M. H. 1979. *Interstate: Express Highway Politics, 1941–1956.* Lawrence: Regents Press of Kansas.

Rydell, R. W., and L. B. Schiavo. 2010. *Designing Tomorrow: America's World's Fairs of the 1930s.* New Haven, CT: Yale University Press.

Schuyler, D. 1986. *The New Urban Landscape.* Baltimore: Johns Hopkins University Press.

Scott, M. 1969. *American City Planning since 1890.* Berkeley: University of California Press.

Seely, B. E. 1987. *Building the American Highway System: Engineers as Policy Makers.* Philadelphia: Temple University Press.

Smith, C. 2006. *The Plan of Chicago: Daniel Burnham and the Remaking of the American City.* Chicago: University of Chicago Press.

Spann, E. K. 1996. *Designing Modern America: The Regional Planning Association of America and Its Members.* Columbus: Ohio State University Press.

Szylvian, K. M. 2000. The Federal Housing Program during World War II. In *From Tenements to the Taylor Homes: In Search of an Urban Housing Policy in Twentieth-Century America,* edited by J. F. Bauman, R. Biles, and K. M. Szylvian, 60–80. University Park: Pennsylvania State University Press.

Tarr, J. A., and C. McShane. 2007. *The Horse in the City: Living Machines in the Nineteenth Century.* Baltimore: Johns Hopkins University Press.

Teaford, J. C. 1990. *The Rough Road to Renaissance: Urban Revitalization in America, 1940–1985.* Baltimore: Johns Hopkins University Press.

Tuason, J. 1997. Rus in Urbe: The Spatial Evolution of Urban Parks in the United States, 1850–1920. *Historical Geography* 25: 124–47.

Upton, D. 2008. *Another City: Urban Life and Urban Spaces in the New American Republic.* New Haven, CT: Yale University Press.

U.S. Department of Commerce, Bureau of the Census. 1992. *Population Trends in the 1980s. Current Population Report: Special Studies,* Issue 175. 1992. Washington D.C.: Bureau of the Census.

Vance, J. 1990. *The Continuing City: Urban Morphology in Western Civilization.* Baltimore: Johns Hopkins University Press.

Walker, R., and R. Lewis. 2004. Beyond the Crabgrass Frontier: Industry and the Spread of North American Cities, 1850–1950. In *Manufacturing Suburbs: Building Work and Home on the Metropolitan Fringe,* edited by R. Lewis, 16–31. Philadelphia: Temple University Press.

Weiss, M. A. 1987. *The Rise of the Community Builders: The American Real Estate Industry and Urban Land Planning.* New York: Columbia University Press.

Wilson, W. H. 1989. *The City Beautiful Movement.* Baltimore: Johns Hopkins University Press.

Wright, G. 1981. *Building the Dream: A Social History of Housing in America.* Cambridge, MA: MIT Press.

Young, T. 1996. Social Reform through Parks: The American Civic Association's Program for a Better America. *Journal of Historical Geography* 22, no. 4: 460–72.

———. 2004. *Building San Francisco's Parks: 1850 to 1930.* Baltimore: Johns Hopkins University Press.

21

Planning and American Urbanization since 1950

Jasper Rubin

The appointment of L. Deming Tilton as San Francisco's first planning director in 1942 marked the beginning of a new era. San Francisco was the last major city in the United States to create a professionally staffed planning department, albeit a small one initially. By the end of Deming Tilton's brief tenure in 1946, planning in the United States was entering what is sometimes referred to as its "golden age," a period of about twenty years when the profession's ranks swelled rapidly, and its practitioners were key to channeling hundreds of millions of dollars in federal funding for urban renewal to cash-strapped cities. Indeed, it was a time when visions of the modern city that had been percolating for decades could actually be implemented, or so it was thought. But if these were planning's brightest years, they were also perhaps the darkest.

For most of the first half of the twentieth century, planning was largely a profession of intellectuals and visionaries, of architects, landscape architects, and lawyers. Its numbers were few, and only a handful of universities offered master's degrees in planning.[1] But this was to change radically in the early postwar years. World War II had demonstrated the efficacy of planning—the need to manage resources and logistics and to envision scenarios and strategies. City planners offered a similar approach to addressing an increasingly pressing set of urban problems. There were three main challenges, all related. The first was to increase housing production for returning veterans and a growing population. America was also fast becoming not just an urban nation but a suburban one. This shift underscored the need to plan for resources, services, and infrastructure as metropolitan areas expanded.

Second was the pressure to accommodate the automobile. Populations fleeing to new bedroom communities wanted and needed the freedom of mobility, however illusory, that the car offered. The wheels of commerce also turned more and more frequently on asphalt as opposed to rails, leading places small and large to pursue the construction of highways, ring roads, and expressways, endeavors that had scarred many cities by the 1950s and 1960s. Third, central cities were losing population, with jobs soon to follow, as the white middle class fled the density, congestion, pollution, and disorder associated with the urban core. The suburbs offered the safety of homogeneity (imposed partly through redlining and restrictive covenants) and the relative predictability of Euclidian zoning. The attraction of a self-contained, neopastoral life of barbeques, manicured lawns, built-in GE appliances, and carports was powerful.

Suburbanization drained cities of resources by reducing their tax base and created a growing concentration of people with fewer choices and resources and who were more in need of social and economic support. As industrial work, largely in distribution, warehousing, and manufacturing, left the city for suburban locations, many jobs employing entry-level or less educated and skilled workers vanished, leaving significant segments of central-city populations in distress.[2] Shrinking budgets meant cities found it more difficult to provide critical services. All this in combination with lowered property values, declining family incomes, and federal tax structures that encouraged construction of new commercial buildings as opposed to maintenance of older ones sowed the seeds for what geographers John Jakle and David Wilson (1992) have called "derelict landscapes."

The word "landscape" is an important descriptor. On the one hand, as John Fraser Hart (1995, 23) has said, the landscape is "the things we see." But the built environment does not usually reveal the processes of its creation, at least not just through observation of its material features. That an area of idyllic, rolling countryside dotted with imposing farmhouse-like homes and horse stables has resulted from exclusionary zoning practices and the machinations of the power elite is not necessarily obvious when driving through (Zukin 1991; Duncan and Duncan 2004). Moreover, not everything important about a landscape is physically present in it. If there is no skyscraper to see, how does one know that neighborhood activists were able to prevent its construction? Thus, an urban landscape is not just the physical character of an area but the processes and conditions that created it (Rubin 2011). Indeed, the simple spatial dichotomy of central city and suburb presented here belies a complex mix of economic restructuring, technological change, social and cultural transformation, and public policy adopted and implemented at various scales. And one of the most critical, but not always clearly visible, forces involved in the process of American urbanization has been planning.[3]

COGS IN THE MACHINE

So, a fundamental aspect of urban transformation from the mid-1940s to the end of the 1960s was the dysfunctional pattern of suburban growth and central-city decline. What was planning's role in this dynamic? To some degree the answer depends on where in the urban realm the planner worked—or, more accurately for some places, where the planning function was in operation—in part because there were few trained planners. This distinction also reflects the widely varying capacity (or desire) of towns, cities, and counties to perform planning as a governmental activity. In smaller, less populated jurisdictions, planning was barely a presence and rarely—if ever—carried out by stand-alone departments or agencies.[4] And even in larger or more populous places, much of the work to establish zoning and related building controls was done by consultants or by planning commissions or boards whose members may or may not have had any exposure to, let alone training in, planning or even architecture or law. For instance, the day-to-day operations of hearing grievances, evaluating requests for zoning variances, or approving permits were also often carried out not by a professional staff but by the commission itself or by building, engineering, or other departments, such as they existed.

But in midsize cities and larger urban areas, where suburbanization was most prevalent, planning was more prominent. To organize and manage development spreading outward from core towns and cities into the urban periphery took more effort. The most essential requirement for suburban growth in this regard was that planners create zoning schemes to ensure that land uses considered incompatible did not mix, that property values be maintained, and that sufficient land be identified for basic activities such as housing, commerce, and industry. Planners also had some direct, if modest, impact on development through the subdivision approval process. In some places—California is a prime example—subdivision regulation predated zoning as a means of influencing development. The early impetus for adopting controls was to prevent the most egregious platting practices, for instance, laying out parcels for sale on slopes too steep to build on or without access to a right-of-way. Subdivision regulations evolved into a way for planners to enforce some basic standards such as minimum lot sizes, building setbacks, and street widths. They might also require developers to provide street lighting or install sidewalks or make other improvements as part of the conditions of approval for the subdivision.

Planners also participated in other basic matters of suburban development, such as identifying needs for sufficient infrastructure, especially roads, power, water, and sewage, and community facilities and services such as schools and fire protection. More and more frequently, they accomplished this by applying new quantitative methods to the reams of demographic and economic data becoming available. Sometimes reports formed the basis for a land-use plan, a map-based graphical depiction of what should go where, often accompanied by a minimal amount of text in the form of basic policy statements. Generally, however, planners left details, specific implementation, and financing to experts in the respective areas—engineering departments, school district officials, and administrators, for instance.

Zoning and subdivision regulation are intrusions into the free market of capitalist land development. They are exercises of the police power supported by Supreme Court decisions and legislation. They are an imposition on property rights and can be hotly contested. But in most places, planning and its basic tools helped manage the process of suburban development, to allow it to unfold in a relatively orderly fashion, not to impede it. Growth and expansion were an almost unquestioned good, and planning could be seen more or less as a cog in the machine, an element of the mass production of suburbs. Some would say that in such circumstances, in the suburbs and elsewhere, planning acts as a state apparatus supporting capitalist strategies for the accumulation of wealth. And for this, planning and planners have been deeply criticized, proposals for new towns and greenbelt cities notwithstanding.[5] The analogy of planning to something machinelike and mechanical is fitting, given its engagement with modernist ideas. And it was in the central cities, not the suburbs, that dreams of a modern future city became most tangibly realized, if only in fractured ways.

PLANNING THE MODERN CITY

Whether from among the small but growing cadre of seasoned professionals or from the ranks of newly minted architects and bureaucrats, planners in the 1940s to 1960s were, on the whole, heavily influenced by modernism. Generally speaking, the modernist ideal embraced technology, believed that physical design could improve social welfare—a well-ordered built environment would produce equity and encourage rational behavior—and asserted that form should follow function. The high priests of architecture at the time, such as Le Corbusier, Frank Lloyd Wright, Walter Gropius, and Mies van der Rohe, inspired concepts that found their way into the sketches and diagrams of land-use plans and educational pamphlets intended for the public. For example, in a document summarizing the master plan of San Francisco, planners intoned, "A city is like a machine. It should run smoothly, like a ball bearing, with all its parts fitting and working together in harmony" (San Francisco Planning Department 1946). The Bauhaus and the Congrès International d'Architecture Moderne were powerful forces in both urban theory and professional practice. Such movements and organizations shaped not just buildings but also an approach to urbanism, perhaps most widely evinced in urban renewal.

The Housing Act of 1949, the legislative beginning of urban renewal, marked a new dawn for planners and the planning profession.[6] Among the act's many provisions was the dictate that redevelopment projects using federal grants must conform to a comprehensive plan for the locality. Then, the Housing Act of 1954 went a step further in its well-known Section 701, which detailed the elements such a document should include. For example, it called for plans for land use, circulation, and community and public facilities. Together the acts resulted in an unprecedented demand for planners. Indeed, the need for planners outstripped the capacity of educational institutions to train them, and so cities hired architects, public administrators, and engineers into planning positions to learn on the job. Many new planners found themselves working to produce general plans to support the purposes of urban renewal or were directly involved in designing proposals for redevelopment.

Urban renewal was a top-down approach to addressing urban problems in that the impetus to engage in redevelopment projects came from the federal government, with federal officials working directly with local agencies to implement programs; residents and local organizations were not brought into the process.[7] Its core goals were to provide housing for low-income populations and to support slum clearance and redevelopment of blighted areas (Roth 2003). As an official set of programs initiated by acts of Congress, urban renewal had a life of only about twenty-five years, but its impacts were lasting.

Although urban renewal did result in the construction of housing, it was also used to support a variety of large-scale commercial developments carried out by private developers. Urban renewal projects bulldozed large chunks of scores of cities, displacing hundreds of thousands of people, most of them poor, and destroying the physical and social fabric of many communities (figure 21.1). That neighborhoods could be permanently sundered, that urban renewal was, as writer James Baldwin put it, "negro removal," did not result, at least until the mid-1960s, in any change in course (Baldwin, Standley, and Pratt 1989).

The modernist visions of redevelopment planners and architects often took shape in superblocks and included elements such as monumental office buildings, convention centers, entertainment facilities, parking structures, and upscale apartments. These might be fitted with plazas and concourses and connected to freeway ramps, as in Baltimore's Charles Center, San Francisco's Golden Gateway and Embarcadero Center (figures 21.2 and 21.3), and Pittsburgh's Golden Triangle area (Bauman and Muller 2006; Rubin 2011). But perhaps the most notorious expression of modernist design was found in public housing projects ineptly built as Le Corbusian "towers in a park." Examples include

Figure 21.1. Western addition neighborhood identified for urban renewal, 1954. Known as the Fillmore neighborhood, this would become the redevelopment area toured by James Baldwin. Photo by Eddie Murphy, courtesy of the San Francisco History Center, San Francisco Public Library.

Figure 21.2. The completed Golden Gateway, 1965. Photo courtesy of the San Francisco History Center, San Francisco Public Library.

Pruitt-Igoe in St. Louis and the Cabrini-Green housing project in Chicago; both have been demolished.

Ultimately, however, the impact of urban renewal on the physical development of cities was modest in terms of acres of urban land affected. Some projects never came to fruition, and many others resulted in the demolition of more housing units than were constructed. A pocked and pitted urban landscape was thus not an uncommon result of urban renewal. In Philadelphia's Eastwick neighborhood, large areas were cleared, but most of the planned development never occurred. In Cleveland, architect I. M. Pei fashioned a high modernist scheme for 163 acres of the city's waterfront; only one office building had been constructed by 1964, and the project was subsequently scaled back and reprogrammed. In Manhattan, the Lincoln Center project undertaken in the mid-1960s displaced seven thousand families, many Puerto Rican, and built only forty-four hundred apartments, the vast majority of which were market-rate units (Roth 2003). Despite the hopes and efforts of bureaucrats, mayors, and city boosters, federally supported urban renewal came nowhere close to eradicating blight or rebuilding the nation's slums; nor did it reverse central cities' fortunes. But it did have three other, perhaps more significant impacts.

First, the promise of federal funding through urban renewal was the impetus for most states to pass enabling legislation that led to the creation of redevelopment agencies. Many states did this before the 1949 act, anticipating its eventual

Figure 21.3. Urban renewal in San Francisco: construction of the Golden Gateway near the waterfront, 1963. Photo courtesy of the San Francisco History Center, San Francisco Public Library.

passage. Tasked with engaging in federal urban renewal programs, these agencies received permanent powers, such as eminent domain and the ability to employ tax increment financing, and local jurisdictions across the country have used them frequently, although not without controversy. Even at the height of urban renewal, some cities pursued redevelopment projects without seeking recourse to federal funding. Philadelphia's Penn Center and most of Pittsburgh's Golden Triangle, for example, were completed entirely by local public-private partnerships with some assistance from the state (Teaford 1990). In such cases, the partnership usually consisted of the locality exercising eminent domain to acquire land cheaply and then selling it to developers at below-market rates. Second, as indicated above, urban renewal helped make planning a common and permanent governmental function of urban America—put another way, planning became institutionalized. The third and perhaps most significant impact may have been in the reactions it eventually provoked, which called into question not only the efficacy of urban renewal in general but also specifically the activities and responsibilities of planners.

Apart from issues of urban renewal, planners were busy writing down and sketching the direction their cities should take to reverse incipient decline. Whether or not redevelopment funding was in the offing, cities recognized the benefits of planning in the face of rapid change, and the plans produced through the 1960s and even into the 1970s took on a decidedly modernist sheen. They targeted waterfronts, dilapidated industrial and warehousing districts, and abandoned rail yards in an intensive search for the "highest and best uses" for moribund urban land. Planners were also aware of the need to manage transportation systems, to provide for recreation and open space and for community facilities and services, and to support retail corridors. But almost always their documents were primarily physical plans with only scant verbal policy direction and little on implementation. They suffered from the same problems as suburban plans and urban renewal schemes: they were unitary plans, the articulation of a rational approach to managing the built environment prepared by experts and technocrats.[8] Establishing objective physical standards and a well-laid-out pattern of land uses, the thinking went, could achieve the better city of tomorrow.

This approach to planning did not help revive suffering central cities, especially their downtowns. Instead it stultified many places by discouraging a mix of active uses at different scales. Older cities saw their traditional downtown areas become office districts that lost all life after 5:00 p.m. Streets were all but abandoned to the automobile. Department stores and centers of retail activity were forsaken. However, the more serious flaw in much planning during this period was its general neglect of, or at least failure to redress, the social impacts created by changes to the built environment and by the loss of resources to the suburbs. Many planners treated the urban landscape as a physical thing demanding only physical alteration to create better places. They did not tackle issues of race and class, gender and age, equity and justice either systemically or directly. As I hint in the introduction, this was arguably planning's darkest period.

PLANNING FOR PEOPLE AND PLACES

The 1960s and 1970s were a time of upheaval in American society. Foreign wars, demands for equal rights, urban riots, a distressed environment, an oil crisis, and a recession contributed to a deep sense that things were not moving in the right direction. In universities, reaction to the times generated an engagement with more radical economic and political analysis and critical theory. Social and political activism spread from neighborhood to state capital. Criticism of the modernist approach to urbanism grew more intense and biting. Planning education, while still influenced by the quantitative revolution and its statistics and models, engaged more with leftist thinkers and with sociologists, geographers, and other social scientists sensitive to the human condition. These circumstances produced a new breed of "social planners" who were more grassroots in orientation and pursued new approaches to solving urban problems through advocacy and community-based planning.

Kevin Lynch's (1960) *The Image of the City* was one of the earliest and most important planning studies of the relation between people and their built environment. It focused primarily on what makes cities navigable, memorable, and comfortable—the cohesiveness of their image. Based on field research and interviews, Lynch identified what he deemed the basic physical elements of the city. His nodes, paths, edges, districts, and landmarks helped create a vocabulary that citizens—not just professionals—could employ, and it is still used today. His work helped sensitize people to the physical qualities that help produce a positive urban experience. Although it was decidedly not modernist, nor was it a call to arms. That was the purpose of Jane Jacobs's *The Death and Life of Great American Cities* (1961)—perhaps the most influential book on planning of the twentieth century.

Jacobs's book was a broadside aimed at planning and urban renewal, a keenly observed study in defense of the city. She lambasted modern architects and planners as "irrelevant to the workings of cities," which "have served as sacrificial victims" (1961, 25). Inspired by her neighborhood, Greenwich Village in New York, Jacobs identified the features and characteristics of places that make them urban, that make cities lively, safe, and attractive: active sidewalks, densely populated mixed-use neighborhoods, diversity, small blocks, structures of various ages, and so on. The wrecking ball of redevelopment had eradicated all these qualities. Jacobs was also an activist who took on Robert Moses, the most powerful city builder in the country at the time, helping to prevent the construction of a freeway through lower Manhattan. Jacobs's activism and writing became a clarion call for planners and activists, but it came from outside the profession. In a 1965 article titled "Advocacy and Pluralism in Planning," Paul Davidoff, a lawyer and planner, raised a banner from the inside, exhorting his colleagues to abandon their stance as neutral bureaucrats. Rather, planners should identify values and advocate for them. He attacked the idea of the unitary plan, arguing that planning should be conducted by and with the community, not for it. He warned that land-use planning as practiced could not address issues of equity or of access to places and resources. Thus, planners needed to learn how to evaluate the socioeconomic impact of development and to develop familiarity with the social, cultural, and political practices and institutions that make up urban life.

Identifying what makes a city urban, as well as what planners should do to enlarge the scope of their profession and change its position in society is one thing; realizing the latter two objectives is another. But by the end of the 1960s and the beginning of the 1970s, practitioners indeed began to have an impact on the course of urban development in ways clearly different from modernist approaches. In 1971, under the direction of Allan Jacobs, the San Francisco Planning Department published the watershed Urban Design Element of its general plan. The document was a balanced mix of maps, graphics, goals, and policies that emphasized "the relationship between people and their environment" (1971, 1). It was, and remains, a strong statement about the importance of managing development in ways that reflect human needs and preserving those qualities that establish a strong sense of place. In Savannah, planners made historic preservation a priority and worked with various stakeholders to ensure that its implementation reflected a progressive social agenda. By the 1980s, black residents could use the process of establishing historic districts to preserve neighborhoods important to their communities (Hodder 1996). In Cleveland, planning director Norman Krumholz embarked on a series of projects during the 1970s that helped to establish what has been called "equity planning." He and his staff maintained a professional ethic that emphasized helping the disadvantaged—for instance, by fighting for affordable public transit. They also argued against public subsidization of private investment in downtown development (Krumholz 1982).[9]

Generally speaking, planners in cities across the country were becoming more involved with the communities that they were planning in, for, and with. Planning became a way to help provide more equitable results from development and to ensure better access to things that improve the quality of life in cities for a broader range of citizens. This occurred for two main reasons. First, planners began to make efforts to educate people about the role or potential of planning in shaping cities. Simultaneously, savvy citizens and activist organizations recognized that they could affect the outcome of planning-related decisions through political action. Second, in many cities planning matured into a process; that is, it became a fully systematic function of government, at the nexus of politics, economics, and law. For instance, codes and statutes mandated requirements for public notification of projects of nearly any size, for the analysis of a project's potential impact on the environment, for public hearings, and for processes of appeal. It was expected that planners would hold neighborhood meetings to solicit input on planning proposals and engage more routinely with other agencies as part of any significant planning effort, whether initiated by staff in the form of a new community development plan or as part of vetting major development projects. The main document of the planner—the comprehensive or general plan—evolved into a more robust articulation of what kind of place the city should become, addressing topics such as equitable housing opportunities, access to jobs, neighborhood character, and non-auto-based transportation improvements.[10]

In many cities by the end of the 1970s, planning had transformed into a public process that, often concerned with social and economic issues, had the potential to alter or halt development and to improve the conditions of cities for their less powerful residents. But pursuing these goals clearly meant that planning's role was to intervene in the market. Some came to see planners and planning not as just cogs in the machine but as monkey wrenches in the works. So, at the same time that planning was evolving in its purpose and sharpening its tools, it was becoming an embattled endeavor.

The postindustrial economy, driven by the rise of the service sector in the 1960s and 1970s, required offices, restaurants, shops, and other amenities for the increasing legions of white-collar workers. The chambers of commerce, mayors, building trades, real estate professionals, developers, land-use attorneys, and local media who agitated to accommodate this economic transformation were part of the "city as growth machine" (Logan and Molotch 1987). This coalition of the powerful and the elite pressured planning to allow for uninhibited expansion of downtown upward and outward. For geographer Edward Relph, "Indeed, corporations seem to be engaged with planning departments in a great dialectical process of confrontation, compromise, and construction" (1987, 167). But on the other side, resident-activists, environmentalists, and neighborhood groups believed that unfettered growth would block sunlight, create windy sidewalks, overly burden public transportation, generate pollutants, and increase the cost of housing. This clash enmeshed planning in the daily political life of many cities: planners found themselves in the difficult position of being urged to serve two, if not more, masters.

PLANNING AND THE POSTMODERN CITY

Not long after architect and cultural critic Charles Jencks famously declared that the 1972 demolition of Pruitt-Igoe marked the end of modern architecture, cities began to sprout postmodern buildings characterized by a mix of styles, materials, historical references, and, often, whimsy. The modernist emphasis on form following function gave way to aesthetics, whereby architects might include design flourishes simply for effect. Because such qualities might take the form of "funny hats" on refrigerator box–shaped buildings, or a similar pastiche, critics have lambasted some postmodern architecture as superficial and arbitrary.

In the urban realm, the "postmodern turn" entailed more than just a reaction to modernist structures. Indeed, it encapsulated wider changes, seen especially in an economy based on post-Fordist production, globalized financial markets and producer services, and the rise of a new bourgeoisie bent on conspicuous consumption.[11] The built environment reflected the impact of such societal shifts deeply enough to constitute what some geographers dubbed the "postmodern urban landscape" (Knox 1991; Ley and Mills 1993; Dear and Flusty 1998). This landscape was especially apparent in central cities, which continued to struggle to compete with the suburban dynamo. Cities and their boosters realized they had to do more than focus on office development in their downtowns; they needed to accommodate well-heeled workers and coax along a nascent "back-to-the-city" movement. In what became a common urban strategy, cities capitalized on resources unique to them: a varied building stock, cultural institutions, a diverse population, accessibility, and the not-yet-dead sense that cities were still "where it's at." The leveraging of these qualities in the search for urban competitiveness signaled that many places by the 1980s were stitching together a postmodern urban fabric.

One result was the rapid spread of urban spaces focused on spectacle, entertainment, and flights of fancy. James Rouse, a maverick shopping mall developer, is sometimes credited with creating the quintessentially postmodern festival mall or market, first realized in 1978 in Boston's Faneuil Hall. By the 1980s, he had completed similar projects in New York City, Baltimore, St. Louis, and Miami, among others. Such projects relied not on the typical large anchor tenants like department stores but rather on a diverse collection of small, often local shops, supported by programmed entertainment intended to create a carnival atmosphere. But creating a city of consumption and mass spectacle did not stop with "Rousification," as it became known. Cities also established historic districts anchored in adaptively reused buildings, held street festivals, festooned ethnic neighborhoods with banners and signs, built downtown sports stadiums and entertainment complexes, revitalized their waterfronts, and willingly turned over disused warehouse districts and older inner-city neighborhoods to loft living and gentrification (Zukin 1982; Mills 1988). Cities emphasized variety and diversity that could be consumed, literally and figuratively, in a collection of connected but fragmentary neighborhoods. Indeed, according to some observers, by the end of the 1980s the American urban scene could be summarized by Los Angeles—a fractured metropolis of bits and pieces, including gated communities, defended/militarized spaces, theme parks, ethnoburbs, and command-and-control centers (Soja 1989; Davis 1990; Dear and Flusty 1998).

According to some urbanists, planning in the postmodern mode was reemphasized as a function of government geared to enabling capitalist investment in the urban environment (Beauregard 1989; Harvey 1990). Planners and the planning process became "increasingly geared to the needs and wants of specific producers and consumers rather than to overarching notions of rationality or public good" (Knox 1991, 188), as had been the case in the modernist era. But planning was, and is, more complicated than that. It plays a variable role in urban transformation, and the direction of planning and the extent of its power reflect local urban politics to a significant degree.

During the 1980s and into the 1990s, many cities focused their planning efforts on their downtowns and adjacent areas seen as fit for "revitalization"—a euphemism meant to create distance from the negative associations generated by the phrases "urban renewal" and "urban redevelopment." Such plans were intended to help harness, support, and direct investment in core areas; the importance of jobs and economic development trumped social welfare, as in Cleveland and Denver (Keating and Krumholz 1991). But planning did not bend completely to the purposes of developers and the downtown power elite. To be sure, planners were often in a defensive mode, reduced to tempering a project's "most egregious negative externalities" as opposed to considering "the broader framework of urban development" (Beauregard 1989, 387). Yet planners could squeeze concessions from developers and other capitalists. Where planning enjoyed the support of vocal advocates, in places like Seattle and San Francisco, planners could establish a nexus between projects and their impacts on the city, allowing them to argue successfully that some public benefit be extracted from the sponsor as an offset or mitigation. These could be inclusionary housing policies requiring that a percentage of units in a new development be affordable to those with lower incomes; transportation impact fees, which require contributions to funds that support public infrastructure; provision of open space and public art; design controls; and socially supportive programs such as child-care provision and first-source hiring. On the one hand such modest concessions can be viewed as rearguard actions that do not address systemic problems and only succeeded in some cities. On the other hand they are impressive because never before had modern American society imposed exactions on private development to support the public good as a matter of policy.

Beginning in the 1970s and commonly by the 1980s, planners were also active in neighborhoods outside the core. There, they worked with residents and businesses to establish historic districts, support or revive neighborhood commercial areas, improve streets, and work with communities to develop their visions for the future. Beyond the central cities, a new approach to suburban development was taking root. A small group of architects and planners, a number of them in private practice, including Peter Calthorp, Andres Duany, and Elizabeth Plater-Zyberk, founded the Congress for New Urbanism in 1993. The proponents of new urbanism espouse an approach that harkens back to traditional towns in scale and mix of uses but also embraces more urban qualities. These include increased density, a variety of housing types and affordability, and arrangement of land uses that support walkable neighborhoods and transit use. New "towns," such as Kentlands in suburban Maryland and Seaside in Florida, exhibit design features that emphasize the mix of old and new: neocolonial town houses with front stoops, single-family homes with gabled roofs, garages on alleyways with in-law units above, brick sidewalks, central squares, and access to transit. Although the progressive and wry Howard Kunstler has been a vocal supporter, new urbanist projects have also been criticized as being simply dressed-up subdivisions. Perhaps new urbanists can be forgiven their pretensions—Peter Katz (1994) subtitled his book *Toward an Architecture of Community*—because at least their work has elevated the discourse on what makes places livable and accessible to a range of incomes.

PLANNING IN THE AGE OF NEOLIBERAL URBANISM

Growth in the suburbs was not the only reason that many central cities adopted the competitive strategies that contributed to the evolution of postmodern urban landscapes. Federal funding for urban revitalization had all but dried up by the mid-1980s. This meant that cities had to find other sources of stimuli to foster growth and change, which entailed entering into competition not just with suburbs but with other cities for job-and tax-generating activities. Many cities adopted what David Harvey has referred to as an "entrepreneurial" stance. Urban governments began to focus on investment and development that helps to bring about a reimagined city rather than working directly to improve conditions for a city's inhabitants (Harvey 1989). This is one result of the neoliberal ideology at work. Broadly speaking, neoliberalism is characterized by government devolution, rollbacks in welfare state policies, free market fundamentalism, and the privatization of public resources (Rubin 2010). In the urban context, neoliberal policies helped to create the climate for producing many of the features of the postmodern city. By the 1990s, neoliberalism was affecting the character of many places, particularly central urban areas. It remains a powerful influence as of this writing, especially given the 2008 recession's impact on state and local finances.

Cities have responded to neoliberal pressures by providing tax breaks to lure high-tech industries, pursuing public-private partnerships to attract sports teams, cultural institutions, and mixed-use development, and marketing themselves to the "creative class" with sleek condominium towers, good urban design, and "consumable cultural diversity" (Rubin 2010). The city is offered up as an elite job creator and ultimate playground for the well-heeled. There is some feeling that a rising tide, perhaps, will lift all boats: the more taxes a city can generate by attracting successful firms and wealthy residents, the more it can fund social programs for the needy and disenfranchised. But in reality many of the proverbial boats are washed out to sea as gentrification becomes methodical and widespread, affecting even middle-class redoubts and commercial and industrial areas. It is a form of displacement quite different from the more "organic" process that transforms neighborhoods incrementally through sweat equity. Hackworth (2007) has described this kind of super-gentrification as the "knife's edge" of neoliberal urbanism. Furthermore, in the process much that is public about cities, their civic character, is eroded. Public land is handed over to developers, government functions are performed by private contractors, parks and open spaces suffer as budgets for maintenance shrink, and surveillance is increased as the poor and the "other" are criminalized.

Planners are engaged, and often complicit, in this process because, in some ways, recent urban transformations reflect basic planning goals. Many of these goals are laudable. It is clearly important to encourage the kind of density that supports public transportation and more sustainable places. One way to do this is to build new tower-based residential neighborhoods in and near traditional downtown areas and financial districts, as can be seen in big cities like New York, Baltimore, Washington, D.C., Chicago, Seattle, and San Francisco. Improvements to the public realm that create active, pedestrian-friendly environments through sidewalk widening, traffic calming, and installation of pocket parks, street-level retail, and buildings with porous first stories are almost unarguably beneficial. Maintaining neighborhood character and preserving important historic buildings and cultural sites can be a civic good. But all of these things also make cities more attractive, and this is the crux of a crisis in contemporary planning. The only way to preserve a less wealthy person's "right to stay put" or "right to the city" is to ensure that affordable housing is available and that places for industries that generate blue-collar employment—well-paying jobs for people with less education and few skills—are preserved (Hartman 1984; Lefebvre). And to foster cities as democratic places requires that public spaces and places be protected and expanded. As mentioned above, some cities do have policies that address these issues—but none are sufficient to attain what Susan Fainstein and others call "spatial justice" (Fainstein 2009). Bringing these things about requires that planners fight for them, but they should not struggle alone.

So, while planning has come a long way from its modernist origins, it remains an unfulfilled promise. The neo-utopian ideas of the modernist project proved insensitive and misguided. The push for advocacy and equity, while still a core principle for many planners and the planning profession by and large, has met with the reality of urban politics and the power of the growth machine. In more recent decades, during which effective advocacy has strengthened planners and the planning process, some advances have been made with respect to physical form and social life. Since the 1990s, although urban design and sustainability have been central to the urban agenda, neoliberal forces have distracted planning from a sustained engagement with issues of equity and justice. And suburbs continue to expand willy-nilly.

All told, the impact of planning on the process of contemporary urbanization, on the physical form of cities and their social, cultural, and political lives, is not clear or consistent. Nevertheless, the success or failure of planning is intrinsically related to the life and death of cities. And yet, geographers, particularly historical geographers, have not paid much attention to urban planning. The urban landscape is a deeply spatial concept and is about processes as much as physical, material things. Process is fundamentally something that occurs over time. It would seem then that historical geographers would do well to turn their attention to planning. There is much work to do before we have a thorough understanding of its role in shaping cities and, more broadly, in the evolving urban condition of North America. And unless we understand it, bring evidence to bear that supports that understanding, and spend time to inform others about what is at stake, making planning work for us in the way that it could and should will be difficult.

NOTES

1. In 1935, according to Violich (2001), nineteen universities offered master's degrees in planning, graduating about two hundred students. In 1949, the American Institute of Planners had about six hundred members, although not all practicing planners were part of that or other related organizations (Scott 1969).

2. This shift in location of industry resulted from a variety of factors, including changes in production technology (for instance, from vertically integrated manufacturing to horizontal assembly-line methods requiring large floor plates), the prominence of trucking, tax incentives, and a somewhat less powerful union presence.

3. Of course many cities were engaged in planning, even if nascent in form, from the turn of the century, if not earlier. See chapter 20 by Edward Muller in this book and, for instance, Bauman and Muller (2006), who date planning in Pittsburgh to 1889.

4. However, the 1954 Housing Act provided some direct grants to support planning in smaller jurisdictions.

5. See, for instance, Jacobs (1961). In fact, planning's complicity in suburbanization (and urban renewal, discussed later in the chapter) has haunted the field for decades, making it the subject of a sustained criticism, especially from the left. On histories of suburbanization and forces at work in their creation, see Jackson (1985) and Hayden (2004).

6. For a full account of the origins and impacts of the various urban renewal–related acts, including the Housing Act of 1954 and the Housing and Urban Development Act of 1965, see Mel Scott (1969).

7. This differed from the Community Development Block Grant (CDBG) program created by the 1974 act. CDBG was considered a bottom-up approach to direct aid to cities because, for instance, it required input from community members and organizations and employed formulas to control more closely how funding was spent.

8. Paul Davidoff (1965) used the term "unitary" to describe plans produced from a single source, typically a planning department, that did not represent or take into account multiple perspectives.

9. Krumholz points out that the development in question, Tower City, was not built for reasons other than their opposition—but planners were able to make clear in a public way critical issues that may otherwise have been swept under the rug.

10. To some degree the new emphasis on community-based planning was a result of new federal urban programs, especially Model Cities and the Community Development Block Grants (CDBG) program, that encouraged grassroots, neighborhood-based improvement. Acts funding mass transit were also passed in 1964 and 1970.

11. In essence post-Fordism literally refers to methods of production that contrast with the production-line work made common by Henry Ford. It is characterized by, among other things, specialization, flexibility, small batch, and "just-in-time" production and more varied cross-firm relationships.

REFERENCES

Baldwin, James, F. L. Standley, and L. H. Pratt. 1989. *Conversations with James Baldwin.* Jackson: University of Mississippi Press.

Bauman, J. F., and E. K. Muller. 2006. *Before Renaissance: Planning in Pittsburgh, 1889–1943.* Pittsburgh, PA: University of Pittsburgh Press.

Beauregard, R. A. 1989. Between Modernity and Postmodernity: The Ambiguous Position of U.S. Planning. *Environment and Planning D* 7: 381–95.

Davidoff, P. 1965. Advocacy and Pluralism in Planning. *Journal of the American Institute of Planners* 31, no. 4: 544–55.

Davis, Mike. 1990. *City of Quartz: Excavating the Future in Los Angeles.* New York: Vintage Books.

Dear, Michael, and Steven Flusty. 1998. Postmodern Urbanism. *Annals of the Association of American Geographers* 88, no. 1: 50–72.

Duncan, J., and N. Duncan. 2004. *Landscapes of Privilege.* New York: Routledge.

Fainstein, S. 2009. Spatial Justice and Planning. *Justice Spatiale/Spatial Justice* 1: http://www.jssj.org/wp-content/uploads/2012/12/JSSJ1-5en1.pdf.

Hackworth, J. 2007. *The Neoliberal City: Governance, Ideology, and Development in American Urbanism.* Ithaca, NY: Cornell University Press.

Hart, J. F. 1995. Reading the Landscape. In *Landscape in America,* edited by G. F. Thompson. Austin: University of Texas Press.

Hartman, C. 1984. The Right to Stay Put. In *Land Reform, American Style,* edited by C. Geisler and F. Popper, 302–18. Totowa, NJ: Rowman & Allanheld.

Harvey, David. 1989. From Managerialism to Entrepreneurialism: The Transformation in Urban Governance in Late Capitalism. *Geografiska Annaler* 71, no. 1: 3–17.

———. 1990. *The Condition of Postmodernity.* Cambridge, MA: Blackwell Publishing.

Hayden. D. 2004. *Building Suburbia: Green Fields and Urban Growth, 1820–2000.* New York: Vintage Books.

Hodder, R. 1996. Savannah's Changing Past: Historic Preservation Planning and the Social Construction of a Historic Landscape, 1955 to 1985. In *Planning the Twentieth-Century American City,* edited by M. Sies and C. Silver, 361–82. Baltimore: The Johns Hopkins University Press.

Jackson, K. T. 1985. *Crabgrass Frontier: The Suburbanization of the United States.* New York: Oxford University Press.

Jacobs, Jane. 1961. *The Death and Life of Great American Cities.* New York: Vintage Books.

Jakle, John A., and David Wilson. 1992. *Derelict Landscapes.* Savage, MD: Rowman & Littlefield.

Katz, P. 1994. *The New Urbanism: Toward an Architecture of Community.* New York: McGraw-Hill.

Keating, D., and N. Krumholz. 1991. Downtown Plans of the 1980s: The Case for More Equity in the 1990s. *Journal of the American Planning Association* 57, no. 2: 136–52.

Knox, Paul L. 1991. The Restless Urban Landscape: Economic and Sociocultural Change and the Transformation of Metropolitan Washington, D.C. *Annals of the Association of American Geographers* 81, no. 2: 181–209.

Krumholz, N. 1982. A Retrospective View of Equity Planning. *Journal of the American Planning Association* 52, no. 2: 163–74.
LeFebvre, Henri. 1996. *Writings on Cities.* Translated by E. Kofman and E. Lebas. Oxford: Blackwell Publishing.
Ley, David, and Caroline Mills. 1993. Can There Be a Postmodernism of Resistance in the Urban Landscape? In *The Restless Urban Landscape*, edited by P. Knox, 256–78. Englewood Cliffs, NJ: Prentice Hall.
Logan, J. R., and H. L. Molotch. 1987. *Urban Fortunes: The Political Economy of Place.* Berkeley: University of California Press.
Lynch, K. 1960. *The Image of the City.* Cambridge, MA: MIT Press.
Mills, C. 1988. Life on the Upslope: The Postmodern Landscape of Gentrification. *Environment and Planning D* 6: 169–89.
Relph, Edward. 1987. *The Modern Urban Landscape*. London: Croom Helm.
Roth, L. 2003. *American Architecture: A History.* Boulder, CO: Westview Press.
Rubin, J. 2010. San Francisco's Waterfront in the Age of Neoliberal Urbanism. In *Transforming Urban Waterfronts: Fixity and Flow,* edited by G. Desfor et al., 143–65. New York: Routledge.
———. 2011. *A Negotiated Landscape: The Transformation of San Francisco's Waterfront Since 1950.* Chicago: Center for American Places, in association with the University of Chicago Press.
San Francisco Planning Department. 1946. *The Master Plan of the City and County of San Francisco: A Brief Summary of the Master Plan as Adopted by the City Planning Commission on December 20, 1945, with an Outline of the Task Ahead.* San Francisco: San Francisco Planning Department.
———. 1971. *The Urban Design Plan*. San Francisco: San Francisco Planning Department.
Scott, M. 1969. *American City Planning since 1890*. Berkeley: University of California Press.
Soja, Edward. 1989. *Postmodern Geographies*. London: Verso.
Teaford, J. C. 1990. *The Rough Road to Renaissance: Urban Revitalization in America, 1940–1985.* Baltimore: Johns Hopkins University Press.
Violich, F. 2001. "Intellectual Evolution in the Field of City Planning: A Personal Perspective toward Holistic Planning Education, 1937–2010." Working Paper 2001–07, Institute of Urban and Regional Development, University of California, Berkeley.
Zukin, Sharon. 1982. *Loft Living: Culture and Capital in Urban Change.* New Brunswick, NJ: Rutgers University Press.
———. 1991. *Landscapes of Power*. Berkeley: University of California Press.

22

Justice and Equity in the City

Christopher G. Boone

Cities have always been centers for extremes of wealth and poverty, health and disease, safety and crime, tranquility and chaos, power and vulnerability, privilege and disadvantage. In New York City in the mid-nineteenth century, multiple families sometimes slept and worked in a single room, many windowless, in Lower East Side tenements, whereas the Astor family occupied stately mansions on Fifth Avenue just a few miles away. French Canadian families in Montreal in 1900 endured an infant mortality rate significantly higher than their Irish Catholic or Anglo Protestant neighbors (Thornton and Olson 2001). Today, life expectancy for African American males in Baltimore is just sixty-five years compared to seventy-two for white males, and life expectancy by neighborhood within the city ranges from sixty-three to eighty-three years.

When such disparities are brought to light, governments, civic bodies, and individuals may or may not choose to address or even acknowledge them as concerns or problems. Fear can inspire motivation to change, such as following the Civil War Draft Riots in New York City in the 1860s, which were linked to the extremely poor living conditions for the majority of the city's residents (Plunz 1990). Moderate reform to tenement housing resulted from the mob riot along with a detailed study of deplorable living conditions by the Council of Hygiene and Public Health. Jacob Riis's (1890) photographs of tenement dwelling twenty years later, however, showed that the reforms had resulted in only marginal improvements (figure 22.1). Many cities in the nineteenth century adopted reforms to improve sanitation because of fear of disease, including its effects on commerce (Melosi 2000). In the late nineteenth century, some ships stopped calling in Baltimore's harbor, especially during summer months, because of its reputation as unsanitary and disease ridden. Fear of losing commerce because of the prevalence of illnesses like yellow fever and typhoid spurred the city council to finally begin building sanitary sewers in 1905 (Boone 2003).

A sense of justice can also motivate efforts to do something about disparities. When Jacob Riis illustrated in stark images and text how the other half lived in

Figure 22.1. Bohemian cigar workers at home in their tenement, ca. 1890. Photo by Jacob Riis. Reproduced with permission of the Museum of the City of New York.

New York, he inspired a series of reforms driven partly by the need to right some serious wrongs. For the immigrants, impoverished, and ethnic and racial minorities occupying the deplorable tenements, he reckoned that change would come either by the knife (violent uprising) or by justice. "I know of but one bridge that will carry us over safe," Riis argues in the final pages of his book, "a bridge founded upon justice and built of human hearts" (1890, 296).

This chapter focuses on historical-geographical research in cities that relates to questions of justice and equity. It begins with a brief discussion of the meanings of those terms and then examines ways that these concepts form the basis for analyses and interpretations of social and spatial disparities in the city, including ideas of the right to the city, gender equity, environmental justice, and sustainability.

JUSTICE AND EQUITY

Justice refers to the fair treatment of people based on moral principles of rightness. It may be achieved through impartial evaluation of information and arguments, such as in a court of law, but it ultimately rests on societal values regarding what is right and wrong. Justice is often associated with formal legal systems. One can seek fair outcomes or treatment through the courts, especially when existing rules or regulations do not adequately address a complaint or when arbitrary or unclear situations require judgment. The justice system can also hear appeals or challenge existing rules and regulations if one finds them unfair. In addition to allocating rewards, the justice system can punish unlawful behavior and use judgment to determine the severity of the punishment.

However, justice is often defined outside formal systems of law, especially when legal systems are unwilling or unable to deal with unfair and wrong treatment of people. The environmental justice movement, discussed later in the chapter, arose in part out of activists' frustration that the courts were not adequately addressing the problem of uneven environmental burdens experienced by racial and ethnic minorities. Instead, many environmental justice activists found it more effective to appeal to common notions of justice, sometimes called social justice, through such mechanisms as protests to achieve just outcomes.

A good deal of geographical writing draws on the concept of distributive justice, the idea that the distribution of goods should be just and fair. At a basic level, just distribution can be defined as equal distribution of benefits and burdens among individuals or groups. For instance, we could say that the idea that all people should enjoy the same air quality regardless of where they live in a city calls for a just distribution of an environmental good. Although the idea of equality in distribution is often laudable, in some cases unequal distribution may be more just than equal outcomes. For example, a just distribution of public transportation may justifiably provide more services to people who do not own cars or are physically disabled. This example illustrates the concept of equity, which takes into account the needs, choices, and merits of individuals or groups in defining just distribution. Subsidizing public transportation for seniors and children is a widespread example of equitable distribution of a social good (Hanson and Giuliano 2004).

Many geographers draw on the writings of John Rawls (1971) for theories of distributive justice, or the socially just distribution of goods in society. Rawls argued that inequality in the distribution of goods is just only if the unequal distribution is to the greatest benefit of the least advantaged members of society. His ideas of justice as fairness also included the notions that people should have equality of opportunity based on comparable merits and that all individuals have equal rights to basic liberties. Fairness should thus be judged in terms of not only outcomes but also opportunities or processes, differentiated in the geographical literature as outcome equity and process equity.

John Rawls was not without his critics. Influential scholar Amartya Sen questions Rawls's liberal notions of justice, especially his emphasis on the right to basic liberties. For Sen, an economist who has written extensively on the structural roots of poverty and famine, the basic liberty of an equal right to vote is meaningless if people do not have the capacity to vote due to any of a number of reasons, from having no means to get to a polling station to lacking the basic education necessary to understand the voting process. For Sen and others, liberty carries little real meaning for justice if people are simply trying to survive. A second critique questions Rawls's belief that just institutions will lead to just outcomes. Sen (2009) does not believe institutions are sufficient in themselves to achieve social justice or that we should measure actions on their ability to achieve good social outcomes. His work has been influential in the geographical literature, especially in development studies (Corbridge 2002; Barnett 2011).

For the political theorist Iris Marion Young, Rawls's concept of distributive justice does not go far enough. She does not discount the importance of distribution in a just society but argues it is limiting because it tends to focus on the just allocation of material resources (e.g., income) and to ignore the social structures (e.g., gender relations, power and privilege) that determine the distributive patterns in the first place (Young 1990). Geographers who draw on her work emphasize the importance of understanding social structure and processes in examining questions of justice, especially with regard to decision making and capacity for action.

In *Social Justice and the City* (1973), David Harvey, perhaps the most influential scholar on justice issues in geography, explores the idea of distributive justice from a spatial perspective, noting that although justice is ultimately about the welfare of an individual, just distribution can also be evaluated in terms of groups, regions, and territories. Two key points regarding justice are that (1) just distribution should be justly achieved, and (2) the three primary criteria, in order, for evaluating just distribution should be need, contribution to the common good, and merit. Like Sen and Young, Harvey argues that justice should not rest on universal ideas of morality but should rather be viewed as "contingent upon the social processes operating in society as a whole" (1973, 15). For Harvey, a Marxist geographer, the key social process that inhibits just distribution is the capitalist market structure.

SOCIAL AND SPATIAL DISPARITIES

A fundamental concern in the geographical literature is the spatial expression of disparities between groups or individuals. By mapping the distribution of household income or incidence of disease, scholars are usually able to show that these characteristics are spatially clustered, meaning that wealthy families tend to live near one another, and some neighborhoods are more likely than others to have high rates of certain diseases. The 1889 Booth maps of London are an early and influential example of spatially defining the characteristics of a city. Following careful fieldwork conducted by walking the streets and alleys of London, Charles Booth and his team produced detailed maps that color-coded each block of the city according to his social classification—from "lowest class, viscous semi-criminal" to "upper-middle and upper classes; wealthy" (Booth 1889).

A contemporary of Booth, Herbert Ames, published a similar study on Montreal in 1897 focused on conditions in the "City below the Hill," the low-lying area close to the St. Lawrence River where most of the poor and manual laborers lived, in contrast to the wealthy who lived in the upper city. By city block, Ames provides data on family income, housing characteristics, occupation, nationality, religion, death rates, and other information. Ames conducted the study in part due to his observation that "most of the residents of the upper city know little and at times seem to care less regarding their fellow men in the city below"

(1897, 4), and he believed that ignoring conditions would be dangerous to the whole.

People like Booth, Ames, and Riis witnessed the profound changes in cities and urban life that accompanied industrializing economies. In 1800, North America was a continent of farmers, fishers, and hunters. At that time, only 6 percent of people in the United States lived in cities, but by 1900 nearly 40 percent of Americans (30 million) and 37 percent of Canadians (2 million) were urban dwellers. Over the course of the nineteenth century, New York City grew from a small city of 60,000 to a metropolis of 3.5 million people. For cities such as New York or Montreal, the growth in nonfarm and primary-resource jobs provided new opportunities that drew people from the countryside (and immigrants from around the world) to the burgeoning urban centers.

In this era of rapid urbanization, institutions to plan urban development or protect the health and well-being of residents were relatively weak, resulting in the gross inequities that Riis and others witnessed. By the latter part of the nineteenth century, cities had embraced the idea of sanitary reform, such as clean water, refuse collection, and modern sewers, as a means of improving health (Melosi 2000; Bauman and Muller 2006), but dealing with other city ills often fell to charities, which did not have the capacity to handle the magnitude of civic problems like affordable and decent housing, unemployment, children's education, food safety, and labor protections (Rosen 2003).

Ward politics of the nineteenth century contributed to stymying efforts to build institutions for the modern city that could deal comprehensively with social justice issues. While ward bosses, such as Boss Tweed of Tammany Hall in New York City, provided benefits to poor and immigrant residents in their home wards in return for votes, the system was rife with corruption. In response, the so-called Progressives began calling in the 1890s for sweeping changes in the governance and functioning of cities, with an emphasis on modern, efficient, and fair practices. The building of playgrounds in poorer parts of cities rather than grand bucolic landscape parks in well-to-do neighborhoods was one expression of Progressive ideals (Tuason 1997; Young 1995). However, although charitable ideas of justice gave rise to the playground movement, some saw them as a form of social engineering for moral improvement, a way to soothe the seething masses to avoid class conflict and violence (Kirschner 1975; Young 1996; Pipkin 2005).

The Progressives counted among their ranks Jane Addams, who labored to lead by example, and the settlement house she established in Chicago in 1889, Hull House, became the test bed for innovations in child and adult education, a center for the scientific study (including statistical mapping) of social conditions such as disease and overcrowding, and the intellectual source for child labor laws, improved sanitation laws, and stricter building codes, among other legislation (Bridge 2008). Nevertheless, disparities persisted in Chicago and other North American cities along lines of race, ethnicity, class, religion, and gender. The segregation of groups (and concomitant land use) made possible the famous concentric zone maps of Chicago authored by University of Chicago sociologists Robert Park and Ernest Burgess in the 1920s. Their theory of urban ecology, informed by ecological processes of invasion and succession, suggested that the

ON MENTORS AND ACTIVISM
Karen M. Morin

Perhaps like most people, I became interested in historical geography through inspirational mentors and advisors—in my case, professors at the University of Nebraska, Lincoln, in the 1990s: Jeanne Kay Guelke and David Wishart (geography) and Frances W. Kaye (English and Center for Great Plains Studies). Jeanne, in particular, was a pioneering intellect in feminist historical geography. In the 1980s and 1990s, she offered some of the most incisive critiques of the masculinism of American historical geography. Thanks to scholars like her, we can now take for granted altered notions about which places, scales, processes, and especially people count in and for historical geography. Much of my earlier contribution to historical geography focused on the nexus between gender relations and travel writing as colonialist discourse, especially as these relate to American expansionism in the nineteenth century (see my *Frontiers of Femininity: A New Historical Geography of the Nineteenth-Century American West*, 2008).

Subsequently my research has spanned several historical geography tracks, all of them foundationally linked to the social justice vision of feminism and critical social theory. These include the history of geographical thought and literacy in North America, British and American postcolonialisms, the historical geography of religion, and, most recently, critical prison studies.

Whom do we include in our histories of geography and why? My book *Civic Discipline: Geography in America, 1860–1890* (2011) attempts a response in offering an intellectual history of post–Civil War American geography. In it, I examine the role of geography in American commercial empire building in the nineteenth century via the influential New York–based American Geographical Society and the many ties its members—mostly wealthy businessmen—had to American railroad development, colonialism in Africa and the Arctic, and canal building in Central America. The basic argument—that the roots of American geography are specifically commercial in nature—not only raises questions about why and how geographical knowledge was produced as such in the past but also offers a way to consider the sometimes questionable purposes for which geographical knowledge is produced today, such as for American commercial, political, or militaristic advantage overseas.

In this and other ways, my work has begun to feel more scholarly-activist in nature. I specifically became interested in critical prison studies as an activist—as a volunteer and now decadelong executive board member of a local nonprofit prisoner rights group called the Lewisburg Prison Project. I am presently at work on a number of projects related to historical geographies of mass incarceration in the United States and the "spatial violence" of late-modern American prisons and jails. My focus on the conditions of confinement stems from the position that although we need to work hard to challenge the basic pathology of mass-incarceration trends, we also need to advocate for incarcerated inmates' civil and human rights.

segregation of urban form by land-use and social class followed a predictable pattern with a simple ecological and economic logic (Park, Burgess, and McKenzie 1925). It ignored, however, the forces of discrimination, racism, unfair decision making, and other key social processes that help to shape the city. In other words, it did not acknowledge that unjust practices underpinned the patterns of urban growth in Chicago and elsewhere.

One legal scholar called the forced segregation of blacks and whites in early-twentieth-century Baltimore "apartheid" (Power 1983). In 1910, Baltimore was the first city in the nation to pass a legal ordinance restricting where blacks and whites could live. The ordinance was precipitated by violence against a black lawyer and his family when they moved across a de facto color line into a residence they had purchased. Homeowners groups, called neighborhood improvement associations, promoted restrictions based on race and religion and helped to draft the initial legislation (Buckley and Boone 2011). The Baltimore ordinance inspired similar segregation legislation in Louisville, Kentucky, which the Supreme Court eventually ruled unlawful in 1917. Even after the ruling, segregation persisted because deed restrictions (stipulating whom a property owner could sell to) remained in effect (Schein 2006). On the West Coast, Chinese in San Francisco were hemmed into distinct neighborhoods and blamed for the spread of diseases like smallpox and syphilis (Craddock 2000). Similar claims were made against the Chinese in Vancouver, British Columbia, where officials described Chinatown as an "ulcer" on the larger Anglo community (Anderson 1987).

A critical point is that segregation did not grow out of complete freedom of choice. Although people from similar backgrounds may have wished to live close to one another for a variety of reasons—sharing a common language, maintaining social networks and opportunities, building a sense of security—attempts to move outside their communities could meet with hostility, as well as unfair housing and real estate practices, and, in some cases, violate the law.

Until passage of the Fair Housing Act in 1968, property owners could choose whom they wished to sell to, including by race, ethnicity, skin color, religion, sex, and national origin. Often, property owners were complying with restrictive covenants established by developers, home owners' associations, or real estate agents. In Kansas City, racial segregation became more pronounced in the twentieth than the nineteenth century as real estate boards promoted the idea of racially homogenous neighborhoods—meaning the exclusion of blacks from white neighborhoods—to boost property values. One major developer in Kansas City made home owners' associations mandatory to ensure that neighbors did not breach the restrictive covenants and sell or rent to blacks (Gotham 2000).

Similar to the earlier segregation ordinances, racially restrictive covenants were challenged in the courts, and in 1948 the Supreme Court ruled that such covenants were not legally enforceable. However, developers and home owners' associations continued to write and implement restrictive deeds, in some cases into the 1970s. More racially restrictive covenants were recorded in Kansas City after the 1948 Supreme Court ruling than in the forty years before the decision (Gotham 2000). In the 1960s, the civil rights movement vehemently challenged these and other forms of discrimination. The Fair Housing Act, Title VIII of the

Civil Rights Act, gave the federal Department of Housing and Urban Development stronger authority to fight discriminatory housing practices. Revelations about discriminatory practices with subprime mortgages, predatory lending, and the subsequent foreclosure crisis after 2006 make clear that unfair housing practices continue, despite legal institutions to protect people from discrimination (Barwick 2010).

RIGHT TO THE CITY

In 1968, the same year that the U.S. Congress passed the Fair Housing Act, French sociologist Henri Lefebvre published an influential volume titled *Le droit à la ville* (Right to the City). Lefebvre wrote his book during a series of student revolts in Paris, and to this day scholars and activists alike continue to associate the phrase "right to the city" with radical uprisings, including the Occupy movements (e.g., Occupy Wall Street) in the United States. Lefebvre argued that those who inhabit the city should have decision-making power over the production of urban space and the right to use or appropriate it. In this view, the state does not enfranchise people based on their national citizenship; rather, that decision-making authority belongs to those who inhabit the city. For a city like Phoenix, in a state that has passed controversial anti–illegal immigration measures, this would mean that U.S. citizenship had little bearing on a person's right to be and live there. Furthermore, decisions about the production of urban space would not be entirely in the hands of corporations or the national government; urban inhabitants would have an equal or greater say in any determinations. This view also holds that people have the right to be physically present in the city, not to be excluded from its spaces, and to occupy and use those spaces (Purcell 2002). The privatization of urban spaces, such as gated communities or private parks, where rights such as freedom of speech are constrained or taken away, goes very much against the principle of appropriation (Davis 1992; Kirby 2008).

People's Park in Berkeley, California, has been a site of activism since the 1960s. Owned by the University of California, Berkeley, the park was slated for development as housing in the 1960s, but students and community members fought to keep it as a public park. It now houses a large homeless population, among the most marginalized groups in urban spaces. From a right-to-the-city standpoint, homeless people in People's Park should have as much or more decision-making authority as the Regents of the University of California and the right to appropriate the space because they inhabit the park and, through their daily activities, produce the urban space (Mitchell 2003; Mitchell and Heynen 2009). In the Occupy movements, many groups called for their right to the city, to appropriate space (notably camps in parks), and to protest (as the 99 percent) against the disproportionate authority of the wealthiest and most powerful 1 percent (figure 22.2).

GENDER EQUITY

A great deal of writing on justice and the city focuses on issues of class and race/ethnicity. Yet the world is profoundly gendered, and gender inequity is persistent

Figure 22.2. A sign at an Occupy movement demonstration. The Occupy movement declared its right to the city by calling for stronger decision-making power for the "99 percent" and by appropriating urban space. "Leaders of the Occupy Wall Street Movement Gives [*sic*] a Speech to the People of New York City, November 12, 2011." Marcio Jose Bastos Silva/Shutterstock.com.

and pernicious. Patriarchy has long attempted to prescribe where women are allowed to be, to define "appropriate" behaviors and occupations, and to dictate the daily roles that constrain women's opportunities (Rose and Ogborn 1988). At the same time, women have contested these injustices through a variety of strategies and mechanisms (Cope 1998; Hayden 2000).

In the early twentieth century, a key goal of the Progressive movement was women's suffrage, inspired partly by the belief that a woman's vote would be "pure" and not susceptible to corrupt political machines. However, women in the United States did not get the vote nationally until the ratification of the Nineteenth Amendment in 1920. Women in Canada won the right to vote in federal elections in 1919. The long-fought battle for enfranchisement put many suffragettes in jail or in harm's way and subjected women to ridicule, humiliation, and harassment.

Growing economic opportunities for women, including property ownership, which in some municipal jurisdictions was a requirement for voting privileges, bolstered the suffrage movement. In New York, the suffrage movement found strong support among immigrant, unionized, working-class women, particularly those working in the garment industry (Mead 2006). Although cities opened up new job prospects for women workers, the gender division of labor was strong, limiting opportunities to such areas as domestic service, the garment industry, and later clerical work. In 1900, only one in five women (over age sixteen) held paying jobs in the United States, although 43 percent of African American women were in the paid workforce, especially in domestic service (Department of Commerce and Labor 1907). In Canada, women worked mostly in domestic services and manufacturing and earned on average a little less than half of male incomes in 1900 (Fortin and Huberman 2002). At this time, more women began to move into clerical positions but worked under scrutiny by supervisors. One study of female clerical workers in Montreal at the turn of the twentieth century notes that women were "tethered" to their typewriters, while men received more freedom in offices and worked under less scrutiny and supervision than women (Boyer 2003).

Over the succeeding decades, women moved away from manufacturing jobs (typically in the textiles and garments sector) especially to clerical work but continued to earn less than their male counterparts. In the United States, by 1950 the median income for women was only 37 percent of that for men (in 2011, it was 64 percent). Even counting only full-time employees, clear discrepancies persist; in 1960, women earned sixty-one cents for every dollar that men earned (in 2011, that figure was seventy-seven cents). In Canada in 1961, women earned on average fifty-four cents for every dollar that men earned, and by 2008 the median earnings for women working full-time were 76 percent of men's (Fortin and Huberman 2002; Cool 2010). These disparities continue despite pay-equity legislation passed in both countries.

Pervasive gender roles mean that women usually work a "second shift" of unpaid labor at home, taking on more household chores and caregiving than male partners. These gender roles have had an influence on the geography of North American cities. Post–World War II suburbanization, which restricted transportation and employment options and led to the flourishing of back-office data-processing centers as well as the suburbanization of retail to tap a (lower-paid) female workforce (Pacione 2009), reinforced pressures for women to work close to home. Constraints on mobility limited women's economic opportunities (Hanson 2010), contributing to the "feminization" of poverty, as women represent the majority of impoverished people (Goldberg and Kremen 1990). One consequence is that single-mother families are more likely to live in neighborhoods with poor air quality and hazardous facilities, meaning that gender is an important dynamic for explaining environmental injustice (Downey and Hawkins 2008).

ENVIRONMENTAL JUSTICE

In a suburb in upstate New York in the late 1970s, one woman faced a difficult environmental challenge—buried toxic chemicals that were affecting the health of her family and others. In 1978, alarmed by the strange health problems afflicting her son and her neighbors, Lois Gibbs began a petition to close down the local school situated on a toxic chemical dump, the former Love Canal in Niagara Falls, New York. The school board initially refused to acknowledge any danger, but when the case drew national attention, eventually the board demolished the school, even though neither the board nor the chemical company that buried the toxic wastes would admit liability. Lois Gibbs's efforts and the incidents at the Love Canal inspired new legislation in the United States, the 1980 Comprehensive Environmental Response, Compensation, and Liability Act (commonly known as Superfund), to hold polluters responsible for contamination (Colten and Skinner 1995). A self-proclaimed "accidental activist," Gibbs went on to found the Center for Health, Environment and Justice, an organization that helps people voice their concerns about hazardous pollutants to decision-making bodies.

About the same time that Lois Gibbs was battling the school board and the chemical company in Niagara Falls, Professor Robert Bullard was working on a case with his spouse in Houston, where African American residents were resisting plans to locate a landfill in their neighborhood. In researching the case, Bullard found that all of the city's public landfills (and the vast majority of incinerators and private landfills) were located in black neighborhoods. Other research in the 1980s found similar disturbing patterns of environmental injustice. A nationwide study conducted by the United Church of Christ (1987) showed that hazardous waste and disposal facilities were far more likely to be in racial/ethnic minority zip codes than in white zip codes. The most surprising conclusion was that race and ethnicity were more significant than income in explaining the location of hazardous waste sites. This suggested that the location of unwanted land uses stemmed from more than market forces; rather, it pointed to racism, intended or unintended, as a key factor driving the observed pattern.

Another watershed moment in the history of environmental justice was the release of information to the public about the location and practices of toxic facilities in the United States. In 1986, the U.S. Congress passed the Emergency Planning and Community Right-to-Know Act (EPCRA). This piece of legislation gave the Environmental Protection Agency the authority and mandate to collect information from facilities that released known toxins into the air, land, or water. Most important, the legislation provided people and organizations with information they could use to "shame" polluting industries (Fung and O'Rourke 2000). Many scholars saw this database as a way to test environmental justice theories, and most found that race and ethnicity were indeed the best predictors of toxic facility locations (Mohai and Saha 2007). Others showed that the distributive justice patterns were the result of long-standing dynamics that marginalized people into neighborhoods where they were likely to live with unwanted or hazardous land uses. In Los Angeles, for instance, social privilege afforded to whites (Pulido 2000) repelled most toxic industry from majority-white neighborhoods, while as early as the 1920s, zoning patterns, informed by racist notions, shaped where industry and Latino populations were destined to concentrate on the city's east side (Boone 2005). In turn-of-the-twentieth-century New Orleans, white privilege extended water and sewer infrastructure first to white neighborhoods, leaving black communities exposed to floods and higher rates of malaria and typhoid. Segregation ordinances and restrictive deeds limited where African Americans could live in New Orleans, even as new infrastructure opened up new areas for residential development (Colten 2002). In 2005, the tragic events of Hurricane Katrina, which hit minority and low-income communities in New Orleans hardest, shows how long-standing, entrenched segregation created acute vulnerabilities to the environmental hazard of floods (Colten 2005, 2007).

Environmental justice is an analytical framework for understanding environmental problems, but it is also a social movement. Under the banner of environmental justice, communities have railed against unwanted or unhealthy land uses (distributive justice) and demanded fair treatment (procedural justice) and recognition in decision making and applications of the law (Schlosberg 2007). Many environmental justice movements draw on struggles from the civil rights era for inspiration and strategy. In New York City in the early 1990s, Latinos and Hasidic Jews working together successfully opposed the building of a giant incinerator to burn New York's garbage in their Brooklyn communities. Reconciliation between the Latino and Hasidic communities, which was instrumental to the protest, was initiated by a former activist for the Young Lords, a largely Puerto Rican group that fought for civil rights in the late 1960s and early 1970s (Gandy 2002). Environmental justice groups have used language from the Civil Rights Act to fight against racial discrimination and to hold the federal government accountable. In 1994, President Bill Clinton issued an executive order requiring all federal agencies to develop environmental justice strategies that reduce inordinate environmental burdens and health effects on low-income and racial/ethnic minority communities.

Environmental justice gained traction through local struggles in the United States, but the language and strategies have been used to address social and environmental issues on the global scale. In the 1980s, some high-profile cases of hazardous waste being shipped from rich to poor countries (to avoid costly handling and disposal charges in countries with stringent regulations) led to calls for environmental justice at home and abroad (Pellow 2007). Environmental justice has also effectively framed issues regarding recycling of electronics waste, threats to biodiversity, and climate justice, making sure they do not remain just technical challenges but become moral issues as well since they disproportionately affect vulnerable populations in developing countries (Shepard and Corbin-Mark 2009).

SUSTAINABILITY AND JUSTICE

Sustainability seeks to reduce environmental degradation and improve human well-being by maintaining and strengthening the social and ecological systems that support us. Justice and equity are core principles of sustainability for practical and ethical reasons. When the Brundtland Commission published *Our Common Future* (WCED 1987), which popularized the idea of sustainability, it argued that persistent poverty and other social inequities would undermine any efforts to sustain earth's life-support systems. Poverty, illiteracy, inadequate health care, and other social ills make it difficult to think and act in the long term and to build the human capital necessary to support sustainable environmental practices.

A powerful message of sustainability is that our children should enjoy the same social, economic, and environmental benefits as the current generation. This is known as intergenerational equity. Typically, proponents of intergenerational equity and sustainability focus on environmental stewardship, or ensuring ecological integrity over the long term. This is based on the notion that we need to prioritize ecosystem management over human development; otherwise, we will exceed the ability of the planet to support humans and other species. However, sustainability also means addressing intragenerational equity, or reducing inequities within the current generation. The environmental justice movement has tended to focus on intragenerational equity and also to remind us that urban areas are environments, with functions and characteristics similar to other ecosystems.

Over the last decade, an increasing number of cities have adopted sustainability plans that address intra- and intergenerational equity. One of the boldest is New York City's PlaNYC (http://www.nyc.gov/html/planyc2030), which asked New Yorkers to envision what their city should be like in 2030. In addition to preparing for sea-level rise, a more intense urban heat island, and other expected environmental changes, New York's sustainability plan also calls for affordable housing, better access to parks, improved public health, and access to meaningful employment. In New York and other cities, sustainability means preparing for an uncertain future in ways that reduce present and future inequities.

CONCLUSION

Urbanization has profoundly altered the human experience. In the early twentieth century, the United States and Canada shifted from an agrarian to an urban society, and now we live in a world where cities are home to the majority of the global population. People continue to flock to cities because urban life offers hope and opportunity, but cities can also bring gross disparities and injustice into stark relief. This chapter has touched on some of the ways that geographers and others have employed justice and equity to make sense of urbanization and urban life, as well as on how individuals and groups have employed these ideas to fight for better and fairer outcomes and practices. The historical geography of cities shows that justice and equity have served as guiding normative principles, helping to define what is right and what we should do. Sustainability has reignited questions about justice and equity within the larger goal of a desirable future that sustains earth's life-support systems. Global sustainability will depend on urban sustainability, and as this chapter shows, we cannot ignore justice and equity as powerful motivators and agents of change in cities.

REFERENCES

Ames, H. B. 1897. *The City below the Hill: A Sociological Study of a Portion of the City of Montreal, Canada*. Montreal: Bishop Engraving and Printing Co.

Anderson, K. J. 1987. The Idea of Chinatown: The Power of Place and Institutional Practice in the Making of a Racial Category. *Annals of the Association of American Geographers* 77, no. 4: 580–98.
Barnett, C. 2011. Geography and Ethics: Justice Unbound. *Progress in Human Geography* 35, no. 2: 246–55.
Barwick, C. 2010. Patterns of Discrimination against Blacks and Hispanics in the U.S. Mortgage Market. *Journal of Housing and the Built Environment* 25, no. 1: 117–24.
Bauman, J. F., and E. K. Muller. 2006. *Before Renaissance: Planning in Pittsburgh, 1889–1943*. Pittsburgh, PA: University of Pittsburgh Press.
Boone, C. G. 2003. Obstacles to Infrastructure Provision: The Struggle to Build Comprehensive Sewer Works in Baltimore. *Historical Geography* 31: 151–68.
———. 2005. Zoning and Environmental Inequity in the Industrial East Side. In *Land of Sunshine: An Environmental History of Metropolitan Los Angeles*, edited by W. Deverell and G. Hise, 167–78. Pittsburgh, PA: University of Pittsburgh Press.
Booth, Charles. 1889. *Labour and Life of the People.* Vol. 1: *East London.* London: Macmillan.
Boyer, K. 2003. "Neither Forget nor Remember Your Sex": Sexual Politics in the Early Twentieth-Century Canadian Office. *Journal of Historical Geography* 29, no. 2: 212–29.
Bridge, G. 2008. City Senses: On the Radical Possibilities of Pragmatism in Geography. *Geoforum* 39, no. 4: 1570–84.
Buckley, G. L., and C. G. Boone. 2011. "To Promote the Material and Moral Welfare of the Community": Neighborhood Improvement Associations in Baltimore, Maryland, 1900–1945. In *Environmental and Social Justice in the City: Historical Perspectives*, edited by G. Massard-Guilbaud and R. Rodger, 43–65. Cambridge, UK: White Horse Press.
Colten, C. E. 2002. Basin Street Blues: Drainage and Environmental Equity in New Orleans, 1890–1930. *Journal of Historical Geography* 28, no. 2: 237–57.
———. 2005. *An Unnatural Metropolis: Wresting New Orleans from Nature.* Baton Rouge: Louisiana State University Press.
———. 2007. Environmental Justice in a Landscape of Tragedy. *Technology in Society* 29, no. 2: 173–79.
Colten, C. E., and P. N. Skinner. 1995. *The Road to Love Canal: Managing Industrial Waste before EPA*. Austin: University of Texas Press.
Cool, J. 2010. Wage Gap between Women and Men. Report no. 2010–30-E. Canada, Library of Parliament. http://www.parl.gc.ca/Content/LOP/ResearchPublications/2010–30-e.pdf.
Cope, M. 1998. "She Hath Done What She Could": Community, Citizenship, and Place among Women in Late 19th Century Colorado. *Historical Geography* 26: 45–64.
Corbridge, S. 2002. Development as Freedom: The Spaces of Amartya Sen. *Progress in Development Studies* 2, no. 3: 183–217.
Craddock, S. 2000. *City of Plagues: Disease, Poverty, and Deviance in San Francisco.* Minneapolis: University of Minnesota Press.
Davis, M. 1992. *City of Quartz: Excavating the Future in Los Angeles.* New York: Vintage.
Department of Commerce and Labor, Bureau of the Census. 1907. *Statistics of Women at Work: Based on Unpublished Information Derived from the Schedules of the Twelfth Census, 1900.* Washington, D.C.: Government Printing Office. http://www.census.gov/prod/www/abs/decennial/1900.html.
Downey, L., and B. Hawkins. 2008. Single-Mother Families and Air Pollution: A National Study. *Social Science Quarterly* 89, no. 2: 523–36.
Fainstein, S. S. 2010. *The Just City.* Ithaca, NY: Cornell University Press.

Fortin, N. M., and M. Huberman. 2002. Occupational Gender Segregation and Women's Wages in Canada: An Historical Perspective. *Canadian Public Policy/Analyse de Politiques* 28: S11–S39.

Fung, A., and D. O'Rourke. 2000. Reinventing Environmental Regulation from the Grassroots Up: Explaining and Expanding the Success of the Toxics Release Inventory. *Environmental Management* 25, no. 2: 115–27.

Gandy, M. 2002. *Concrete and Clay: Reworking Nature in New York City.* Cambridge, MA: MIT Press.

Gilliland, J., and S. Olson. 2010. Residential Segregation in the Industrializing City: A Closer Look. *Urban Geography* 31, no. 1: 29–58.

Goldberg, G. S., and L. Kremen. 1990. *The Feminization of Poverty: Only in America?* Westport, CT: Praeger.

Gotham, K. F. 2000. Urban Space, Restrictive Covenants and the Origins of Racial Residential Segregation in a U.S. City, 1900–50. *International Journal of Urban and Regional Research* 24, no. 3: 616–33.

Hanson, Susan. 2010. Gender and Mobility: New Approaches for Informing Sustainability. *Gender, Place and Culture: A Journal of Feminist Geography* 17, no. 1: 5–23.

Hanson, S., and G. Giuliano. 2004. *The Geography of Urban Transportation.* New York: Guilford Press.

Harvey, D. 1973. *Social Justice and the City.* London: Edward Arnold.

Hayden, D. 2000. *The Grand Domestic Revolution: A History of Feminist Designs for American Homes, Neighborhoods and Cities.* 8th ed. Cambridge: Cambridge University Press.

Kirby, A. 2008. The Production of Private Space and Its Implications for Urban Social Relations. *Political Geography* 27: 74–95.

Kirschner, D. S. 1975. The Ambiguous Legacy: Social Justice and Social Control in the Progressive Era. *Historical Reflections/Réflexions Historiques* 2, no. 1: 69–88.

Mead, R. J. 2006. *How the Vote Was Won: Woman Suffrage in the Western United States, 1868–1914.* New York: New York University Press.

Melosi, M. V. 2000. *The Sanitary City: Urban Infrastructure in America from Colonial Times to the Present.* Baltimore: Johns Hopkins University Press.

Mitchell, D. 2003. *The Right to the City: Social Justice and the Fight for Public Space.* New York: Guilford Press.

Mitchell, D., and N. Heynen. 2009. The Geography of Survival and the Right to the City: Speculations on Surveillance, Legal Innovation, and the Criminalization of Intervention. *Urban Geography* 30, no. 6: 611–32. doi:10.2747/0272-3638.30.6.611.

Mohai, P., and R. Saha. 2007. Racial Inequality in the Distribution of Hazardous Waste: A National-Level Reassessment. *Social Problems* 54, no. 3: 343–70.

Pacione, M. 2009. *Urban Geography: A Global Perspective.* 3rd ed. New York: Routledge.

Park, R., E. Burgess, and R. McKenzie. 1925. *The City: Suggestions for the Study of Human Nature in the Urban Environment.* Chicago: University of Chicago Press.

Pellow, D. N. 2007. *Resisting Global Toxics: Transnational Movements for Environmental Justice.* Cambridge, MA: MIT Press.

Pipkin, J. 2005. The Moral High Ground in Albany: Rhetorics and Practices of an "Olmstedian" Park, 1855–1875. *Journal of Historical Geography* 31, no. 4: 666–87.

Plunz, Richard. 1990. *A History of Housing in New York City.* New York: Columbia University Press.

Power, G. 1983. Apartheid Baltimore Style: The Residential Segregation Ordinances of 1910–1913. *Maryland Law Review* 42: 289–328.

Pulido, L. 2000. Rethinking Environmental Racism: White Privilege and Urban Development in Southern California. *Annals of the Association of American Geographers* 90, no. 1: 12–40.

Purcell, M. 2002. Excavating Lefebvre: The Right to the City and Its Urban Politics of the Inhabitant. *GeoJournal* 58, no. 2: 99–108.
Rawls, J. 1971. *A Theory of Justice*. Cambridge, MA: Harvard University Press.
Riis, J. 1890. *How the Other Half Lives: Studies among the Tenements of New York*. New York: Charles Scribner's Sons.
Rose, G., and M. Ogborn. 1988. Feminism and Historical Geography. *Journal of Historical Geography* 14, no. 4: 405–9.
Rosen, C. M. 2003. *The Limits of Power: Great Fires and the Process of City Growth in America*. Cambridge: Cambridge University Press.
Ruddick, S. 1996. Constructing Difference in Public Spaces: Race, Class, and Gender as Interlocking Systems. *Urban Geography* 17, no. 2: 132–51.
Schein, R. H, ed.. 2006. *Landscape and Race in the United States*. New York: Routledge.
Schlosberg, D. 2007. *Defining Environmental Justice: Theories, Movements, and Nature*. Oxford: Oxford University Press.
Sen, A. K. 2009. *The Idea of Justice*. Cambridge, MA: Belknap Press.
Shepard, P. M., and C. Corbin-Mark. 2009. Climate Justice. *Environmental Justice* 2, no. 4: 163–66.
Thornton, P., and S. Olson. 2001. A Deadly Discrimination among Montreal Infants, 1860–1900. *Continuity Change* 16: 95–135.
Tuason, J. 1997. Rus in Urbe: The Spatial Evolution of Urban Parks in the United States, 1850–1920. *Historical Geography* 25: 124–47.
United Church of Christ, Commission for Racial Justice. 1987. *Toxic Wastes and Race in the United States: A National Report on the Racial and Socio-economic Characteristics of Communities with Hazardous Waste Sites*. New York: Public Data Access.
World Commission of Environment and Development (WCED). 1987. *Our Common Future*. New York: World Commission on Environment and Development.
Young, I. M. 1990. *Justice and the Politics of Difference*. Princeton, NJ: Princeton University Press.
Young, T. 1995. Modern Urban Parks. *Geographical Review* 85, no. 4: 535–51.
———. 1996. Social Reform through Parks: The American Civic Association's Program for a Better America. *Journal of Historical Geography* 22, no. 4: 460–72.

Index

About the Contributors

Derek H. Alderman is professor and head of the Department of Geography at the University of Tennessee in Knoxville. He was born and raised in the American South—the land of Confederate monuments and Martin Luther King Jr. streets. Moved by the politically charged nature of southern public memory, he has undertaken a study of the historical geographies of African American life and the relationship between landscape and racial control and resistance.

Timothy G. Anderson is an associate professor in the Department of Geography at Ohio University. He attributes much of his interest in historical settlement geography to an understanding of experiences growing up in the winter wheat belt of northwestern Oklahoma refined and sharpened under the guidance of his master's and doctoral advisors at Oklahoma and Texas A&M.

Kevin Blake is a professor in the Department of Geography at Kansas State University. His attempts to pierce the veil of mythic landscapes build upon the insights of his graduate school mentors, Dr. James R. Shortridge and Dr. Daniel D. Arreola.

Christopher G. Boone is dean of the School of Sustainability at Arizona State University. As a graduate student at the University of Toronto, he was supervised and inspired by Jock Galloway, a historical geographer of Latin America. Boone had the good fortune to be educated by a large group of historical geographers at the University of Toronto and Queen's University.

Geoffrey L. Buckley is professor of geography at Ohio University. Introduced to the field of historical geography by Alexander Murphy and Edward Price at the University of Oregon, he went on to work with Robert Mitchell and Paul Groves at the University of Maryland. His research interests focus on urban environments, state forestry, environmental justice, and the evolution of mining landscapes.

Karl Byrand was raised in Pittsburgh, Pennsylvania. His research interests include the cultural landscapes of national parks and the migration of the Hmong from the Southeast Asian highlands to the United States and the cultural landscapes they have formed. Currently, he is a professor in and chair of the Department of Geography and Geology for the University of Wisconsin Colleges.

Craig E. Colten is the Carl O. Sauer Professor at Louisiana State University. After dropping out of college to raft down the Mississippi River in the 1970s, he suddenly found himself without his crew and abandoned the adventure. By good luck, he returned to his studies and stumbled into a great historical geography program at the university where he now teaches.

Michael P. Conzen is professor of geography at the University of Chicago. Educated at the Universities of Cambridge, Wisconsin, and Giessen, he began his teaching career at Boston University before moving to Chicago. His research and teaching interests span historical, cultural, and urban geography, historical cartography, and landscape history. He has published widely in these fields, including *A Scholar's Guide to Geographical Writing on the American and Canadian Past* (1993), *Mapping Manifest Destiny* (2008), and *The Making of the American Landscape* (2nd ed., 2010; Korean ed. 2011). His current research includes fieldwork on the physical evolution of Italian cities; comparative studies of urban structure in Brazil, China, and the United States; and the early history of the California wine industry.

Dydia DeLyser is an associate professor in the Department of Geography and Anthropology at Louisiana State University. She began her geography career interested in ecology/biogeography but soon found herself more compelled by people than plants and pursued graduate studies in cultural-historical geography, a field that has kept her challenged and engaged ever since.

Lary M. Dilsaver is professor emeritus of geography at the University of South Alabama. Sitting by the campfire one evening in Kings Canyon National Park, he told his fellow hikers, "I should figure out a way to work in the national parks." So he did.

Mona Domosh is professor of geography at Dartmouth College. After spending much of her childhood traipsing through battlefields with her Civil War–obsessed father, she became fascinated with landscapes as action-packed sites of men, machines, and maneuvers. Influenced by the women's movement and the emerging women's studies discipline, she turned to uncovering the importance of everyday "life and death" in the making of American geography and history.

William E. Doolittle is Erich W. Zimmermann Regents Professor of Geography in the Department of Geography and the Environment at the University of Texas, Austin. Details about his professional activities can be found at http://www.utexas.edu/courses/wd.

Steven Hoelscher is professor of American studies and geography and former chair of the Department of American Studies at the University of Texas, Austin.

His primary research interest centers on the historical geography of the United States, both domestically and transnationally. His books include *Heritage on Stage* (1998), *Textures of Place* (2001, coedited with Paul Adams and Karen Till), *Picturing Indians* (2008), and, most recently, *Reading Magnum* (2013).

Stephen J. Hornsby is director of the Canadian-American Center and professor of geography and Canadian studies at the University of Maine. A lover of maps since an early age, he is currently finishing up editing a historical atlas of Maine and writing a book on American pictorial maps.

Joshua Inwood is assistant professor of geography and affiliated faculty with the Africana Studies Program at the University of Tennessee. As an undergrad in history and geography at Michigan State University, he drove several girlfriends to drink by insisting that they stop at every historical marker in the state. At that time he decided to follow his passion and engage in geography graduate work at Kent State University and the University of Georgia.

Anne Kelly Knowles is a professor in the Geography Department at Middlebury College. She discovered historical geography while editing a new American history textbook for which Michael P. Conzen was hired as map consultant. There was no looking back.

K. Maria D. Lane is an associate professor in the Department of Geography and Environmental Studies at the University of New Mexico. She fell in love with historical research as an undergraduate at the University of Virginia, where she spent many hours prowling the stacks and archives at Alderman Library. She decided to study the history of water resources management after moving away from the eastern seaboard and discovering that the Southwest is extremely dry.

Ines M. Miyares is professor of geography at Hunter College–CUNY. She developed her research passion for understanding historical geographies of ethnic change while working her way through college as a paramedic in California's San Joaquin valley and experiencing firsthand the impacts of immigration and refugee resettlement on both the immigrants and the local communities in which they settled.

E. Arnold Modlin Jr. is the lone geographer in the History Department at Norfolk State University, a historically black university in southeastern Virginia. As an undergraduate history major at East Carolina University, he took life-changing geography courses that opened his eyes to how he could combine his interests in history and travel with his desire to understand and challenge the ongoing issues of racism and social injustice in the United States.

Karen M. Morin is associate dean and professor of geography at Bucknell University in Lewisburg, Pennsylvania. Her volunteer work with a local nonprofit prisoners' rights group led to her current interest in the American carceral past.

Edward K. Muller studied historical geography at the University of Wisconsin, Madison, which required extensive participation in the graduate history program. This interdisciplinary training influenced his eagerness to join the Department of History at the University of Pittsburgh, where he is a professor. Immersion in history for many years as a teacher and scholar has deepened and enriched his understanding of historical geography as an essential way to comprehend the world around us.

Michael D. Myers directs an archaeological consulting firm and plans to develop a nonprofit focused on sustainable agriculture and energy. His discovery of geography as a discipline began late in his undergraduate training, following a casual conversation about research interests on a boat off the Yucatán coast, when a fellow student inquired, "Have you thought about taking geography?"

Karl Raitz is Provost's Distinguished Service Professor of Geography at the University of Kentucky. Born and raised on the black dirt prairie of west-central Minnesota, he developed an interest in landscape and the geographies of infrastructure based on the writings and teachings of John Borchert, Grady Clay, John Fraser Hart, Warren Hofstra, J. B. Jackson, Peirce Lewis, Fred Lukermann, E. Cotton Mather, Thomas Schlereth, Joseph Wood, Wilbur Zelinsky, and many others.

Jasper Rubin, trained as an urban and urban historical geographer, is chair of the Urban Studies and Planning Department at San Francisco State University. Before escaping to academia, he spent more than a dozen years as a planner at the San Francisco Planning Department, working on complex land-use policy issues.

Chie Sakakibara is a member of the Department of Geography and Environmental Sustainability at the University of Oklahoma, Norman. Her love of animals eventually led her to pursue academic degrees in the United States, where she specialized in the geography of human-animal-environment interactions. A Japanese native, she lives in Oklahoma, the proud mother of a Shiba Inu mix, Giro, and of her own biological daughter, Kaya (whose Iñupiat name is Iñutuq, meaning "baby whale").

Joan M. Schwartz became a historical geographer when, as a second-year math and physics major at the University of Toronto, she was daunted by the reading list for an elective in Canadian history. So, instead, she enrolled in a course on the historical geography of Canada taught by Cole Harris, who subsequently supervised her master's thesis at the University of British Columbia. After working as a photo archivist at the National Archives of Canada, she completed her doctoral dissertation at Queen's University, Kingston, Ontario, where she is now associate professor of the history of photography.

Steven Silvern is associate professor of geography at Salem State University, where his teaching and research interests focus on indigenous peoples, environmental sustainability, and sustainable food systems. His interest in the historical geographies of Native Americans developed during his graduate work at the University of Wisconsin in the late 1980s, when the legal and political conflict over Ojibwe treaty rights in northern Wisconsin was making national headlines.

Andrew Sluyter's fascination with the history of the Atlantic world seems inexplicable, given his birth on the far northern shores of the Pacific Ocean, but it probably relates to being Dutch by parentage, Argentinean by marriage, and Louisianan by luck. He was a Digital Innovation Fellow of the American Council of Learned Societies in 2012–2013, has published *Colonialism and Landscape* (2002) and *Black Ranching Frontiers* (2012), and currently teaches at Louisiana State University.

Jeffrey S. Smith is associate professor of geography at Kansas State University. His historical/cultural research on the American Southwest among the Nuevomexicano population has opened many doors to new research opportunities in Mexico, Central America, and the Caribbean.

Robert Wilson developed his fascination with landscapes as a boy while backpacking in the Sangre de Cristo Mountains and traveling the back roads of New Mexico. He is an associate professor in the Department of Geography at Syracuse University and author of *Seeking Refuge: Birds and Landscapes of the Pacific Flyway* (2010).

William Wyckoff is professor of geography in the Department of Earth Sciences at Montana State University in Bozeman. A California native, he has written widely on the historical geography of the American frontier and on the evolution of the western American landscape. Today, he and his family make their home in southwestern Montana.

Terence Young is professor of geography in the Department of Geography and Anthropology at the California State Polytechnic University in Pomona. He earned his PhD at the age of forty-one and has consistently pursued research topics related to his pre-academic life in plants, parks, and camping.

Yolonda Youngs is an assistant professor in the Department of History at Idaho State University. Her passion for historical and cultural geography in the western United States developed over a decade of exploring the mountains and rivers of Wyoming, Utah, Arizona, and Montana as a professional river and kayak guide. These experiences shaped her commitment to geographical research and inspired her return to teaching in a university program.